W9-ADN-164

EUROPEAN NATIONS

SPAIN AND PORTUGAL

A REFERENCE GUIDE
FROM THE RENAISSANCE TO THE PRESENT

Julia Ortiz-Griffin
and
William D. Griffin

Facts On File
An imprint of Infobase Publishing

Spain and Portugal: A Reference Guide from the Renaissance to the Present

Copyright © 2007 Julia Ortiz-Griffin and William D. Griffin

All rights reserved. No part of this book may be reproduced or utilized in any form or by any means, electronic or mechanical, including photocopying, recording, or by any information storage or retrieval systems, without permission in writing from the publisher. For information contact:

Facts On File, Inc.
An imprint of Infobase Publishing
132 West 31st Street
New York NY 10001

ISBN-10: 0-8160-4592-5
ISBN-13: 978-0-8160-4592-1

Library of Congress Cataloging-in-Publication Data

Ortiz-Griffin, Julia.
Spain and Portugal : a reference guide from the Renaissance to the present / Julia Ortiz-Griffin and William D. Griffin.—1st ed.
  p. cm.
Includes bibliographical references and index.
ISBN 0-8160-4592-5 (hc : alk. paper)
1. Spain—History. 2. Portugal—History. I. Griffin, William D. II. Title.
DP66.O78 2007
946.0009′0303—dc22   2006026951

Facts On File books are available at special discounts when purchased in bulk quantities for businesses, associations, institutions, or sales promotions. Please call our Special Sales Department in New York at (212) 967-8800 or (800) 322-8755.

You can find Facts On File on the World Wide Web at http://www.factsonfile.com

Text design by David Strelecky
Cover design by Semadar Megged
Illustrations by Dale Williams

Printed in the United States of America

VB Hermitage 10 9 8 7 6 5 4 3 2 1

This book is printed on acid-free paper.

CONTENTS

Foreword   iv

Introduction   v

History of Spain and Portugal   1

THE LANDS AND PEOPLES OF IBERIA   3

HABSBURG SPAIN   9

SPAIN AND PORTUGAL IN THE EIGHTEENTH CENTURY   25

THE AGE OF REVOLUTION IN SPAIN AND PORTUGAL   33

THE NEW DEMOCRACIES   57

Historical Dictionary A–Z   67

Chronology   417

Appendixes   441

RULERS AND STATESMEN OF SPAIN AND PORTUGAL   442

MAPS   451

Bibliography   463

Index   467

FOREWORD

This series was inspired by the need of high school and college students to have a concise and readily available history series focusing on the evolution of the major European powers and other influential European states in the modern age—from the Renaissance to the present. Written in accessible language, the projected volumes include all of the major European countries: France, Germany, Great Britain, Italy, and Russia, as well as other states such as Spain, Portugal, Austria, and Hungary that have made important intellectual, political, cultural, and religious contributions to Europe and the world. The format has been designed to facilitate usage and includes a short introduction by the author of each volume, a specialist in its history, providing an overview of the importance of the particular country in the modern period. This is followed by a narrative history of each nation from the time of the Renaissance to the present. The core of the volume consists of an A–Z dictionary of people, events, and places, providing coverage of intellectual, political, diplomatic, cultural, social, religious, and economic developments. Next, a chronology details key events in each nation's development over the past several centuries. Finally, the end matter includes a selected bibliography of readily available works, maps, and an index to the material within the volume.

—Frank J. Coppa, General Editor
St. John's University

INTRODUCTION

Spain emerged as the dominant power in Europe at the beginning of the modern era. Like France Spain became a centralized nation-state and defeated that country in the struggle for mastery that left Spain's rulers dominant from the North Sea to the Mediterranean through a combination of arms and diplomacy. Spain became a cultural leader as well through its writers, artists, and even styles of dress. Moreover, Spain was not only the first European Great Power, it was the first European global power. Its proudly named *conquistadores* were indeed the "conquerors" of a New World that they had found in the Western Hemisphere and explored. Subsequently Spain imposed its language, its religion, and much of its tradition on North and South America. In the Old World Spain took the lead in what would become a centuries-long clash of civilizations between Christianity and Islam. The sheer wealth and power wielded by Spain would decline through economic and political reverses, however. During the 19th century its European and global standing diminished and its colonial empire shrank. Civil war and dictatorship engulfed its during most of the 20th century. Yet the restoration of democracy in 1975 and its return to full membership in the international community in subsequent decades have restored Spain to much of the rank and respect formerly commanded by its position as one of the largest and most populous countries in Europe.

Portugal, only a fraction of Spain's size, has been called an "accidental country." Its success in driving out the Islamic invaders who overran the entire Iberian Peninsula during the early Middle Ages 300 years before the Spaniards accomplished the same feat of liberation and unification gave her special advantages that compensated to some extent for its smaller size. Even though Spaniards would continue to complain that Portugal had no more justification for separate nationhood than any of Spain's provinces, the Portuguese soon forged ahead in global outreach. Portugal's navigators and traders found an all-water route to the riches of Asia, made decisive contacts with sub-Saharan Africa, and even staked its claim to a part of South America before Spain had effectively begun its colonial conquests. After a "Golden Age" that lasted only a few generations, Portuguese resources were stretched too thin. Portugal would eventually have to surrender control over a commercial empire that stretched from the Cape of Good Hope through South Asia, the Spice Islands, the China coast, and Japan. Even Portugal itself would, between 1580 and 1640, be subjected to the direct rule of its powerful neighbor. During the 18th century Portugal would occasionally be at war with Spain but during the 19th century would more characteristically share an epoch of decline. During the 20th century there were the parallel experiences of depression and dictatorship ending at almost the same moment. For Portugal the new era of democracy and optimism dawned in 1974 with the so-called Carnation Revolution.

The Iberian Age of European history encompasses more than 400 years, stretching from the High Renaissance to the onset of the Industrial Revolution (c. 1450–1850) with its harsh discrimination between "modern" and "agrarian" nations. The significance of the Iberian countries is to be found, however, not merely in their paucity of natural resources and their lagging production figures but in a history that transcends mere comparative statistics. Spain and Portugal reached out to circumnavigate the globe while others cowered in Europe fearing the unknown. They created the cultural heritage that encompasses a large part of the Western Hemisphere in terms of language and religion. They filled the art galleries and the library shelves with masterpieces. Reinventing postcolonial relations, they have established diplomatic and economic bonds with the peoples of America, Africa, and Asia in a spirit of mutual respect and cooperation. Finally, having entered a new millennium as good citizens of a united Europe, they have contributed the work of their statesmen and thinkers to the collective prosperity of the Continent.

HISTORY OF
SPAIN AND PORTUGAL

THE LANDS AND
PEOPLES OF IBERIA

Spain and Portugal are inescapably linked to one another by their geographical position and their historical experience. That these two countries have preserved their separate identities within the Iberian
Peninsula is due to a complex array of physical, political, economic, and
cultural factors and, at times, unpredictable accidents of fate.

Modern Spain and Portugal emerged from more than 2,000 years of
life on the periphery of Western civilization. Like most of the Mediterranean peoples, the Iberian and Celtic inhabitants of the peninsula
experienced Greek, Phoenician, Carthaginian, and Roman influence in
varying degrees. Roman rule, as elsewhere, yielded to the triumph of
Christianity and the ascendancy of Germanic tribes.

The arrival of Muslim invaders in the Iberian Peninsula in 711 created a distinct dimension of European history. For the next eight centuries Islam, Christianity, and Judaism coexisted in a relationship that
was often financially and intellectually enriching but periodically disrupted by religious tensions and civil strife.

During the Middle Ages a number of Christian kingdoms arose, pursuing a "Reconquest" of the territory lost to the "Moors." Of these,
Castile and Aragon gained dominance over lesser realms to become the
progenitors of a united Spain. By 1147 the Portuguese had expelled the
Muslim overlords from Lisbon and secured effective independence.

THE SIGNIFICANCE OF THE RENAISSANCE

In the conventional periodization of European history, the Renaissance
has long been viewed as the shift between "medieval" and "modern."
All the major European states are described as making this fundamental
transition some time in the second half of the 15th century. A more
sophisticated understanding of their respective experiences reveals that,
for most of them, modernity came later. In Germany and Italy it was

associated with the unification struggles of the 19th century; in France, with the great revolutionary turmoils of the late 18th; in England, with the Glorious Revolution of 1688 or the Industrial Revolution a few generations later. In the case of Spain and Portugal, however, the Renaissance was truly the formative and decisive experience of their whole modern existence. Their transition from insignificance to global dominance; their political, military and cultural glory; and their onset of decay were concentrated within the Renaissance era. They would spend much of their modern history looking back upon their Golden Age, periodically striving to recapture past greatness but perpetually frustrated by their failure to live up to the achievements of their ancestors. In a sense the Iberian kingdoms would be shaped for the whole of their modern existence by the memory of what they had been in their earlier days. For this reason it is necessary, if one is to understand the history of Spain and Portugal during the last five centuries, to form a clear picture of what they were in this moment when they began to assert themselves, for their respective characters would be permanently linked to the identities then established.

OLD BOUNDARIES AND NEW FRONTIERS

The physical geography of the Iberian Peninsula limited options and presented opportunities for its inhabitants. The Pyrenees walled them off from northern Europe, while the long stretch of Mediterranean coastline encouraged contact with Italy, the Levant, and North Africa. The shores of Portugal and northwestern Spain presented tantalizing vistas of the Atlantic and what might lie beyond. The mouths of the Douro and the Tagus at Porto (Oporto) and Lisbon, respectively, gave Portugal maritime potentials that were echoed in Spain by the Guadalquivir for Seville and the Ebro for the northeast coast. Yet none of these rivers were naturally navigable routes into the interior. Instead, like the mountain ranges, they contributed to the compartmentalization of the peninsula and the dominance of localized social groupings as well as political alliances. The great central plateau that dominated the pastoral economy and shaped the human personality of Castile reinforced its love-hate relationship with the lush southern lands of Andalusia and the ruggedly independent dominions of Galicians and Basques in the north. On a far smaller scale Portugal exhibited regional distinctions and even antagonisms that manifest themselves in the mountainous terrain and conservative attitudes of the region north of the Douro, the proud assertiveness of the central provinces and the Alentejo, and the more easy-going environment of the Algarve.

By the mid-1400s the options and opportunities of the Iberian states might have interacted in several different ways. With the Muslim power shrinking to a soon-to-disappear remnant around Granada, the Iberian peoples were poised to move beyond the physical and political limitations that had been imposed upon them by the Cruzada (the war waged by Christian Iberian kingdoms against the Muslim states). Would they pursue the retreating Moorish enemy into Morocco and beyond? Would they venture beyond early Atlantic outposts established in Madeira and the Azores? Would they renew old ties with Italy? As late as 1476 Portuguese rulers sought to seize the throne of Castile and become the dominant force on the peninsula. Aragon, on Castile's eastern flank, had similar ambitions. Castile, through a combination of superior size of territory and population, would eventually triumph over the reckless military adventurism of the Portuguese and the guileful diplomacy of the Aragonese to emerge as the dominant player and the molder of Iberia's future.

UNIFICATION AND EXPANSION

In 1469 Isabella, sister of the reigning monarch of Castile, married Ferdinand, son and heir of the king of Aragon. In 1474, on the death of her brother, she ascended the Castilian throne after defeating a challenge from the king of Portugal, who had previously courted her himself and who now supported the claims of her niece in another attempt to gain control. In 1479 Ferdinand succeeded his father as king of Aragon. Thus, within 10 years the future direction of the peninsula had been decided. Portugal would remain a separate and unequal player. Spain would move toward unity, but not as the old king of Aragon had envisioned when he secured the hand of Isabella for Ferdinand. Wily though the Aragonese rulers might be, they were doomed to subordination by the sheer weight of Castile. Castile's landmass and population far outweighed those of Aragon. Furthermore, the *cortes* of Castile, which represented all the components of the kingdom, was a much more manageable parliamentary instrument than the three separate legislatures of the autonomous kingdoms of Aragon proper and Valencia and the principality of Catalonia. Each of these had not only its own *cortes* but its own administration, and laws and prerogatives that had to be manipulated (often with difficulty and delay) by their shared sovereign. By the terms of Isabella's marriage Ferdinand became coruler of Castile, but many restrictions were placed upon his freedom of action, and numerous barriers were set up against Aragonese interference with Castilian property and privileges. As long as the two maintained a true partnership in matters of policy as well as personal relationship, all would go smoothly. Unification, however, was very much a work in progress throughout the 35 years of their marriage. This being said, the process was much more rapid than the slow, agonizing business of bringing France together—a labor that took more than twice as long.

Isabella and her consort agreed to a remarkable degree about priorities, such as breaking the power of the great nobles in Castile, restoring security on the highways of the kingdom, working with the *cortes* to guarantee reliable tax revenues, and building up a central bureaucracy and royal authority in the municipalities. This latter concern was met by the reshaping of the old royal council into a cluster of committees, each charged with a particular sphere of government business (finance, military affairs, external relations, and so on), and by the appointment of *corregidores* to supplant the power of local magnates in town government. These tasks were assigned to newly created officials drawn from the ranks of lawyers, merchant families, and petty nobility (hidalgos). Like the "new men" who fulfilled a similar mission for the Tudor kings in England, such individuals owed everything to their royal patrons and could be counted upon for loyal service—unlike the traditionally unreliable and self-serving aristocrats of Castile's great noble houses. In matters of religion, Ferdinand may simply have accepted Isabella's demand that the alien element be purged from Castile (a concern that he did not share with regard to the Aragonese realms). It has also been suggested that they both submitted to popular hostility in Castile toward Muslims and Jews. In any event, the conquest of Granada in 1492 was immediately followed by an expulsion order directed against the kingdom's Jews, and initial promises of personal and religious liberty to the "Moors" were supplanted by a decree of banishment.

Militant Christianity had become a characteristic of crusading Castile and would envelop the whole of Spain as it unified. Ferdinand and Isabella were designated "the Catholic Kings" (los Reyes Católicos) by the pope in 1496, and the religious orthodoxy enforced through the Inquisition became state policy. Ferdinand was, of course, ready to exploit any advantage in religious affairs. He secured the revenues of the old crusading orders for the royal treasury, obtained the right to designate bishops and other high-ranking ecclesiastics, and integrated the Inquisition (established in 1478) into the civil administration. Nevertheless, for all his cynicism he was clearly impelled by popular fervor and what some have described as a Castilian fanaticism, shared by his wife and her subjects, to champion the faith against infidels. This identification between the Crown and Catholicism would be reinforced during the reigns of Isabella and Ferdinand's successors as Spain became the leader of the Counter-Reformation.

Almost incidental at first amidst the excitement of the final act at Granada was the departure of the Genoese navigator who had been promoting his concept of a transatlantic route to the trade treasures of Asia. Whether known as Cristoforo Colombo, Cristóbal Colón, or Christopher Columbus, he appears on the scene in 1492 as a minor player in the great events that were unfolding in the Spain of Ferdinand and Isabella. And for all his subsequent fame his establishment of the possibility of crossing the Atlantic to what turned out to be a new pair of continents rather than Asia remained a subordinate concern at the court of the Catholic Kings. Subsequent voyages of Columbus and others gradually created a sense of a New World that invited exploration and further discovery. But it remained jealously reserved to the Castilian queen and her subjects, even as the Aragonese response to France's invasion of Italy in 1494 drew Spain's attention firmly into European politics. Until there was treasure to be had from this new transatlantic territory, Ferdinand remained preoccupied with Mediterranean concerns and his subjects in Catalonia and Valencia were not particularly jealous of Isabella's vassals and their exclusive rights to venture into the Americas. Ultimately, to be sure, the divisions between the subjects of the Catholic Kings would be ended, and the Castilians would dominate both the European and overseas spheres of action. In the meantime, up to the 1540s the conquest of the New World would be left largely to adventurers and the private initiative of soldiers and priests. For all the delay this caused in creating a coherent Spanish colonial policy, it at least avoided many of the distractions of bureaucratic management.

Long before Columbus had received his belated commission to sail under the Castilian flag, Portugal had been pursuing its own route to the wealth of the "Indies." It had surely been unrealistic for a kingdom that occupied a mere corner of Iberia and had a population of no more than a million to aspire to a dominant role in the peninsula. Yet by the time the marriage of Isabella and Ferdinand brought an end to that particular dream, the House of Aviz was well advanced on an even more grandiose plan. Beginning in the late 14th century Portuguese seamen had ventured out into the near Atlantic to lay claim to Madeira and the Azores. Under the oversight of Prince Henrique (Henry) the Navigator—son, brother, and uncle of successive monarchs—voyages of exploration had been dispatched down the west coast of Africa. By the time of the prince's death, in 1460, the probing process had taken his captains far along on the quest for a route to Asia that would turn the southern tip of Africa and cross the Indian Ocean. On the way the

Portuguese had established their dominance over the Cape Verde Islands (while conceding the Canaries to Castile) and secured alliances with many African rulers. By 1485, while Columbus was still promoting his transatlantic route (he had solicited Portuguese support unsuccessfully before going to Castile), Bartolomeu Dias had reached and rounded the Cape of Good Hope, proving the feasibility of the Portuguese project. By 1498, while Columbus and his cohorts were extracting trivial returns from the off-shore islands of what they still thought was Asia, Vasco da Gama was leading a Portuguese trading fleet to the shores of India. Longer voyages and bolder trading adventures would soon follow. When the Portuguese announced the "discovery" of what would become Brazil in 1500 as an accidental by-product of their African voyages, it appeared almost as a mocking gesture directed at their old Castilian rivals. So wealthy had the Portuguese dynasty become that they could afford to leave this foothold in Spain's New World unexploited for the next 30 years.

Manuel I (reigned 1469–1521) was appropriately known as "the Fortunate." Presiding over Portugal's ever-expanding seaborne empire, he extended his own wealth and assured that of his successors as the global reach of his sailors and merchants extended his dynasty's fame. The gold of Africa, the spices of the Indies, the silks of East Asia flowed into Lisbon creating an affluent aristocracy and a flowering of culture. Nevertheless, Manuel understood that on the European scale of things Portugal could not stand as a great power alongside Spain. He sought cooperation rather than confrontation and successively married two daughters and a granddaughter of Ferdinand and Isabella. While he periodically yielded to pressure from his in-laws by, for example, following their lead on the expulsion of the Jews, his statecraft secured his interests overseas and the long-term stability of his kingdom. Several generations would pass before the extinction of Manuel's line would reveal how deeply dynastic diplomacy had undermined Portuguese independence.

HABSBURG SPAIN

In addition to the Portuguese marriages, two other daughters of the Catholic Kings had also married strategically. Catalina (Catherine of Aragon) wed the Prince of Wales and after his death his brother, who became Henry VIII of England, creating an alliance that ended when he repudiated her and took his country into the Reformation. Joanna, as the bride of Philip the Handsome, duke of Burgundy, became the ancestress of a new Spanish ruling house—the Habsburgs. Inheriting the Netherlands from his mother and heir to the Austrian lands of his father, Holy Roman Emperor Maximilian I, Philip linked Spain with a whole new range of European domains and commitments. After the death of Isabella the Catholic in 1504, he was briefly cosovereign of Castile with Joanna, as Philip I. On his death two years later, Castile passed to their eldest son, Charles I. Although Ferdinand was now theoretically only king of Aragon, Joanna's mental incapacity and the youth of his grandson (born in 1500 and still living in the Netherlands) left Ferdinand with effective control of the Castilian realm until his own death in 1516. As evidence of his increasing regard for Castilian pride, he arranged for the hitherto independent kingdom of Navarre to be attached to Castile rather than Aragon when he snatched it from French dominance in 1512. He continued to concentrate on intermittent warfare with France over Italian territory, securing the position of what was now effectively a united Spain as one of the three great centralized despotic monarchies dominating Renaissance Europe. In securing this position, Spain would thus become a contender in the struggle for mastery of the Continent for the next 200 years.

The adolescent Charles I made his first visit to Spain as an outsider, surrounded by foreign advisers and insensitive to regional traditions. Neither his Castilian nor his Aragonese subjects were particularly pleased with his desire to obtain as much of their money as possible in pursuit of his larger goals. Nor were they impressed when he secured the title of Holy Roman Emperor as Charles V upon Maximilian's death in 1519. Gradually, however, Spaniards warmed to this wide-ranging ruler, who fought the French in Italy, the Turks in the Mediterranean, and the Lutherans in Germany yet found time to cultivate their good-will and develop an appreciation of their culture. They willingly supplied men to wage his battles and began to refer to him gladly as "the emperor," taking pride in the fact that Spanish power was now being displayed everywhere in Europe. Their king was also king of Naples, Sicily, and Sardinia, duke of Milan and Burgundy, and bearer of a multitude of other titles. The Habsburg network of alliances and marriages extended from Portugal to Denmark and even for a few years included England again, while placing Charles V's brother Ferdinand upon the twin thrones of Hungary and Bohemia.

The grandeur of Spain's king-emperor was not confined to the Old World. Building on the preliminary work of Ferdinand and Isabella; Columbus, the pioneer of the Caribbean discoveries; Vasco Núñez de, Balboa, who discovered the Pacific Ocean; and all those other authors of empire, Charles V (the name by which he is generally known) consolidated Spanish rule in the Americas. Hernán Cortés conquered the Aztec Empire in Mexico and dispatched his subordinates to push its boundaries south through Central America and north into what would become the southwestern United States. As these deeds were redounding to the glory of Spain in the 1520s, Francisco Pizarro was planning a parallel conquest of the Inca realm in the Andes. During the 1530s Peru and its dependencies fell to a new cohort of conquistadores, while other adventurers pushed through Amanzonian jungles and probed the shores of the Río de la Plata (River Plate). By the 1540s Charles V was king of New Spain (in effect, everything north of Panama) and Peru (all of South America minus the Portuguese foothold in Brazil). Moreover, between 1519 and 1522 the ships of Fernando de Magallanes (Ferdinand Magellan, formerly a captain in the Portuguese service) crossed the Atlantic, rounded the southern tip of South America, boldly traversed the uncharted Pacific, planted the Spanish flag in the Philippine Islands (named after Charles's son) and engaged Portuguese forces in what is now Indonesia. The surviving ship and its handful of crew continued on across the Indian Ocean and up the African coast to complete the first circumnavigation of the globe. Although Magellan had been killed in the Philippines, he had secured the archipelago for his master, and by the Treaty of Saragossa (Zaragoza) in 1529 Portugal recognized this Spanish foothold in Asia.

Fifty years after the child of King Philip I had succeeded to the throne of Castile, the weary global monarch Charles V abdicated his multiple crowns and withdrew to the tranquillity of a Spanish monastery. Not all of his enterprises had been successful, and he left the management of the Habsburg concerns in central Europe and the Balkan perimeter to his brother as Holy Roman Emperor Ferdinand I. The Spanish Habsburg line and its vast dependencies would now be headed by Philip II, only son of Charles V, and a thoroughly Castilian king both in temperament and priorities. Proceeding methodically, Philip II confronted and crushed Spain's longtime rival, France, in 1559. It would be well into the next century before this rival could again dream of challenging Spain for the mastery of Europe. The alien challenge from Islam was next confronted. A Turkish defeat at the siege of Malta in 1565 and the death of the aggressive sultan Suleiman the Magnificent in the following year slowed the advance of Spain's Ottoman adversary in the Mediterranean. At the Battle of Lepanto in 1571 Spain's naval forces delivered what amounted to a death blow against the "infidel." Coming after the defeat of a rebellion in Aragon by crypto-Muslims who had been spared in earlier purges, the triumph at Lepanto elevated Philip II to the position of champion of Christendom. Even Protestant Europe applauded his victory.

But Philip was no respecter of Protestantism. He had already focused the attention of the Inquisition upon the extirpation of heresy. Founded in Castile in 1478 and soon extended to Aragon and then to all of the Spanish possessions, the Spanish Inquisition had diminished its early persecutions of Jewish and Muslim suspects in favor of vigilance against *"luteranos."* Employing a small army of police, judges, and jailers and relying on paid informers as well as the denunciations of "loyal Christians," it maintained a constant safeguarding of orthodoxy that was viewed abroad as a hallmark of Spanish political and religious identity. During the reign of Philip II the Inquisition became the centerpiece of the "Leyenda Negra" ("Black Legend") about the sinister and oppressive nature of Spanish society that shaped its image throughout the world for centuries to come. Although harassment of unorthodox thinkers—religious or secular—was common to all regimes, and although relatively few of the Inquisition's prisoners were subjected to torture or execution, Spain became known as the stronghold of intolerance. Descriptions of the *auto de fe*—the public burning of heretics—were a commonplace in anti-Spanish propaganda.

Other elements of the Leyenda Negra included portrayals of Philip as a gloomy misanthrope and his massive palace-monastery residence, El

Escorial, as the center of a spider web of international intrigue. He was seen as the implacable enemy of Christian reconciliation who had prevented the Council of Trent from instituting meaningful Catholic reforms. He was believed to be the true overlord of the Jesuit order (founded in 1540 by the Spaniard Ignatius of Loyola), which was thought to be a subversive force in all corners of Europe. His colonial administration was reported to be rigid, repressive, and insatiable for wealth extracted from the sufferings of the native peoples. Even the relatively casual enforcement of the Inquisition in Portugal and that country's notoriously careless management of its colonies were held up in positive contrast to the ruthless efficiency of the grim black-clad Spaniards.

Philip II would soon make the Counter-Reformation his principal project, but there was the matter of Portugal. By the third quarter of the 16th century Portugal's expansion overseas had attained dimensions vast enough to satisfy the greediest imperialist. Portugal's outposts included forts and trading settlements in West and East Africa, as well as the stronghold at what is now Capetown, the entrances to the Red Sea and the Persian Gulf, and ports in India. The Portuguese also dominated present-day Sri Lanka, Malaysia, and Indonesia, while having a trade monopoly with China based at Macao and Japan based at Nagasaki. Given the small size of Portugal's population (perhaps one-tenth of Spain's), all of these outposts amounted to a lightly held commercial empire rather than a secure overlordship.

The always-strained relationship between Spain and Portugal reached the ultimate crisis in 1580, after the extinction of the House of Aviz precipitated a Spanish invasion of the smaller country. With most of the Portuguese aristocracy supporting Habsburg claims that were based on marriage ties to the former rulers, a popular resistance was quickly crushed, and Portugal and its vast empire became a dynastic appendage of Spain. This integration of the Iberian states and their territories abroad would last from 1580 to 1640 and become known in Portuguese history as the "Sixty Years' Tyranny."

It was during the period of Spain's total control of the Iberian Peninsula that its power reached its apogee on the Continent. Philip's empire, like that of Britain's Victoria in the 19th century, had become one on which the Sun never set. In the latter part of his reign he became absorbed in the great enterprise of rolling back the Reformation and restoring the dominance of Catholicism, whose outreach was already being furthered by missionaries in Spanish and Portuguese America.

The champion of the Counter-Reformation, he was also the champion of Spanish mastery in Europe. Since the 1560s he had been fighting a rebellion in the Netherlands that was both a nationalistic resistance to Spanish repression of traditional rights and an assertion of Calvinist Protestantism. Spain would eventually split the Catholics of the southern provinces (modern Belgium) away from the Dutch Calvinists of the north. French Calvinists had been aiding the Dutch rebels and threatening to take over the weakened French monarchy, turning it into a serious threat to Spain once again. In this complex of political and religious antagonists, Philip saw Elizabeth of England as the ultimate enemy, who not only aided international anti-Catholicism but sponsored piratical raids in the Spanish Caribbean. Philip formed a grand design, which originally involved the replacement of Elizabeth by her captive cousin, Mary Queen of Scots. This would have resulted in a Catholic regime in England, Scotland, and Ireland under Spanish control. When Mary was executed, Philip decided to replace her with his own daughter, Isabella, and to combine the invasion of England with a decisive onslaught against the Dutch rebels and the capture of Paris by his Catholic allies, who would govern France in conformity with Spanish guidance. His plan centered on the so-called Invincible Armada, a Spanish-Portuguese fleet, supplemented by vessels from allied countries that would combine warships with transports carrying thousands of elite troops. After sweeping the English Channel clear of resistance, the Armada would discharge its invasion force to carry out the capture of the British Isles, while coordinated actions in Holland and France would achieve total victory. When launched in the summer of 1588, the Armada suffered a series of mischances and abandoned the invasion; the other segments of the plan were equally unsuccessful. Philip attempted to re-create his scheme but without success. He was obliged to accept the victory of his old enemy Henri de Bourbon, the Calvinist leader, as King Henry IV of France (albeit after conversion to Catholicism) in 1595. Three years later, on his deathbed, the monarch whom Spaniards called "the Prudent King" swore his son, about to become Philip III, to carry on the fight against the English and the Dutch.

Philip II, taciturn, conscientious, and hard working, had been driven throughout his reign by a sense of historical mission. It is said that upon gazing at a portrait of Ferdinand the Catholic, Philip murmured, "We owe it all to him." Certainly he was committed to preserving all that Charles V had achieved and building an even greater Spanish empire upon the existing foundations. Yet he had overstrained the nation's resources and provided only a weak heir to the throne. Even as Renaissance Spain reached its peak of glory, the first signs of decay were beginning to appear.

THE DECLINE AND FALL OF HABSBURG SPAIN

Spain's war with England had sunk to such a level of futility by 1598 as to appear pointless to many of Philip III's senior councillors. But two developments in 1599 seemed to offer both provocation and an opportunity that the prowar party at the Spanish Court could exploit. Damaging English raids on Spanish territory demanded revenge, and English rejection of peace proposals from the Irish rebels offered a means of inflicting it. Philip II had given intermittent support to a series of Irish opponents of the Elizabethan conquest as far back as the 1570s. A new, formidable leader had emerged in Ireland when Hugh O'Neill, earl of Tyrone, launched an insurrection in 1595 and inflicted a series of startling defeats upon the English. When O'Neill's offer of accommodation in return for the restoration of confiscated property, semi-autonomy for his country, and freedom of religion for Catholics was rebuffed by Elizabeth, he and his fellow lords promised to recognize Philip III as king of Ireland if Spain would aid in the war of liberation. Attracted by the idea of afflicting Elizabeth in the same way she had vexed his father by aiding the Dutch rebels, yet fearful of involvement in such a precarious cause, Philip hesitated. Spanish lay and clerical militants insisted that he must go to the aid of this Catholic population isolated among the Protestants of northern Europe. English Jesuits, eager to end their exile on the Continent, assured him that Ireland would yield him an easy victory and a stepping stone to the conquest of England. Persuaded at last, Philip committed his troops, and in the summer of 1601 Don Juan del Águila and a force of some 5,000 men seized the port of Kinsale on the southeastern coast of Ireland and attempted a conjunction with the rebels. The opportunity was lost, however. The Irish were slow to move, and the English, all too quick. Besieged in Kinsale, del Águila attempted to break out in December but was forced to withdraw when Tyrone's army sustained a reverse and retreated back to its stronghold in the north. After the surrender of the Irish and the death of Elizabeth in 1603, her successor, James I, made an offer of peace that Philip was quick to accept. For nearly 50 years after the 1604 peace treaty, Spain and England continued to avoid full-scale war, despite periodic tensions. The religious question remained alive, for James I had soon confiscated the lands of Tyrone and the other Irish leaders, flooding Ulster with Protestant settlers and guaranteeing perpetual strife in Ireland. Irish Catholic refugees continued to seek shelter in Spain, providing a useful source of mercenaries for that country and easing the conscience of the Spaniards, who would provide sanctuary if not liberation for their coreligionists.

The war in the Netherlands was an even more painful issue for Philip III. His father had sworn never to reign over heretics, thus vowing a permanent conflict with the Calvinists who were trying to snatch his Burgundian heritage away from him. Although the old king had made headway in the southern provinces by the time of his death, the Dutch Calvinists of the north not only continued to challenge Spanish authority but began harassing the sea-lanes and threatening colonial possessions of both Spain and Portugal. Although Philip III continued operations against the Dutch, his generals sustained a series of defeats, and his administrators in the Netherlands began pressing for a cease-fire in order to renew Spanish strength and consider alternative approaches. Finally in 1609 a 12-years' truce was agreed upon, to the indignation of the war party and the relief of those who insisted that Spain needed time to put her internal affairs in order.

Thus, with the English and Dutch enemies no longer in the field and the worrisome revival of France interrupted by the death of Henry IV in 1610, Philip III found himself presiding over a nation at peace. To be sure Spain had achieved no victories; moreover there were still skirmishes going on in northern Italy under the direction of local commanders, and diplomatic initiatives against the Ottoman Empire, including attempts to incite the shah of Persia to attack the sultan. Philip III was now the most powerful monarch in the world, presiding over a vast empire, won by force during the reigns of his grandfather and father and now subject to a Pax Hispanica such as they had never been able to impose. The last half of his reign offered him an opportunity to focus his attention on desperately needed internal reforms.

An outbreak of the plague in Castile in 1599 and a steady immigration to the colonies diminished the population during the first years of Philip's reign, a situation exacerbated by the expulsion of the Moriscos between 1609 and 1614. These "new Christians" were the survivors of two earlier purges of Spain's Islamic elements, in the reigns of Ferdinand and Isabella and Philip II, respectively. Avowedly Catholic, the Moriscos were still regarded in the early 17th century as "the enemy within." They were generally believed to adhere secretly to Islam and to regard the Ottoman sultan as their true sovereign. Although many of them were laborers, mule drivers, and small craftsmen, their sheer numbers (some 250,000 scattered across Castile and Aragon in a total population of 7 million) represented not merely a political danger but a potential economic loss. Nevertheless, public opinion, urged on by the clergy, demanded their expulsion. As soon as the fighting in the Netherlands was over, a royal decree was promulgated ordering all those of Muslim descent to depart from the peninsula. In a process that stretched over five years, Spain was ethnically cleansed, despite pleas by the Moriscos for mercy and offers of cash payments to secure exemptions or at least deferments. While some old Christians argued in their favor, the general will of the people was reflected in the king's orders. He remained unmoved by stories of exiled families being slain upon their arrival in North Africa because they refused to abjure Christianity, and he seemed equally indifferent to the departure of so many productive subjects, just as his predecessors had been by the expulsion of the Jews and earlier contingents of Muslims. Philip, devout and totally under the influence of an ardent clerical elite, took pride in ruling a now completely Catholic state.

A depleted population was merely one dimension of Spain's problems. Its agriculture was minimally productive, its once-great pastoral activity (reflected in the great herds of sheep moving annually across the Castilian plains) was much diminished, and its urban manufactures were strangled by an archaic guild system. Dependent on foreign imports, encumbered by foreign debt, and constricted by a large yet unequal tax burden, the country was increasingly compared to the biblical "whited sepulchre," externally splendid but inwardly filled with "rottenness and corruption." The 32 families of grandees and the hundred or so lesser nobles, who owned much of the land, were exempt from taxes. So, too, in large part, were the hidalgos, who numbered in the thousands. Many others enjoyed tax exemption, including a multitude of clergy and a swarm of hangers-on who benefited from clerical patronage. The highways in the rural areas and the crowded streets of the towns teemed with uprooted peasants, vagabonds, bandits, and those picturesque but unproductive figures known as picaros, who lived by their wits and mingled with smugglers, swindlers, and other petty criminals. The weight of taxation fell upon honest folk: the tradesmen, farmers, and laborers who were stripped of all but a bare living in order to fund the idleness of the rest and the fantastic extravagance of a royal court that was maintained on an imperial scale, although the revenues of the empire were pledged for decades in advance to foreign bankers.

To foreigners, Spain appeared to be a country of insane contrasts, where lords and bishops lived in regal state while beggars lived off the scraps they discarded. It seemed a nation of parasites, where everyone who possessed credentials or connections (such as the graduates of the 32 universities producing an unending stream of useless scholars) sought employment at court or council chamber. It was not only outsiders who recoiled from the spectacle. One commentator declared that Spain had become "a republic of the bewitched, living outside the natural order of things." It seemed to some observers that Don Quijote, pursuing his chivalric fantasies amidst the mundane realities and brutalities of the present, symbolized the exalted fantasies of the country's ruling class. Thoughtful Spaniards spent these years in an agony of introspection. Like many who would come after them, they looked back from a period of decline and disarray at a past full of splendid and noble achievements and asked how their country had come to the degradation it was now undergoing. What could be done to redeem these errors? Could Spain, while it still possessed the outward characteristics of majesty, put its affairs in order? Scores of writers published books and pamphlets recommending reforms ranging from equalization of taxes or government subsidies to promote trade and industry to massive projects that would make the rivers navigable into the interior or reorganize the system of land tenure. Some even ventured to suggest that the clergy ought to be transformed in a more productive class or that the Court should return to the austerity of medieval living. Few of these ideas received more than passing attention, nor were most of them within the bounds of practicability even had they found patronage at a sufficiently high level of government. The regime's exertions were limited to debasing the currency and flirting yet again with bankruptcy in order to maintain its imperial facade.

The flaws of 17th-century Spain were numerous. But in an absolute monarchy the most dangerous flaw of all was the absence of royal capacity to rule. In his last days Philip II is reported to have lamented to a trusted adviser that his heir seemed destined not to govern but to be governed. Successor to a line of autocratic and ferociously energetic kings, whose constant attention had been devoted to the business of kingship, Philip III totally lacked the character and fortitude of his ancestors. His father had attempted to train him in the management of the realm and the principles of statecraft, but the 20-year-old prince who succeeded the Prudent King was never more than an aimless, weak-spirited sovereign. He possessed the virtues of a faithful husband and a kind father, sober and devout. He was amiable enough by all accounts, though lacking much awareness of life outside the Court. Such a man was, indeed, fated to be governed rather than to govern. A strong chief minister might have remedied his deficiencies or supplied those qualities lacking in the monarch. Unfortunately, Philip chose for his adviser the duke of Lerma, a Valencian aristocrat whose weakness of character and lack of resolve matched those of his patron. Like the king, Lerma preferred to avoid difficulties and to put off decisions. Instead of being governed by the king, he allowed himself to be dominated and even bullied by the Castilian grandees whose great estates constituted the political and economic stronghold of the kingdom. Under such leadership, all was arranged to perpetuate a situation that favored the elite, and nothing could be undertaken by way of reform that threatened the status quo. The *cortes* of Castile, once capable of influencing royal decisions, were routinely ignored, while the ancient realms of Aragon, Valencia, and Catalonia (which still preserved certain rights even after the harsh rule of Philip II) were unable to influence events. An outsider himself in Castile, Lerma spent the greater part of the reign placating his Castilian colleagues and shielding his royal master from disturbing truths. Little changed after Lerma was finally cast out of office, for the king had become accustomed to confiding the affairs of state to others. In his last months on the throne he dedicated himself not to the rehabilitation of Spain, but to the renewal of war in the Netherlands (upon the expiration of the truce) and involvement in the politico-religious adventures of his Austrian Habsburg kinsmen who had launched a war against the German Protestant princes. Even a belated state visit to Portugal, long disillusioned with Spanish overlordship, was mishandled. Philip antagonized many of the key figures in his western realm, preparing the way for the secession that lay ahead. On the way home from this hapless expedition he fell ill. Still a comparatively young man, he sensed that he would not recover. But even in the classic deathbed advice to his heir, Philip III failed to offer more than platitudes, the more sensible of which would be ignored as soon as he was gone. Thus ended the reign of Philip III, who was not truly a failure, for he had attempted virtually nothing.

The signs of decay and disarray, already evident during the reign of Philip III, became desperately clear as Philip IV began his long tenure. More aggressive and self-confident than his father, he was little more clear headed and competent, with the result that the business of government was soon confided to the management of another favorite. This minister, the count of Olivares, was made of stronger stuff than Lerma, for he was both intelligent and energetic. Furthermore, as a high-ranking nobleman of Andalusia, he had no fear of the Castilian aristocrats and did not avoid confrontations with them as had his Valencian predecessor. Unfortunately both Olivares and the king shared an unrealistic view of Spain's greatness in the world and of its ability to project power. Neither monarch nor minister ever fully understood the limitations imposed upon Spain by its internal political and economic weakness. In true Castilian fashion they relied on miracles to carry the day in a succession of crises that by any rational standard should have been avoided or dealt with through negotiation and compromise. Both men, immortalized in numerous paintings by Diego Velázquez, display an air of arrogant bravado that came to be thought of throughout the rest of Europe as typical of Spaniards. The grim, silent, somewhat sinister but undoubtedly efficient aura projected by Philip II had given way to a far less impressive tendency to threaten and bluster.

Although freedom from the distractions of war was what his county most needed, the late king had permitted Spain to become involved in renewed conflict with the Dutch Republic and in the adjacent territory of the Holy Roman Empire. Philip IV lacked the good sense to extricate himself from these commitments and, indeed, became even more entangled in them during the 1630s. Olivares, recognizing the damage done by political corruption and administrative extravagance under Lerma, had made a sincere effort to implement reforms during the first five years of his ministry. A flurry of decrees abolished this office, forbade that practice, and, in general, conveyed an impression of a new broom sweeping clean. Although he succeeded in replacing the power of the archaic council system by creating a series of committees (juntas) under his personal supervision to manage various aspects of government business, most of his efforts at reform failed. Lacking the follow-up necessary to prevent backsliding, the decrees were allowed to become almost dead letters, and the offenders soon returned to the corrupt practices of the past. By 1626 Olivares was concentrating on new, grander schemes of rescuing Spain from its difficulties. Inevitably these involved ingenious methods of raising taxes to cover the ever-increasing cost of war. But Olivares also grasped the underlying reality that Spain had never attained complete unity.

In a memorandum addressed to Philip in 1626 Olivares warned his master that he would never succeed in his purposes unless he truly became king of Spain, rather than king of Aragon, prince of Catalonia, king of Portugal, Naples, and the rest. While all of these realms had been brought under Castilian overlordship during the previous century, they had, in fact, separate constitutional arrangements, administrative structures, fiscal peculiarities, and, perhaps most serious of all, a strong sense of their own traditional identities. Olivares maintained that unless the tensions between the Castilian center and the other lands of which Philip was overlord could be assuaged, the Spanish Empire could not be made to work as a coherent whole. There is much truth to this perception, and Olivares was not the first to arrive at it. While the other two centralized despotic monarchies that emerged during the Renaissance—France and England—also suffered from problems of consolidation and restlessness in their outlying territories, Spain's problems in this regard were far more serious and persistent. Regionalism within Spain herself—even after the imperial realms had been lost—would remain a grave problem for centuries to come. By tackling this problem head on Olivares demonstrated both his intelligence and his recklessness. His attempt to reorganize the Spanish Empire in wartime was simply more than could be achieved. The centerpiece of his plan was an Unión de Armas (Union of Arms) intended to create a unified armed force drawn from all of Philip IV's military resources. A total of 140,000 men was envisioned, with specified contingents ranging from 44,000 from Castile and the Americas to 6,000 from the Duchy of Milan. These contingents were to be made available on call from each of the dozen realms that made up the empire and would be deployed to any area that required reinforcements. Unlike many of his earlier reforms, which were negated by passive noncompliance, Olivares's concept of an imperial army was thwarted by outright refusals, springing from regional legislatures and interest groups ranging from merchants to peasants. In the end Spain's military commitments continued to be borne disproportionately by Castile.

The situation worsened after 1635, when Spain and France began to confront each other directly on the battlefields of northern Europe. France had previously played a role in the great war between the Austrian Habsburgs and their Protestant enemies by subsidizing German and Scandinavian armies. Now the duc de Richelieu and Olivares became direct antagonists, and the Spanish minister found himself outclassed by the French cardinal who subordinated religious zeal to national advantage. Not only did Richelieu commit French troops on the major battlefields, he intensified political intrigue and incitement among Philip's vassals. Rebellions against the king in Portugal (1637) and Catalonia (1639) were put down, but both regions launched formidable insurrections in 1640, which they were able to sustain with French aid. The Catalans were not finally subdued until 1652. The Portuguese, proclaiming the end of the dynastic union with Spain, continued their independence war until 1668, when Madrid formally recognized their sovereign status. A relatively short-lived revolt in the kingdom of Naples was crushed in the mid-1640s, though not without diversion of badly needed units from other areas. In the meantime the northern war continued to go badly as Spain's navy sustained a major defeat off the Dutch coast in 1639, and the once-invincible Tercios (infantry units) were beaten by the French at Rocroi in 1643. In that year the aristocratic enemies of Olivares succeeded in persuading the king to "retire" the minister on the grounds of declining health. Although Olivares was succeeded as the king's chief councillor by his nephew, Luis de Haro, his broad vision and bold designs soon faded from the minds and hearts of the Spaniards. In 1648, as a by-product of the negotiations that ended the Thirty Years' War, the independence of the Dutch Republic was recognized. For another 11 years Philip continued the struggle against France, until, his resources exhausted, he concluded peace in 1659 (exactly one century after his grandfather had triumphed over France). Not only did he cede Cerdagne and Rousillon on the Pyrenean frontier, he agreed to give his daughter María Teresa in marriage to the young French monarch, Louis XIV, as a pledge of dynastic reconciliation.

As the fortunes of the dynasty withered, so did the actual Spanish branch of the House of Habsburg. By the end of the war with France Philip IV had no surviving sons. A new marriage, to an Austrian kinswoman, brought him the male heir he desired, a sickly child born in 1661. Four years later the boy succeeded his vexed and troubled father under the name of Charles II. Throughout the remaining 35 years of his life this monarch would suffer from a multitude of physical and mental illnesses, his life frequently in jeopardy and the future of his country perpetually in doubt. Until he was 14 his mother served as regent, assisted by her German father confessor, whose skills in statecraft were scarcely more developed than those of the queen mother. Declared of age at 14, Charles relied heavily upon the advice of others, pulled this way and that by rival factions in the Court. Although France had fought another two brief wars with Spain over territory in the Low Countries claimed by Louis XIV on behalf of his Spanish wife, it was eventually agreed that Charles II would marry a French princess. The bride soon died, allegedly poisoned by Austrian agents, and a successor was chosen from that country which now moved into the ascendancy at Madrid. Childless in both of his marriages, the morose and confused king wandered aimlessly about the palace when he was not confined to bed by one of his frequent illnesses. On his better days he sought to take counsel from his advisers and to understand the complexities of the international maneuvers that drew Spain into yet another war with France between 1688 and 1697. By now the country was no longer playing a leading role in European affairs but merely functioning as a subservient ally to others.

The contending European monarchs concluded the Nine Years' War in 1697 largely in order to focus on the fate of the moribund Charles II and his much decayed empire. Although still a vast complex of far-flung territories, the inheritance passed on from Philip II was no longer capable of mobilizing its resources to determine its own destiny. Two successive partition treaties (in 1697 and 1699) in effect divided the spoils among the major European political players, with the kingship of Spain itself designated for Archduke Karl of Austria. In response to the insults and humiliations that were heaped upon him, the now-dying Charles II roused himself in a last gasp of indignation and pride to dictate a will that left all of Spain's territories in Europe, Africa, Asia, and America to his great-nephew Philippe, duke of Anjou (the grandson of Louis XIV and the Infanta María Teresa). The last king of Spain's Habsburg monarchy died in November 1700, amidst attempts to exorcise demons and accusations by the Inquisition that renegade members of the clergy were trying to seize control of the royal sickroom. The sad end of the man whom his pitying subjects called "Charles the Bewitched" seemed all too tragic a metaphor for the fate of a country that had once sought to rule the globe and dictate the terms upon which Christianity would survive. Now Spain was about to become a prey of her oldest and most bitter enemies.

PORTUGAL REGAINS ITS INDEPENDENCE

When Portugal rose against the Spanish overlordship in 1640, seeking to end 60 years of tyranny, the people could scarcely have imagined that it would take them 28 years of struggle to attain their liberation. It would, indeed, be a people's war, for the impetus toward independence came from the lower classes in 1640, just as the rank and file had resisted Philip II's initial occupation. The nobles, higher clergy, and merchant elite had welcomed the union then and only gradually moved into a posture of antagonism. Many aristocrats and prelates, as well as the Portuguese Inquisition, remained loyal to Spain well into the 1650s, even after other segments of the upper class followed the popular lead. The decisive commitment came from the duke of Bragança, a descendant of Portugal's medieval kings. His family had originally acknowledged Philip II and were ostentatiously loyal in Philip III's day. But when Duke João permitted himself to be proclaimed King John IV in 1640, he became the rallying point of the insurrection and remained its leader for the next 16 years. He projected the image of the people's choice, by accepting the acclamation of the *cortes* with the stipulations that power came from God to the people and through them to the king and that the king was answerable to the nation and might legitimately be removed if he failed to govern in the national interest. While the overseas territories quickly rallied to John, the independence fight was a bitter one on the Iberian Peninsula, and the military weakness of a country with a population of only 2 million contending against an enemy three times its size resulted in a series of near-desperate moments. At one point, the Portuguese government considered evacuating Lisbon and carrying on the fight from Brazil. Eventually, however, the declining strength of Spain and assistance given, however intermittently, by Spain's antagonists tipped the balance.

By the time formal recognition of Portuguese independence was gained in 1668, both Philip IV and John IV were dead, the former having been succeeded by the feeble Charles II, and the latter, by the mentally defective Afonso VI. Each country pursued a policy of survival and recovery under regencies. In the case of Portugal the rule of the queen mother was terminated in favor of a ministerial government that managed to keep the unbalanced young king in check while seeking to restore political and economic order. This was not an easy task, for even the supposed benefit of marrying the Princess Catalina to King Charles II of England was largely illusory, and the goodwill of France was always unreliable. The Dutch, who had become Portugal's enemy when it was linked to Spain, agreed to a settlement in Europe once that link no longer existed but persisted in pursuing their seizure of Portuguese territory overseas. The situation improved when in 1668 the king's brother, Prince Pedro, replaced the incompetent monarch who was confined in the Azores until his death in 1683. First as regent, recognized by the *cortes,* and then as King Peter II, the new ruler and his chief ministers settled the outstanding international issues and presided over a period of stability much needed by their country.

Unlike Spain, whose status was declining into that of an international victim, Portugal spent the closing years of the 17th century on a rising trajectory of enhanced prestige and growing prosperity. It avoided any further military or diplomatic entanglements and maintained domestic tranquillity and social harmony. Portugal had suffered the loss of most of its empire in Asia because of its affiliation with Spain (in contrast to Spain, which had given up only Jamaica and the western part of Hispaniola). Even in the colonial sphere, however, Portugal was about to experience a happy reversal of fortune, for the turn of the century saw the discovery of gold and diamond deposits in Brazil that led to a huge influx of wealth and a new age of grandeur during the early 1700s.

SPANISH AND PORTUGUESE CULTURE IN THE GOLDEN AGE

Between 1500 and 1700 Spain and Portugal had achieved a level of fame and fortune without parallel in the Western world since the fall of the Roman Empire. In the centuries to come they would look back upon this, their own imperial epoch, as their time of greatest achievement. This was particularly true for Spain, which became the admiration and model of all Europe. By the 18th century, however, the South American mines might still, on occasion, yield treasure trove, but in a larger sense the Golden Age of Iberia (Siglo de Oro) was over.

Even today Spaniards unhesitatingly proclaim Miguel de Cervantes, creator of the immortal Don Quixote, their greatest literary figure. Cervantes was but one of a galaxy of literary geniuses that included Mateo Alemán, master of the picaresque genre; the Renaissance poets Juan Boscán and Garcilaso de la Vega; the baroque poets Luis de Góngora and Francisco de Quevedo; and the mystically oriented Juan de la Cruz (St. John of the Cross), Teresa de Ávila (St. Teresa), and Luis de León. Drama, too, flourished with special glory in the 17th century in the work of Lope de Vega, Pedro Calderón de la Barca, and Tirso de Molina (who gave the world that eternal archetype, Don Juan). Among Europe's greatest painters of the 1600s were El Greco, Velázquez, Bartolomé Murillo, and Francisco de Zurbarán. Portugal enjoyed a flowering of its distinctive culture in the 1500s, when painters such as Nuno Gonçalves and the great poet-historian of exploration and adventure Luis de Camões gave luster to their nation before the Spanish annexation and the protracted war of liberation diverted the national creative energies. Many Iberian artists and writers in the generations to come would tacitly accept the judgment of other Europeans that the great days were over. They felt themselves to be pygmies standing on the shoulders of giants. For others, however, the challenge to reclaim lost laurels would inspire distinguished achievements.

SPAIN AND PORTUGAL IN THE EIGHTEENTH CENTURY

At the beginning of the 18th century Spain appeared to have reached its nadir. The extinction of the Habsburg dynasty after a long period of declining political and military strength left their inheritance prey to the ambition of Europe's major powers. There was a grave question as to whether Spain could ever again aspire to that title for itself. And yet Spain would make a remarkable recovery, preserve its colonial empire, and experience a significant degree of long-needed reform. By the end of the century it would be poised for genuine recovery. And then, a new series of misfortunes would overtake the nation.

Portugal, too, began the 18th century on an upward path of stable government, increased domestic prosperity, and enhanced colonial revenue. It would also enjoy a period of enlightened reform by mid-century. Yet like Spain, Portugal would end the century overwhelmed by unresolved weaknesses and unforeseeable external forces.

THE EARLY BOURBON REGIME IN SPAIN

The War of the Spanish Succession (1701–14) was the first of a series of international squabbles (Polish Succession, Austrian Succession, even Bavarian Succession) that would preoccupy the European states during the first three quarters of the century as they snatched, like a flock of vultures, at whatever wounded prey offered itself to their greedy onslaught. The Austrian Habsburg claimant, Archduke Karl, backed by England, the Dutch Republic, and lesser allies, sought to overturn the will of Charles II and secure the whole of the Spanish Empire. Although much of the fighting took place in distant parts of Europe, or even overseas, there was periodic warfare in Spain itself, with France supporting the "rightful" claimant, Louis XIV's grandson the duke of Anjou, now known as Philip V. Although most Spaniards rallied to the Bourbon prince, the Catalans backed the Austrian archduke. For a time Karl held Barcelona and several other eastern cities. Portugal intervened to stir up trouble for its old persecutors in Madrid but failed to achieve any permanent benefit. More significant, England captured Gibraltar in 1704 and turned this fortress at the entrance of the Mediterranean into a stronghold that it would retain for the next 300 years. As early as 1711, however, the British and Dutch were becoming weary of their exertions on behalf of the archduke, and by 1713 they had negotiated a separate peace with the Bourbons, to which the abandoned Austrians had to give reluctant agreement a year later. By the Treaties of Utrecht and Rastadt Philip V was recognized as king of Spain (including Catalonia, but not Gibraltar) and the colonies in America, Africa, and Asia. The Austrians obtained the southern Netherlands (Belgium) and the Italian realms, while further concessions were made to other interested parties.

Far from being reduced to a mere ruin, as some were already anticipating in 1700, Spain was, in a sense, invigorated by the War of the Spanish Succession. Philip had proved himself an energetic and brave leader in defense of his new home, restoring a sense of national pride and fighting will that had been sapped in the closing decades of the previous century. Moreover, the loss of European dependencies actually freed Spain of encumbrances that had become more trouble than they were worth. In a practical calculation, as distinguished from one of mere prestige, Spain was better off without these relics of Renaissance expansion. Once peace had been restored Philip was free to devote himself to the introduction of salutary reforms, many of them modeled on administrative and economic arrangements that had been introduced into France by his grandfather's able advisers. A number of French and other foreign officials undertook to revivify the Spanish state, making more progress than Olivares, native son though he was, had been able to achieve a hundred years earlier. Philip circumvented the old system of councils, creating secretaries of state and controllers of finance who functioned according to the modern system of ministerial responsibility for particular functions of government. Jean Orry, Giulio Alberoni, and Jan Ripperda, though holding office only briefly, went far beyond the accomplishments of the traditional *privado* (confidential political adviser). The French financier Jean Orry, as early as 1702 provided a complete plan for the fiscal and administrative reorganization of Spain; Giulio Alberoni, a native of Parma, directed Spanish foreign policy in 1717–18; and the Netherlander Jan Ripperda was given direction of military, naval, and financial affairs during the early 1720s.

Unfortunately for the progressive trends initiated under the first Bourbon king of Spain, Philip soon allowed himself to become distracted by his desire to meddle in the affairs of France. Despite the fact that the two countries were pledged to remain separate, Philip sought the regency when his young kinsman, Louis XV, succeeded "the Sun King" in 1715. Even after these pretensions had been abandoned, Philip was subjected to the Italian ambitions of his wife, Elizabeth Farnese. This formidable stateswoman calculated that Spain would surely go to her husband's sons by his first marriage and therefore set herself, over the course of more than 20 years, to secure prizes for her own two children. As the sister of the last of the Farnese dynasty in Parma, she envisioned a throne in northern Italy for one son and a domain in Naples for the other. By the time Philip V died in 1746 she had succeeded in both ambitions, although at the price of involving Spain in several unnecessary wars. These subsidiary Bourbon monarchies—the kingdom of Naples ruled by Charles and the Duchy of Parma ruled by Philip—were technically not Spanish possessions, but they did something to repair the humiliation sustained in Italy during the War of the Spanish Succession.

In the meantime King Philip V had gone through several periods of depression and recovery and actually abdicated in 1724 in favor of his eldest son, who became Louis I. This virtually forgotten Spanish monarch occupied the throne only six months before his death, by which time his father had grown weary of retirement and resumed his reign for another 22 years. Although probably not as severely unbalanced as contemporary rumor suggested, Philip V was certainly far less effective in his later years than he had been in his youth. The early impetus for reform had petered out in the distractions of foreign adventurism and the all-too-familiar reluctance of entrenched interest groups to cooperate in the reduction of their own power.

The following monarch, Ferdinand VI, inherited some of his father's instability and if left to himself would probably have succumbed to a natural preference for inertia. Spain was fortunate, however, in securing the service of a new crop of reform-minded officials who pushed and pulled the king along the path of progress. Undoubtedly the most important of the institutions created during the reign of Ferdinand VI was the position of *intendente* (intendant). Originating in France, this was a title bestowed upon professional administrators, usually lawyers by training. Their task essentially was to manage a wide variety of financial, logistical, and infrastructural matters within a designated jurisdiction. They became the pragmatic men of affairs who held the real responsibility for running the Spanish provinces at home and overseas, while civil or military governors fulfilled the ceremonial positions that were traditionally accorded to nobles on the basis of birth rather than competence. The Bourbon Reforms, which had begun with many stops and starts during the reign of Philip V and had continued more promisingly during that of Ferdinand VI, came to a full flower after the latter's death in 1759.

Childless, Ferdinand was succeeded by his half brother as Charles III. For more than 20 years this serious and conscientious sovereign had been learning his trade and promoting his ideas on the Italian peninsula, first in Parma, which he eventually turned over to his brother, Philip, and then as king of Naples. He seems to have been happy during this prolonged absence from Spain and to have enjoyed the affection of his Neapolitan subjects. But he had long anticipated succeeding to the Spanish throne and had developed ideas he wanted to implement there. When he arrived at Madrid he brought with him not only his elder son, who would eventually become Charles IV (while leaving the next son, Ferdinand, to carry on a separate line of Bourbons in Naples), but a group of Italian administrators, including Bernardo Tanucci and, most famously, the marquis of Squillace. Unfortunately, his choice of helpers got the new regime off on the wrong foot. Squillace, or Esquilache as the Spaniards called him, soon aroused opposition by his high-handed decrees that trampled on Spanish customs and long-established, if questionable, practices. The ultimate confrontation came over the somewhat absurd issue of the broad-brimmed slouch hats and enveloping cloaks favored by many citizens of Madrid. These, Esquilache decided, could be used to conceal identities and facilitate illicit activities. Spaniards might, up to a point, endure higher taxes, but they would not be deprived of their preferred garments. Riots broke out in Madrid and spread to other towns. Conservative factions among the nobility and the clergy were rumored to be inciting the malcontents in order to challenge the broader policy changes that the king was thought to be contemplating. Shaken by the vehemence and rapid growth of these riotous outbreaks, Charles removed his Italian advisers and made conciliatory gestures to popular protests. Once he had recovered from the immediate crisis, however, he resolved to act with consistent firmness and to pay particular attention to the troublemaking proclivities of the privileged classes.

CHARLES III AND ENLIGHTENED DESPOTISM

Charles III was no intellectual, yet he shared the commitment of many of his brother and sister rulers to the practical benefits of modernization and efficiency. While not a student of the Enlightenment, he was prepared to employ enlightened despotism. Devout, although not to the extreme lengths of some of his predecessors, he was prepared to curb what he regarded as the excessive power and tendency to meddle in the business of government displayed by some of the clergy. Among the earliest targets of his housecleaning were the Jesuits who had been implicated in the attacks on his ministers. By 1767 he had expelled them from Spain and all her dominions, and a few years later he joined together with other Catholic monarchs who resented the intrigues of the Society of Jesus to bring about its dissolution. Thus the most formidable of modern Catholic religious orders, founded by a Spaniard and long identified in a special way with Spain, was the victim of Bourbon authoritarianism and jealousy, not to be reestablished until 1814.

Charles III also crushed the power of the Spanish Inquisition, guaranteeing its subservience to the state, a subordinate role that had been laid down at its foundation in the 15th century but sometimes evaded in more recent generations. In addition, the king tightened his government's control on the Spanish hierarchy so as to make the bishops and priests of the Spanish church more reliable instruments of state power.

Addressing the long-neglected internal economy of Spain, Charles III undertook measures to develop domestic industry, import new techniques and technology in agriculture, and exploit the country's mineral resources. Particularly in this last sphere, the king drew upon the expertise of mining specialists from northern Europe and mineralogists who could assess Spain's hidden wealth. Local administrators were encouraged to work for the development of trade and commerce and to apply incentives to overcome apathy.

The program of reform was extended to Spain's American colonies. Rationalization of territorial boundaries and jurisdiction led to the creation of two new viceroyalties in South America, in the areas of modern-day Venezuela and Argentina. These and other modifications of boundaries laid down during the first decades of colonization reduced the burdens of overextended central administrators and aided the development of new projects on what had hitherto been the outer fringes of the Viceroyalty of Peru. Periodic border wars with the Portuguese over the region known as Colonia were ended (at least for a time), leaving an area between Brazil and the Buenos Aires Province that would ultimately become Uruguay. Transatlantic trade was reorganized, easing the grip of Spanish metropolitan bankers and merchants over colonial shipping. These experiments in greater flexibility and responsibility came too late, however, to satisfy the long-accumulated grievances of the Creoles. Particularly among South American businessmen and professionals, the centuries of alternating repression and neglect had weakened ties of loyalty to the mother country. While great landowners and the administrators who came over from Spain for a few years' service clung to the king and accepted whatever changes he decreed, a spirit of discontent was already on the rise at the middle level of colonial society. When, in the coming generation, it moved downward and outward among the masses, the force of rebellion would prove too strong to resist.

In shaping and implementing his domestic reforms Charles III had invaluable help from the conde de Aranda and the conde de Floridablanca, who were with him during most of his reign. Regrettably neither the king nor his ministers could accept the need for a strong focus on progressive developments in Spain and her colonies, even at the expense of a policy that amounted to relative isolation in Europe. Charles III had allowed himself to be drawn into the Seven Years' War (1756–63). His shrewd minister of foreign affairs, Richard Wall, advocated (despite his Irish ancestry) a pro-British position in the diplomatic maneuvers of the period, but the king instead renewed the French alliance. As a result, at the end of the war Spain lost Florida and the Balearic island of Minorca, a valuable naval base close to Spain. It did take custody of Louisiana when the defeated French surrendered the rest of North America to Britain, but this would not prove of much long-term advantage. After Wall retired in 1763, there was little incentive for a rapprochement with London, and Spain was soon drawn into French schemes for a new Bourbon family compact that would pay back the British for their previous triumph. The opportunity came during the American Revolution when France gave decisive assistance to the rebels. Spain bided its time until 1779, then began naval operations in the Caribbean and mounted a siege of Gibraltar. Although the "Rock" remained unconquered, Spanish troops triumphed at Pensacola. At the peace settlement of 1783, Spain regained Florida.

Charles III died in 1788, five years after the conclusion of his intervention against Britain. There might have been time in these years to concentrate his government's attention on firm establishment of progressive reforms at home and, above all, on conciliation of Spain's colonial subjects. In the larger picture, there was no hope of Spain reestablishing European hegemony, but there was a possibility of transforming its still vast overseas empire into a foundation for economic power and prosperity that might have led it into a new era of respect and influence. Perhaps it was too late for the long abuse of Spanish America to be remedied. Even the spirit of Enlightenment, to the extent it had penetrated Spanish minds, was probably not strong enough to overcome centuries of Eurocentric visions and unapologetic colonial exploitation. More fundamental than these considerations was the fact that Charles III was destined to be succeeded by an heir who possessed none of his ability or commitment to the full-time business of being a king. In an absolute monarchy, the king must be of the highest caliber or at the very least supplement his own shortcomings with the selection of first-rate ministers and sincere collaboration with them. The situation in the Spanish monarchy was particularly perilous because of the stagnation into which its institutions had fallen by 1700 and the weight of inertia that demanded constant struggle from all of those who recognized the need for reform. At the beginning of the century Louis XIV had remarked that the Spanish Habsburgs seemed dedicated to the destruction of their country. After some 80 years of Bourbon reform initiatives, the count of Campomanes, a shrewd observer of his compatriots' natural inclinations, remarked that anyone who thought it was possible to bring about reform in Spain by mere proclamations and decrees was deluding himself. The force of inertia in Spanish society was so great that almost superhuman efforts were needed to effect salutory change.

Like Philip II, who had tried to prepare his successor and died fearing that he had not done enough, Charles III passed his crown to a son in whom, despite his best efforts, he could have little confidence. The genetic lottery that was absolute monarchy had passed the succession to Charles IV. Within a few years he and his monstrously corrupt minister Manuel de Godoy would lead Spain into a crisis of disastrous proportions.

PORTUGAL'S EXPERIMENT IN ENLIGHTENED DESPOTISM

Portugal's relative prosperity in the 18th century resulted largely from prudent diplomacy abroad and efficient management at home. The Methuen Treaty of 1703 guaranteed a favorable market for Portuguese wines and strengthened the ties between Lisbon and London. Although the political implications of the alliance drew Portugal into the War of the Spanish Succession, her participation in that conflict as the cobelligerent of Britain was relatively brief and caused little lasting damage. Peter II's son, John V, enjoyed a long and tranquil reign (1706–50), during which he expended the treasure that flowed in from Brazil's newly discovered gold and diamond mines on lavish building projects. Mafra Palace was hailed as the Portuguese Versailles and John's self-indulgent lifestyle was mimicked by the Portuguese nobility, just as he himself sought to mimic Louis XIV of France.

John's successor, Joseph I, placed the effective management of the kingdom in the hands of Sebastião José de Carvalho e Melo, known to history as Pombal (although the title of marques de Pombal was not bestowed on him until 1770). A disciple of the French philosophes but utterly ruthless and brutal in his administrative tactics, this minister was one of Europe's most ardent exponents of enlightened despotism. His energy and resourcefulness in rebuilding Lisbon after the devastating earthquake of 1755 were paralleled by his merciless repression of an aristocratic conspiracy in 1758 and his expulsion of the Jesuits in the following year on the general ground that some of them had aided the conspirators. Pombal thus preceded the Spanish onslaught against the Jesuits during the next decade and was a major advocate of the order's dissolution by the pope in 1773. Although the need to preserve good relations with Britain drew Portugal into another short-lived war with Spain during the Seven Years' conflict, Pombal's main concern was with strengthening his country's economy. This policy was reflected in promotion of agriculture and industry, support for education, and development of new approaches to trade, particularly in the colonial sphere. Pombal was even more heavy handed in Brazil than in Portugal, with the result that salutary reforms in America did not create a legacy of goodwill but contributed to rising discontent among the colonists. When Joseph I succumbed to insanity in 1774, his Spanish wife, María Ana, assumed the regency and began to undermine Pombal's authority. The dictator was dismissed in 1777 after the king's death and the accession of his daughter Maria I. During the next decade the nobility reclaimed much of its old power, and many of Pombal's reforms were weakened, although few were completely abolished.

Maria I also went mad, in 1792, and her son John took control of the country. Fearful that the virus of revolution would spread from France into Portugal, he joined the anti-French coalition led by Britain and remained loyal to it even after his powerful neighboring state defected. Portugal's new time of troubles began in earnest as the century ended with an attack from Spain, egged on by Napoléon Bonaparte because the smaller Iberian realm refused to close her ports to the British. The so-called War of the Oranges lasted only a few months and resulted in Portugal's adherence to the policy of trade exclusion. But its troubles were just beginning.

THE AGE OF REVOLUTION IN SPAIN AND PORTUGAL

Within a year of his accession, Charles IV of Spain was confronted by the outbreak of the French Revolution. The ministers whom he had inherited from his father, notably Aranda, strove to keep what they perceived as a dangerous infestation from spreading across the Pyrenees. Even commentaries hostile to the direction of developments in France were banned from Spain lest the mere knowledge that a revolution was in progress might stir up evil thoughts. By 1792, however, the inept king had been persuaded to dismiss his competent ministers in favor of the upstart officer Godoy. This paramour of Queen María Luisa was accepted by the naive monarch as a good friend to the dynasty and a shrewd statesman. Profoundly corrupt and skilled at nothing but intrigue, he led Spain from its initial armed opposition to the French Republic into an alliance that by 1797 had led to a major naval defeat. Scarcely had this humiliation been sustained than the Bonaparte dictatorship compelled Spain to hand over Louisiana (soon sold by Napoléon to the United States). In 1805 another joint naval venture with the French led to the destruction of the Spanish fleet at Trafalgar. In addition to these dismal results of Godoy's diplomacy, his master had been obliged to yield the strategically positioned island of Trinidad to Britain in order to regain Minorca.

Stronger than ever in his allegiance to France and in the acquiescence of Charles IV to his ruinous policies, Godoy schemed with Napoléon to stage a joint invasion of Portugal in 1807, the aim being to exclude Britain once and for all from any access to that stretch of continental coastline. The victim was to be divided into three parts, with a "Kingdom of Northern Lusitania" in the north going to a Bourbon prince and a personal realm in the south for Godoy, while central

Portugal was left to a later disposition, probably direct annexation to France.

Portugal was quickly overrun in 1807, although the Bragianças succeeded in escaping to Brazil aboard a British naval squadron. French occupation remained tenuous, and the partition scheme could not be implemented. In the meantime Napoléon wearied of working through intermediaries, and the French troops who had been welcomed into Spain turned upon and disarmed their hosts. Charles IV and his defiant son (who had gone so far as to proclaim himself Ferdinand VII) were taken into custody, along with the rest of the royal family, and imprisoned in France. Joseph Bonaparte, brother of the French emperor, was proclaimed King Joseph I of Spain in 1808.

For Britain, the Peninsular War of 1809–14 was merely one segment of a worldwide struggle against France. It included an abortive campaign in northwestern Spain, the invasion and clearing-out of Portugal, and a series of spectacular victories under Arthur Wellesley's (soon to be created duke of Wellington) command in which his expeditionary force was merely supplemented by Portuguese and Spanish irregulars. But for Spain, the "war of independence" was a national crusade in which remnants of the old royal army, reinforced by volunteers from every walk of life, systematically expelled the "intrusive king," his French army of occupation, and the minority of Spaniards who had accepted him. Moreover, in the southern part of the country, which had never been overrun by the enemy, a junta loyal to Ferdinand VII summoned the Cortes to create, as a national body, a constitution. Produced in 1812, the liberal document granted wide franchise and personal freedoms unprecedented in Spanish history. Far more than a mere military experience, the struggle against Napoléon would profoundly affect the political and cultural future of the Spanish nation.

For the restored Bourbon king, Ferdinand VII, the constitution and all that it represented were to be swept away. Spain was to return to what it had been before the taint of revolution crept across the Pyrenees. His supporters among the aristocracy and the clergy concurred in his refusal to acknowledge that a new era had dawned. Around the king and his supporters, a conservative movement took shape celebrating the glories of Spain's past, denying its decline over recent generations, and refusing to accept the possibility of any change for the future. They equated the supporters of liberal reform with the "traitors" who had welcomed the godless and radical doctrines of the French invaders, ignoring the shared struggle against the foreigners that had just come to an end. In the environment of uncompromising reaction created by the restoration, it was hardly surprising, although profoundly shocking, that the Inquisition, which had been abolished by Joseph Bonaparte, was reinstated. Scarcely a month passed without new evidence of the king's commitment to archaic ritual and oppressive policy. His behavior was all the more reckless because of the deep division that had developed in the army between modernizers and reactionaries. Even before the French invasion a significant number of officers in the technical branches, such as artillery and engineering, had come from middle-class, progressive backgrounds. During the struggle to expel Bonaparte many volunteers had joined the ranks, bringing with them attitudes and experiences entirely outside the traditional professional sphere. Necessity and imprudence led Ferdinand to retain many of these outsiders in the officer corps. The inevitable result was a sequence of conspiracies, with at least one major military plot to overthrow the government being discovered each year between 1815 and 1820.

The tensions within the army were particularly ominous, given the monarch's determination to regain control over the colonies. From Mexico City to Buenos Aires the nationalism that had been simmering among Spain's American subjects since the mid-18th century surged up in the aftermath of the French invasion. Local administrations, claiming to be loyal to Ferdinand VII and insisting that they were protecting his dominions against the Bonapartist usurper, pursued their own agendas. When the king resumed his throne in Madrid, he soon found protestations of loyalty replaced by demands for autonomy. Here again Ferdinand and his advisers would accept nothing short of the reestablishment of absolute sovereignty. Had Spanish conservatives been able to negotiate some form of compromise in the individual territories, a relationship mutually beneficial to Spain and the Americas might have evolved. Instead, the king demanded total submission, the colonies proclaimed their independence, and a decade of war followed. The mounting of transatlantic military expeditions proved a tremendous strain on Spain's material and human resources. Spaniards, barely recovered from their own liberation struggle, now found themselves conscripted to repress the liberation movements overseas. Many of them lacked any real sympathy with the inhabitants of those distant lands yet were reluctant to face death by bullet or tropical disease in a meaningless conflict.

In 1820 military discontent and the rising toll of the colonial wars combined to generate a mutiny among soldiers at Cádiz who were about to embark for South America. Their commander, Colonel Rafael del Riego, led them on a march toward Madrid that was joined by other rebellious units. The insurrection turned into a successful revolution, as the mutineers joined with liberal politicians to install a reformist government, with Riego as minister of war. Ferdinand VII was permitted to retain his throne but only as a constitutional monarch, under the provisions of the 1812 document. A virtual prisoner of his ministers, the king was obliged to make speeches praising the new political order in Spain and to experience such personal humiliations as walking in a state funeral procession behind the coffin of a liberal conspirator whom he had executed two years before. Ferdinand's sufferings came to an end in 1823, when the conservative powers of the so-called Holy Alliance (Austria, Russia, and Prussia) sponsored a French invasion force (the 100,000 Sons of St. Louis) provided by the restored Bourbon dynasty in Paris. Ferdinand offered to negotiate an honorable surrender for the defeated liberals but betrayed them to the French, who executed Riego and many others. Back in full power again Ferdinand resumed his absolutist regime at home and his anti-independence operations in America, although these came to an effective end when the Spanish forces were defeated at the Battle of Ayacucho in 1824.

A new crisis arose for Ferdinand VII in 1830 when he precipitated a confrontation, not with the liberals, but with his own conservative adherents. The latter had pursued a consistent line ever since 1812 when they had opposed the constitution voted by the Cortes at Cádiz, arguing for preservation of traditional institutions such as the Inquisition and press censorship. As soon as the French had been expelled, they had rallied behind Ferdinand in his abolition of the odious constitution. The ultraconservatives (who commonly referred to themselves as "traditionalists") supported the king in all his difficulties and triumphs until it became a question of their principles colliding with his ego. Having failed to produce a son through several marriages, Ferdinand decided to name his daughter Isabella as heiress to the throne, thus abandoning the Salic law, the ancient Germanic rule of succession brought into Spain by the Bourbons. The traditionalists insisted that not even the king had the absolute power to change so fundamental a rule, with its exclusion of all but male inheritance. Even though there was a Spanish custom of female inheritance that far predated the coming of the Bourbons, the ultraconservatives now asserted that they were more traditionalist than the king and declared that his brother Carlos was the rightful heir. They maintained this position until the death of Ferdinand in 1833, when the Carlists, as they were now known, rejected the succession of the king's daughter as Queen Isabella II and proclaimed his brother as King Charles V. What followed was a civil war (First Carlist War) that resembled the dynastic bloodletting that had vanished from the rest of Europe centuries before, even though it was disguised by modern political labels. The child queen was supported by liberal factions and recognized by the newly installed liberal regimes in Britain and France. Charles was championed by Spanish conservatives and their ideological peers in Austria and Russia. Within the country, the Carlists drew their strength from the northern regions (the Basque provinces, Catalonia, and Aragon), which had a long history of autonomist ambition.

In nearly five years of war (1834–39) the material assistance provided by the French Foreign Legion and the volunteers of the "British Legion" proved more valuable to Isabella's camp than the moral support of the conservative monarchs was to Carlos. Although the Carlist field commanders were often more skilled and energetic than their opponents, they finally became estranged from their political colleagues and demanded a negotiated settlement. The rebels were allowed to lay down their arms and go home in peace, while their officers were confirmed in their commissions. Carlos withdrew to Austria without formally renouncing his claims.

An even more complex set of dynastic follies enveloped Portugal during this period. The royal family had fled to Brazil in 1807 to escape the Napoléonic invasion. Following the ouster of the French, a regency council ruled the country until 1820. In that year Portuguese liberals, inspired by the Riego uprising in Spain, deposed the council, proclaimed a democratic constitution, and demanded the return of the absentee king. Leaving his elder son, Pedro, to govern Brazil, John VI returned to Portugal with his younger son, Miguel. Although the king replaced the constitution with a more moderate one in 1823, conservatives remained discontented. The absolutist faction, which rejected a constitution of any sort, looked to Miguel as its leader. He attempted a coup against his father in 1824 and after its failure was banished to Austria.

On the death of John VI in 1826, Pedro, by now emperor of an independent Brazil, succeeded to the Portuguese throne. He decided to remain in Brazil and hand over the sovereignty of Portugal to his seven-year-old daughter, Maria da Glória (Queen Maria II). Pedro reaffirmed the British-style constitution but sought to appease conservatives by offering his brother, Miguel, the regency during the minority of Maria da Glória, on the condition that Miguel marry her as a gesture of commitment. Miguel at first seemed willing to accept this arrangement, returned to Lisbon in 1827 and took an oath of loyalty. But he soon rallied his old supporters and early in 1828 persuaded a majority of the parliament to repudiate the young queen and proclaim him King Miguel I. The stage was now set for a civil war, pitting liberal backers of the constitutional monarch against the champions of absolutism, who declared the female succession to be invalid and the whole religious and social tradition of Portugal to be at stake. In this conflict the liberal side would receive the support of Britain and France, and the conservative position would be endorsed by Spain and Austria.

With the constitution abolished and the queen finding sanctuary in Britain, the absolutists carried out a triumphant persecution of their opponents during the next several years. All avowed liberals were declared "atheists, traitors and thieves." But then, in April 1831, Pedro abdicated the Brazilian throne in favor of his son and returned to Europe to fight for Maria da Glória's restoration. With the aid of Britain and France he secured a foothold for his campaign in the Azores, where many sympathizers of the young queen had taken refuge. The civil war soon spread to the mainland, with skirmishes between the two factions in several northern provinces. Pedro struck a decisive blow in July 1832 when, again with foreign backing, he captured Oporto. The Miguelite troops were badly defeated in a belated attempt to retake Portugal's second city. The war continued to go against the conservative forces during 1833. A naval squadron (on "loan" from Britain) crushed the royal Portuguese fleet in a confrontation off Cape St. Vincent, and liberal volunteers routed the Miguelites in a series of land battles that tightened the noose around Lisbon. At the beginning of 1834, with his resources exhausted, Miguel surrendered and was allowed to go into exile. His followers were given amnesty, and civil servants and clerics who had supported Miguel were pensioned, though not restored to their positions.

SOLDIERS AND THE STATE IN LATE NINETEENTH-CENTURY SPAIN

The end of the First Carlist War was followed by three decades of political maneuvering and socioeconomic stagnation. Two antagonistic factions emerged from the old liberal movement (the *moderados* and the *progresistas*) to vie for power, while absolutists and republicans on their respective right and left flanks intervened periodically. Constitutions came and went, with the famous 1812 document variously incised and subtracted from or even abolished for a time. There were abortive revolutions and successful military coups with the military holding effective power throughout. Generals Baldomero Espartero, Ramón Maréa Narváez, Leopoldo O'Donnell, and their collaborators or rivals rotated in office as chief minister or regent, all under the nominal rule of Isabella II.

Although there were some generally successful military operations in Morocco, a series of interventions in the former American empire were unprofitable. There were short-lived wars with Peru and Chile and a landing in Mexico, as well as the renewed occupation of the Dominican Republic (1861–65). All of these were undertaken while the United States was caught up in its own civil war, but even with the Monroe Doctrine inoperative Spain could not sustain itself in these endeavors. Even those outposts that had survived the tumults of the 1820s, Cuba and Puerto Rico, were becoming increasingly restless in the 1860s, as were the far-off Philippines.

Spain's prestige in Europe fared no better during this period. The complex diplomatic negotiations surrounding the marital prospects of the queen and her younger sister, Luisa Fernanda, led to a crisis in Anglo-French relations ("the affair of the Spanish marriages"), but in these matters Spain was a mere bystander. Isabella eventually married her cousin Francisco, which satisfied the competing Great Powers, if not the queen herself.

The ever-growing antagonisms among political and military leaders came to a crisis in 1868, fed by the scandalous stories about the queen's alleged amours and the appointment of her latest favorite, a former actor, as minister of state. Declarations of public indignation and repudiations of loyalty by senior commanders made it impossible for Isabella to sustain her position, and she departed into exile.

The next eight years were as disordered and destructive as anything Spain had seen since the 1830s. While a newly ascendant leftist majority in the Cortes passed a series of anticlerical and populist laws, a clique of generals enforced the retention of constitutional monarchy. They then began hunting for a new monarch. A series of offers to various European princes and even to the veteran general Espartero were all rejected. Prince Leopold of Hohenzollern-Sigmaringen accepted, but he subsequently withdrew (though the affairs of Spain once again precipitated a European crisis and brought on the Franco-Prussian War of 1870–71). In the meantime the duke of Aosta, son of Italy's newly established king, was persuaded to accept the throne of Spain. His resolve was undoubtedly shaken when the leading member of the junta in Madrid, General Juan Prim, was assassinated on the day of the new sovereign's arrival. King Amadeo I endured two years of hostility, abuse, and even outright danger before abdicating. His departure from Spain was followed almost immediately by the proclamation of a republic and the outbreak of revolt in the north, where the supporters of another Carlos saw their opportunity. The First Republic and the Second Carlist War came to an end, successively, by 1875, although now without much bitterness and bloodshed. Republicanism had not been stamped out in Spain, but the episode had clearly revealed the problem of reconciling centrists and anarchists to a common republican policy. Carlism, too, was by no means given a death blow, even though most of the regular army commanders repudiated it. Their decision to install Isabella's son as king ended the matter for most of them. Political Carlism was even more gravely wounded, however, when the pope was persuaded to abandon his recognition of Charles VII by Madrid's concessions on the special status of the church. Both republicans and Carlists would be heard from again in the coming century.

The brief reign of Alfonso XII (1875–85) brought a degree of much needed political stability to Spain, albeit at the expense of anything that could be called a genuine parliamentary system. The Liberal Party under Práxedes Mateo Sagasta and the Conservative Party under Antonio Cánovas alternated in power, managing the elections so as to prevent any authentic expression of public will. Under the latest revision of the constitution the ministry was entirely dependent upon the monarch, who was thus able to exercise considerable personal power when he chose to do so. Alfonso XII was, however, a mixture of good intentions and self-indulgent impulses. Although prosperity rose, especially in the northern regions, due to an increase in industrial activity, it was accompanied by growing labor unrest. Combined with the revival of anarchism in the south, this produced frequent outbursts of violence and massive police repression. As he dissipated much of his initial popularity, the king lost both the ability and the inclination to promote national harmony and renewal. Following his sudden death in 1885 he was succeeded by his only son, born posthumously, Alfonso XIII, who remained under the regency of his mother Queen Maria Christina until 1902. During the vacuum of leadership that persisted over the last decades of the 19th century, the domestic issues that bedeviled Spain were rendered even more baffling by another outbreak of colonial warfare. Both Cuba and the Philippines were shaken by insurrections that began in 1895 and persisted until the war between Spain and its subject peoples turned into a confrontation with a far greater antagonist, the United States of America.

As the 19th century drew to a close a passion for overseas expansion gripped the major powers. Britain, France, and Germany sought colonies in Africa and Asia. The United States looked both to the Caribbean and to the Pacific Basin. In both of these latter zones of ambition the obvious target was the remnants of the once-great Spanish Empire. It was only a matter of time before Spain's difficulties provided America's opportunity. Early in 1898 the long-simmering antagonisms between Cuba's colonial master and American advocates of Cuban "liberation" exploded when the battleship *Maine* sank to the bottom of Havana's harbor. Whether destroyed by Spanish officers who resented the ship's intrusive presence or by Cuban rebels seeking to provoke a confrontation that would aid their cause or even by an accidental boiler explosion, the sinking of the *Maine* and the loss of more than 200 American lives precipitated a declaration of war by a reluctant president under the urging of an aroused Congress and passionate public opinion. Most Spaniards, from the ministers in Madrid to the soldiers in the field, were far less eager for the war. From its very inception a mood of fatalism hung over the conduct of this "affair of honor."

By early summer 1898 an American expedition had landed in Cuba and, ignoring Havana, marched across the island brushing aside half-hearted resistance. After a fierce assault on the landward defenses of Santiago, the Americans captured the city. The Spanish naval squadron sheltering there sailed out to its doom under the guns of the "Northern Colossus." Another U.S. expeditionary force had meanwhile sailed across the Pacific, captured the Marianas on the way, and joined forces with the American ships that had annihilated the Spanish vessels in Manila Bay. Already besieged by Filipino rebels, the defenders of Manila quickly surrendered. All that remained was to scoop up Puerto Rico. The "ever-loyal island" that had been rewarded by Spain for its fidelity by a statute of autonomy only a year before was now abandoned by the mother country. As its legislature convened to hold its first and last exercise in self-government, the garrison laid down its arms and yielded the inhabitants to a new colonial overlord. By December 1898 the final dispositions had been made by a peace treaty that recognized Cuban independence under the oversight of the United States while transferring the Philippines, Guam, and Puerto Rico to direct American sovereignty. Aside from a few fragments in Africa, the Spanish Empire was at an end.

PORTUGAL: THE LAST BRAGANÇAS

Portugal, during the middle years of the 19th century shared with Spain many of the consequences of economic and social backwardness although spared the degree of political instability and domestic violence that plagued the larger country. A series of untimely deaths and short reigns weakened the influence of the monarchy. By the time Charles I ascended the throne in 1889 most of his subjects were unready for the kind of heavy-handed regime that he introduced and unwilling to accept it. His reign saw a significant growth in industry, public works, sponsorship of cultural activities, and a belated effort to exploit the rich resources of the African colonies. Energetic and arrogant, the king made far more enemies by his activism than his predecessors had ever raised by their idleness. A growing republican movement focused on removal of the monarchy as the salvation of the Portuguese people without a very coherent ideological or practical plan for what was needed or what should be done. In 1908 the king and the crown prince were shot dead as they rode through Lisbon. Although the surviving younger son became Manuel II, his regime became an insignificant footnote to the history of the Braganças. Swept away in the upsurge of republicanism, he went into exile in 1910, and Portugal ended nearly 800 years of monarchy.

SPANISH AND PORTUGUESE CULTURE IN THE EIGHTEENTH AND NINETEENTH CENTURIES

The collapse of Spanish political dominance in Europe at the end of the 17th century was accompanied by the deterioration of its cultural hegemony. Just as the French Bourbons imposed their principles and practices in the political realm, so French cultural models became the norm in 18th-century Spain. Royal academies of language and history and the National Library in Madrid now replicated those in Paris. Playwrights, of whom the most distinguished was Leandro Fernández de Moratín, essayists, and poets all took their lead from the powerful neighbor north of the Pyrenees. In art, as well as literature, there were few pretenders to the distinction attained by the great men of the Golden Age. Only Francisco de Goya with his shrewd portraits of the royal family and their courtiers and his shocking drawings illustrating the horrors of war raises Spanish culture of this period from a mediocre level.

Despite their heroic struggle against Napoléon's military dictatorship in the first decades of the 19th century, Spaniards remained under the cultural mastery of France during succeeding generations. Romanticism, exemplified by the poets José Espronceda and Gustavo Adolfo Bécquer was followed by the realism favored in the novels of Benito Pérez Galdós (*Doña Perfecta, Episodios nacionales*), Emilia Pardo Bazán (*Los pazos de Ulloa*), Juan Valera (*Pepita Jiménez*), and Vicente Blasco Ibáñez (*La barraca, Los cuatro jinetes del Apocalipsis*). Spain, ironically had now become a source of picturesque settings for French dramas such as *Hernani* and operas such as *Carmen*.

Portugal, too, succumbed to the French cultural predominance in the 18th and 19th centuries. Only in the late 1800s, in the novels of José Maria Eça de Queirós (*Os Maias* and *O crime do Padre Amaro*) did Portugal offer a truly significant contribution to European literature.

SPAIN, FROM THE AMERICAN WAR
THROUGH THE CIVIL WAR

The events of 1898, often referred to simply as "the Disaster," produced a profound reaction among Spaniards that varied according to their political, socioeconomic, and cultural status. For those with a degree of historical sophistication it was perceived as yet another stage in the recurring pattern of convulsion that seemed to mark the end of each successive century: the discovery of the New World in 1492 and the launching of the struggle for mastery of the Old, the crises that followed Philip II's death in 1598, the end of the Habsburg dynasty and the succession struggle that commenced in 1700, and the onset of the revolutionary upheaval that engulfed the Iberian Peninsula at the beginning of the 19th century and destroyed Spanish rule in the Americas. Now at the end of the 19th century the symbolic remains of empire were gone (save for a few stretches of sand and jungle in Africa), and the armed forces were humiliated as never before. Intellectuals asked whether this was truly the end of Spain or an opportunity for a new, better way of thinking and acting. Capitalists called for a long-delayed modernization now that Spain was no longer mired in reveries about past glory. Politicians attempted to reposition themselves according to their ideological commitments and personal ambitions. The Conservative Party split into a faction that clung to traditional values as the salvation of the country and a moderate wing that accepted the need for change without being too clear about how to achieve it. Its old rival, the Liberal Party, claimed to have a "progressive" solution to the nation's needs. Newer parties multiplied, often as the result of the class warfare that had developed in the 1880s and '90s and the perception that the Disaster had come about because they had not been in charge at the critical moment. These parties or pseudoparties included Socialists, anarchists (each with its own affiliated trade union movements), Radicals, and Republicans, to say nothing of a Catalan nationalist movement and even the remnant of Carlism holding out in Navarre. All of these would have their role to play in the tumultuous events of the next four decades. Nor was the Catholic Church reluctant to prescribe its own remedies for the national malaise or the army to insist that its own brand of self-interested patriotism was essential to national survival.

Amidst the chorus of blame, critical analysis, and militant opportunism that rose up at the beginning of the 20th century, a surprisingly wide variety of Spanish commentators still looked to the monarchy as an anchor in the great storm that threatened to engulf the country and a beacon that would guide Spaniards to a harbor in which they would preserve their distinctive identity while adjusting to the winds of change.

Alfonso XIII, born a king in 1886, was proclaimed of age in 1902. Although his mother, the regent, continued to guide and assist him for a time, his marriage in 1906 (to a granddaughter of Queen Victoria of Great Britain) marked his definitive assumption of full royal authority. Trained both in political and military institutions and imbued with a sense of his role and responsibility as king, Alfonso was a well-intentioned sovereign, although neither his intellectual gifts nor his judgment would prove equal to the task that lay before him. Under the latest version of Spain's many constitutions, he still held powers that had disappeared from the repertoire of many "limited" monarchs. By temperament and his own understanding of duty he would have no hesitation in exercising such power, either openly or by indirect means.

If the young king required any dramatic introduction to the situation in which he found himself, it came during the festive procession of royal carriages and mounted guards that carried him and his bride from the cathedral to the royal palace after their wedding in 1906. A bomb hurled at the royal couple exploded short of its target, covering the English princess with the blood of soldiers and horses. Anarchists, to whom this outrage was ascribed, had found in Spain a particularly fertile ground for their doctrines ever since the 1860s and had already applied their "propaganda of the deed" to a prime minister and many other dignitaries in recent years. They made a twin appeal to the downtrodden peasantry of Andalusia and to the industrial workers of Catalonia. During Barcelona's "Tragic Week" in 1909 they would confront the security forces with a mixture of straightforward violence and anticlerical atrocity that shocked the country and the world. Although their insurrection at the time frightened off many Catalan businessmen who had hitherto supported disruptive regionalism, neither this outcome nor the brutal behavior of the Civil Guard and army prevented further outbreaks.

While the twin specters of socioeconomic disorder and regional separatism were perhaps the most serious problems on the domestic front, Alfonso also was faced by the need to shape a foreign and colonial policy. The Liberal ministers whom he chose to cope with internal issues did not provide him with much relief. In matters of European policy their advice and Alfonson's own links to Britain drew Spain into friendship with London and its new ally, Paris. While this tendency threatened to draw Spain into the Allied camp during World War I, the countervailing sympathy of army leaders for Germany ended in preserving Spain's neutrality.

France had overlapping interests in Morocco that might have created tensions with Spain, but from 1912 onward (with some encouragement from Britain) the two Mediterranean states were able to work out a division of North African claims that left the Spanish protectorate intact and linked to a larger stretch of desert land—known originally as Ifni and Río de Oro and later, more grandly, as Spanish Sahara—that eased some of the pain of colonial deprivation. Though these lands, as well as the recently acquired Spanish Guinea, cost more than they were worth, they would be jealously preserved long after other European powers had given up their realms. Spanish Morocco was regarded as the jewel in the crown, and its preservation was the particular obsession of Alfonso's generals. They had been heavily engaged against the local tribesmen of the Rif region since the beginning of the century, and fighting there intensified after the European war ended. The French, in their neighboring territory, experienced a string of successes and reverses in dealing with their own "natives," yet nothing in the French zone compared to the catastrophe of 1921 during the so-called Anual campaign when thousands of Spanish troops, mostly raw conscripts (the number is estimated as anywhere from 8,000 to 20,000), were killed in a desperate retreat that turned into a bloody rout.

The parties of the Left soon demanded an inquiry into the origins of the North African catastrophe and clearly intended to use it to weaken the power of the army and the monarchy. They would not have far to look, for the king had recklessly incited General Manuel Fernández Silvestre to launch the operation that brought so many men to their death and nearly cost Spain control of the protectorate. When no other evasion or delaying tactic seemed likely to keep the Cortes from pursuing its inquiry, a coup saved the generals and their king from embarrassment. After 50 years of civilian and parliamentary government, a new *pronunciamiento* returned Spain to military dictatorship. The captain general of Barcelona, Miguel Primo de Rivera, declared that he was acting to save his country from terrorism, financial incompetence, communist threats, impiety, regional extremism, the Moroccan problem, and reckless political opportunism in the Anual investigation. Although he was initially supported only by his own troops, no other commanders would offer resistance, and the king made it clear that he would not support his ministers in the crisis. By the end of September 1923 the government had resigned, Alfonso had welcomed Primo de Rivera to Madrid and appointed him head of a military directorate with broad powers, and the dismantlement of the Cortes and the very structure of constitutional law was under way. Although Primo de Rivera rejected the designation of dictator and insisted that he and his nine fellow military directors would serve only a few months, the regime would last for more than six years. The king gave Primo de Rivera his full support throughout, reportedly introducing him to the Italian monarch as "my Mussolini." A hearty, seemingly good-natured individual (despite a long record of intrigue and ambition), Primo de Rivera won popularity with the church, major landowners, and leading capitalists by his identification with the traditional ruling class (he was a member of a dynasty of soldiers and inheritor of a title of nobility). Conversely he roused the immediate antagonism of professional politicians by his oft-stated contempt for their "selfish and unpatriotic" actions.

Among Primo de Rivera's positive achievements were the initiation of numerous programs of modernization both in the bureaucracy and the public works sector, fiscal reform, an attack on the abuses of the cacique system (control by local political bosses), and a compromise solution of the Moroccan problem. Not willing to resort to the degree of brutality employed by contemporary dictators, Primo de Rivera eventually made concessions, such as the inclusion of civilians in his directorate, that encouraged the opposition rather than conciliated it. Several local uprisings were put down, but after Spain began to experience the impact of the global economic decline in 1929, the general's position became increasingly difficult. Deteriorating health finally led him to submit his resignation in January 1930, and he withdrew to Paris where he died two months later. Alfonso XIII attempted to continue the directorate under another senior officer, but the rising tide of dissatisfaction led him to abandon the dictatorship by the latter half of 1930. Restored parliamentary life now focused on the demand for a totally new system. The Radical and Republican Parties led the cry for the king's ouster. After they won massive support in local elections at the beginning of 1931, the discredited sovereign announced that he was leaving the country for a time to give his people the chance to arrive at a calm, balanced judgment about their future. Alfonso XIII had passed through a series of initiatives and experiments during the last three decades, all aimed at using his prestige for the rehabilitation and restoration of Spain as it entered the new century. The final gamble with military dictatorship had failed and sealed his own fate. Alfonso XIII never abdicated, but the call that he awaited never came. He died in exile 10 years later.

The Second Republic, however, died even before the monarch whom it had replaced. Between 1931 and 1936 the republic struggled through a succession of crises that reflected the social and political divisions that had plagued the first three decades of the 20th century. A relatively moderate opening phase reassured conservative elements whose natural allegiance to the king had been worn thin by his vacillating and unproductive policies. Even the military, traditional bulwark of national order and restorer of the Bourbons in 1875, remained quiet. Their concept of honor seemingly did not require them to act until their own interests were affected. But within two years the illusion of stability had been shattered. Voices of moderation were drowned out by strident demands from the Left, lamentations from the establishment arose, and plans to reduce the numbers and prerogatives of the officer corps precipitated a revolt that failed without exhausting the army's capacity for mischief. A shift toward the Right precipitated widespread strikes that were put down with severity and bred a spirit of class rage that would guarantee revenge seeking in later days. By 1935 the pendulum had swung back toward radicalism, and anticlerical, anticapitalist legislation had roused the deepest fears of the old elite. The first half of 1936 seethed with conspiracies, groupings and regroupings of factions and assassinations. Rhetorical accusations of "communism" and "fascism" provided new labels for bitter enmities whose origins lay far back in Spanish history.

The man and the hour had met. Francisco Franco, born in El Ferrol to a Galician dynasty of naval officers, had changed his career path after the Disaster of 1898 had swept Spain from the seas. As a young soldier in Morocco, he had distinguished himself by personal bravery and a capacity for quick thinking. One of the principal organizers of the hard-fighting Foreign Legion (modeled on the famous French unit), he had become by the late 1920s the youngest general in Europe and a national hero. Intensely ambitious and a skillful manipulator of favorable publicity, he masked his lust for power under a facade of modesty and honesty. During the escalating troubles that beset the Second Republic, he avoided entanglements, intrigued adroitly, and bided his time.

On July 17, 1936, army leaders, including Franco, began a revolt against the leftist government that had gained power in the February elections. Their aim was to halt the extremism of social revolutionaries who threatened the three pillars of the state: the military, the church, and the men of property. Initial successes in various cities were reinforced by the arrival of Franco's troops (including Foreign Legion and Moorish units) from Morocco on board transport planes lent by his German and Italian friends. Much of the west and and northwest came under their control. The rebels (generally designated as the Nationalists) included most of the army, air force, and Civil Guard, as well as volunteers raised by conservative groups. Among the latter were monarchists (both Legitimists, or supporters of Alfonso XIII and Carlists, the majority of whom also acknowledged the rights of Alfonso), the Catholic party the Spanish Confederation of the Autonomous Right (CEDA), and the fascist-oriented political organization known as the Falange. Backing the government were some officers and men of the regular military, much of the navy, the Assault Guards (created as a Republican counterbalance to the army-dominated Civil Guard), and militias drawn from unions that adhered to the Socialist, Anarchist, Trotskyite, or Communist Parties, as well as Basque and Catalan regionalists. Although their general designation as Loyalist or Republican forces gave them a semblance of unity, their resistance to a common enemy would often be impaired by their antagonism to one another.

On September 29 the so-called Committee of National Defense (Junta de Defensa Nacional) named General Franco as head of the government and commander of the armed forces. These positions he would retain, in essence, for nearly 40 years, and very early in the war those of his co-conspirators who represented a potential rivalry disappeared from the scene. The Republican government withdrew to Valencia, which enabled it to exercise control within the eastern part of the country, with an outlying stronghold in the Basque provinces, where the Catholicism of the Basques was outweighed by their commitment to ethnic autonomy. Regional semi-independence was accorded to both the Basques and the Catalans by the Second Republic, condemning it still further in the eyes of the Francoists.

The opening weeks of the Spanish civil war were characterized by horrendous atrocities, most of them inflicted by an inflamed working class upon conservatives in general and Catholic clergy in particular. Ultimately 12 bishops and hundreds of priests, nuns, and seminarians were slaughtered. The reprisals taken by the Nationalists were as brutal, though usually less picturesque in their cruelty. Europe looked on in horror as a country once recognized as the center of Western civilization descended into bloodshed on a scale not seen since the ghastly events surrounding World War I. Some countries saw opportunities to further their own political agenda. Germany and Italy sent troops and planes to assist Franco, while the Soviet Union supplied tanks and technicians to the Republicans. Western democracies, including Britain, France, and the United States, pledged themselves to nonintervention, though thousands of volunteers made their way to Spain to fight for the republic in the International Brigades.

During 1937, having consolidated their initial triumphs, the Nationalists concentrated on attacks in the north. Guernica, the traditional seat of Basque political identity, was bombed in April by German Luftwaffe pilots acting under Franco's direction. Bilbao, the great Basque port, was taken in June, while Santander fell in August, followed by Gijón in October. From the spring through the end of the year, the Loyalists struck all along the rebel perimeter trying to divert their northern campaign, but to no lasting effect. For all their efforts the defenders of the republic found themselves pushed back and during early 1938 losing control of Aragon, and seeing their territory cut in half by July. Digging in along the Ebro, the Loyalists tried to draw in and destroy as many as possible of Franco's troops during a prolonged struggle between July and November. Instead, they lost as many as 70,000 men and all real hope of victory.

With the line along the Ebro broken, defenders began streaming back toward the French frontier. Catalonia was completely overrun by February 1939, and Madrid, the last isolated hold-out, fell in March after a grotesque struggle for power among the Communists and their rivals within the beleaguered capital. Franco was, at last, truly master of the nation.

The Spanish civil war had cost that nation somewhere between 600,000 and 800,000 lives, counting deaths in battle and executions, as well as civilians killed by bombing, starvation, and disease. Under the new regime thousands more would be condemned to death, imprisoned, or forced into exile. The world was confronted with the full array of horrors about to engulf it as commentators warned that it had just seen the rehearsal for what Edgar Allan Poe had called the tragedy "Man." After centuries off the center stage of history Spain had once again gained universal attention.

PORTUGAL: THE EMERGENCE OF THE
SALAZAR DICTATORSHIP

The Portuguese republic that emerged from the revolution of 1910 had limited support at home and scanty respect abroad. It soon entered into a pattern of rapid changes in political leadership that would plague it for more than a decade. Those in charge during World War I decided that joining the French-British alliance would enhance Portugal's prestige. The country's participation in the fierce fighting on the western front achieved little beyond the death of several thousands of its sons. By 1926 factional rivalries, class conflict, and economic disarray impelled the president to seek a savior.

António de Oliveira Salazar was born on April 28, 1889, into a modest, ardently religious family in northern Portugal. Originally intended for the priesthood, he shifted his path to the law and had a distinguished career both as student and instructor. In 1926 he was well known as a professor at the University of Coimbra with a number of publications on abstruse fiscal matters and strong opinions on economic policy issues. When asked to take over the Ministry of Finance, he declined because he could not obtain the guarantee of a completely free hand that he demanded. Within two years the offer was renewed, with all his conditions fully met. Thus in 1928 Salazar, the most bureaucratic of dictators, began a 40-year regime in the most bureaucratic of manners. He was, in effect, hired to manage a government that could not manage itself. Although his accession to power was in prosaic contrast to Benito Mussolini's flamboyant march on Rome a few years earlier, the emergence of this new ultraconservative nationalist leader on the European scene soon led journalists to link them in an ill-assorted phalanx of dictators that briefly included Primo de Rivera in Spain and some exotic characters farther to the east. Moving with all deliberate speed, Salazar established an official party, the National Union, in 1930, took the office of prime minister in 1932, and crafted a new constitution in 1933 to enshrine his so-called New State. The corporate models upon which these institutions were based fall short, however, of full fascism.

Salazar was, in fact, no Mussolini or Adolf Hitler. He was a pragmatic dictator, who understood the situation in which Portugal found herself and the limits of her possibilities. Salazar realized the significance of such social institutions as the Catholic Church and the landowning aristocracy but granted them respect rather than power. Similarly he set the limit of the generals' ambitions by emphasizing budgetary limitations that curtailed military adventurism or foreign policy initiatives. With no personal military experience (unlike the aforementioned Italian, German, and Spanish dictators), Salazar had no empathy with soldiers and considered them merely well-paid civil servants. Perhaps because they mistrusted one another, the military men accepted this relationship with their civilian national leader. While Salazar's new secret police harassed leftists and his censors muzzled intellectuals, the great part of the population, however, found increased efficiency, development of the infrastructure, and modest growth in industrialization sufficient justification for the professor's blend of austerity and repression.

By the time Spain plunged into civil war in 1936 Portugal had already experienced the overthrow of its monarchy, an unhappy experiment with a republic, and the stress of dictatorship. But it had at least avoided the kind of fraternal bloodletting that was about to sweep over its larger neighbor. During the war Salazar became increasingly cooperative with the insurgents, whose conservative principles largely resembled his own. Yet he remained mistrustful of military men and avoided being too closely identified with Franco. Lisbon dealt harshly with some Spaniards who fled across the border from the rising tide of Falangist victory, but in isolated rural areas Portuguese villagers often gave shelter to desperate refugees. As so often in the past, relations between the two countries remained ambivalent, even after authoritarianism had established itself on both sides of the frontier.

IBERIAN NEUTRALITY IN WORLD WAR II

During World War II both Spain and Portugal remained neutral. For Franco this status represented a much more complicated relationship with the belligerents. When the great conflict began in September 1939, he had been master of Spain for only six months and was still deeply engaged in consolidating his control, punishing his enemies, and trying to restore some degree of normality to the country. Yet Germany and Italy (the latter would enter the war in June 1940) had been invaluable allies and expected him to repay his debt to them. Hence it was necessary for him to spin a game of feigned cooperation while avoiding formal commitments. Furthermore he had to conserve what remained of his badly damaged human and material resources. After a year of dealing with Franco, during which the Germans had overrun France and become, in effect, neighbors of Spain, Hitler met Franco at the border town of Irún, where the Generalísimo had professed his greatest respect and solidarity but evaded any real agreements. French and other anti-Nazi refugees had been slipping across a border that was nominally closed. A proposal to permit German forces to cross Spain for an assault on Gibraltar had gone nowhere. What can one expect, the Führer complained to an aide, of a leader who appoints the Virgin Mary to the rank of captain general in his army? When Germany launched its invasion of the Soviet Union in 1941, Franco renewed his protestations of friendship, vowed to a shared loathing of Bolshevism, and authorized Spanish "volunteers" to join a special force that would fight in Russia. Spain's División Azul (Blue Division) and a contingent from its air force served on the eastern front until the tide began to turn against Hitler. They were then withdrawn for "rest and rehabilitation." As the fortunes of the Axis sank, Franco's adherence to the strict letter of neutrality rose.

In Portugal Salazar had been even more canny about his relationship with countries with whom he had obvious ideological links but no previous comradeship in arms. His neutrality was formally manifested, although his capital was infested with spies, diplomats of dubious loyalty, refugees, and self-proclaimed journalists. Lisbon's greatest intriguer remained, however, the prime minister himself. Even before the fascist powers had begun to collapse he negotiated an arrangement with the United States and Britain for the use of air bases in the Azores, thus positioning himself as a friend of the soon-to-be-victorious democracies. Portugal was able to slide away from its negative wartime image with relative ease. It would be much harder for Spain to escape the stigma of Nazi connections after 1945.

THE FRANCO REGIME: 1945–1975

As the world emerged from war Franco had already exercised nearly a decade of dictatorship. Ahead of him lay 30 more years of ruling Spain under the title of El Caudillo (the Leader), combining the functions of chief of state, head of government, and commander in chief of the armed forces. It was an absolute monarchy without a king, for those who had expected a royal restoration remained frustrated until the very last.

In the aftermath of its internal bloodletting Spain learned the price paid by those who had lost—and by those who had won. For the defeated Republicans there was exile, execution, imprisonment, or vengeful repression. For the triumphant Nationalists there was isolation, deprivation, cold, and hunger in an economy that failed to recover. The ambitions of all the other right-wing parties were curbed, as the Falange, founded by the martyred José Antonio Primo de Rivera, son of the former dictator, was transformed into the National Movement, a cult-like instrument for controlling thought and focusing adoration upon the supreme leader. The army, the church, and the magnates, "saved from communism," enjoyed no real power—merely the privilege of singing El Caudillo's praises. Franco, who had borrowed so much else from his fascist allies, also learned the techniques of internal tyranny, although only the methodology of state terrorism was new, for his secret police drew upon a heritage well understood in Spanish history.

The first half of the dictator's postwar regime, from approximately 1945 to 1960, was sustained at home by a combination of political propaganda and morale-building fantasy. Under harsh censorship journalists and broadcasters were restricted to endorsing the official line of denouncing everything that lay outside the regime as "godless communism." At the same time Spaniards (especially students) were endlessly reminded of their country's great past and the deeds of bygone heroes. Amidst faded pomp, Franco reenacted patriotic rituals, celebrated the approved forms of national culture, and crushed all manifestations of "divisive" regionalism. Past glories from the days of Ferdinand and Isabella onward were constantly evoked, while the uncertain future was obscured in clouds of rhetoric. Spain continued to cling to the remnants of the colonial empire like an impoverished hidalgo clutching about him tattered rags that were once a splendid cloak.

Abroad Spain at first paid the full price of her Nazi connections, excluded, for example, from the United Nations and most other international bodies. Spanish citizens were also kept at arm's length throughout the world unless they could produce credentials certifying their status as dissenters or escaped political prisoners. The onset of the cold war brought about a gradual change. During the 1950s Franco was able to play the anticommunist card with increasing effect. Many in the United States, including leading political figures, now endorsed him and hailed his country as a firm bulwark against Soviet penetration of Western Europe. As a wide variety of dictators began to be taken into the service of the "free world," Franco appeared less isolated and less odious. American air and naval bases presently appeared on Spanish soil, and membership in international institutions, with the United States acting as patron, became increasingly possible. Privation at home and rejection beyond the frontiers gave way to a new sense of possibility.

The last 15 years of Franco's rule were characterized by a promotion of foreign involvement and increasing liberalization of domestic economic controls. Although still a poor country, Spain began to take on some appearance of prosperity, especially in the coastal regions favored by tourists. Yet industry lagged, and the rural areas remained backward. Unemployed countrypeople migrated to Madrid and other major cities, introducing complex urban problems. Some Spaniards continued to seek work in other parts of Europe, sustaining their hungry families at home by a flow of remittances that made up a significant portion of the country's revenue. Old wealth and new entrepreneurial fortunes preserved the existence of a social elite, whose fear of proletarian discontent assured their loyalty to the regime.

All of this change was viewed with a mixture of satisfaction and apprehension by members of the governing circle. Those who considered themselves progressives and reformers urged El Caudillo to greater political as well as economic openness while hard-line conservatives warned of danger ahead and insisted that he should rule and change nothing, even rescinding some of his earlier modifications of the authoritarian system. Franco, whose fundamental concept of rule was to encourage rivalry among his principal supporters while keeping his own counsel, allowed these factions to compete and alternate in small victories while pursuing an essentially liberalizing line. Even in matters of state control over the media, political discussion, and labor policy, the regime slowly moderated its regulations. Censorship became more relaxed, although intellectuals found it absurdly arbitrary and still fundamentally opposed to "modernism."

The late 1960s and especially the early 1970s were a time of increased stress and confused expectations for Spaniards. The economic "boom" had receded, a terroristic response to oppression had surfaced among Basque nationalists (leading to the spectacular assassination of Franco's right-hand man), and arguments about the parameters of reform raged. The question of leadership was, however, clearly the most urgent of all. Franco was evidently in declining health and the murder of his deputy, Admiral Luis Carrero Blanco, by the Basques opened the question of future control of the state. But the old man had already provided for that. Some years before he had initiated the process of training a successor. His intention was to restore the monarchy as a stabilizing force. His safeguard, however, was to pass over the direct heir of Alfonso XIII, the count of Barcelona, in favor of the latter's son Prince Juan Carlos. The prince, who had lived most of his life abroad, would be brought to Spain for his higher education, including attendance at the academies of the three armed services. He would also serve apprenticeships in key civil ministries. Having thus prepared himself for the kingship through a thorough training in the workings of government, he would, in effect, sit at the side of El Caudillo, gaining practical experience in decision making. As this plan evolved to its completion, various interests became increasingly nervous. Reactionaries of all stripes feared the persistence of liberal ideas in the prince's thinking. Reformers suspected that the nature of the young man's education would produce a mere Francoist cypher. Others frankly did not know what to make of him, for he preserved a certain reserve under a veneer of affability. Whether Franco intended, in his final years, to render a patriotic service to the country that he had so long exploited for his own benefit or whether this plan of succession was intended as a bitter joke will probably never be known. Franco died, after a long illness, on November 20, 1975, and Spain was left to work out its destiny.

THE LATER SALAZAR REGIME AND ITS AFTERMATH: 1945–1975

In Portugal the Salazar regime emerged relatively unscathed from World War II, with little of the odium attached to the Spanish dictatorship. By 1955 Salazar had secured membership in the United Nations and was ready to embark on the career of elder statesman. He was prepared to work with some of his more progressive advisers to transform the resources of the colonial empire into a basis for Portuguese economic development on a scale not attempted since the late 19th century. Investment of capital and encouragement to settlers in the African territories were key elements in extracting the latent riches of some 800,000 square miles for the benefit of the 35,000 square-mile mother country. Unfortunate for his plan, the dictator was confronted with an upsurge of anticolonialism that had already forced Britain and France to surrender much of their overseas domain. Inevitably the oldest empire of all became the target of international denunciation, and Salazar's response of a revised constitution that made the "overseas provinces" an integral part of Portugal was greeted with derision. As early as 1961 India snatched back Goa and its dependencies, which had been Portugal's earliest footholds on the subcontinent. Beginning in 1964 revolt spread across Angola, Mozambique, and Guinea, presenting Salazar with the stark question. Should Portugal defy world opinion and the prospect of bankruptcy to confront the colonial insurrections? Answering in the affirmative he levied conscription on a scale that put one of every four young Portuguese men into uniform and sent nearly a quarter of a million troops to Africa. The master economist, who had rescued his country from its fiscal woes 40 years earlier through shrewd, prudent calculations, now seemed ready to risk everything on a gigantic gamble against the tide of history. He was not to see the end of the game, for he suffered a paralyzing stroke in 1968 that obliged him to surrender power to a deputy. Salazar died in 1970 and was accorded a state funeral on a scale worthy of a national hero, but the war went on.

Marcelo Caetano, the dictator's longtime associate, who had served as university president, cabinet minister, and party official, took up the reins of government when the prime minister became incapacitated and retained them after his death. While maintaining the structure of dictatorship he sought to convey an impression of moderation by easing some of the regime's more repressive practices. He would recount in his memoirs how he strove to keep a balance between conservatives and progressives by adroit gestures that alternated between a hard line and a glimmer of hope. Whether Caetano was simply not capable of sustaining this complex balancing act or whether the situation in Africa was simply too ruinous to continue, he did not long survive the death of his predecessor. As in the U.S. struggle in Vietnam, the Portuguese employed warships to halt arms smuggling along the coasts and probe the interior waterways, planes to scout for troop movement in the rugged interiors, and infantry to trek through swamps and jungles pursuing an elusive enemy. At home civilian support waned while disillusion spread among both politicians and military men. In April 1974 an insurrection broke out among junior officers and conscripts destined for colonial campaigning. The rebels denounced the ruinous expense, heavy loss of life, and moral evil generated by the regime's policies. General António Spinola, a former commander in Africa who had turned against the government, was called to assume control in Lisbon, while Caetano and his minions gave up without a fight. Soldiers walked the streets of Lisbon with flowers in their gun barrels, and the Carnation Revolution swept away decades of dictatorship with scarcely a shot fired.

THE NEW DEMOCRACIES

THE TRIUMPH OF DEMOCRACY IN SPAIN: 1975–2000

Between 1975 and 1982 the Spaniards amazed the world and, most of all, themselves. A nation that for centuries had won a reputation for arrogant confrontation and, more recently, murderous political strife carried out a peaceful transition from dictatorship to democracy. Despite all of the journalistic predictions and well-founded apprehensions, the Spanish people bade farewell to Franco and followed his designated successor into the mainstream of modern life.

Moving cautiously but steadily, the moderate reformers who had guided the process of change during the last years of the old regime prepared the ground for constitutional revision. With even more remarkable self-restraint and patience the various opposition groups refined their programs to meet the common interests of the country as a whole. Even the most reactionary and potentially most dangerous elements in Spanish society, including the military and security forces, permitted what could only result in a steady erosion of their power. During this period of transition, as everyone seemed to be holding his or her breath, wondering when an inevitable crisis would come, King Juan Carlos played a vital role in balancing the special interests and fears that divided Spanish society. He encouraged, rebuked, and negotiated, at all times reminding his people of the need to preserve stability and unity. Far more than a mere figurehead the monarch proved to be a man who could rally support from all quarters, convincing them of his honesty and personal regard while always keeping his eye on the ultimate prize—the triumph of Spain.

By 1978 the intense debates over the new constitution had produced a document that guaranteed an authentic representation of the people and the preservation of the national heritage in conjunction with due recognition for regional autonomy. An orderly political process had been initiated, as the transition from one-party authoritarianism to functioning democracy guided Spain toward the political center. The old Falangists yielded with little more than grumbling, while the newly-enfranchised Communists displayed surprising restraint.

What seemed to be the moment that most Spaniards had dreaded came in 1981 as a contingent of the paramilitary Civil Guard seized control of the legislative chamber in Madrid, fired shots into the ceiling, and proclaimed over national television that they would hold the deputies hostage until unspecified changes were made. Amid fears that this was merely a prelude to a full-fledged military coup, the king went on the air to reassert the primacy of law and constitution and call upon his people to stand by the new Spain in this crisis. Most important of all he addressed a special message to the armed forces reminding them of their oath of loyalty to him and the nation and commanding them to refrain from any illegal action. Whatever support for a coup existed in the army quickly evaporated, and several generals who had issued preliminary orders for action hastily revoked them.

In 1982, confirmed in their commitment to democracy, Spaniards went to the polls in a parliamentary election fought on issues of economic policy and sociocultural evolution and gave a majority of their votes to the Socialist Party. For the first time in nearly half a century they had freely chosen a government of the Left. Many among them could scarcely believe what had been achieved, for they had not only moved their nation in a political direction long repudiated by its leaders but those who adhered to parties of the Right calmly accepted the majority decision and prepared to work within the normal political process for their own goals during the next electoral cycle. Spain had, in short, assumed its place in the modern European system. It had not only abandoned the Franquist past; it had essentially abandoned its whole tradition of authoritarianism.

Felipe González, leader of the Socialist Workers Party of Spain (PSOE), had established his credentials as a dynamic and charismatic politician in the southern region of Andalusia. These positive qualities, added to the sheer excitement generated by the first complete victory for the Left in so many decades, created a momentum that took some time to grind to a halt. New freedoms in cultural life, affiliation with international bodies such as the North Atlantic Treaty Organization (NATO) and the European Union, and schemes for nationalization and social welfare were generally welcomed. Conservatives might denounce them as, respectively, godless immorality, subordination to foreign interests, and creeping communism, but they remained in a minority, at least for the time being. It was rather from the Left itself that the

most damning complaints would eventually come. As foreign investment raised the level of domestic prosperity, socialist ideals seemed to
give way to capitalist ambition. Cronyism and corruption generated
scandal after scandal within the González administration. The prime
minister alternated between unconvincing reassurances and blustering
denials. While he traveled abroad enjoying plaudits as the new hero of
international socialism, socialism was beginning to lose its luster at
home among his compatriots. The government made compromise after
compromise, generating embarrassment among its supporters and contempt among its rivals. González, in the 10th year of his premiership,
attempted to refurbish his image and celebrate the "New Spain." The
quincentenary of Columbus's voyage to the New World in 1992 was
marked by lavish construction projects, an international exposition in
Seville, and the staging of the Olympic Games at Barcelona. The results
were decidedly mixed. Although circumstances ranging from financial
problems to the diminished prestige of Columbus and his colonial heritage undercut much of the quincentenary celebrations, González himself
was the principal loser due to the perceived irrelevance of his priorities.

Regionalism had come back to haunt the government after the hasty
and improvisational efforts made to dispose of the issue in the 1978
constitution. The Socialist regime had wavered between concessions to
the lesser pretensions of opportunistic autonomists and unproductive
negotiations with the Catalans and Basques. The country was now
morselized into 17 regions, many of which had no serious claim to
autonomy and merely complicated the administrative process by their
endless complaints. The only autonomists who really mattered, those
of Catalonia and the Basque Country, were even more troublesome but
could not be silenced by minor favors. In his attempts to curb terrorist
violence by the militant Basque nationalists of the ETA (Euskadi Ta
Askatasuna, or "Basque Homeland and Freedom"), González authorized brutal actions by his police. Prisoners were in a number of instances
tortured or even murdered. The prime minister may not have specifically approved of these actions, but his defense of his underlings amid
judicial inquiries and mounting public outcry hastened his downfall. In
the election of 1996, the PSOE was defeated by the Popular Party, under
José María Aznar. A solemn, even gloomy conservative, Aznar represented a turn back toward the Right, although by no means a reversion
to Franquist principles. Aznar favored the continuation of most of his
predecessor's programs of interactive outreach, economic modernization, and cultural freedom, albeit at a more cautious pace. Above all he
was committed to the unity of the nation, and some of his most ardent
combats would be with regionalists rather than with trade unionists

(although the latter did not care for his labor policies). A temporary cease-fire was reached with the Basque militants in 1998 but had collapsed by late November 1999, and political violence accelerated, steadily approaching the level of 1,000 deaths since 1969. Despite ending the century as the leader of 40 million Spaniards who enjoyed a new sense of prosperity and respect in Europe, Aznar could not hope for ultimate success until the Basque problem was settled. He might have a renewed mandate in the democratic process that had now established itself firmly in his country, but ballots were still incapable of defeating bullets.

THE TRIUMPH OF DEMOCRACY IN PORTUGAL: 1975–2000

Portugal's dictator, unlike Franco, made no provision for a designated successor and the improvisational nature of Caetano's regime never allowed it to be seen as more than a transition to an unknown future. Amid the confusion that followed the Carnation Revolution of 1974, many Portuguese may have wished that they had not been so eager to discard the monarchy back in 1910. There was no king available to provide the balance and disinterested patriotism the situation required. Perhaps it was Portugal's long association with Great Britain that enabled the country to adopt Britain's well-known tactic of somehow muddling through crises. After several years of attempted coups, quarrelling generals, communist threats, and regional upheavals, the Portuguese republic emerged in the early 1980s intact and confident. Although the constitution adopted in 1975 seethed with antifascist rhetoric, the extreme Left won surprisingly few votes in the 1976 elections. Despite an initial program of nationalization in banking, insurance, and some aspects of industry, as well as the expropriation of certain landed property, most of these manifestations of marxism were repealed by 1986. The military, which had reached a strength of more than 200,000 in the last days of the dictatorship, sank to little more than 60,000, and the capacity of those who remained for domestic mischief making had disappeared. Portugal had arrived at essentially the same middle ground attained by Spain in the 1980s, having evaded the dangers of counterrevolution from the Right and unrestrained radicalism from the Left.

Mário Soares, the Socialist leader who had provided desperately needed good sense as prime minister during the most critical period, moved on to the presidency, the first civilian to occupy that post in 60 years. His party evolved a practical collaboration with the Social Democrats, constituting a center-Left coalition that guided the country into the '90s. The last decade of a century that had seen Portugal through such profound transformations provided it with a breathing space. Membership in the European Union secured much needed support for economic modernization and facilitated both foreign investment and a profitable growth of tourism. Improved relations with its often unfriendly neighbor led to collaboration, both within the European Union and on Ibero-American projects. Spain, like Portugal, had given up most of its remaining colonies in 1975 but had soon launched a program of cultural and financial outreach. Portugal now followed this example by forming what amounted to a Lusitanian Commonwealth that linked it with Brazil and its former dependencies in Africa. Portugal also gave belated support to the liberation of its abandoned colony, East Timor, from Indonesian oppression in 1998–99. In the latter year the Portuguese flag was lowered in the ultimate remnant of her once globe-girdling empire as Macao was handed over to China.

Five hundred years after the valor and ambition of Portuguese navigators had carried them to the shores of America in the same grand sweep of empire building that was mapping the coast of Africa and opening the trade of Asia, the empire was gone. But the Portugal of 2000 was at least free of the divisive regionalism and on-going terrorism that tormented Spain. Moreover Portugal, too, had secured a functioning democracy. Even though her principal political parties were sometimes on shaky ground and her economy, after the expiration of European Union subsidies, was not entirely sound, there was every reason to believe that her best days were not all in the past.

SPANISH AND PORTUGUESE CULTURE IN THE TWENTIETH CENTURY

For Spain, the 19th century had ended with a conjunction of failures and frustrations that seemed to go beyond even those experienced during the preceding 200 years. Yet the "Generation of '98" would prove to be remarkably resilient. Rather than continue the familiar lamentations about lost greatness, Spaniards would henceforth show themselves willing to confront a daunting array of challenges, endure the bitterest sufferings, and persist in reforming their worst shortcomings.

Nowhere was there determination to break free from the preoccupation with the past more evident than in their cultural achievements of the 20th century. Indeed, some observers would speak of this century as representing a new "golden age."

Spain produced five winners of the Nobel Prize in literature—José Echegaray (1904), Jacinto Benavente (1922), Juan Ramón Jiménez (1956), Vicente Aleixandre (1977), and Camilo José Cela (1989)—and emerged at the end of the Franco dictatorship with a whole new crop of young writers as well as a "found generation" of those who had evaded the censorship and harassment of the regime. Once again there were great poets such as Antonio Machado and Federico García Lorca and profound philosophers such as Miguel de Unamuno, José Ortega y Gasset, and the transplanted George Santayana. Pablo Picasso, a founder of cubism, towers above his contemporaries, though other sons of Spain such as the painters Joan Miró and Salvador Dalí and the sculptor Eduardo Chillida made major contributions to the evolution of modern art. There was a new flowering of music, with composers such as Enrique Granados, Manuel de Falla, Isaac Albéniz, and Joaquín Rodrigo, not to mention the brilliant cellist Pablo (Pau) Casals and Andrés Segovia, who transformed the guitar into an instrument of high art. Singers of the greatest distinction included the tenors Plácido Domingo, José Carreras, and Alfredo Kraus and the sopranos Montserrat Caballé and Victoria de los Ángeles. The 20th century's most distinctive art form—cinema—flowered in Spain, particularly in the work of Luis Buñuel, an international giant. He was followed in the post-Franco era by the acute Carlos Saura and the outrageous Pedro Almodovar (winner of Hollywood's Academy Award).

Portugal, laboring for most of the 20th century under the burdens of cultural isolation and political repression, rose in the post-Salazar period to a heightened level of individuality and dynamism among its artists and writers. The neglected genius of Amadeo de Souza Cardoso, a pioneer of modernist painting, was not fully acknowledged until the 1990s, many decades after his death. The country's most notable novelist, José Saramago, a foe of fascist dictatorship and clerical censorship, was awarded the Nobel Prize in literature in 1998, crowning (though not ending) a career that enhanced his country's prestige around the world and emphasized the significance of Portuguese as a global language.

INTO THE TWENTY-FIRST CENTURY

On September 11, 2001, a series of attacks by Islamic militants destroyed the World Trade Center in New York City with its landmark Twin Towers; ravaged the Pentagon building, headquarters of the Defense Department, in Washington; and was barely thwarted in the destruction of the U.S. Capitol or White House. Planes hijacked by members of a militant fundamentalist group called al-Qaeda were used as flying bombs, and the 19 perpetrators killed some 3,000 passengers and building occupants. There had been some preliminary evidence of growing Islamic militancy during the preceding 10 years but response and even strategic planning to deal with it in the United States or elsewhere had been minimal. In answer to the events of what became known as 9/11/01 the United States launched an invasion of Afghanistan, where the al-Qaeda headquarters was located under the hospitality of its affiliate, the Taliban. With the militants routed and the country taken over by the American forces, the crisis seemed at an end. Members of NATO were generally willing to support the United States in its "liberation of Afghanistan." Spain dispatched a token force to join the occupying troops. However, Washington declared that a "global war on terrorism" had now begun, identified Iraq as an enabler of al-Qaeda, and called upon right-minded nations to join in a confrontation with that country. During the year 2002, arguments raged over American allegations that Iraq was preparing weapons of mass destruction. Both the United States and the European Union divided over whether to pursue the war that Washington declared had been launched against civilization and democracy by the agents of terror.

In Spring 2003, Portugal's island province, the Azores, hosted the president of the United States and the prime minister of Great Britain. Standing beside them, the leaders of Spain and Portugal pledged solidarity with those countries that chose to launch military action against the regime of Saddam Hussein, dictator of Iraq. The invasion and occupation of Iraq followed with the same rapidity and seemingly total victory that had been achieved in Afghanistan. By May 2003, President George Bush proclaimed "mission accomplished." Then, on March 11, 2004, terrorists set off bombs in Madrid's principal railroad station and on board trains carrying commuters into the city. Nearly 200 passengers were killed. Prime Minister Aznar, already widely criticized for supporting the United States, hesitated to point the finger of guilt at Islamists, suggesting that his old foe, ETA, had been responsible. This tactic has been blamed by many analysts for his party's loss of the parliamentary election that took place a few days later. The Socialist opposition was swept into power by voters who evidently believed that Aznar had tried to disguise the fact that he had brought Spain into a bloody confrontation with militant Islam that most Spaniards had never wanted. The Socialist leader, José Luis Rodriguez Zapatero, upon assuming office as prime minister withdrew the Spanish contingent from Iraq. During the next few years, U.S. relations with Spain deteriorated. The Spanish government prosecuted those alleged to have "punished" Spain for its initial support of the Iraq invasion but made it quite clear that Spain wanted nothing more to do with that enterprise, although maintaining a NATO commitment in Afghanistan.

Spain's ambivalence over the question of Islamic terrorism was increased by a steadily mounting flow of illegal immigrants into Spanish territory. Spain's geographical location as the closest part of the European Union to North Africa had long made it a favorite entry point for foreigners seeking to make their way across the Mediterranean. Some of these crossing the Strait of Gibraltar on improvised rafts sought to move north of the Pyrenees, but others were content to remain in Spain and establish an economic foothold for themselves. By the year 2006, more that 100,000 "refugees" had opened a new flank in the informal invasion by landing on the Canary Islands and demanding accommodation on the mainland. Although some originated in distant countries and had made their way with great exertion to the borders of Spain, many were North African Muslims who represented a potential complication to the already vexed state of affairs. Some commentators pointed out that a demographic shift was in process. The birthrate among the traditional population of Spaniards was in decline and the number of "exotic" residents in the country was rising. Although this phenomenon was clearly discernible in a number of other European countries, Spain's position on the "borderlands" of Western civilization made its situation particularly disturbing.

Although the ongoing quarrel between Spain and ETA had presented an alternate scenario to explain the Madrid train bombing of 2004, Basque terrorism had quickly been discarded by most Spaniards in favor of an Islamic source. A few conservatives continued to insist that ETA had at least worked in conjunction with Muslim militants. Their theories evaporated in 2005 when ETA made a sweeping proposal for a cease-fire and negotiations with the Madrid government. Prime Minister Rodriquez Zapatero responded with initial caution but then showed himself more receptive to the proposal. Little actual progress toward serious discussion of the Basque question could take place during 2006 because various Basque political groups weighed in with complex points involving Basque "nationhood" and even suggestions that France had to be involved in any discussion because part of the Basque homeland lay within France. Further complications were presented by Catalan nationalists who were not to be outdone in seeking even greater special status concessions for their nationality within Spain than had already been granted in previous concessions. Spanish nationalists, ever on guard against separatism, were quick to warn against creeping erosion of Spanish unity. Several voices from the Francoist past were heard to the effect that the time had come to take a hard line against anyone and any minority that threatened the survival of the Spanish nation. It had long been the dream of many Spaniards to regain the status of great power in Europe and the world. As they moved on into the 21st century they were learning, as had Spaniards of earlier centuries, that glory does not come without cost.

HISTORICAL
DICTIONARY
A–Z

A

adelantado

First used on the frontiers of medieval Spain in lands recently reconquered from Islamic invaders, this title was introduced into the New World in 1497 and continued to be employed throughout the period of discovery and conquest. Granted to the man who undertook the initial exploration and mastering of new territory, it included political, judicial, and military authority within a defined area. Signifying "one who goes before, or is ahead," the designation was intended both as recognition and reward to the pioneering conquistador who established the boundaries of an expanding Spanish empire. The title was usually granted for the lifetime of the pioneer or, in some cases, that of his immediate heir and only rarely became a hereditary title. In any case the term *adelantado* soon became regarded as merely honorific and would be replaced by a formal administrative structure as soon as effective Spanish control was established in a region.

Afonso VI (1643–1683)
king of Portugal

The son of JOHN IV, Afonso suffered from physical and mental disabilities that made his conduct unstable or, at best, useless for the exercise of government. During a series of regencies and ministerial dominations, the war of independence from Spain was brought to a successful conclusion, and Afonso was given the designation (ironic under the circumstances) "the Victorious." His nominal marriage to a French princess precipitated a conspiracy by his brother, Pedro, and the bride, who had formed an instant attachment to her new brother-in-law. Afonso was deposed in 1667 and sent to reside under supervision in the AZORES. His marriage was annulled, and his wife married Pedro, who exercised the regency until Afonso's death when he assumed the crown as PETER II.

Aguirre, Lope de (1510–1561)
Spanish soldier and rebel

Reportedly of noble birth but with a reckless and violent temperament, Aguirre arrived in the New World in the early 1530s, took part in the pacification of the Caribbean and Central America, and then journeyed to PERU. An adherent of the Pizarro family, he took part in the civil war between the conquerors and was accused of numerous atrocities. He was, however, granted amnesty by the royal government that was imposed after the conflict ended and held several administrative posts.

In 1560 the viceroy of Peru organized an expedition to the east with the chief purpose of ridding his territory of its numerous idle and troublemaking adventurers. Pedro de Ursúa was charged with verifying the persistent legends of El Dorado, a fabulously wealthy native ruler who supposedly lived in the interior of the Amazonian jungles and whose name referred to his practice of coating himself in gold dust. While this story had been in circulation for decades and El Dorado's residence variously designated as the deserts of North America or the islands of the Caribbean, it was still enough to arouse the enthusiasm and greed of many criminal types. Ursúa set out to sail down the Marañón and Amazon Rivers with some 300 soldiers and numerous civilian servants and hangers-on. Aguirre was third in command.

As on previous expeditions into this region, nothing of value was discovered and the party became disillusioned and angry, enabling Aguirre to instigate a mutiny in which Ursúa and his closest associates were murdered. Aguirre then proclaimed a new commander, the former deputy leader Fernando de Guzmán, subsequently enticing him to renounce his allegiance to Spain and declare himself "prince of Peru." As the downstream voyage continued, it degenerated into a sequence of increasingly insane and bloody clashes provoked by Aguirre and his picked cohort of thugs, who eventually slew the deluded Guzmán and all of those who did not transfer their allegiance to Aguirre. Diverting their course down the Orinoco River, they reached the Venezuelan coast, laid waste to Indian villages and Spanish settlements, crossed over to the island of Margarita, and carried out a reign of terror there while Aguirre planned his next move. This evidently involved crossing the Isthmus of Panama, sailing back south on the western shore of South America, and seizing control of Peru. A manifesto addressed at this time to King PHILIP II of Spain repudiates Aguirre's allegiance to the monarch, whom he charges with various fancied misdeeds and declares Aguirre to be the rightful ruler of the Spanish dominions in Peru and adjacent lands. Retreating from forces that were being mustered against him and abandoned by most of his surviving comrades, Aguirre was eventually trapped in VENEZUELA and according to various accounts either assassinated by one of his own men or executed by Spanish authorities.

The career of Lope de Aguirre illustrates the descent into madness and massacre that was always a threat to conquistadores as they endeavored to maintain their often-proclaimed commitment to honor and religion amidst the incitements of greed, jealousy, and warrior rage. Aguirre's story would be told in later days as a cautionary tale but unfortunately did not always have the desired deterrent effect.

Alarcón y Mendoza, Juan Ruiz de (1580–1639)
Spanish dramatist

Born in Mexico to an administrator of mines and a mother descended from the noble house of Mendoza, Alarcón studied for the law in Spain and then returned to Mexico hoping to secure a position. Failing to do so he settled in Madrid to pursue his career ambition. It was chiefly to support himself during this period that he began writing plays, including some of his best-regarded work. After receiving an appointment on the staff of the Council of the Indies, he enjoyed a secure and well-paid position for the rest of his life.

Particularly after he became professionally established in the law Alarcón produced numerous plays, although few were as well regarded as his earlier achievements. He was much derided by jealous rivals, who mocked his pretentiousness, his colonial origin, and his physical deformities. LOPE DE VEGA was particularly scathing, as was the satirist FRANCISCO DE QUEVEDO.

Despite the negative reaction of his contemporaries Alarcón was undoubtedly among the ablest of Spanish dramatists. As a lawyer he was especially conscious of questions relating to false ideas, trickery, and veracity. His point of view is particularly evident in his best-known play, *La verdad sospechosa* (The suspicious truth), written during Alarcón's period of straitened circumstances in 1618. The protagonist, Don García, is an appealing young man whose only vice is a tendency to invent stories. As the plot develops, what seems at first to be a comic tangle ends sadly with García losing the girl he loves and forced into an undesirable marriage. Alarcón thus makes the point that truth telling is not only moral but likely to lead to the best result. When Pierre Corneille appropriated this play some years later under the title *Le Menteur* (The liar), he emphasized the farcical elements and gave it a falsely happy ending—a resolution more satisfying to French audiences than to Spaniards. Also illustrating Alarcón's concern with the sad outcome of character defects is *Las paredes oyen* (The walls have ears), dating from 1617. Here, too, the polite relationships of urbane society are disrupted by the protagonist's inability to resist a particular form of behavior, in this case, slander. Another moral flaw is confronted by Alarcón in *La prueba de las promesas* (The proof of the promises) where the

all-too-familiar sin of ingratitude destroys happy relationships.

In these and two dozen other plays, Alarcón presents striking characters, clever dialogue, and an adroit revelation of the fatal deficiencies that underlie a civilized social setting. Although his total literary output is far smaller than that of his major contemporaries, Alarcón has left an impressive dramatic legacy and one that has been an inspiration to playwrights in other countries as well as his own.

Alas, Leopoldo (Clarín) (1852–1901)
Spanish writer

Best known under his pseudonym "Clarín," this Asturian studied law at the Universities of Madrid and Oviedo and became a professor at the latter. His 1884 novel, *La regenta* (The regent's wife), is an unsparing depiction of the provincial bourgeoisie, set in the fictional town of Vetusta (actually Oviedo). Along with *Su único hijo* (His only son), published in 1890, it established him as one of the major novelists of late 19th-century Spain. Some compared him with Emile Zola (although he disdained what he considered the crudities of the French writer) and regarded Alas, rather than EMILIA PARDO BAZÁN, as the prime exponent of Spanish naturalism (although he was an admirer and defender of Pardo Bazán).

Alas was perhaps even better known as a literary critic, whose numerous essays on contemporary literature were often so biting and personal as to terrorize the authors who came under his scrutiny. Despite his reputation as a ferocious reviewer and his harsh depiction of small-town hypocrisy in his best-known novels, Alas was, above all, a conservative moralist, who held writers to a high standard of probity and dignity. He was convinced that Spain, for all its ills, had a distinctive cultural identity and capacity for regeneration. In this sense he was unwilling to yield to the self-flagellation popular with the GENERATION OF '98.

Clarín was the author of a number of admired short stories, but his later novels were perhaps not truly up to his own high critical standards. Those standards and the judgments that he levied on contemporary writers are what preserve his name and fame.

Alba, Fernando Álvarez de Toledo, duque de (duque de Alva)
(1508–1582)
Spanish soldier and statesman

Descendant of a noble Castilian family that had provided many warriors and counselors to the Spanish Crown, the third duke of Alba followed a military career that led him to his greatest victory in 1547 when he defeated the German Protestant forces at the Battle of Mühlberg. As the culmination of nearly 30 years' struggle by Spain to put down the Reformation, this victory represented a triumph for Alba's master, King CHARLES I (Holy Roman Emperor Charles V), and was suitably rewarded. Alba was also victorious in the 1550s over France and her Italian allies in the final stages of the ITALIAN WARS, which had been waged by Spain since 1494. Although this victory like that in Germany, was ultimately undercut by later political developments, Alba retained his status as Spain's most distinguished general.

During the 1560s, under the new king, PHILIP II, Spain became embroiled in a new conflict with the people of the Netherlands who resisted the political and religious dominance of Spain. Alba was given command of the Spanish forces in these provinces in 1567 and subsequently was designated as regent of the area. Exercising total control, he pursued a policy of repression, instituting a special court (the so-called Council of Blood) that decreed the execution of many prominent Netherlanders. Further harsh measures, far from quelling resistance, drove the territory into full-scale rebellion, and by 1573 Alba was recalled to Spain and replaced by an administrator who was ordered to pursue a more conciliatory policy. Blamed by some members of the king's entourage for the worsening of the situation, Alba was not further employed until 1580, when the extinction of the ruling dynasty of Portugal precipitated a crisis in the Iberian Peninsula. Alba was called out of retirement to command the troops, who invaded the smaller country, defeated partisans of a native pretender to the throne, and captured LISBON. Although Philip II was thus able to annex the Portuguese empire to his realms, the characteristically uncompromising tactics of Alba as he enforced Spanish control created an initial antagonism that persisted among the Portuguese during the 60 years of Spanish overlordship.

The duke of Alba was undoubtedly a military commander of great skill and determination, but he totally lacked the ability to curb his battlefield ferocity when charged with overseeing an occupied country. His brutal tactics in the Netherlands have remained the object of execration for centuries, and throughout Europe his name has been a by-word for a bloodthirstiness that has often been attributed to all Spaniards.

Albéniz, Isaac Manuel Francisco (1860–1909)

Spanish composer

When little more than a boy, Albéniz left home to pursue a passion for playing the piano and supported himself during his wanderings by his facility with that instrument. When he was in his 20s he returned to a more orderly and disciplined life and studied with Franz Liszt and the advocate of a distinctively Spanish school of music, Felipe Pedrell (who was also the teacher of ENRIQUE GRANADOS and MANUEL DE FALLA). In Paris Albéniz met with leading French composers of the day and developed his own style, incorporating contemporary pianistic approaches with traditional Spanish folkloric themes. He was prolific in his compositions, producing the suites for piano *Iberia* and *Catalonia,* the "Tango in D Major," and a series of *Cantos de España*. On a larger scale his work ranged from the comic opera *The Magic Opal* to the grand opera *Pepita Jiménez,* based on the celebrated novel by JUAN VALERA. The career of Albéniz was cut short by illness, and he produced little in the years up to his death.

Alberoni, Giulio   (1664–1752)

Spanish statesman

Born to a humble family in the Italian duchy of Parma, Alberoni was recognized by the Jesuits for his natural abilities, educated in their schools, and ordained to the priesthood, subsequently becoming a canon of the cathedral of Parma. Shifting from an ecclesiastical to a diplomatic career, he represented the duchy at the headquarters of the duke of Vendôme, the principal French commander during the WAR OF THE SPANISH SUCCESSION. Traveling with Vendôme as adviser both in France and Spain, he continued to represent his own sovereign, becoming the latter's personal agent in MADRID after the close of the war. He played a major role in arranging the marriage of the duke of Parma's daughter, Isabella Farnese, to the widowed PHILIP V.

Between 1716 and 1719 Alberoni was prime minister of Spain in everything but name, serving both the interests of his adopted country and the political ambitions of the queen consort. His most important achievements in domestic policy were the promotion of trade, the enhancement of manufacturing by encouraging the immigration of foreign craftsmen, and the abolition of the archaic system of royal councils. Although in these matters he essentially followed the line advocated by Philip's French advisers during the earlier part of his reign, he was drawn into an increasingly anti-French program by pressure from the queen. While Alberoni sought only to reestablish the diminished prestige of Spain and preferred to concentrate on it strengthening the American empire, the king's new wife demanded an aggressive challenge to Austria's new predominance in Italy. This would, in later years, lead to the queen's obsession with securing Italian thrones for her sons, particularly the future CHARLES III. Despite Alberoni's arguments that such actions were premature, he was compelled to launch invasions of Sardinia and Sicily, territories that had been lost by Spain in the succession war. This merely provoked a massive counterattack from a coalition of France, Austria, Britain, and the Dutch Republic. By 1719 Spain had been defeated on land and sea, and Alberoni, blamed for the disaster, was forced to withdraw to Rome. Thanks to his status as a cardinal, obtained while he was still in Spain, he was able to secure a place for himself in papal service, eventually governing, successively, Ravenna and Bologna. He died at an advanced age in his native town, Piacenza, his brief but significant role in Spanish history long since past.

Alberti, Rafael (1902–1996)
Spanish poet

A native of CÁDIZ, Alberti shared his friend FEDERICO GARCÍA LORCA's passion for the landscape and environment of ANDALUSIA. Some critics consider these two the finest lyric poets of modern Spain. They were part of a group of poets and other intellectuals known as the GENERATION OF '27 that gathered in MADRID in the years just before the proclamation of the republic and dedicated themselves to a new cultural direction for their country. Alberti defended the Second Republic during the SPANISH CIVIL WAR both as a combatant and a writer of propagandistic material. After the triumph of FRANCISCO FRANCO, Alberti chose exile, living in various countries until settling in Rome, where he and his wife, also a writer, maintained a rendez-vous for Spanish expatriates opposed to the dictatorship. Alberti returned to Spain in 1977 and was elected as a Communist member of the legislature. He soon gave up this political post to devote himself to public poetry reading. The literary awards that were conferred upon him, including the Cervantes Prize and the National Theater Prize (1980), were a recognition of cultural achievements that transcended any lingering political antagonisms.

Alberti's *Marinero en tierra* (Sailor on land), published when he was only 23, reflected his enduring love for the sea as viewed from his native Cádiz and marked him as a rising poet. Among the poetical works that he published in subsequent years, perhaps the most striking was *Sobre los ángeles* (About the angels, 1929), which showed surrealist influences. As a member of the Generation of '27, he never ceased to assert his idealistic vision for a new and better Spain in his plays, such as *Noche de guerra en el Museo del Prado* (Night of war at the Prado Museum, 1935), and his autobiographical writings, which included *La arboleda perdida* (The lost grove). When he died in 1999 he was the last survivor of that generation, but he had lived long enough to see the birth of a truly democratic Spain.

Albuquerque, Afonso de (1453–1515)
Portuguese admiral and colonial administrator

After a naval-military career, including battles with the Turks in the Mediterranean, Albuquerque was dispatched by King MANUEL I to be his viceroy in Portuguese Asia. Arriving in the Indian Ocean, he asserted Portuguese control over the rulers of southern Arabia but failed to establish his authority on arriving in India. After spending a year in confinement (1508–09), he was liberated upon the arrival of a fleet from Lisbon and installed as viceroy. In a brilliant series of campaigns he conquered GOA, which was to become the center of the Portuguese Empire in Asia; the great island of Ceylon; the strategic straits of Malacca; and the Sunda Islands, key to the Eastern spice trade. By capturing Hormuz at the entrance to the Persian Gulf, he further disrupted Arab attempts to challenge Portugal's new ascendancy in the region. As his fleet was returning from its latest triumph, he received word that the king had been persuaded by jealous rivals at court to dismiss him. Albuquerque loyally declined his followers' urgings to rebel against this injustice and died a few days later.

Referred to by his contemporaries as the "Great Albuquerque" or "Afonso the Great," a warrior-statesman who wielded a strict command but was esteemed by his subjects, Albuquerque was the true founder of the Portuguese realm in the East whose remnants endured for nearly five centuries.

Alcazar of Toledo, siege of the
(July 21–September 27, 1936)
Of all the alcazars, those Moorish combinations of palace and fortress that were constructed throughout Spain, the most famous is undoubtedly the Alcazar of Toledo. It acquired its fame during a more than two-month siege that it endured at the beginning of the SPANISH CIVIL WAR. This citadel stood on a hill overlooking the historic city that lies some 40 miles south of MADRID. Its massive walls and two looming towers gave it the aspect of an impregnable medieval castle, while its vast subterranean storehouses provided shelter for a large garrison, a repository for huge quantities of ammunition, and (even more important during a siege) an internal water supply. The Alcazar had been modernized and reinforced in the early 1900s and served as the army's infantry school. In 1936 its commander, Colonel José Moscardo, had attempted to seize control of TOLEDO in the opening hours of the Nationalist uprising, but like his colleagues in Madrid, he had been thwarted by Loyalist militia. He withdrew into the Alcazar,

accompanied by some 1,500 fighting men and nearly 600 women and children, mostly dependents of soldiers and police. There were also an undetermined number of civilian hostages (whose fate, it appears, was never of particular concern to the Loyalists). Between mid-July and late-September Moscardo held out in expectation of being relieved by the rebel forces advancing from the south.

The most famous episode of the siege occurred during the first few days when the commander of the Loyalist forces who had encircled the citadel informed Moscardo by telephone that they were holding his son and would execute him unless the coronel surrendered the fortress. When they put the youth on the line to verify that he was indeed their captive, his father told him that he must make his peace with God and die proudly shouting *"¡Viva España!"* The two then exchanged fond farewells. The Loyalist commander came back on the line to hear Moscardo state, "The Alcazar will never surrender" and hang up. His son was shot some days later.

Lacking adequate artillery and the ability to make use of that which they had, the besiegers were unable to bombard the Alcazar effectively, and the trained marksmen under Moscardo's command were much more deadly with their rifle and machine-gun fire than the militia men were. As the weeks wore on, the attackers launched a number of assaults that were beaten off by the defenders with numerous displays of personal valor by individual cadets and officers. Eventually mines were planted by tunneling under the towers, and both were brought down by explosions that reduced them to rubble. By late September the besiegers had put their hopes on starving out the garrison, who beat back every attempt to drive them out of their improvised positions. Starvation and disease were setting in with almost nothing left to eat but the putrefying flesh of butchered cavalry horses and mules. Then Moscardo and his staff, who had received virtually no news about the progress of the uprising, saw evidence of battles raging on the hills surrounding the city and realized that relief was at hand. Troops from the Army of Africa broke through the Loyalists' outposts during the last days of September. The Republicans proved no match for the Foreign Legion and Moorish battalions who swarmed into Toledo. The siege came to an end with Moscardo stepping forward from the ranks of his soldiers, saluting the leader of the rescuing army, and reporting laconically with the standard phrase *"Sin novedad"* ("Nothing new").

The siege of the Alcazar of Toledo became the iconic event of the Nationalist movement during the civil war. Although the struggle would continue until early 1939, with tens of thousands of lives lost on both sides, the image of determination, valor, and sacrifice embodied the highest principles of the Spanish army. Even their enemies, while they might despise the professional ideals of the rebels, were often secret admirers of the very "Spanish" way in which Moscardo and his men had conducted themselves.

Alcazarquivir, Battle of (1578)

No event in Portuguese history was more catastrophic than the Battle of Alcazarquivir, for it brought to an abrupt halt the trajectory of good fortune that had taken the lesser of the two Iberian kingdoms to a level of global empire paralleling that of Spain. King SEBASTIAN, ever since coming of age and emerging from the tutelage of his elders, had aspired to military glory. In particular he was determined to lead a great crusade against the Muslims of North Africa. Against the advice of his uncle, PHILIP II of Spain, the young monarch assembled all the available resources of Portugal, hired German mercenaries, and even diverted a force of Italian soldiers sailing under papal mandate to aid Catholic rebels in Ireland. This army he conveyed to the Moroccan coast where he intended to support one candidate for the sultanate against a rival. The entire campaign was not only ill conceived but poorly planned and executed. Having marched into the desert to a point near the town of Alcazarquivir, Sebastian and his 17,000 men encountered a superior force of Moroccans. On August 4, 1578, after a hard-fought battle, virtually all of the Portuguese and their allies were slain or carried off as slaves. The exact fate of Sebastian has never been determined, and tales of his survival and ultimate return to save his country from adversity long persisted. The only remaining member of the Aviz dynasty, the elderly cardinal Enrique succeeded his great nephew, but following his death in 1580, the disarray into which Portugal had fallen after the defeat at Alcazarquivir laid the way open for invasion and annexation by Spain. Philip II, whose wise counsel to Sebastian had been ignored, now reaped the benefit of the young king's folly. He was proclaimed Philip I of Portugal, and the two kingdoms were joined in a personal union for the next 60 years. It was more than a century before Portugal recovered from the consequences of the North African disaster, and even then the country never regained the high status that it had achieved during its Golden Age.

Aleixandre, Vicente (1898–1984)
Spanish poet

Born in SEVILLE, the son of a railway engineer, Aleixandre was trained for the law and briefly taught that subject. After 1925 his poor health led him to quit his profession and devote the remainder of his life (with several interruptions due to recurring bouts of illness) to poetry. Although evidently a supporter of the Second Republic, he took no active part in the SPANISH CIVIL WAR and remained in Spain during the Franco era. While his poetry was banned for a time, he was elected to the Royal Academy in 1949, having already won major literary prizes. In 1977 he was awarded the Nobel Prize in literature in recognition of the whole body of his work.

Despite his fragile health Aleixandre lived a long and remarkably productive life, authoring dozens of volumes of poetry, including an anthology that ran to more than 800 pages and was by no means the sum total of his work. A pioneer in the surrealist approach to poetry and in the use of free verse, he was a living link between the poets of the GENERATION OF '27 and those who emerged in the post-Franco period. Aleixandre's work, from *La destrucción o el amor* (Destruction or love, 1935) and *Sombra del paraíso* (Shadow of paradise, 1944) to *Poemas de la consumación* (Poems of consummation, 1968) and *Diálogos del conocimiento* (Dialogues of knowledge, 1974) had as its recurring themes the great questions that have absorbed philosophers and theologians as well as poets—the essence of human nature, the destiny of humans, and the meaning of the cosmos. While younger poets might dismiss some of his work as ponderous and overly cerebral, he earned a well-deserved respect until the very end of his literary career.

Alemán, Mateo (1547–1614)
Spanish novelist

The son of an attending physician in a prison hospital in SEVILLE, Alemán originally intended to follow his father's profession but evidently either did not finish his studies or did not practice. Instead, he became a government accountant but nevertheless had to face debtor's prison. After taking up residence in NEW SPAIN, he had a more prosperous later life. The principal reason for his changing fortunes was the novel *Guzmán de Alfarache* (first part, 1559; second part, 1604). Although not the first picaresque novel, *Guzmán* scored an instant triumph and was promptly translated into most of the major European languages. The protagonist, Guzmán, relates the story of his life and of how he has lived by his wits, pursuing a long series of deceptions, frauds, and outright crimes under many guises. Alemán's vivid depictions of criminal types may owe their origin to his youthful encounters with the inmates he met while accompanying his father on his rounds. The idea of the picaro (rogue) as hero or antihero became so appealing to readers that scores of writers in Spain and other countries produced their own version of Guzmán or created characters inspired by this archetype. Alemán inserted in his novel philosophical and moral reflections and pious warnings by the aging Guzmán not to follow his roguish path, passages which some commentators have called distractions and flaws in Alemán's style. Other critics have suggested that these homilies were deliberately inserted to disarm the shocked responses of conventional readers or to save the book from formal censorship. The motivations of Alemán have been variously analyzed by modern scholars, some of whom say that as a member of a converso family (one that had converted from Judaism to Catholicism under fear of persecution), he transferred his own sense of being a marginal figure in Spanish society into identifying with the antisocial behavior of Guzmán. Others dismiss this notion and conclude that Alemán was simply pursuing a theme whose boldness he felt would be unusual and titillating enough to win him readers and income. Whatever the source of his story, Alemán's novel remains one of the major works of Spanish literature, completely overshadowing his minor writings.

Alentejo

This Portuguese province (divided in modern times into Upper and Lower Alentejo) lies between the Atlantic and the Spanish frontier. Its location guaranteed a prominent place in the political and military events of the nation from the Middle Ages onward. The flat and unpromising terrain was rendered productive by irrigation, drawing upon the Guadiana and several other streams. The cultivation of wheat, as well as various other cereals and fruits, made the Alentejo region Portugal's "bread basket," and the extensive growth of cork trees provided a source of income in an era when virtually every wine bottle in the world was stopped by a cork derived from the Alentejo's forests. Long the seat of an absentee landlord class that exploited the labor of an impoverished peas-

antry, the region was the object of special attention by the radical reformers who took power after the 1974 revolution. Many of the great estates were confiscated by the government and divided up into small holdings for individual farmers. Those lands that were reorganized as cooperatives usually fared the best. The total area of Upper Alentejo (capital at Évora) and Lower Alentejo (capital at Beja) is approximately 9,000 square miles and includes a number of productive quarries as well as small-scale copper and sulfur operations. Although not as picturesque as other of the country's regions, Alentejo continues to play, as always, a vital part in Portugal's existence.

Alexander VI (Rodrigo de Borja [Borgia]) (1431–1503)
pope

Born Rodrigo de Borja of a noble family from VALENCIA and nephew of an earlier Spanish-born pope, Calixtus III, this Spanish occupant of the papal throne enjoyed the patronage of his uncle and other members of the family who were highly placed in Rome. Archbishop of Valencia and cardinal at an early age, he successively occupied major offices in the Papal States. In 1492 Rodrigo de Borja (now known under the Italian form of his name, Borgia) was elected pope in a notoriously corrupt conclave. As Alexander VI he conducted an active political and military policy in Italy aimed at strengthening the secular powers of the papacy and the personal advantages of his family. During the opening phase of the ITALIAN WARS (1494–1503) he alternately favored France and Spain, although generally preferring the interests of the latter. In 1494 he exercised the papal prerogative to decree the division of newly discovered lands outside of Europe between Spain and Portugal (TREATY OF TORDESILLAS, revised in 1497). Although endlessly denounced as the most corrupt and amoral of Renaissance popes, Alexander VI was not without redeeming virtues and occasional manifestations of a reforming spirit. His greatest weakness was his support for the political adventures of his son Cesare, whose schemes collapsed after the death of Alexander VI in 1503.

Alfonso XII (1857–1885)
king of Spain

The son of ISABELLA II and her consort, Francisco de Asís, Alfonso accompanied his mother into exile in 1868. The queen renounced her rights to the throne in his favor in 1870, and while the youth attended schools in France and Britain, royalists strove to restore the monarchy during the subsequent period of turmoil in Spain. In 1875 Alfonso XII returned to his homeland with the aid of a number of generals who saw him as the solution that divided their country the least. He presided over the resolution of the Second Carlist War and the first Cuban rebellion. Throughout his reign Alfonso continued to be a conciliator, working for the establishment of a stable society in an era of growing disruption both at home and abroad. An affable and outgoing young man, he gained popularity among the common people that helped to counterbalance the incessant rivalries between Liberals and Conservatives. The king's first marriage to his cousin Mercedes ended tragically within a few months. His second wife, Archduchess Maria Christina of Austria, bore him two daughters, presenting the possibility of a renewed dispute over female

King Alfonso XII *(Library of Congress)*

succession echoing that which had divided the country in the 1830s. The premature death of Alfonso XII in the 10th year of his reign threatened to bring on a political crisis avoided by the posthumous birth of a male successor. Although a promising young sovereign, a tubercular affliction and his conscientious determination to carry out his duties despite their impact on his health doomed him to be merely a transitional figure.

Alfonso XIII (1886–1941)
king of Spain

The posthumous son of ALFONSO XII, he was born a king and passed his childhood

King Alfonso XIII *(Library of Congress)*

catastrophic defeat of Spanish colonial forces at ANUAL (Morocco) in 1921. Pressure from leftist parties in the parliament threatened to embarrass the army leadership and, perhaps, to disclose the king's own incitement of a reckless offensive against Moroccan rebels. Whatever his motives, Alfonso encouraged General MIGUEL PRIMO DE RIVERA to rebel against the government in 1923 and confirmed this officer as head of a military council that supplanted the cabinet, the legislature, and the whole constitutional apparatus. Between 1923 and 1930 Primo de Rivera exercised a dictatorship in Spain achieving various "reforms" desired by the king. Whatever benefits were gained under this authoritarian collaboration were, however, outweighed by popular discontent as well as the decline of economic stability throughout Europe. When the general resigned and the king could not sustain the dictatorship, he called for elections early in 1931 in an attempt to rally public support. Failing in this, he left Spain, promising to return when the situation had resolved itself. The prompt proclamation of a republic and the subsequent onset of the SPANISH CIVIL WAR made his resumption of the throne impossible. Alfonso XIII was fated to spend the rest of his life in exile.

under his mother's regency during an era of disaster overseas (the loss of the remaining colonies) and growing disorder at home (attacks from anarchists and republicans). The regency ended in 1902, and Alfonso XIII's full coming of age was marked by his marriage to a granddaughter of Queen Victoria of Britain in 1906. His attempts to play a strong role within the scope left to the sovereign by the constitution proved ineffective, though his pro-British inclinations may have counterbalanced the military's sympathy for Germany and thus helped keep Spain neutral in World War I.

Alfonso XIII's most dramatic intervention in Spanish politics took place after the

Algarve

A province located in Portugal's Mediterranean coastal region and encompassing nearly 2,000 square miles, Algarve is known for its mild climate and abundant harvests, particularly of citrus fruits. Settled by Phoenicians in antiquity, Muslim conquerors held on to the Kingdom of Algarve as their last possession in Portugal. Afonso V captured it in mid-13th century and assumed the double title of king of Portugal and Algarve.

Almansa, Battle of (1707)

What proved to be the decisive battle of the WAR OF THE SPANISH SUCCESSION was fought on April 25, 1707. The conflict had begun nearly six years earlier with the designation of Louis XIV's grandson, Philippe, as king of Spain in the will of CHARLES II, the last Spanish HABSBURG. Most Spaniards had rallied to the young duke of Anjou, Charles's great nephew, as his successor PHILIP V. The Austrian Habsburgs, however, had insisted that Archduke Karl, younger son of Emperor Leopold I, had a better claim to the Spanish throne and won support from some Spaniards, chiefly in the northeastern provinces. The Austrian pretender made this region his stronghold, aided by an alliance that included Britain, Portugal, and the Dutch Republic. These forces had success in the earlier years of the war, but by 1707 the rising fortunes of the House of BOURBON threatened the alliance. Their rival armies moved toward one another on the plain of Almansa in Albacete province near VALENCIA.

The troops of Archduke Karl, numbering 26,000 infantry and 7,000 cavalry, advanced upon those of the duke of Berwick, which were slightly stronger in horsemen and artillery. Berwick, a natural son of James II of England, was a marshal of France, his adopted country, and an experienced commander despite his relative youth. He was particularly gifted in his ability to obtain and evaluate intelligence. On the eve of the battle scouts informed him that the enemy was advancing, doubtless seeking to precipitate a clash before French reinforcements arrived. Positioning his forces so as to take advantage of such structures as an old Moorish fort and a former monastery, he provoked an attack by English troops under the earl of Galway and then launched a fierce assault on the opposite flank that totally routed the unstable Portuguese infantry. The result was a retreat of the alliance forces and their subsequent loss of most of northeastern Spain. After the fall of BARCELONA Austria's allies withdrew from the war and signed the Treaty of Utrecht in 1713. Archduke Karl was compelled to abandon his claim to the Spanish succession in 1714. The strategy and tactics of the duke of Berwick at Almansa were much admired by the leading generals of the day, including Frederick the Great of Prussia, who declared him to be a "scientific" commander. His victory at Almansa assured the future of the Bourbon dynasty in Spain.

Almeida, António José de
(1866–1929)

Portuguese statesman

Active in the republican movement that achieved the overthrow of the Portuguese monarchy in 1910, Almeida served as minister of the interior in the provisional government established in the aftermath of the revolution. He was leader of the centrist group known as the Republican Evolutionist Party. During World War I (in which Portugal suffered grave losses), he formed a coalition government and served as prime minister. He was president of the republic from 1919 to 1923 during a period of great political and social instability.

Almeida, Francisco de (1450–1510)
Portuguese soldier and colonial administrator

Member of a noble family, Almeida began his military career in Portugal's Moroccan campaigns and subsequently volunteered for the final stage of the Castilian capture of Muslim territory that culminated in the CONQUEST OF GRANADA (1492). He was chosen in 1503 to lead the first great Portuguese expedition to conquer land and trade in the Indian Ocean region. With a fleet of some two dozen warships he pursued a tactic of destroying rival trading posts and establishing new Portuguese strongholds along the East African coast. Crossing to the western shores of India, he set up headquarters at Cochin from which he negotiated treaties with local rulers and launched naval expeditions against rivals. His most spectacular victory was achieved in 1509 when he destroyed a large combined fleet of Egyptians, Arabs, and Indians outfitted by Venice, which feared the loss of its domination of the Indian Ocean trade. Almeida was evidently the first European to visit Mumbai (Bombay) and to open trade with what is presently known as Malaysia. His son led the first expedition to what is now Sri Lanka.

Almeida was suspended in his position as first viceroy of Portugal's Estado da India and set out for home late in 1509. On reaching the area near present-day Capetown, South Africa, his ships stopped to take on freshwater, and Almeida was killed in a skirmish with the local population.

Almeida Garrett, João Baptista da Silva Leitão, visconde de (1799–1854)
Portuguese writer and statesman

A graduate in law from the University of Coimbra and a supporter of the Liberal (Constitutional) Party, Almeida Garrett was forced into political exile in 1823. Residing at first in England, he became fascinated by the work of Sir Walter Scott, which influenced his epic poem *Camões* (1825) in which he dwells upon the 16th-century Portuguese poet's longing for home. Later, in France, he fell under the spell of romanticism, a commitment that would lead to his becoming the founder of the romantic school of Portuguese poetry. Almeida Garrett returned to Portugal in 1832 to aid in the struggle against the Miguelites and after the victory of 1833 was appointed minister of the interior and began a long period of service in the national legislature. In addition to his political activities, he took a major part in the creation of the National Theater. In support of this theater he wrote a number of historical dramas, including *Um auto de Gil Vicente* (A short play of Gil Vicente, 1838) and *O alfageme de Santarém* (The armorer of Santarem, 1841). His 1843 play *Frey Luís de Sousa* is considered by many to be the greatest achievement of Portuguese drama. Still another contribution of major importance was his *Romanceiro* (1851–53), a collection of medieval Portuguese romances and ballads. As he drew near the end of his life, Almeida Garrett produced a collection of love poems, *Folhas caídas* (Fallen leaves, 1853), considered to be the finest poems in the Portuguese language.

Altamira Crevea, Rafael (1866–1951)
Spanish historian

Rafael Altamira was one of the generation of Spanish intellectuals who became active in public life just before the great crisis of 1898. Like so many of his peers, he was trained at the Institución Libre de Enseñanza under the guidance of GINER DE LOS RÍOS. Like them, too, Altamira participated in a wide variety of activities relating to national affairs, ranging from journalist to labor arbitrator. He continued this commitment to a broader role in society even after becoming a professor at the University of Oviedo and later at the University of Madrid. Altamira's range of concern was international as well as national. As an advocate of educational development and an increasingly recognized historian, he frequently traveled abroad, becoming particularly well known in the United States, where he lectured at Johns Hopkins University, Rice University, and other institutions. Although he favored the official policy of neutrality during World War I, he was sympathetic to the Allied cause and aided in the foundation of the League of Nations. Altamira, whose recognized expertise included law, was invited to take part in shaping plans for the International Court of Justice and later served as a judge on that tribunal.

As early as 1891 Altamira brought out his influential book on the teaching of history, *La enseñanza de la historia,* which guided Spanish teachers for decades. He subsequently established the *Revista crítica de historia y literatura,* a history and literature journal to which most of the leading scholars of the day were regular contributors. Altamira's own writings were published in some 60 volumes, including collections of articles and essays. Undoubtedly the best known of his works is the *Historia de España y de la civilización española* (History of Spain and the Spanish civilization), which he originally wrote between 1900 and 1911 and subsequently appeared in a number of revised editions. Working on a grand scale, Altamira here traced not only the political history of Spain but the evolution of Iberian institutions, law, and social structures over the centuries. He also took care to place his country's experience within the larger European and world frameworks. Although dedicated to objectivity and free from nationalist preoccupations, Altamira's history clearly exhibits an underlying moral sense that promotes compromise and cooperation as an alternative to war. Less distinctively Spanish in his perspective than some other historians of his time, Altamira clearly had a sense of the pan-European or even global environment that would continue to emerge in the latter half of the 20th century.

Alvarado, Pedro de (1485–1541)
Spanish explorer

Of a large noble family known for its aggressiveness, Alvarado was committed from an early age to a life of military activity and exploring. In 1510 he arrived in HISPANIOLA and a year later took part in the conquest of CUBA, where he was joined by half a dozen brothers and cousins and established himself as a plantation owner. Not content with a sedentary life he took part in the GRIJALVA expedition in 1518, and this probe into the coastal regions of Central America gave him a familiarity with the area. Although he was a candidate to lead the subsequent major advance into MEXICO and was passed over in favor of HERNÁN CORTÉS, Alvarado accepted the position of his second in command and served him loyally. During the next three years Alvarado was in the forefront of every battle as the small army of Cortés fought its way to the heart of the Aztec Empire and entered Tenochtitlán, the capital of its emperor, Moctezuma. Left in charge of Spain's interests in Tenochtitlán while Cortés returned to the coast to deal with a rival force, Alvarado soon provoked a confrontation with the Aztec and had to withdraw his small garrison under attack. Angered by his subordinate's violent and willful behavior, Cortés could not dispense with his leadership abilities. Alvarado took the forefront in recapturing the Aztec capital and crushing all resistance. In 1523, perhaps as much to keep Alvarado out of the way as to reward him for services rendered, Cortés sent him to undertake the conquest of what is now GUATEMALA and EL SALVADOR. During the next 10 years Alvarado and his soldiers (led by his many kinsmen) overthrew the remnants of the Maya civilization and established a dozen towns and missionary outposts. He was confirmed as governor of Guatemala but had frequent disputes with the ever-growing bureaucracy in Mexico City and was obliged to visit Spain on two occasions to protect his status. Ever more restless than the average conquistador—all a roving breed—Alvarado sailed to what is now ECUADOR in 1534. His plan to seize a portion of the Inca Empire, then about to collapse under PIZARRO's assault, was thwarted within a year. Back in Guatemala Alvarado conceived a plan to sail across the Pacific and challenge the Portuguese for control of the Spice Islands (in present-day Indonesia). While preparing for this voyage he was drawn into a local war with Indian tribes in northwestern Mexico and was killed in battle in 1541. His widow succeeded him as governor of Guatemala.

Alvarado deserves to rank among the most formidable of the conquistadores. Although he gained neither the fame nor the power of Cortés, he carved out his own dominion at the expense of Cortés and made a serious challenge to Pizarro's Inca domain. As violent and bloody as any of his peers, he was shrewder than the average in matters of organization and administration. Had he not allowed himself to be distracted by the campaign that led to his almost chance death, he might have found the ultimate fulfillment of his large ambition in the East Indies.

Amadeo I (Amadeo Ferdínando Maria di Savoia) (1845–1890)
king of Spain

Younger son of King Victor Emmanuel II of Italy, Amadeo had a military education and served with distinction in his native country's 1866 war with Austria, sustaining a severe wound in frontline combat. A year later he married a noblewoman of high rank with whom he had several children. They were transformed into Spain's new royal family in 1870 when the lengthy search for a new monarch to replace the deposed ISABELLA II came to an end.

Amadeo arrived in Spain in December 1870, just as General JUAN PRIM, the man who had sponsored his choice by the Cortes (see CORTES), was assassinated. This unhappy event was just a taste of his experience in his adopted homeland. During the next several years Amadeo was beset by rebellions all over the country, factional disputes within the only political grouping that gave him even nominal support, and conspiracies formed by republicans, Carlists, and partisans of the Bourbon pretender, the titular ALFONSO XII. Despite his proclaimed devotion to Spain and his obvious good intentions the young king was unable to win over any important segment of Spanish society. The political situation deteriorated everywhere, from BARCELONA to the Basque provinces, not to mention CUBA, and Amadeo decided to abdicate in February 1873. Ignoring protests that it was illegal for him to do so without permission of the Cortes, he promptly departed with his wife and children (including a newborn son) and returned to Italy. There he remained for the rest of his comparatively short life.

Although some historically minded commentators were struck by Amadeo's resemblance to the long-departed Spanish Habsburg kings (whose distinctive jaw he inherited from his Austrian mother), Amadeo had little else to recommend him to the attention of Spain in a time of turmoil. Amiable but incapable of dramatizing his ideas or attracting popular support, he quickly faded from the scene and was soon forgotten.

Andalusia (Andalucía)

Stretching across the whole southern width of Spain, with an area of more than 33,000 square miles, Andalusia is as large as Portugal. The size of this region reflects her long-ago status as a separate kingdom. Included within her boundaries are the modern provinces of Almería, CÁDIZ, CÓRDOBA, GRANADA, Huelva, MÁLAGA, and SEVILLE, whose very names recall the former glories of Moorish Spain. Already a center of agriculture and trade in the days of the Romans, the area that eighth-century Muslim conquerors called al-Andalus generated a level of artistic and intellectual activity that made it a by-word for sophistication during the Middle Ages. As the Christian reconquest of Spain (RECONQUISTA) spread southward, the Caliphate of the West, with its seat at Córdoba, and the other regimes located within

Andalusia fell, until Granada alone retained its political independence. After its annexation by CASTILE in 1492, (see CONQUEST OF GRANADA), Andalusia began to lose its luster, with only Seville and Cádiz retaining prosperity through their commercial links with the New World. Throughout later centuries Andalusia has experienced periodic revolts both from aristocratic opponents of MADRID and anarchist peasants seeking to overthrow their semifeudal overlords. In quieter times Andalusia's rich variety of resources and the picturesque character of its natural and human-made landscape have continued to preserve the appeal of this most distinctive of Spanish regions.

Andorra

This sovereign state, located in the eastern Pyrenees between Spain and France, traces her existence to a decree by Charlemagne in the early ninth century. From 1278 to 1993 Andorra maintained a feudal tradition of government under which the Spanish bishop of Urgel and the French sovereign (later the president of the republic) were co-suzerains of the principality. Since 1993 Andorra has been governed through a democratic parliamentary system. Among the population 43 percent is of Spanish origin, and 33 percent is of native Andorran descent, with the remainder of Portuguese or French extraction. The total population of nearly 70,000 represents a tenfold increase since the mid-20th century, chiefly attributable to business opportunities.

The official language is Catalan, and the principal cultural, commercial, and traditional links are with Spain. The lofty mountains and deep valleys that constitute most of Andorra's territory have favored a pastoral rather than an agricultural economy, though smuggling was long the most lucrative occupation. In more recent times the promotion of tourism, linked to a free trade zone, has been responsible for most of the country's economic activity. Within Andorra's 180 square miles, the capital, Andorra la Vella, and the half-dozen other small towns provide venues for limited, specialized industrial activity. Since altering her relationship with the neighboring states, Andorra has joined the United Nations and maintains a representative at that body's headquarters in New York City.

Ángeles, Victoria de los (Victòria dels Àngels) (1923–2005)
Spanish singer

Born in BARCELONA as Victòria Gómez Cima, the future diva was trained there at the conservatory. She began her career in a choral group, moved on to individual recitals, and then began a series of operatic debuts: 1949 (Paris), 1950 (Salzburg, London's Covent Garden and Milan's La Scala), 1951 (New York's Metropolitan Opera), 1957 (Vienna State Opera), and 1961 (Bayreuth Festival). During the 1950s and '60s, in addition to these debuts, she was a performer during each season or a regular visitor at all of these venues as well as a guest artist at many others. Her most frequent roles included Mimi in *La Bohème,* Carmen, Cio-Cio-San in *Madama Butterfly,* Desdemona in *Otello,* Violetta in *La Traviata,* Marguerite in *Faust,* and Elisabeth in *Tannhauser.* After taking time off to raise her two sons, she brought her much admired lyric soprano voice chiefly to the concert stage, where she performed for several decades. In addition to a wide variety of Italian, French, and German songs and arias, her repertoire always included Spanish songs, reflecting not only her wide knowledge of the music of her native land but her intense patriotism. During interviews she often spoke feelingly of Spanish character and tradition and how it was necessary to understand a role such as Carmen in the social context of the individual's place and time.

Throughout her long life, de los Ángeles was noted for the personal charm that she brought to all of her performances, particularly those in the concert hall, where she could "be herself" rather than an operatic character. At her first concert in New York City's Carnegie Hall in 1950, after the formal program ended, she sat on the closed lid of the stage piano and performed a number of Spanish songs while playing the guitar. The *Herald Tribune*'s critic, Virgil Thomson, praised her artistry and her beautiful voice, but it was clear that the woman herself had won the hearts of all the audience.

Angola
This West African territory became known to Portugal during the 15th-century voyages that led to the creation of Portugal's Asian empire. By the 1480s Portuguese outposts had been established along the coast, and relations with local chiefs led to alliances and missionary activity. During the 16th century the transatlantic slave trade had its base in Angola and remained a Portuguese monopoly thereafter. The interior was not, however, explored or mastered until the 19th century, when Portugal was obliged to formalize her sovereignty over a vast dominion ultimately amounting

to some 400,000 square miles. Boundary disputes with British and German colonies continued until the early 1900s, and there were periodic uprisings among the indigenous population until the eve of World War I. The Salazar regime, building upon initiatives commenced during the BRAGANÇA period, endeavored to increase the number of Portuguese colonists and to exploit the natural resources that Angola possessed in abundance. In 1951 the territory was proclaimed an "overseas province" of Portugal. These measures were not sufficient to preserve unchallenged sovereignty, and by 1961 an anticolonialist revolt had begun. A massive deployment of troops and a heavy expenditure of funds to sustain Portuguese control proved ruinous to the "mother country" as well as devastating to Angola herself. Finally in 1974 revolution in Portugal, precipitated in large part by frustration with the African war, toppled the regime. In 1975 the new Portuguese government recognized the independence of Angola.

Anual, campaign of (1921)

In spring 1921 Spain launched a major offensive against the Moroccan resistance forces in the interior of its North African protectorate. A total of 27,000 men was deployed from the base at MELILLA, with an attack force sent into the interior to strike at the major rebel leader, Abd el-Krim. By July the bulk of this force, some 8,000 troops, was encamped at Anual (about 45 miles from Melilla). Poorly entrenched, inadequately equipped, and lacking in supplies of food, water, and ammunition, the garrison at Anual found its situation increasingly untenable. The commander of the

Melilla region, General Manuel Fernández Silvestre (who had repeatedly told superiors that he had no need of help in conquering the "Moors"), made his first visit to Anual in the last days of July to find the situation rapidly deteriorating. After personally leading a failed cavalry attack to relieve a nearby outpost he reluctantly came to the same conclusion that Anual was untenable. Word that a major rebel force was advancing on the camp led to a panicky flight by all but the general, who apparently committed suicide rather than leave his post. In the desperate and disorderly flight toward Melilla, most of the Moroccan colonial troops deserted their Spanish masters, who were overtaken and slaughtered by the thousands. Melilla itself was threatened by a rebel attack with only an exiguous remnant of Spanish soldiers to defend it. The prompt arrival of reinforcements, notably a battalion of the Spanish Foreign Legion under FRANCISCO FRANCO, averted a final disaster.

The total collapse of the Anual campaign, with all of its attendant circumstances of poor planning, incompetent leadership, and inadequate support at every level of authority, became a national scandal. The Spanish political parties, from Left to Right, denounced the government and demanded inquiries into the inadequacies of the army. There were increasing hints that King ALFONSO XIII himself might be publicly blamed for having encouraged the reckless colonial adventure. Before the full story of Anual could be laid bare, a coup d'état was approved by the king and carried out by General MIGUEL PRIMO DE RIVERA. His dictatorship during the later 1920s preserved the prestige of the army and, thanks to the cooperation of France, ultimately reestablished European predominance in Morocco.

Aragon (Aragón)

Lying in Spain's northeast, along her Pyrenean frontier, the region that was formerly the kingdom of Aragon includes the present-day provinces of Zaragoza, Teruel, and Huesca, with a total area of some 18,000 square miles.

It has been the fate of Aragon to remain perpetually overshadowed. During the medieval era Aragon was variously linked with NAVARRE, CASTILE, and VALENCIA. Its Renaissance rulers carved out a domain in the Mediterranean, particularly in Italy. At the beginning of the modern era it entered into a dynastic union with Castile that proved fatal to its pretensions. FERDINAND V (who died in 1516) was the last and greatest of its kings. His heir, PHILIP II, crushed Aragon's attempt to assert its traditional autonomy during the late 1500s. A final attempt to assert Aragonese freedom during the WAR OF THE SPANISH SUCCESSION resulted in the abolition of the kingdom's remaining rights by PHILIP V. Some Aragonese historians maintain that the region's finest hour came during the Napoleonic Wars, when Aragon's capital city, ZARAGOZA, withstood a siege that demonstrated the enduring stubbornness and bravery of its people.

Aranda, Pedro Pablo Abarca de Bolea, conde de (1719–1798)

Spanish statesman

Member of an Aragonese noble family, Aranda trained for a military career in Prussia as part of a wide-ranging tour of Europe. He subsequently distinguished himself in battle, rising to the rank of general. In 1766, while serving in a diplomatic position, he was judged, due to his harsh uncompromising temperament, to be the right man for suppressing a rebellion in and around MADRID. On his return to Spain he carried out this assignment with ruthless efficiency. Named president of the Council of State in 1767, he presided over the expulsion of the Jesuits from Spanish territory and encouraged the subsequent abolition of the order by the pope. Aranda's animus against the clergy (which some historians feel has been exaggerated) is said to have originated during his European tour when he became a friend of Voltaire and other philosophes. Despite his reputation as a disciple of the Enlightenment, Aranda seems to have been of two minds about reform. He undertook many salutary measures in economic and administrative areas but pursued authoritarian policies with such rigor as to antagonize many progressive Spaniards. His critics finally persuaded CHARLES III to remove him from office in 1733, but the monarch, as a mark of gratitude for past services, named him ambassador to France. During the crucial years leading to Spain's declaration of war against Britain in 1779 Aranda supported the French alliance, while FLORIDABLANCA who had supplanted him in Madrid, favored preserving the peace with Great Britain. Although Aranda's preference prevailed, his negotiations with British representatives over the treaty that ended the American Revolution (1783) did not give Spain everything she had hoped for. Aranda returned to power briefly early in the reign of CHARLES IV but soon clashed with the new favorite at the royal court, MANUEL DE

GODOY. As a result Aranda was stripped of his offices yet again and vanished to internal exile. Allowed to spend the last years of life in his family home in ARAGON, he died there in 1798.

Argentina

The region that later emerged as the modern country of Argentina was first explored by Spanish navigators who sailed up the Río de la Plata in 1516 and during the next two decades. A permanent settlement was established at Buenos Aires in 1536. This languished but was resettled in 1580, as were several other outposts in the region. Originally placed under the jurisdiction of the Viceroyalty of PERU in 1620, the area around Buenos Aires as well as more distant settlements in present-day URUGUAY, PARAGUAY, and BOLIVIA were formed into the Viceroyalty of La Plata in 1776. Buenos Aires was the object of British military and naval assaults in 1806–07 while Spain was still allied with Napoleonic France. The role played by the local population in beating off their assaults contributed to a rising sense of self-sufficiency and were followed by a declaration of independence from Spain in 1816. Over the next 10 years recognition of the United Provinces of the Río de La Plata was granted by both the United States and Great Britain, and Spanish colonial control came to an end. Prolonged disputes between various regions and factions were resolved by the establishment of a federal republic in Argentina in the mid-19th century.

Arias de Ávila, Pedro   See PEDRARIAS DÁVILA.

Arias Navarro, Carlos (1908–1989)
Spanish politician

Trained in the law, Arias Navarro joined the Ministry of Justice in 1929 and pledged his allegiance to the new republic in 1931. Suspected of disloyalty, he was arrested on the outbreak of the Franco uprising in 1936 but soon liberated by fellow conservatives. During the SPANISH CIVIL WAR he served as a military judge advocate. Having demonstrated his loyalty to the new order, he was rewarded with a series of administrative appointments: civil governor of LEÓN (1944–49), governor of NAVARRE (1949), director general of security (1957–65), mayor of MADRID (1965–73), and minister of the interior (1973).

In 1973 Basque terrorists assassinated Admiral Luis Carrero Blanco, the prime minister and expected successor of FRANCISCO FRANCO. Arias Navarro was named to replace him as prime minister, the first civilian to hold this position during the dictatorship. Many observers understood this appointment as representing the triumph of moderate elements in El Caudillo's administration and a signal that Franco was preparing to hand over power to the designated heir, Prince JUAN CARLOS, rather than to a military clique. It fell to Arias Navarro to announce Franco's death in 1975 and to preside over the transition that effectively reestablished the monarchy during the next few months. By the time Arias Navarro resigned the prime ministership in 1976 Spain's return to democracy was well under way. Arias Navarro lived quietly for the remainder of his life, his earlier alignment with authoritarianism forgiven in light of his vital work in easing the rebirth of Spanish civil society.

Arizona

This area lying to the west of the present-day state of NEW MEXICO in the United States, shares much of its history. Arizona was not severed from the territory of New Mexico until 1912 when it was admitted to the Union as a separate state with a size (113,000 square miles) almost as large as its eastern neighbor. Arizona was first visited by Spaniards in 1539 and first settled as an extension of NEW SPAIN in 1598. Missionary activity during the 1600s was followed by the creation of military outposts to deal with Apache raids. The city of Tucson was founded in 1775 by Colonel Rodrigo O'Connor as part of this defensive network. Arizona ceased to be a Spanish dependency in 1821, when New Spain became independent MEXICO and, in turn, was surrendered to the United States in 1848. During the late 19th century there were protracted lawsuits laying claim to Spanish land grants, particularly that made to the Peralta family, which originally covered most of Arizona.

Armada (the Invincible)

With a mixture of arrogance and optimism Spain gave the designation "Invincible" to the great force of ships and troops assembled for a decisive victory over her enemies in 1588. The plan, approved by PHILIP II and his advisers, was to gain control of the English Channel with an overwhelming naval force, land thousands of troops in England, and depose Queen Elizabeth I, the leader of an anti-Spanish coalition that included the Dutch Republic and major political factions in France. Coordinated attacks against the Dutch, who had rebelled against their Spanish overlords, and the French were to complete the simultaneous defeat of Philip II's enemies and restore Catholic dominance in Europe.

English raids on the Spanish coast had damaged vital supplies, but the king insisted on pursuing his timetable and assembled hundreds of ships (Portuguese and Italian as well as Spanish) and thousands of troops at LISBON, from which they sailed northward in July 1588. While the Spanish were preparing at Calais for the cross-channel onslaught, English fireships were launched into the harbor destroying a number of Spanish vessels. The remnants of the Armada ventured forth and were attacked by English warships, whose greater mobility and longer range guns counterbalanced the heavier galleons and massive artillery of the Armada. While the issue was still in doubt, the Spanish commander in chief, the duke of MEDINA SIDONIA, ordered a withdrawal. Although the experienced subordinates who had been sent with him to supplement his own ignorance of naval matters urged a continuation of the attack, the duke, fearing to be caught in the channel by an impending storm, led his fleet north, ultimately rounding northern Scotland and sailing south along the Atlantic coast of Ireland. His ships were scattered by gales, many being wrecked on the rocky coasts, others being driven far out to sea; crews who fell into the hands of the local population were killed or handed over to English authorities. Due to unanticipated setbacks in Holland and France the intended coordination of the entire grand design failed.

The "Enterprise of England"—in which Philip had contemplated making his daughter queen of England, Scotland, and Ireland—was the centerpiece of the great Counter-Reformation triumph that would have changed the course of Spanish and European history. Philip II accepted the defeat of the Armada, despite its heavy loss of ships and men, with his usual stoicism and did not even reproach the admiral upon his belated arrival back in Spain. Instead the king continued his schemes to defeat the English, crush the rebellious Dutch Republic, and put a puppet king on the French throne during the remaining years of his reign. He passed this mission on to his son, PHILIP III, who proved more interested in the religious than the political aspect of his father's vision.

Asencio Torrado, José (1892–1961)
Spanish soldier

This leading Loyalist commander during the SPANISH CIVIL WAR fought against his military academy classmate FRANCISCO FRANCO. A veteran of campaigns in MOROCCO and an officer of the General Staff, Asencio was widely regarded as the most brilliant mind among the officers who remained loyal to the government. With the rebel Nationalist forces advancing on several fronts during the summer of 1936, Asencio was selected to organize the defense of MADRID. He was able to divert the Nationalists toward TOLEDO and gain the time necessary to reinforce the capital, which subsequently withstood a 28-month siege. Due to the heightened level of suspicion in Madrid Asencio was transferred from field command to the nominal position of undersecretary of war. He was returned to command in the field later in 1936, but what was originally described as the "heroic" retreat of his forces from the area around MÁLAGA during the following year was made the basis for his removal and impris-

onment. Overcoming charges of "conspiracy against the republic," Asencio was appointed in the summer of 1938 to lead a series of successful flanking attacks against Nationalist forces. With the civil war drawing to a close, Asencio was sent to the United States to seek support for what was still recognized as the legitimate government of Spain. After the triumph of the Nationalists he settled in New York, supporting himself by editorial work, giving lectures, and teaching Spanish.

An able tactician and a respected military leader, Asencio was hampered throughout the civil war not only by the shortcomings of his ill-equipped and largely amateur soldiers but by the factional disputes and obsessive suspicions that denied him the consistent backing of the Loyalist regime.

asiento

A Spanish term for a contract or royal patent granted by the government to an individual or group of interested parties for the exclusive provision of certain goods or services. The best-known *asiento* was that granted by the Crown for the delivery of slaves to the American colonies between approximately 1543 and 1834. The practice of enslaving captives had been introduced in Spain during the wars of the Christian kings against the Muslims during the Middle Ages. When Spain began to develop her colonial system in the New World various forms of compulsory service were imposed among the Amerindians (including the *ENCOMIENDA* system), but proved unsatisfactory and was opposed by certain of the clergy who viewed the native peoples as potential Christians protected by their status as subjects of the sovereign.

By the middle of the 16th century contracts had been assigned to slave traders operating along the west coast of Africa. Most of these traders were Portuguese who drew upon their connection with African rulers in the interior of the continent. Their captives were brought to the so-called Slave Coast and sold there to traders, who delivered them to the American colonies. With the deterioration in Spain's relations with Portugal these arrangements had broken down by the late 1600s, after an estimated 800,000 enslaved persons had been delivered to the markets of America.

The *asiento* was transferred to France during the early 1700s and then to Britain as part of the settlement made in 1713 at the conclusion of the WAR OF THE SPANISH SUCCESSION. Although the *asiento* had previously included various concessions of the right to provide commodities such as tools, clothing, and weapons in addition to slaves, English traders illegally ignored the fact that their *asiento* rights were limited to conveying African slaves. Many of them smuggled a wide range of goods into Spanish colonial waters, and by the 1730s Anglo-Spanish disputes led to actual warfare between the two countries (1739). At various times, specifically in the later 18th century, the term *asiento* was also applied to the right granted to various individuals and companies, some foreign some Spanish, to extract and transport certain categories of natural resources from Spain's American colonies. These included precious metals, coral and other marine resources, tobacco, herbs, sugar, and certain types of wood.

A series of temporary concessions was followed by the general decline of slavery in the New World growing out of the spread of enlightened ideas. With the collapse of the Spanish-American empire in the 1820s and international agreements to eliminate the slave trade, the *asiento* system was at an end in 1834, although slavery within the surviving colonies of CUBA and PUERTO RICO remained legal until 1875.

Asturias

A picturesque mountainous region of northwestern Spain made up of some 4,000 square miles, Asturias's chief claim to fame is her dramatic resistance to the Moorish invasion that swept over the peninsula in the early eighth century. Almost alone among Spanish Christians in the first years of the Muslim conquest, Asturias, under the noble warrior Pelayo, routed the intruding armies, who turned aside to seek easier prey. Pelayo and his victory at the Battle of Covadonga (718) became an iconic inspiration for the subsequent 700-year-long RECONQUISTA. Asturias, a small kingdom, was eventually absorbed into LEÓN and then into CASTILE. In 1838 she was redesignated as the administrative district of Oviedo (her principal city). The proud Asturians have, however, continued to assert their own identity, notably in the coal miners' revolt in 1934, crushed by the Second Republic, and in the resistance to the Franco forces during the SPANISH CIVIL WAR. Poets and other intellectuals insist upon the status of Asturian as a separate language and contribute to its distinctive literature. Since the late Middle Ages the title prince of Asturias has been borne by the heir to the throne of Castile and then of Spain. In May 2004 Philip, Prince of Asturias (heir to King JUAN CARLOS) married Letizia Ortíz, a native of Asturias.

Aviz, House of (Avis)

The order of warrior knights based at the town of Aviz (Avis) in Portugal played an important role in the country's liberation from Moorish rule and its consolidation as an independent state during the 12th to 14th centuries. In 1383 the death of King Ferdinand I of Portugal precipitated the seizure of the throne by his illegitimate brother, João, the master of the order, to block claims by the ruler of CASTILE. As John I he founded a dynasty whose successive monarchs built a powerful presence on the Iberian Peninsula and by the early 1400s were engaged in overseas exploration and discovery. The most notable member of the line was MANUEL I (reigned 1495–1521, known as Manuel the Fortunate) who reaped the rewards of his predecessors' energy and initiative. During his reign Portuguese navigators, traders, and warriors created for him a seaborne empire that included colonies in Africa, Asia, and America. The Golden Age of Portuguese wealth and cultural achievement came to an end when King SEBASTIAN I recklessly led a "crusade" into MOROCCO, where his expedition was destroyed in 1578. An elderly great-uncle (Henrique I) reigned briefly as the last of the dynasty. On his death in 1580 PHILIP II of Spain took the throne of Portugal for himself and ruled the country as a Spanish dependency. After an uprising in 1640 to reassert Portuguese independence the nation turned to a new dynasty, the House of BRAGANÇA. In a strange epilogue to the once-glorious story of the House of Aviz, a mystical belief persisted for many centuries that the crusader king Sebastian would return from his unknown resting place to bring back lost glory. This cult of "Sebastianism" persisted in Portugal and some of her colonial dependencies (particularly BRAZIL) until the 1890s.

Ayacucho, Battle of (1824)

This climactic battle of the War of Independence in South America was fought on December 9, 1824. It took place near the town of Ayacucho in south-central PERU. Under the overall command of the South American Liberator, SIMÓN BOLÍVAR, ANTONIO JOSÉ DE SUCRE, Bolívar's principal lieutenant, had been maneuvering for some weeks to avoid a full-scale battle with the royalist forces. Finally, instructed by Bolívar to confront the troops of the viceroy of Peru, José de la Serna, Sucre attacked. His army, numbering approximately 5,500 men, consisted of numerous volunteers from NEW GRANADA, ARGENTINA, and CHILE as well as local militia. The Royalist forces, aside from a few hundred Spaniards, amounted to 7,000 men almost entirely Peruvian. After initial success the royal forces began to fall back in disarray when the viceroy himself was wounded. They were rallied by his deputy and delivered a fierce counterattack, which led to a hard-fought contest and heavy casualties on both sides. At the end of the day, with their strength and ammunition nearly exhausted, the royalists yielded to the rebels. The viceroy signed a capitulation that included the surrender of the Viceroyalty of Peru and by implication the remainder of Spanish America. Although several Spanish generals refused to accept this order and continued to resist, the events of December 9, 1824, amounted to the downfall of what was left of Spain's imperial power on the continent.

Azaña, Manuel (1880–1940)
Spanish statesman

A lawyer and civil servant who gained attention as a journalist and author, Azaña found his true vocation in politics. During the 1920s he rose to prominence as an antimonarchist and took part in the ousting of ALFONSO XIII in 1931. He was war minister in the first cabinet of the republic, during which his antimilitarist and anticlerical rhetoric antagonized conservatives but endeared him to the parties of the Left. As prime minister from October 1931, he pursued a wide range of reforms, only to be defeated by moderates in the 1933 elections.

Out of office Azaña fended off repeated charges of fomenting conspiracy, endured a period of imprisonment, and constructed a new radical coalition, the Frente Popular (Popular Front), which won control of parliament in February 1936. Azaña soon forced the resignation of Niceto Alcalá Zamora, whom he succeeded as president of the republic. The accession to power of Azaña and his leftist allies precipitated a long-planned military uprising in July 1936. The SPANISH CIVIL WAR that followed pitted Spanish conservatives of many factions against even more fragmented Loyalists defending the republic. Azaña attempted to persuade international opinion that Spain was being attacked by the forces of fascism but won little help from abroad. When the military situation deteriorated his regime fell steadily into the hands of more extreme elements, and he found it impossible to regain control. As the war drew to a close in early 1939 Azaña resigned, declaring that he had no wish to prolong the suffering of his nation. Across the Pyrenees, with the remnant of his followers, he took up residence in France, where he died in November 1940.

Aznar López, José María (1953–)
Spanish politician

Although destined to lead Spain away from its post-Franco experiment in socialism, Aznar advocated a more moderate conservative line than that which the Franco regime had followed. His family had worked for that regime, and he himself had served as a tax inspector after his graduation from the University of Madrid. As the country strove to come to terms with its political heritage during the later 1970s and early 1980s and finally brought FELIPE GONZÁLEZ MÁRQUEZ of the Socialist Party to power in 1982, Aznar chose to join the right-wing Popular Alligiance (later known as the Popular Party). He rose steadily in its ranks, becoming its national leader in 1989. He continued to advocate a centrist line, easing out the old-guard Franco supporters and bringing in younger activists, including women whose role in conservative politics had hitherto been limited. Both in the Cortes (see CORTES) and as regional president of Castile-León he emphasized sober, prudent policies, deliberately contrasting himself, as a solid ordinary Spaniard, with the flamboyant González.

As the economic failures of the later Socialist period were compounded by corruption, scandals, and abuse of power, González lost public support and was finally ousted from the premiership in 1996. Aznar, falling short of a parliamentary majority, was forced to form an alliance with the nationalists of CATALONIA. It was Basque nationalists, however, who proved the greatest thorn in this side (see

BASQUE NATIONALISM), and a cease-fire negotiated with them in 1999 soon collapsed. Despite the ongoing civil strife with the terrorists of the Basque ultramilitant group ETA, Aznar did make progress on the economic side and reassured many Spanish voters who had been alarmed by the excessive libertarianism of the González period. Aznar also sought to enhance his country's role in world affairs by joining the U.S.-led coalition that invaded Iraq in 2003, contributing several thousand Spanish troops to the occupation force. Although this commitment was vehemently criticized in Spain, he insisted that his country must take part in a global struggle against terrorism that included the ETA insurgency as well as attacks on the United States by militant Islamists and the support alledgedly given to such forces by Iraq. In designating the expeditionary unit sent to the Middle East as the Plus Ultra brigade, Aznar deliberately evoked the memory of Spain's former military glory and his belief that it must rise once again to the status of a respected power. As he approached the completion of his second term, Aznar confidently prepared to hand over the party leadership to a hand-picked successor.

Only days before the scheduled election, on March 11, 2004, a series of explosions in the principal railroad station of MADRID and aboard several suburban train lines killed nearly 200 people. The government at first blamed this terrorist assault on ETA, but evidence almost immediately revealed that it was the work of Islamic extremists punishing Spain for her presence in Iraq. The parliamentary election that followed became a repudiation of what was thought to be an attempt by Aznar to protect his Middle Eastern policy and falsely divert blame to the Basques. The Popular Party was defeated, and the new Socialist leader, JOSÉ LUIS RODRÍGUEZ ZAPATERO, with support from other parties on the Left, became prime minister. One of the new administration's first actions was to withdraw the Spanish troops from Iraq. This was followed by a promise to work more closely with European Union members rather than maintaining Aznar's close friendship with America. Aznar, for his part, announced that he would be spending some time in the United States as a visiting professor at Georgetown University.

Azores (Açores)

This Portuguese-ruled archipelago in the North Atlantic lies 800 miles from Portugal's coast. It comprises nine large islands and a number of islets. The Azores constitute an autonomous region of Portugal, and the capital is Ponta Delgada. The total area of the archipelago is 900 square miles, and its population amounts to approximately a quarter of a million. The chief products are fruits, grains, and wine.

Portugal established settlements on these islands one by one during the 15th century and was confirmed in the possession of the entire archipelago in 1479. As the islands became an assembly point for Spanish treasure ships sailing to and from the Americas during the period of Spain's overlordship of Portugal (1580–1640), they were frequently the site of battles with English raiders. Ruled as separate colonies, the islands were united under a single governorship in 1766 and given their own legislature in 1895. They played a part in the MIGUELITE WAR when they were seized by the supporters of

Queen MARIA II and in World War II when the Salazar government ended its posture of neutrality by welcoming British air units (1943). The Azores subsequently became a base for the North Atlantic Treaty Organization (NATO), used by U.S. forces from the 1950s onward.

Azorín   See MARTÍNEZ RUIZ, JOSÉ.

B

Bahia (Salvador)

The full name of this city, in English translation, was City of the Holy Savior on the Bay of All Saints. It was erected on the coast of BRAZIL at the point sighted by PEDRO ÁLVARES CABRAL in 1500 and on the bay that was visited by Amerigo Vespucci a few years later. After years of comparative neglect of the land that it claimed in the Americas, Portugal commenced the colonization of the region in the 1540s. The city and its adjacent interior were assigned to the *donatário* (proprietor) Tomé de Sousa. Under the terms of his land grant he brought over Portuguese settlers and established a town on the bay, from which it was informally known as *Bahia* throughout the colonial period. Although the *donatário* system proved ineffective and was soon abandoned in favor of direct government from Portugal, Bahia grew to be a substantial city and the seat of government for all the Portuguese dependencies in the Western Hemisphere. It reached its apex of commercial dominance and architectural splendor during the 18th century, in the so-called Golden Age of Brazil, when discovery of gold and diamonds in the interior sustained an affluent class of traders and officials. A less dramatic but steadier supply of sugar and coffee from the plantations of the interior constituted, along with other natural products, the main exports from Bahia. Its geographical position and political policy led to the transfer of the new viceregal regime to Río de Janeiro in 1763. Despite a consequent falling off of Bahia's prestige and power, it remained a significant outpost of the Portuguese Empire until the Brazilian declaration of independence in 1823. Bahia, in fact, did not recognize the declaration at first and did not formally sever its ties with Portugal until 1824. The city is now known as Salvador, capital of the state of Bahia.

Bailén, Battle of (Baylen) (1808)

Following Napoléon's invasion of Spain in spring 1808 and the occupation of MADRID by his brother Joseph Bonaparte, who was proclaimed King JOSEPH I, French forces moved southward. ANDALUSIA and adjacent regions were still under the control of a junta loyal to the imprisoned FERDINAND VII. This de facto government in the south appointed General Francisco Castaños (1756–1852), the commander of troops at GIBRALTAR, as captain general of Andalusia and ordered him to repel the enemy's advance. Gathering a large force of regulars and volunteers, Castaños quickly planned the splitting of the French expedition and the isolation and defeat of its separate components. The French commander, General

Pierre Dupont, played into the hands of the Spaniards by himself dividing his forces. One brigade, after a clash with the Spaniards near the town of Bailén on July 16, withdrew. The remaining body, under Dupont in person, arrived at Bailén, found it abandoned, and set out to link up with Dupont's subordinate, Jean Vedel. On July 19, Castaños's principal lieutenant, the Swiss-born general Theodor von Reding, blocked the advance of Dupont with a large and well-positioned mixture of infantry and artillery, which beat back a succession of French attacks to break through the Spanish lines. Growing increasingly desperate, Dupont promised his exhausted and near-mutinous soldiers that Vedel would soon join them and then launched an all-out attack that was repelled with even greater losses. In despair Dupont opened negotiations for surrender, which occurred on July 23, and the veteran imperial troops experienced the humiliation of laying down their arms at the feet of an army whom they had expected to sweep away with scarcely any effort. Castaños's men had suffered some 500 casualties all told, while the French had been mowed down by the thousands in their repeated attempts to smash their way through the implacable royal army.

The victory at Bailén amazed and thrilled all the nations of Europe, who had come to accept Napoléon as invincible. His brother Joseph fled from Madrid, and for a time it appeared that the French would completely evacuate Spain. Although the emperor would cross the Pyrenees with a new army to reimpose his tyranny for another five years, the Battle of Bailén had rallied Spaniards of all classes and regions to oppose the invaders, and the memory of Bailén sustained them throughout what came to be known in Spain as its war of independence (PENINSULAR WAR). Castaños was created duke of Bailén, held many political offices during his long life, and remains a national hero.

Balboa, Vasco Núñez de (1475–1519)
Spanish explorer

Part of the first wave of conquistadores that followed the "discoveries" of CHRISTOPHER COLUMBUS, Balboa arrived in the New World in 1501, while Columbus was still active. He took part in several unproductive ventures to the coast of what is now VENEZUELA and COLOMBIA, then took up farming in HISPANIOLA. By 1510 he had accomplished little except the accumulation of debts, which he attempted to evade by stowing away on board a ship carrying the new governor to the outpost of Darien (the Isthmus of Panama). Governor Martín Fernández de Enciso, on finding Balboa, at first threatened to throw him overboard but then permitted him to complete the voyage. This proved a mistake, for Balboa soon organized a mutiny among the settlers, supplanted Enciso, and sent him back to Hispaniola.

During the next few years Balboa displayed his latent genius for organization and leadership by fending off various rivals and establishing effective relationships with the local indigenous population. The latter inspired him to cross the isthmus, and Balboa thus became the first European to gaze upon the Pacific Ocean (1513). Calling this body of water the South Sea, he claimed it and all the lands that touched upon it for the Spanish Crown. Balboa's report of his discovery gained him initial backing from King FERDINAND V who granted him titles of governorship and the honorific ADELANTADO of the South Sea in recognition of his pioneering achievement. However, due to his irregular means of taking control in Darien, Balboa continued to be viewed as an outlaw in some circles. His authority was soon challenged by the newly arrived administrator PEDRARIAS DÁVILA, who began a lengthy campaign of calumny and manufacture of false evidence against the impulsive conquistador. Balboa was, meanwhile, preoccupied by grand visions of new explorations—he had already glimpsed the peaks of the Andes as he probed toward the Colombian shore of South America—and ignored the political threats gathering around him. He assembled craftsmen and Indian laborers at Acla, on the Pacific coast of the isthmus, and began constructing a fleet intended either to venture forth into the Pacific or to sail southward, following up stories of the gold of PERU. Pedrarias interrupted these dreams by arresting Balboa and his principal henchmen on charges of treason and malfeasance and decreed their execution. Balboa was beheaded in January 1519 near where he first landed in PANAMA.

Reckless and obsessive, like so many conquistadores, Balboa had skills that some of them lacked, such as his talent for improvisation and his ability to win over indigenous peoples by a combination of initial forcefulness and subsequent benevolence. Furthermore he seems to have possessed a visionary impulse that transcended the purely materialistic motivations of most of his contemporaries. His discovery of the Pacific assures him a place in the direct line of major explorers stretching from Columbus to FERDINAND MAGELLAN who opened

the European mind to an awareness of a wider world.

Balearic Islands (Islas Baleares)

This Mediterranean archipelago, lying several hundred miles to the east of the Spanish coast, includes four larger islands—Majorca, Minorca, Ibiza, and Formentera—and several smaller ones, having a total area of 1,936 square miles. A mild climate suitable for agriculture and abundant harbors for shipping have drawn a stream of conquerors to these islands through the centuries. They finally passed to the rule of ARAGON in the 14th century and now constitute an "overseas" province of Spain, with special regional status. Minorca was under British rule for most of the 18th century and not finally returned to Spain until 1801. Despite their tumultuous past, the Balearics are now esteemed as a tranquil vacation resort by mainland Spaniards (including the royal family) and sun-seeking northern Europeans. The remarkable megalithic remains of prehistoric settlements attract the interest of scholars and scientists. Catalan is the predominant language on all of the islands.

Barcelona

The second city of Spain, with a population of 2 million, and the capital of its CATALONIA region, Barcelona is located in the northeast of the country, some 300 miles from MADRID, the city's traditional rival. A major Mediterranean port since ancient times, Barcelona became the center of a far-flung commercial network during the Middle Ages, with connections extending to Italy and Greece. Its subordination to the Crown of ARAGON by the beginning of the 16th century was followed by a period of decline and stimulated Catalan antagonism to the emerging centralization of Spanish government. Barcelona rebelled against the Madrid regime during the mid-1600s and again in the WAR OF THE SPANISH SUCCESSION. The deterioration of its Mediterranean commerce and its exclusion from Spanish-American trade until 1778 contributed to Barcelona's decline as a financial center.

Barcelona experienced a renewal of fortune thanks to the Industrial Revolution, and by the late 19th century had become a thriving center of manufacturing and a place of great wealth and political influence. Catalan industrialists, though usually at odds with the thousands of workers who swelled the city's population and who often espoused anarchism, were joined with them in sympathy for Catalan nationalism. The revival of the region's distinct language and culture, combined with the city's increasing tendency toward radicalism, generated conflict between Barcelona and Madrid throughout the 20th century. The bloody repression of a leftist uprising in 1909, the proclamation of an autonomous government during the Second Republic, and the city's prolonged resistance to the forces of FRANCISCO FRANCO during the SPANISH CIVIL WAR doomed Barcelona to repression under the Franco regime (1939–75). Since 1975 Barcelona has enjoyed a renaissance in both its commercial and cultural life. The dynamism of the new Barcelona was on display to the world during the Olympic Games held there in 1992. While Barcelona continues to be a major center of intellectual life, its ambivalent relationship with the Spanish state due to seemingly endless debates over Catalan autonomy present an ongoing problem.

Baroja, Pío (1872–1956)
Spanish novelist

A Basque born in San Sebastian and trained as a physician, Baroja gave up his rural practice before age 30 to devote himself to social issues. After two unsuccessful campaigns for parliament as a Republican and an unsuccessful period in the family business, he became a full-time writer. His output in this career choice was prodigious, totaling nearly 100 volumes. Baroja's favorite format was the trilogy of linked novels, of which he produced 11. He also achieved identification as the "heir" to BENITO PÉREZ GALDÓS, the 19th-century historical novelist. Baroja chronicled, in a series of no less than 22 volumes called *Memorias de un hombre de acción* (Memoirs of a man of action, 1913–28), the adventures of a hero who participates in all of the wars and upheavals in Spain from the onset of the First Carlist War to the fall of ISABELLA II. The sheer mass of his writing has led some commentators not only to hail him as the new Galdós but as Spain's greatest novelist of the 20th century, or even as Spain's greatest modern writer. More restrained critics have focused their praise on the consistency of Baroja's preoccupation with social issues, particularly the repression and degradation of the lower classes. The multiplicity and variety of his scenes and characters draw the reader on, but often without a coherent plot. His protagonists, moreover, have been found wanting in individual traits or inner motivations. Many of them, it has been said, are simply excuses to follow a thread of action from one moment or one scene to another without much resolution of the issues presented.

Baroja's ability to pursue a long literary career through the changing sociopolitical environment that encompassed the SPANISH CIVIL WAR and the first phase of the Franco regime might seem remarkable in that he was consistently an enemy of the established powers, particularly the church, the military, and the privileged classes. Baroja was, however, accepted as a kind of universal critic, who attacked and rejected everyone and everything. Although he claimed to be motivated by his desire to point out the evils of society and to inspire reform, he gives the impression of having no sympathy with anyone. Unlike other members of the "GENERATION OF '98," who called for the renewal of Spanish life, Baroja perceived Spain as irredeemable and detested virtually everything about his country and its people. His many admirers among foreign readers regarded him as the quintessential Spanish writer of his time and thought of him as a voice of opposition to dictatorship. Many Spaniards, on the other hand, seem to have regarded him as a kind of ultimate manifestation of their national traits of ill temper and perennial suspicion. This colossal crankiness and his fondness for picturesque, adventurous situations gained and held a vast readership.

Perhaps the most acclaimed of Baroja's trilogies is *La lucha por la vida* (The struggle for life, 1904). Among his individual novels, *El arbol de la ciencia* (The tree of science, 1911), which contains significant autobiographical elements, has remained consistently the most widely read.

Basque nationalism

The world has long since moved beyond the French writer Voltaire's dismissive definition that the Basque are "a small people who sing and dance in the Pyrenees." Other submerged nationalities in Europe who resorted to armed violence to assert their claims during the 1960s and '70s have faded from view. But whether denounced as terrorists or praised as freedom fighters, Basque militants have remained at the center of Spain's politics into the 21st century.

Many theories have been advanced as to the origin of the Basque, their distinctive culture, and their mysterious language. They made their first appearance in history some 2,000 years ago in the northwestern Pyrenean corner of what is now Spain; remained unconquered by Romans, Visigoths, and Muslim invaders; and established a presence on the other side of the Pyrenees in southwestern France (Gascony takes its name from them) during the early Middle Ages. Although their heartland south of the Pyrenees eventually acknowledged the overlordship of the kings of CASTILE, the Basque retained considerable autonomy, the last of which was not formally abolished until the 1870s. They never ceased to think of themselves as a nation apart.

When they were in a cooperative mood, the Basque rendered good service to Spain as seamen and soldiers, sheepherders, and farmers. Their principal city, BILBAO, became a center of manufacturing, shipbuilding, and maritime trade. Their kinsmen north of the mountains proved equally valuable subjects to France. Their contrary, independent temperament led them to fight for the losing side in the Carlist wars and to support the doomed Second Republic during the SPANISH CIVIL WAR. Their adherence to the republic was all the more incongruous because of their ardent Catholicism, as contrasted with the anticlericalism of most Loyalists. They were promised self-government by the republic and famously endured the bombing of their ancient political center at Guernica as punishment. Worse punishment came during the dictatorship of FRANCISCO FRANCO, when the Basque were denied most of their cultural manifestations, including the use of their language.

In the later years of the Franco regime, as attempts were being made to develop a compromise between moderate leaders in the region and a progressive cadre in the MADRID government, a militant movement emerged among the younger Basque generation. They rejected compromise, proclaimed their commitment to independence, and launched an armed struggle in 1968–69. By 1973 when these militants staged a spectacular assassination, they were clearly in the vanguard of what observers were calling a worldwide rising tide of terrorism. Admiral Luis Carrero Blanco, Franco's deputy and his presumptive political successor, was slain as he drove through the streets of the capital by a bomb so powerful that it hurled his limousine onto the balcony of an adjacent building. International analysts as well as Spanish security forces sought to learn more about this rising force. It was called Euskadi Ta Askatasuna (Basque Homeland and Liberty), or ETA. It had loose association with various Basque political groups and would change those associations from time to time, although most frequently perceived as tied to a party called Batasuna (Unity). A relatively small organization, ETA may have had fewer than 100 active members, relying on supporters and sympathizers to facilitate its operations. Its goal, however, was large, for it claimed all of Vizcaya, Guipúzcoa, Álava, and NAVARRE (the latter of which is only part Basque in population). In addition to the 2 million

inhabitants of these four provinces, ETA also envisioned reclaiming three former provinces now mostly contained within the French department of Basses-Pyrénées (renamed Pyrénées-Atlantiques in 1969), where another half-million Basques lived.

After the death of Franco in 1975 and the establishment of a democracy as well as a popularly endorsed constitution, the "new" Spain sought to win over Basque sympathizers. Without abandoning its fundamental commitment to Spain's unity, the Socialist ministry of FELIPE GONZÁLEZ agreed to more than a dozen autonomous regions, one of which was to include the Spanish BASQUE PROVINCES. While welcomed by moderate Basques who formed legal nationalist parties and elected a regional parliament, this plan was totally repudiated by ETA. The war of liberation that they pursued against the post-Franco state involved bombings, shootings, and other attacks upon civil society. Although most of their targets were members of the security forces and public officials, many of those who perished were innocent bystanders. As the armed struggle continued and the death toll rose past 800, authorities denounced the ETA militants as "terrorist murderers" and documented their ties to the practitioners and sponsors of terrorism around the world from the Irish Republican Army in Ireland to the Qaddafi regime in Libya. Several particularly outrageous killings brought hundreds of thousands of Spaniards into the streets of Madrid and other major cities to denounce ETA and demand an end to the killings. On a less open level of response Prime Minister González authorized counterterrorist units that evolved into death squads that carried out their own extralegal murders of captured ETA operatives. The revelation of these deeds helped to bring down the González government in 1996. The administration led by JOSÉ MARÍA AZNAR of the conservative Popular Party vowed a commitment to legal measures, at the same time promising vigorous action. Yet a partial truce in 1998–99 failed to resolve the Basque question. Spain was by this time receiving help from the French government. Paris had begun rounding up key leaders of the ETA movement who had built up a network of supporters in France. Most of these captives were handed back to the Spanish courts. Increasingly hard pressed in the first years of the new century, ETA seemed to be losing its momentum.

The events of March 2004 introduced a whole new dimension. The Aznar administration at first blamed the bombings of Madrid-bound commuter trains that killed nearly 200 people on Basque terrorists. The parliamentary elections that were already scheduled for that week resulted in the return of the Socialists to power, for many voters believed Aznar and his associates had lied about Basque involvement. As the true authors of the Madrid atrocity were proved to be Islamists angered by Spain's support of U.S. intervention in Iraq, the role of ETA in Spanish affairs seemed almost forgotten. The new prime minister, JOSÉ LUIS RODRÍGUEZ ZAPATERO, concentrated on Spain's relations with Muslims abroad and within his own country. ETA seemed almost obliged to set off bombs and fire guns in subsequent months to remind Spaniards that Basque demands still needed to be addressed. During 2005, however, even debates about regional autonomy were largely diverted to new claims made by Catalan nationalists. In March 2006 the leader-

ship of ETA announced a "permanent cease-fire," later rescinded in September.

Basque provinces (Provincias Vascongadas)

Located in northwestern Spain, the provinces of Guipúzcoa, Álava, and Vizcaya, with a total area of 2,800 square miles, constitute an autonomous region, the Basque Country, possessing an unusual sense of distinct identity. The Basque, a people of mysterious origin and with a language that cannot be linked to any other European tongue, have preserved cultural traditions that have set them apart for centuries, despite their political subjugation to the Castilian monarchy since the late 14th century. Their prudent overlords left them in possession of their highly democratic laws and local government institutions until the late 19th century. In more recent times, however, the process of centralization has brought repeated confrontations. Granted de facto sovereignty by the Second Republic at the beginning of the SPANISH CIVIL WAR, the Basque fought against the followers of FRANCISCO FRANCO and were consequently partially repressed during his dictatorship (1939–75). Since 1969 militant nationalists have carried on a campaign of political violence in the name of independence (see BASQUE NATIONALISM). Although the democratic regime that succeeded Franco has made concessions to Basque regional autonomy, extremists have carried on their struggle with few interruptions for more than 25 years. Nearly a thousand people have been killed in this conflict, which has occasionally spilled over into the Basque-populated districts of southwestern France.

Despite the impact of terrorism upon their society the Basque have sustained a prosperous economy with its industrial base in the area around BILBAO. They have also safeguarded their love of liberty, individualism, and (even though Franco banned Basque-language publications) a distinct literary tradition. Cheerful, energetic, and for the most part opposed to extremism, the Basque still hope to preserve their special place in Europe despite the currents of unification moving across the continent.

Bécquer, Gustavo Adolfo (Gustavo Adolfo Domínguez Bastida)
(1836–1870)
Spanish poet

Born in SEVILLE and orphaned at an early age, Bécquer, who later adopted an old family name by which he is known, abandoned an unpromising apprenticeship in art to seek a literary career in MADRID. In the capital he acquired a wife and several children but earned only a precarious living and a reputation as a poet that was limited to publication in newspapers. In retrospect Bécquer would be seen as the most tragic, as well as the last, of the romantic school. Unlike JOSÉ DE ESPRONCEDA who was full of activity and bravado, Bécquer was thwarted by domestic unhappiness, a failed love affair, and deteriorating health. Some of his most admired work was produced during a prolonged residence in a monastery during the 1860s where he evidently found the tranquillity and relief from the consumption that haunted him. His poems and stories were collected and published in book form only after his early death through a subscription raised by friends and admirers who had not been able to save his life but guaranteed him a posthumous reputation that has grown with time. Bécquer's major poetical works are included in the 80 or so lyrics of *Rimas* (*Rhymes*). Continuing themes in *Rimas* include his striving to achieve pure poetry of form and image and his frustration over the inability to attain perfect love. The prose writings contained in *Leyendas* (*Legends*) are set in a world of golden moonlight, vine-covered castles, and vague locations in which tragic figures pursue their dreamlike destinies.

Bécquer is now regarded as one of Spain's finest poets, whose evocations of poignant longing represent a lyric romanticism that some critics find to be, in fact, a new departure in poetry. Many 20th-century writers have proclaimed their admiration of him and acknowledge him as their inspiration.

Belalcázar, Sebastián de
(1479–1551)
Spanish explorer and conqueror

An early participant in the conquest of the New World, Belalcázar accompanied CHRISTOPHER COLUMBUS on his third voyage (1498) and participated in the occupation of Darien and NICARAGUA. He then took part in the conquest of PERU under FRANCISCO PIZARRO (1532) and established control over present-day ECUADOR by capturing Quito and founding Guayaquil. He subsequently marched into the southwestern part of what is now COLOMBIA, where he founded the city of Cali in the course of searching for the fabulous El Dorado. Afterward he became embroiled in a three-sided dispute with rival conquistadores GONZALO JIMÉNEZ DE QUESADA and NIKOLAUS FEDERMANN, an argument that was not resolved until all three had returned to Spain to settle their claims. Back in South America in 1541 as governor of the Colombian province of Popayán, Belalcázar threw himself into disputes among the heirs and allies of Pizarro. As a result of one of his more violent actions Belalcázar was tried and convicted of an unauthorized execution and died on route to Spain to plead for reversal of this judgment.

Benavente y Martínez, Jacinto
(1866–1954)
Spanish dramatist

In the seemingly endless parade of political revolutionaries that marches through Spanish history, Benavente stands out as an authentic revolutionary in literature for he not only demolished the old-fashioned theatrics that had long dominated his country's stages but did much to spread dramatic realism throughout turn-of-the-century Europe. His achievements were appropriately recognized by the award of the Nobel Prize in literature in 1922.

Widely traveled and a keen observer of society, with an acute ear for the conversation of bourgeois drawing rooms and an occasional provincial farmhouse, he produced nearly 200 plays, to say nothing of an abundance of essays and anecdotal memoirs. Benavente's literary fecundity, inevitably compared to that of LOPE DE VEGA, has led some to draw a sharp distinction between his writings before World War I and those of his later years. His first play, *El nido ajeno* (Somone else's nest, 1894) was too "different" from what the playgoing public was used to to be popular, but commercial and critical success soon greeted a series of dramas, many of a satirical character, such as *Gente conocida* (People one

knows, 1896), *El marido de la Téllez* (Mrs. Téllez's husband, 1897), *La comida de las fieras* (The beasts' dinner, 1898), *El primo Román* (Cousin Román, 1901), *Señora ama* (Mistress of the house, 1908), and *La malquerida* (*The Passion Flower,* 1913). From this period also date two of his undoubted masterpieces: *La noche del sábado* (*Saturday Night,* 1903) and *Los intereses creados* (*The Bonds of Interest,* 1907). The former is a mixture of fantasy, satire, and "ideas" in which his emphasis on the power of the will reflects prevailing Nietzschean concepts. In the latter, borrowing the style of the commedia dell'arte and employing heavy sarcasm, Benavente presents an unusually bitter satire of the way in which personal interests govern and deform all elements of society.

World War I brought a series of political crises that affected Benavente's popularity. Already a member of the Royal Academy (1912), his public utterances, which favored Spain's support for Germany and reflected the point of view expressed by the church, army, and aristocracy, alienated many of his previous admirers, who felt he had betrayed his critical and reformist credentials. Benavente, shocked by this overt antagonism, ceased to write for a time, until the award of the Nobel Prize stimulated him to new work. However, in the increasingly embittered environment of the 1920s and early '30s he continued to meet with criticism that was as much a reflection of personal animosity as of artistic concerns. The SPANISH CIVIL WAR and World War II sapped his creative imagination, if not his dramatic output. The last decade of Benavente's life saw a resurgence of his inspiration and reputation. Numerous well-received plays emerged from his pen, three of them in the months before his death, although critics did not rate them equal to his finest work.

Whether talk of Benavente's creative decline during the last half of his creative life represents political prejudice, a shift in fashion, or an authentic loss of imaginative power continues to be in dispute. What cannot be doubted is that at his best Benavente is one of the great masters of Spanish drama, who transformed it from the mere moving about on stage of cardboard characters into an achievement in which his countryfolk could again take pride.

Bilbao

Principal city of the Basque Country in northern Spain, this major port and industrial center began its rise to prominence in the 14th century when it became a major commercial link between CASTILE and northern Europe. In modern times it suffered from prolonged sieges in the First and Second Carlist Wars and was a center of resistance to the Franco forces during the SPANISH CIVIL WAR (1936–39). Although Bilbao enjoyed rising prosperity from the late 19th century onward and was the business and banking center of the region, many dismissed it as a grimy, polluted place, resembling the industrial cities of northern England rather than the physically attractive towns in other parts of Spain. During the late 20th century an urban renaissance marked by environmental and cultural renewal reached its peak in 1997 with the opening of the Museo Guggenheim de Arte Contemporáneo (an extension of the famous Guggenheim Museum in New York City), housed in a remarkable structure designed by the American architect Frank Gehry. With a population (including sub-urbs) reaching 1 million and a pivotal position in Spain's most volatile region (see BASQUE PROVINCES), Bilbao has emerged as one of the country's major urban centers.

Blasco Ibáñez, Vicente (1867–1928)
Spanish writer

Born in VALENCIA, the setting of some of his most admired writings, Blasco Ibáñez was employed in his youth as secretary to the popular and prolific novelist MANUEL FERNÁNDEZ Y GONZÁLEZ, an experience from which he undoubtedly derived his own facility and productivity. During the politically tumultuous period preceding and immediately following the SPANISH-AMERICAN WAR, he was deeply involved in criticism of the government, forming his own party and winning election to parliament. By 1890 he had made himself the object of threats and harassment and left Spain to become a permanent traveler abroad. A long residence in South America and other journeys overseas inspired many of his essays and stories. His last years were spent in the French Mediterranean resort town of Menton.

Blasco Ibáñez's most critically acclaimed works belong to his early period when he examined aspects of Valencian society. These include *Arroz y tartana* (*Rice and boats*) from 1894 in which he probes the aspirations and conflicts of lower class life in the city of Valencia, paying particular attention to tradesmen and petty merchants. He moves into the Valencian countryside in *La barraca* (The cabin, published in 1898) to portray clashes between landowners and tenant farmers as well as the tensions among the farmers themselves. In *Cañas y barro* (Reeds and mud, published in 1902) he again presents social conflict, this time among dwellers on the Mediterranean coast of Valencia.

The diminished standing of Blasco Ibáñez among contemporary Spanish critics has much to do with the very success of his best known novels, *Sangre y arena* (*Blood and Sand*) published in 1908 and *Los cuatro jinetes del Apocalipsis* (*The Four Horsemen of the Apocalypse*, from 1916). Both were international best-sellers in translation and became even better known in cinema productions. In each case Blasco Ibáñez is blamed for creating stereotypes and over dramatizing family confrontations. Although some of the blame for these impressions may attach to the films rather than the novels themselves, commentators complain that for many people outside of Spain, Blasco Ibáñez is the only Spanish writer whose name they can remember and his bullring images have become clichés.

Blue Division (División Azul)

This Spanish military unit was the means by which Spain, although nominally neutral, participated in World War II, supporting Germany in the fight against the Soviet Union. Adolf Hitler's regime had provided substantial military support (mostly through air power) to the Nationalists during the SPANISH CIVIL WAR. When the German dictator launched his war with Britain and France, a few months after the end of the Spanish conflict, he clearly expected both gratitude and assistance from General FRANCISCO FRANCO, the new ruler in MADRID. El Caudillo was able to make the plausible excuse that his country needed time to recover from recent hardships. Even a personal meeting between the two men at the Spanish-French frontier in summer 1940

failed to achieve Hitler's immediate goal, free passage for German forces through Spain to attack the British fortress of GIBRALTAR. However, after Hitler's invasion of the Soviet Union in June 1941 and the proclamation of a so-called Great Anti-Bolshevik Crusade, considerable enthusiasm arose among the Spanish people. Those who resented Russian aid to the Loyalists during the civil war or who regarded communism as a threat to Christian civilization were eager to join in the fight (as were many in Nazi-occupied Europe). Franco announced that volunteers would be accepted from the Spanish armed forces and from the civilian population. Although his original intention envisioned a few thousand men, more than 18,000 came forward within a month, and it was estimated that several times that number could easily have been raised. The majority of these volunteers were professional soldiers (including some 2,000 officers) or veterans of the civil war. Even some who sympathized with the republic volunteered in the hope of winning release for imprisoned relatives. Under the command of General Agustín Muñoz Grande, a division comprising three brigades of infantry (named after the cities of BARCELONA, VALENCIA, and SEVILLE) with supporting units of armor and artillery was formed. In addition, several squadrons of German aircraft manned by Spanish fliers were formed.

By August 1941 most of the initial Spanish contingent was en route to Russia. Until late 1942, Spanish soldiers and airmen played an active role in the siege of Leningrad and in operations near that city. More than 5,000 were killed, and a comparably high proportion, wounded. Many earned major decorations, including some of the highest honors bestowed by the Reich. While in combat they wore the standard field gray German uniform with the distinguishing shoulder patch of the red and yellow Spanish colors and the word *ESPAÑA*. As they were officially not part of the Spanish regular army their uniform on home leave included the red beret and blue shirt of the Falangist militia, thus inspiring the designation "Blue Division." In the later months of the Russian campaign many of the annual draft of conscripts were required to join the originally all-volunteer force. At least one-third of the 45,000 men who were rotated into the division may have been serving under compulsion.

By early 1943 Franco was under considerable pressure from those governments who questioned his neutrality to remove the "volunteers." Moreover Hitler was clearly sustaining a reversal of fortune on the eastern front. The Blue Division was, therefore, withdrawn—even though Franco quietly allowed those who wished to remain in action against the Soviets to do so. These determined anti-Bolsheviks were distributed among a number of the Nazi SS (intelligence and security) units, some specifically designated as Spanish volunteers and others composed of multinational personnel. A detachment of Spaniards served to the bitter end in the battle for Berlin as part of the Nordland SS Division, which was entirely destroyed in May 1945.

Böhl von Faber, Cecilia   See
CABALLERO, FERNÁN.

Bolívar, Simón (1783–1830)
Spanish colonial rebel
Born in Caracas, to a wealthy Spanish family, Bolívar was sent to MADRID to study

law. He subsequently traveled in Europe. His experience in France in the climactic days of the French Revolution as well as his readings of the French philosophes inspired a strong sympathy with the new spirit of the age. Further travels in the United States confirmed his revolutionary instincts and converted him to the cause of colonial independence. Back in his native province of VENEZUELA, he joined the revolt against the Spanish authority that broke out in 1811.

Although Bolívar had little political experience and no military training, his enthusiasm and intelligence soon led him to positions of leadership. During the next 10 years he became, in effect, the George Wash-

Simón Bolívar *(Library of Congress)*

ington of much of South America. Like his North American counterpart, who was also self-taught in revolutionary struggle, Bolívar experienced alternating victories and defeats and was at times reduced to desperate straights. Also like Washington, he overcame adversity through self-confidence and indomitable persistence and inspired his followers to carry on the cause of freedom even after crushing reverses in battle. Bolívar was inexhaustible in his commitment to the cause of American independence from Spain, even during periods of exile in Curaçao, JAMAICA, and Haiti, which merely added to his hemispheric perspective. In 1819 he united what is now Venezuela, COLOMBIA, PANAMA, and ECUADOR into the republic of Greater Colombia, under his own presidency. He, then, moved against the Spaniards in PERU, freed that country, and created in its southern district the republic of BOLIVIA, which took his name as its own. By the late 1820s Bolívar was de facto ruler of much of the continent but challenged by local rivals in most regions. Even after resigning his presidency and proclaiming himself dictator he was unable to mobilize enough power to sustain his rule or fulfill his dream of a great, united, and progressive nation. Once again he went into self-exile but died on the journey to an uncertain destination.

The reverse of Bolívar's heroic image as a great leader and the Liberator was an authoritarian egotism that was incompatible with his original democratic principles. Ultimately his goals proved unattainable, for in destroying the Spanish regime he unleashed the forces of localism and rivalry that made it impossible for Spanish South America to become both free and a single great country. Nevertheless, his dream of a united Spanish America is still honored by

many under such modern concepts as the "Bolivarian revolution."

Bolivia

The area encompassing much of present-day Bolivia, which lies to the east of PERU, was ruled by the Aymara people until the early 14th century when it was subjugated by the Inca Empire. The Spanish conquerors of the Inca gained control of the so-called Upper Peru region during the 1540s and '50s. The area was ruled under the name Charcas as part of the Viceroyalty of Peru until it was transferred to the Viceroyalty of La Plata (see ARGENTINA) in 1776. An uprising against Spanish rule began in 1809, but it was not until 1825 that total independence was achieved under the new name of Bolivia, assumed by the republic in honor of SIMÓN BOLÍVAR, the great South American Liberator.

Borja (Borgia) Rodrigo de   See ALEXANDER VI.

Bourbon (Borbón)

Following the extinction of the HABSBURG line (Casa de Austria) in 1700, most Spaniards recognized Philippe, duke of Anjou, as King PHILIP V of Spain. The accession of this grandson of Louis XIV of France and great-nephew of CHARLES II of Spain marked the beginning of the Spanish House of Borbón, which has (with interruptions) ruled ever since. Initially, however, a rival claim was raised by the Austrian Habsburgs, and a subsequent WAR OF THE SPANISH SUCCESSION (1701–14) was fought among the European powers over the disputed inheritance.

Although it had been agreed that the Spanish and French branches of the family would never lay claim to each other's lands, there were numerous territorial disputes across the centuries, both in Europe and overseas. During the middle years of the 18th century the so-called Bourbon Family Compact brought the countries into continuing military alliance.

Philip V and succeeding Bourbons FERDINAND VI and CHARLES III attempted, with varying degrees of success, to introduce French methods of administration and economic development—"the Bourbon Reforms"—in Spain and many of the colonies. After the French Bourbons were temporarily ousted by the great revolutionary upheavals of 1789–1815, CHARLES IV and FERDINAND VII of Spain became entangled in the grand politics of the era, with disastrous results for their country. The restoration of the Bourbons on both sides of the Pyrenees after the fall of Napoléon provided only intermittent stability. In the case of ISABELLA II her unhappy reign came to an end with a military coup in 1868. Restored in 1875 under ALFONSO XII, the Spanish Bourbons soon saw a new era of ill fortune that coincided with the reign of ALFONSO XIII. Military defeats abroad and political turmoil at home led to his departure from his country in 1931. The remarkable durability of the Spanish Bourbons was demonstrated more than 40 years later when his grandson, JUAN CARLOS I, ascended the throne at the end of the Franco dictatorship and ushered in a period of democracy and rising prosperity.

Boyacá, Battle of (1819)

This battle on August 7, 1819, ended in a decisive victory for the forces of independence in the Viceroyalty of NEW GRANADA and the fall of Spanish rule in what is now COLOMBIA and VENEZUELA. The South American Liberator, SIMÓN BOLÍVAR, had for some time been building up his forces and simultaneously exhausting those of his enemy by constant deceptive maneuvers. Late on the afternoon of August 7, he attacked a large body of Royalists (mostly colonials) as they were attempting to cross a bridge near Boyacá, in south-central Colombia. After several hours of fighting his rebel forces, numbering about 2,000, forced the surrender of some 1,600 soldiers and the senior Spanish officers. The way now lay open to Bogotá, from which the viceroy fled and Bolívar rapidly advanced to the city. There, a few days later he proclaimed the independence of the Viceroyalty of New Granada. This victory tipped the scales in favor of the Spanish American revolution. It encouraged the rebels in MEXICO and Central America, who won independence two years later. By 1824 Bolívar was able to personally participate in the final downfall of Spanish rule in South America following the last battle at AYACUCHO in the highlands of PERU.

Braga, Teófilo (1843–1924)
Portuguese writer and statesman

Born in humble circumstances in the AZORES, Braga managed to secure admission to the University of Coimbra where he became associated with the Portuguese disciples of positivism. Subsequently, as a teacher at the University of Lisbon, he promoted the philosophical doctrines of the French thinker Auguste Comte. Gradually, however, Braga became less interested in philosophical analysis and more ardently committed to a militant nationalism that was reflected in his voluminous writings. His work included history, literary criticism, and poetry and exhibited a steady growth of anticlericalism and antimonarchism. By 1910, recognized as one of his country's leading intellectuals, Braga was called upon to become the first president of the newly proclaimed republic of Portugal. His tenure was almost as brief as that of King MANUEL II, who had reigned only two years. Braga left the presidency in 1911 and was obliged to endure the domestic tumults and the disastrous results of entry into World War I that led his county into so many sufferings during the next two decades.

Bragança (Braganza)

This district in northern Portugal and the town from which it derives its name were formerly held by the dukes of Bragança, a line of nobles descended from an illegitimate son, Afonso, of King John (João) I, who had conferred the ducal title upon his son in 1442. Duke John (died 1583) briefly opposed PHILIP II of Spain when the latter claimed the Portuguese throne in 1580 but was persuaded to abandon his claim. His grandson was proclaimed King John IV in 1640 when Portugal broke away from Spanish rule at the end of the so-called Sixty Years' Tyranny. The descendants of John IV ruled Portugal during the 18th and 19th centuries, with the line being ousted in 1910 by a republican revolution. MANUEL II died in exile, bringing an end to the Bragança dynasty, although claimants to the throne remain in Europe and a Brazilian branch descended from JOHN VI still resides in that country.

Bravo Murillo, Juan (1803–1873)
Spanish statesman

Intended for a position in the church and for a time a professor of philosophy, Bravo Murillo instead pursued a career in politics. By the early 1830s he had settled in MADRID and taken a leading role in the controversies that grew out of the confrontation between conservatism and liberalism. He was elected to the Cortes (see CORTES) as a deputy from SEVILLE, in 1837, and from Ávila in 1840, but his opposition to the dominance of General BALDOMERO ESPARTERO forced him into exile in France until the general had surrendered power. Bravo Murillo's adroit maneuvering and subtle political manipulations led to his nickname "the Lawyer," which reflected the hostility of those who saw him as a cunning and unprincipled politician. For others his insistence on an orderly civilian process of constitutional law represented a welcome contrast to the incessant military coup-making of the period. During the 1840s he was successively minister of justice, public works, and finance, and by 1850 he had become president of the Council of State. Bravo Murillo, convinced of the rightness of his ideas and plans, became increasingly authoritarian, insisting upon his own wishes and refusing to accept political compromises. Although he was not a strong supporter of ISABELLA II, her opponents marked him for removal in the crisis of 1854, and he again left the country. He accepted a number of diplomatic assignments in subsequent years, but the revolution of 1868 effectively ended his political career.

Bravo Murillo is posthumously honored by statues and streets named for him but suffered the fate of many strong and determined politicians who could not win the support of lesser men. His policies represented a progressive program of public development and financial discipline that most of his contemporaries found inconvenient, as it threatened their special interests. His self-righteous and bullying approach deprived him of necessary support. Although even his enemies recognized his integrity, he failed in most of his attempts to modernize Spain, and it has been left to historians to grant him the recognition that contemporaries denied him.

Brazil (Brasil)

Portugal laid claim to this eastern part of South America in 1500. The land may have been sighted by Europeans several years earlier. Agreements with Spain had assigned new discoveries in Asia and Africa to Portugal while reserving the rest of the world to FERDINAND V and ISABELLA I. A revised dividing line proclaimed in 1497 created a foothold for Portugal on the southern continent. The resulting linguistic and cultural separation of what would become Brazil from Spanish America has endured for more than five centuries. Although the Portuguese made periodic visits to the coast to harvest brazilwood (after which the country was named), the red dye derived from this tree did not seem to justify a permanent settlement until the 1530s. Several attempts were made to secure Brazil against foreign encroachment, including her division into proprietary domains whose grantees assumed the costs of colonizing and defending their respective territories. Some of these "captaincies" evolved into the provinces of the future, but many were abandoned, and the royal government had

to find a way of managing the colony. Little was done during the period of Spanish rule of Portugal (1580–1640), but after regaining independence Portugal was able to turn its unprofitable possession into a source of wealth during the late 1600s and early 1700s by the fortunate discoveries of gold and diamond in the interior.

During the 18th century (sometimes referred to as Brazil's "golden century") a central administration was established at Rio de Janeiro, monopoly trading companies were created to manage the economy, new settlers were sent from Portugal, and the boundaries of Brazil were extended westward and southward. Large numbers of African slaves continued to be shipped from ANGOLA during this period, the large Amerindian population of the interior having been found unsuitable or uncooperative for work on sugar plantations. By the beginning of the 19th century Brazil contained a large, complex population with a growing sense of a separate identity. In 1808 the Portuguese royal family arrived at Rio de Janeiro after fleeing the French invaders of their homeland. The prince regent, Dom João, (later King JOHN VI), was delighted with his new residence and proclaimed Brazil an equal partner with Portugal in a united kingdom. This situation persisted even after the liberation of Portugal at the end of the Napoleonic Wars (1814). By 1821 political leaders in Portugal demanded the monarch's return to LISBON. Recognizing the growing spirit of independence in Brazil, the king appointed his son Pedro as prince regent of Brazil with the advice that he should join rather than resist the movement when it became inevitable. In 1822 the prince took control of the nationalist upsurge and proclaimed himself

PEDRO I, emperor of a sovereign Brazil. Portugal's colony thus joined the wave that was already sweeping Spanish America. The adroit House of BRAGANÇA had, however, avoided the process that transformed Spain's colonies into republics. Instead, an imperial Bragança dynasty planted the exotic flower of monarchy in American soil, where it flourished until 1889. Although Pedro I would pass on the Portuguese succession to his daughter MARIA II, he eventually returned to Portugal to play a role in his homeland's politics. His son, Emperor Pedro II, ruled Brazil throughout a long life with a facile mixture of Brazilian patriotism and European sophistication. It was not until the end of the 19th century that a bloodless revolution introduced a republic and marked the true end of Portugal's colonial presence in Brazil.

Breda, siege of (1625–1626)

The city of Breda, long a center of Netherlandish opposition to Spanish rule, had remained in control of the Dutch rebels when the Twelve Years' Truce was signed in 1609. This cessation of hostilities between Spain and the Dutch Republic ended in 1621, when the new king, PHILIP IV, abandoned the peaceful policy of his father and attempted to reimpose Spanish rule over the Low Countries. Breda became a symbolic target of his initially unsuccessful plan. His forces laid siege to the city in 1625, employing bombardment and blockade to reduce it and thereby break the will of the rebels. The Dutch defenders resolutely endured a siege of more than 10 months, finally capitulating in 1626. The commander of the garrison, Count Justin of Nassau, was finally authorized by his kins-

man, the prince of Orange (head of the Dutch Republic) to surrender. The ceremony of capitulation, in which the count handed the keys of the city to the Spanish general AMBROGIO SPINOLA was immortalized in DIEGO VELÁZQUEZ's famous painting, *The Capitulation of Breda*. The two noblemen are seen in postures of mutual respect before a backdrop of Spanish soldiers, whose tall lances held at rigid attention resemble a forest of weapons, giving rise to the painting's popular name, *Las Lanzas* (The lances). The capture of Breda, which came after a series of military setbacks, raised Spanish pride and self-confidence, but it proved a false dawn.

Buero Vallejo, Antonio (1916–2000)
Spanish dramatist

A young painter of considerable talent, Buero left his art studies to join the Republican forces during the SPANISH CIVIL WAR, in which he served as a medical orderly. At the end of the conflict in 1939 he was prevented from resuming his career by a term of confinement in a Nationalist prison. By 1949, when he was again at liberty, he had turned his interests to drama and debuted his first play, *Historia de una escalera* (Story of a staircase), which won him the distinction of the Lope de Vega Prize. He continued to write for the stage throughout the period of the Franco dictatorship and on into the era of democratic revival, winning the National Drama Prize in 1980 and the Miguel de Cervantes Prize in 1986. Having been opposed by Nationalists, who resented the success of a man who had fought against them, and in later years by Republican exiles, who suggested that he had "sold out" by continuing to work under the

Franco regime, Buero commented, "If you are a good writer, you will write, no matter what stands in your way. Only those who had no real talent blamed the dictatorship for their silence. With the onset of democracy, they still had nothing to say." In addition to *Historia de una escalera*, Buero is well known for *En la ardiente oscuridad* (In the burning darkness, 1951), in which he uses the device of blind characters to hint at the political environment then prevailing. His plays *Un soñador para un pueblo* (A dreamer for a people, 1959) and *El sueño de la razón* (The sleep of reason, 1970) were among a series of plays that maintained an undercurrent of dissent during the Franco years. More awards and accolades for his dramatic output followed and even membership in the Spanish Royal Academy in 1971. His work for the theater continued unabated until a week or so before his death, in May 2000.

bullfighting

Bullfighting is one of the most distinctive cultural phenomena of Spain, and mention of the one invariably summons thoughts of the other throughout the world. Whether bullfighting is a sport or an entertainment has been disputed endlessly. So, too, has its origin in Spain. Legends connect it with the bull vaulters of ancient Crete and with the "games" passed on by the Etruscans to the Romans. The Romans may well have introduced some form of bull baiting into Spain, but virtually nothing is known about their role in the process, nor are there any clear indications of Muslim influence. What is known is that medieval Spanish nobles raised fighting bulls and trained some of their vassals to battle with the animals in order to stage combats before royalty. Such encounters between man and beast grew more ritualized and elaborate during Spain's Golden Age and survived the decline of national fortunes as well as the attempts at reform by the new BOURBON dynasty. By the end of the 18th century, the corrida, as the spectacle of the bullring was called, had attained, if anything, a greater popularity than ever. Breeders controlling landed estates provided the bulls, and matches were arranged with the cooperation of professional entrepreneurs who trained young men as matadors (killers). The greatest of these matadors was undoubtedly Pedro Romero, who between 1771 and 1799 killed no less than 5,000 bulls. The corridas were by now public spectacles staged in bull rings before large and enthusiastic audiences, who cheered on or hooted at the performers. Between the end of the Napoleonic intrusion and the start of the SPANISH CIVIL WAR, bullfighting became a major industry in which breeding of bulls was a scientific process aimed at producing bloodlines that would yield natural-born fighters. Shrewd proletarian managers did the dirty work of creating bullrings in all the major cities and recruiting youthful enthusiasts who were taught not merely the skills of a "killer" but the elegant style of an art form: The matador was now generally known as a "torero" (bullfighter). He was a hero to his home province and, potentially, to the entire country.

Disrupted by the civil war (1936–39), bullfighting both as an industry and as an art form fell into decline. FRANCISCO FRANCO attempted to revive it in order to raise national morale and to contribute to a positive image for Spain during the era of his dictatorship (1939–75). He had only mini-

Matador Emilio Redondo holds his cape before an injured bull, which has been stabbed several times. *(Library of Congress)*

mal success due to the degradation of the breeding stock and the disappearance of many training academies. The bulls, aficionados complained, had become lethargic and timid, while the toreros were often clumsy youths unworthy of the name. There were, to be sure, some notable bullfighters during this period, and foreign authors such as Ernest Hemingway perpetuated the idea of the bullfight as an almost spiritual exercise.

During the last quarter of the 20th century democratic Spain experienced a surprising revival of what had seemed a doomed institution. Animal-rights crusaders were disappointed to see the revival of

public enthusiasm for this iconic tradition. Aficionados were delighted by the development of new "brave" bloodlines in the breeding farms, and they have been impressed by the quality of a new generation of toreros. These young bullfighters, including the occasional woman and foreigner in their ranks, were attracted to the burgeoning new training schools and to the glamour associated with the glittering "suit of lights" that is the highly ornamented outfit of the torero. The vast bullring of MADRID is merely the most impressive of the *plazas de toro* to be found in every major Spanish town. Substantial crowds gather as they did in generations gone by during each bullfighting season. They applaud the stirring music that accompanies the march of the bullfighter and his entourage of assistants into the sandy arena, and they are thrilled by the blare of trumpets that heralds the menacing arrival of a large and clearly murderous beast whose confrontation with the torero leads to the "moment of truth": It can end in the fatal goring of the bullfighter and will always be concluded with the bull's death. The corrida appears to have survived into the 21st century.

In Portugal bullfighting followed a somewhat similar pattern of development to that in Spain. However, because it became a form of training for warrior knights during the Middle Ages, it remained a contest between the bull and a fighter on horseback. Perhaps more significant is the Portuguese requirement that the bull's horns be sheathed so that it cannot gore its opponent. This decree was imposed in 1799 after a nobleman was hideously killed by a bull before the shocked eyes of the Portuguese royal family. Aside from these variations the Portuguese *tourada* is distinguished from its Spanish equivalent by a greater role for the entourage that accompanies the bullfighter. Instead of the Spaniard confronting the bull on foot after his helpers have weakened the animal, the Portuguese horseman exhausts the bull, and only then do his helpers (young men who have volunteered for this role to demonstrate their bravery and strength) rush upon the bull and wrestle it to the ground, even though some may be flung aside in the process. The fact that neither bull nor bullfighter is killed is a source of scorn among Spanish enthusiasts. Ironically bullfighting, which had long been discontinued in MACAO, Portugal's last colony, was revived shortly before the 1999 handover to China, although its survival there is unlikely. As for Portugal, the bullfight, for all its "tameness" and its predominantly regional popularity, appears to have retained its traditional status.

Bullring in Mijas, Spain *(Getty)*

Buñuel, Luis (1900–1983)

Spanish filmmaker

A student of the Jesuits, whose training initiated his life-long detestation of the Catholic Church, Buñuel contemplated a career as a writer but then became fascinated by the possibilities of the new art of filmmaking. In Paris he served an apprenticeship with French filmmakers, but personal differences soon sent him off on his own. Collaborating with the surrealist painter SALVADOR DALÍ, he made *Un chien andalou* (An Andalusian dog) in 1928, followed in 1930 by the fiercely anticlerical *L'age d'or* (The golden age). Despite his growing reputation (or notoriety) in France, he chose to continue his work in the promising environment of the new republic in Spain. His work during the next few years ranged from grim portrayals of rural poverty to propagandistic support for the Loyalist cause during the SPANISH CIVIL WAR. He went abroad to promote the Republican cause in 1938 and spent much of the next decade in exile. He met with mixed success in the United States but inevitably fell under suspicion for his left-wing views.

Buñuel settled in Mexico in 1947 and lived by a mixture of serious (and even surrealistic) experimentation and straightforward commercial filmmaking. By the end of the 1950s his reputation was on the rise again, and he was invited to make a film in Spain. Evidently the result of a dispute between "progressive" and "conservative" elements within the regime of FRANCISCO FRANCO, this invitation gave Buñuel not only the opportunity to revisit his homeland but to make a film essentially reflecting his own attitudes. The result, *Viridiana* (1961), was promptly banned in Spain for its anticlericalism and awarded a prize at the Cannes Film Festival in France.

Buñuel now began a new phase of his career. While retaining his base in Mexico he became an international filmmaker, obtaining financial support, cinematic talent, and appropriate locations on the strength of his reborn fame. His films, often a mixture of realistic and surrealistic effects, included *The Exterminating Angel* (1962), *Diary of a Chambermaid* (1964), *Belle de Jour* (1967), *Tristana* (1970), *The Discreet Charm of the Bourgeoisie* (1972), *The Phantom of Liberty* (1974), and *That Obscure Object of Desire* (1977).

By the time of his death, in 1983, the genius of Buñuel was universally recognized, and for all his irritating qualities Spaniards of all political persuasions basked in his reflected glory.

C

Caballero, Fernán (Cecilia Böhl von Faber) (1796–1877)

Spanish writer

Daughter of a noted German Hispanist and his Spanish wife, Böhl von Faber was born in Switzerland and wrote fluently in German and French as well as Spanish. Three times widowed, she was left with a title of nobility (marquesa de Arco Hermoso) but very little money. Turning to the writing of novels she revealed, under the pen name Fernán Caballero, a talent for romantic characters, playing out sometimes melodramatic plots in picturesque settings. Her best and undoubtedly most famous work is *La gaviota* (The sea gull), first published in 1849. Compared by contemporary critics to authors as varied as Sir Walter Scott and Charles Dickens, she exhibited traits of both romanticism and realism. She is most frequently praised, however, for her success in conveying the lifestyle and character of Andalusian society in the mid-19th century. Like many of her contemporaries—particularly women—who wrote to support themselves or their families, she was inevitably affected by the demands of productivity over artistry. Nonetheless, although her once great reputation has diminished, her signature tale of the country girl who rises to fame as a singer and ends by returning to her native place has retained its popularity over many generations. Among her many other works are *Clemencia* and *La familia de Alvareda* and the short stories about local life called *Cuadros de costumbres.*

Cabarrús, Francisco conde de (François Cabarrus) (1752–1810)

Spanish financier and statesman

Born in Bayonne, France, Cabarrús spent most of his life in Spain. He was a major financial adviser to CHARLES III and was the founder and president of the Banco de San Carlos, which became a significant factor in Spanish banking operations. He also launched the Compañía de Comercio de Filipinas, which was very successful in promoting colonial trade. He was a leading figure in the promotion of enlightened despotism and a close friend of progressive Spanish thinkers such as JOVELLANOS and FLORIDABLANCA. A promoter of the Sociedad Económica de Amigos del País, he delivered there the funeral oration for Charles III in 1788.

In the political intrigues following the accession of CHARLES IV Cabarrús was charged with fiscal irregularities and detained for a time, only to be exonerated and honored by the king with the title of count. He served the new monarch in a number of diplomatic assignments but abandoned him in 1808 to enter the service of the French-appointed usurper JOSEPH I, who made him minister of the treasury. This decision led to his repudiation by Jovellanos and other patriotic leaders.

Cabeza de Vaca, Álvar Núñez
(1500–1557)
Spanish explorer, colonial official, and chronicler

After serving as an officer in the ITALIAN WARS, Cabeza de Vaca was appointed treasurer to the expedition under PÁNFILO DE NARVÁEZ that sailed to FLORIDA in 1528 to establish Spanish rule in that region. A series of disasters culminated in the shipwreck of the last remnants of the expedition on the coast of what is now Texas. Cabeza de Vaca, prisoner of various Indian tribes, survived by a combination of improvisations as a faith healer and wandering across Texas as a peddler. After encountering three other survivors of his expedition he led them along the coast of the Gulf of Mexico, experiencing many hardships but always pushing westward in the direction of presumed Spanish settlements. As the wanderers crossed from Texas into what is now the American Southwest, Cabeza de Vaca noted the distinctive characteristics of the various native bands and made the first sighting of bison (which he described as a "hump-backed cow"). Finally, after eight years, during which he had achieved the first transcontinental crossing of North America, Cabeza de Vaca and his comrades reached Spanish outposts near the Pacific.

Following a festive reception in Mexico City, Cabeza de Vaca returned to Spain in 1537. Far from settling down at home he sought the governorship of a territory cor-responding to the present-day PARAGUAY in South America, embarked for the La Plata estuary in 1541, and traveled into the interior of South America. After further adventures, including clashes with hostile Indians and a penetration of the unexplored Chaco region, Cabeza de Vaca was deposed from his governorship by hostile residents of Asunción. Sent back to Spain to answer charges of exceeding his authority, he was sentenced to detention in a fortress in North Africa. Following several years in the city of Oran, the sentence was revoked, and Cabeza de Vaca returned to Spain, occupying a judgeship in SEVILLE until his death.

In many respects Cabeza de Vaca was the quintessential Spanish adventurer. While less aggressive than many conquistadores and certainly not as spectacularly successful, he exhibited remarkable endurance combined with bold initiative and restless curiosity. An intelligent, observant individual, he was the author of *Naufragios* (Shipwrecks) and *Comentarios* (Commentaries), which describe, respectively, his experiences in 1528–36 and 1541–44 and are filled with geographical data and ethnographic information. His sojourns in four continents represent the peculiarly Spanish dimension of the Renaissance, which was as much a reconnaissance of the world as it was an intellectual phenomenon.

Cabral, Pedro Álvares   (1457–1520)
Portuguese navigator

Recommended for the second Portuguese expedition to India by his friend VASCO DA GAMA and briefed by him on the best sailing route, Cabral, an officer and member of the minor nobility, was dispatched by MANUEL I in 1500 with 13 ships and 1,000 men to

Pedro Álvares Cabral, engraving from c. 1943 *(Library of Congress)*

lay a solid foundation upon the tentative base that da Gama had established two years earlier. Varying his predecessor's route down the West African coast to obtain more favorable winds, he found himself driven across the narrowest part of the Atlantic and arrived on the shores of South America. Cabral claimed this newly discovered land for King Manuel under the designation "Island of the True Cross," which would later be changed to BRAZIL. Some historians have suggested that Cabral was not actually the first Portuguese to reach this coast and that his supposed accidental discovery was actually intended to secure his country's control over an area originally assigned to Spanish exploration. In any event Cabral returned to his original sailing plan and

crossed the Indian Ocean, as had da Gama, to arrive at Calicut. There he fell into disputes with the local potentate and Muslim clergy over Portuguese plans for commercial and missionary activity. Cabral's ships (only eight of which had survived) bombarded the city but then withdrew for fear of losing the trade goods they had already taken on board. On returning to LISBON Cabral was reprimanded for being neither successful as a diplomat nor triumphant as a soldier, and he does not seem to have been considered for any further command. Despite his ultimate misfortune Cabral retains the double distinction of being a pioneer of Portuguese empire-building in Asia and the presumptive discoverer of Brazil.

Cabrillo, Juan Rodríguez (João Rodrigues Cabrilho) (?–1543)
Portuguese-born Spanish explorer

A native of Portugal with maritime experience, Cabrillo (as he was usually known in Spain) traveled to CUBA shortly after it was brought under Spanish rule. In 1520 he accompanied the force of PÁNFILO DE NARVÁEZ that was sent to arrest HERNÁN CORTÉS for exceeding his authority. When Narváez was defeated, Cabrillo, like most of his men, joined the army of Cortés. During the next few years he participated in the conquest of MEXICO and then moved on to Oaxaca and GUATEMALA. In these operations he became a close friend of PEDRO DE ALVARADO. When that conquistador developed his plan for an expedition to the East Indies, he appointed Cabrillo as his navigator. Proceeding to the Pacific coast of Mexico, they put their men to work building several ships. The voyage to the Moluccas was postponed after Alvarado made an agreement with the viceroy of New Spain to survey the unknown Pacific coastline to the north. When Alvarado was killed in a skirmish with Indians in 1541, Cabrillo assumed command of the project and sailed along the western shore of Baja California. Beyond the peninsula he touched upon the coast of what is now U.S. territory near the present site of San Diego. His landing place is now included in the Cabrillo National Monument. He then continued northward and passed the entrance of San Francisco Bay.

After his death fellow Portuguese navigator Bartolomé Ferrelo led the ships on to a point in the coast of what is now Oregon. Before returning to Mexico Ferrelo gave the name of Juan Rodrígues Island to the spot on the Santa Barbara coast of California where his compatriot had died and was buried, preserving the name by which he was known to the Portuguese. A minor figure among the conquistadores, Cabrillo nevertheless has the distinction of being the first European to gaze upon the western coast of the North American continent.

Cadalso, José (1741–1782)
Spanish writer

A widely traveled and sophisticated observer of foreign languages and mores, Cadalso followed the profession of arms in his younger days, rising to the rank of cavalry coronel during the Seven Years' War, although he later claimed to have learned to detest all wars. Like many contemporary intellectuals, he dabbled in several fields of literature, including poetry and drama, both in the neoclassic style, without great success. His reputation as a precursor of the romantic school derives from his almost manic reaction to the death of his beloved,

an actress whom he literally sought to rescue from the tomb. His *Noches lúgubres* (Somber nights), posthumously published in 1789, commemorates this experience and the depression that followed it. Cadalso is most significant, however, as a keen observer of Spanish society in an age of decline. His most notable works in the genre of satire and critical commentary are *Los eruditos a la violeta* (Men of false learning, 1772) and *Cartas marruecas* (Moroccan letters, 1788–89). In the former he cleverly exposes the pretensions and absurdities of those who claim to instruct and lead Spain. In the latter he employs the device of a foreign traveler, in this case a Moroccan, writing to his friends about the peculiarities and shortcomings of Spanish society. Although Cadalso's tone is often bitter and even contemptuous of Spaniards' shallowness, his Moroccan alter ego finds enough instances of surviving honesty and character in out of the way places to prove that the author was still hopeful for a revival of his nation's greatness.

Disillusioned though he might be over the glories of war, Cadalso was at heart a patriot. He returned to active duty during the American Revolution and was killed in action at the siege of GIBRALTAR, fighting against the British. His *Cartas marruecas* were published posthumously on the eve of Spain's entry into the great European revolutionary struggle that would reveal the truth about so many of Cadalso's criticisms of his country's weakness.

Cádiz

Believed to be the oldest city in western Europe—settled by Phoenicians in 1100 B.C.—Cádiz was a center of Mediterranean trade throughout antiquity and was held by the Moors until the 13th century. With the "discovery" of the New World this port that linked the Mediterranean to the Atlantic entered its greatest era. It gradually supplanted the other Andalusian port, SEVILLE, that had originally dominated transatlantic trade. Cádiz paid the price of her prominence as the object of periodic raids by the English and other enemies from the 16th to the 18th centuries. As the stronghold of Spanish resistance to the French invaders during the PENINSULAR WAR, Cádiz housed the legislature, or Cortes (see CORTES) that produced the famous Constitution of 1812. This document was the reference point for all subsequent attempts to establish liberal governments in Spain and many other European countries. Diminished in its commercial importance in more recent times, Cádiz has lately acquired a new significance with the growing influx of immigrants entering Spain during the age of globalization.

Calatrava, Santiago (1951–   )

Spanish architect and engineer

Born in VALENCIA and trained in engineering and architecture in Spain and Switzerland, Calatrava established his office in Zurich and carried out his earliest commissions in that city, such as the Stadelhofen Railway Station (1983). A series of projects in Europe followed, including Alamillo Bridge and La Cartuja Viaduct, in SEVILLE (1987–92); the Campo Volantín Footbridge and the Sondica Airport, in Bilbao (1990–99); the Oriente Station, in LISBON (1993–98); and Alameda Bridge and Underground Station, the City of Science Museum and Planetarium, and the Palace of Arts, in Valencia (1991–2001).

Calatrava's achievements led to his induction in November 2000, into the Royal Academy of Fine Arts. As might be expected, he broke with tradition by omitting the usual speech of modest respect for his elders in favor of the self-made film titled *Movimiento* (Movement), in which he discussed his work as engineer, architect, and sculptor as part of an integrated approach that linked him to all of the fine arts, including painting and music. While some of the academicians at the ceremony were reportedly baffled or annoyed, others considered his approach "brilliant" and appreciated his attempt to let a breath of fresh air into the stuffy atmosphere of the academy.

As the new millennium began, Calatrava had already attained a global reputation. He became a natural choice for some of the key work connected with the Athens venue of the 2004 Olympic Games. In designing a roof for the existing Velodrome (the stadium constructed in 1982 for cycling competitions) Calatrava's conception of what suggested an overarching structure of curved tubes and arches revealed once again his ability to integrate the strength of engineering techniques and the abstract quality of architectural vision. His critics— of whom there are still many—inevitably suggested that the design was too complex and would never be finished on time, or conversely that after it was put in place it would fall down upon the audience gathered within. Neither of these prophesies came true. Calatrava also designed additional features of the Olympic site, including a tubular metal wall of nations that undulated according to a computer program and a covered walkway that evoked the Agora, the public meeting place of ancient Athens.

Calatrava's activities during this period also took him not only to scenes where ancient history had been made in the Old World but to pristine locations in the New. His work on such varied projects as the expansion of the Milwaukee Art Museum and the Sacramento River Bridge, both daringly innovative in design, made him well known in the United States. When the destruction of the World Trade Center in New York City in September 2001 opened the way for new construction and new thinking, Calatrava and his associates were selected to play a major part in the great enterprise with a commission to design and construct the transportation center on the site. His plans revealed a grand concept of a physical and spiritual gateway to the city, with soaring arches and grand vistas far beyond the mundane, utilitarian concepts usually favored in such venues. His admirers spoke of how earlier work on air and rail facilities in Portugal and France had foreshadowed this approach. They spoke, too, of how Calatrava's design for the two dozen bridges that he had created in various parts of the world reflected his deep artistic vision of bridges linking past and present and bringing people together. His ideas for this great project made its completion the most eagerly anticipated of all his work.

Calderón, Rodrigo (marqués de Siete Iglesias) (1570–1621)

Spanish politician

Born the son of a Spanish nobleman and garrison commander in what is now Belgium, but was then part of the Netherlands, Calderón was educated at the University of Valladolid and served as private secretary to several high-ranking officials, eventually becoming the assistant and confidant of the duke of LERMA. Exercising increasing influence over his master, Calderón became the "man behind the throne," for Lerma was the *privado,* or most trusted adviser, of King PHILIP III. Calderón's fortunes (both figuratively and literally) rose with those of Lerma during the early 1600s. The king so appreciated Calderón's intelligence and good judgment that he showered him with estates and titles. Calderón returned as envoy to his native Netherlands for a time and was rewarded for his diplomatic services with the title marques de Siete Iglesias.

The reign of Philip III was increasingly characterized by a carnival of corruption in which Lerma and all of his associates lived lavishly at the public expense, but Calderón exhibited a level of arrogance and ostentation that made him the greatest target of criticism. The queen, Margarita of Austria, was convinced by her clerical advisers that Calderón needed to be curbed, and she urged the king to distance himself from the Lerma-Calderón clique. The sudden death of the queen provoked a flood of rumors that she had been poisoned by order of Calderón. Although there was no evidence to support this allegation, it stimulated a new outburst of criticism and led to the arrest and detention of Calderón for a period of several months (1619–20). Just when Philip III had come to the conclusion that Calderón had suffered sufficiently for any misdeeds he might have committed, the monarch died, preventing Calderón's release. PHILIP IV, wishing to avoid the opprobrium that had been heaped upon the previous reign, ordered Calderón to stand trial for a number of capital offenses. Although the more serious accusations were probably false, Calderón was made the scapegoat for all of the excesses of the Lerma regime. The duke sheltered himself by acquiring ecclesiastical status, and it was his henchman who paid the supreme price. Calderón's calm and dignified bearing at his execution gave rise to a phrase that became proverbial: *Tener más orgullo que Don Rodrigo en la horca* (Prouder than Rodrigo on the scaffold).

Calderón de la Barca, Pedro
(1600–1681)
Spanish dramatist
Born of a good family and educated at the University of Salamanca, Calderón de la Barca gained a reputation for dramatic skill while still in his 20s. Following the death of the hitherto dominant playwright LOPE DE VEGA, in 1635, Calderón was appointed court dramatist to PHILIP IV and remained associated with the royal court for the remainder of his life. Following a varied and sometimes violent career (including active military service) he was ordained a priest in 1650.

Both in his earlier secular plays and in the *autos sacramentales*, plays of religious symbolism that he created for the royal court in his later years, Calderón concerned himself with profoundly moral issues, such as the conflicting demands of honor and virtue or predestination and free will. Among the most highly esteemed of his more than 150 works is undoubtedly *La vida es sueño* (*Life Is a Dream*), published in 1635. It is a philosophical-theological drama in which contrasting perceptions of reality offer a perennial appeal to modern audiences. Set in a fantasy version of Poland, the play finds Prince Segismundo impris-

oned in a tower and reduced to an animalistic state of rage. His reaction to changing circumstances, his subjection to drug-induced sleep, and his reawakening to the uncertainty of whether he has dreamed all or part of his experiences eventually lead him to the conclusion that in an ever-changing and elusive reality, all that matters is doing good. Also pursuing a moral theme is the *Alcalde de Zalamea* (*The Mayor of Zalamea*), from 1646. It touches upon issues of abuse of authority, competing concepts of honor, and pursuit of justice that resonate over the centuries. His most impressive *auto sacramental, El gran teatro del mundo* (*The Great Theater of the World*, ca. 1635) displays a breadth of vision and a sense of the universality of the mystery of the Eucharist that transcends the boundaries of court pageantry.

Just as Lope de Vega towers over the earlier part of the century, Calderón is generally acclaimed as the greatest dramatist of the latter half of the 17th century, each playwright exhibiting particular strengths that make his achievements complementary. Some critics have sought to limit Calderón's distinction to an embodiment of Spanish religiosity, but more acute commentators, notably the distinguished A. A. Parker, insist that Calderón is not merely a dramatist who was forced by his situation to distort his work to conform to religious clichés but instead a "theological poet and dramatist in a deep and legitimate sense."

California
Soon after HERNÁN CORTÉS's conquest of the Aztec Empire in modern MEXICO, in the 1520s he began probing the outer limits of

what came to be known as NEW SPAIN. By the 1540s expeditions organized by him or his successors were moving along the Pacific coast. During the next two centuries Spanish ventures into what is now northwestern Mexico and the West Coast of the United States were sporadic. The name *California*, taken from chivalric romances, was applied to the region, and Spanish expeditions sailed along the peninsula known as Baja (Lower) California and probed the shores of Alta (Upper) California all the way to the present-day state of Oregon. The hostility of the indigenous peoples and the lack of gold in accessible areas diminished incentives for intensive exploration or settlement. Periodic appearances in the region by English, French, and Dutch mariners and, much later, Russian settlers were enough, however, to renew Spanish concern from time to time. It was not until the latter half of the 18th century that a serious commitment to settle, defend, and evangelize California was undertaken.

A major part of the effective occupation of California was led by the Franciscan missionary JUNÍPERO SERRA. During the 1770s he founded a series of mission stations along the California coast. They included San Diego, San Luis Obispo, San Juan Capistrano, San Francisco de Asís, Santa Clara de Asís, and San Buenaventura. Many of these missions grew into flourishing outposts for the instruction of the local Indians, their training in productive labor, and the implantation of Spanish culture. Aside from military garrisons, the growth of a Spanish settler population was tentative, but under Serra's successors, some of his early foundations grew into what would become the major cities of modern California.

By the end of Spanish colonial rule in 1822 this last area of Spanish exploration and conquest in the New World was still a relatively remote and underdeveloped region. It continued to be so under the rule of the independent Mexican government, and it was only after the area of Alta California was ceded to the United States in 1848 and gold was discovered that the region moved into the spotlight of world attention.

Calleja del Rey, Félix María (conde de Calderón) (1750–1826)
Spanish general and colonial official

Following an active combat career that included the Algerian campaign of the 1770s and the siege of GIBRALTAR in 1780–81, Calleja demonstrated his capacity as a "scientific soldier" by service as director of studies at the military college of Puerto de Santa María. He accompanied the new viceroy to NEW SPAIN in 1789 and rose in rank and responsibility during the next 20 years. In addition to military operations along the northern frontier Calleja undertook an extensive program of mapping the coastline of the viceroyalty and made other contributions to the strategic planning of MEXICO's defenses. When the first stage of the Mexican war of independence began in 1810, Calleja, already a brigadier general, threw himself vigorously into thwarting the insurrection and was largely responsible for the defeat of the promoter of the rebellion, Father Miguel Hidalgo. When the war was continued by the priest José Morelos and other Mexican nationalists, Calleja played an increasingly important part in raising a royalist militia to fight alongside the regular troops. This demonstration of his initiative and organizational skill was also responsible for dividing the country into two sharply defined factions, leaving no room for neutrals or noncombatants. Calleja was in almost constant action against the rebels during the next several years, winning several major victories and earning further promotion as well as the title count of Calderón. The insurgents proved resilient, however, and the conflict continued throughout the period when Spain herself was struggling to throw off the French occupation that Napoléon had imposed in 1808. When the Regency Council at CÁDIZ realized that Calleja was being hampered rather than supported by the incumbent viceroy, it appointed the general to the viceregal office in September 1812, permitting him to combine full military and civil power. With a free hand to shape his own policy of suppressing the rebellion, Calleja dealt harshly with armed rebels, who were executed when captured, while promising leniency to those who surrendered. To prominent rebel leaders he showed no mercy, but he was ready to implement progressive policies regarding courts, legislative representation, and other matters decreed by the Cortes (see CORTES) in Cádiz.

With the restoration of FERDINAND VII in 1814, Calleja became fully committed to monarchical absolutism and prosecuted the war in Mexico with all his resources. With an army now totaling more than 50,000 regulars and militia, he recaptured the major towns still in rebel hands, disrupted the attempts of nationalists to organize a Mexican government, and finally succeeded in capturing Morelos, the national hero, whom he tried and executed in 1815. Calleja was not unaware

of the ambivalent loyalties of his commanding general in the northern provinces, Agustín de Iturbide, and stripped him of his duties in 1816. For the moment the Royalists were in the ascendancy, although Iturbide would later abandon his status as a Spanish officer and unite the fragmented rebel bands into a second wave of revolution. Calleja returned to Spain in 1816 to applause and honor as the man who had saved New Spain for the empire. Appointed captain general of ANDALUSIA, he was charged with preparing an expeditionary force to regain control of South America but was dismissed from office and detained in MAJORCA by the liberal revolutionaries who controlled Spain between 1820 and 1823. Having declined to betray the absolutist principles to which he had become totally committed, Calleja was not reinstated in his military rank until Ferdinand VII was back in full control. During his last years the veteran general enjoyed a post of honor at VALENCIA, where he died in 1826. If any one man can be said to have saved Mexico for Spanish rule during the first phase of revolution in the Americas, it is Calleja. Indefatigable in his military operations and implacable in his exercise of governmental power, he succeeded, as long as he was entrusted with the means of confronting the nationalists, in maintaining colonial rule. Ultimately all his efforts would be swept away by the irresistible forces of history.

Camões, Luíz Vaz de (Camoens) (1524–1580)

Portuguese poet

Born into a family of minor nobility and, according to tradition, educated at the University of Coimbra where he acquired a broad knowledge of classical literature, the young Camões served with Portuguese troops in MOROCCO, where he lost an eye in battle. Although precise facts about his life are few, it appears that a brawl in LISBON led to what amounted to banishment to the Portuguese Far Eastern empire, where he served from 1553 to 1570. Returning home after many travels and dangerous adventures, he spent the last decade of his life in the literary work that has earned him his status as Portugal's greatest Renaissance poet.

Camões wrote nearly 200 lyric poems in many forms as well as several verse dramas inspired by the comic plays of ancient Greece. He is best known, however, for his epic poem *Os Lusíadas* (*The Lusiads*), published in 1579. Inspired by the epics of antiquity and the Middle Ages and taking its name from the Roman designation for Portugal—*Lusitania*—this poem grew naturally out of Camões's own long service in the distant lands won by Portuguese conquerors. It tells the story of VASCO DA GAMA's voyage to India at the end of the 15th century. Camões incorporates a good deal of Portuguese history as well as descriptions of exotic lands and peoples but also follows long-standing convention by giving the ancient gods a role to play as helpers or opponents of da Gama's mission. The poem ends with the safe completion of the passage to India, essentially the commencement of Portugal's great imperial achievement. Ever since its publication *Os Lusíadas* has been revered as Portugal's great national epic and hailed by critics as the finest work in the epic form created during the Renaissance.

Campoamor y Campoosorio, Ramón de (1817–1901)
Spanish poet

Born in ASTURIAS, Campoamor moved to MADRID to pursue studies, first for the church, then for medicine. He finally settled on a career in politics and by the age of 30 had already secured the first of a series of civil governorships in various provinces. He also held seats in the legislature and was a frequent contributor to journals of opinion. In all of these activities Campoamor was a staunch conservative. Clearly, however, he considered himself first and foremost a man of letters, producing a number of plays and prosework and, most important, a large quantity of poems. Although he would be referred to by his admirers as the "Spanish Homer," his style was not the epic but rather a short pithy type of verse in which he sought to create an immediate impact. Campoamor had dabbled in romanticism in some of his early verse, but that style was losing favor in utilitarian Spain after mid-century, and Campoamor abandoned it without regret, declaring that he favored art for ideas' sake. During the later years of his life, when he was a well-established public figure as well as a much-published writer, Campoamor was the particular favorite of middle-class Spaniards, who enjoyed his mixture of cynicism and recognition of the realities of life with wry humor. Literary commentators held differing views: RUBÉN DARÍO spoke well of him, while JOSÉ MARTÍNEZ RUIZ (Azorín) fulminated against him. In the century that followed his death his reputation steadily declined, with academics dismissing his faulty and uninspired execution, while emotionally driven poets dismissed him as a mere dispenser of quips and clichés. His reputation became, in fact, that of a poet for the "middle brow" reader. A more just view would see him as the natural product of his time and place, in which he was grossly overpraised but a poet by no means as despicable as many later observers have suggested. Among the best known of Campoamor's writings are *Doloras* (1845), *Pequeños poemas* (1871), and *Humoradas* (1886).

Canary Islands (Islas Canarias)

This Atlantic archipelago, lying southwest of Spain and northwest of Africa (about 60 miles from the continents's coast at its nearest point), became a training ground for the exploration and conquest of the New World. The islands were known to the ancients, including the Romans, who gave them the name "Canis Islands" for the wild dogs that roamed there. However the Canaries were generally neglected by Europeans until the late 14th century and were not definitively claimed by Spain until the 1470s. During the next two decades the larger islands, inhabited by people of North African origin called *guanches,* were successively conquered by Castilian expeditions. The Spaniards' tactics and techniques would soon be employed against the Amerindians, and some of the conquistadores of the Americas learned the art of mastering an indigenous population in the Canarian campaigns. By the early 1500s the entire archipelago had been mastered, and the *guanches* were virtually extinct. The subsequent history of the Canary Islands has been comparatively tranquil, with their importance considerably diminished since they ceased to be a way station on the trade route to Spanish America. In 1927

the archipelago was administratively divided into two provinces: Las Palmas (including the islands of Gran Canaria, Lanzarote, Fuerteventura, and some uninhabited islets) and Santa Cruz de Tenerife (comprising the islands of Tenerife, La Palma, Gomera, and Hierro). These provinces have an area of 1,279 square miles, and 1,528 square miles, respectively.

Although the Canary Islands have been recognized since the 1970s as one of Spain's autonomous regions, the central government has firmly repressed most of the extreme elements who have demanded independence and have intermittently

El Teide volcano on Santa Cruz de Tenerife *(Getty)*

Las Palmas Cathedral on Gran Canaria Island *(Getty)*

resorted to terroristic tactics. For the most part Spain and this "overseas" realm have enjoyed mutual benefits from a prosperous tourist trade thanks to the archipelago's salubrious climate, which supports a rich variety of flora and a lively commerce based upon numerous natural products.

Cánovas del Castillo, Antonio
(1828–1897)
Spanish statesman and writer
A native of MÁLAGA, belonging to a "good family" but without much money, Cánovas earned enough as a journalist to complete law school in Madrid. Hoping to pursue a career as a historian, he found himself increasingly drawn into legal and political affairs during the 1850s. Nevertheless, some of his best studies on Spanish history belong to this early period, including his account of the country's decline during the late 17th century. A moderate Conservative, Cánovas allied himself with LEOPOLDO O'DONNELL and held many offices, including several ministerial positions. Disapproving of the 1868 revolution, he was unimpressed by the choice of AMADEO I to replace ISABELLA II.

During the early 1870s Cánovas again put aside his literary activity to work for the Bourbon restoration and was the principal agent in effecting the return of ALFONSO XII to Spain in 1875. During the next two decades Cánovas alternated in the office of prime minister with the Liberal leader PRÁXEDES MATEO SAGASTA under an agreement to share power by "rotation" in office. When his Conservative Party held control of the government Cánovas pursued a policy of protectionism, restriction of press freedom, and other measures designed to keep Spain under firm control. At the same time he was by no means the most reactionary representative of the political Right. Many commentators denounced his maintenance of a balance with Sagasta as a cynical "deal" that preserved the personal advantages of a ruling elite without true ideological commitment.

When a new revolution broke out in CUBA in 1895 Cánovas proclaimed a hard line of no concessions and no reforms. His dispatch of massive troop reinforcements to the island and his approval of General WEYLER's harsh methods of eliminating support for the rebels aroused widespread condemnation, and in 1897 he was assassinated by an anarchist.

In his ability to pursue the alternate careers of prolific writer and active politician Cánovas represented a type of multitalented statesmen not uncommon in mid-19th century Europe. By his day, however, men like Thomas Babington Macaulay in Great Britain or François Guizot and Adolfe Thiers in France were disappearing. In his last years the sheer complexity of Spain's problems made it impossible for Cánovas to preserve the posture of detached intellectual that had characterized his earlier career. In the aftermath of his death he was blamed for most of the disasters that befell his country in 1898.

Cape Verde Islands (Ilhas do Cabo Verde)

This archipelago off the west coast of Africa was reached by the Portuguese in 1456 and formally declared a royal possession in 1495. Comprising 10 major islands and a number of smaller islets, it was a stopping point on the route to Portuguese possessions in Asia and produced coffee and tropical fruits for European markets. By the time of its independence in 1975 more than 300,000 people were contained within its total landmass of slightly more than 1,500 square miles.

Carlism

Rising out of a succession dispute between two BOURBON pretenders, Carlism became a social philosophy and a political movement that endured in Spain for more than a century. It derived its name from Don Carlos (1788–1855), younger son of CHARLES IV. His status as heir apparent was undercut in 1830 when his elder brother, FERDINAND VII, put aside the Salic law that limited the royal succession to males in favor of his daughter Isabella. Don Carlos became the rallying point for Spanish conservatives who had hitherto regarded Ferdinand as the very model of a modern absolutist. These traditionalists, as they preferred to call themselves, insisted upon a strong government, a strong church and a subordinate Cortes (see CORTES,) strict censorship, and a tight social framework maintained by unchanging customs. Upon the death of Ferdinand VII in 1833 and the espousal of his daughter's claim by Spanish liberals, the Carlists rose in revolt. Between 1833 and 1839 Spain was torn by the First Carlist War. Calling himself Charles V, the pretender was supported by the aristocracy, the church, and the landowning gentry as well as the rural masses of the north, including the BASQUE PROVINCES, CATALONIA, and ARAGON. He was also recognized by Vienna, St. Petersburg, Berlin, and Rome, where apprehension had been raised by the revival of Europe's revolutionary spirit. The young ISABELLA II was championed by Spain's liberals, who were in turn aided by military forces dispatched from Britain and France, where liberal governments had recently taken power. After years of bitter fighting key Carlist generals were won over by promises of integration into the regular army and other material rewards. They abandoned their political leaders in 1839, and Don Carlos was forced to go into exile, without abandoning his claim.

After three decades of scandal, military coups, and at least one Carlist plot to overthrow her, Isabella II was herself driven out of the country. The generals who overthrew her proved incapable of forming a new government or finding a new leader, and by 1873 the Second Carlist War had begun. The current claimant, the titular Charles VII, raised his standard in NAVARRE, the remaining stronghold of a movement that had been marginalized by economic modernization in other regions of the north. The restoration of Isabella's son as ALFONSO XII in 1875 gave focus to the legitimist forces who defeated the Carlists decisively in 1876.

By the death of Charles VII in 1909 Carlism had become a theoretical rather than a practical cause whose philosophies spoke of absolute monarchy as an essential center of the nation and of an "integral" society rooted in history. The new pretender, Don Jaime, attempted to promote a more liberal approach for his movement but was opposed, to the point of a de facto split in Carlism, by the old guard, and the pendulum swung back to "authentic" traditionalism when Don Jaime was succeeded by his elderly uncle, Don Alfonso Carlos in 1931. The latter provided Navarese militia men who supported the Franco side in the SPANISH CIVIL WAR but refused to join in a unified monarchist front.

During the Franco regime (1939–75) Carlist claims were theoretically transferred to the Bourbon-Parma line led by Don Carlos Hugo, but their significance, both under the dictatorship and since the restoration of democracy, has been minimal.

Carlos I of Portugal   See CHARLES I (PORTUGAL).

Carlos I of Spain   See CHARLES I (SPAIN).

Carlos II   See CHARLES II.

Carlos III   See CHARLES III.

Carlos IV   See CHARLES IV.

Carmona, António Óscar de Fragoso (1869–1951)
Portuguese soldier and statesman
In a successful military career that led him to the rank of general (and later marshal) Carmona came into his own as a political figure after the 1910 revolution that ended

the Portuguese monarchy with the overthrow of MANUEL II. The disturbed political climate of the new republic led to the seizure of power by General Manuel de Oliveira Gomes da Costa in 1926. Carmona was appointed foreign minister but soon ousted Gomes da Costa and headed a provisional government until assuming the presidency for himself in 1928. He was reelected to this office in 1935, 1942, and 1949. Incapable of managing Portugal's disordered finances, the regime turned to the economist ANTÓNIO DE OLIVEIRA SALAZAR, who demanded and received unrestricted power to restructure all aspects of the Portuguese state. What was in external appearance a military dictatorship under Carmona thus became in reality a civilian dictatorship under Salazar, who outlived President Carmona and, as prime minister, reduced the latter to a mere figurehead.

Carnation Revolution (1974)

Although mild enough to be given the name of a flower, the revolution that brought an end to dictatorship in Portugal actually began in violence and bloodshed. Between 1961 and 1964 outposts of Portugal's still far-flung empire (from Dahomey to GOA) were lost to the rising tide of nationalism that swept across the globe after World War II. The old European colonial realms collapsed one after the other, sometimes after a struggle, sometimes with a handshake and polite exchange of "good luck" and "thank you." The Dutch, the Belgians, the French departed, and Britain, the greatest empire of all, had led the way by giving independence to India. Indeed, newly sovereign India lost no time in expelling Portugal from Goa and DAMÃO AND DIU. But the great mass of land and people that made up the bulk of Portugal's colonial realm would not be yielded without a stiff fight. Prime Minister SALAZAR regarded the African colonies as the essential source of his plan for economic development and national renewal. Moreover ANGOLA and MOZAMBIQUE, PORTUGUESE GUINEA, and the West African archipelagoes of SÃO TOMÉ AND PRÍNCIPE and the CAPE VERDE ISLANDS were equally important as assertions of his nation's historical achievements and its right to be accorded respect in the future. He flatly rejected international opinion and pressure from the United Nations, as though a parliamentary declaration that these colonies were now "overseas provinces" would be taken seriously. These territories were not merely jewels in the crown; they were, in his estimate, essential to the survival of Portugal herself.

Between 1964 and 1968 Salazar mobilized the resources of Portugal to hold the mainland African colonies (while the offshore islands simmered in potential revolt). More than 200,000 Portuguese men were called into military service and dispatched to the battlefronts. One man in every four was in uniform, and almost the entire Portuguese labor force was subjected to a civilian mobilization to support the combat forces. When the dictator suffered an incapacitating stroke in 1968, the war to preserve the empire continued unabated. When he died in 1970, he was entombed in the Pantheon that commemorated the explorers and conquerors—and the war went on.

Marcelo Caetano, a longtime associate of Salazar, assumed the premiership after his colleague's death, having been the acting prime minister since the dictator's stroke.

Although he, too, exercised dictatorial powers in this one-party state with its rubber-stamp parliament, Caetano made occasional gestures toward political reform and domestic public opinion. But he was as much the captive of his circumstances as the rest of the population. Salazar, the doctrinaire professor who had created the "New State" of Portugal had chosen this fellow academic as his deputy because he lacked the cunning and ruthlessness to challenge him. For that very reason Caetano was incapable of making more than weak gestures toward reform. Having no personal base of support, he was obliged to accept the assurances of the elite among war ministry generals and staff officers who enjoyed the privileges of LISBON that they could see the light at the end of the tunnel. Contingent after contingent of young men sailed off to Africa, and Caetano repeated the bland assurances of his predecessor and his advisers.

Yet dissent was growing, and not only among the civilian population, as they paid an ever-higher price in blood and treasure. Conscripts and young officers were also complaining about the endless marches through jungles and swamps, the fruitless struggle against elusive guerrilla forces who enjoyed the support of "liberation movements" in neighboring countries, and the bombardments and burnings they were ordered to inflict upon the civilian population. Even in the higher ranks field commanders were beginning to speak out against a war that had no end in sight. By spring 1974 the blood and venom had flowed back to Portugal itself. The armed forces movement had emerged among captains and majors disgusted with the corruption of their superiors, both civilian and

military. Many of these young men shared the radical perspectives of banned leftist parties, including the Communists. Their plan was, however, for a nonviolent revolution. Key units stationed in Lisbon and other cities were ready to act, and a system of signals and a plan of action emphasizing rapidity of movement as well as an appeal to peaceful patriotism were agreed upon. On April 25, 1974, radio stations began broadcasting coded messages, often in the form of popular songs containing metaphorical allusions. Detachments of troops moved to designated government buildings and took charge of operations there. Key government officials, including senior officers at the army headquarters were placed under arrest. The entire seizure of control passed off without violence or opposition. Members of the government were described as surrendering almost wearily, as if the inevitable had arrived. Armed soldiers posted at key points in Lisbon were cheered by civilians, many of whom placed flowers in their rifle barrels as a gesture of goodwill and a symbol of the fact that no shots had been fired. Such scenes gave the nickname "the Carnation Revolution" to the fall of the dictatorship.

Caetano and his principal associates were detained for a time but eventually were allowed to go quietly into retirement. General ANTÓNIO DE SPINOLA, an outspoken critic of the war who had secretly signaled his support to the revolutionaries, took the lead of a provisional government. Negotiations were soon opened to end the fighting in Africa and to grant independence to the colonies. Portugal would still have many problems to solve in the years ahead, but with the Carnation Revolution it had taken the first steps on the road to democracy.

Casals, Pablo (Pau Casals)
(1876–1973)

Spanish musician

Trained in composition, piano, and cello in BARCELONA and Brussels, this Catalan musician chose to concentrate on the cello and was soon recognized for his mastery of the instrument. He developed personal techniques for extracting distinctive tones from the instrument and acquired a reputation as being among the finest musicians of his time. Perhaps his most important achievement was his revival of the neglected cello pieces of Johann Sebastian Bach, his favorite composer. From the 1890s through the end of World War I he toured widely, performing in the United States as early as 1901. Far from being an introverted virtuoso, Casals formed a famous collaboration with the pianist Alfred Cortot and the violinist Jacques Thibaud, devoted time to conducting, and took part in the establishment of a music school in Paris. Proud of his Catalan heritage, he became, in 1920, the founder and conductor of the Orquestra Pau Casals in Barcelona.

Appalled by the results of the SPANISH CIVIL WAR, he took up residence in France in 1939, vowing never to return to Spain as long as the regime of FRANCISCO FRANCO was in power. For a time he actually gave up performing in public as a protest against "fascism." By 1950, however, he was again performing and recording. In 1956 he moved to PUERTO RICO, where he established an annual music festival that helped focus international attention on this former Spanish colony. He also became a celebrity in the United States and performed at the White House during the term of President John F. Kennedy. Casals, true to his vow, remained permanently in his new home,

dying two years before the fall of the dictatorship in Spain.

Castelar y Ripoll, Emilio
(1832–1899)

Spanish statesman

Born in CÁDIZ and trained in philosophy and law at the University of Madrid, Castelar became a professor of history at this institution. He soon earned a reputation as an advocate of republicanism and was dismissed from his position in 1866 after a particularly bold denunciation of ISABELLA II. Implicated in several conspiracies against the monarchy during that year, he fled to France and did not return until the deposition of the queen in 1868. During the political turmoil of the next several years he served in parliament and earned a reputation for moderate republicanism, even accepting the short-lived kingship of AMADEO I as a temporary measure. When that monarch left Spain in 1873, Castelar took part in the formation of the First Republic, playing an active and valuable role as minister of state. He emerged from the faction struggles that disrupted the republic to accede to the presidency in September 1873 but resigned in January of the following year as the administration broke down completely amid military coups, regional insurgencies, and the outbreak of a new Carlist war.

After ALFONSO XII took the throne in 1875, Castelar returned to parliament and played a constructive moderating role during the next decade. He continued to support such democratic principles as universal suffrage and the abolition of slavery in the Caribbean colonies. Castelar gradually moved away from any short-term prospect of restoring the republic, advising his adherents to work in collaboration with the Liberal bloc in the legislature. In his last years Castelar concentrated on the literary activities that he had pursued intermittently throughout his career. He wrote extensively on Spanish history and politics, the subjects of his famed oratorical achievements that had made him the most admired public speaker of his day. Despite the failure of his republican dreams, Castelar's integrity, reasonableness, and sweeping vision of Spain's destiny made him an admired figure whose legacy would survive until the founding of the Second Republic in 1931.

Castelo Branco, Camilo (visconde de Correia Botelho) (1825–1895)
Portuguese novelist

The life of Castelo Branco reads like the plot of one of his own novels, although none of them quite reaches the same level of complexity and melodrama. The illegitimate son of a provincial family, he was orphaned at an early age and raised indifferently by relatives. Despite a spotty education he attended university with the aim of becoming a physician but abandoned this career goal in favor of casual journalism and a bohemian lifestyle. Among many romances his preferred mistress was Ana Plácido who jilted him to marry a more substantial suitor. It was at this interval, apparently, that he decided to enter the religious life. That career path he also abandoned without attaining ordination. Ana, having wearied of her husband, ran off with Castelo Branco, but he was arrested and imprisoned for adultery. Shortly after he was released, Ana became a widow, and they married. Their life together was not entirely smooth.

Their children were more of a problem than a blessing, particularly the son who became insane (supposedly a hereditary affliction of the paternal line). Castelo Branco, who had already achieved some literary recognition, now became a full-time writer in the most literal sense. Most of his 58 novels were written during the later decades of his life, often under intense pressure from publishers, who dictated the subject matter as well as the due date of the manuscript. Finally worn out by family problems, old age, and deteriorating health, Castelo Branco committed suicide.

Despite the impression of being both a picaro and a hack writer, conveyed by his personal biography, Castelo Branco was well regarded by his contemporaries and sufficiently esteemed by the Portuguese establishment to be awarded the title of visconde. Almost all of his books, although disfigured by the circumstances under which they were written, contain elements of real merit. He possessed a casual and engaging style, a familiarity with all levels of society, and a shrewd eye for character depiction. His easy manner, light satirical tone, and sympathetic tolerance for human foibles gave little evidence of the troubles he had (and still) experienced.

Among Castelo Branco's best-regarded novels are *Onde Está a Felicidade? (Where Is Happiness?* 1856), *Vingança* (Revenge, 1858), and *Amor de perdição (Love of Perdition,* 1862). This last work was evidently inspired by his own experience of passion and imprisonment. Despite the disorderly state of his affairs and his successive resort to whatever literary genre would sell best at the time— from his early gothic stories to romance to realism—Castelo Branco evidently settled upon a consistent level of plotting and writing that satisfied his readers. Unfortunately the income he was able to command from the endless task he had accepted became not so much a mark of success but a form of enslavement.

Castile (Castilla)

As the petty kingdoms of northern Spain began their struggle against the Muslim invasion during the early Middle Ages that would grow into the RECONQUISTA, Castile emerged to a position of leadership. Her aggressive sovereigns and warrior lords would gradually elbow aside rivals such as ASTURIAS, LEÓN, and NAVARRE. They would overrun moorish territory to the east and the south, finally capturing GRANADA in 1492. In the course of this great enterprise Castile not only became the political unifier of Spain but absorbed much of the ever-expanding frontiers. In time it became necessary to distinguish between Castilla la Vieja (Old Castile), the original kingdom, and Castilla la Nueva (New Castile), which included the later acquisitions. This distinction between Old and New Castile was preserved in the regional reorganization of Spain during the 1970s: The region known as Old Castile—including the provinces of Ávila, Burgos, Logroño, Palencia, Santander, Segovia, Soria, and VALLADOLID with a total area of 25,523 square miles and its capital at Burgos—was set apart from the region of Castile–La Mancha—including the provinces of Ciudad Real, Cuenca, Guadalajara, MADRID, and TOLEDO with an area of 28,010 square miles and its capital at Toledo.

Although Castilians still regard themselves as the most authentic Spaniards and their Castilian language as the purest form of Spanish, the size and centrality of their territory has, after 500 years, failed to completely overawe the other regions of the country.

Castro, Eugénio de (1869–1944)
Portuguese poet

Like so many Portuguese men of letters before him, Castro sought to reanimate what he considered the uninspired and archaic poetry of his nation by introducing new ideas and new forms from abroad. He returned from a visit to Paris in 1889 full of enthusiasm for the Symbolist movement that was then flourishing in France. Portuguese poetry was, he told all who would listen to him, little more than vapid nationalism. What was needed was a bold and emotional outpouring of deep thoughts and profound realities. He provided inspiration for the rising generation in Portugal and offered them a series of examples in the collections of poetry that he published at regular intervals for several decades. These included *Horas* (1891), *Belkiss* (1894), *Sagramor* (1895), *Salomé* (1896), *Saudades do Ceú* (1899) *Constança* (1900), *Depois da Ceifa* (1901), and *Camafeus Romanos* (1921).

Castro's standing as Portugal's preeminent poet was recognized by his appointment as director of the Faculty of Letters at the University of Coimbra and by his election to membership in the academies of Portugal, Spain, and Brazil.

Castro y Bellvís, Guillén de (1569–1631)
Spanish dramatist

Born to a family of Valencian gentry, Castro served as an army officer, attained the rank of knight of Santiago, and through his connections among the elite was appointed governor of Seigliano in the Kingdom of Naples in 1607. Also active in intellectual circles from an early age, he became a close friend of LOPE DE VEGA and a member of several literary groups in VALENCIA, a city second only to MADRID in its cultural activities.

Castro was the author of a wide variety of plays in such categories as mythological, autobiographical, and "cape and sword." His most notable work was drawn directly from the popular tradition of the *romancero*, a collection of ballads growing out of the medieval epics of warriors and heroes. His *Las mocedades del Cid* (*The Youthful Deeds of the Cid*, c. 1599) presents the Spanish national hero at the commencement of his career as he is forced to choose between his love for Jimena and the demands of family honor, which eventually force him to confront and kill her father. This episode served as inspiration for *Le Cid* (1637) by Pierre Corneille and has been retold in opera and motion pictures. The dramatist also drew upon the *romancero* for *El conde Irlos* (Count Irlos) and *El conde Alarcos* (Count Alarcos), both striking depictions of the chivalric codes and published between 1614 and 1625.

Castro drew his dramatic inspiration not only from medieval themes but from the creative writings of his contemporaries. Three of his plays were inspired by the recent (1605) novel by MIGUEL DE CERVANTES; the most notable of these is *Don Quijote de la Mancha*. As in later adaptations for the stage from this work, *El curioso impertinente* (The impertinent curious one) and *La fuerza de la sangre* (The force of blood), he chooses particular incidents and characters from Cervantes's sprawling panorama of Don Quixote's pursuit of a noble vision among the realities of 17th-century life.

Catalina of Aragon   See CATHERINE OF ARAGON.

Catalonia (Cataluña, Catalunya)

Catalonia is a region in northeastern Spain comprising the provinces of BARCELONA, Gerona, Lleida, and Tarragona, each based on the city of the same name. Catalan, still widely spoken there, is a romance language more closely allied to the Provençal of southern France that to the Castilian that is the official language of modern Spain. During the Middle Ages Catalan literature and art flourished as did a Mediterranean trade that reached out to Italy and the Middle East. Through a dynastic union with ARAGON in 1137 Catalonia was joined to the Aragonese crown, while retaining a considerable degree of autonomy. Its political and cultural traditions were undercut by the merger of Aragon with CASTILE during the early Renaissance, and Catalonia's commercial outreach was likewise submerged into the general policies of the Spanish state.

Catalan nationalism was never far below the surface, despite the diminution of special privileges and the constant insistence upon the unity of "imperial Spain." During the 1640s, with the support of France, Louis XIV was proclaimed prince of Catalonia, and the authority of King PHILIP IV was restored only with difficulty. This "revolt of the Catalans" was echoed some 60 years later during the WAR OF THE SPANISH SUCCESSION, when the new BOURBON dynasty of Spain was rejected in favor of the rival claims of Archduke Karl of Austria. Barcelona welcomed the Habsburg pretender and his English allies, but after the triumph of PHILIP V in 1713–14 the Catalans were punished for their defiance by loss of virtually all their remaining regional privileges.

Catalonia did not go unscathed by the Napoleonic invasion or the Carlist wars, but by the late 19th century it had experienced a massive growth in industry and trade that created socioeconomic issues. Class conflict developed between the urban working class, which had swelled by the movement of job seekers from less developed parts of Spain, and Catalan industrialists, business magnates, and their supporters in the Barcelona middle class. While the newcomers flocked into the socialist and anarchist movements and the unions that supported radicalism, the better-off elements staunchly defended the interests of capitalism. On the question of Catalan nationalism the urban elites favored autonomy, or even independence, while the urban workers generally had no interest in purely Catalan matters. The rural population of Catalonia, on the other hand, preserved their regional language and culture and were prepared to fight for autonomy should the opportunity arise. During the first years of the 20th century these overlapping aspirations created a series of clashes between the various interests in Catalonia and the central government. Politicians in MADRID were as much baffled as angered by the complex situation in Barcelona. Following the proclamation of the Second Republic in 1931 Catalan nationalists were able to obtain a considerable degree of autonomy. By 1934, however, misunderstandings with the central authorities led to an armed insurrection in the region that was not resolved until 1936.

Needing the support of every potential ally in the SPANISH CIVIL WAR, the republic restored the rights that had just been withdrawn from the Catalan rebels and increased their autonomy. The Catalan nationalists had little time to celebrate. Although they fought hard for the republic and even provided a temporary capital at Barcelona, the cause of Loyalism was doomed by early 1939. The victorious general FRANCISCO FRANCO was determined to make an example of the Catalan dissidents as well as assert the absolute priority of Spanish unity. He, therefore, not only once again stripped the region of political autonomy but virtually banned all manifestations of Catalan language and culture.

With the death of Franco in 1975 and the constitutional reconstruction that was undertaken soon thereafter, autonomy once again became a subject open for discussion. The new Spanish constitution attempted to compromise by guaranteeing the identity and self-expression of nationalities within the larger context of Spanish unity. For the Catalans, who were now allowed to create their own parliament and regional government and to have free use of their language, this seemed at first to be sufficient. Jordi Pujol, who became the leading Catalan politician of the next two decades, succeeded in developing a regional administration that maintained a balance between various political tendencies in Catalonia while keeping lines of communication open with Madrid. A relatively small group of Catalan nationalists pursued their militancy to the point of armed violence during the 1980s but never reached the threat level achieved by Basque terrorists (see BASQUE NATIONALISM). The extremists, who seemed almost moderate by comparison with the Basques, eventually abandoned the course of violence.

In 2005 a new Spanish government headed by JOSÉ LUIS RODRÍGUEZ ZAPATERO was in power. It faced the problems created by Islamist terrorism and the perennial danger of ETA attacks still to be feared on the Basque flank. It was now that Catalan nationalism once again posed a clear and present danger. Following Pujol's retirement from politics a new set of Catalan leaders emerged in Barcelona and touched off a new political firestorm by announcing their intention to reopen the whole question of Catalan status. The most alarming point made in their initial statement was that Catalonia must be recognized as a "nation." Prime Minister Zapatero promptly responded that the constitution was clear on the matter of autonomy and that no alteration could or should be made. The constitution referred to the rights and interests of "nationalities" and did not speak of any "nation" except the Spanish nation, whose unity was asserted as a fundamental fact. While outsiders might regard the distinction between *nationality* and *nation* as a mere legalistic quibble, it was a far more serious matter to the disputants. Madrid considered *nationalities* to be essentially another term for ethnic minorities, but the Catalans seemed to be asking for virtual independence. Some Catalan politicians even spoke of Catalonia as a sovereign state, linked to Spain by a form of association. Others talked of a kind of melting away of traditional boundaries into a shared membership in the European Union that made traditional labels irrelevant.

By early 2006 a new element had entered the debate as officers of the Spanish army with clear ties to ultrarightist groups spoke out on the threat that Catalan aspirations posed to the unity of Spain. The two generals were given early retirement. Even more disturbing was the statement that came from a lower-ranking retired officer, the lieutenant colonel who had led the abortive military coup in 1981: When he and his men seized the parliamentary chamber in Madrid and held the legislators hostage for hours, the country seemed on the brink of ruin. These armed members of the Civil Guards were perceived as the agents of a military conspiracy that was poised to overthrow democracy and restore a Franquist dictatorship in the name of "unity and stability." After King JUAN CARLOS intervened to halt the insurrection Spain had seemed to have escaped the specter of militarism. Now here was a voice from the past suggesting that Spanish patriots should be prepared to use military force to preserve unity. Political scientists had previously judged that Basque nationalism was essentially self-isolating and therefore could not hope to fulfill its broadest dreams. They had argued that Catalan nationalism was more inclusive and would, in any case, be crushed by the large non-Catalan speaking population of Barcelona. Both these soothing analyses suddenly seemed less realistic. Most urgently, the course of Catalan nationalism might well provoke a more immediate backlash from Spanish nationalists than that of the Basque.

Catherine of Aragon (Catalina)
(1485–1536)
Spanish queen-consort of England
Catherine was the daughter of FERDINAND V of ARAGON and ISABELLA I of CASTILE. Her marriage to Arthur, Prince of Wales, in 1501

Catherine of Aragon *(Library of Congress)*

was arranged by his father, Henry VII, to promote political and commercial ties for the Tudor dynasty with the increasingly powerful Spanish monarchy. When Arthur died in 1502 it was immediately proposed to marry Catherine to his younger brother, Henry, but the matter was delayed over the question of a papal dispensation required to celebrate a marriage between a man and his brother's widow. It was not until the prince succeeded his father in 1509 that he and Catherine were wed. The marriage was at first a happy one, but of Catherine's six children only one survived infancy. That child, the future Queen Mary I, was considered by her father to be an insufficient guarantee for the survival of the Tudor dynasty in an era of political instability. As

relations between the monarch and his consort cooled, Henry sought to have the marriage annulled on the ground that even a pope had lacked the authority to authorize a marriage under such fundamental divine prohibitions. From 1526 onward Henry VIII's attempts to secure the nullification of his marriage were thwarted by Catherine's refusal to cooperate and the interference of her nephew, CHARLES I of Spain, to keep the pope from granting Henry's wishes. Finally in 1533 Henry repudiated papal authority and obtained a decree of divorce from an English court. He thus was freed to marry his mistress, Anne Boleyn, who bore him yet another daughter (the future Elizabeth I). Throughout this process Catherine had maintained her personal dignity and a firm regal insistence upon her rights. She continued to maintain her long-established popularity among the English people, even as she was forced to live in a minor royal residence until her death.

The bitter dispute over Catherine of Aragon's rejection by Henry VIII was the precipitating issue in the English Reformation. It also disrupted the Anglo-Spanish alliance that had strengthened Spain's hand in the opening phase of the ITALIAN WARS. That alliance would be renewed briefly during the reign of Catherine's daughter, Mary Tudor (1553–58), England's last Catholic ruler.

Catherine of Bragança (Catherine of Braganza, Catalina) (1638–1705)
Portuguese queen-consort of England
Daughter of JOHN IV, the first king of Portugal's new BRAGANÇA dynasty, Catherine married Charles II of England in 1662.

Most of the English nation welcomed the restoration of the Stuarts after prolonged civil war and Oliver Cromwell's military dictatorship. They were disappointed, however, by the choice of a Catholic bride and her failure to bear an heir to the throne. Protestant hostility peaked in 1678 when the queen was accused of supporting the so-called Popish Plot. She was protected, nevertheless, by the king, who remained fond of her despite her lack of children and his own numerous infidelities. After the death of Charles II his widow was given hospitality by his brother, James II (1685–88), but she left England after his overthrow. Catherine spent the remainder of her life in Portugal, serving for a time as regent for her brother, PETER II.

Catherine's dowry included the Portuguese colony of Bombay, which became the foundation for England's Indian empire. Her marriage influenced ongoing friendly relations between Portugal and England, enhanced by the Methuen Treaty of 1703, which she helped facilitate, and Portugal was long known as "England's oldest ally."

Cela, Camilo José (1916–2002)

Spanish writer

Born in Iria Flavia, Galicia, Cela was very conscious of his Galician links as well as his English connection, through his mother's family, Trulock. After tentative studies in medicine and law he was caught up in the SPANISH CIVIL WAR, fighting on the Franco side and later serving briefly as a censor. It has been said that he spent the rest of his life making up for that choice. His most famous novel, *La familia de Pascual Duarte* (*The Family of Pascual Duarte*), was published as early as 1942 and has appeared in countless editions and a multitude of translations over six decades. Some have called it the best known, if not the greatest, Spanish work of fiction since CERVANTES's *Don Quijote*. An unsparing self-revelation by the murderous peasant of the title, it shocked by its mixture of brutality and humanity. In *La colmena* (*The Hive,* 1951), he offered an intricate portrayal of contemporary life in MADRID, interweaving some 300 characters struggling with the frustrations and oppressions of the Franco dictatorship. Variously called the founder of a new school of social realism or the father of *tremendismo,* an emphasis on violence and grotesque imagery, Cela disdained categories and labels, turning over the years to a wide variety of themes and approaches. A self-confidence amounting at times to arrogance and the audacity that seemed always to escape the usual fate of the reckless fascinated the public and kept the authorities off balance. It might have been said that there were two Celas. One was the author of the travel account *Viaje a la Alcarría* (*Journey to the Alcarría,* 1948), the member of the Spanish Royal Academy (1957), and the founder and editor of the respected literary review *Papeles de Son Armadans* (1956–79). The other was the author of the multivolume *Diccionario secreto* (Secret dictionary), whose 11th volume appeared in 1972, a compilation of "unprintable" but well-known words and phrases, described by some contemporaries as "disgusting" and "appalling."

After the death of Franco, King JUAN CARLOS marked the esteem in which Cela was held by inviting him to join the drafting committee for the constitution. As Cela told it his proposals were too democratic (or perhaps too outrageous) to win acceptance from his more staid colleagues, but within a few years the monarch honored him again with a title of nobility, marqués de Iria Flavia.

Cela continued his prodigious output of novels, short stories, and essays, which would total more than 100 books, including *Rol de cornudos* (Catalogue of cuckolds, 1976); *Mazurca para dos muertos* (*Mazurka for Two Dead People,* 1983), a novel for which he received the National Prize for Literature; *El asno de Buridán* (Buridán's donkey, 1986); *Nuevo viaje a la Alcarría* (New journey to the Alcarría, 1986); *Cristo versus Arizona* (Christ versus Arizona, 1988); *El asesinato del perdedor* (The assassination of the loser, 1992), *La cruz de San Andrés* (The cross of Saint Andrew, 1994), and *Madera de boj* (*Boxwood,* 1999).

Frequently interviewed by the media, he could always be counted on for the provocative opinions and unorthodox perspectives that alternately delighted and shocked his fellow Spaniards. When asked about his reputation as "enfant terrible" and "nonconformist," Cela insisted that nonconformity is in the best tradition of the greatest Spanish writers. QUEVEDO, one of the masters of the SIGLO DE ORO (Golden Age), raised the flag of nonconformism, according to Cela, and he saw himself, not as a rebel, but as a traditionalist in that splendid tradition.

Cela was awarded the Nobel Prize in literature in 1989. When an interviewer asked him about his plans, following receipt of the prize, Cela replied, "I am going to keep writing, which is what really matters to me. Winning the prize was an important step for me, but not the end in itself; the only end is death."

Cerignola, Battle of (Battle of Ceriñola) (1503)

Fought in April 1503, this battle marks Spain's first great victory in the ITALIAN WARS (1494–1559). Essentially one long war between Spain and France for the domination of the Italian peninsula, interrupted by truces or peace treaties, this struggle had revived in 1500. Louis XII of France, having gained control of the northwestern region, had initially agreed with FERDINAND V to allow him domination of the south. The French king then decided to seize the Neapolitan realm as well. Attacked in Apulia by the French, Ferdinand's general, GONZALO FERNÁNDEZ DE CÓRDOBA, broke free from the siege of Barletta and withdrew to the heights near Cerignola. There he constructed a defensive line that included trenches and a barrier of pointed stakes. The pursuing French forces launched a precipitous cavalry charge, which was halted by or, in some cases, impaled upon the barrier of stakes. At the same time an accidental spark exploded a Spanish gun powder depot, sending flames high into the air. The quick-witted Spanish commander is reported to have shouted to his men that the heavens were illuminating their moment of victory and launched his infantry into a counterattack. His opponents were thrown into disarray by their sudden reversal and by the near-simultaneous deaths of the duke of Nemours, the French commander, and the leader of his Swiss auxiliaries.

Cerignola marks the first triumph of Fernández de Córdoba, known to Spaniards as El Gran Capitán, and the TERCIO, the Spanish infantry force that would dominate European battlefields for generations to come. A new French army was sent south to regain control of the Neapolitan kingdom but was beaten back during the summer in several fierce battles along the Garigliano River. After months of maneuvering the Gran Capitán secured a surprise envelopment of both flanks that the French had previously established on the north bank of the river and his Tercios completely overwhelmed King Louis's troops. By early 1504 France had temporarily abandoned its claim on Italy.

Cervantes Saavedra, Miguel de
(1547–1616)

Spanish writer

Born in Alcalá de Henares, the son of a barber-surgeon, Cervantes traveled about Spain with his family and seems to have resided in MADRID in his youth and to have attended school there, although information about his eduction is lacking. In 1570 he enlisted in the Spanish regiment stationed at Naples and in the following year took part in the decisive naval battle of LEPANTO. He was proud throughout his life of the wound he sustained in this great victory over the Turks and regarded the permanent impairment of his left hand as a badge of honor. The letters of recommendation that he earned from the commander JOHN OF AUSTRIA (Don Juan de Austria), the king's half brother, testified to his zeal and would have perhaps earned him rewards had he not subsequently been captured by corsairs and carried off to five years of slavery in Algiers (from which captivity he made repeated attempts to escape). By the time he was ransomed and made his way back to Spain in 1580 his patron was dead, and his prospects were much diminished. Cervantes spent most of the remainder of his life in Madrid, holding several minor appointments in government service but perennially short of money and involved in several disputes with the authorities, which led to brief imprisonment. It was during these years, however, that he began a series of literary endeavors that would ultimately earn him his place as Spain's greatest writer.

Although Cervantes, with typical self-deprecating humor, would later admit that his vision of himself as a poet far exceeded his capacity in that genre, as a playwright writing in verse he produced a number of works, and those that survived from the 1580s—*Numancia* (*Numantia*) and *El trato de Argel* (*The Commerce of Algiers*)—have some

Miguel de Cervantes *(Library of Congress)*

merit. It was, however, as a novelist that Cervantes achieved his reputation. As early as 1585 he wrote a pastoral novel (*La Galatea*), a form very much in vogue. Although rather imitative, *La Galatea* apparently retained a place in his regard, for he was still contemplating a sequel in the last years of his life. His 12 *Novelas ejemplares* (*Exemplary Tales,* 1613) were both popular in their day and critically admired in later generations. They reflect an understanding of the varieties of human experience and a positive response to its vicissitudes that clearly grew out of his own physical wanderings and emotional ups and downs. But it is, of course, his masterpiece, *El ingenioso hidalgo don Quixote de la Mancha,* that has raised him to the stature of one of the world's greatest writers and, in the estimation of many, the first true novelist.

Published in what are usually referred to as two parts in 1605 and 1615, respectively, *Don Quixote* (or *Don Quijote* in modern Spanish) is actually two separate novels. In Part I a small-town middle-aged gentleman, Alonso Quijano, overexcited by his endless reading of chivalric tales, assumes the name Don Quixote de la Mancha (his home province) and sets out as a knight errant in what was believed to be the medieval tradition of righting wrongs and rescuing damsels in distress. He persuades a peasant named Sancho Panza to accompany him as his squire (a role in which Sancho has become virtually as famous as his master) and dedicates himself to exalting the name and fame of his chosen lady, Dulcinea del Toboso (who is, in fact, a glorified version of a young woman of a neighboring town to whom he has never actually spoken). Don Quixote's encounters and adventures as he and Sancho travel across the countryside

are a mixture of tragicomic blunders, high-minded exhortations by one whose mind is clearly out of joint, and populist pragmatism from Sancho. Don Quixote encounters bemused courtesy from some of those whom he meets and violence from others who have no time to waste on what they regard as a madman. He is also trailed by sympathetic friends who attempt to banish his delusions and bring him safely home. Eventually, after an odyssey that has given to the reader a remarkable picture of 17th-century Spain, the don is lured back to home and family. So enthusiastically received was this account of Don Quixote's misadventures and wisdom both in Spain and abroad (where English, French, and Italian editions soon appeared) that Cervantes became a famous and respected writer, whose *Novelas ejemplares* won serious attention, although he never became a wealthy man from his writings.

Success brought with it problems, notably imitations and even theft of characters by other writers, including a bogus sequel published by a man using the pseudonym of Alonso Fernández de Avellaneda in 1614. Cervantes was so indignant over this theft of his literary creation that he brought out his own Part II in 1615. The story finds the older but still potentially obsessed HIDALGO slipping back into his chivalric fantasies. Sancho, who has become more articulate but still susceptible to grand promises, again joins Don Quixote, and they set out on a journey across Spain that is in some ways more tightly plotted, with their adventures pursuing a more orderly sequence (although some readers prefer the free-wheeling action of the first novel). Once again Don Quixote is followed by those who wish to restrain him and return him to his home, sometimes by playing along with his mad ideas. In one notable episode Sancho at last has his reward as a faithful squire when a nobleman, who is in on the "game," appoints the peasant governor of a district, where he amazes everyone by the common sense and compassion of his administrative decisions. After a week Sancho has to be driven out by a fake enemy attack before the local folk become too attached to him. Ultimately the don and his companion arrive in BARCELONA where a ship-board battle finally persuades the now aged Quixote that it is time to quit his chivalric mission. Back home at last he accepts that the age of knight errantry is over, returns to a tranquil sanity, and dies peacefully.

The story of Don Quixote gave the world the word *quixotic* to describe the sort of pursuit of ideals in the face of inevitable frustration and centuries of amused perception of the truths that underlie the hidalgo's quest for honor and beauty. While the novel fell out of fashion during the Age of Reason, by the late 19th century it was being hailed for its "realism." During the 20th century it grew steadily in the admiration of readers and writers throughout the world and was transformed into many new versions including works for opera and ballet, cinema, musical comedy, and children's illustrated books. Virtually every major Spanish novelist of the modern era has avowed his or her esteem for, and indebtedness to, the achievement of Cervantes.

Cervera y Topete, Pascual
(1839–1909)
Spanish admiral

Cervera's naval career brought him experience in every corner of the diminished Spanish Empire. He took part in naval operations in support of the Moroccan War of 1859–60, served in the Philippines and adjacent Far Eastern seas, and did patrol duty in the West Indies. He also distinguished himself on the coasts of Spain during the Second Carlist War and the other civil conflicts of the 1870s. Steadily promoted and repeatedly decorated for valor and steadiness under fire, Cervera won a reputation for honesty and frankness as well as professional skill. By 1892, having attained the rank of rear admiral, he was named minister of marine. He resigned from the cabinet, however, when he found his colleagues unwilling to support the administrative reforms or the budgetary allocations that he considered absolutely necessary for the proper maintenance of the navy.

At the outbreak of the SPANISH-AMERICAN WAR in 1898 Cervera was ordered to take command of a squadron consisting of four cruisers and auxiliary vessels that was being dispatched to the West Indies. On joining his ships, and again as he reached the CANARY ISLANDS, Cervera notified the government about severe shortages in supplies including coal and ammunition. Ordered to press on to his destination, he entered the harbor of Santiago, CUBA, and, in effect, waited to be attacked. During the U.S. assault on the landward defenses of the city he lent artillery pieces and sailors to the commanders who were resisting the siege, but after Santiago fell he had no option but to undertake a doomed sortie from the harbor against a fleet three times as strong as his own. On July 3, 1898, in a running fight along the Cuban coast, the entire squadron was sunk or driven aground. Cervera was plucked from the sea by the Americans and detained at Portsmouth, New Hampshire, until the end of the war. On his return home he was subjected to a board of inquiry, which exonerated him of blame for the defeat. In 1901 he was promoted to vice admiral and the following year named chief of the naval staff. He was a member of the Senate from 1903 until his death.

Cervera was the last in a long line of Spanish admirals who created and defended their nation's seaborne empire. It was his misfortune to be sent on a hopeless mission by a government that failed to provide adequately for its soldiers and sailors and demanded virtual suicide from them in order to protect its political interests.

Ceuta

One of the last outposts of the Spanish Empire, Ceuta is a port in North Africa, across the Strait of GIBRALTAR from Spain. It encompasses just under seven square miles, containing a population of approximately 75,000. The site of a Phoenician trading post, the city was held successively by Romans, Vandals, and Arabs. Captured from its Muslim rulers in the late Middle Ages by Portugal, Ceuta was acquired by Spain in 1580. Periodically besieged by Moroccan rulers and still claimed by them, Ceuta is nevertheless uncompromisingly retained by Spain. During the early 21st century Ceuta, along with her sister enclave MELILLA, became the target of many African migrants seeking to gain entry into Europe. A cosmopolitan city with a large ethnic Berber Muslim minority, Ceuta is known officially as an autonomous city, having a rank between a standard Spanish city and an autonomous community.

Ceylon (Sri Lanka)

This island off the southern tip of India, with an area of just over 25,000 square miles, was the seat of an ancient Sinhalese civilization and a Buddhist culture when the Portuguese made their first landfall there in 1505. They quickly grasped its strategic significance as an extension of their emerging power base in the western Indian Ocean and a way station in their ever-expanding Asian empire. The political divisions within Ceylon facilitated Portuguese tactics of divide and conquer and enabled them to control the island with a relatively modest military and naval presence. The situation altered in the early 17th century with the emergence of the Dutch Republic. This former Spanish dependency in Europe transformed itself into a colonial empire builder, and Portugal, having become attached to the Spanish Crown, became a target of Dutch ambitions. Like many other Portuguese outposts, Ceylon was repeatedly invaded by Dutch forces. The Portuguese and their local allies put up a dogged resistance but were obliged to yield the island in 1658. Ceylon was in turn captured by British troops in 1796 and remained a British possession until the coming of independence in 1948.

Charles I (Carlos I) (1863–1908)
king of Portugal

Soon after succeeding his father, LOUIS I, in 1889, Charles displayed the contradictory elements of his nature. Perceived by some as extravagant and licentious, he was widely admired as a patron of the arts, a studious amateur scientist (with particular commitment to oceanography), and the promoter of handsome public works throughout the country. He was also eager to defend and expand the long-neglected Portuguese colonies in Africa. His overseas projects were, however, a threat to British and German ambitions, and his inability to meet the challenge of these powerful rivals diminished him in public esteem at home. In addition, Charles was the inheritor of decades of bad government, for the corrupt deals made between liberals and conservatives during the preceding reign had stimulated a republican movement. Attempting to take a strong line against his critics, Charles supported the repressive tactics of Prime Minister João Franco, but this merely provoked a revolutionary upsurge culminating in 1908 with the assassination of the king.

Charles I (Carlos I, Holy Roman Emperor Charles V) (1500–1558)
king of Spain

Born in Gent (now in Belgium), he was the son of JOANNA, heiress and later queen of Castile, and Archduke Philip of HABSBURG, later PHILIP I). He was, thus, the grandson of FERDINAND V and ISABELLA I, the Spanish monarchs, and of the Holy Roman Emperor Maximilian I and Duchess Marie of Burgundy. As the ultimate inheritor of his grandparents' realms, he was destined to become the ruler of much of Europe. Charles paid his first visit to Spain in 1517 following the death of Ferdinand in order to take formal possession of Castile and Aragon. His high-handed manner and the rapacious arrogance of the Burgundian advisers who accompanied him created antagonisms that burst forth in a series of popular revolts after his departure. When Charles returned in 1522, having become

Holy Roman Emperor Charles V in 1519, he put down the disturbances with military force but also paid attention to the sensibilities and traditions of his Spanish subjects. Remaining in Spain for the next seven years, he became thoroughly familiar with the land and its culture and developed bonds of mutual affection between himself and the Spaniards. His identification with the Iberian Peninsula intensified when he married Princess Isabella of Portugal (1526), and their growing family was brought up exclusively in this corner of his dominions.

Charles, for all that he was king of Spain, could not remain there for any extended period after 1529. He was constantly pursuing the demands of international politics, which included an ongoing war with France (fought everywhere from Italy to the Low Countries), the challenge posed by the Protestant Reformation in his German territory, and the constant menace of Turkish expansion both in the Balkans and the Mediterranean. At times Charles took personal charge of military operations in North Africa or diplomatic negotiations such as those with England or the Scandinavian kingdoms. Through marriage alliances he was linked to most of the dynasties of Europe and took his obligation seriously, whether in supporting his niece's claim to the Danish throne or seeking to protect the remnant of Hungary after his brother-in-law, the king, was killed during the Turkish invasion.

While Charles, whom even his Spanish subjects came to call simply "the emperor," was preoccupied with European affairs, his concerns were global as well. The New World discovered under the patronage of his grandmother, Queen Isabella, and claimed for Castile by CHRISTOPHER COLUMBUS and his successors had been merely a subsidiary dimension of Spanish policy until the reign of Charles I. It was in his name that HERNÁN CORTÉS conquered the Aztec and FRANCISCO PIZARRO the Inca, opening up the vast mineral world of the Americas to finance Spanish military enterprises. It was under the banner of Charles I that Spanish ships completed the first circumnavigation of the world and established an imperial foothold in Asia. Reports from conquistadores of new terrain explored and new outposts founded flowed into Charles I and mingled with the coded dispatches from his ambassadors and the triumphant bulletins from his generals.

Fifty years after the child Charles had become nominal king of Castile, the prematurely aged king-emperor decided to lay down his multiple burdens. Again and again he had sought to stabilize the situation in Europe only to be challenged by a new Turkish onslaught or the latest French repudiation of a peace treaty. The Religious Peace of Augsburg (1555), by conceding equality between Catholics and Protestants in Germany reflected his inability to reestablish papal and imperial dominance in the Holy Roman Empire. Exhausted and frustrated, Charles abdicated his multiple titles in 1556, leaving the central European territories to his brother Ferdinand (who would continue the Austrian Habsburg line) and the Spanish inheritance to his son PHILIP II. Choosing to spend his last days in his adopted country, Charles took up residence at the monastery of Yuste in EXTREMADURA and died there in 1558.

As befitted a monarch who was essentially an adopted Spaniard, Charles I remained a truly cosmopolitan figure. His perspective was European. Neither his base in Spain nor the newly discovered extensions of Spain around the world were the prime concerns of his policy. Charles did not view his vast and complex dominions as components of a Spanish empire. Instead he thought of them as distinct territories, for which he had assumed the responsibility of a sovereign. Although there were bureaucratic attempts to consolidate and rationalize the management of the lands under his jurisdiction, there was no genuine imperial government. Some of his advisers (who themselves were of various nationalities) favored the concept of an empire of individual units linked by the possession of a common monarch. Other counselors promoted the idea of a spiritual empire, in which Catholicism, fully restored in Europe and constantly expanding overseas would be the universal bond. If anything, Charles seems to have favored the latter concept. His attitude, so far as can be ascertained, was more influenced by medieval Catholic traditions than by "modern" anticipations of a "United States of Europe" or even a "global Spanish Empire." Charles was not a political sophisticate but a prince who felt that he must preserve what had been confided to him by God and his ancestors. To fail in that task of preservation would be a betrayal of a sacred trust. It was perhaps a sense that he had at least partially failed in his duty, rather than mere weariness, that compelled him to pass on the mission to the next generation.

Charles II (Carlos II) (1661–1700)
king of Spain

The only surviving legitimate son of PHILIP IV, Prince Charles was sickly from the time of his birth and an object of great concern when he succeeded his father in 1665. While his mother's regency officially ended when he was 14, he remained under her influence for most of his life. Various noblemen, including his illegitimate half brother, Don Juan José, also dominated the royal government at various times, with varying degrees of effectiveness. Although Charles was surprisingly alert to the issues of the day, his perennial poor health and neglected education made it impossible for him to be master of his country. Political factions serving the interest of France and Austria shaped national policy at various times.

The changing ascendency of cliques at court was reflected in the king's two marriages, but neither his first wife, a French princess, nor his second, a kinswoman of the Austrian emperor, produced an heir.

King Charles II *(Library of Congress)*

Charles became a helpless bystander in a series of wars with France that cost Spain territory along her frontiers. The last of these conflicts, the War of the League of Augsburg, was brought to a close by the French king Louis XIV, in 1697, primarily to clear the way for the division of spoils among the European monarchs when the hapless Charles should finally expire. Two successive partition treaties allocated most of Spain's dependencies to France or Austria, with smaller benefits allotted to England, the Dutch state, and others.

Forced to look on as his heritage was disposed of without his approval, Charles II produced a will just before his death in 1700 that left his entire realm in Europe and overseas to Philippe, duke of Anjou, a grandson of Louis XIV who would rule as PHILIP V. While the young man was Charles's great-nephew and there was some geopolitical logic to an independent Spanish state tied to France by dynastic alliance, the ultimate reason for this decision may have been a desire to preserve the integrity of the Spanish inheritance that Charles, during his life, had been able to do nothing to protect. The last Spanish HABSBURG thus delivered the empire created by his ancestors to a BOURBON.

Charles III (Carlos III) (1716–1788)
king of Spain

Son of PHILIP V by his second marriage, Charles secured the Duchy of Parma (his mother's ancestral home) by international agreement in 1731 and left it three years later when he conquered the Kingdom of Naples from its Austrian overlords. During his time in Italy the young monarch came under the influence of the Enlightenment, a movement of reform that he would later introduce into Spain.

Following the death of his half brother, FERDINAND VI, in 1759 Charles succeeded to the Spanish throne (leaving a younger son to maintain the Neapolitan line of the Bourbons). During the early years of his reign, still under the influence of Italian advisers, he aroused opposition from various interests in Spain including the Jesuits and had to put down a number of conspiracies. During the latter part of his reign, however, he enjoyed growing popularity and was given credit for increased national prosperity.

The least successful of this king's policies lay in the area of foreign relations, for he allowed his personal antagonism toward Britain (dating back to experiences in Naples) to draw him into the final stages of the Seven Years' War, 1761–63, which cost him FLORIDA. He also supported the American revolutionaries between 1779 and 1783. Although this intervention regained Florida for Spain, it created a dangerous new neighbor in the Western Hemisphere who would play a major role in the ultimate downfall of the Spanish Empire.

The domestic policy of Charles III was far more positive both in its inspiration and execution. Applying the tactics of enlightened despotism, he forced an often-reluctant population to modernize the management of national resources, improve transportation and communications, and accept a more rigorous government supervision of local administration and taxes. Foreign experts were brought in to assist progressive ministers such as ARANDA and FLORIDABLANCA in guiding Spain's development. Critics of backward traditions, such as JOVELLANOS and the count of Campomanes, were given scope for their recommendations. Educa-

tion was improved, public works undertaken, and commerce both on land and sea supported. Agriculture and, to a lesser degree, industry were transformed from their neglected state.

The mentality of Charles III was that of a practical rather than an intellectual sovereign. He had few interests other than hunting and was not a patron of literature or the arts. Simple and sober in his private life, he was a devout Catholic. Nevertheless, he retained his mistrust of the Jesuits from what he believed was their involvement in opposition during the first days of his reign and continued to harass them, banning the order from his European and overseas possessions in 1767 and joining with other rulers a few years later to procure the papal dissolution of the Society of Jesus around the world. Charles III was also generally suspicious of the church's overall influence in Spanish affairs, which he tried to limit, and he greatly curtailed the influence of the SPANISH INQUISITION.

The record of Charles III in management of Spain's New World colonies is mixed. Inspectors and investigators were required to send him copious reports on everything from the Islas Malvinas (Falkland Islands) in the Atlantic to the California coast on the Pacific (first settled during his reign). Fortifications and garrisons were increased in the islands of the Caribbean, and trade in that region, developed. The structure of government was reorganized both by increasing the number of viceroyalties and by enhancing the effectiveness of local government. Spanish America remained plagued, however, by two serious problems. The old inability to transform decrees issued in Madrid into practical results on the ground continued regardless of reform efforts. But in addition, the patience of many Spanish Americans with their colonial subordination was wearing thin, especially after the example of Britain's rebellious colonies on the Atlantic seaboard stimulated the long-standing grievances of the criollos.

Charles III has been variously described as the greatest of the Spanish Bourbons and a disorganized, random reformer who achieved no lasting results. A true judgment probably lies somewhere between these extremes. But there is no doubt that his inability to prepare his successor, CHARLES IV, for the demands of kingship left Spain without either enduring enlightenment or effective despotism as it entered the Age of Revolution.

Charles IV (Carlos IV) (1748–1819)
king of Spain

The son of CHARLES III, whom he succeeded in 1788, this monarch was unable either to continue his father's policy of enlightened despotism or to secure the country against the cataclysmic forces generated by the French Revolution of 1789. During most of his reign he was dominated by his wife, Maria Luisa of Parma, and her paramour, MANUEL DE GODOY. Godoy, who was named chief minister in 1792, at first tried to keep Spain neutral in the spreading revolutionary warfare, then joined an anti-French coalition, and finally formed an alliance with France. After more than a decade of misfortunes, including Spain's abandonment of LOUISIANA and the naval defeat at TRAFALGAR, Charles IV found himself virtually subject to the will of the emperor Napoléon I. After the intrigues of Godoy brought a French army into Spain, supposedly to seize and divide Portugal, Charles

King Charles IV *(Library of Congress)*

was overthrown by his son the prince of Asturias. When the ousted monarch petitioned the emperor for help, the entire royal family was invited to Bayonne to confer about their problems. Once in Napoléon's presence, both Charles IV and the prince were taken prisoners, the Bourbon dynasty was declared deposed, and Napoléon's brother Joseph was named King JOSEPH I of Spain. While the fate of his country was being decided during the subsequent years of struggle against the French occupiers, Charles IV was held captive in France, along with his queen and his minister, Godoy. After the collapse of the Bonaparte regime, the former prince of Asturias, now FERDINAND VII, returned to Spain, and his father spent the remaining years of his life drifting about Europe, eventually dying in Italy.

A pious, amiable, and well-intentioned monarch, Charles IV lacked the cunning, or even the common sense, to handle the demands of kingship in tumultuous times. His apparent ignorance of his wife's relationship with Godoy was merely one aspect of his inability to grasp the domestic and international situations with which he was confronted. Totally out of his depth, Charles IV eventually drifted away from Spain and was essentially forgotten long before his actual demise.

Chile

A subordinate region of the Inca Empire by the early 15th century, Chile was invaded by Spaniards in the course of their conquest of the Inca during the 1530s. Permanent settlements were established in Chile by the 1550s, although the southern region would remain in contention for many generations. Chile's character as an active military frontier zone was emphasized by the creation of the Captaincy General of Chile in 1778 as a dependency of the Viceroyalty of PERU. Chileans revolted against Spain in 1810 but did not secure their full independence until 1818.

Chillida, Eduardo (1924–2002)
Spanish sculptor
Hailed as "one of the three pillars upon which 20th-century sculpture rests"

(together with Constantin Brancusi and Alberto Giacometti) and undoubtedly the most esteemed Spanish sculptor of his time, Chillida was trained as an architect at the University of Madrid but turned to sculpture in the 1940s. Drawing upon the craftsman tradition of his Basque heritage, he drew attention with his ability to combine the solidity of iron with an openness and lightness of technique in his abstract work, later bringing similar skill to larger sculptures in granite. By the late 1960s he had attracted sufficient international attention to be included in the Franco regime's support of modern art as a vehicle for gaining overseas prestige. Controversies provoked by the clash between political and artistic priorities led to an unprecedented flare-up of cultural protest against the reactionary regime and marked the opening of a new era in Spanish public art.

Chillida's awards and the recognition they confirmed included the Japanese Imperial Prize for Art, the Sculpture Prize at the Venice Biennale, the Kandinsky Prize, and the Mellon Prize. By the time the Guggenheim Museum opened its shrine to modern art at BILBAO in the late 1990s, Chillida's renown earned him a grand retrospective show as part of the opening ceremonies.

Chillida was not only an international master but also among Spain's most prolific and popular artists, earning multiple commissions at home as well as elsewhere in Europe and in the United States. Although some of his creations were on a modest scale, he had a clear preference for monumental work. The best known of these sculptures is *Peines del viento* ("Wind combs," 1977). Set dramatically on the Basque coast near his native Donostia–San Sebastián, its outstretching combs or fingerlike projections evoke an interaction between land and water, wind and wave.

Chillida's final project was his most monumental in scale. It involved nothing less than the hollowing out of a mountain and the opening up of passageways on its peak that would permit beams of light to flow into its interior. A suitable mountain had been found in the CANARY ISLANDS, and local authorities, flattered by the choice, had endorsed the great sculptor's concept. Environmentalists raised objections, however, and the passage of time proved the ultimate enemy of Chillida's grand vision.

Cisneros, Francisco Jiménez de
(1436–1517)
Spanish clergyman and statesman

Born to a minor HIDALGO family in CASTILE and educated at the University of Salamanca, Cisneros visited Rome and subsequently held a number of administrative positions in the Castilian church. He would later say that a period of ascetic life as a Franciscan friar was, however, the happiest and best time in his life. His character was such that he could not allow shortcomings in the order to go unnoticed, and he became a major force for reform of the Franciscan communities. Having acquired a reputation for rigorous and uncompromising actions, he was recommended in 1492 for the position of confessor to Queen ISABELLA I. Within three years he had been named archbishop of Toledo and primate of Castile. In this capacity he applied his reforming principles to the clergy in general and interfered with many of their privileges, although he had to overcome strong opposition. Impressed by his zeal, Isabella asked him to undertake an intense program of conversion among the Moors of GRANADA, who had initially been left largely undisturbed in their faith. Cisneros undertook an aggressive approach that provoked the outrage of the Muslim community, and he actually had to flee the city in 1499 to avoid physical attack. This confrontation was followed by a general uprising among the Moors of the Alpujarras region that lasted for several years and had to be put down by force of arms. Unabashed by the results of his excessive zeal, Cisneros persuaded the Crown to issue a decree in 1502 ordering the expulsion of all Muslims who did not promptly convert to Christianity.

During the last few years of the queen's reign Cisneros spent much of his time at the royal court, strengthening the operations of the SPANISH INQUISITION and promoting new standards of public behavior and morality while organizing the establishment of a new university at Alcalá. This institution became a center of learning that played a major role in the development of the Renaissance in Spain. Cisneros's most notable achievement in this dimension was the project for creating the Complutensian Bible. Taking its title from the Latin name of the town of Alcalá, this was the first major polyglot edition of the Bible to be produced in the new age of humanistic scholarship.

When Isabella died in 1504, Cisneros took part in the political maneuverings around the succession question, rallying nobles who were likewise loyal to the memory of the queen and protecting the interests of her husband, FERDINAND V of Aragon. As soon as the latter recognized his son-in-law as PHILIP I of Castile, Cisneros accepted the arrangement. Following Philip's sudden death in 1506, however, Cisneros intervened once more to thwart plotters who wanted to impose a regency by Philip's father, Holy Roman Emperor Maximilian, and again managed the situation in favor of Ferdinand. Ferdinand reciprocated by obtaining the title of cardinal for Cisneros.

Cisneros, now regent of Castile, persuaded Ferdinand to support a long-cherished project: a crusade against the Muslims of North Africa. Between 1507 and 1509, Cisneros not only organized the financing and equipping of an invasion force but accompanied Castilian troops during their capture of Oran. Ferdinand's heart was never truly in this scheme, and the cardinal's dream of a Christianized North Africa soon faded. The two men did not ever fully trust each other. Yet Ferdinand could not deny the rigorous, uncompromising character of the cardinal and saw the value that lay in keeping a man so unlike himself in a position of trust. Cisneros was continued in the regency of Castile until Ferdinand's death and oversaw the accession of CHARLES I. The faithful servant laid down his burden only when the young king had at last set foot on the soil of Spain. They did not meet, however, for Cisneros died a few days before Charles could reach the cardinal's deathbed.

Cisneros had lived the first 60 years of his life in an essentially ecclesiastical environment where his activities would scarcely have earned him the attention of historians, yet during the last 20 years he became one of the most active and involved personalities in the public life of Renaissance Spain. His concern for the triumph of Catholicism extended to the New World as well, for he demanded the establishment of the Inquisition in CUBA as well as Oran. A loyal supporter of the Castilian dynasty, he protected the orderly succession that ultimately brought the rightful prince to the throne, but his willingness to work with Ferdinand of Aragon showed that he well understood the political dynamics that were creating a new Spanish state. A harsh, unbending individual, Cardinal Cisneros thus shared with the cunning and flexible Machiavellian king Ferdinand a major role in Spain's rise to dominance.

Clarín   See ALAS, LEOPOLDO.

Colombia

The coast of this region in the northern corner of South America was explored by Spaniards in the early 1500s, and permanent settlements were made in the 1520s. The indigenous Chibcha people were conquered by GONZALO JIMÉNEZ DE QUESADA, who founded Bogotá, later the capital of Colombia, in 1538. Colombia was the nucleus of the Viceroyalty of New Granada (which also included VENEZUELA, ECUADOR, and PANAMA), founded in 1718. After an eight-year struggle for independence from Spain, Colombia finally achieved victory under SIMÓN BOLÍVAR in 1819. The old structure of New Granada was swept away when Venezuela and Ecuador separated from Colombia in 1830, although Panama remained a Colombian province until 1903.

Columbus, Christopher (Cristóbal Colón) (1451–1506)
Italian navigator and explorer in the Spanish service
Born in Genoa, Italy, according to tradition, Columbus's place of birth, ethnic

Christopher Columbus, kneeling in front of Queen Isabella *(Library of Congress)*

origin, and the details of his early career have been disputed by historians. He seems to have had considerable experience in practical navigation and is believed to have made voyages to northern Europe as well as to the west coast of Africa and evidently made an extensive study of maps and accounts of voyages to distant lands. After residing for a time in MADEIRA and absorbing knowledge of Portuguese voyages, he developed a proposal for establishing a transatlantic route to Asia. Portuguese authorities, already committed to a route circumnavigating Africa that would bring them to the trade centers of India and East Asia, showed little interest in Columbus's ideas.

Having shifted his efforts to Spain, Columbus spent a number of years promoting his transatlantic project before securing sufficient support to obtain a hearing from ISABELLA I, queen of CASTILE. Benefitting from the positive mood generated by her CONQUEST OF GRANADA in 1492, Columbus won royal backing for a voyage to seek out the wealth of the Indies and departed in that same year with three ships and 120 men. After a voyage of some two months uninterrupted by bad weather but vexed by the restlessness of his sailors, he made landfall on October 12, 1492, at an island in the present-day Bahamas, which he called San Salvador.

Columbus subsequently sighted CUBA and sailed on to reach a large island that he named "La Española"—HISPANIOLA—now Haiti and the DOMINICAN REPUBLIC. Here he established friendly relations with the inhabitants and built a fort to be occupied by some of his men.

Although these islands in the Caribbean clearly did not correspond to the images of advanced civilization and great riches conveyed by medieval writers such as Marco Polo, Columbus claimed his "New World" discoveries for Castile, planted the banner of the cross there, and returned to Spain early in 1493 to present an enthusiastic account of his experience to the queen and her consort, FERDINAND V. Even the latter was intrigued by the evidence of Columbus's accomplishments, including several "Indians" and a quantity of gold brought back with him. Columbus made three subsequent voyages, seeking to vindicate his claim that he had indeed established a transatlantic route to Asia.

In 1493, only a few months after his return to Spain, Columbus sailed west again, this time with a far larger contingent of men and ships owing to the excitement aroused by his report. On this second voyage he touched at still more islands, notably JAMAICA and PUERTO RICO. His fort on Hispaniola had been destroyed, and the garrison had apparently perished in a clash with hostile Indians. Nevertheless, he created a new settlement and left colonists to build a base for future exploration. On a third voyage, in 1498, Columbus reached the coast of South America, in present-day VENEZUELA, and discovered the mouth of

the Orinoco River. Back in Hispaniola he found that his brother Diego, whom he had left in charge, had made enemies among the colonists, and the subsequent disputes led to Columbus and members of his family being sent back to Spain in chains on charges of undermining royal authority. After being exonerated Columbus made a fourth voyage, in 1502. Still searching for the mainland of Asia he sailed along the coast of Central America sighting PANAMA, COSTA RICA, NICARAGUA, and HONDURAS. He still found nothing that corresponded to his grand vision and no route that would carry him into the interior of what he still firmly believed to be Asia.

Back in Spain the self-confidence and aggressiveness that had enabled Colum-

Christopher Columbus and sons Diego and Ferdinand
(Library of Congress)

bus to win support for his original plan and to carry it to fulfillment in 1492 had by now made enemies. Just as among settlers in Hispaniola, so at the royal court there were those who resented the titles and powers extracted from the Crown by this foreign-born upstart. With the death of Queen Isabella in 1504 Columbus lost his supporter and protector. By the time of his own death in 1506 Columbus had been reduced to relative obscurity. His descendants would enjoy the titles of nobility that he had earned by his achievements, but the proudest title of all—Admiral of the Ocean Sea—had become something of a mockery, and the nominal governorship of his discoveries was quickly taken over by royal bureaucrats.

Although Columbus probably died still believing that he had reached Asia and that the wonders of the Chinese imperial palace lay just over the horizon, the calculations that led him to propose the transatlantic route underestimated the distance to Asia and failed to anticipate a vast landmass and a great unknown ocean that lay between his starting point and his goal. He had, in fact, discovered the Americas, although they would later be named for someone else. To be sure, other Europeans touched upon the coast of North America before him, and the Amerindian population that had spread from its Asian point of entry throughout both North and South America had clearly been on the ground long before him. Nevertheless, Columbus was the effective discoverer of the Americas, and the New World to which he had opened the way became a magnet for European explorers and the basis for Spain's imperial greatness for centuries to come.

Conde, Carmen (1907–1996)
Spanish writer

Already an active teacher and writer by the time of the SPANISH CIVIL WAR, Conde later said that the shock and horror of this great Spanish national trauma lifted her from persistent naïveté to true adulthood. Unlike many other intellectuals who fled the country, Conde and her husband, fellow poet Antonio Oliver Balmas, stayed on in their country throughout the Franco era. They refused, she would later declare, to leave the spoils to the enemy. Her work as an educator and as the author of more than 50 books (primarily of poetry but also including novels, biographies, and a memoir) established her as an elder stateswoman of Spanish literature. Her status was recognized by her induction into the Spanish Royal Academy in 1978, as its first female member.

Carmen Conde's poetical work spans more than six decades. Her collections include *Brocal* from 1929, *Júbilo* (Joy), *Empezando la vida* (Starting to live), *El Arcangel* (The Archangel), and *Mientras los hombres mueren* (While men are dying), all published in the 1930s. The two latter ones were inspired by her own anguish regarding the Spanish civil war. In 1967 she won the national prize for literature for her collection *Obra poética* (Poetic work), which includes the greater part of her writings. Among her most recent works are *Del obligado dolor* (Enforced pain, 1984), *Por el camino viendo estrellas* (On the road and looking at the stars, 1985) and *La calle de los balcones azules* (The street of the blue balconies, 1986).

Córdoba (Cordova)

Like the other ancient cities of ANDALUSIA, Córdoba overwhelms with the sheer grandeur of its history (and perhaps is

The Mezquita mosque and cathedral, in Córdoba
(Getty)

reconquest (RECONQUISTA) in the 13th century. Impressed by the sheer vastness of its principal mosque, Christian rulers spared it and encapsulated a cathedral within its huge structure. French looters were less respectful of the city's dignity during the PENINSULAR WAR. In more recent days, though trade and manufacturing have reestablished a population that approaches that of its heyday (some 400,000), modern Córdoba lives in the shadow of its past glories.

Coronado, Francisco Vázquez de (1510–1552)
Spanish explorer and soldier

A protégé of the viceroy of NEW SPAIN, whom he had accompanied to the New World, Coronado was appointed governor of NEW GRANADA, in northwestern MEXICO, in 1539. Shortly thereafter a probe led by a monk, Fray Marcos de Niza, was sent into the wilderness to the north to investigate reports that had been given by CABEZA DE VACA of rich Indian towns. Fray Marcos returned saying that he had been within sight of a vast city, merely one of the "Seven Cities of Cíbola" inhabited by highly civilized Indians. Dreaming of conquests on the grand scale of CORTÉS's and PIZARRO's, the Spanish authorities organized an expedition by land and sea under the overall command of Coronado. His ship sailed up the Gulf of California, discovered the mouth of the Colorado River, and followed its course in small boats as far as the southern end of the Grand Canyon. Meanwhile, a detachment from Coronado's main force had traveled westward through the desert to reach the rim of the canyon farther up its length. Some of the soldiers made a partial descent

overwhelmed by it). Capital of Hispania under the Roman Empire, the city became the greatest achievement of the Arab empire after its conquest of Iberia. The seat of the Caliphate of the West, Córdoba was a center of the learned arts and sciences during the 10th century, compared by many to ancient Athens. The leading scholars of medieval Islam and Judaism taught and wrote there, amid a splendid array of shrines and palaces. As the Moors sank into civil strife, Córdoba lost its dominance and succumbed to the Christian but could not climb more than a third of the way down. These were the first Europeans to reach this great terrain feature of North America, and their reports would astound the Old World.

Coronado's main force had marched directly to the designated location of Cíbola only to discover that it was no more than a collection of poverty-stricken Indian villages. Cursing the deceitful friar they trekked wearily back to the banks of the Rio Grande where they remained until 1541. The following spring Coronado led a part of his cavalry into what is now eastern Kansas pursuing yet another tale of rich Indian settlements at a place called Quivira. This, too, proved to be nothing more than an overgrown village. Mortified and depressed, Coronado led his men back into Mexico where he was received with chagrin and hostility by the viceregal administrators. Although he was allowed to resume his governorship of New Granada for a time, he was soon made the object of political persecution, accused of mismanagement, and even sentenced to house confinement. Eventually released, he lived quietly, receiving only minor assignments until his death.

By the standards of high expectations set for conquistadores Coronado was a failure. Yet his expedition opened up whole new areas of western North America, including much of NEW MEXICO, and provided valuable information about what would later be the states of ARIZONA and Kansas, the course of the Colorado River, and the astounding dimensions of the Grand Canyon. If not rich in material gains, his enterprise enriched the Spanish fund of information about the perimeters of the empire.

cortes

As its name implies, this Iberian legislative institution derives from courts that exercised judicial functions under the authority of the crown in all of the Iberian kingdoms, including Portugal. In some of the Spanish realms an assembly known as the *cortes* existed as far back as the early 13th century. Originating as gatherings of noblemen whose purpose it was to advise and support the king's policies, or to restrain his excesses, these bodies eventually expanded to include representatives of the common people. The latter were seen as the tax base and source of rank-and-file manpower upon which all royal power ultimately rested. As this representation was usually provided by delegates selected by town councils and urban elites, they were democratic only in a limited sense. By the middle of the 14th century most of the Iberian *cortes* contained these representatives of the "communes." There was also usually a house of the clergy, and some kingdoms had an additional *brazo* (arm) in which the lower nobility, or "gentlemen," sat separately from the *ricos hombres* (rich men) of the upper nobility. With the consolidations carried out during the later medieval period, the *cortes* were reduced to those of Portugal, CASTILE, and the lands of the crown of ARAGON, although separate, subordinate *cortes* in VALENCIA, CATALONIA, and Aragon proper survived through the 16th century. NAVARRE, too, preserved nominal *cortes* of its own, meeting occasionally until the mid-19th century.

For all practical purposes the history of the Iberian *cortes* followed a parallel course with that of France, on a rising arc during the Middle Ages when the Crown needed support for its growing ambitions, then on a descending arc as the Crown attained absolute authority. The *cortes* withered in Spain and Portugal during the 18th century. It had a brief revival in both countries during the early 19th as it challenged royal power. This was particularly true in Spain when the Cortes met as a national body at CÁDIZ during the French intrusion to ratify the liberal constitution of 1812.

The greater part of the 19th century saw this institution functioning in a perfunctory manner, and it was only during the brief heyday of Republicanism (Spain, 1931–39; Portugal, 1910–30) that anything like a democratic process either in elections or procedures was followed. Since the fall of the FRANCO and SALAZAR dictatorships, the parliamentary life of both Iberian nations has moved into the European mainstream and the heritage of the word *cortes* has attained a new respect.

Cortés, Hernán (marqués del Valle de Oaxaca) (1485?–1547)
Spanish explorer and soldier

The son of an officer, Cortés was nevertheless intended by his parents to pursue "a learned profession"; however, he left the University of Salamanca without taking a degree, driven by a restless nature and excited by tales of discovery and adventure in the New World. He made his way to the Americas while still in his teens and combined his literary skills and bold temperament to make himself useful to the conquerors of the West Indian islands. He acquired land in CUBA but was bored by the life of a gentleman-farmer. Having acquired influential friends and the patronage of Governor DIEGO VELÁZQUEZ DE CUÉLLAR, Cortés secured command of an exploratory mission to the Central American mainland. Earlier probes into this region had raised rumors of a powerful Indian realm in the interior, and Cortés was determined to let nothing stand in the way of transforming his dreams into reality. In 1519 he landed on the Yucatán Peninsula with a force of some 500 men and soon made contact with the local tribes, whom he won to his support by a combination of combat and conciliation. The most important of these native allies would be the Tlaxcalans of central Mexico, longtime enemies of the Aztec Empire, which never successfully conquered them. They told him of the vast wealth amassed by these dwellers in the heart of what is now MEXICO and of the bloody tyranny that they maintained over other tribes from their splendid capital at Tenochtitlán (present-day Mexico City). Aided by the Indian woman Malintzin, whom the Spaniards called Doña Marina, Cortés's interpreter and adviser as well as mistress, the conquistador developed a policy of aggressive diplomacy that took advantage of Aztec legends about the return of a "fair god" whose predicted arrival happened to coincide with that of the Spanish adventurer.

Marching into the heart of the Aztec Empire, Cortés met and gained dominance over its ruler, Moctezuma, and the Spaniards were invited to take up residence as honored guests amid the splendid palaces and temples of Tenochtitlán. While Cortés was absorbed in strengthening his position and amassing gold, he received word early in 1520 that Velázquez had turned against him. The governor's anger had been aroused by Cortés's legal maneuvers in establishing a town council at Veracruz (a settlement he had founded upon landing on the coast of the Gulf of Mexico) and having himself designated by that body as captain general with independent authority to pursue his own designs. Cortés hastened back to the coast with half of his troops where he was confronted by a large force under PÁNFILO DE NARVÁEZ, who had been authorized to arrest him. Adroitly spinning out negotiations about how to resolve the situation, Cortés lured away most of the new arrivals with tales of Aztec gold. He then attacked and defeated Narváez and marched back to Tenochtitlán. However, the state of affairs in the Aztec capital had deteriorated under PEDRO DE ALVARADO, with Moctezuma now rejected by his own people as a collaborator and the Spaniards hated as oppressive and greedy invaders rather than messengers of the gods. Attempting to escape from the city with their loot, Cortés's men were attacked and suffered heavy losses as they crossed the leading causeway over the lake that surrounded the city. The Noche Triste (sad night) of June 20, 1520, brought heavy losses to the Spaniards, who finally fought their way through to the safety of Tlaxcalan territory.

Resilient as ever, Cortés rebuilt his army with Spanish soldiers and Indian auxiliaries and laid siege to Tenochtitlán. With Moctezuma dead, his successor weakened by rivalries within his own ranks, and the population of the city stricken by famine and disease, Tenochtitlán fell (August 13, 1521) and with it the Aztec Empire.

In the years that followed Cortés received titles of nobility and accumulated a great fortune. Expeditions organized by him explored much of Mexico, GUATEMALA, and HONDURAS and conquered remnants of the Aztec elite, seizing their wealth. Cortés himself crossed to the Pacific shore and

Combat between Hernán Cortés and Pánfilo de Narváez *(Library of Congress)*

sailed into the Gulf of California. The Spanish Crown nevertheless refused to grant him full recognition of the rights he claimed as discoverer and conqueror. Administrators were sent out to displace and dominate him, leaving him with honors that were largely ceremonial. Cortés encountered a similar denial of the full respect he felt was owed to him when he returned to Spain in the 1540s. He attempted to ingratiate himself with King CHARLES I (Emperor Charles V) by taking part in an expedition against the Muslim rulers of Algiers, but his days as a soldier and a conqueror were over.

Although Cortés experienced the sort of anticlimax that befell so many of his fellow conquistadores once their services to Spain were over, he at least emerged from his adventures with his life and a goodly share of material rewards. Moreover he earned the lasting fame that motivated men of his breed. From his overthrow of the Aztec Empire sprang the conquest of the vast territory of NEW SPAIN and the Spanish claim to rule North and Central America. His name would be execrated in postindependence Mexico, but for generations of Spaniards he would be a national hero and the epitome of the conquistador.

Costa Gomes, Francisco da
(1914–2001)
Portuguese soldier and politician

As president from 1974 to 1976, this general oversaw the dismantling of Portugal's colonial empire when independence was granted to ANGOLA, MOZAMBIQUE, CAPE VERDE ISLANDS, and SÃO TOMÉ AND PRÍNCIPE. Born in Trás-os-Montes, Costa Gomes rose through the ranks to high military assignments at home and abroad. He was chief of military command in MACAO, served on the North Atlantic Treaty Organization headquarters staff in England, and later was undersecretary of state for the army, rising to brigadier general. From 1972 to the end of the Salazar-Caetano regime he was the head of the Joint Chiefs of Staff. After the overthrow of the dictatorship General Costa Gomes served as president for two years, during which he implemented his policies of independence for the colonies and domestic tranquillity. Following his retirement in 1981 he was awarded the title of marshal, his country's highest military rank.

Costa Rica

The coastline of this region was first observed by CHRISTOPHER COLUMBUS during his 1502 voyage and further explored by an expedition sent in the 1520s by PEDRARIAS DÁVILA, governor of PANAMA. Costa Rica was occupied by Spanish settlers in the late 1530s and remained subject to the Spanish Crown until the breakup of the empire in the region in 1821. Briefly linked to the Mexican regime under AGUSTÍN DE ITURBIDE, Costa Rica transferred its alignment to the United Provinces of Central America but left that group in 1838 and pursued an independent destiny thereafter.

Cuba

This large island (44,000 square miles) in the Caribbean was claimed for Spain by CHRISTOPHER COLUMBUS in 1492. Conquest was begun in 1509 by DIEGO VELÁZQUEZ DE CUÉLLAR, and the virtual extinction of the Amerindian population led to the importation of large numbers of slaves from Africa, whose presence became a major factor in the island's development. Cuba was the major staging area for the exploration and conquest of the mainland Americas. Part of the viceroyalty of NEW SPAIN and the island itself a captaincy general within the Spanish military and administrative structure, Cuba was also a transit point for the shipment of mineral wealth to Spain. Its capital, Havana, was captured by the British in 1762 but regained a year later. With its defenses strengthened Cuba withstood the revolutionary movement that swept away most of Spain's other possessions in the early 19th century and continued to be a prosperous agricultural colony, exporting sugar and tobacco, even after the abolition of slavery in 1876. A revolutionary movement was suppressed (the Ten Years' War) in 1868–78. A new independence struggle was launched in 1895. In 1898, following the destruction of the USS *Maine* in Havana harbor, the United States, which for many decades had maintained a strong interest in the island, declared war, invaded Cuba, defeated the Spanish forces, and compelled their evacuation from Cuba. Following the conclusion of the SPANISH-AMERICAN WAR, Cuba remained under the protection of the United States until she was proclaimed a sovereign republic in 1902.

D

Dalí i Domènech, Salvador (1904–1989)

Spanish painter

Born in CATALONIA and educated in BARCELONA and MADRID, Dalí went to Paris in the mid-1920s where he met fellow Catalan artists PABLO PICASSO and JOAN MIRÓ. He

Salvador Dalí *(Library of Congress)*

soon abandoned his earlier representational art inspired by various painters, both classical and contemporary. Instead, he turned to surrealism, under the particular influence of Sigmund Freud's writings on dreams and sexual symbolism. He proclaimed his dedication to the "paranoic critical" technique that enabled him to look within the inner meanings of images. This enabled him to create a dream landscape such as that of *The Persistence of Memory* (1931) with its melting watches, each set to a different time and displayed in a harsh landscape resembling that of Dalí's Catalan childhood. He gained further approval from the surrealists through his collaboration with the Spanish director LUIS BUÑUEL on two films, *Un chien andalou* (An Andalusian dog, 1928) and *l'Âge d'or* (The golden age, 1930). The mixture of the grotesque and even repulsive with startling perceptiveness won further plaudits from the dominant school of modern art.

During the late 1930s Dalí underwent a rapid fall from the heights of esteem to which he had been raised. This was due to a number of factors: his increasing emphasis on sexual and violent themes (which had offended the puritanical morality of the doctrinaire Left), his flamboyant egotism, and jealousy of his ability to attain international notoriety through self-promotion. He was denounced as a fascist when he refused to take a stand during the SPANISH CIVIL WAR, proclaiming an abhorrence of war no matter who waged it. In addition Dalí turned increasingly in these years to a more naturalistic style (although with frequent intrusions of surreal elements), and he even drew upon religious themes. He resided in the United States during World War II and made frequent trips back and forth between that country and Spain thereafter. Accepting commissions from both theatrical producers and commercial enterprises, Dalí ventured into every field from ballet to interior design and was increasingly denounced by other artists as a charlatan. To these criticisms he remained blandly indifferent, delivering eccentric pronouncements, publishing provocative writings, and producing whatever form of art struck his fancy at a given time. Although he continued to be discussed and even to be honored by retrospective exhibitions until the late 1970s, he increasingly appeared to the general public as a strange figure whom they could scarcely imagine as having dominated the artistic scene in the long-ago era of surrealism.

Damão and Diu (Daman and Diu)

Annexed by Portugal in 1559, these cities and their hinterland included a total area of approximately 39 square miles. They provided strategic and commercial support to the nearby city of GOA, the capital of Portuguese Asia. Damão, in particular, afforded a useful harbor, with shipbuilding facilities and access by river to the interior of western India. Like Goa, Damão and Diu remained Portuguese possessions until 1962 when, after being invaded by the recently independent "Union of India," they were ceded by Portugal.

Darío, Rubén (Felix Rubén García Sarmiento) (1867–1916)

Spanish-American (Nicaraguan) writer

Darío's stature is equally great on both sides of the Atlantic. His poetry has influenced both Spanish and Spanish-American writers. Born in NICARAGUA, Darío's family circumstances led to a somewhat irregular youth and a haphazard education, but his wide and perceptive reading in Spanish and French literature fostered both sophistication and innovation. He traveled in Spanish America, undertaking diplomatic and consular missions for a number of countries. It was his appointment as correspondent for the Buenos Aires newspaper *La Nación* that provided the basis for most of his work in Europe and the foundation of his income. Although he had already visited Spain in 1892, his return there in 1898 had a special significance. In the first place he had in the interim established himself as the creator of *modernismo* in Spanish poetry and introduced a whole new appreciation of symbolism. He had earned the respect of the older generation of the literati in 1892. In 1898 he was hailed as a virtual member of the rising generation. In the second place his maturing awareness of the world had carried him beyond purely aesthetic concerns. In the aftermath of Spain's defeat by the United States in 1898 he recognized the menace that the "Colossus of the North" posed to all of the peoples of Latin America. He understood more clearly, too, the global outreach of colonialism. His writings, both in prose and poetry, took on a more serious tone as he dealt with the dark side of the human experience.

Darío had already begun to experience the "dark side" in his own personal life. Marital problems had tormented him in his earlier days, and it was only after he formed a happy relationship with Francisca Sánchez in Spain that domestic stress diminished. But Darío's artistic temperament increasingly drove him to excesses as he veered between an elegant and aristocratic lifestyle and his inability to manage his finances and his drinking problem. As the gathering clouds of World War I cast their pall over Europe, he made his way back to his birthplace where he succumbed to physical and emotional exhaustion in 1916.

In a comparatively short life Darío produced a substantial volume of poetry, along with prose fiction and effective journalism. His work was published in a series of collections, the most important being *Azul* (Blue, 1888), *Prosas profanas* (Profane prose, 1896), and *Cantos de vida y esperanza* (Song of life and hope, 1905). More than 30 years after Darío's death, Francisca Sánchez donated to Spain a large collection of his papers, including unpublished work, which constitute the Rubén Darío Archive, an invaluable source of knowledge about the author's ideas and aesthetics.

There is almost universal agreement among 20th-century Spanish critics that Darío is a towering figure in their literature. One of them declared that he was among the greatest masters of Castilian rhythms and the one who has most enriched the language among all its recent poets. Darío, who introduced the forms and meters of the French Symbolist school at the end of the 19th century, has been compared to GARCILASO DE LA VEGA of the 16th, who introduced the forms and meters of the Italian Renaissance to Spanish poetry. Virtually all Spanish poets who accepted the *modernista* identity acknowledge him as their guide and inspiration. While some members of the GENERATION OF '98 and their successors drifted away from Darío, many others remained committed to his approach to poetry throughout their careers. Moreover, despite his advocacy of "reform," Darío was aware of the deeper roots of Spanish culture and respectful of the very forms and traditions that he was reworking in his poetry. The strength and beauty of his writings comes not only from the "newness" of his style but from his consciousness of what had gone before. In sum Darío is the undisputed creator of the new wave in Spanish poetry that swept across the Americas after the publication of *Azul* and broke upon the shores of Spain, changing the whole course and character of Spanish-language poetry from the late 19th century onward. Those who clung to the sentimentalist school that had hitherto predominated used *modernista* as an epithet to dismiss the enthusiastic imitators of Darío who rose up in Spanish America. But they were unable to repulse the power of *modernismo* when it attained its ascendancy as the 20th century dawned in Spain. Reflecting a panoply of new perceptions variously celebrated by French poets as Symbolism, Parnassianism, or even decadentism, Spanish *modernismo* remains, nearly a century after Darío's death, a force powerful enough to change the character of Spanish-language poetry forever.

Dias, Bartolomeu (1450–1500)
Portuguese navigator

This seaman, who played a historic role in the long Portuguese search for a water route to Asia, took part in the series of voyages that gradually charted a course down the coast of West Africa. In 1481 he captained a ship that reached the Gold Coast (present-day Ghana), and by 1486 the Portuguese government was ready to push to new lengths in its search for proof that Africa's southern tip could be rounded, opening the way into the Indian Ocean. Dias was given command of a squadron charged with this mission. Early in 1488 Dias was able to verify that he had in fact turned the tip of the continent and was sailing northward. As his instructions were to confirm the possibility of entering the Indian Ocean rather than to sail on to India, he headed home. Reaching LISBON in December 1488 after exploring nearly 1,300 miles of previously unseen African coast, he concluded his report to the king with a description of the perilous waters near Africa's southern end by stating that he had given it the name of *Cabo Tormentoso* (Cape of Storms). King MANUEL I, not wishing to frighten off future travelers, renamed it *Cabo da Bõa Esperança* (Cape of Good Hope).

After a period of less dramatic activities Dias was assigned to accompany PEDRO ÁLVARES CABRAL on a major expedition to extend Portuguese trade in the Far East. In the course of the voyage, apparently driven by contrary winds across the Atlantic, the Portuguese reached South America and took possession of what would later be called BRAZIL. Sailing back toward their original objective they encountered fierce gales that sank four ships at the entrance to the Indian Ocean. One of them was Dias's. The Cape of Storms, which he had discovered and originally named, had claimed his life, and his passage to India remained incomplete.

Domingo, Plácido (1941–   )
Spanish singer

Born in MADRID, the son of well-known ZARZUELA (light opera) performers, Domingo moved with them to Mexico City at the age of eight and grew up in a musical ambience. He originally studied piano and conducting at Mexico's National Conservatory of Music but committed himself to an operatic career in his early 20s, appearing in Mexico, the United States (Dallas), and Israel. He made his debut with the Metropolitan Opera in New York City in 1968 and at Milan's La Scala in the following year. During the next few decades his combination of vocal and dramatic skills made him a successful performer throughout the opera world. His memoir, *My First Forty Years*, published in 1983, in retrospect seems merely a preliminary sketch for an increasingly active and complex career that showed no sign of ending as he entered his 60s. In addition to mastering more than 100 operatic roles and becoming acknowledged as the most popular and admired tenor of his time, Domingo also appeared in cinematic and television productions based on major operas, recorded both classical and general songs, and did concert tours with his countryman José Carreras and the Italian star Luciano Pavarotti as the internationally applauded Three Tenors. Domingo, a world traveler, was to be found at one moment aiding in the recovery of his old hometown, Mexico City, after the 1985 earthquake and at another presiding as artistic director over the 1992 exposition in SEVILLE. He has served as musical director of opera companies in BARCELONA, Washington, D.C., and Los Angeles, among other cities. Domingo has also returned to an early interest in conducting, periodically leading major symphony and opera house orchestras in various countries. With a durable and well-managed tenor voice and a remarkable combination of stamina and eagerness to test new dimensions, Domingo has moved beyond the familiar French and Italian repertoire to become fluent as a performer in Wagnerian and Russian operas. He has become, some have contended, the best-known Spaniard of his time.

Dominican Republic (República Dominicana)

When CHRISTOPHER COLUMBUS founded a settlement on the island that he named HISPANIOLA in 1493, he was establishing the first Spanish colony in the New World. It would be the first of a series of "lost colonies" on that island. The discoverer's men left behind on that occasion had disappeared by the time he returned on his second voyage (presumably slain in a dispute with Amerindians). Spain's next outpost on the island was established at the opposite end of Hispaniola, in what is now the Dominican Republic. Within a short time it languished to the point of near disappearance as the tide of conquest rolled on to the North and South American mainland. By the late 1600s Spain's presence in Hispaniola had become so enfeebled that it was neither staunchly defended nor greatly regretted when France, newly triumphant in the Caribbean, took control of the western end of the island. During the 18th century Saint-Domingue (present-day Haiti) prospered while the Spanish-ruled eastern two-thirds of the island continued to decline in economic and military vitality.

The era of the French Revolutionary and Napoleonic Wars (1789–1815) saw a series of convulsions in the region, with slave revolts, the proclamation of Haitian independence, and gradual loss of Spanish control in what had come to be known as Santo Domingo. An ephemeral Dominican Republic emerged when the Spanish colonists sought to follow the pattern established throughout the Spanish-American empire during the early 1820s. Haitian invaders quickly unified the island under their control, and it was not until 1844 that an independent Dominican Republic emerged in the area formerly ruled by Spain. Internal political rivalries and the threat of a renewed Haitian invasion impelled the Dominican leaders to make a startling offer in 1860 when they proposed to reenter the Spanish Empire. MADRID was now given the unprecedented opportunity of regaining control of a dependency that it had been forced to surrender decades earlier. The offer was not a completely attractive one, for the situation in Santo Domingo was far from prosperous, and the Haitian threat remained present. Furthermore the United States had proclaimed its opposition to new colonial enterprises in the Western Hemisphere. Spain nevertheless undertook to reestablish its presence in Santo Domingo and remained in possession until 1865. The end of the American Civil War (which also precipitated France's abandonment of its puppet regime in MEXICO) made Spain's position in Hispaniola untenable. Moreover the persistence of nationalism among Dominicans and the fact that Santo Domingo cost Spain more than it could earn from its presence there led to its final departure. Spain's perennially lost colony was now permanently lost. The Dominican Republic resumed its separate existence in 1865.

E

Eanes, António dos Santos Ramalho (1935–)

Portuguese military leader and statesman

Son of a middle-class family, Eanes graduated from the military academy in 1956 and pursued a military career almost exclusively spent in colonial outposts of Portugal's vast but steadily shrinking empire. He served in GOA from 1958 to 1960, during the years when that first outpost of Portugal's expansion was yielding to the demands of Indian nationalism. In 1962 he was reassigned to MACAO, yet another fragment of the Asian realm. Moving to Portuguese Africa he spent some months in 1964 and from 1966 to 1968 in MOZAMBIQUE, where new anticolonial forces were rising. Eanes went on to lead the fight against other rebels in PORTUGUESE GUINEA from 1968 to 1973 under the governorship of General SPINOLA. Eanes led another campaign in ANGOLA during 1973 and 1974, where the African rebels were supported by foreign intervention. During this period Eanes became convinced that Portugal's struggle against the tides of history was hopeless.

Profoundly disillusioned with the policies of the Caetano regime, Eanes joined the conspiracy of younger officers who brought down the government in April 1974 (see CARNATION REVOLUTION). As director of the nation's television system under the provisional government established by the revolutionary officers, Eanes played a major role in communicating the ideas and ideals of the new era. During the unstable period that saw abortive coups launched by both the Right and the Left, Eanes sustained a moderate commitment to democratic principles and was rewarded for his opposition to the radical revolt of November 1975 by promotion to the highest rank in the army and designation as chief of staff. Recognized as a champion of democratic socialism, Eanes became Portugal's first popularly elected president in 1976 and continued to hold that office until 1986, playing an essential part in the transition to full parliamentary stability during the postrevolutionary era.

East Timor (Portuguese Timor)

This Portuguese colony was originally part of the vast empire established in the Far East during the 16th century. Timor, one of the South Sunda Islands, became Portugal's last outpost when all the remaining territory of what is now Indonesia was lost to the Dutch. In 1618 it was agreed that Portugal would retain only the eastern half of the island. After various boundary adjustments in the late 19th century, Portuguese Timor consisted of an area of 5,763 square miles, whose chief product was coffee. When Portugal withdrew from this "overseas province" in 1975, a short-lived republic was invaded and annexed by Indonesia. After decades of struggle culminating in the United Nations's intervention East Timor established its independence in 1999 and began the work of reconstruction with aid from various countries, including Portugal.

Éboli, Ruy Gómez de Silva, prince of (1516–1573)
Portuguese nobleman in the Spanish service

The closest friend and adviser of PHILIP II of Spain, Gómez de Silva was born in Portugal of aristocratic lineage. He came to CASTILE in his youth with the entourage of the Portuguese princess Isabella when she arrived to marry CHARLES I (Holy Roman Emperor Charles V). The son born to this regal marriage, Prince Philip, was known to Gómez from birth. As page, companion, and mentor, Gómez was the virtual "big brother" of Philip and his inseparable associate, both before and after the latter's succession to the throne in 1556. The monarch's shrewd, prudent approach to the business of government reflected the temperament and policy inclinations of his faithful associate. To the extent that Philip knew much of the European scene outside Spain, it was largely the result of his early travels to England, Germany, and Italy accompanied by Gómez de Silva. Philip conferred numerous honors upon him, including membership in the Councils of State and War as well as titles of nobility of which the designation prince of Éboli (in the Kingdom of Naples) was customarily employed. Philip was, however, wise enough to maintain a creative tension in his royal court between the prince of Éboli and the duke of ALBA. The *"ebolistas"* were supporters of a more cosmopolitan and diplomatic approach to the affairs of Europe. The *"albistas"* were seen as aggressive and "prowar." Alba, in contrast to Éboli, possessed a militaristic spirit that advocated blood and fire to dispose of the country's enemies. Ultimately the *ebolistas* gained the upper hand, and Alba was, for the time being at least, sent away from court. Despite his occasional concern about the manipulative tactics of his best friend, Philip was profoundly grieved by Éboli's death, sitting by his bedside during the prince's last illness.

Much has been made by both historians and contemporary rumormongers, of the influence of the princess of Éboli (Ana Mendoza de la Cerda, 1540–79), who took the lead of the Éboli faction after her husband's death and was involved in the intrigues of ANTONIO PÉREZ. Whatever the relations, romantic or political, that existed among the Ébolis, Pérez, and even Philip himself, it was the death of Gómez de Silva that precipitated some of the most complex and destructive events in late 16th-century Spanish history.

Eça de Queirós, José Maria (José Maria Eça de Queiroz) (1845–1900)
Portuguese writer

Portugal's leading 20th-century novelist and, by some accounts, its greatest literary figure, Eça de Queirós was trained for the law but soon abandoned his practice in LISBON. He attracted attention with a steady stream of short stories, many of a surprising or even shocking character. Simultaneously he supported the social reform movement that advocated a new order in Portugal. Ironically he chose ultimately to pursue his social criticism from overseas, joining the consular service and residing successively in Cuba, Britain, and France. His novels, most of which were written abroad, depict the abuses and hypocrisies of Portuguese aristocratic and upper-middle-class society, particularly the influence of the Catholic Church. In *O crime do Padre Amaro* (*The Sin of Father Amaro*, 1875) a young priest begins an affair with a naive girl. The resulting pregnancy ends in abortion and her death. The character of Amaro, combined with what Eça de Queirós regarded as the pernicious rule of celibacy, destroys lives in a society that is obsessed with covering up "scandal" and preserving reputations. A bitterly satirical view of the absurdities of passion pursued according to "romantic" convention and its potentially disastrous results shaped his next novel, *O primo Basílio* (*Cousin Bazilio,* 1878). *Os Maias* (*The Maias,* 1885) is generally regarded as Eça de Queirós's finest novel. In it he presented, with unsparing detail, the degeneration of an elite family, whose intrigues and hypocrisy bring ruin upon their youngest generation. They are representative of the ruling class whose false values and corrupt practices have brought about the decay of contemporary Portuguese society. These novels established Eça de Queirós as the writer who introduced realism and naturalism to Portuguese literature and introduced his country to progressive currents of thought that had already affected the cultural life of other parts of Europe. He was almost certainly the best-known Portuguese of his day. Living in Paris from 1888 onward, however, Eça de Queirós, with his affluent lifestyle and fashionable connections,

seems to have lost faith (or, perhaps, interest) in the reform movement. His last novel, *A cidade e as serras* (*The City and the Mountains,* 1901) is more sentimental than critical. It is the work of a writer who is content to rhapsodize over the charm of Portuguese rural scenery and the easygoing ways of country living.

Echegaray y Eizaguirre, José
(1832–1916)
Spanish playwright

Successively an engineer, professor of mathematics, and cabinet minister, Echegaray turned his hand to playwriting (under a pseudonym) in 1874 with *El libro talonario* (The checkbook). During the next 30 years the name of this already highly regarded scientist and financier—who was chiefly responsible for the creation of the Banco de España—became known as that of Spain's most successful contemporary dramatist. In 1904 his increasing reputation abroad was confirmed by the Nobel Prize in literature, which he shared with the Frenchman Frédéric Mistral. Echegaray's plays were generally melodramatic, full of charged situations and vehement characters whose crises were frequently resolved by suicide. He was clearly indebted to the old romantic tradition but ventured into thesis drama from time to time, reflecting an awareness of Ibsen's work, for instance, without any of the Norwegian master's subtleties. Tremendously popular with Spanish audiences, he was denounced by rivals and critics as the author of contrived, crowd-pleasing work that he turned out with indecent haste. It was even rumored that his secretary fed him a series of "catchy" titles for which Echegaray then dictated plots and dialogue more or less on the spot. Inevitably his Nobel Prize provoked a storm of protest by those who insisted that Echegaray was a degrader of the playwriting art.

Although the plays of Echegaray have become a by-word for outmoded rhetoric and obvious posturing, his work is not entirely without merit. His *O locura o santi-dad* (*Folly or Saintliness,* 1877), for instance, offers a clever portrayal of the hypocrisy and greed of those who want to prevent an honest man from disposing of what they regard as their rightful inheritance by having him declared mad. *El gran Galeoto* (rendered in English as *The World and His Wife,* 1881)—which was well received in London as well as Madrid—deals, with considerable realism, with the effect of slander and character assassination upon honorable individuals. Neither of these plays, which are generally esteemed as Echegaray's best, are mere romantic entertainments, but they do not escape his tendency to melodramatic resolution of conflict. Echegaray, who drove out the work of MANUEL TAMAYO Y BAUS from Spanish playhouses, was himself fated to be ousted by that of JACINTO BENAVENTE. It is noteworthy that Benavente himself never joined in the widespread denunciation of his competitor, seeing in him, perhaps, a transitional figure worthy of respect if not imitation.

Ecuador

An Amerindian kingdom centered on the city of Quito (a name apparently once applied to the whole Peruvian region), this area in western South America was subordinated to the Inca Empire shortly before the arrival of conquistadores, who brought the whole Inca realm under Spanish colonial rule from 1534 onward. Ecuador, as the Spaniards christened this territory, was part of the Viceroyalty of PERU until 1718, when it was transferred to the Viceroyalty of New Granada. Along with the other components of that viceroyalty, Ecuador fought for and won its independence from Spain, with the decisive battle for Ecuadoreans taking place at Monte Pichincha in May 1822. Ecuador proclaimed its full sovereignty in 1830. Intermittent wars throughout the 19th and early 20th centuries have greatly reduced the country's original boundaries.

El Greco   See GRECO, EL.

El Salvador

As HERNÁN CORTÉS conquered the Aztec Empire and laid the foundation for the Viceroyalty of NEW SPAIN, his subordinate, PEDRO DE ALVARADO, occupied the territory named for the Savior (el Salvador) in 1523. Following the occupation of GUATEMALA in 1524, these two provinces were incorporated into the Captaincy General of Guatemala, which controlled all of Central America until the withdrawal of Spanish rule in 1821. During the next two years El Salvador adhered to the independent Mexican empire and then to the United Provinces of Central America until 1839. Although it became sovereign in the latter year, its leaders long continued to advocate various plans for Central American confederation.

Encina, Juan del (1469–1530)
Spanish playwright and composer
Often described as the "father" or "patriarch" of Spanish theater, Encina was the

recipient of both a classical education at SALAMANCA, and training in church music and choral presentations. He subsequently became a composer and choral conductor at the court of the duke of ALBA, whose patronage in later years would free him to pursue his literary activities. By the age of 30 he had already created well over 100 musical and dramatic pieces. After 1500 he spent extended periods in Rome where he became a confidant of Popes ALEXANDER VI and Leo X. Having received minor orders in his youth, he was now ordained and journeyed to the Holy Land where he celebrated his first Mass. Encina's residence in Italy also brought him into contact with the new dramatic techniques of the Renaissance, and his later work reflects a departure from the pastoral and religious themes that had originally inspired him. His later work contains a considerable number of secular themes, although many of the plays are filled with the gods and goddesses borrowed from classical tradition. In his last phase Encina makes use of an even wider range of innovations, including the introduction of dance as well as music to his plays.

Although Encina has been presented by some critics as the virtual creator of Spanish drama, he clearly shares the title with several other major Renaissance figures; nevertheless, he pioneered in the transition from the medieval emphasis on religious subjects to at least a partial acceptance of "profane" themes and characters. Furthermore, while his *églogas* (pastoral poems modeled on Virgil's eclogues) are clearly derived from established formulas, his free and humorous use of the peasant dialect known as *sayagués* for the simple-minded dialogues of shepherds would evolve into a regular feature of Span-

ish comedy in subsequent generations. Some commentators have even suggested that the use of dance to accompany musical "numbers" by this former chorister represents the origins of the Spanish musical comedy known as ZARZUELA. Among the notable works of Encina are *Égloga de Plácida y Victoriano* (1513), *Égloga de Cristino y Febea,* and *Auto del repelón.*

encomienda

A system of allocation of land and labor made by the Spanish Crown from the earliest period of settlement in the New World. Originally introduced in HISPANIOLA (present-day Haiti and DOMINICAN REPUBLIC), it was later extended to the entire colonial area. Spaniards favored by the authorities or deserving of rewards were assigned jurisdiction over the life and labor of indigenous peoples living within a certain district. The holder of the *encomienda,* the *encomendero,* would be entitled to "tribute" from the Indian population, to be paid in goods or services. In practical terms this arrangement led to a system of compulsory labor by Indians who became vassals of a particular *encomendero* or even their virtual slaves. The related practice of *repartimiento,* a form of distribution of Indian tribute obligations, enabled certain Spaniards to become masters of plantations and mines worked by hundreds of compulsory laborers. Originating in similar grants made in Spain during the conquest of the Muslim population, these institutions were balanced by the obligation of each *encomendero* to safeguard the health and material well-being of the subjects entrusted to him under his *encomienda* and to see that they received religious instruction.

Designed as a system for managing the economic development of the New World as well as the transformation of the indigenous population into orderly Christian subjects of the Spanish Crown, the *encomienda* plan all too often degenerated into a system of forced labor that was scarcely distinguishable from slavery. Despite the complaints of such clergymen as BARTOLOMÉ DE LAS CASAS and the protective decrees that they persuaded the Crown to issue during the first 50 years of the conquest in America, greed and self-interest among the colonists persistently thwarted salutary efforts. Negative by-products of efforts to reform or abolish the *encomienda* system included the introduction of African slavery into the New World and the perpetuation of a pattern of debt peonage that survived in Spanish America for centuries.

Enrique IV   See HENRY IV.

environmental issues in Spain and Portugal

The Iberian Peninsula was famed in ancient times for its harsh, sun-baked landscape, and this image was not much altered during the Middle Ages when Europeans dwelling north of the Pyrenees thought of their continent's southwestern corner as an isolated war zone in a centuries-long struggle between Christendom and Islam. Even those who possessed a better-informed awareness of the gardens of ANDALUSIA and the forests of northern Portugal were also conscious of the arid central plateau and the lack of good harbors along most of the coastline. Driven as much by hard conditions at home as by the lure of foreign lands,

Castilians and Portuguese of the Golden Age launched a global conquest that created vast empires and dazzling fortunes. With the collapse of their colonial achievements the reality of Iberian poverty was starkly presented at the beginning of the 20th century. Spain could sustain no more than a modest and austere existence, while Portugal was derided as the "poorhouse" of western Europe.

These perceptions were not merely the grumblings of disillusioned intellectuals or the fruit of foreign prejudice. Nature had, in fact, given the Iberian Peninsula a poverty of resources. Large stretches of infertile land, insufficient internal waterways to fill the needs of irrigation and transportation, and a paucity of fauna or even of flora were paralleled by limited mineral resources, particularly of the iron, coal, and oil essential for industrial development. During the FRANCO and SALAZAR dictatorships, denial of these realities continued to be accompanied by evocations of past glories that became ever more fantastical.

The establishment of democratic governments and market economies after 1975 in both Spain and Portugal compelled both nations to look at their economic situation with a clear eye. Subsidies from the European Union and solicitation of foreign investment could only be counted upon up to a certain point. For both countries, but especially Portugal, the preferred solution seemed to be the promotion of tourism. The adoption of this tactic has, however, led to severe environmental damage in many areas. Moreover neither government has been willing to deal seriously or consistently with fundamental questions including drying-up of water resources, extinction of native species, and massive pollution on land and coasts. A growing environmental movement in Spain and Portugal has repeatedly called for reform. Environmentalists have pointed to such episodes as inadequate responses to oil spills that have ruined fishing zones and the destruction of Spain's Doñana nature preserve and Portugal's Malcata wildlife refuge. They complain that sluggish and irresponsible bureaucracy makes promises but fails to fulfill them and that the institutions of the democratic state seem little better at doing the needed work than those of the dictatorships. Whatever the truth about the much-debated phenomenon of global warming, the climatic extremes of 2005 struck Spain and Portugal with undeniable impact. Drought overwhelmed much of the peninsula. Lakes were reduced to dust bowls, and crops perished. Cork, olives, grapes, and other agricultural mainstays of Spain's and Portugal's survival were profoundly, if not permanently, ruined. Faced with what seemed to be the ultimate intersection of natural disaster and human-made pollution, Spain and Portugal have been forced to confront the catastrophic implications of putting off fundamental decisions.

Equatorial Guinea   See SPANISH GUINEA.

Escorial, El (Royal Monastery of San Lorenzo de El Escorial)

Residence of the kings of Spain since 1584, this massive structure is located some 30 miles west of MADRID in the foothills of the Guadarrama mountain range. It owes its creation to PHILIP II who intended it as a final resting place for his father, CHARLES I, and subsequent monarchs, as well as a suitably grand seat for the dominant rulers of Europe. Wishing to honor San Lorenzo (St. Lawrence), on whose feast day—August 10, 1557—Spanish forces had won a decisive victory over the French at the Battle of St. Quentin, in Flanders, Philip conceived the idea of combining a great church and monastery that would visibly link the power of church and state in the same structure. A committee to explore possible locations near the newly chosen capital, Madrid, recommended a site with a grand prospect to the south and east and a splendid mountain background to the north and west. The tiny village near the site took its name, *Escorial*, from the iron-smelting operation that had formerly been carried on there. Begun in 1563, with a plan drawn up by one Juan Bautista de Toledo, the structure, with its huge dome and its hundreds of rooms, courtyards, and fountains, was laid out to resemble the grid upon which St. Lawrence had supposedly been martyred by pagan Romans. The monastery and palace of San Lorenzo de El Escorial was completed under the direction of Juan de Herrera more than 20 years after its commencement. The dimensions of the nine-towered granite building led visitors to call it everything from "the eighth wonder of the world" to a "gloomy prison-like colossus." In addition to the modest rooms occupied by Philip II from which he could gaze down into the splendid chapel with its daily round of religious services, later monarchs fitted out a whole complex of lavish apartments. Over the centuries El Escorial became the repository of a great collection of art and one of the world's most magnificent libraries. In keeping with the wishes of Charles I, he and nearly all of his successors have been buried in the royal pantheon that lies beneath the central chapel, flanked by the remains of their consorts and children.

Española   See HISPANIOLA.

Espartero, Baldomero (duque de la Victoria, conde de Luchana) (1792–1879)
Spanish soldier and statesman

Born into a humble family whose great ambition was for him to enter the priesthood, Espartero fought as a young volunteer against the French invaders supporting JOSEPH I. He subsequently secured a commission in the regular army and served in Spanish America until the final collapse of the royal forces there. Returning to Spain as a colonel, Espartero, like all who had fought the South American rebels, was under something of a cloud during the 1820s. On the death of FERDINAND VII in 1833 he supported the succession of ISABELLA II. Rising steadily in rank and command responsibility, Espartero became the most successful and admired adversary of the Carlist forces and ultimately negotiated the 1839 settlement that ended the prolonged civil conflict. Already an elected member of the Cortes, (see CORTES), he became involved in politics on the left wing of Liberalism, and this in turn led to his opposition to the regent, Queen MARIA CHRISTINA. After her withdrawal from Spain Espartero, who had been created *duque de la Victoria* (duke of victory) for his triumph over the Carlists, served as regent until 1843.

As virtual military dictator, Espartero dealt harshly with dissent and repressed several rebellions with such ruthlessness that public opinion turned against him and he was forced out of office in 1843, spending the next five years in Britain. He then returned to Spain but lived quietly until 1854 when Isabella II called upon him to resist the revolt of General LEOPOLDO O'DONNELL.

Espartero achieved a temporary compromise with O'Donnell, who served as minister of war under his premiership until 1856. Once again out of power Espartero withdrew into the role of elder statesman. After the downfall and banishment of Isabella II in 1868 he was included, along with several foreign princes, among those proposed as new king of Spain. Seeking to promote stability he successively supported the Italian AMADEO I, the short-lived republic that followed him, and the Bourbon restoration of 1875 that brought Isabella's son ALFONSO XII to the throne.

In the breadth and variety of his military experience, as well as his triumph over the Carlists, Espartero was undoubtedly the most notable Spanish soldier of his era. As a political leader he lacked the suavity that was demanded by complex negotiations. Fundamentally a man of the people who sympathized with radical reforms, he tended to lose patience when in office, employing strong methods that alienated potential supporters. In the last decades of his life he emerged as a more balanced actor on the national stage, earning respect as a disinterested and patriotic guardian of Spain's well-being.

Espronceda, José de (1808–1842)
Spanish poet

The epitome of early 19th-century romanticism, Espronceda has long been called "the Spanish Byron." The melodramatic details of his life support this image. Born on the road down which his father and mother and thousands of others were fleeing from Napoléon Bonaparte's advancing army during the PENINSULAR WAR, Espronceda grew up strongly motivated by both patriotic and revolutionary impulses. Although the product of a respectable military family, he early enlisted in radical movements and, before he was 20, was obliged to flee to Portugal. It is said that as he crossed the frontier he took his few remaining Spanish coins from his pocket and hurled them into the river declaring that he could not enter such a fine city as LISBON with only a few pennies. He subsequently made his way to Britain, later lived in France (where he took part in the revolution of 1830), and became a founding member of the Spanish republican movement. In the course of his wanderings he formed an ardent but conflicted relationship with the equally impulsive Teresa Mancha (to whom he dedicated at least one of his poetic works) and raged against all of the pillars of the Spanish establishment including the church. Despite his roving and controversy-filled life Espronceda was a prolific poet and the author of several plays and a novel of epic length. Toward the end of his life, having secured a diplomatic appointment and a parliamentary seat in a more stable Spain, he succumbed to a minor throat infection.

Espronceda's longer works are *El diablo mundo* (The devil world), which includes his enduringly popular "Canto a Teresa" (Song to Teresa) and *El estudiante de Salamanca* (The student of Salamanca), which uses the Don Juan theme. Both are from the last two years of his life. Espronceda is best remembered, however, for shorter poems about groups marginalized by society, which include "La canción del pirata" (The pirate's song), "El verdugo" (The executioner), "El mendigo" (The beggar), and "El reo de muerte" (Death's culprit).

Extremadura

This region of Spain, consisting of the provinces of Badajoz and Cáceres, lies along the Portuguese border, adjacent to that country's province of the same name (but spelled *Estremadura*). Much of Extremadura's 16,000 square miles constitutes a flat and unproductive terrain with only limited crops produced in the areas watered by the Tagus and Guadiana Rivers. Recaptured from Moorish conquerors in the late 12th and early 13th centuries, the region served chiefly as grazing land for Castilian sheep. Its proverbial poverty drove many inhabitants to migrate, and many of the conquistadores of the Americas (including CORTÉS and PIZARRO) abandoned their homes in this region to seek fortune abroad. Long a battleground in the wars between Spain and Portugal, Extremadura was fought over in the PENINSULAR WAR and was rapidly conquered by the Nationalists in the SPANISH CIVIL WAR. In the late 20th century a number of initiatives were launched to promote fertility and productivity in this region.

F

Falange Española

Founded in 1933 by José Antonio Primo de Rivera, this organization became the predominant movement within the Nationalist forces that triumphed in the SPANISH CIVIL WAR of 1936–39. Primo de Rivera was a 30-

Poster of the Falange Española. It reads, "In Spain it is dawning: Arise, Spain." *(Library of Congress)*

year-old lawyer, possessing considerable personal charm and political fluency (if not profound originality of thought). As the son of General Miguel PRIMO DE RIVERA, dictator of Spain from 1923 to 1930, he was shaped in his values and political attitudes by an exalted image of his father, whose mission of "saving" Spain from the extremes of "degenerate liberalism" was the younger man's prime inspiration. He preached a doctrine of national unity, preservation of traditional values, loyalty to the Catholicism that had shaped Spanish history, and ultimately to the restoration of the monarchy that had been replaced by the 1931 proclamation of the Second Republic. From the founding of his party Primo de Rivera, who avowed himself a fascist, was rivaled by a number of other activists (mostly of middle-class bureaucratic and academic background) who had come under Italian and German fascist influences as far back as 1928. Their emphasis on socioeconomic syndicalism whose vertical structure repudiated marxist class-conflict ideology was fused with the more specifically Spanish concepts of Primo de Rivera in an amalgamation of parties that took place early in 1934. The result was the Falange Española de las Juntas de Ofensiva Nacional-Sindicalista. From the Juntas of National-Syndicalist Offensive, or JONS, the Falange acquired its emblem of the yoke and arrows, its black and red flag, its party uniform (featuring blue shirts), and a semi-military organization. Despite its grandiose political rhetoric the movement was primarily designed for direct confrontation with the Socialists, assorted anarchists, and other leftists parties that dominated the republic during the period 1934–36. Street battles involving hundreds of militants became common in the major cities. The coalition government feared a full-scale insurrection. In their attempts to prevent such a development they imprisoned Primo de Rivera and other Falangists in early 1936. This action merely guaranteed the support of the party for the army revolt launched in July of that year.

During the Spanish civil war, which lasted until early 1939, the emergence of General FRANCISCO FRANCO as the political as well as military leader of the Nationalist "crusade" at first fulfilled Falangist ambitions but ultimately guaranteed the party's virtual extinction. Just as he disposed of all of his rivals within the army high command during the course of the war, Franco repressed or consolidated the various right-wing groups that were his natural allies in the revolt against the republic. The Carlists were forced to merge with the Falange, which added their red beret to its party regalia. Monarchists, Catholic activists, and other factions were likewise absorbed by the organization. The party created by Primo de Rivera (who was executed by the republic in 1936) now found itself firmly under the dominance of Franco: He transformed it into the single approved political organization of Spain after his victory, under the new name of Falange Española Tradicionalista y de las Juntas de Ofensiva Nacional-Sindicalista (usually abbreviated as FET y de las JONS).

He sidelined most of the old Falangist leaders and adroitly maintained a jealous competition between the "National Party" and the army. This balance of power within the Franco regime, which controlled Spain from 1939 till El Caudillo's death in 1975, had the effect of concentrating all real power in the hands of the dictator. Long before his death, however, the Falange was reduced to a mere shadow of its former self, totally dependent on Franco for any prestige or nominal influence that it still possessed. In the years that followed the restoration of democracy, several splinter groups sought to preserve their versions of the Falange but commanded only minimal support.

In its theoretical foundations laid down by Primo de Rivera and his early colleagues the Falange was clearly a part of the fascist wave that spread across much of Europe as a reaction to marxism and other perceived dangers to "European traditional civilization." Spanish fascism was distinctive, however, not only in its obvious lack of anti-Semitism but also in a greater commitment to an inward-looking nationalism. Its preoccupation with distinctively Spanish values led it to emphasize the importance of Catholicism to a unique degree, and its ambiguous relationship to monarchism caused many problems. Like the army, the Falange had an obsessive hostility to separatism but was never able to resolve the fundamental contradictions that set the Falangist "upstarts" at odds with the military leaders' claim to be the natural defenders of the Spanish state.

Falcón, Lidia (1935–)
Spanish writer and political activist
The leading figure in modern Spanish feminism, Falcón was the daughter of a radical

journalist, and she combined journalism with the practice of law. She was imprisoned twice during the Franco era, once for distributing antigovernment pamphlets and the second time on a false charge of aiding Basque terrorist bombers. These experiences led her to write a series of exposés about the shocking conditions in women's prisons. Her early career as a lawyer specializing in women's and family issues generated a series of books on feminist issues between 1969 and 1975.

Far from being satisfied with the end of the Franco oppression, she redoubled her activities with a feminist assault on the patriarchal institutions that survived the transition to political democracy. Her writings of this period include half a dozen books and major articles on the role and rights of women in Spain.

A poet, playwright, and novelist, as well as lawyer, politician, and international champion of women's issues, Falcón summed up her public life in *Memorias políticas* (Political memoirs) *(1959–1999)* an autobiographical narrative in which she recalls her early struggle against censorship, the persecution and tragic exile of her comrades, and her own imprisonment and then moves on to the still-flawed environment of Spain today, a country in which the repressive power of elites and the irrelevant trappings of monarchy still stir the indignation of this unreconstructed revolutionary.

Falla, Manuel de (1876–1946)
Spanish composer
An Andalusian pianist, Falla studied composition under Felipe Pedrell, an advocate for a distinctive Spanish music based on national themes, who also exerted his influ-

ence on another pupil, ENRIQUE GRANADOS. In Paris, between 1907 and 1914, Falla came under the additional influence of Claude Debussy and Maurice Ravel whose "impressionistic" approach he adapted to his own ideas. What resulted was a stream of composition that did not re-create Spanish traditional themes but rather created original work inspired by them. Among his most notable achievements were the composition for piano and orchestra *Noches en los jardines de España* (*Nights in the Gardens of Spain*, 1909–15), the opera *La vida breve* (The brief life, 1914), the folk songs *Siete canciones populares* ("Seven popular songs," 1914), and the ballets *El amor brujo* (*Love, the Magician*, 1915) and *El sombrero de tres picos* (*The Three-Cornered Hat*, 1919). In addition, he composed a concerto for harpsichord, as well as chamber music. By the 1930s he was acknowledged as the leading Spanish composer and enjoyed international recognition. He left Spain at the end of the SPANISH CIVIL WAR and spent the rest of his life in Argentina. His principal work in these last years was *Atlántida* (Atlantis). This massive composition was left unfinished at his death but was completed by others and presented in Madrid in 1961.

Farnese, Alessandro (1545–1592)
Spanish general
As the son of MARGARET, DUCHESS OF PARMA (daughter of CHARLES I), Farnese was a nephew of PHILIP II and of JOHN OF AUSTRIA (Don Juan de Austria). Educated in Spain and a combatant at LEPANTO in 1571, Farnese was thoroughly identified with that country's grand designs. He was particularly attached to Don Juan de Austria under whom he had served at Lepanto and accom-

panied him to the Netherlands. By the time of his uncle's death in 1578, Farnese, despite his youth, had demonstrated his military genius in a number of independent commands and was designated as the new governor general of the troubled region. He succeeded his father as duke of Parma in 1586 but never returned to Italy. Having demonstrated his diplomatic and political skills by splitting the southern Netherlands from their original support of the Dutch-speaking Protestants of the north (1579), Farnese carried on a series of brilliant campaigns against the forces of the Dutch Republic. Philip II fully appreciated his kinsman's skills but never entirely trusted him, an attitude that derived more from the monarch's suspicious nature than from any conduct by his subordinate. Farnese frankly and wisely opposed several of Philip's imprudent projects but loyally did his best to carry them out. In 1588 he was prepared to launch his troops in an invasion of England during the ARMADA campaign. In 1590–91 he led his troops into France to disrupt Henri de Bourbon's siege of Paris and save Rouen, although he considered Philip's stripping of the Netherlands for this purpose to be militarily reckless. Returning to repair the damage caused by the Dutch during his excursion into France, Farnese was fatally wounded in 1592.

Farnese was universally acknowledged as one of the greatest generals of his era. His military brilliance was matched by his skill in the management of people and politics. It was Spain's misfortune that this adopted son was denied the fulfillment of his abilities by a sovereign who alternated paranoid timidity in practical matters with reckless grandiosity in the creation of international policy.

Fátima

This village in central Portugal, named after a Moorish princess, has become one of the most notable pilgrimage sites in Catholic Europe since a series of apparitions reportedly occurred there in 1917. Three peasant children stated that a "lady," understood to be the Blessed Virgin Mary, appeared to them over a period of months asking that a shrine be erected and prayers offered and promising revelations about the future of the world. When, in October 1917, a large gathering of local people declared that they had witnessed inexplicable movements of the Sun, church authorities began a slow, cautious investigation of these manifestations, culminating in a declaration that a true divine apparition had taken place. In 1927 construction began on a basilica at the site (not completed until 1953), and Fátima became an increasingly important gathering place for pilgrims seeking miracles. The "revelations" by the Virgin were long kept secret by the church. The first two are believed to relate to the end of World War I and the outbreak of World War II, and the fall of communism, respectively. The third, prophesying the assassination attempt directed against Pope John Paul II in 1981, was finally announced in 2000 during a beatification ceremony for the children who had received these "revelations" in 1917.

Federmann, Nikolaus (1501–1542)
German explorer in the Spanish service
Born in Ulm, Germany, Federmann was employed by the Augsburg banking house of Welser, which had made large loans to CHARLES I of Spain (Holy Roman Emperor Charles V), in compensation received vast land grants in what is now VENEZUELA, and

dispatched German agents to survey its property. Federmann joined this contingent in 1529 and was appointed captain of a company of Spanish soldiers sent out on reconnaissance. He quickly demonstrated his qualities of audacity and endurance as he confronted vast stretches of unknown territory with great determination. Clearly, however, his energy was as much fueled by personal ambition as by a sense of duty. After this initial probe into the wilderness he was involved in several disputes with superiors and was denied a free hand for some time thereafter. Nevertheless, his usefulness could not be denied, and he was put in charge of a large party of exploration, including some 300 soldiers as well as native auxiliaries, that set out from the Welser base at Coro, on the Caribbean shore, in 1537. They traveled for nearly 1,000 miles over wide plains, regions of swampy terrain, and ultimately into the Andes. In a remarkable instance of chance encounter three Spanish expeditions, coming from different bases and obedient to different commanders, arrived at the same spot in this great wilderness and put in their rival claims to the surrounding territory in 1539. Federmann negotiated a cash compensation from GONZALO JIMÉNEZ DE QUESADA, but their arrangement was disrupted by the sudden appearance of a force under SEBASTIÁN DE BELALCÁZAR, who demanded to be admitted to their compact. The three leaders at length agreed to refer their issues to the Crown, and on returning to the nearest Spanish port they embarked for Europe. Federmann, the junior member of the triumvirate, lost out to the arguments of the other two. Feeling that the Welser bank had failed to give him due support, he filed charges before Spanish magistrates accusing his employer of massive theft from the share of American treasure that was due to the king-emperor. Losing this case as well, he was charged with numerous offenses against higher authority and confined in a prison at VALLADOLID, where he died while awaiting trial.

Amid the Spanish and Portuguese explorers of the New World (as well as the occasional Italian), the German presence initiated by the Welser claims in Venezuela stands out. And among these transplanted Teutons, Federmann deserves special note for his reckless, tireless pursuit of whatever version of El Dorado he could obtain. A memoir attributed to him reveals a striking mixture of naïveté and fascinated curiosity about the strange sites and peoples he encountered on his marches across the plains, jungles, and mountains of Venezuela, COLOMBIA, and PERU. He was tough, resourceful, and seemingly inexhaustible in his energy but at the end proved an odd man out in the struggle to win fame and fortune in the Americas.

Feijoo, Benito Jerónimo (1676–1764)
Spanish essayist

A Benedictine who spent most of his long life as a professor at the University of Oviedo, Feijoo was an incongruous figure in the narrow-minded setting of his time and place. Proudly proclaiming himself a *"ciudadano libre de la republica de las letras"* (free citizen of the republic of letters), he wrote on a wide variety of subjects. Encyclopedic in his interests and opinions, he was less an expert in any one of the natural sciences and human institutions that he discussed than a champion of free investigation and debate. He has been called "the Spanish Voltaire," and it was necessary for

King FERDINAND VI to protect him specifically from interference by ecclesiastical authorities. Feijoo was not, however, an enemy of the church or a heretical thinker. He was rather an advocate of progress who derided the superstition, bigotry, and censorship that afflicted 18th-century Spain. In this sense, he was not only a humanist with a universal perspective but also a patriotic Spaniard who shared with a small band of his compatriots the mission of bringing the Enlightenment across the Pyrenees. Among the most important writings of Feijoo are *Teatro crítico universal* (Critical universal theater), a collective title for eight volumes of essays written between 1726 and 1739, and *Cartas eruditas y curiosas* (Letters on learned and curious subjects), five volumes written between 1742 and 1760.

Felipe I   See PHILIP I.

Felipe II   See PHILIP II.

Felipe III   See PHILIP III.

Felipe IV   See PHILIP IV.

Felipe V   See PHILIP V.

Ferdinand V (Fernando V)
(1452–1516)
king of Aragon and first king of a united Spain

Son of John (Juan) II of Aragon, Ferdinand was betrothed to the heiress of Castile in pursuit of his father's plan to unite the kingdoms. After marrying the infanta Isabel in 1469, and more aggressively after she became Queen ISABELLA I of Castile in 1474, he pursued a policy of strengthening her power and eliminating rivals for control of her realm. When Ferdinand became king of Aragon in 1479 (under the designation Ferdinand II), the project of unification began in earnest. He was obliged to deal with recalcitrant nobles, a decentralized government, lawlessness bred by years of civil strife, and the need to create an effective military, civil, and fiscal structure. Furthermore, as king consort of Castile, he was limited by the need to work in collaboration with his wife, who was determined to preserve her own personal sovereign status in Castile. Nevertheless, a steady advance in strengthening the power of government was pursued during the last two decades of the 15th century.

The title *"los Reyes Católicos"* bestowed by the pope in 1494 recognized not only Ferdinand and Isabella's commitment to the faith but also their ability to work together for common goals. Ferdinand was, however, not as interested in some of Isabella's projects as in others. His use of the SPANISH INQUISITION (established as an instrument of state power in 1483), for instance, was more motivated by a desire for control of dissidents than by his wife's zeal for religious purity. Although he joined with her in waging war on GRANADA, the last Muslim stronghold in Spain (which she annexed in 1492), he was less preoccupied with the expulsion of Jews and Muslims that began soon after. Similarly the voyages of CHRISTOPHER COLUMBUS and the subsequent settlement of the New World were reserved to Castilian management, without much interference from Aragon.

Christopher Columbus addressing Ferdinand V and Isabella I at court *(Library of Congress)*

Having achieved the stabilization of Castile and the enhancement of his power that the effective unification of Spain brought, Ferdinand devoted the latter part of his reign to European politics, displaying both a readiness to make war and a skill in diplomacy that brought Spain to the forefront of the new state system. The ITALIAN WARS (1494–1559), despite a seemingly endless process of shifting alliances, truces, and changing leaders, represent Ferdinand's consistent recognition that the struggle for mastery in Europe would be settled by the ultimate triumph of either Spain or France. Throughout his reign he used dynastic marriages as a means of linking his family with the Aus-trian Habsburgs, the English Tudors, and lesser royal houses. He progressively tightened his grip on the Italian states, postponed any confrontation with the Turks, and displayed an amazing dexterity in the use or abuse of treaties. Ferdinand clearly adhered to the principle that among rulers there were no permanent friends or permanent enemies, merely permanent interests.

After Isabella's death in 1504 Ferdinand thwarted an attempt by his son-in-law, Philip of Habsburg (PHILIP I of Castile) to control the larger of the two Spanish kingdoms. After Philip's death in 1506 Ferdinand used the mental instability of his daughter, JOANNA, to maintain his own de facto control of Castile. His recognition of the crucial importance of that kingdom was emphasized by his conciliatory gestures, such as the transfer of NAVARRE (conquered in 1512) to Castilian control. Even to the last, however, Ferdinand's personal love of power led him to manipulate the question of succession. His marriage to the French king's niece, Germaine de Foix, shortly after his first wife's death, and his expectation of having a new family revealed his addiction to political gamesmanship. Unfortunately for his plans, Germaine gave him no surviving children. His death early in 1516 put an end to his schemes and left the way open for his and Isabella's grandson CHARLES I to inherit the whole of Ferdinand's dominions.

More than any other Renaissance statesman Ferdinand V embodies the political skills and amoral cunning of Machiavelli's Prince. His perennial intrigues, his readiness to continue diplomacy by means of war, and his mixture of egotism and realism make him one of the most sinister, yet fascinating rulers of the era. Above all he was the founder of modern Spain and Spain's empire, the greatest that the world had ever seen. As his descendant PHILIP II said, "We owe it all to him."

Ferdinand VI (Fernando VI)
(1713–1759)

king of Spain

Son of PHILIP V, he succeeded to the throne upon his father's death in 1746. His reign was notable for the beginning of the "Bourbon Reforms," which had been anticipated for nearly half a century but never effectively pursued by his predecessor. Ferdinand discontinued the preoccupation with European high politics that had character-

ized the first half of the century and initiated programs of economic development. He also began the reevaluation of Spain's seaborne empire as a source of prosperity rather than mere prestige. While not a man of great intellectual gifts, Ferdinand chose well among potential advisers, preferring men with modern ideas and practical abilities to those who merely boasted aristocratic pedigrees. He also became a patron of the arts, encouraging a cultural revival in Spain. In this latter concern he had the strong collaboration of his consort, the Portuguese-born Queen Bárbara, who was particularly interested in music and brought many notable musicians and performers to the royal court.

Unfortunately for the success (and even the duration) of his reign, both Ferdinand and Bárbara were of a sickly constitution and a melancholy temperament so that their great affection for one another, instead of having a positive effect, reinforced a mutual tendency to hypochondria. When his wife died the king fell into a mood of profound gloom that soon degenerated into madness and ended in death within a year of the queen's passing. As the couple had no children, the succession went to Ferdinand's half brother, the king of Naples, who became CHARLES III and pursued many of the initiatives that dated from the abortive reign of Ferdinand VI.

Ferdinand VII (Fernando VII)
(1784–1833)

king of Spain

The ninth but eldest surviving son of CHARLES IV, Ferdinand became the focal point of opposition to the pro-French policy of his father and the opportunistic chief minister MANUEL DE GODOY. Having organized a band of supporters, he staged a coup d'état in 1808 and was proclaimed Ferdinand VII. Shortly thereafter Emperor Napoléon I summoned the entire Spanish royal family to a meeting at Bayonne that was supposed to resolve all their differences. Instead the French ruler proclaimed the termination of the BOURBON dynasty and imposed his brother Joseph Bonaparte as King JOSEPH I of Spain. During the following six years Ferdinand, his brother Charles, and members of their entourage were confined in France, separate from the former king and queen.

Following the downfall of the Bonapartes and the end of the Napoleonic Wars,

King Ferdinand VII *(Library of Congress)*

Ferdinand VII returned to Spain and was widely welcomed as the country's rightful monarch. However, during his absence loyal subjects had acted largely on their own initiative to defend and liberate their country. Furthermore a governing committee that retained control in the south had convened a legislature, the Cortes (see *CORTES*) that gave Spain its first written constitution in 1812. This Constitution of Cádiz created a limited monarchy and established "liberal" institutions that would be the subject of debate for generations to come. Ferdinand, who wished to rule as an absolute monarch, rejected these developments. In addition to reestablishing the SPANISH INQUISITION, which had been abolished during his absence, he launched a persecution of reformers of all persuasions. Between 1815 and 1820 at least one major conspiracy was uncovered and crushed each year, with the conspirators imprisoned or executed.

By 1820 independence movements that had emerged in the Spanish-American colonies during Ferdinand's absence had developed into full-scale revolts, and although the king seemed to pay more attention to his domestic enemies than to his rebellious subjects abroad, he did dispatch several military expeditions to the Americas. It was among troops destined to depart for the colonies that a mutiny broke out and spread across the country in that year. Overwhelmed by the forces of liberalism within both military and civilian sectors, Ferdinand preserved his crown by making profound apologies for past mistakes and passionate promises to be a leader of a new, more humane Spanish society. After three years of liberal government Spain's position amid the prevailing counter-revolutionary conservatism of European regimes provoked an invasion sponsored by the reactionary powers grouped in the Holy Alliance and carried out by the restored Bourbon dynasty of France. The invading army (the "One Hundred Thousand Sons of St. Louis") soon overcame the Spanish forces and restored Ferdinand to absolute authority. He took harsh and vengeful reprisals against those who had humiliated him between 1820 and 1823.

The final 10 years of Ferdinand VII's reign were dominated by disputes over the question of the royal succession. Childless after several marriages, Ferdinand had, by his fourth wife, Maria Christina of Naples, two daughters. This circumstance led him to insist on the right of female succession to the throne. There were contradictory precedents and laws involved, as well as objections raised by the king's brother, Charles, who argued that as the nearest male relative he had a preemptive right to succeed Ferdinand. With conservative interests, including the church, supporting the "traditionalist" position, the right of female succession inevitably drew the support of the reviving liberal forces. Ironically, in his dying months Ferdinand was in alliance with his old enemies to assure that his elder daughter would be recognized as sovereign. Upon his death the three-year-old princess was proclaimed Queen ISABELLA II, and Spain moved rapidly toward civil war.

Ferdinand VII, largely an unknown quantity when he returned from his exile in France in 1814, had become a symbol of national identity and patriotic resistance during the struggle against the French. He soon revealed himself as a committed reactionary. Although he was capable of personal affability that won him significant support among the common people, his absolutist conception of monarchy antago-nized all the forces of reform that had built up over the previous decades. He was forced to accommodate himself to the liberals during the 1820–23 period, but his display of hypocrisy and cruelty once he was free to follow his own inclinations again guaranteed him the hatred of a growing proportion of his people. Moreover his obsession with enforcing his will in Spain diverted his attention from the situation in the Americas and made the collapse of the transatlantic empire a certainty. This colonial catastrophe and the dynastic-political war that he brought upon his country make his reign one of the most tragic in Spanish history.

Fernandes, Vasco (c. 1475–1542)
Portuguese painter
Perhaps the principal artist produced by Portugal during the reign of MANUEL I, Fernandes is often referred to as "Grão Vasco" (Great Vasco). His early work (1506–11) was much influenced, like that of other Portuguese artists, by the early Flemish masters. Lucas van Leyden, whose prints had found their way to Portugal by the 1520s made a particularly strong impression on him. Fernandes's greatest achievements belong to the period of 1535 to 1541, when he integrated a wider range of Renaissance awareness and inspirations in producing the paintings that adorn the cathedral at Viseu.

Fernández de Córdoba, Gonzalo (1453–1515)
Spanish soldier
Known even in his lifetime as el Gran Capitán (the Great Captain), this commander

rose steadily in the esteem of FERDINAND V and ISABELLA I as he took part in the wars with Portugal and the Moors that surrounded their ascent to the mastery of Spain. By the time the French invasion of Italy in 1494 precipitated what would become a decades-long struggle for control of that peninsula, Fernández de Córdoba had become the obvious choice to lead the Spanish response to France (see ITALIAN WARS). Positioning himself in the Kingdom of Naples as the rescuer of Ferdinand's kinsmen there, Córdoba fought a series of actions that completely dislocated the plans of the enemy. The death of Charles VIII in 1498 led to a temporary withdrawal of French forces from Italy and a treaty of friendship with Spain. Córdoba, back in CASTILE, busied himself with raising and training new forces for what was perceived to be the inevitable renewal of hostilities. He had already developed a new approach to battlefield tactics that marked the transition from medieval warfare, based on cavalry, to the modern methods that transformed infantry into the "queen of battle." El Gran Capitán's use of highly flexible bodies of pikemen and musketeers formed in squares would be developed by subsequent generations of Spanish leaders into a consistently winning instrument well into the 17th century. Even the term *infantry*, derived from the Spanish word for prince (*infante*), endures as a reminder of how armies led by subsequent Spanish princes built and maintained military ascendancy. The league formed in 1500 between Ferdinand and the new French ruler, Louis XII, soon collapsed. The Spanish monarch, who had agreed to the division of Naples into two spheres of influence, claimed the entire kingdom with the extinction of the old Neapolitan dynasty. The El Gran Capitán

met and mastered a series of French and Italian rivals, displaying both his skill at rapid movement of forces and the trick of withstanding a siege to delay the enemy while awaiting reinforcements. By 1503 his victory CERIGNOLA, soon followed by that at Garigliano, put an end to French designs on Naples. Ferdinand appointed him constable of the kingdom, and Córdoba demonstrated his skills as an administrator while ingratiating himself with the Neapolitans. His very success and popularity may have excited the suspicion or jealousy of Ferdinand. In any event the king demanded a full report of his expenditures and then, claiming that it was faulty, summoned him back to Spain. Some historians insist that Córdoba's accounts, still preserved in the archives, are in normal format and properly balanced, but the traditional story that Córdoba sent back a pile of jumbled records and resigned in disgust has survived in the proverb about the "accounts of the Gran Capitán," signifying a faulty report. Ferdinand did not choose to employ his greatest general again. He seems to have considered summoning him from retirement during a crisis in 1512 but then abandoned the idea.

Fernández de Córdoba was undoubtedly the author of Spain's military greatness and one of the premier commanders in European history. His downfall demonstrates a principle that would persist throughout the centuries, that military genius is always at the mercy of political intrigue.

Fernández y González, Manuel (1821–1888)
Spanish writer

One of the most popular Spanish writers of the 19th century, Fernández y González drew upon his fertile imagination and creative energy to produce some 300 novels, in approximately 500 volumes, thus recalling the literary fecundity of LOPE DE VEGA during the SIGLO DE ORO (Golden Age). Much of his work was originally distributed in the form of installments following the contemporary practice of French and British authors (including Alexandre Dumas and Charles Dickens). His output was aided by his use of secretaries who went on to become writers themselves, notably VICENTE BLASCO IBAÑEZ.

Fernández y González specialized in the romantic-historical style of Sir Walter Scott. His novels were largely the product of his vivid imagination rather than historical research. They were full of sharply contrasting heroes and villains in a picturesque world of castles and pageantry that left little room for plot or character development. After launching his career at the age of 16 he went from success to success, becoming legendary for his egotism and extravagant lifestyle. Although he became extremely wealthy from his writings, his lavish taste eventually reduced him to poverty.

Among the best-known novels of Fernández y González are *Rodríguez de Sanabria* (1851), *El condestable don Álvaro de Luna* (1851), *El pastelero de Madrigal* (The pastry maker from Madrigal, 1862), *El cocinero de su majestad* (His majesty's cook, 1857), *El Conde Duque de Olivares* (1870), and *Don Miguel de Mañara. Memorias del tiempo de Carlos V* (Don Miguel de Mañara. Memoirs from the time of Charles V, 1877).

Fernando V   See FERDINAND V.

Fernando VI   See FERDINAND VI.

Fernando VII   See FERDINAND VII.

Fernando de Noronha (Fernão de Noronha)

Discovered in 1503 by the navigator whose name it bears, this island of 10 square miles was one of a number of landfalls made by the Portuguese during their 16th-century voyages between their dominions in Africa and America. Unlike Tristão da Cunha, which was annexed by the British in 1816, this island and its smaller dependencies remained under Portuguese rule until BRAZIL proclaimed her independence. Located some 225 miles northeast of the Brazilian port in Natal, it has variously served as a penal colony and a military base. With somewhat more than 1,000 inhabitants, it acquired the status of a Brazilian federal territory in 1942. During the height of the cold war, from 1950 to 1962, it served as a missile tracking base.

Ferrer, Francisco (1859–1909)
Spanish educator

Born of a prosperous Catalan farming family, Ferrer was the product of a conventional upbringing and schooling. By the time he was in his 20s, he had come under the influence of radicalized coworkers, and as a clerical employee of a railroad company, he became a courier for anarchist groups. In 1886 unwelcome attention from the police forced him to settle in France. In Paris he earned his living by teaching Spanish and extended his circle of radical contacts. The ineffectuality of anarchism led him to describe himself henceforth as a "libertarian" and humanist. A legacy from a former student enabled him to return to Spain in 1901 and open the Escuela Moderna (Modern School) in BARCELONA. His goal in this progressive institution was to build character and to transform his students into humane and responsible citizens. He sought, in his own words, to shape individuals who were consistently devoted to a set of ideals and principles without displaying a public character at odds with their true feelings. In his school Ferrer not only mingled boys and girls but mixed young people of working-class and middle-class origins in order to promote understanding and solidarity. Ferrer also printed a series of pamphlets that were widely distributed to students, factory hands, farmers, and shop assistants. Simply written from a reformist perspective, these booklets were often the first pieces of serious literature that ordinary Spaniards had ever read. Ferrer's unconventional ideas about the organization of his school and the emphasis of its teachings alarmed conservatives, particularly among the leaders of the Catholic Church. His espousal of republicanism, antimilitarism, and anticlericalism made him a marked man, although attempts to interfere with his teaching and writing proved unsuccessful.

In 1906 a member of the Escuela Moderna staff attempted to assassinate the king and queen as they were riding in a public procession in Madrid. The unsuccessful assassin committed suicide, leaving papers in which he denounced Ferrer for his abandonment of anarchism and his moderate views. The educator was arrested on suspicion of complicity and detained for nearly a year until judges ruled that he had no prior knowledge of the attack and ordered his release. Ferrer returned to teaching, but in 1909 he was arrested again following the radical revolt, primarily fomented by anarchists, in BARCELONA. After a week of fierce fighting, with many deaths among both rebels and bystanders, the military rounded up all the usual suspects. There was no specific evidence of Ferrer's complicity in the events of this "Tragic Week," and testimony even placed him far from the scene of the uprising. Despite these facts he was convicted of insurrection and treason. Although there were protests from all over Spain and western Europe, Ferrer was condemned to death and executed.

The judicial murder of Ferrer, as many termed it, was long a focal point of anticonservative and anticlerical rhetoric throughout the Western world. The schoolmaster who had offended the powerful by his advocacy of unpopular ideas was hailed as an anarchist martyr, with buildings adorned with his name and statues dedicated to his memory in many cities. Only the coming of the Great War and then Spain's brutal civil struggle in 1936 would gradually dim the memory of his life and death.

Fialho de Almeida, José Valentim
(1857–1911)
Portuguese writer

A native of Vila de Frades in the ALENTEJO region, Fialho de Almeida attended medical school in LISBON during which he first turned to short story writing to cover his expenses. He published collections in 1881 and 1882 and attracted attention by his use of fantastic and poetic themes. Between 1889 and 1893 he published a series of stories under the overall title *Os gatos* (The cats). In these pieces he combined a satirical view of Lisbon's life and contemporary mores with a denunciation of the abuses of the monarchy that suggested republican sympathies. Frustrated by financial difficulties and his lack of a consistent literary patron, the author concentrated on winning the hand of a wealthy woman. Her death, not long after their 1893 marriage, left him with a fortune of his own. His *O país das uvas* (Country of the grapes, 1893) presents a sunnier image of Portuguese life in which the simple rural patterns of existence contrast favorably with the urban images presented in his earlier stories.

Florida

Evidently sighted by the early Spanish explorers and later visited by JUAN PONCE DE LEÓN (1513), PÁNFILO DE NARVÁEZ, and HERNANDO DE SOTO, this southeastern corner of the present-day United States was not settled by Spaniards until 1565 when San Agustín (St. Augustine) was built after the expulsion of French colonists from the area. Unprofitable owing to its dearth of natural resources, the peninsula was henceforth garrisoned by Spain in order to guard against French and English encroachments and to protect the maritime trade route that passed her shores. East Florida (essentially the modern state of that name) and West Florida (coastal Alabama and Mississippi) were acquired by Britain in 1763 but recovered by Spain in 1783 after her troops seized Pensacola while supporting the American revolutionary cause. Relations with the newly independent United States soon deteriorated, however, and boundary disputes continued until 1819, when the sparsely populated territory was ceded to the Americans for a payment of $5 million.

Apparently named after the feast of Pascua Florida (Easter) upon which day it was discovered in 1513 and long believed to contain the Fountain of Youth and other fabled wonders, Florida had proved a deathtrap for many Spaniards over the centuries and brought few of them anything but grief.

Floridablanca, José Moñino, conde de (1728–1808)
Spanish statesman

A lawyer with experience in business administration, Moñino began his rise to power with the accession of CHARLES III. Appointed treasurer of the Council of Castile, he led an inquiry into matters involving church property that established his credentials as a supporter of royal authority, and he was thereafter involved in the king's moves against the Jesuits.

When Charles III accelerated his confrontation with the clergy by expelling the Jesuits from Spain and her overseas possessions in 1767, Moñino was sent as envoy to the Vatican to persuade the pope to support the growing movement against the Society of Jesus. The mission was successful, the pope dissolved the order, and Moñino was rewarded in 1773 with the title *conde de Floridablanca*. Appointed chief minister in 1776, Floridablanca intensified the development of enlightened despotism, encountering much opposition to his authoritarian program of reform but effecting a number of significant improvements in the Spanish economy. In foreign policy he was successful in improving relations with various old antagonists, including Portugal and the Ottoman Empire. He was not able, however, to overcome the pro-French elements at court who secured a Spanish declaration of war on Britain in 1779. Spanish support of the American Revolution did lead to the recovery of FLORIDA (lost in 1763), but the joint Franco-Spanish siege of GIBRALTAR ended in failure. Floridablanca's waning influence was accelerated by the death of Charles III in 1788, and the rise of MANUEL DE GODOY (already a favorite of CHARLES IV) assured his downfall in 1792. Floridablanca was imprisoned on dubious charges for three years. After his release he remained relatively inactive until the Napoleonic invasion of 1808 provided dramatic justification of his consistently anti-French policy. Floridablanca was named president of the Junta Central (Central Committee) of the loyalist government but died soon after.

Fonseca, Juan Rodríguez de
(1451–1524)
Spanish prelate and colonial administrator
A confidant of ISABELLA I of CASTILE, who presided over Spain's initial discoveries in the New World, Fonseca was born in Toro into a family with important political and ecclesiastical connections. His own clerical career—even before ordination to the priesthood—brought him into the service of the queen and gave him great influence at court. He held four bishoprics in succession and eventually became archbishop of Rossano, in the Kingdom of Naples. From 1493 to his death he served as president of the Council of the Indies and head of the Casa de Contratación (Board of Trade). As such he was essentially Spain's first minister of colonial affairs and presided over the formation of policy during the first phase of discovery and conquest. He was charged with organizing CHRISTOPHER COLUMBUS's later voyages and HERNÁN CORTÉS's expedi-

tion to Mexico, although he was suspicious of and obstructive to both men. He also had a hostile relationship with BARTOLOMÉ DE LAS CASAS. Other conquistadores were favored and assisted by him because they were less innovative and more accepting of complete royal authority.

Fonseca was recognized as a master of world business who lacked either the spiritual or imaginative qualities that might have set Spain's conquest of the New World on a more positive course. However, as a faithful servant of the Crown whose work continued into the early days of CHARLES I, he laid a solid foundation for imperial expansion. Fonseca was also a patron of the arts whose lavish adornment of the principal churches and shrines in such cities as Palencia and Burgos (in both of which he served as bishop) reflected his religious and artistic enthusiasms. Fonseca has been hailed by some contemporaries as a noble and virtuous statesman but condemned by others for his harsh and narrow judgments.

Franche-Comté, Spain in the
The "free county" of Burgundy was a separate offshoot of the French duchy of Burgundy and was bounded by French territory, the Swiss Confederation, the Italian duchy of Savoy, and the independent duchy of Lorraine. In the early 1500s, Franche-Comté began to play an important part in the grand politics of Spain, whose HABSBURG rulers had inherited this strategically located region. CHARLES I and his successors drew upon the material wealth and the intellectual capital of their French-speaking subjects in Franche-Comté, employing many of them as diplomats and state councillors.

Furthermore Franche-Comté provided a part of the "Spanish Road" along which troops could be moved from Italy up into northern Europe without having to venture into disputed territory on land or sea. Inevitably, as Spanish power declined in the late 17th-century, France asserted her claim to Franche-Comté and in a series of negotiations culminating in 1678 Spain surrendered the "free county" to King Louis XIV.

Francis Xavier, Saint (Francisco Xavier [Javier]) (1506–52)

Spanish missionary

A younger son of a Basque noble family, Francisco was born in the castle of Xavier in the kingdom of NAVARRE shortly before it was incorporated into CASTILE. Destined for the church, he was sent when in his early 20s to pursue priestly studies at the University of Paris. There he fell under the influence of IGNATIUS OF LOYOLA. This fellow Basque and former soldier had already experienced a profound spiritual transformation, and the previously lukewarm Xavier soon became an ardent convert to his fellow student's plans. With five other students they took solemn vows to undertake a mission of conversion among believers and nonbelievers alike. These men became the nucleus of the Society of Jesus. While waiting for an opportunity to travel to the Holy Land they were ordained in Venice in 1537. Although Loyola would spend the rest of his life in Rome as the first general of the Jesuits, Xavier was soon dispatched to LISBON, where a Portuguese expedition to the East Indies was being readied. During the next decade he preached, baptized, and founded churches in India, MALACCA, the SPICE ISLANDS (pres-

ent-day Indonesia), and Japan. After a time in GOA, the center of Portugal's Asian empire, Xavier set out for China, the greatest challenge to Christian evangelization then remaining. While preparing himself to undertake this challenge he fell ill and died on an island off the Chinese coast.

Xavier has been rightly called the "Apostle of the Indies." In little more than 10 years he traveled thousands of miles and brought his faith to thousands of people belonging to scores of ethnic groups. A charismatic personality possessed of dauntless determination and seemingly inexhaustible energy, he combined spiritual enthusiasm with practical good sense. Saint Francis Xavier was canonized in 1622. A host of churches and educational institutions throughout the Catholic world bear his name and testify to his status as one of the greatest of missionaries.

Franco Bahamonde, Francisco (1892–1975)

Spanish military leader and chief of state

Born in El Ferrol, GALICIA, the descendant of a long line of naval officers, Franco was himself destined for a naval career. The virtual destruction of the Spanish fleet in the war with the United States (1898) led to his entering the military academy. Between 1912 and 1926 he spent virtually all of his active duty in MOROCCO, rising by rapid promotion from lieutenant to brigadier general (the youngest general in Europe). During these years Franco earned a reputation for bravery under fire and strategic as well as tactical skills. His genius for organization led to several notable victories over the Moroccan resistance forces, and his training of the new Foreign Legion won

Francisco Franco *(Library of Congress)*

him respect in the army and the status of popular hero at home.

Despite being removed from command of the military academy at ZARAGOZA following the establishment of the Second Republic in 1931, Franco maintained the image of the loyal professional soldier, avoiding identification with any of the political intrigues of the early 1930s. Although the harsh repression of the miners' revolt in ASTURIAS (1934) was carried out by others, his role in its planning gave evidence of his increasing commitment to ruthless defense of what he regarded as the best interests of Spain. The left-wing coalition that controlled the republic in early 1936 assigned him to the command of the CANARY ISLANDS, not daring to dismiss him,

but clearly preferring to have him out of the way.

When the insurrection of the so-called Nationalist forces began in July 1936, Franco, by then back in Morocco, proclaimed his adherence and took command of the Army of Africa (comprising the Foreign Legion and colonial troops). Undeterred by the navy's support of the government, Franco arranged with his friends in the German and Italian fascist regimes to transport his soldiers to Spain in cargo planes. The arrival of Franco's forces was decisive in regaining momentum for the uprising, as many of the military rebels had been defeated or contained by the Loyalists, who supported the republic. Franco soon emerged as the undisputed leader of the rebellion thanks to his success on the battlefield and the elimination of generals who might have competed with him. On October 1, 1936, he was proclaimed commander of the armed forces and chief of state of the government that was gradually being installed throughout "liberated" territory. The SPANISH CIVIL WAR was presented by Franco's propagandists as a new *reconquista* (see RECONQUISTA), a crusade of traditionalists and Catholic patriots against godless marxism. Early in 1939, with the republic defeated, Franco was able to assume the absolute control over his country that he would maintain until his death.

Franco's dictatorship may be divided into three periods: 1939–50, 1950–65, and 1965–75. During the first of these he had to develop the structure of his domestic administration while shaping a foreign policy that preserved Spain's neutrality in World War II. At home Franco crushed all dissent, imposed censorship, manipulated public opinion, and created a brutal police apparatus that caused the death, torture, or imprisonment of thousands. By creating the "Spanish State" with himself as El Caudillo (the Leader), he reduced the monarchists, conservative Catholics, and even the army from the status of wartime partners to that of supporting players. The FALANGE ESPAÑOLA, a right-wing party that he had selected as his political instrument, became the nucleus of the National Movement that supplanted all other parties. Chauvinistic rhetoric and historical distortions formed an official doctrine of Spanishness that justified the total elimination of regional autonomy.

Having received substantial military and financial assistance from Germany and Italy during the civil war, Franco was expected to return the favors during their conflict with the Allies. Despite much oratory and diplomatic maneuvering, however, Franco preserved his country's neutrality and enhanced his reputation for cunning and obfuscation. Adolf Hitler declared he would rather have three or four teeth pulled than go through any more negotiations with the El Caudillo. The Spanish "volunteers" who were sent to take part in the great anti-Bolshevik assault on Soviet communism were withdrawn as soon as Russia began to drive the Germans back. A few years of ostracism by the victors added to the economic stress that Spain was already enduring but permitted Franco to consolidate his grip on the country while awaiting the opportunities that the cold war would soon bring.

Between 1950 and 1965 Franco gradually led Spain out of international isolation and into a situation that permitted both the easing of its economic woes and the relaxation of its domestic despotism. After persuading Washington that he was a natural ally in the confrontation with Moscow, he secured the establishment of U.S. bases in his territory, with all the financial benefits and personal prestige this guaranteed. By 1955 he had gained admission to the United Nations, despite the antagonism of governments that found the Franco of the 1950s just as odious as the militarist of the 1930s and the tyrant of the 1940s.

For all his authoritarian methods Franco had never fully embraced the fascist doctrines of his erstwhile friends. His ideology, if it could be so designated, was a mixture of Catholicism and Spanish nationalism with historical fantasy and personal egotism. After borrowing the Nazi concept of autarky (economic self-sufficiency) and nearly wrecking Spain with its heedless application during the 1940s, he reverted to the pragmatism that had come to his rescue during earlier crises in his career. In the late 1950s Spain began to experience the stimulus of foreign investment conjoined with the remissions sent home by millions of Spaniards working abroad. Commentators spoke of an economic "boom," and MADRID took on an unaccustomed air of prosperity. "Moderate" voices began to be heard in the Councils of State recommending a relaxation of the dictatorship. Franco played these advisers off against the hard-liners while preserving the ultimate power for himself. At the same time he began arranging for a succession that would preserve his vision of Spain once he was gone.

During the last 10 years of his rule, Franco permitted an increasing amount of "reform" that led to greater freedom in the daily routines of Spanish life without abandoning the essentially undemocratic character of the Spanish state. He gave growing prominence to Prince JUAN CARLOS (grandson of ALFONSO XIII) while seeking to establish the concept of a future monarchy shaped in the Franquist image. Both the prince and the public were constantly told that nothing would really change when El Caudillo was gone. Franco had always maintained a distance from his subjects and kept his innermost thoughts secret, even from close associates, while preserving an aura of mysterious power. This habit also isolated him from reality—especially in his later years. Franco had long identified himself with the great figures of Spain's past: El Cid, CHARLES I, PHILIP II. Sycophantic propaganda that had engulfed Spain for nearly 40 years eventually convinced even its protagonist that he was all knowing and all powerful. When he finally succumbed to the infirmities of old age (although only after a hard struggle), Franco undoubtedly imagined that all would work out as he had planned. Instead he was succeeded by a king who embraced the concept of democracy and won a mass following that protected Spain against both the old specter of marxist revolution and the chance of a Franquist military coup. Ironically, the soldier who had waded to power through a sea of blood and ruled for decades with an iron hand was destined to fade rapidly into the ranks of historical phantoms.

G

Galicia

A region in northwestern Spain (with an area of more than 11,000 square miles) possessing a strong sense of its distinctive historical and cultural identity, Galicia preserves Celtic traditions and a language rich in distinctive literature. A separate kingdom under Teutonic invaders from the fifth century A.D., Galicia was subsequently ruled by Muslims, linked to the adjacent kingdom of ASTURIAS, then incorporated with LEÓN and CASTILE. Galicia and her southern neighbor, Portugal, have many linguistic ties and historical affinities that have led some observers to suggest—overly simplistically—that their populations possess a single ethnicity. Modern Galician nationalism, however, rejects such an analysis and maintains that Galicia, like CATALONIA and the BASQUE PROVINCES, deserves a special status of autonomy within Spain. Galicia's location on the Atlantic coast and the importance of the port at La Coruña have also served to encourage in the Galicians a greater sense of the wider world than is found among some other Iberians. This has led many of them to venture abroad as seamen or immigrants.

Gálvez, Bernardo de (conde de Gálvez) (1746–1786)
Spanish colonial administrator

One of Spain's most able and active representatives in the New World, Gálvez began his military career with service in North Africa and the Portuguese campaign during the Seven Years' War. He then accompanied his uncle JOSE DE GÁLVEZ to NEW SPAIN, where he gained further experience fighting the Apache on the northern frontier. After a brief stay in MADRID he was sent to New Orleans to take command of the Spanish garrison there and by 1777 had been promoted to governor of LOUISIANA.

Gálvez demonstrated his administrative skills and talent for public relations by facilitating trade, winning over the local Indian population, and easing tensions between the French and Spanish residents in New Orleans. With an eye to the British presence in Spain's former territory in FLORIDA he initiated covert support for the American rebels. After Spain formally recognized the independence of the United States Gálvez launched a series of military operations that gradually won control of West Florida (the coastal regions of present-day Mississippi and Alabama) and in 1781 captured Pensacola, leading to the retrocession of the entire colony of Florida to Spain. Gálvez had already extended Spain's presence to the west with the establishment of new settlements, including the city that now bears his name, Galveston, in Texas.

Returning in triumph to Madrid in 1783, Gálvez was promoted to lieutenant general, given the title of count, and named governor of CUBA, a position that was subsumed into that of viceroy of New Spain when his father, Matías de Gálvez, died in 1784. Although his tenure in MEXICO was brief, the new viceroy won great popularity in much the same way he had earned it in Louisiana—by a combination of personal charm and progressive administrative policy. His conduct in both his major assignments proved Gálvez to be a disciple of the philosophes, committed to the Enlightenment philosophy not merely because it was favored by CHARLES III but because he was personally convinced of its value. Gálvez not only improved the commerce and secured the defenses of Mexico; he relieved food shortages, improved health care, and demonstrated his personal sympathies with the needs of the population. His sudden death precipitated an outpouring of grief among the Mexican people rarely seen during the colonial era.

Gálvez, José de (marqués de Sonora) (1720–1787)

Spanish colonial administrator

The most prominent member of a family from MÁLAGA that served the enlightened despot CHARLES III with exemplary zeal, Gálvez was trained as a lawyer at the University of Salamanca and Alcalá. He had his first taste of colonial administration in the Philippines in the early 1750s and later served as a fiscal director in the royal household. This combination of experience and expertise led to his appointment as visitor in NEW SPAIN in 1765. His duties in this capacity were to investigate the sluggish flow of revenues from the wealthy realm of MEXICO. Finding the incumbent viceroy not only uncooperative but suspect in the diversion of funds, Gálvez procured his replacement by a more compliant nobleman who allowed him to function as virtual ruler of New Spain until 1772. During that period Gálvez undertook a program of reform and development that would be continued during subsequent decades to the great benefit of the Mexican people and the enhancement of Spain's income. During these same years Gálvez also pushed the effective zone of Spanish control northward into what is now the southwestern and far western United States through a combination of military operations and missionary activity. In the so-called Provinces of the Interior of New Spain and along the coast of CALIFORNIA he initiated the last great expansion (or exploration) in the history of the Spanish Empire.

Returning home in 1772 Gálvez was recognized for his accomplishments with a whole new range of duties on various councils and committees and, most important, was given the newly created Ministry of Colonies. Although his work during the remainder of his life was rewarded with the title marqués de Sonora, a man of his character, indefatigable in his dedication to business and relentless in his pursuit of goals, undoubtedly found practical accomplishments more gratifying than mere dignities. He introduced salutary changes in virtually every aspect of Spanish colonial administration, from the encouragement of economic growth on the ground to the promotion of maritime trade. He commenced an efficient oversight of revenues by the implementation of the *intendente* (intendant) system (borrowed from France), which gave each colonial governor an expert manager to assist him in balancing the books and extracting maximum income from his jurisdiction. Gálvez enhanced and extended royal power throughout the colonies, showing the same rigor that he had displayed in Mexico during the 1760s when he mercilessly repressed several outbreaks of indigenous or proto-nationalistic resistance.

Among the group of devoted and dedicated statesmen who made Charles III perhaps the most successful of enlightened despots, Gálvez was an outstanding executor of royal policy. Moreover, in his brother, Matías de Gálvez, and his nephew, BERNARDO DE GÁLVEZ, he found and employed men who were not mere beneficiaries of nepotism but active agents of Enlightenment. They demonstrated their abilities in GUATEMALA and LOUISIANA, respectively, and then served, father succeeded by son, as viceroy of New Spain. Together these three members of the Gálvez family contributed much to the preservation of imperial Spain. Unfortunately their intervention came too late to preserve what so many predecessors had built and what a few unworthy monarchs would soon destroy.

Gama, Vasco da (1469–1524)
Portuguese navigator

The son of a Portuguese official who had been designated originally to undertake the voyage, Gama was sent, after his father's death, by MANUEL I to initiate Portuguese trade with the Indies. Departing in 1497 with four ships, he followed the route marked out by a succession of earlier Portuguese maritime pioneers along the western coast of Africa, rounded the Cape of Good Hope, and sailed up the east coast. Crossing the Indian Ocean from Malindi to Calicut, he established friendly relations with local rulers and returned home in 1499 to report that he had accomplished the mission that had been started nearly a century earlier by Prince Henry the Navigator. Gama laid out the plans for the 1500 voyage of PEDRO ÁLVARES CABRAL but was sent back to India in person in 1502 when the king determined that stronger measures were necessary to establish Portuguese primacy in the East. With a fleet of 20 ships Gama enforced the submission of important African chiefs, clashed with Arab traders who felt their regional monopoly threatened, and procured the cession of bases on the west coast of India. He thus secured the establishment of what grew into the Portuguese Empire in Africa and Asia. Although his methods were harsh the results were vastly profitable, and the Portuguese crown awarded him numerous honors, including the title *count of Vidigueira*. Returning to the scene of his earlier triumph in 1524 with the rank of viceroy, Gama died soon after his arrival. His first voyage was elevated by the poet CAMÕES to the level of heroic mythology in the epic *The Lusiads*. Gama has remained the ultimate exemplar of those navigators and adventurers who shaped Portugal's Golden Age.

Ganivet, Ángel (1865–1898)
Spanish writer

Born in GRANADA, Ganivet was educated there, specializing in foreign languages. He later received his doctorate at the University of Madrid. He represented the Spanish government as consul at Antwerp, Helsingfors (Helsinki), and Riga. In this latter city, depressed by a failed romance and by the onset of a serious illness, he committed suicide at the age of 33. During his brief life Ganivet produced a relatively large number of books, including several novels and a play. It was his essays and commentaries, however, that won him the greatest attention and still marks him as a precursor of the GENERATION OF '98. Although some literary historians have included him in that group of writers who responded to the catastrophic defeat in the SPANISH-AMERICAN WAR, his literary stance, as well as the actual date of his death, make it inappropriate to include him within the group, several of whose members were under his posthumous influence. Ganivet's friendship with MIGUEL DE UNAMUNO grew out of a broadly shared perspective on the historical evolution of Spain and certain flaws in the Spanish character. Like the members of the Generation of '98, these two recognized that many of Spain's problems grew from its own weaknesses. Ganivet and Unamuno, in their philosophical analysis, drew hope from the distinctive positive traits that their country had preserved and believed that a true Spanish renaissance was possible without resort to revolutionary upheaval.

The most important and influential of Ganivet's works is *Ideárium español* (usually translated as "The idea of Spain," 1897). Organized in three parts, it compresses an overview of Spain's historical experience, the country's chief contributions to Western civilization, and the reasons for its decline. An edition of his correspondence with Unamuno, *El porvenir de España* (The future of Spain), was published posthumously in 1912. Unamuno, who first met Ganivet in 1891, would probably not have approved of his friend's suicide, for the philosopher was adamantly committed to the primacy of life, to be preserved even amid the greatest adversity. Their correspondence nevertheless shows a meeting of the minds on many issues and provides an extension of themes introduced in *Ideárium español*. Ganivet's other nonfiction works are chiefly accounts of his travels and observations in northern Europe and contain some interesting insights on the cultural contrasts and occasional similarities that this Spanish thinker encountered there. Much of 20th-century commentary on Ganivet has analyzed his thought, for all its occasional inconsistencies, as a stimulating anticipation of the great debate over Spain's destiny that has continued during the more than 100 years since his death.

García Lorca, Federico (1898–1936)
Spanish poet and dramatist

García Lorca was born in ANDALUSIA and retained an intense identification with his birthplace and its distinctive spirit and culture throughout his life. He said that he felt himself a representative of the Mozarabic history of the region, the fusion of Spanish and Islamic traditions that gave a special character to Andalusia. After a perfunctory study of the law he settled in MADRID to pursue a literary career though intensely interested in art and music as well. His first work was dismissed by the critical establishment, but he soon gained praise and recognition from the more open-minded members of the arts community. By the time he was in his 20s he had already attained a considerable reputation and won praise for his poems and plays. A sojourn in the United States, mostly in New York City, was a stimulating experience, though his poetry of this period (1929–30) was not published until after his death. He returned to Spain after the proclamation of the Second Republic in 1931 and was commissioned by the new government to organize and stage a series of dramatic performances, particularly oriented toward youth. Like the festival of *cante jondo* (the flamenco songs associated with the gypsy traditions of Andalusia) that he had created some years earlier, this enterprise was highly successful and added to his recognition among popular and progressive elements. García Lorca, by the very nature of his art and personality, was however a marked man among reactionary forces in Spanish society. When he returned from Madrid to his home city of GRANADA at the outbreak of the SPANISH CIVIL WAR, he was almost immediately assassinated.

García Lorca is certainly the best-known Spanish literary figure of the 20th century, particularly among the wide circle of admirers in other countries, where his plays are regularly produced, although at least one notable American critic has said that they could only be fully understood and appreciated in Spain. His distinctive style, his striking personality, and the circumstances of his death, cutting short his achievements at so early an age, have perpetuated his iconic stature. Separating García Lorca's plays from his poetry is more a matter of arbitrary distinctions of format than of content or style. While some of his stage works are light or even farcical, his three masterpieces—*Bodas de sangre* (*Blood Wedding*, 1933), *Yerma* (1934), and *La casa de Ber-* *narda Alba* (*The House of Bernarda Alba*, 1936)—constitute a grim trilogy of harsh rural society. Each deals with matters of honor, stifling isolation, desperate passion, and death. While foreign audiences may see them as "quintessentially Spanish," Spanish audiences have recognized their mixture of symbolism and realism as far removed from the florid melodrama with which playwrights such as JOSÉ ECHEGARAY presented such themes.

Among the best known and most controversial of his poetical work is that contained in the *Romancero gitano* (*Gypsy Ballads*, 1924–27), which despite its name, is less a collection of gypsy ballads than a celebration of his Granada. García Lorca's poetry is full of recurring symbolism—the horse, the bull, the moon, the inexorable passage of time—and it is also intensely reflective of the society that he found both fascinating and menacing. The finest example of his poetry among the collections of verse he authored is his elegy on the death of a personal friend, the matador Ignacio Sánchez Mejías, fatally gored in the Madrid bullring in 1934. The ritualistic repetition and the sense of mounting doom that advances with the ticking away of the hours are interwoven with a larger sense of inescapable human destiny and, perhaps, with a premonition of García Lorca's own not-too-distant fate.

Garcilaso de la Vega (1503–1536)
Spanish poet

Revered as the perfect courtier possessing in equal measure all the skills of a noble gentleman, from mastery of musical instruments to bravery on the field of battle, Garcilaso was a native of TOLEDO whose distinguished lineage guaranteed him a position as page to CHARLES I. His intelligence and enthusiasm won him appointment as one of his sovereign's most trusted aides de camp. Garcilaso's good looks, charm, and wit became legendary, and his early death in a reckless attack on the French fortress of Nice enshrined him in the patriotic pantheon. But Garcilaso's claim to fame rests on more distinctive and enduring achievements, for he was the principal exponent of the literary techniques of Renaissance Italy in a Spain that was still old fashioned and somewhat stolid in its poetry at the beginning of the 16th century. Garcilaso's mastery of all the major Italianate forms was demonstrated in a slim volume of his work published a few years after his death and guaranteed his position as the first poet of the SIGLO DE ORO. He was not merely an adroit versifier, with a gift for transforming the new Italian style into the Castilian language, but also a master of deeply felt emotions and images. All the great writers who followed him, down to CERVANTES and beyond, acknowledged their debt to him and the inspiration provided by his life and work, however brief both of these were.

Gaudí i Cornet, Antonio (Antoni Gaudí i Cornet) (1852–1926)

Spanish architect

Born of an artisan family in CATALONIA, Gaudí obtained his diploma as an architect in 1878. His early work was important in preparing his understanding of the deeper roots and broader meanings of architecture in the modern world. At the same time it enabled him to steep himself in the Catalan nationalism that challenged Castilianism both in the political and cultural dimen-

sions during the late 19th century. Paradoxically the man who many regard as the greatest Spanish architect of the 20th century not only opposed many characteristic manifestations of Spanish culture but stood apart from the mainstream of Spanish life.

All of Gaudí's work was executed in or near BARCELONA, frequently under the patronage of wealthy Catalan families who committed themselves to the support of an individual who might, by conventional standards, be considered eccentric. Gaudí passed through several stages of architectural inspiration, drawing from neogothic and, later, Middle Eastern models, and was for a time influenced by the baroque. All of these, however, were increasingly transformed and dominated by his preoccupation with materials and forms derived from nature, including plants, trees, and marine life. Among his most notable and strikingly "different" works were the Güell Estate and the Palau Güell (from the late 1880s), Casa Calvet (1890–1904), Casa Batlló (1904–06), and Casa Milà (1905–10). Each of these was designed by Gaudí down to the last detail, including ornamentation, lighting systems, and furniture, and could be truly described with the much-overworked term *unique.*

In 1883 Gaudí was selected to design and build the church of the Sagrada Familia (Holy Family), which was intended to be a "penitential temple." The building was conceived by devout Catalans as a reparation to God for the violence and irreligion that they perceived to have dominated much of modern Spanish history. Like the medieval cathedrals that often required centuries for completion, this project would continue throughout the remainder of Gaudí's life and remains to date unfin-

La Sagrada Familia, Antonio Gaudí's masterpiece, in Barcelona *(Getty)*

ished. After the early 1900s he pursued no other work, spending all of his time on sketching his designs, consulting with the craftsmen who were capable of carrying out his complex visions, and supervising the handling of materials. The exotic appearance of the structure excited awe and amazement at first, but the passing of the years and changes in taste led many to regard it as the folly of the reclusive architect, who lived on the building site, pestered potential donors to contribute to the cost of the enterprise, and pursued an ever more ascetic obsession with spiritual val-

ues. Although additional features of the structure were completed after Gaudí's death in an accident, the outbreak of the SPANISH CIVIL WAR effectively halted the construction of the Sagrada Familia. His posthumous reputation went through periods of praise by surrealists and abstract expressionists (who saw him as a kindred spirit), derision by advocates of the "international style" (who ridiculed his theory of "equilibrium" and championed a clean architectural line and freedom from ornamentation" and those who took more interest in Gaudí's aphorisms than the strange buildings he had created in pursuit of his visionary philosophy. His name has been put forward at intervals for canonization, but those who celebrate his piety find his reactionary politics and baffling flights of fancy harder to deal with.

Generation of '27 (Generación del 27)

Inspired by the 1927 observances of the tricentenary of the death of poet LUIS DE GÓNGORA, this group of poets acquired an image of common inspiration and motivation resembling that of the GENERATION OF '98. Indeed they have been referred to as the "Grandsons of '98." They are generally considered to have included RAFAEL ALBERTI, FEDERICO GARCÍA LORCA, and the Nobel Prize winner VICENTE ALEIXANDRE, and by extension the filmmaker LUIS BUÑUEL and even the surrealist painter SALVADOR DALÍ. While paving homage to Góngora, they insisted that their primary respect was due to "the word." They insisted that their mission was to find new modes of expression and rejected the doctrines of both romanticism and realism.

Generation of '98 (Generación del 98)

The cultural movement designated by this term incorporates a group of writers who deeply felt the defeat of Spain in the SPANISH-AMERICAN WAR with the resulting loss of the last vestiges of empire and analyzed this catastrophe while trying to find ways to create a new Spain. The phrase is generally attributed to the writer JOSÉ MARTÍNEZ RUIZ (Azorín), who used it in his *Clásicos y modernos* (1913), although it had probably been used by others for some years. In fact, there had been lamentations over the decline of Spain's stature in the world and questions raised about the deterioration of her moral fiber as far back as the late 1600s, and these had grown in frequency since the early 19th century due to the initial loss of her colonial possessions and the deterioration of the domestic economy.

Assignment of particular novelists, essayists, and even poets to this cohort has been much disputed but those most commonly listed as members of the generation include Azorín himself, PÍO BAROJA, RAMÓN DEL VALLE INCLÁN, ANTONIO MACHADO, and MIGUEL DE UNAMUNO, as well as, perhaps, the playwright JACINTO BENAVENTE.

Gerona, siege of (1808–1809)

Gerona, a fortified city in CATALONIA, withstood a prolonged siege during the opening phase of Napoléon's invasion of Spain. As in the siege of ZARAGOZA in the neighboring region of ARAGON, the heroism of Gerona's defenders provided inspiration throughout the long subsequent struggle of the Spanish people to liberate themselves from French occupation.

The siege actually consisted of three phases. During the first, in June 1808, some 5,000 French soldiers were beaten back by defenders. A second attack, in July, with double the number of troops, was similarly repelled. The third and major phase of the siege began in August under the direct oversight of Marshal Gouvion-Saint-Cyr and continued for nearly a year as the French tried every expedient, from heavy bombardment to frontal infantry assault, to break through the defenses. Under the military governor Mariano Álvarez de Castro the resistance was carried on by regular troops, including a large contingent of Spain's Irish Brigade, and civilian volunteers, among whom women grouped in the Company of St. Barbara handled artillery with great zeal and effect. As the siege dragged on into early 1809 Gouvion-Saint-Cyr called for still more troops, much to the disgust of Napoléon, who replaced him with one of his most trusted officers, Marshal Augereau. Increased pressure was applied to the outlying forts, which were successively overwhelmed by the French. General Joaquín Blake, who had managed to bring a detachment into the city to reinforce his Irish compatriots some weeks earlier, was beaten back in a second attempt. The walls and major buildings of Gerona began to crumble, and hundreds of dead bodies lay among the rubble. Disease began to spread, particularly affecting the civilian population. As early as June 21 Gouvion Saint-Cyr had urged the defenders to capitulate. Álvarez de Castro had responded that he would not negotiate with the enemies of his country and warned that any more attempts to propose talks would be met only by bullets. By late September, despite another sortie by Spaniards and a massive counterattack by the French, the situation seemed unchanged. But to the commander's deputy, who had taken charge of the defense when Álvarez de Castro fell gravely ill, Gerona had reached the end of its resources. Both sides agreed that all had been done that could possibly be demanded by military honor, and Gerona yielded to Augereau. Spain's casualties amounted to 9,000 and those of France to 20,000. The siege of Gerona demonstrated the determination of the Spanish nation to defend its sovereignty against the invaders and the obstinate willingness of the French emperor to pour blood and treasure into the struggle for the Iberian Peninsula. The courage and valor displayed at Gerona would continue for another five years to inspire the Spaniards.

Gibraltar

At the southernmost extremity of the Iberian Peninsula, the mountain known in antiquity as Calpe, one of the legendary Pillars of Hercules that marked the exit from the Mediterranean, has stood for the last 300 years as a reminder of certain painful moments in Spain's history. It was here that Muslim invaders led by Tarik launched the first phase of their conquest of the peninsula in 711, since which the mountain has been named for him, *Gibraltar* being a contraction of *Gebel al-Tarik* (the mount of Tarik). Recaptured by the forces of CASTILE in 1462, it was taken in 1704 by England and recognized as one of her colonies at the end of the WAR OF THE SPANISH SUCCESSION (1713). By the time Spain launched an unsuccessful attack in 1779 the new masters of Gibraltar had already begun to construct defenses that would eventually turn it into one of the strongest fortresses in the world. British ships patrolled the Mediterranean during World War I from the mas-

sive harbor facilities that were constructed there, and during World War II the Rock's formidable gun batteries overawed every challenge from Axis enemies. By 2004 the population of Gibraltar stood at a little less than 30,000 and enjoyed British citizenship and a large degree of local government. Spain's periodic efforts to secure the retrocession of Gibraltar were routinely rebuffed by the colony's voters who preferred to retain the advantages of being British (despite the fact that most of them were of Spanish, Italian, or Maltese origin). Although Spain has presented her case in every guise, from demands for historical justice to concerns over environmental pollution, the 2.5-square-mile enclave at the foot of the great fortified mountain seems destined to remain an alien intrusion on Spain's rocky extremity.

Giner de los Ríos, Francisco
(1839–1915)
Spanish philosopher and educator

Giner was the chief Spanish promoter of the doctrines of the German philosopher Karl Krause, whose disciple Julián Sanz del Río had been Giner's teacher. *Krausismo* underlay the movement of educational and moral reform that Giner and his circle attempted to introduce in Spain during the late 19th century. A professor of the philosophy of law at the University of Madrid, Giner became involved in the tumultuous political and social disturbances that followed the deposition of ISABELLA II in 1868. He was imprisoned for his perceived radicalism in 1875 but by 1876 was organizing likeminded educators who founded the independent school known as the Institución Libre de Enseñanza (Institution for

Independent Teaching) in the same year. Opposed to the rigid program of the state and church-run schools, Giner and his associates favored an opening of the students' mind to free thought and individual realization of the connection between life and learning. The institute's program encompassed training for youth through the elementary and secondary levels and involved open-air hiking and sports as well as visits to significant rural and urban locations. The fundamental concept was the development of practical skills and self-motivated awareness rather that rote learning and blind following of traditions. Giner's pedagogical and methodological principles echoed practices followed in various European countries, including Germany and Britain, as well as the United States. In those countries and even more so in Spain they met with criticism on theoretical grounds and because of the challenge they posed to special interests. These educational reforms were never widely successful in Spain. They were further hampered by dissension and defections among the original founders of the institute. Nevertheless, they continued to inspire innovation and experimentation well into the 20th century. Giner, a man of high moral principles and austere dignity, won respect even among his opponents, and his wide-ranging knowledge was reflected in his writings on many subjects, well beyond the conventional bounds of pedagogy. Spain's leading modern intellectual, MIGUEL DE UNAMUNO, called Giner "the Spanish Socrates" and praised him as the "great agitator of spirits."

Goa

Captured from her native rulers in 1510 by AFONSO DE ALBUQUERQUE, this ancient city on the west coast of India became the capital of Portugal's eastern empire. During the height of the imperial period (1575–1625) Goa enjoyed an unparalleled prestige as the symbolic center of trade, missionary activity, military expeditions, and colonial expansion. Popularly known as "Golden Goa," the city was awarded the same political status as LISBON, and her chief prelate was granted the ecclesiastical title of *patriarch*. A significant number of conversions to Christianity were made among the local inhabitants, and a Goanese population of mixed Indian-Portuguese descent grew up in the adjacent region. Repeatedly attacked by Dutch raiders and Indian rulers during the 17th century, the original city was largely abandoned after 1759 due to the outbreak of cholera. While Velha Goa (Old Goa) retained a cathedral and other church buildings dating back to the earliest days, "New Goa" developed at nearby Panaji.

As British-dominated India gained its independence in 1947, a separate Portuguese India, covering some 1,400 square miles with a population of nearly 500,000, continued to exist. The new Indian government began demanding the termination of the Portuguese colonial presence as early as 1948 when it actually occupied certain border areas. It was not until 1962, however, that an invading army overcame brief Portuguese resistance and formally annexed Goa and its subsidiary territories of DAMÃO AND DIU.

Godoy, Manuel de (príncipe de la Paz, duque de Alcudia)
(1767–1851)
Spanish politician
Born into a minor HIDALGO family in EXTREMADURA, he was appointed to the

royal Guardia de Corps (bodyguard regiment) in 1784. He attached himself to the Prince and Princess of Asturias and began a rapid rise to power when the prince succeeded as CHARLES IV in 1788. Although the handsome young guardsman was reputed to be the lover of the new queen, María Luisa, he was considered by Charles IV to be his best friend and wisest adviser, with the result that Godoy soon supplanted the ministers inherited from the previous reign. He rose rapidly in military and civil rank, being created duke of Alcudia and chief minister in 1792. Regarded by the royal couple as a virtual political genius, Godoy was merely a man of more personal charm than formal education, affable in temperament but mediocre in judgment, and no less overwhelmed by the great international crises precipitated by the French Revolution than were his sovereigns.

After initially taking Spain into the anti-French coalition Godoy signed a treaty with France in 1795 that reversed the alliance. This confirmed the king's high opinion of his statesmanship and won him the title *"príncipe de la Paz"* (prince of the peace), a designation which many Spaniards found near-blasphemous. Opposition to the royal favorite increased after Spain sustained a number of defeats at the hands of her new antagonist, Britain. The loss of Trinidad and the return of LOUISIANA to France merely intensified dissatisfaction. Even his inclusion of able and independent public figures within the administration merely provided him with strong opponents inside his own ministry. Forced by French manipulations into a war with Portugal, Godoy led the army in person, the first commander in Spanish history to assume the title of *"generalísimo."*

In 1805 the next stage in Spain's entanglement with France (now ruled by Emperor Napoléon I) cost her the destruction of her fleet at the BATTLE OF TRAFALGAR, and even Godoy was seeking an alternative. His secret plan to join in the latest anti-French coalition collapsed when Prussia was defeated in 1806 and Russia soon sought a settlement with Napoléon. Godoy now seriously contemplated having Charles IV proclaimed emperor of the Americas and withdrawing the royal family to the New World where they could be personally secure and at the same time strengthen Spain's weakening ties with her colonies. When nothing came of this scheme Godoy entered into a new round of negotiations with Paris to partition Portugal, reserving the southern region for himself as sovereign prince of ALGARVE.

By 1808, with French troops already in Spain pursuant to their invasion of Portugal, Godoy was almost universally detested by Spaniards of all ranks, except for his regal patrons. Although generally believed to have fathered several of the queen's children, he was still trusted and esteemed by Charles IV. Finally a band of military and civilian conspirators, supporting the infuriated and disgusted prince Ferdinand, deposed the hapless sovereign in March. Godoy was close to being killed by the mutineers, and only the intervention of a French general saved him. Soon after, the ousted Charles IV and the newly installed FERDINAND VII, along with the rest of the Spanish Bourbons, were lured to Bayonne for a conference with the French dictator. There they were declared superfluous to Napoléon's needs, and his brother was designated JOSEPH I, king of Spain.

Godoy later joined Charles and María Luisa in exile. None of them ever returned to Spain. When María Luisa died in 1819 (shortly before her husband) she left most of her possessions to Godoy. The vengeful Ferdinand VII prevented the implementation of this will, just as he had already abolished the title *príncipe de la Paz*. Godoy, having purchased a papal title, henceforth called himself "prince of Bassano" and devoted his later years to writing his memoirs. He died in Paris just as a new Bonaparte dictator was taking power.

Execrated in his own day as an arch villain and described by later commentators as the first modern dictator, Godoy was essentially something much more commonplace. He was merely the latest in a long line of *privados* (royal political favorites), whose greedy ambition had afflicted the nation over the centuries. His apologists have pointed out that he maintained the system of enlightened despotism practiced under CHARLES III. He continued or even initiated many reforms and improvements in cultural, educational, and economic matters and diminished the ability of the church to restrict free inquiry. He also curtailed the power of the SPANISH INQUISITION. There is no evidence, however, that he pursued a deliberate policy or even possessed a coherent understanding of the Enlightenment. Random and opportunistic in his decisions, he was obsessed with his own enrichment and self-gratification. His relationship with the queen, though lasting, was paralleled by connections with other women, all equally shallow in the depth of affection. After decades of statesmanlike leadership Spain had the misfortune, during a period of international crisis, to fall under the sway of Godoy, a worthless upstart, whose regime brought his country to the brink of ruin.

Golden Age   See SIGLO DE ORO.

Góngora y Argote, Luis de (1561–1627)

Spanish poet

Born in CÓRDOBA, the son of a judge, Góngora obtained an ecclesiastical benefice as a secure source of income. Although he qualified for this position by taking minor orders in his youth, he was not ordained to the priesthood until the age of 55 when he secured a chaplaincy at the royal court. Both at the University of Salamanca (from which he failed to graduate) and in his early clerical career he was notorious for his

Queen María Luisa of Spain *(Library of Congress)*

devotion to gambling, bullfights, and other recreational activities. Góngora possessed a quick and capacious mind that enabled him to accumulate a vast store of learning and to display an amazing range of religious, mythological, and natural references in his poetry. In his later years the enemies he had made in literary controversies and those who were the objects of his satires plagued him, as did his numerous debtors. He was also tormented by deteriorating health (apparently arteriosclerosis), which caused loss of memory and ultimately a fatal stroke.

Góngora has been one of the most controversial figures in Spanish poetry, with his reputation and critical standing changing over the centuries. In his younger days he was admired for light and popular themes and seemed to have a special affinity to the average reader and mundane life. From about 1610 or 1611 onward he produced increasingly complex poetical works featuring elaborate metaphors and loaded with arcane, learned references. His interweaving of allusions that baffled all but the most acute reader led to accusations that he was inventing a self-referential vocabulary. The term *gongorismo* (Gongorism) was increasingly applied to his poetic style by hostile contemporaries, such as FRANCISCO DE QUEVEDO, who made Góngora the butt of many satires. This image of Góngora as a ponderous pedant or perhaps even an incipient madman persisted over many generations, and it was not until the tercentenary of his death that his style began to find support among the rising poets known as the GENERATION OF '27. Critics now favor the idea that Góngora's work did not suffer a sharp break in its inspiration after 1612 but rather evolved from a simpler style of expression into one that was more complex in its expression yet consistent with his earlier themes and concepts.

In his earlier period Góngora was a successful author of numerous lighter poems in several formats including *letrillas* (brief lyrical or satirical poems divided into symmetrical stanzas that end in one or two verses expressing the same thought), sonnets, and romances. His later, more complex creations include *Fábula de Polifemo y Galatea* (Fable of Polyphemus and Galatea, 1612) and *Soledades* ("Solitudes").

González, Julio (1876–1942)
Spanish sculptor

Born in BARCELONA of a family of metalworkers, he learned the craft in his father's workshop but also studied painting at night at the Institute of Fine Arts. When the family moved to Paris in 1900 González renewed his acquaintance with PABLO PICASSO and taught him the techniques of welding that enabled Picasso to experiment with metal sculpture. González was, himself, already investigating the potential of this medium and was undoubtedly influenced by Picasso in a cubist direction, one of several influences evident in his art. Emotionally wounded by the death of his brother in 1908, González retreated to a reclusive life in the suburbs of Paris, emerging during World War I to work on a production line in the Renault factory. When he returned to artistic preoccupation after the war it was with the determination to focus on sculpture rather than painting. His iron sculptures became increasingly well known during the 1920s, and he was recognized as a dominant figure in the use of metal sculpture as a field of abstract art.

During the 1930s González increasingly introduced figurative forms into his sculpture and, for a time at least, drew upon surrealism for ideas.

During the late 1930s, as his homeland was racked by the SPANISH CIVIL WAR and the prospects of a new general conflict threatened all Europe, González was deeply affected in both his emotions and his art. His iconic creation of this period is the bust titled *Montserrat*. A woman with a head scarf, face contorted in agony, is emitting a howl of anguish. The figure's name, frequently borne by women in CATALONIA, is also that of a site in the region. The sculptor evidently sought to evoke not only the suffering of the individual caused by the war but also the devastation brought upon a whole country. The piece had a powerful effect on visitors to the Spanish Pavilion at the Paris World Exhibition of 1937. Depressed and dislocated as the inevitable conflict overwhelmed his adopted country as well as his native land, González died during the darkest moments of the war. His legacy was, however, a significant and powerful one and is particularly evident in the metalwork of EDUARDO CHILLIDA.

González Márquez, Felipe (1942–   )
Spanish politician

Born in SEVILLE, the son of a cattle handler, González was the only member of his family to attend college. Soon after attaining a law degree he began a defense of labor organizers and other activists of the Left, demonstrating his growing commitment to the Socialist cause, although the party itself—Partido Socialista Obrero Español, or PSOE (Spanish Socialist Workers' Party)—was still outlawed under the Franco regime.

During the relaxation of repression that preceded Franco's death in 1975, González rose steadily in the esteem and confidence of his fellow party members and was elected secretary general in 1974, just in time to participate in the flowering of post-Franco democracy. He was elected to the Cortes (see *CORTES*) in 1977 and led the PSOE to a majority in 1982. It would be the first of his four successive terms as prime minister.

The González era was marked by a growing outreach to the world, including membership in the European Union and, somewhat more cautiously, the North Atlantic Treaty Organization. At home he followed a moderate socialist path by promoting education and health care for all, strengthening the judiciary, and curbing the military but also encouraging a freewheeling capitalism. Over time his administration began to lose its luster as his economic policies failed to sustain the initial surge of prosperity that had contributed to his success. González's virtual elimination of censorship in all the media was at first welcomed after decades of dictatorship but eventually opened such floodgates of libertarianism as to antagonize many elements in Spanish society. While his own charisma would survive nearly to the end of his tenure, corruption among ministers and political advisers diminished public support. Other negatives accumulated during the early 1990s, including mixed results from the lavish expenditure on the twin celebrations of the Columbus Quincentenary at Seville and the 1992 Olympic Games at BARCELONA. Far more serious were the accusations that his government had employed police death squads to kill Basque nationalist leaders. González, who had held on to power during the last term only with the support of the nationalists of CATALONIA, was abandoned by these allies in 1995 and defeated in the parliamentary election that he was thereby forced to hold in March 1996. Although he continued as leader of the Socialist opposition for a time, criticizing his successor, the conservative JOSÉ MARÍA AZNAR, González, embittered and increasingly weakened within the PSOE's ranks, surrendered the leadership and by 2000 had essentially retired from politics.

González Pérez, José Victoriano See GRIS, JUAN.

Goya y Lucientes, Francisco José de (1746–1828)

Spanish painter

The son of a gilder, he was committed at an early age to a career in art. He studied painting in ZARAGOZA and later in MADRID; he also spent several years in Italy. His early paintings were mostly commissioned by the church, but he later passed into the service of the Crown, rising to the rank of principal painter to the royal court. An illness in the early 1790s left him deaf but did not significantly affect his prolific output of paintings and prints. After producing portraits of CHARLES IV, his family, and his courtiers he fell out of favor, due, perhaps, to his liberal tendencies. During the French occupation (1808–13) he served as court painter to King JOSEPH I (Joseph Bonaparte). Although he was not persecuted for his service to the usurper, after the restoration of FERDINAND VII he was never entirely trusted by that monarch and left Spain in 1824 when the regime became more

intensely conservative. Goya lived in France (chiefly in Bordeaux) for the remainder of his life, artistically active until the very end.

Goya was undoubtedly the greatest Spanish artist to appear in the 100 years following the death of VELÁZQUEZ. During the 18th century, critics generally agree, Goya had few competitors and no peers. His artistic output paralleled the fecundity of such Spanish writers as LOPE DE VEGA, PÉREZ GALDÓS, FERNÁNDEZ Y GONZÁLEZ, and BENAVENTE, amounting to 700 paintings, 900 drawings, 300 prints, and two major mural cycles. Among his most notable works were unsparing portraits of the elite and more sympathetic portrayals of humbler folk. His drawings reveal a sometimes horrifying realism, both in the early series known as *Los caprichos* (*Caprices,* 1799), with their harsh revelation of social vice, and *Los desastres de la guerra* (*The Disasters of War,* 1810–20), in which the ghastly cruelties perpetrated during the Franco-Spanish conflict present humankind at its most degraded. His most shocking work (not known to the public until long after his death) was contained in the so-called *Black Paintings* of the 1820s, depicting an appalling array of demonic figures.

While certain critics have interpreted Goya largely in terms of his growing pessimism and disgust with the ultimate vileness of human nature, most have preferred to interpret him without psychological analysis and concentrate on his bold innovations in art. He has been widely recognized as the "father of modern art," avowing his personal debt to Velázquez and Rembrandt but leaving the classical tradition behind as he plunged into brilliant experimentation that was not fully understood until the late 19th century, when artists of many schools claimed him as their inspiration. Although Goya is generally ranked with the greatest masters of Spanish painting—Velázquez, EL GRECO, PICASSO—he stands out both as the most intimidating and the most accessible of all. Unlike Velázquez, who reveals almost nothing of himself; El Greco, who ascends to a spiritual plane; and Picasso, who is so often incomprehensible to the uninitiated, Goya strikes the viewer with the immediacy of his passion.

Gracián, Baltasar (1601–1658)

Spanish writer and philosopher

Baltasar Gracián, who published most of his writings under the rather transparent pseudonym of Lorenzo Gracián, was the son of a respectable but impecunious Aragonese family who began his membership in the Jesuits at the age of 18. Having completed his progress through the order's extended training, he took his final priestly vows in 1635. He was at first admired and successful, becoming rector of the Jesuit college at Tarragona in 1643. Within a few years, however, he became embroiled in a series of disputes with his superiors because of his distinctive mode of expressing his ideas and was even accused of anti-Christian attitudes. He sought to resign from the order but was held under its discipline and repeatedly censured throughout the remainder of his life. Fortunately Gracián had a wealthy and cultured patron who funded most of his publications and a circle of intellectual friends who sustained him in his disputes.

Gracián's earlier writings were largely concerned with the principles of conduct that would lead individuals to worldly success while remaining within the bounds of morality. Resembling the works of Castiglione and Machiavelli, these handbooks of conduct included *El héroe* (The hero, 1637), *El político* (The politician, 1640), and *El discreto* (The discreet One, 1646). Blending the philosophical with the literary, Gracián demonstrated his mastery of the principles of *conceptismo* (conceptism). This style of writing involves the use of concise and subtle wit, often employing unsettling metaphors that capture the attention of the reader by their shock effect. His principal exercise in *conceptismo* is *Agudeza y arte de ingenio* (Wit and the art of genius, 1642). His use of this approach links him with his contemporary, FRANCISCO DE QUEVEDO, whose poetry is influenced by the same bitterly satirical and disillusioned sensibility.

Gracián's final achievement was the philosophical novel, published in three parts between 1651 and 1657, *El criticón* (The critic). In this narrative a sophisticated traveler guides a naive "natural" youth—who prefigures the noble savage of 18th-century writers—on a journey of discovery to the various lands and peoples of the "civilized world." The warnings and dismissive comments that the critical traveler makes to his companion reveal a profound disgust with the crimes, follies, and vices of humankind but transcend total pessimism by suggesting that there are higher moral principles that can redeem all of these faults. The author's mentality as revealed in this work displays his deep contempt for the vulgar materialism that afflicted contemporary society and explains how his consistent belief in developing the best potentials of superior men saved him from total cynicism.

Gracián's *El criticón* has been compared with earlier and subsequent works of European literature, sometimes on minor points of resemblance, such as Defoe's *Robinson Crusoe*, and sometimes on a broader scale, particularly in the structure and satirical viewpoint of Voltaire's *Candide*. The 19th-century German philosopher Arthur Schopenhauer was so impressed by *El criticón* that he declared it the best book ever written. In the late 20th-century United States, however, it was the earlier writings of Gracián that were deemed worthy of revival, when an English-language version, *The Art of Worldly Wisdom*, was put together as a manual for successful politicians and businessmen.

Granada

Among the cities of ANDALUSIA Granada occupies a special place. Capital of the Moorish kingdom of the same name, she was the last stronghold of Muslim Spain. After falling to the armies of FERDINAND V and ISABELLA I in 1492 Granada lost its Muslim and Jewish populations and over subsequent centuries became known chiefly as a picturesque setting for the monuments of a bygone era. The American writer Washington Irving, in his *Tales of the Alhambra*, made this fabled palace of long-vanished sultans a reference point for the English-speaking world. The Spanish writer FEDERICO GARCÍA LORCA (slain in 1936 at the beginning of the SPANISH CIVIL WAR) brought a new visibility to his native city. Granada has preserved a sense of its history and mystery in a way unmatched by any other place in Spain.

Pool in front of the Alhambra in Granada *(Getty)*

Granada, conquest of

The struggle for mastery in Iberia that had begun with the Muslim invasion of 711 continued with varying degrees of intensity until the early 13th century, by which time a number of independent Christian kingdoms had established themselves on the Iberian Peninsula. Muslim control had been reduced to the extreme south, roughly equivalent to the old Caliphate of CÓRDOBA. From approximately 1232 to 1492, the kingdom of GRANADA constituted the last surviving Muslim state. During this period of more than two centuries CASTILE and ARAGON (with occasional interference by

Portugal) consolidated their control over the lesser Christian principalities and engaged in dynastic maneuvers that culminated in the marriage of FERDINAND V of Aragon and ISABELLA I of Castile in 1469. Once both of these Reyes Católicos (Catholic Kings) had been recognized as fully sovereign at home they became, in effect, co-sovereigns of a united Christian Spain. They lost no time in preparing for the ultimate confrontation with the "Moros," as the Muslims were commonly called. Yet the Catholic Kings and their advisers were not precipitate in their actions. They took ample time in building up a large military force, drawn chiefly from Castile but under the overall personal command of Ferdinand. Their initial move against Granada, with which they had essentially been at peace for 200 years, was preceded by a legalistic barrage of border adjustment claims. When these were rejected Christian forces launched a series of attacks, only to be repulsed. It was not until 1483 that a reversal of fortune permitted the Spaniards to gain the upper hand when they captured the ruler of Granada, Muhammad XI, called Boabdil by the Spaniards (and in private *"el rey chico"*—"the little king"). Ferdinand treated the young monarch courteously but forced him to accept vassalage in order to regain his personal freedom. This would give Ferdinand the justification for all his military and political actions during the next eight years.

The ultimate fall of Granada was not, however, due solely to the prowess of the Spaniards. It owed much to the internal divisions among the Muslims of the kingdom. The ruling dynasty, the Nasrids, were driven by personal hatreds, and the principal aristocratic families were constantly shifting their allegiance to advance their own presumed advantage. The kingdom had prospered tremendously during two centuries of peace, and its commercial and agricultural wealth had created a concentration of Islamic culture that was reflected in the splendor of its buildings and the confidence of its leaders. But prosperity had bred corruption and luxurious self-indulgence at the highest levels. King Muley Hassan, who had boldly defied Ferdinand's original claims in 1481, was also caught in harem intrigues that led him to execute his elder son and to drive the younger, Boabdil, into revolt. The struggle between Muley Hassan and Boabdil continued to divide their subjects until 1485 when the elder man was driven into exile, shortly followed by his death. Yet this did not bring Boabdil into sole control of the kingdom, for his uncle El Zagal (as he was called by the Spaniards) had been named as presumptive successor by the late king. A virtual civil war between uncle (ruling as Muhammad XII) and nephew continued for the next five years, even as Ferdinand continued to capture Muslim outposts while his fleet blocked the coastal towns to prevent reinforcements being brought in from North Africa. Some Spanish commentators have contrasted the martial virtues of the North African Moors of this period with what are dismissed as the effete and cowardly efforts of the Spanish Muslims to fight for their territory. The latter description can hardly be applied to the forces commanded by El Zagal, who obstinately defended those parts of the kingdom under his control, particularly the city of MÁLAGA, which valiantly withstood a prolonged siege by Ferdinand's troops. Boabdil, by contrast, boldly denied his previous submission to Ferdinand yet failed to mobilize an adequate resistance to the Spanish ruler. In fact Boabdil's only military success in the last years of this three-sided war was to annihilate a relief force marching to the aid of Málaga because it might have strengthened his rival, El Zagal.

By 1490, with Málaga finally captured and all but a handful of outposts in possession of the Reyes Católicos, the splendid city of Granada itself was encircled by a besieging Christian army. The arrival of Queen Isabella, come to join her regal presence to the military energy of her husband, inspired her soldiers to even greater demonstrations of chivalrous and spiritual energy. Boabdil could find no recourse but to open negotiations for surrender in fall 1491. On January 6, 1492, Granada was yielded to the Catholic Kings. Boabdil was once again treated courteously by the victors, and his subjects who did not choose to follow him to North Africa were guaranteed political and personal rights within the city, including preservation of their religion and culture, although these pledges would later be broken. According to tradition Boabdil stood weeping as he gazed upon Granada for the last time but was rebuked by his stern mother who said that if he had fought like a man instead of weeping like a woman they would not have lost the kingdom. The age of the Cruzada (the crusade to recapture Spain for Christianity) had ended. A new era in Spanish history was about to begin.

Granados, Enrique (1867–1916)
Spanish composer
A student of Felipe Pedrell, who is regarded as the founder of the Spanish school of music, Granados also dedicated himself to national themes and after further studies in Paris established a steadily growing reputation as a pianist and teacher in BARCELONA. His 12 *Danzas españolas* (Spanish dances) won him particular attention, but his most notable work was a suite of piano pieces, *Goyescas,* composed between 1911 and 1913. His public performances drew enthusiastic attendance, and his collaborations with such musicians as PABLO CASALS and Camile Saint-Saëns increased the number of his admirers throughout Europe. He also composed seven operas, the last of which was based upon and also titled *Goyescas.* He attended its New York premiere in 1916 at the height of World War I and was about to return to Spain on board an American ship (the United States at that time being neutral) when an invitation from President Wilson to perform at the White House drew him to Washington. Obliged to reschedule his return home on a British ship, he was killed when it was torpedoed by a German submarine.

Gravina y Nápoli, Federico Carlos (1756–1806)
Spanish naval officer
Beginning his naval career in the coast guard Gravina earned successive promotions by a combination of reliability and bravery. He took part in the siege of GIBRALTAR in 1781 during Spain's campaign of support to the American revolutionaries and subsequently carried out a series of important assignments ranging from the eastern Mediterranean to the Caribbean. During the early stages of the French Revolutionary War he commanded a squadron in the assault on Toulon. Within a few

years, after Spain's change of alliances, he was once again fighting the British. By 1803 he was senior admiral of the Spanish fleet and in the following year served as ambassador to France. He was recalled to active sea duty to collaborate with the French in the operations that culminated in the BATTLE OF TRAFALGAR in 1805. In that fierce contest his flagship *Príncipe de Asturias* was engaged with as many as five British warships at once. The admiral, who had already sustained many wounds in the course of his career, was severely injured and had to be brought ashore. He never fully recovered from these wounds and died in CÁDIZ a few months later.

Greco, El (Doménikos Theotokópoulos, Doménicos Theotocópoulos) (1541–1614)

Spanish painter

Born in Crete (then a possession of Venice) and trained in the Byzantine tradition of icon painting, Theotokópoulos worked and studied in Venice from 1558 to 1570, then spent several years in Rome before returning to Venice. During his Italian sojourn he was influenced by the paintings of Titian and Tintoretto. He moved to Spain in 1576/7, hoping to take part in the embellishment of EL ESCORIAL but apparently was rejected by PHILIP II because of what the king considered eccentricities of style. Theotokópoulos settled in TOLEDO where he found frequent commissions for the adornment of religious edifices, as well as for portraits. The designation "El Greco" ("the Greek") was commonly applied to him in Spain, although he continued to sign his paintings with his personal name, using Greek letters. He spent the rest of his life in Toledo rather than returning to Italy, having established a circle of friends and fellow intellectuals in the city as well as a relationship with Jerónima de las Cuevas. Their son, Jorge Manuel Theotocópoulos, became an artist and architect who had a successful (though not brilliant) career in early 17th-century Toledo.

Although El Greco's *The Adoration of the Holy Name of Jesus* had won him initial favor with Philip II in 1578, that monarch ended their contact in 1582 when *The Martyrdom of St. Maurice* exhibited a departure from conventional imagery that offended Philip's conservative taste. Despite royal disapproval and his own personal commitment to pursuing his own ideas and his own visionary style of painting, El Greco found patrons well into the 1600s, working with assistants, turning out many paintings, and living in comfortable circumstances. His most notable achievements included such religious subjects as *The Assumption* (1577), *The Disrobing of Christ* (*El espolio,* 1577), *The Trinity* (1577–79), *Christ Carrying the Cross* and *The Crucifixion* (1580s), *The Holy Family* (1590–95), *The Resurrection* (late 1590s), *The Pentecost* (c. 1596–1600), *The Virgin and Child with Sts. Martina and Agnes* (1597–99), *The Baptism of Christ* (1600), *The Agony in the Garden* (c. 1600–05), *The Nativity* (1603–05), *The Immaculate Conception* (1608–13), *The Adoration of the Shepherds* (1612), *The Visitation* (1610) and *The Marriage of the Virgin* (1613–14), as well as *The Opening of the Fifth Seal* (1608). He also painted portraits of luminaries of his time, such as the poet LUIS DE GÓNGORA, Fray Hortensio Félix Paravicino, and Cardinal Niño de Guevara. He occasionally touched upon mythological themes as well, as with *Lacoon* (1608), and became one of the first true landscapists with several versions of *View of Toledo* (1597–99). His masterpiece is undoubtedly *The Burial of Count Orgaz* (1586), a painting of grand proportions preserved in the church of San Tomé in Toledo.

When El Greco's paintings involved specific persons, such as his portraits, the execution is realistic, but he gives free rein to his spiritual impulses when moving beyond literal representation. For example, in *The Burial of Count Orgaz* the lower portion of the canvas, representing the earthly plane, contains natural figures (including, it is believed, El Greco himself and his son); the upper portion of the canvas, offering a view of heaven, takes greater liberty with the imagery, particularly in the elongated manner in which bodies are painted. Similarly the *View of Toledo* does not offer a literal landscape but a mixture of symbolism and mysticism. Despite the popular notion that the distortions of perspective and figure in many of his paintings resulted from astigmatism, there is no reliable evidence that El Greco had any visual abnormality. Rather his links to medieval Byzantine tradition, modified by his experience of Italian figure painting, interacted with his intense personal spirituality to create an artistic impulse that often transcended the norms of imagery.

El Greco was, according to contemporary records, an arrogant, contentious, and opinionated individual who followed his own inclinations and notions of the way to present exalted situations on canvas. Fortunately for his career his approach found favor among the more open-minded members of Toledo's elite.

The respect in which El Greco was held until the end of his life gave way to antagonism and later neglect during the mid-17th century, as tastes changed. It was not until the 19th or even the beginning of the 20th century that he accumulated the endorsements of modern painters that helped to elevate him to the stature he has since enjoyed. He is now firmly established as one of the three or four greatest painters that Spain can claim.

Grijalva, Juan de (1480–1527)
Spanish explorer

Grijalva owed his opportunity for fame and fortune and the loss of any prospect of attaining them to the same man, his fellow Segovian DIEGO VELÁZQUEZ DE CUÉLLAR. Arriving in HISPANIOLA in 1508, Grijalva joined Velázquez in the conquest of CUBA, in 1511. During the next few years he partnered with the brutal soldier PÁNFILO DE NARVÁEZ and the benevolent clergyman BARTOLOMÉ DE LAS CASAS in bringing the interior of the island into submission. By 1517 Velázquez, now governor of Cuba, had grown impatient with the failure of earlier probes sent out toward the North American mainland. He commissioned Captain Grijalva, with four ships and several hundred soldiers, to explore the unknown coast that lay to the west. Between January and September 1518 Grijalva became the first Spaniard to touch the coast of what is now MEXICO, an area to which he gave the name Santa María de las Nieves. He also negotiated with several Indian tribes and through them received messages from Moctezuma, the ruler of the Aztec Empire. Grijalva also surveyed the coast of the Yucatán Peninsula. However, although he had been authorized to initiate a settlement, he deemed it imprudent to establish a Spanish colony without a fuller knowledge of the area. For this excess of caution he was harshly criticized by the aggressive soldier PEDRO DE ALVARADO, who was one of his officers and who denounced him to Velázquez. Grijalva was stripped of his authority to continue the exploration and was replaced in command of the next expedition, which left Cuba at the end of 1518, by HERNÁN CORTÉS, with Alvarado as his deputy. Grijalva remained marginalized during the conquest of Mexico and was denied any opportunity to emerge from disgrace by the spite of Cortés and his allies. It was not until 1527 that Grijalva found an opportunity to advance himself by securing an appointment under the command of PEDRARIAS DÁVILA. He made his way to a gold-rich district where he might have made his fortune had he not been, almost immediately, killed in an Indian uprising.

Grijalva is one of those lesser figures in the story of Spain's conquest of the Americas. Like the majority of the conquistadores, he did not cover himself with glory nor did he gain riches or titles. Even his failures were more pathetic than spectacular. Yet he had the distinction of being the first to gaze upon the land that others would conquer, to communicate with the indigenous peoples of Mexico, and, thus, to be the precursor of a century of conquest.

Gris, Juan (José Victoriano González Pérez) (1887–1927)
Spanish artist

González Pérez, who adopted the name Juan Gris, was born in MADRID and studied painting, illustration, and drawing there. He moved to Paris in 1906, where he became associated with such leading painters as Georges Braque, Fernand Léger, and his compatriot PABLO PICASSO. Under their influence he joined the cubist movement. Possessing a strongly disciplined mind and influenced by his scientific training, Gris found the geometric and logically ordered patterns of cubism particularly appealing. Gris moved beyond the Analytic School of Cubism, whose techniques he quickly absorbed, and entered the so-called Synthetic School, making use of an analysis of geometrical forms and planes and the additional dimension of collage. His *Still-Life* (1911) shows his preoccupation with the pictorial visualization of time and space through a physical representation of the possibilities of human perception. His presentation of fundamental elements in a simplified form created a high degree of abstraction. This approach found its natural expression in his preference for still-lifes; nevertheless, Gris did occasionally venture into figurative painting, most notably in *The Smoker* (1913), in which he invites comparison with the analytic approach of Picasso, Braque, and others, while asserting his own precise approach in the geometrical division of the painting into distinct areas devoted to particular aspects of the figure. This picture has been compared to a jigsaw puzzle in which the viewer is required to reassemble the separate elements of the painting into a meaningful whole.

The artistic career of Gris was a relatively short one. Having continued his study of drawing in Paris and supported himself by working as an illustrator, he did not begin to exhibit publicly until 1912. After the outbreak of World War I (1914) he moved to the south of France, where he attracted the admiration of Henri Matisse, although he was not necessarily influenced by the better-known painter. Shortly after the war (1919) he had a major exhibition (in Paris), again attracting favorable comment for the discipline of his structures and the sober tone of his coloring. During the early 1920s, as his work expanded to include a number of sculptures, critics continued to pay attention to his control of material and structures. In addition to further exhibitions of painting and sculpture he accepted design commissions from the Ballets Russes and returned to his early career as an illustrator for books by important authors.

Gris is generally esteemed to be one of the great cubists, not perhaps ranked with Picasso and Braque, but having his own distinctive understanding of geometric forms and possibilities offered by the intersections of art and science.

Guatemala

One of the earliest offshoots of the conquest of the Aztec Empire by HERNÁN CORTÉS, the area of present-day Guatemala was occupied by his lieutenant, PEDRO DE ALVARADO, in 1524, and the administrative center, known as Ciudad de Guatemala, was established. By 1527 Guatemala City had become the seat of the Captaincy General of Guatemala, which included within its jurisdiction all of the modern Central American republics. Guatemala renounced Spanish rule in 1821 and subordinated itself to the empire of AGUSTÍN ITURBIDE until 1823. Subsequently it was part of the short-lived United Provinces of Central America, which broke up in 1839, and thereafter remained an independent republic.

Guevara, Antonio de (1480–1545)
Spanish clergyman and writer

Born of an aristocratic family, Guevara was a page at the court of ISABELLA I and FERDINAND V. Subsequently ordained as a Franciscan priest, he served as a court preacher, as chaplain to CHARLES I (Emperor Charles V), whom he accompanied on his expedition against Tunis, and as royal chronicler. Although later appointed bishop of two Spanish sees, he was not primarily interested in religious affairs and his designation as an inquisitor was largely nominal. Guevara was in fact obsessed by language, and many of his numerous works are intended to display his elaborate prose style rather than to convey serious ideas. His most important publication was the *Reloj de príncipes o libro áureo del emperador Marco Aurelio* (1529), published in mid-16th-century England as *The Golden Boke of Marcus Aurelius* or *The Diall of Princes*. This volume was presented as a philosophical study of the proper role and conduct of monarchs based on the newly recovered meditations of the Roman emperor Marcus Aurelius. Like several other contemporary authors, including Machiavelli, Guevara was admired by his contemporaries for his sophisticated analysis of a ruler's duties. After it was subsequently discovered that much of what he had attributed to the emperor was in fact invented by Guevara himself, his reputation faded and his *Reloj* became little more than a historical curiosity.

H

Habsburg

The consolidation of Spain's regional kingdoms was completed between 1469 and 1479 by the marriage of FERDINAND V and ISABELLA I, her accession to the throne of CASTILE, and his to the throne of ARAGON. These two royal cousins both belonged to the House of Trastamara. In 1495 the marriage of their daughter JOANNA to Philip, the heir to the Austrian ruling house of Habsburg prepared the way for the start of a new dynasty in the newly established kingdom of Spain. Although Joanna was queen in her own right from 1504, her husband was designated co-sovereign as PHILIP I. Their son ruled as CHARLES I, but his accession to the throne of the Holy Roman Empire as Charles V emphasized Spain's Habsburg connection, and the ruling family would generally be referred to as the "Casa de Austria." After Charles I abdicated his multiple thrones in 1556, the imperial title passed to his brother, Emperor Ferdinand I, and, through him, to subsequent Austrian rulers until 1918. PHILIP II succeeded his father Charles I as king of Spain and its worldwide dominions. The relationship between the two branches of the House of Austria remained close, and there would be frequent intermarriages. The Spanish house of Austria was continued by PHILIP III, PHILIP IV, and CHARLES II from 1598 to 1700.

Support given to their Austrian kinsmen drew the Spanish rulers into the Thirty Years' War (1618–48). Spain's decline as a great power was paralleled by the physical and mental deterioration of her last Habsburg king, and, on his death in 1700, his will conferred the Crown on his great-nephew, a prince of the French ruling house of BOURBON.

Haro, Luis de (marqués de Carpio) (1598–1661)

Spanish statesman

Of noble birth (he succeeded his father as marqués de Carpio in 1648), his most important relationship was with his mother's brother, the count duke of OLIVARES. Although on good terms with this chief minister of PHILIP IV, Haro facilitated the end of his uncle's tenure in office and succeeded him as *privado* (political favorite) of the king in 1643. During the latter half of the reign Haro was Philip's principal adviser in foreign and domestic affairs. Although the king had learned from the failure of Olivares's policy how dangerous it was to confide total authority to a single politician, his own attempts to play a more direct role in ruling his country proved sporadic and unsuccessful. Haro lacked the gifts to either fill his uncle's shoes or remedy the king's failings. An affable man who did not arouse the opposition that Olivares had provoked among the magnates, Haro made no real attempts to pursue his predecessor's reform program. In foreign affairs he pressed ahead with the imperial program that had already begun to unravel and continued to struggle against France, even after the end of the Thirty Years' War in 1648 removed many of the issues that had drawn the two powers into confrontation. Despite one reverse after another Haro and his master raised new forces, with the *privado* even taking personal command in the field. By 1659 there was clearly no hope of victory, and Haro performed his last service by arranging a dignified peace conference. There was no escaping the fact, however, that in the Peace of the Pyrenees Spain had given up its claim to be master of Europe.

When Haro died in 1661 his son launched an abortive revolt against Philip IV, demanding that he be accorded the same power and respect that his father had enjoyed. The king did not punish him for this piece of folly, evidently out of affection he still held for his late minister. Yet the era of the *privado* as the true ruler of Spain, like the era of Spain as the true ruler of Europe, was undoubtedly over.

Henry IV (Enrique IV) (1425–1474)
king of Castile

Son of John II of CASTILE, he joined in widespread opposition to the dictatorship exercised by his father's henchman, the notorious Álvaro de Luna. However, Henry soon changed sides in the conflict, beginning a pattern of vacillation that would characterize his behavior in Castile's ongoing civil strife. Despite his youthful partici-

pation in various battles Henry developed into a weak, indecisive prince whose essentially quiet, kindly disposition proved ill suited to the rough politics of his realm. The disrespect that many of his subjects came to feel for him was intensified by his wife's successful petition for an annulment of their marriage on the ground of nonconsummation. Henry married a second time but remained childless for several years, and when his consort gave birth to a daughter, rumor held that the infant, Juana, was actually the child of a courtier named Beltrán de la Cueva. Although Henry recognized Juana as his daughter, she was popularly given the derisive nickname *La Beltraneja* (Beltran's kid).

From the time when Henry IV ascended the throne (1454) the question of succession lay at the heart of all Castilian political activity. The old king had complicated matters by producing two children from a later marriage. Alfonso and the future ISABELLA I of Castile, Henry's young half brother and half sister, were inevitably supported by cliques within the nobility and clergy. Henry's reign became a series of defeats and humiliations. The most notable of these (1465) involved a ritual of deposition, when an effigy of the king was set up on a public platform, denounced for his shortcomings, stripped of the royal regalia, and kicked to the ground while Prince Alfonso was proclaimed sovereign.

The hapless Henry continued to play one faction against the other and ultimately renounced Juana's right to succession on the condition that she marry Alfonso. Before this solution could be seriously considered Alfonso died, and Isabella became the de facto heiress, a position reinforced by her marriage to FERDINAND V of Aragon

(1469). After Henry's death in 1474, the king of Portugal, having married La Beltraneja, invaded Castile to support her claim to the throne. Within a few years this enterprise failed in turn. The Portuguese ruler abandoned his campaign, and La Beltraneja, like Henry, faded away, although she would live on in dignified retirement for many decades. The question of her parentage has remained unresolved by all the arts and sciences of modern times. Isabella emerged as the unchallenged queen of Castile, joining her kingdom with that of her husband, Ferdinand of Aragon, in a united Spain.

The reign of Henry IV has continued to be the subject of endless fascination for Spanish historians, with its mixture of court intrigue, political maneuvering, and recurrent warfare. From its medieval anarchy emerged the strong monarchy that would build a Spanish empire. For this reason, at least, the enigmatic figure of King Henry has in latter days been accorded the sympathy that he never received in his own unhappy lifetime.

Herculano de Carvalho e Araújo, Alexandre (1810–1877)

Portuguese historian and novelist

Portugal's literary heritage owes much to Herculano, whose work ranged from the poetical through the historical romance to a multivolume authoritative history. Consistently a champion of liberal causes, he opposed the reactionary regime of Dom MIGUEL in the early 1830s and left Portugal to join the opposition forces mustering abroad. Returning as a member of the liberation army in 1832, he participated in the defeat and ouster of the Miguelite forces. These harsh political and military experiences transformed the youthful poet into a serious journalist committed to advancing Portugal's cultural standing in Europe and safeguarding her intellectual freedom. Herculano founded the journal *O Panorama*, which monitored the international scene for his countryfolk and was personally involved in overthrowing a new authoritarian regime that challenged constitutional liberties in 1851.

Working with other intellectuals, such as ALMEIDA GARRETT, Herculano furthered the growth of cultural institutions and from 1839 was head of the Royal Library, which became a center of scholarship. Like many of his literary associates, Herculano initially approached history as a romantic art and published a number of novels modeled on those of Sir Walter Scott. This tendency was not entirely banished from the early chapters of his historical magnum opus. His *History of Portugal* appeared in four successive volumes between 1847 and 1853, and it gave a very detailed account of Portugal's origin and growth. The first volume, which carried the story up to the middle of the 13th century, was based on a mass of hitherto neglected documents that he employed to emphasize the rise of the middle class and the growth of democratic institutions. A similar liberal bias was evident in his other major historical work, *Da origine e establecimento da inquisicão em Portugal* (*History of the Origins and Establishment of the Inquisition in Portugal*, 1854–59). Although less notorious than its Spanish counterpart, the Portuguese Inquisition was to men of Herculano's principles a sinister and dangerous force whose deeds must be recorded and criticized by the historian. In his breadth of activities, his international contacts, and his progressive activism, Herculano became one of the most influential figures in the Portugal of his time.

Herrera, Fernando de (1534–1597)
Spanish poet

Esteemed the greatest poet of the Spanish Renaissance and hailed by his contemporaries as El Divino (The Divine One), Herrera was a native of SEVILLE who founded the Sevillian school of poetry. Having taken minor orders to secure an ecclesiastical benefice that would support him, he devoted his life to poetry. Herrera was preoccupied by the form, content, and scope of the poetic art, constantly making notes on images and ideas that he might introduce into his own work. He was in a sense a promoter, as well as a practitioner, of poetry. The literary circle over which he presided at the mansion of the conde de Gelves was Spain's first tertulia (literary salon). His preferred form was the epic, and his verses celebrating the achievements of JOHN OF AUSTRIA (Don Juan de Austria) and the victory over the Turks at LEPANTO are merely the best known of repeated excursions into this genre. He clearly aspired to be Spain's great epic poet, as LUÍZ DE CAMÕES was that of Portugal. But Herrera was also capable of tender emotions, and his poems celebrating the virtues of the condesa de Gelves clearly reflect the warm feelings that lay beneath his rather cold and sometimes hostile personality. Perhaps the most striking characteristic of Herrera's work is his preoccupation with original and striking images and metaphors. His richness and even novelty of language would be much imitated by subsequent generations of SIGLO DE ORO poets, culminating in the verbal excesses of LUIS DE GÓNGORA.

hidalgo (Portuguese: *fidalgo*)

Title of a subordinate class of nobles, roughly equivalent to the gentry or country gentleman in England, this term is derived from *hijo de algo*, signifying "son of something." It came into use during the early Middle Ages and survived until the 19th century. Conferring certain legal protections and privileges, it entitled individuals who were recognized as members of this class to representation in a distinct chamber of the CORTES (a form of Spanish parliament), separate from the nobles and the commoners. Traditionally distinguished by the right to display a coat of arms and wear a sword, the hidalgo was generally an object of respect or derision, depending on whether he had the financial means to support his pretensions. By the 19th century the term had become essentially customary or rhetorical.

Hispaniola (Española)

This island in the central West Indies (encompassing nearly 30,000 square miles) was reached by CHRISTOPHER COLUMBUS on his first voyage of discovery in 1492. He named it *La Española* (for "the Spanish [Island]") and left a small settlement on his departure in 1493. This had disappeared by his return voyage in 1494 but was succeeded by a permanent settlement named Santo Domingo in the eastern end of the island. This town became the seat of Spanish administration in the New World and the launching place of the first phase of expeditions to the American mainland. The influx of Spaniards soon led to the virtual extinction of the original Amerindian population, but the need for a labor force led to the importation of a large numbers of African slaves.

After protracted struggles Spain ceded the western half of the island to France in 1697 and retained the eastern part under the designation Santo Domingo. The western part was called St.-Domingue by the French, but the name *Haiti* eventually became associated with the French-speaking western area, although the same name was sometimes applied to the whole island, both before and after 1697. The slave revolts that began in 1791 under the stimulus of the French Revolution eventually replaced all European government with a series of rebel leaders. Spanish rule was reestablished between 1807 and 1821 but was abandoned once again when a new president in Haiti proclaimed the unification of the whole island. In 1844 the erstwhile colony of Santo Domingo proclaimed its independence as the DOMINICAN REPUBLIC (República Dominicana). Dissidents invited Spain to resume her sovereignty over this eastern region of Hispaniola in 1861. By 1865 the arrangement had proved mutually unpopular, and Spain ended the relationship, leaving the Dominican Republic to resume her interrupted existence.

Honduras

First sighted by CHRISTOPHER COLUMBUS on his last voyage to the Americas in 1502, this region was subsequently explored and claimed for Spain by the lieutenants of HERNÁN CORTÉS. The first significant Spanish settlements were made at Trujillo and Puerto Cortés in 1525. During the remainder of the colonial period Honduras formed a province under the Captaincy General of GUATEMALA. Honduras declared its independence in 1821, adhered to the United Provinces of Central America until 1839, and thereafter remained a sovereign republic.

I

Ibárruri, Dolores (1895–1989)
Spanish politician

Born to a working-class family in the Basque province of Vizcaya, Ibárruri left school at an early age to earn her living. She nevertheless displayed eloquence in articles for labor union publications and was already well known as an agitator when she joined the newly formed Communist Party in 1920. Under the pseudonym La Pasionaria (the Passion Flower), she was already famous as a street orator and proponent of class warfare when she was elected to the Cortes (see CORTES) after the establishment of the Second Republic. The SPANISH CIVIL WAR of 1936–39 brought her international notoriety as she exhorted the Republican forces with such slogans as *"No pasarán"* ("They shall not pass") and *"Es mejor morir de pie que vivir de rodillas"* ("It is better to die on your feet than to live on your knees"). Following the collapse of the republic, Ibárruri was welcomed by the Soviet Union as Spain's most prominent Communist leader. She remained there during World War II (in which her son was killed while serving in the Red Army). With the end of the Franco dictatorship in 1975 and the subsequent legalization of the Communist Party, Ibárruri returned to Spain where she was reelected to the Cortes. Within a few years her advancing age led her to withdraw from active politics, but she was named honorary president of her party. A dynamic and outspoken champion of her cause, La Pasionaria was undoubtedly the best known Spanish woman of the 20th century.

Ignatius of Loyola, Saint (Ignacio López de Loyola) (1491–1556)
Spanish religious leader

Born in the Basque province of Guipúzcoa, the youngest son of a noble family, Ignatius (later to be known as Ignatius of Loyola) spent his youth as a page in noble households and, for a time, at the court of King FERDINAND V. He then followed a military career until badly wounded at the siege of Pamplona in 1521. While recovering from his injuries, spiritual books, which were his only available reading, turned his mind to the religious life. A year of hermitlike isolation and meditation confirmed him in his decision.

Ignatius spent more than a decade repairing the defects of his early education, studying in BARCELONA and at the Universities of Alcala and Salamanca, where his intensity and enthusiasm won him a following among pious students but led to his interrogation by the SPANISH INQUISITION, presumably on the ground that he was caught up in the heretical movements of the day. A similar rebuff during a pilgrimage to Jerusalem led him to complete his studies, secure ordination as a priest at Venice in 1537, and place himself along with a new band of followers under the personal authority of the pope. In 1541 his spiritual confraternity was confirmed as a religious order under the designation of the Society of Jesus, with Ignatius as head, or general, of the order.

Later identified with the struggle that was now developing between the Catholic Church and the Protestant Reformation, the Jesuits, as they were commonly known, were at first intended by Ignatius for work in the foreign missions, and they played a major part in the introduction of Catholicism to Japan, India, and BRAZIL. Ignatius agreed, at first reluctantly, to accept the additional special task of educating the social and intellectual elite of Catholic Europe with the result that Jesuit secondary schools and universities became widely diffused and increasingly influential.

Much has been made of the Jesuits' military model of organization, and their enemies inevitably asserted that they followed a secretive policy to subvert rival organizations and influence secular governments, as well as adhering to the doctrine that "the end justifies the means." None of these characterizations correspond to the thinking of Ignatius as revealed in the *Spiritual Exercises,* which are the fullest expression of his own religious feelings and commitments. The Constitutions that he drew up for the governance of the order and have remained its basic foundation ever since his time offer little evidence of authoritarian impulses. Far from exercising autocratic rule over the thousand-member order that

grew within a dozen "provinces" in Europe and overseas, Ignatius seems to have remained both humble and committed to his early acceptance of Christ as his personal model of life. Due to declining health he sought to resign his leadership in 1551, but his followers insisted that he must not leave them, and he continued as general until his death.

Ignatius was canonized in 1622, and on the 300th anniversary of that occasion he was proclaimed universal patron of religious retreats. As Saint Ignatius of Loyola his name has been given to churches, schools, and universities all over the world.

immigrants in Portugal

For centuries Portugal was a country that exported its people. During the imperial era they traveled to the far corners of the world, as traders and fighters in Asia, as settlers in BRAZIL, and, in the last decades of the Salazar regime, as colonial "planters." There was also, particularly in the latter half of the 20th century, an exodus to other European countries in search of employment. Even the United States welcomed a modest flow of Portuguese expatriates. Since the CARNATION REVOLUTION of 1974 the movement has been reversed. Among the causes of this shift have been the relative improvement in the domestic economy, offering increased job opportunities and a sense of general optimism generated by the restoration of democracy. The granting of independence to the African colonies after the prolonged fighting of the 1960s and early '70s placed the Portuguese residents of those colonies in an impossible situation. There was no serious prospect of remaining in an African environment that had become totally antagonistic to their presence, even if they had been willing to consider such an option. As a result scores of thousands of ex-colonial Portuguese returned to the "mother country," which, for many of them, was an unfamiliar place of residence with an unfamiliar way of life to which they found it difficult to adapt.

Adaptation was, however, far more difficult for Africans who chose to take up residence in the territory of their former overlord. They were driven, in most cases, by the collapse of the local economy in their homeland or the continuation of violence there. In particular, factional or tribal strife among rival political and ethnic groups continued almost without interruption after the end of the colonial regime. Although not precisely welcomed in Portugal, these people from the former "overseas provinces" had certain legal claims to enter and few prospects of finding homes elsewhere. By 2001 there were some 45,000 immigrants from the CAPE VERDE ISLANDS living in Portugal, as well as 20,000 Angolans and 15,000 from Guinea Bissau (formerly PORTUGUESE GUINEA). The total number of immigrants—aside from Africans, mostly people from eastern Europe and the former Soviet Union—amounted to nearly 250,000. When one considers that the population of Portugal is about 10 million, this is a considerable proportion of aliens to be absorbed. Inevitably social tensions grew during the 1990s. In LISBON there have been clashes between Cape Verdian youths and police, Cape Verdians and white civilians, and Cape Verdians and blacks from other African colonies. Eastern Europeans, for their part, have been accused of playing a role in the trafficking of drugs and prostitutes and of turning Portugal into a participating country in a growing criminal network stretching from Russia into western Europe. The government, however, speaks confidently of positive achievements in racial and ethnic assimilation. Yet one commentator remarked, "During the diaspora one asked where are the Portuguese? Now one asks who are the Portuguese?"

Inquisition   See SPANISH INQUISITION.

Isabella I (Isabel I, Isabella of Castile, Isabella the Catholic) (1451–1504)
queen of Castile, first queen of a united Spain

Daughter of John (Juan) II of CASTILE by his second wife, she was not in the immediate line of succession until the death of her brother Alfonso and the failure of her half brother HENRY IV to produce a recognized legitimate heir. By the time she was 18 Isabella was at the center of a power struggle between Castilian factions and was pressed by suitors from Portugal and France. Her marriage in 1469 to Fernando (FERDINAND V), heir to the throne of ARAGON, secured her position and set the future course of Spanish history. She claimed the title of queen on the death of Henry IV but was still obliged to defeat competitors, and it was not until her husband became king of Aragon in 1479 that the couple were truly rulers of their realms. Isabella and Ferdinand worked together to establish good order and strong government in Castile after years of civil war and weak administration. A well-functioning central government, a royal army, and dominance over both nobles and clergy were among the

Queen Isabella I *(Library of Congress)*

her family and soldiers, Isabella enjoyed a moment of intense personal triumph.

The terms under which Granada had been yielded obliged the queen to extend tolerance and a generous degree of self-management to the Muslim population after their native ruler went into exile. At first Isabella abided by these commitments, impatient though she was for Granada to be integrated into Christian Castile. The priests employed by Archbishop Talavera to hold discussions with Muslim clergy engaged in the sort of polite, scholarly, and gradualistic dialogues that might have continued a regime of benign tolerance indefinitely. However, under the influence of her new confessor, FRANCISCO JIMÉNEZ DE CISNEROS, whom she appointed in 1492 and named archbishop of Toledo in 1495, Isabella undertook a more urgent timetable and a more aggressive approach to conversion. These measures provoked violent attacks upon Cisneros and, ultimately, a general revolt in the region. By 1499 Cisneros had persuaded Isabella to order the prompt departure from Castile of all Muslims who would not embrace Christianity. Having already decreed a similar banishment of her Jewish subjects, in 1492, Isabella could now rejoice in presiding as a truly Christian monarch over a truly Christian realm.

Although the conquest of Granada had preoccupied the attention of the Castilian queen in 1492, she had spared time to fund the bold project of a transatlantic expedition to Asia laid before her by the navigator CHRISTOPHER COLUMBUS. By 1493 Columbus was back from what was eventually recognized, not as Asia, but a New World of two continents and a multitude of islands. Ferdinand remained preoccupied with the ongoing crises in the Old World, particu-

fruits of their collaboration. Ferdinand also shared with his wife the CONQUEST OF GRANADA (1492), the last Muslim stronghold on the Iberian Peninsula.

The expulsion of the Moors was a project particularly dear to the heart of Isabella. Not only did the continued presence of this alien foothold in Spain offend her pride as a monarch; it also represented a challenge to the universality of what she devoutly believed to be the one true faith. The war that was waged for nearly 10 years and culminated in the fall of GRANADA was a crusade that preoccupied her, while it never engaged the full attention of Ferdinand who had far more interest in the main currents of European affairs. Entering the captured city of Granada in January 1492 amid larly the Italian Wars, for the wealth of the "Indies" was yet to be proven to him.

Isabella, however, was fascinated by the prospect of whole new realms being laid at her feet through the successive voyages of Columbus and his followers. She reserved these new discoveries as an exclusively Castilian preserve, excluding Aragon from them. Her greatest enthusiasm was aroused not by regal pride but by the opportunities that these new lands presented for extending her religion to untold multitudes of "pagans." She gave a significant role in planning the acquisition and management of new territories to her clerical advisers and in her last testament shows a mixture of pride, humility, and joy at being able to spread the gospel of Christ to hitherto unknown lands. She also asks her successors, to be sure, that her "Indians" are well and justly treated, receiving no harm in their person or property.

While Isabella and Ferdinand were the parents of five children (whose marriages were factors in dynastic diplomacy), their partnership had more of the pragmatic than the romantic about it, despite popular legend. Unlike her essentially amoral consort, Isabella was a woman of obsessive principles and unswerving commitments. Intelligent but not an intellectual, she was less of a Renaissance personality than was Ferdinand. Her prime concerns were the renewal of Castile after generations of destructive warfare and the triumph of the Christian faith. Her title "the Catholic," although shared with her husband, was a far more appropriate recognition by the pope of what she had done for the faith in completing the RECONQUISTA. During the 12 years following Isabella's death in 1504 Ferdinand was able to draw more freely upon the resources of Castile. While she was alive, she had remained a jealous guardian of the rights of Castile and her own role as sovereign. In Spain Isabella remains a revered figure, one who commands affection in a way that Ferdinand never could. In Spanish America she is still remembered as the true initiator of the transatlantic empire with a language and culture that have survived more than five centuries. Although her religious zeal reflected the intolerance of her time, the ardor of her faith has made her among Catholics an iconic figure for whom the honor of sainthood would be almost superfluous.

Isabella II (1830–1904)
queen of Spain

Born to King FERDINAND VII and his fourth wife, Maria Christina of BOURBON, princess of the Two Sicilies, Isabella represented, in effect, her father's last chance to leave a direct heir. Having lost all the sons of his previous marriages, he now proclaimed that his daughter should be his successor, a provision that was consistent with earlier Spanish custom but inconsistent with the Salic law introduced by the French Bourbons, under which only males could rule. Although this royal decree was approved by the Spanish legislature, conservatives insisted that so fundamental a law could not be altered and argued that the rightful succession must pass to the king's brother Carlos. When Ferdinand died in 1833 the three-year-old Isabella II was hailed as queen by those who supported a "liberal" direction for Spain. Conservatives (including most churchmen and many groups in the northern provinces) recognized Carlos as the rightful sovereign. The dispute rapidly escalated into a civil war, the first of a series of ongoing struggles associated with the cause of CARLISM. Although the First Carlist War came to an end in 1839, with the victory of the *cristinos* (as the supporters of the regent Maria Christina were called), divisions in Spanish society, both political and social, would continue for generations. Forced to leave the country in 1840, the queen mother soon returned and continued to dominate Isabella II until a second departure in 1854.

Unrestrained by her mother's presence, the young queen spent the remainder of her reign in pursuit of self-indulgence. Estranged from her husband, Francisco de Asís (who was her first cousin and bore the title of king consort), she pursued a series of romances, reputedly involving everyone from a general to a pastry chef. The scandalous nature of her conduct was paralleled by a seemingly total indifference to the duties of her office. Popular feeling passed from disapproval to bitter resentment to political opposition, resulting in a series of plots and abortive coups between 1854 to 1868. When word of the latest rebellion's victory over her few loyal supporters reached the queen at a country residence far removed from the center of conflict, she reacted, according to one account, with an indifferent shrug, as if her whole reign had been a dream unconnected with reality. Isabella departed for a comfortable exile in Paris, where in 1870 she issued a formal abdication in favor of her son ALFONSO XII. She died there 34 years later, during the reign of her grandson, ALFONSO XIII.

The reign of Isabella II was marked by a succession of wars, frequent changes of government and constitution, military seizures of power, and loosening ties of national unity. However, it was also a period of economic growth and diversification during which Spain became increasingly modernized and introduced at least the foundations of an industrial system as well as networks of transportation and communication. Historians may dispute the degree of progress attained during the period from 1833 to 1868 as compared to what was achieved in other European countries. What they cannot dispute is that Isabella II passed through these 35 years in a state of virtual trance, self-absorbed and self-indulgent, having no real interest in her country and therefore no real influence upon its fate.

Isabella Clara Eugenia (Isabel Clara Eugenia) (1566–1633)
Spanish princess and ruler of the Low Countries, archduchess of Austria

Daughter of PHILIP II by his second wife, a French princess, Isabella was her father's favorite child and remained with him as his constant companion and assistant until his death (1598). Although her father had sought several European thrones for her (France by hereditary claims and England by conquest), Isabella did not benefit from any of his political projects. There had also been several planned marriages that did not materialize, evidently because the king feared a lonely old age. In 1599, however, she was wed to her cousin Archduke Albert of Austria and journeyed with him to Brussels to take up the joint sovereignty of the Netherlands. This territory, which the Spaniards referred to as "Flanders," included the present-day Belgium and part of the modern Netherlands. Philip II had created a pseudo-independent country in the hope of rejoining the rebellious Dutch provinces of the north with those still under Spanish military control. As a device for the unification of the Low Countries, the plan failed, for the seven United Provinces refused to return to the old Burgundian realm.

Albert, who had previously served his Spanish cousins as administrator in the Netherlands, carried on an intermittent campaign against the Dutch until 1609 when the Twelve Years' Truce was concluded. Isabella, in the meantime, won the hearts and minds of her subjects by her personal charm, generosity, and promotion of public services. Her status as *reina* (queen) of a theoretically sovereign nation was curtailed by the inescapable interference of Spain, which also controlled the funds necessary for waging war against the Dutch. When her consort died in 1621, the possibility of their producing a line of succession ended. Under Philip II's original decree the territory known as Flanders reverted to Spain. Isabella stayed on in Brussels, however, as governor on behalf of her nephew, PHILIP IV. The resumption of hostilities with the Dutch Republic and the growing entanglements of the region with the campaigns of the Thirty Years' War made her task increasingly difficult. Devout and dutiful as ever and still enjoying public affection, Isabella succumbed to the fatigues of office in 1633. Belgium would not become a truly independent country for another 200 years.

Isabella Farnese (Isabel de Farnesio, Elizabeth Farnese) (1692–1766)

queen consort of Spain

Daughter of Odoardo Farnese, duke of Parma, Isabella was chosen as second wife of PHILIP V (1714) in the expectation that she would be easily managed by the dominant French clique at the court of Madrid. To the surprise of this group the new consort quickly displayed a natural intelligence and firmness of character that not only gave her dominance over her depressed and melancholic husband but changed the direction of Spain's foreign policy. French influence was supplanted by Isabella's preoccupation with Italian affairs, which grew into an obsession to regain control of the lost Spanish possessions. Her protégé, GIULIO ALBERONI, became chief minister and precipitated a war with France (1718–19). Despite its unsuccessful outcome and the minister's downfall, the queen continued to intrigue during the 1720s and '30s to obtain Italian thrones for her sons. Two more major European wars achieved this desired effect: Charles became duke of Parma in 1731 and then king of Naples in 1735; his brother, Philip, succeeded him in the former Farnese duchy of Parma (1735), founding the Bourbon-Parma line that reigned there until 1860. Inevitably Isabella's power in Madrid ended with the death of her husband in 1746. The new king, FERDINAND VI, sent his stepmother to a dignified but frustrating retirement far from court. This period of internal exile ended in 1759 when the death of Ferdinand VI without children resulted in Charles's leaving Naples to become CHARLES III of Spain. He was greeted joyfully by his mother, who had not only fulfilled her aspirations but now saw her favorite child seated on the Spanish throne, while one of his sons remained in Naples to preserve a Spanish-based line of succession there.

Although Queen Isabella was bitterly resented by some Spaniards for her preoccupation with dynastic affairs in Italy and for delaying the implementation of domestic reforms so desperately needed, many European politicians regarded her as among those remarkable stateswomen, such as Maria Theresa of Austria, the empresses Elizabeth and Catherine of Russia, and France's Madame de Pompadour, who dominated the international scene during the mid-18th century. There is no doubt, however, that the narrow focus of her concerns left the application of enlightened policies both at home and in the colonies to a time when it was probably too late for Spain to benefit from them.

Italian Wars (1494–1559)

A protracted conflict between Spain and France that spanned the years 1494 to 1559, this struggle for mastery in Europe was actually a single war periodically interrupted by truces and rearrangements of alliances. Charles VIII of France invaded Italy in 1494, claiming certain hereditary rights and was opposed by FERDINAND V, who intervened to support his Neapolitan kinsfolk. The struggle was interrupted by the death of Charles in 1498 but recommenced in 1500 under his successor, Louis XII. During the next 15 years the war spread to other parts of western Europe, drawing in such countries as Germany and England. Although Louis XII had accepted his defeat shortly before his death in 1515, his successor, François I, soon took up arms. A decade of struggle with Spain culminated in his loss of the Battle of Pavia (northern Italy) in 1525. Conveyed as a prisoner to Spain by CHARLES I (Holy Roman Emperor Charles V), François signed the Treaty of Madrid in 1526, abandoning his claims in Italy. Upon his release he almost immediately resumed

military operations; however, in 1529 his mother, Queen Louise, and MARGARET OF AUSTRIA, the aunt of Charles I, signed the so-called Ladies' Peace, which seemed to augur a permanent settlement. The French king resumed hostilities within a few years, drawing in a variety of allies, including the Turks and continued to clash with Spain virtually until his death in 1547.

During the reign of Henri II, son and successor of François I, France continued to stir up trouble for the Spanish monarch, not only in Italy but also with the Turks in the Mediterranean and the Balkans and with the German Protestants. These endlessly multiplying issues contributed to the exhaustion and to the abdication, in 1556, of the Spanish ruler, who left his dominions in central Europe to his brother and his Spanish inheritance to his son, PHILIP II. The latter monarch delivered the decisive blow to France in 1557 at the BATTLE OF ST. QUENTIN, near the Franco-Flemish border. The final settlement of the ITALIAN WARS came in 1559 with the Treaty of Cateau-Cambresis. Henri II was killed in a jousting accident shortly thereafter, and France sank into 30 years of civil war. Philip II led Spain on to the long-sought mastery of Europe and the extension of her world-wide empire.

Italy, Spain in

Spain's involvement in Italy grew out of the geographical proximity of the two Mediterranean peninsulas to each other. The lands of the Crown of ARAGON were particularly involved with Sardinia and Sicily, and as early as the 13th century Aragon had established its authority on both islands. The southern third of Italy, which constituted the Kingdom of Naples, had at various times during the Middle Ages been under common rule with Sicily. From the mid-1400s onward both were under the rule of branches of the House of Aragon and were known as the Kingdom of the Two Sicilies. Rival French claims to Naples precipitated a prolonged struggle between France and Spain (1494–1559) known as the ITALIAN WARS. The intervention launched by FERDINAND V of Aragon to support his kin in Naples was transformed into the imposition of his direct rule after the original Neapolitan line died out (1503). Throughout the 16th and 17th centuries the Two Sicilies were an important part of Spain's dominions in Europe, providing a reservoir of money and military manpower as well as important cultural connections. By 1640, however, the Neapolitan subjects of PHILIP IV were sufficiently discontented with Spanish overlordship to launch a revolt. Although put down by force, it represented a continuing element of antagonism during the last decades of Spanish rule.

Over the course of its intervention in the peninsula Spain at first supported local rulers in northern Italy against France but then established its own influence. The most significant of these Spanish intrusions took place in 1535 when the Sforza dynasty was replaced at Milan by CHARLES I's assumption of the ducal title. During the greater part of the next two centuries the kings of Spain were also dukes of Milan and dominated much of Lombardy. Like the Two Sicilies, the Milanese, as the region was sometimes called, was a valuable adjunct to Spain's military and political mastery of Europe, facilitating the movement of Spanish troops and the intrusion of

its diplomacy into central Europe. With the end of the WAR OF THE SPANISH SUCCESSION, in 1714, Spain lost its Italian dependencies, chiefly to Austria. The new ruling family, the Spanish house of BOURBON, made vigorous efforts to regain their country's pivotal role in Italy. Aside from a nominal gain in Parma (which was recognized as an independent duchy under a branch of the Spanish Bourbons from 1720 onward), only the Two Sicilies returned to the Spanish orbit. From 1735 to 1759, when he became CHARLES III, this Spanish prince ruled at Naples. When he succeeded his brother as sovereign of Spain (1759–88), he left behind one of his sons to govern the Italian realm, but it was linked to Spain only by royal kinship, not by legal subordination. The northern area around Milan continued under Austrian rule until the 19th century when all of these monarchies were absorbed into the unified kingdom of Italy.

Iturbide, Agustín de (1783–1824)
Spanish colonial rebel

Born in MEXICO of Basque descent, Iturbide held increasingly important commands in the Spanish army during the period 1810–20 and played a significant role in repressing early Mexican moves toward independence. However, he was not fundamentally opposed to a break between Spain and "New Spain" as long as it could be achieved in a conservative spirit. When the revolt of RAFAEL DEL RIEGO in 1820 precipitated a shift toward liberalism in Spain, Iturbide decided to support a break with the mother country. He secretly made agreements with nationalist leaders while publicly accepting the task of repressing them. By 1821 he had

Agustín de Iturbide *(Library of Congress)*

effectively severed the ties between Spain and Mexico. He headed a provisional government that sought a Bourbon prince to accept an imperial throne in Mexico. When no such candidate could be found Iturbide was proclaimed by his soldiers Emperor Agustín I. His reign was short lived, essentially lasting only from 1822 through early 1823. Iturbide's conservative and authoritarian values were repugnant to liberal nationalists, and he was overthrown by a conspiracy of erstwhile allies (including Mexico's perennial president Miguel López de Santa Ana). Iturbide found sanctuary in Italy but returned to Mexico in 1824 hoping to mobilize conservatives for a restoration on his behalf. He did not know that the legislature of the republic had proclaimed him an outlaw subject to death if he set foot in Mexico. The former emperor was arrested upon his arrival and promptly executed.

J

Jamaica

"Discovered" by CHRISTOPHER COLUMBUS in 1494, on his second voyage to the New World, this island in the Greater Antilles was named *Santiago* by him, after the Spanish saint. This name never came into general use, however. Even the Spaniards referred to it by the Amerindian name Xaymaca more commonly spelled *Jamaica,* signifying "land of forest and water." The island became something of a stepchild among the Caribbean colonies, for Spanish settlers were reluctant to go there from the larger and more prosperous islands of the region, and those who did for the most part were quickly lured away by the prospect of gold on the continental mainland. Formally "conquered" in 1509, the native inhabitants were estimated at 60,000. They offered relatively little resistance and were soon subjected to forced labor, which along with the spread of disease exterminated them by the end of the century. In the early 1600s the population was calculated at approximately 1,500, evenly divided between Spaniards and African slaves imported to provide a new labor force. Neither the colonial administration nor the home government took much interest in Jamaica, either as an economic resource or a strategic position. Warnings from local authorities that the island was becoming the resort of pirates and raiders were routinely ignored. Several initiatives were made toward the fortification of the principal harbors between 1620 and 1640, but these came to little. Warnings about the increasing interest of England in the island were likewise dismissed. Virtually no precautions were taken, therefore, against the inevitable attack. In 1655 English forces captured the island. Belated attempts to hold Jamaica for Spain were repulsed. A major expedition launched from MEXICO proved equally unsuccessful. By the late 1660s Spain had abandoned Jamaica, although formal cession did not take place until several decades later.

Japan, Portuguese presence in

Early in the 16th century, as Portuguese traders and missionaries traversed the Indian Ocean region and reached the Pacific shore of East Asia, they became aware of the commercial potential of Japan, hitherto known only indirectly to Europeans. First contacts were made in 1542–43, and missionary activities promoted by FRANCIS XAVIER took place in 1549–51. Both commercial activity by Portuguese traders.and the preaching of Christianity by Portuguese Jesuits continued in Japan for the next 50 years. After 1571 Portuguese operations were centered at the port of Nagasaki.

Through Portuguese merchants Japanese wares began reaching European markets, and a more informed knowledge of Japanese civilization developed. There were numerous conversions to Catholicism thanks to the efforts of the Jesuits, who concentrated on winning the allegiance of feudal nobles who in turn mandated the conversion of their dependents. Firearms brought in by the Europeans were an increasing factor in the internal warfare of Japanese clans and political factions. After 1603 the consolidation of central government in Japan under the Tokugawa shogunate (military-political leaders who usurped the power of the emperor) undercut the influence of the Portuguese. There were massive persecutions of Japanese Catholics and edicts against the presence of foreigners. By 1642 the Portuguese had been expelled from Japan, and their converts, reduced to a handful of clandestine Christians. As happened in many parts of Portuguese Asia, the rising power of the Dutch Republic filled the gap that Portugal had left. From 1642 to 1854 Japan closed itself to the outside world. Half a dozen Dutch trade agents living on the offshore island of Deshima were the only reminders of Japan's original contacts—through Portugal—with Europe.

Jiménez, Juan Ramón (1881–1958)

Spanish poet

Poems published in the local press of his native ANDALUSIA brought the young Jiménez to the attention of the poet RUBÉN DARÍO and other writers who urged him to move to MADRID. During the early 1900s he became part of the intellectual circle that was shaping the hoped-for transition to a "new" Spain. Although not formally a member of the GENERATION OF '98, he shared in the cultural debates of the early 20th century, often internalizing the conflicts, as when he repudiated his earlier work and actually sought to buy up and destroy all copies of his first two books of poetry. Of a more sensitive temperament than many of his colleagues, he suffered from ill health and melancholia that impelled him to return for several years to his native town. After 1916, however, a much more self-confident and assertive Jiménez emerged. He rejected the "modernist" school of poetry, preferring a pared-down style that eschewed florid verse in favor of what he described as *"poesía desnuda"* (naked poetry). It was at this time, too, that he married Zenobia Camprubí, after paying a short but influential visit to the United States to renew his acquaintance with her. A translator of authors such as the Indian Rabindranath Tagore and the Irish John Millington Synge, she was his psychological support and sometime literary collaborator for the next 40 years.

Jiménez gave some time to teaching and editing but was primarily engaged in the writing and revision of his poems, publishing a steady stream of collected verse, encompassing hundreds of poems. He experimented with various forms and concepts and frequently analyzed the merits or demerits of the shifting tastes in Spanish poetical composition. During the SPANISH CIVIL WAR Jiménez left Spain to travel in Europe and then to reside in the Western Hemisphere for most of his later life. A significant portion of this period was spent in PUERTO RICO, a favorite refuge of self-exiled Spanish intellectuals. In 1956 he was awarded the Nobel Prize in literature, an

achievement clouded by the almost simultaneous death of his wife. He survived her for a mere 18 months.

Jiménez, who was influenced in his youth by Darío and other turn-of-the-century literary lights, himself became the inspiration and stimulus for many leading poets of the later 20th century. Some critics have questioned his designation as a Nobel laureate on the ground that he was too inconsistent in his thinking, and others dismissed him as a light-weight pointing to one of his most popular works, *Platero y yo* (*Platero and I*, 1914) as an example of triviality. *Platero* was, in fact, a poetical memoir of his boyhood home and a recollection of an amiable donkey that listened to his meditations. Its popularity in the United States many decades later was a nostalgic phenomenon and no proper gauge of the author's merits. Jiménez was, like all good poets, a man perpetually in quest of "the word" and the right way to match it with idea and emotion. As such he deserves a respected place in 20th-century Spanish literature.

Among the best-known works of Juan Ramón Jiménez are *Almas de violeta* (Souls of violet, 1900), *Elegías puras* (Pure elegies, 1908), *La soledad sonora* (Sonorous solitude, 1911) *Poemas mágicos y dolientes* (Magical and sorrowful poems, 1911, *Diario de un poeta recien casdo* (Diary of a newlywed poet, 1917), *Eternidades* (Eternities, 1918), *Poesia* (Poetry, 1922), and *Voces de mi copla* (Voices of my song, 1945).

Jiménez de Quesada, Gonzalo
(1499 1579)
Spanish explorer and conqueror

One of the first generation of conquistadores, Jiménez de Quesada was an administrative magistrate in Santa Marta, on the coast of what is now COLOMBIA, in 1535 when he was commissioned by the Spanish Crown to undertake an exploration of the Magdalena River region and pursue a search for the fabled El Dorado. In the course of his expedition he and his followers fought numerous battles against the Chibchas. This highly developed indigenous group, which has been compared to the Maya of Southern Mexico and Central America, was now past its peak but still put up a stiff resistance to the invaders. Jiménez alternated between brutality and generosity in his dealings with them but eventually subdued the region he had been sent to explore, without finding El Dorado, but bringing back great quantities of gold and emeralds. In the course of this quest he encountered several competing expeditions that had come into the territory from other jurisdictions. He persuaded their leaders, BELALCÁZAR and FEDERMANN, to avoid violent rivalry by returning with them to Spain to settle their competing claims. Back in Europe, however, Jiménez was less than successful in pursuing his claims. When he returned to South America in the 1550s, he bore several honorific titles but did not receive the recognition he believed due to the founder of Bogotá (one of many other accomplishments).

Another expedition in search of El Dorado was launched in 1569. The aging warrior and the remnant of his band returned three years later worn, exhausted, and poor but bringing back valuable information on the upper reaches of the Orinoco River. In his final expedition, when he was already almost 80 and carried on a litter, Jiménez rallied his soldiers to beat off a major native onslaught. An indefatigable optimist, who shared many attributes of his fellow conquistadores, he was a typical representative of those terrifying agents of Europe's "civilizing" mission who would rise up again and again during the great age of conquest.

Joanna (Juana) (1479–1555)
queen of Castile

Second daughter of FERDINAND V and ISABELLA I, she married Philip of Habsburg, duke of Burgundy, in 1496. Due to a series of deaths in her family she became the inheritor of CASTILE in 1504. As Joanna had been subject for some years to bouts of mental derangements (hence the nickname *Juana la Loca*—"Joanna the Mad"), her husband and her father disputed control of her inheritance. Following the death of Philip (who had been proclaimed PHILIP I of Castile in 1506), Joanna nominally ruled as cosovereign with her son, CHARLES I. Due to her incapacity she remained under supervision at the Castle of Tordesillas for the rest of her life. During the 1520s rebels against her son's authority briefly restored her liberty and proclaimed her their rightful ruler, but after initial signs of normality she refused to cooperate and was soon returned to her familiar setting where she remained until her death.

John IV (João IV) (1604–1656)
king of Portugal

John, duke of Bragança from 1630, represented a line of claimants to the Portuguese throne that had been excluded in 1580 when the Spanish monarch, PHILIP II, seized the succession in LISBON. By 1640, after the so-called Sixty Years' Tyranny, the Portuguese were ready to throw off the rule of their larger neighbor. John was proclaimed king of Portugal by an assembly of both nobles and commoners and took an oath to be subject to their will. As the first ruler of the House of BRAGANÇA, he was a popular but relatively inactive ruler, leaving the conduct of the independence war to his generals. His main concern was to secure the continuing support of France, whose ongoing conflict with Spain made her willing to assist Portugal and other rebels against Spanish imperial dominance. The struggle for Portuguese freedom was still being waged at the time of John's death, and MADRID would not recognize Portuguese sovereignty for another decade.

John V (João V) (1689–1750)
king of Portugal

The adolescent John V inherited from his father, PETER II, in 1706 both a lucrative trade agreement with England and Portugal's damaging participation in the WAR OF THE SPANISH SUCCESSION. The discovery of gold and diamonds in the previously unproductive colony of BRAZIL enabled him to lead Portugal into a period of prosperity. His generous expenditure of the colonial revenues on public works and the adornment of LISBON led to his being nicknamed "the Magnanimous." In time his extravagance caused lasting damage to the nation's economy. Preoccupied with his grandiose self-image, he attempted to create at his palace at MAFRA a version of Louis XIV's Versailles that wasted resources and earned him much criticism. Although designed as a combination of royal residence, monastery, and basilica, like that which PHILIP II of Spain had created at EL ESCORIAL, Mafra, had in fact much more in common with the French palace and the Sun King's desire to impress his people and the rulers of Europe.

John VI (João VI) (1769–1826)
king of Portugal

The son of MARIA I and her king-consort, PETER III, John began management of the royal household in 1792 at the onset of his mother's mental illness, although he did not formally assume the title of regent until 1799. An opponent of the revolutionary change that was sweeping Europe, he clung to Portugal's long-standing alliance with Britain and was consequently attacked and defeated by Spain in its role as ally of France (the War of the Oranges, 1801). John attempted to avoid further conflict thereafter but was marked for vengeance, ultimately being invaded by a Franco-Spanish force in 1807. John and his entourage escaped aboard British warships and found refuge in BRAZIL. Enjoying a comfortable residence in Rio de Janeiro, John proclaimed Brazil a co-equal kingdom with Portugal and showed no interest in returning to Lisbon, even after his homeland was liberated. As king, following his mother's death in 1816, John VI attempted to oversee his transatlantic realm from a distance, but a liberal revolt in 1821 finally compelled him to return to Portugal where he attempted to undercut the new constitution. John was nevertheless opposed to the extreme reactionary party led by his younger son MIGUEL. John favored the claim of his older son, but the latter had been recognized as the ruler (PEDRO I) of a now-independent Brazil in 1825 leaving him in an anomalous position. These issues of inheritance and political orienta-

tion were left unresolved at the time of John's death.

John of Austria (Don Juan de Austria) (1547–1578)
Spanish prince and military commander

An illegitimate son of CHARLES I (Holy Roman Emperor Charles V), he was formally recognized by his father and confirmed by his half brother, PHILIP II, as a prince of the HABSBURG dynasty (the "House of Austria"). During his 20s he demonstrated his leadership qualities by commanding a naval squadron in the Mediterranean against Barbary pirates and putting down a revolt in ANDALUSIA. In 1571, as admiral of the Holy League fleet confronting a Turkish force at the BATTLE OF

John of Austria *(Library of Congress)*

LEPANTO, he won a decisive victory that made him a Spanish national hero and an admired figure throughout Europe. After serving as governor of Spanish possessions in Italy he undertook a similar position in the Netherlands where he had mixed success against the Dutch rebels (1576). Various rumors arose about John's ambitions, including the accusations that he was planning to assume the lead of the Netherlands's rebellion and that he had concocted a scheme to marry Mary Queen of Scots and make himself king of the British Isles. His sudden death was the object of further speculation and charges that Philip II had caused him to be done away with.

John of the Cross, Saint (Juan de la Cruz) (1542–1591)
Spanish religious reformer and mystical poet

Born Juan de Yepes and admitted as a monk in the Carmelite order in 1563 under the name Juan de la Cruz, he was ordained priest in 1567. Shortly thereafter he met with TERESA OF ÁVILA and was persuaded by her to aid in the reform of the Carmelite order. Their plan was for him to undertake a reform of the monastic communities parallel to that which she had initiated among Carmelite nuns. They aimed at returning the order to its contemplative and spiritual base after centuries of gradual abandonment of the austere and spiritual simplicity of the order's founders. John had initial success with the plan but eventually encountered intense opposition to his reform project similar to that which Teresa had experienced. He was actually arrested and imprisoned during 1576 and again in 1577 on charges of doctrinal and disciplin-

ary irregularities. Confined virtually without access to sunlight or exercise, isolated, and subjected to periodic harsh interrogation, he survived by mental projection of intense mystical emotion that he expressed in poetical form. Managing to escape from his captors in TOLEDO in 1578, he found refuge among sympathizers in ANDALUSIA, where he resumed his reforming mission and became vicar provincial of the order from 1585 to 1587. The Carmelites were wracked by further disputes just before his death, however, and John was obliged to withdraw completely from the world to find both security and peace.

A major figure in the movement for renewal of the religious orders, which was such a significant part of the Catholic Reformation, St. John is even more notable as a mystical thinker and writer. After escaping from the clutches of the reactionaries who had imprisoned him, he reproduced from memory the poetry that he had composed during his confinement to convey his mystical raptures. These verses, accompanied by prose commentaries that sought to open the mystical experience to others, were published in a number of volumes, including *Cantico espiritual* (*Spiritual Canticle*), *Llama de amor viva* (Living flame of love), and *Noche oscura del alma* (*Dark Night of the Soul*). They were published posthumously in 1618. For all their personal intensity and literary complexity these poems remain among the most admired and influential fruits of Spanish mysticism. They have become literary as well as spiritual classics. John was canonized in 1726. Saint John of the Cross was named a doctor of the church in 1926 elevating him to a special status as a magisterial and guiding figure among the intellectual and spiritual mentors of the Catholic Church.

Joseph I (José I) (1714–1777)
king of Portugal

Soon after succeeding his father, JOHN V, in 1750, Joseph turned over most of the business of government to his chief minister, POMBAL. Credited with being an enlightened despot, the monarch merely acquiesced for the most part in his adviser's decisions. The notable events and initiatives of his reign were, therefore, actually more truly associated with Pombal than his master. They included the great LISBON earthquake of 1755, the ruthless repression of a plot against the king's life in 1758, and a series of measures aimed at curbing the power of the church. The enlightened reforms associated with this reign affected both Portugal and BRAZIL. Many of them were short lived due to the opposition of entrenched interests. Joseph also proved unfortunate in foreign policy, being pressured into joining Spain and France in the Seven Years' War (1756–63) against his country's traditional ally, Great Britain. The king's deteriorating health during his later years raised questions about the stability of the succession, which were further complicated by the growing unpopularity of the chief minister. The death of Joseph, soon followed by the fall of Pombal, ushered in a period of decline for the Portuguese monarchy.

Joseph I (José I, Joseph Bonaparte) (1768–1844)
king of Spain

Joseph Bonaparte, elder brother and close collaborator of the French military dictator Napoléon Bonaparte (Emperor Napoléon I), was born in Corsica and had a political career paralleling that of his soldier brother. By 1806 he had served in various important

King Joseph I of Spain *(Library of Congress)*

diplomatic assignments and was rewarded with the Kingdom of Naples when that country's Bourbon dynasty was overthrown. Within two years King Giuseppe was transformed into King José when the emperor removed the Spanish Bourbons and placed his brother on the throne in Madrid. The new king and his Neapolitan subjects apparently had been happy with each other. Such was not the case in Spain. Joseph I had little knowledge or appreciation for his new realm, and only a minority of Spaniards had the least respect for him, preferring instead to circulate diatribes and mocking nicknames (the epithet "Pepe Botella," "Joe Bottles," was a reference to his alleged heavy drinking, which seems to have been inaccurate). Some Spaniards, known as *afrancesados,* supported his regime out of a belief that he would introduce much-needed modernization and reform, but he had little opportunity to satisfy their hopes. Any positive initiatives attempted by King Joseph were promptly vetoed by Napoléon; indeed, French officials and generals ran as much of Spain as they could dominate between 1808 to 1814 essentially as an extension of France. Even Spaniards who were not actively engaged in the irregular warfare carried on throughout much of the country were likely to be passive opponents of the *"rey intruso"* (intrusive king) and secret supporters of the banished FERDINAND VII.

After six years of fruitless effort the French intruders were forced to withdraw from Spain. Joseph resumed his former identity, played a subordinate role in the last months of his brother's rule in France, and then went into decades of exile, much of the time being spent in the United States.

A loyal henchman of his dynamic sibling, Joseph Bonaparte was a mild and self-effacing individual. Often referred to as the "gentle Bonaparte," he seems to have had neither the temperament nor the practical knowledge to deal with the situation into which he was thrust when he became king of Spain. In any case Joseph I, like all of Napoléon's kin, was treated as a branch manager in the family business rather than an autonomous ruler. Unsurprisingly Joseph has left little impression in the annals of Spanish history.

Jovellanos, Gaspar Melchor de
(1744–1811)

Spanish statesman and writer

Jovellanos followed the not uncommon Spanish career path of studying for the priesthood, abandoning that idea in favor of the law, and devoting his early years (after attending the Universities of Oviedo and Alcalá) to poetry. His literary efforts in the neoclassical vein are unremarkable, and he later believed that he and his friends had wasted their time in not doing the serious business that confronted the young men of the rising generation. Jovellanos would more than make up for any such neglect by becoming one of the most active promoters of the Enlightenment in Spain.

The so-called Bourbon Reforms that had been talked about since the arrival of that French dynasty in the early 18th century did not come into full flower until the accession of CHARLES III in 1759. The enlightened despotism of this monarch offered an opportunity to Jovellanos to advocate some of the reforms that he had already been considering. His ideas ranged over the state of the economy, the deficiencies of the educational system, and the need for administrative efficiency. His numerous writings had brought him to the attention of progressive Spaniards and gained him the support of the monarch, although Charles III proved far less consistent and far more distractable than champions of reform might have expected. Jovellanos was given particular encouragement to develop agrarian reform yet found his freedom of action in this regard curtailed by reactionary officials who arranged for him to be sent off into the hinterlands. He nevertheless profited by the chance to make detailed examinations of agrarian life and practices throughout much of the country, resulting in analysis and recommendations that he would later bring together in what may be regarded as his principal opus, *Informe sobre la ley agraria* (Report on the agrarian law, 1795).

After years of orderly study and careful reporting on his conclusions, Jovellanos was plunged into the mainstream of high politics following the accession of CHARLES IV in 1788. The new chief minister, MANUEL DE GODOY, seeking to curry favor with reformers, appointed Jovellanos minister of justice in 1797. The appointment was appropriate, for the polymath had written extensively on subjects such as the treatment of prisoners and the shortcomings of the Spanish judiciary. Too honest to play the political game, Jovellanos was soon out of office and was in fact imprisoned some time later (1801) for his protests over Godoy's improper relations with the queen. He remained confined, again putting his time to good use for reflection and writing until the general breakdown of the country precipitated by the French invasion of 1808. Released from prison, Jovellanos had become a sought-after elder statesman. When the intrusive Bonaparte king, JOSEPH I, invited him to join the puppet government, Jovellanos rejected the offer with indignant patriotism. He was then asked to give his advice to the provisional government being set up in the still-unoccupied southern area of the country. In support of this resistance movement Jovellanos penned his last major work, esteemed by many as his finest, *Memoria en defensa de la Junta Central* (Memorial in defense of the Central Committee, 1810). Unhappily, having devoted so much of his life to the improvement of his country, he would not live to see it emerge from the chaos into which it had been plunged.

Jovellanos has been called one of the finest prose stylists of 18th-century Spain and a literary bridge between neoclassissism and romanticism. Like so many of the philosophes, Jovellanos had such a wide range of interests that he could scarcely contain his enthusiasms and arguments regarding one before moving on to another issue. This breadth of reformist vision as well as his high standards of morality and patriotism made him the target of those whose self-centered focus on their main issue made them successful and led to his frustration.

Juan Carlos I (1938–)
king of Spain

A grandson of ALFONSO XIII, Juan Carlos was born in Rome and had his early education in Switzerland and Britain. Despite the fact that Don Juan, count of Barcelona, was a pretender to the throne after Alfonso's death in 1941, he agreed to send his son to Spain in 1947 to pursue his further education and training under the supervision of the Franco regime. Neither the count of Barcelona nor the Spanish dictator had come to any agreement on the future of the monarchy, but it was assumed that it would be restored at an appropriate time. FRANCISCO FRANCO subsequently made it clear that he had no intention of allowing Don Juan, whom he deemed too liberal, to ascend the throne. Instead he arranged for young Juan Carlos to be trained in all three of Spain's armed forces academies, attend university courses, and carry out internships in various government offices. Designated "Prince of Spain" and acknowledged as Franco's eventual successor, Juan Carlos was thus separated from the traditional line of succession and made dependent on the whim of the general who had won the SPANISH CIVIL WAR and destroyed the republic, but who refused to let the royalists resume power during his lifetime. Franco's political game came to an end with his death in November 1975.

When Juan Carlos was proclaimed king, many thought that he would be a mere figurehead for Franco's associates or enjoy only a short reign. Instead the monarch announced his strong commitment to a democratic, modern, and inclusive society. By 1978 a democratic constitution had been adopted, and the new regime had gained a broad range of supporters leaving the extremes of Right and Left unable to assert their claims to dominance. The king's prompt and decisive response to an attempted military coup in 1981 thwarted any danger of a reactionary reversal and confirmed his popularity with the vast majority of Spaniards.

By the time Juan Carlos celebrated the 25th anniversary of his accession, in 2000, he had achieved a level of popularity that defied all early predictions. Modest in his lifestyle, dignified in his conduct, and respectful of the institutions generated by the "new Spain" over which he presided, he seemed the ideal chief of state for an era in which the country was resuming a place of influence in the affairs of Europe and a wider world. His children by his marriage to Princess Sofia of Greece gave promise of a continuance of the Spanish BOURBON dynasty into the 21st century.

K

Kinsale, Battle of (1601)

The prolonged conflict between PHILIP II of Spain and Elizabeth I of England had periodically involved Spanish attacks on Ireland. None of these had been successful, but in the year of the old king's death (1598) the Irish rebel leader, Hugh O'Neill, earl of Tyrone, had won a major victory over English forces in Ulster. This left him and the coalition of northern lords that he headed in a position of unprecedented power. In 1599 he offered peace to Elizabeth on terms that she rejected. He then offered the crown of Ireland to the new king of Spain. PHILIP III hesitated at first, unwilling to pursue new military adventures. He had, however, promised his father to carry on the struggle against England, and the oppressed condition of the Catholics in Ireland stirred his religious feelings. Accepting O'Neill's offer, Philip ordered the preparation of an expedition to aid his new subjects. Late in 1601, a Spanish fleet conveyed a large force of infantry and artillery to the southeastern coast of Ireland, where they seized the fortified port of Kinsale and placed garrisons in several castles belonging to rebel noblemen. Kinsale lay hundreds of miles away from O'Neill's northern stronghold, and it required much time for him to mass his followers and accomplish the long march south to the county of Cork. Meanwhile the principal English commander in

the region, Sir George Carew, had laid siege to Kinsale. When the earl of Tyrone reached the vicinity of the siege, it was already late December, with the weather fast deteriorating. Nevertheless, he sent a message to the Spanish commander, Don Juan del Águila, that he would immediately launch an attack on the rear of the besiegers. Advancing during a storm with unreliable guides in a terrain unfamiliar to the northerners, the Irish were attacked and routed by Carew, who then turned his troops about and beat back the Spanish sortie from Kinsale. The dispirited Irish withdrew back to their home territory. Deeming the campaign lost, Águila negotiated a surrender, extracted his troops from Kinsale and other outposts, and sailed back to Spain early in 1602.

The Battle of Kinsale marked the end of any serious attempt by Philip III to pursue his father's war with England. In 1603 the Irish rebels came to terms with the government in London, and in 1604 Philip III signed a peace treaty with Elizabeth's successor. Spain gave generous refuge to Tyrone and his adherents and to other Irish exiles for many generations thereafter. The hitherto Catholic province of Ulster was rapidly transformed into a predominantly Protestant stronghold, the seat of the centuries-long religious and political quarrels that have bedeviled present-day Northern Ireland.

L

Labrador, Pedro Gómez Labrador, marqués de (1775–1852)

Spanish diplomat

A native of ARAGON who represented successive Spanish monarchs on diplomatic missions, the marquis of Labrador served CHARLES IV in Florence at the court of the grand duke of Tuscany. When the dispute between Charles IV and his heir led to the latter's proclamation as FERDINAND VII in 1808, Labrador sided with the new king. He accompanied him to the conference at Bayonne in southwestern France to which Napoléon Bonaparte summoned the whole BOURBON family. Upon the arrest and confinement of the entire party, Labrador was among those who accompanied Ferdinand VII to his separate place of detention, where he shared his master's company for the next six years. Having established his fidelity to the ruler and his loyalty to Spain's interests, Labrador was appointed plenipotentiary to the Congress of Vienna (1814). At this international "summit conference" he found his scope for action limited by the recognition that Europe would henceforth be dominated by the so-called Great Powers, which included Great Britain, France, Austria, Russia, and Prussia. In this new concept of European international relations Spain was not included. Although the country had been allied with Britain during the PENINSULAR WAR, its reduced standing did not entitle it to a deciding role at Vienna, and Spain's interests were not respected despite the best efforts of Labrador. The marquis served as envoy to the Kingdom of Naples and to the papacy during the remainder of Ferdinand's reign. His Carlist sympathies excluded him from further employment after the defeat of the pretender in 1838. During his retirement Labrador wrote two books: *Relación del Congreso de Viena* and *Miscelánea . . . de la vida del marqués de Labrador,* both of which give valuable glimpses of Spanish foreign relations in the early 19th century.

La Mancha

Constituting the larger part of Castilla–La Mancha autonomous region, this area is nevertheless largely barren. Its name, signifying "the wasteland," reflects the unprepossesing image that existed even in the Middle Ages, when La Mancha was a kind of border zone or no man's land between Christian and Muslim territory in Spain. In later days La Mancha was chosen by CERVANTES as the site for the adventures of his hero Don Quixote. The image of the deluded knight and his stolid squire roaming about La Mancha added a particular piquancy to the tale for knowledgeable readers, and in later centuries La Mancha has been thought of primarily as the home of fictional characters rather than real people.

La Plata, Viceroyalty of

This Spanish viceroyalty in South America was created in 1775 as part of an evolving reorganization of the vast Viceroyalty of PERU that had begun with the creation of the Viceroyalty of NEW GRANADA in 1718–40. The patterns of international trade and intracolonial management, as well as an enhanced appreciation of geographical factors, led to the grouping of PARAGUAY, URUGUAY, and what is now BOLIVIA (then Upper Peru) with the greater part of what is now ARGENTINA under a viceroy based at Buenos Aires. By the time that city was attacked by British forces in 1806–07, the Napoleonic Wars in Europe and the decline in colonial loyalty to Spain were already eroding the political stability of the viceroyalty. The *porteños* (residents of Buenos Aires) regarded their successful repulse of the British forces as a vindication of their rising self-confidence and independent spirit. The end of Spanish colonial rule soon followed, and the components of the Viceroyalty of La Plata went their separate ways.

Largo Caballero, Francisco
(1869–1946)
Spanish statesman

Originally a stone mason, Largo Caballero became active in the Socialist Party in 1894 and by 1925 was leader of its trade union confederation. He cooperated with the royalist dictatorship of MIGUEL PRIMO DE RIVERA but supported the proclamation of the Second Republic in 1931. He served as minister

of labor from 1931 to 1933 but was forced to resign after the elections of 1934 brought an upsurge of right-wing activity. Active in Socialist politics, he helped to create the alliance of parties of the Left that led to the victory of the Popular Front in 1936. His presence as prime minister of the republic in this regime was a major precipitating factor in the uprising launched by FRANCISCO FRANCO and associated factions in July 1936. An internal power struggle in the Republican government forced Largo Caballero's resignation in 1937, and the deteriorating military situation during the last period of the SPANISH CIVIL WAR made it impossible for him to play an effective public role thereafter. Like many supporters of the republic, Largo Caballero found refuge in France at the end of the war in 1939, but he was taken prisoner by the German invaders of that country in 1940. A notorious symbol of "international Bolshevism," Largo Caballero remained a captive of the Nazis until 1945 and died shortly after his release.

Larra, Mariano José de (1809–1837)
Spanish essayist

Larra belonged to an *afrancesado* family, one which supported the intrusive regime of JOSEPH I (Joseph Bonaparte) and its French influence on Spanish life. His father was a court physician in MADRID until the fall of his patron obliged him to move to France. The young Larra received his early education there and imbibed the liberal ideas that contrasted so strongly with those of the restored BOURBON regime in Spain. Even after the Larra family returned to their homeland both father and son were the objects of suspicion and discrimination, and the young man attributed the interruption of his studies in both medicine and law to conservative officials. Pursuing a journalistic career in Madrid Larra became well known for a series of essays published in a paper of which he was the editor, *El pobrecito hablador* (Poor little chatterer). He combined a lively and acute description of Spanish society with satirical wit. While literary success seemed within his grasp, he was frustrated in his romantic relationships, the probable cause of his suicide.

Larra, who traveled widely and brought a sophisticated as well as critical perspective to his portrayal of his countryfolk's foibles, seems never to have been at home in his native land. Balanced between romanticism and realism, feeling himself something of an outcast yet disdaining vulgar applause, his sensitivity seemed almost to guarantee the brevity of his career and his life. Larra was the author of a novel, *El doncel de don Enrique el Doliente* (The page of Don Enrique the Sorrowful, 1834), and a play, *Macías* (1834), as well as *No más mostrador* (Goodbye to the shop counter, 1831), an adaptation of a play by the French dramatist Scribe. It is, however, for his essays under the pen name Fígaro and various other pseudonyms in papers other that his own that Larra is still remembered and honored.

Las Casas, Bartolomé de (1474–1566)
Spanish priest and humanitarian
Las Casas, after studying law and theology at the University of Salamanca, traveled in 1502 to the New World, where family connections and his own service to the Crown earned him an ENCOMIENDA. His increasing interest in Spain's obligation to evangelize the Indians led to his ordination in 1512 (evidently the first in America) and to his subsequent abandonment of his plantation holdings because they involved the virtual slavery of the Indians.

For nearly 30 years Father Las Casas dedicated himself to the principle that the native population was entitled to the rights and security of all Spanish subjects. He repeatedly argued against those who held that the Amerindians were subhuman, lacked souls, or were without any entitlement to the dignity of human beings. His advocacy earned him the hostility of most landowners in the New World, who wished to exploit the labor of the natives, but he gained the sympathy of King CHARLES I on his repeated visits to Spain and was designated "Protector of the Indians." Royal decrees in the 1520s (later confirmed and extended) forbade mistreatment and uncompensated labor but were repeatedly ignored or evaded by plantation and mine owners. As promoter of model indigenous communities in GUATEMALA and as bishop of Chiapas in MEXICO during the 1540s, Las Casas strove to achieve a self-supporting, self-governing status for native Americans. Despite his persistent efforts and those of some of other clergymen Las Casas was never truly successful in eliminating the distinction most Spaniards made between themselves and those who they regarded as conquered colonials. One unfortunate consequence of his insistence than America's Indians could not legally be enslaved was the importation of slaves from Africa: Portuguese traders purchased captives taken in local warfare and sold them for use in the Americas, where the Africans were not considered to have any claims to human rights. Las Casas would later bitterly regret this unintended consequence of his championship of the Indians and argued that it was also immoral to enslave the Africans.

During the last decades of his long life Las Casas lived in Spain, concentrating on written advocacy, the most notable example of which was *Brevísima relación de la destrucción de las Indias* (*Brief Account of the Destruction of the Indies,* 1552), a work whose horrendous examples of cruelty by Spanish conquistadores in the Americas were sometimes exaggerated and certainly provided ample material for Spain's enemies. The LEYENDA NEGRA (Black Legend) of Spanish infamy would be exploited for centuries in countries whose own colonial behavior was scarcely better than that of which Spain was accused. Although Las Casas's crusade for justice was unsuccessful, he kept alive a debate over human rights and social justice that had no parallel in Europe during the 16th century.

León

Emerging from the first manifestation of Christian resistance to the Muslim conquest of Spain in eighth-century ASTURIAS, a separate kingdom of León dominated the next stage of the RECONQUISTA. During the early Middle Ages this northern realm went through a series of dynastic and territorial interactions with CASTILE. The leaders of León prided themselves on their aristocratic dignity, considering the Castilians as mere foot soldiers in the great crusade against Islam. By 1300, however, the larger and more populous Castile had gained the ascendancy. León would henceforth be a subordinate domain of the Castilian monarchy. This situation was confirmed more recently during the regional reconstruction of the 1970s, when the autonomous region of Castile and León was created in the vast territory of some 36,000 square miles dominating north-central Spain. León is now essentially a historical artifact.

León, Luis de (Fray Luis)
(1527–1591)
Spanish poet and scholar

Member of a family of distinguished jurists, but one marked by the taint of Jewish ancestry, León joined the Augustinian order at an early age, distinguished himself in his studies at the University of Salamanca, and was appointed to a chair at that institution in 1561. Admired for his lectures and writings, he also excited the jealousy of several colleagues as well as the suspicions of those perennially on the lookout for heresy in the troubled Reformation period. In 1572 León was accused of attacking the Latin (Vulgate) translation of the Bible, which was the only officially approved version of the Scriptures. The fact that his great-grandmother had been forced to convert from Judaism was a factor just below the surface in the charge against him. He was imprisoned under harsh conditions (which led to the death of a cellmate) but survived to be exonerated and restored to his teaching duties at the beginning of 1577. Despite—or perhaps because of—his steadily growing reputation of scholarship he was again accused of doctrinal irregularities in 1582 but escaped any serious consequences. The rest of his life was one of relative tranquility.

Fray Luis, as he was commonly called, is one of the most important figures in Spanish Renaissance literature. The depth and thoroughness of his learning, based on a command of Latin, Greek, Hebrew, and

Italian; the range of his biblical studies; and the skill of his exposition set a standard for scholarship that few could attain. His literary style, elegant but free from pedantry, became a model of Castilian prose. His most important works in prose are *De los nombres de Cristo* (*The Names of Christ*, 1583) and *La perfecta casada* (The perfect married woman, 1583). In addition to these learned and didactic works Fray Luis is admired for his poetry. Although not a mystical poet in the strict sense like SAINT TERESA OF ÁVILA or SAINT JOHN OF THE CROSS, his ability to sustain and transform the hardship of his imprisonment into a deep appreciation of the mysteries and majesty of the Christian faith have retained a place in the praise of literary critics and the hearts of the faithful. The best known of these poems are "Vida retirada" (Life of withdrawal) and "Noche serena" (Serene night).

Lepanto, Battle of (1571)

The most famous victory of Spanish arms and one of the decisive battles of history, this naval action was fought on October 7, 1571. It takes its name from a cape at the entrance to the Gulf of Patras in Greece. In adjacent waters a fleet of some 200 galleys, assembled by the Holy League, encountered a Turkish armada of comparable size. Although the forces of Christian Europe that had been assembled to confront their Muslim antagonists included contributions from the Papal States, the Republic of Venice, and some smaller Italian states, the bulk of the force, which carried 30,000 men, was provided by Spain. The entire Holy League coalition was under the leadership of Don Juan (known as DON JOHN OF AUSTRIA because the Habsburg dynasty ruled in

Spain), the brother of King PHILIP II. Spain had been contesting with the Ottoman Empire for mastery of the Mediterranean during the past five decades with little lasting success. The death of Sultan Suleiman the Magnificent, in 1566, had seemed to offer an opportunity owing to the incompetence of his heir, Selim II. The Turkish fleet, which had massed under Ochiali Pasha to halt the Holy League advance, assumed its usual crescent formation. Don John's bold tactics broke the Turkish crescent, scattered the isolated squadrons, and achieved the destruction of all but 40 of the Turkish galleys, which their admiral led in desperate flight. In addition to destroying or capturing the bulk of the Turkish forces, Don John liberated some 10,000 galley slaves and inspired rejoicing throughout Christian Europe. Even the Protestant realms of the north rang bells and lit bonfires to celebrate the triumph of the Catholic fleet.

Although Turkish attacks would continue on land for decades, the myth of the "Terrible Turk" and his supposedly invincible navy was forever shattered. Lepanto proved to be a turning point in the centuries-long struggle between western Europe and the Turkish empire. For Spaniards in particular it was a perpetual source of pride, and CERVANTES reflected the feelings of his compatriots when he spoke of the crippled arm that he sustained in the battle as a badge of honor.

Lerma, Francisco Gómez de Sandoval y Rojas, duque de (1553–1625)
Spanish statesman

Descended from FERDINAND V and the House of Borja (Borgia), his family connections won him a place at court in the reign of PHILIP II. Having gained access to the royal heir, he quickly won an ascendancy over the young man who became PHILIP III in 1598. The new monarch was disinclined to the business of kingship, and his *privado* (political favorite) became the effective ruler or Spain.

In the sphere of foreign affairs Lerma favored the maintenance of peace and encouraged the king to end the conflicts with England (1604) and the Dutch rebels (1609) and to avoid hostilities with France. However, he had no interest in remedying the defects of the government or in improving the economy. As a Valencian nobleman, Lerma could not persuade the Castilian magnates to undertake necessary reforms. Moreover his own avariciousness and nepotism were the source of endless scandal. Ultimately his domestic policy was reduced to holding on to the king's favor, fending off mounting criticism from aristocrats and commoners alike, and letting sleeping dogs lie when it came to national decline.

By 1618 Lerma's corruption had spread throughout the administration, which was packed with his relatives and henchmen. His greed became almost manic as he obtained ever more titles and property for himself and bestowed civil and ecclesiastical offices upon his relatives, particularly his son, the duke of Uceda. When a murder by one of Lerma's underlings threatened to precipitate an irresistible attack on the favorite's position, Uceda persuaded his father to seek the protection of papal investiture as a cardinal, thus securing himself against criminal proceedings. The scheme worked to the extent that it saved Lerma from personal destruction, but his role as all-powerful favorite was over. Uceda

briefly took his father's place, but with the death of Philip III in 1621, PHILIP IV ascended to the throne and installed his own favorite, the count of OLIVARES, as chief minister. In the purge that followed, Lerma's "creatures" were executed, imprisoned, or stripped of their wealth. The cardinal-duke died a few years later amid the ruins of his former grandeur.

Contemporary observers described Lerma as the arch villain of Philip III's reign, suggesting that the young monarch was able and well informed and would have succeeded had he not been dominated by the favorite. Yet Philip was under no obligation to surrender his power to Lerma and freely chose to sign whatever the latter put before him. No single individual, sovereign or statesman, can be blamed for the decline of the country, but Lerma, as a "monster of egotism," remains an enduring symbol of the ruin that was overtaking early 17th-century Spain.

Leyenda Negra (Black Legend)

This term has been applied to the characterization of Spain, its people, and its historical record in general as totally negative and profoundly evil. The precise origin of the phrase in unclear, but it evidently began as a Spanish reaction to a growing flood of denunciation and outright calumny that can be traced back to the 16th century. Elements that contributed to the Black Legend were Spain's harsh treatment of ethnic and religious minorities, its policies in the conquest and rule of the Americas, its persecution of dissenters (particularly the activities of the SPANISH INQUISITION), and its aggressive political-military policies in Europe. Spain's wealth and power and undeniable cultural achievements during the so-called SIGLO DE ORO (Golden Age) added resentful jealousy to moral indignation and patriotic fervor as elements contributing to a deep enduring antagonism toward all things Spanish. During the 18th century, a period of relative decline for the country, Spain was perceived as the opponent of Enlightenment and modernism. The loss of its colonial empire in the 19th century and its socioeconomic backwardness were added to the evidence of its fundamentally flawed character and even of divine punishment for the misdeeds of a corrupt nation, whose material deterioration proved its unworthiness to participate in the mainstream of European society. Spain's long-term antagonists, Great Britain and the Habsburg Empire, provided prolific promoters of the Leyenda Negra. The United States by and large inherited its perspective from Britain. Even such chroniclers of Spain's past glories as William H. Prescott tended to see Spanish achievements outweighed by the bad principles and conduct of its leaders. The negative view of Spain among North Americans was inevitably intensified by the SPANISH-AMERICAN WAR of 1898. French opinion was less consistently hostile to Spain, but France's writers usually cultivated an image in fiction, operatic scenarios, and travel accounts of Spain as a romantic but violent and dangerous place, whose denizens were given to extreme passion and violent action. Spain's relative isolation from the Western mainstream through most of the 20th century compounded ignorance and prejudice to produce a mixture of dismissal and contempt even more lacerating to Spanish pride.

Although some Spanish writers have actually made their own contributions to the Black Legend by emphasizing particular misdeeds (for example, BARTOLOMÉ DE LAS CASAS in his denunciation of Spanish mistreatment of the Indians and ANTONIO PÉREZ in his depiction of PHILIP II), most Spaniards defended their country from its traducers, even while lamenting its shortcomings. The legacy of the Black Legend remains profoundly significant even at the beginning of the 21st century.

Lisbon (Lisboa)

An important seaport from ancient times, Lisbon was held by many rulers, from Romans to Visigoths before becoming a Moorish stronghold in the early Middle Ages. Captured by Christian lords in 1147, it became the capital of the newly independent kingdom of Portugal. A base for transatlantic and circum-African voyages of exploration and trade, it was one of the most important cities of Renaissance Europe until the end of the 16th century, when it fell under Spanish control. It experienced a revival during the reign of JOHN V (1706–50) due to the influx of wealth derived from Brazilian mineral discoveries. After the devastating earthquake of 1755 it never regained its former prosperity, although much was done to reconstruct its public buildings and to restore its historic structures. The decline and fall of the BRAGANÇA dynasty between 1807 and 1910 further diminished links with the historic grandeur of the past. During World War II (1939–45) Lisbon became celebrated as a center of international espionage, as agents from all over the world met and competed for information in this neutral capital. Following the end of the Salazar dictatorship in 1974, Lisbon began to emerge from its isolation and to recover some of its economic and cultural brilliance.

Lope de Vega Carpio, Félix
(1562–1635)
Spanish dramatist

Although of humble origin Lope de Vega, thanks to clerical patronage, received a classical education and attended the University of Alcalá. He soon embarked on a pattern of life that would last for many decades: a restless combination of literary activity, the pursuit of women, and travel about Spain and overseas (including participation in the ARMADA's failed invasion of England in 1588). A bewildering succession of wives and mistresses, legal tangles, and even a period of banishment from MADRID complicated his financial situation. Some of his difficulties were resolved when he entered the priesthood in 1614, although this change in status by no means ended his romantic attachments.

If Lope de Vega's lifestyle was picturesque, his literary achievement was prodigious. Aside from a wide range of works in poetry and prose he was the most fecund of all playwrights. While he speaks in an autobiographical passage of writing 1,500 plays, other sources suggest that the total reached 1,800 or even 2,000. Of these only 500 have survived, due to the careless manner in which texts were distributed and preserved during his era. The author alludes to about 100 plays that he wrote in just one day each. Lope, as he was popularly called by his contemporaries, was variously hailed as a "phoenix," a "marvel," or even a "monster" due to his unnatural facility and productivity.

Although some critics have questioned the worth of an output so vast and so rapidly produced, most scholars of the drama have praised Lope's achievement at the same time that they are obliged to struggle with some organizing principle to categorize his plays. Broadly they may be divided into religious, mythological, pastoral, historical, and comedies of manners. The most important of his plays are those that focus on concepts of honor, justice, and the relations among social classes.

Among Lope's best play is *Fuenteovejuna* (Sheep's well, ca. 1612–14), the story of a village who rises up against the tyranny of its overlord and then assumes the collective guilt for his death. Royal investigators cannot persuade or force anyone to identify the slayer of the *comendador* (commander). Each resident, when asked who killed the tyrant, will only respond *"Fuenteovejuna."* In the end the king decrees that since it would be unjust to punish all and since the citizens are moved by the virtues of a shared love and solidarity, he must pardon them all. Over the centuries the perennial relevance of resistance to oppression and collective responsibility have given this play an ongoing resonance. In *Peribáñez y el comendador de Ocaña* (*Peribañez and the Commander of Ocaña*, ca. 1610) the title character is a respected farmer whom the local *comendador* raises to the rank of HIDALGO with command of a company of peasant soldiers. The villainous commander hopes to get rid of him so as to seduce his bride. Peribáñez, however, confronts and slays the *comendador,* justifying his action on the ground that he has now attained the rank of gentleman and has a right to defend his family honor in a way not permitted to mere peasants. The *comendador,* by promoting Peribáñez, has thus guaranteed his own doom. In this play, as in *Fuenteovejuna,* a *comendador* who has sworn to safeguard the king's subjects placed under his authority has betrayed his trust. Lope, as in other plays, presents the king as ultimately restoring order and dispensing justice in a setting that has been disrupted by abuse of power. The king, to use Lope's own phrase, is "the best magistrate." Distinctly different in theme from *Fuenteovejuna* and *Peribáñez* but striking in its won way is *El caballero de Olmedo* (*The Knight from Olmedo,* 1622). Inspired by medieval folk songs, this play is a highly poetic tragedy in which the knight of the title, Don Alonso, pursues his deep love for a girl who has been betrothed by her father to a villainous rival, Don Rodrigo. Although repeatedly warned by the song of a peasant in the field, sinister dreams, and even the vision of his own ghost, Don Alonso finally meets his doom at the hand of Don Rodrigo, thus fulfilling the saying that love will lead to death.

The perennial appeal of Lope's plays lies in the understanding that he must give his audience what they need and want. In the 1609 essay *El arte nuevo de hacer comedias* (*The New Art of Making Plays*) he declares that he has set free the *comedia* (drama), emancipating it from rigid formulas and boundaries. The people pay to see his work, he says, and he must give them what they want, mixing the tragic and the humorous, the grand and the everyday in the determination to gratify his audience. What some have seen as cynicism is also a professional playwright's pragmatism and an artist's refusal to be bound by long-established conventions. Lope is in fact the creator of a Spanish national drama. Unlike CALDERÓN DE LA BARCA and other playwrights, he does not pursue a preoccupation with special topics and limited themes.

His theater is all encompassing, both in subject and in form.

Lorca, Federico García   See GARCÍA LORCA, FEDERICO.

Louis I (Luís I) (1838–1889)
king of Portugal

Succeeding his brother, PETER V, in 1861, Louis at first partook of some of the popularity and hopeful spirit raised during that youthful monarch's brief reign. With the passage of time, however, a pattern of political corruption and parliamentary fraud set in. As in contemporary Spain liberals and conservatives "rotated" in office reducing the electoral process to a purely nominal operation and taking turns in running the country for the enrichment of their friends and the advantage of a small socioeconomic elite. For most of his life the king was merely a bystander in the governing of Portugal.

Louis I (Luis I) (1707–1724)
king of Spain

Eldest son of PHILIP V, he was unexpectedly called to the throne early in 1724 when his father announced that he was weary of his duties and wished to withdraw to a place of quiet retirement. Some commentators have suggested that Philip V was more interested in pursuing the French crown, which seemed about to become available.

Louis was totally unprepared for the responsibilities of kingship, but progressives in Madrid were hoping to transform this youthful Bourbon into the kind of reformer that his father had never become. Barely six months after his accession, however, Louis was dead. The official cause was stated as smallpox, although some contemporaries alluded to mental stress caused by the deranged behavior of his young wife, and others have attributed the collapse of his health to overindulgence in hectic pleasures encouraged by bad companions. Whatever the cause of his demise, the rapid reign of Louis I (the only king of Spain to have that name) was followed by the return of Philip V to rule for another 22 years. Louis I has been virtually forgotten, and his name is absent from many histories of the country over which he briefly presided.

Louisiana (Luisiana)

Occupying the valley of the Mississippi River and the lands drained by its tributaries, the territory of Louisiana extended over hundreds of thousands of square miles and linked the interior of North America to the Gulf of Mexico. Early Spanish expeditions along the gulf coast established a claim to the area around the mouth of the Mississippi. None of these early voyages, including that of PÁNFILO DE NARVÁEZ, who had been granted the land west of the FLORIDA peninsula, resulted in settlement. During the later 1500s and early 1600s expeditions marching north from Mexico and west from what is now the southeastern United States sought the fabled inland kingdom of Quivira without success. These efforts, which included the attempts by JUAN DE OÑATE, FRANCISCO VÁZQUEZ DE CORONADO, and HERNANDO DE SOTO, were all of value only in establishing a theoretical Spanish claim to the region. French explorers, moving south from their Canadian settlements in the late 1600s, initiated a more effective

colonial presence, and by the time New Orleans and outlying posts were established in the early 18th century, France had essentially usurped Spain's original pretensions, naming the territory after King Louis XIV.

A dramatic alteration in the situation resulted from the French defeat in the Seven Years' War and the cession of the Louisiana territory to CHARLES III. At first hesitant to take on the vast additional burdens that this imperial expansion would impose, the king finally began a tentative process of asserting Spanish rule in the Mississippi valley and at New Orleans. The already-flourishing gulf port proved militantly hostile to the initial arrival of Spanish representatives, expelling Governor Antonio de Ullóa in 1768. His successor, General ALEXANDER O'REILLY, imposed Spanish rule with a harsh hand, and the colonial transformation proceeded smoothly thereafter. Spain proved more flexible than its new subjects might have expected. It realized that people of European stock, already committed to a religious and social system much like its own, could not be treated with the brusque and intolerant tactics it had employed elsewhere in the New World, where the inhabitants had been of a different race and culture. A rational modification of Spanish laws on trade permitted the mercantile population to carry on their business much as before, while accommodations were made to the presence of British and French traders in nearby islands. The governors who succeeded O'Reilly generally made themselves popular with the Creole inhabitants, although the treatment of blacks and Indians was sometimes imprudently rigorous. During the final stage of the American Revolution Spanish forces seized a number of British posts along the disputed frontiers of Louisiana and crowned their achievement by capturing Pensacola. As a result of these operations Florida was retroceded to Spain in 1783, although that area was not placed under the administration at New Orleans. Instead both Florida and Louisiana were made subject to the Captaincy General of CUBA.

The last decade of Spanish rule in Louisiana was troubled by new boundary disputes, in which the United States now joined, having claims to the so-called West Florida district (now coastal Alabama and Mississippi). Just when stability and prosperity seemed to be emerging for Louisiana the impulsive decision of Napoléon Bonaparte to revive French domination in the Caribbean led him to exert pressure on the weak-willed CHARLES IV and his corrupt chief minister, MANUEL DE GODOY. The result of this was an agreement in 1800 to restore the territory to France. The rapid changes in international affairs that occurred during the next few years delayed the effective transfer until 1803 by which time Bonaparte had changed his plans and sold the entire territory, including New Orleans, to the United States.

During the period of nearly 40 years when Spain finally exercised control over a domain that it had been the first to explore and had always claimed as rightfully its own, it had maintained a rule that was usually benevolent and had encouraged the continuing development of the region's economy. New Orleans had become a city of some 50,000 inhabitants with a flourishing commerce that would play a vital role in the ongoing development of the young American republic. The story of Spanish Louisiana constitutes more than a mere parenthesis in the history of French Louisiana.

Luís I   See LOUIS I (king of Portugal).

Luis I   See LOUIS I (king of Spain).

M

Macao (Macau)

This Portuguese colony on the southeastern coast of China was established in 1557. For several centuries it was, with nearby Canton, the only point of entry into China available to European traders. When Britain established its control of Hong Kong, some 40 miles down the coast, Portugal asserted (1849) her sovereignty over Macao, which had been hitherto regarded as leased territory. This claim was not acknowledged by China until 1887. The enclave—with a population of some 300,000 crowded into a few square miles on a peninsula and two islands linked by causeway—remained in Portuguese hands after the rest of her empire had vanished. Although the Communist regime in China sought Macao's surrender in the 1960s, a later policy change encouraged her retention as a useful opening to the outside world. Macao was finally returned to China by mutual agreement and with elaborate ceremonies of mutual respect in 1999. Macao was, thus, the last surviving remnant of Portugal's once globe-girdling empire.

Machado, Antonio (1875–1939)
Spanish poet

The son of an eminent folklorist who had advocated the revival and renewal of Spain's literary traditions, Machado was himself a member of that GENERATION OF '98 that sought to overcome the spirit of defeatism and disarray gripping Spain after her military and political failure in 1898. Machado was, moreover, a product of the Institución Libre de Enseñanza founded by FRANCISCO GINER DE LOS RÍOS, whose graduates were viewed as the potential renovators of their country. Having studied at the Sorbonne and received a doctorate in literature, Machado dedicated himself to the teaching of French at secondary school in CASTILE. During his time there this native of ANDALUSIA became thoroughly imbued with a love and sympathy for the people and landscapes of his adopted region. His happiest years came to an end in 1912 with the death of his adored wife and the necessity of taking up a new teaching position in the south. A serious and solitary figure who avoided the cliques and intrigues of the literary world, Machado was much esteemed by many of the leading figures in contemporary Spanish culture, but it was not in his austere temperament to be close to the men or movements of his time. Loyal to the Second Republic, he remained in its last capital, BARCELONA, until the very end and left for France, escorting his aged mother, only under the compulsion of the retreating Loyalist soldiers. Both he and she died within a few days of crossing the French frontier.

Perhaps more than any other member of the Generation of '98, Machado felt a profound historical revulsion toward the decline of Spain dramatized so starkly by "the Disaster" of 1898. His youth reflected a considerable degree of positive and optimistic feeling, but at the beginning of the 20th century he was speaking of Castile as a symbol of the lost greatness of Spain: "Castile, dominant yesterday, now miserable, wrapped in its rags . . . once the mother of many leaders now the harsh stepmother of mere laborers." In his poems the nostalgia for better days and a sense of true worth lingering on in the provincial villages of Castile mingle affection with sadness. These feelings are embodied in his collection of poems titled *Campos de Castilla* (Plains of Castile, 1912).

Already retreating from the early influences that tempted him to indulge in florid and exuberant stylistics, Machado achieved a mature simplicity of expression in his later works, including *Nuevas canciones* (New songs, 1924) and *Poesías completas* (Complete poetry, 1928). These writings also reveal the existential themes that increasingly attracted him. Throughout his work, however, there is a persistent theme of solitude and a haunting loneliness that goes beyond his personal misfortunes. Machado clearly identifies with the sorrow and seemingly inescapable misfortunes of modern Spain. It is for this reason, above all others, that he is revered as one of the great national poets.

Machado, Manuel (1874–1947)
Spanish poet

In contrast to his brother, ANTONIO MACHADO, Manuel Machado remained deeply involved in the cultural and physical environment of their native ANDALUSIA. For him, not the austerity of CASTILE, but rather the sensuality and voluptuous environment of the south inspired him. Both were influenced by the enthusiasms of their father (also named Antonio), one of Spain's greatest folklorists, but Manuel managed to combine the practical need of a career with poetical egoism. After taking degrees at FRANCISCO GINER DE LOS RÍOS's Institución Libre de Enseñanza, he gave himself over, for a time, to the bohemian life in Paris. In the company of French and international poets he absorbed the spirit of modernism, an approach that influenced him throughout his life, although he moved away from narrowly defined poetical forms.

Marriage and the need for a more stable lifestyle brought Machado into a career as a librarian from 1909 onward, and he also found success as a journalist. In the closing years of the monarchy he became director of Madrid's Municipal Museum and continued in the position during the Second Republic. Changing sides during the SPANISH CIVIL WAR, he was confirmed in this position by the Franco regime and continued as director until 1944. Here again Machado is in sharp contrast to his brother, for Antonio was a Loyalist. In view of their divergent patterns of thought and life, it is somewhat unexpected to find them collaborating on a number of plays, of an essentially comedic character. Machado wrote extensively in the critical vein, commenting on the dramatic productions of the day and retained an acute sense of Spanish traditions in his nonfiction work. It is, however, as a poet that he will be remembered, and above all as a poet who celebrated the moods and emotions of Andalusia, claiming to have "the soul of a Spanish Arab." For him there are no permanent loves, no overwhelming passion, but merely the evocation of sensual pleasures as he drifts through the starlit night or floats on warm buoyant waters. His poems are sensual but essentially light in their emotion. His desire to strike effects or even to shock (as in his early "Mal poema") seems never deeply felt.

Madariaga, Salvador de (1886–1978)
Spanish historian

Born in La Coruña, GALICIA, of a military family, Madariaga was drawn to history and literature at an early age. His father, however, insisted upon a "practical" technical training, and the youth was sent to pursue his higher education in France, earning a degree from the National School of Mines in 1911. Returning to Spain, he obtained a position as technical adviser to a railroad company. After a few years, finding the job uncongenial, he moved to London, where he devoted himself to study and writing. He also continued journalistic work that he had previously combined with his other activities. An interest in Spanish influence on English literature brought about the publication of *Shelley and Calderon* in 1920. This and subsequent books led to his appointment as a professor of Spanish studies at Oxford (1928–31). After the establishment of the Second Republic, an event that he hailed as a great triumph for democracy, he served as his country's representative at the League of Nations, where he had already established numerous contacts, from 1931 to 1936. He also served the republic as minister of justice and education but was impelled by political attacks and ill health to withdraw from public service.

Madariaga left Spain on the outbreak of the SPANISH CIVIL WAR and did not return there until the end of FRANCISCO FRANCO's dictatorship in 1975. During much of this nearly 40-year period Madariaga resided at Oxford where he resumed his academic and literary activities. This period of self-exile was the most prolific of Madariaga's career. In addition to novels and plays he published several general histories of Spain and of Spanish national character, studies of notable individuals in Spanish and Spanish-American history (such as CHRISTOPHER COLUMBUS, HERNÁN CORTÉS, and SIMÓN BOLÍVAR) and literature, and a number of books on Spanish America, including histories of the colonial era. Probably his most important books are *Guide for the Reading of Don Quijote* (1926), *The Rise of the Spanish American Empire* (1942), and *The Fall of the Spanish American Empire* (1945).

Madariaga was the recipient of numerous honorary degrees and of honorary membership in learned societies in Europe and the Americas. His learning and his readiness to discourse upon the largest themes of world history, combined with his sheer endurance, gave him the status of a Renaissance intellectual living up to the closing decades of the 20th century. Having witnessed the end of the Franco regime, he had the pleasure of seeing the restoration of democracy in his native land. Shortly before his death he published his valedictory hailing the triumph of responsible leadership in the person of JUAN CARLOS I and common sense among the people at large who overwhelmingly approved the 1978 constitution. He tempered his optimism by warning of the danger still posed by communism, a danger that would soon be dissipated both in Spain and the rest of the world. He proved more prophetic, however, when he suggested that militant BASQUE NATIONALISM would continue to undermine the sound regionalist solutions set forth in the constitution.

Madeira

This overseas province of Portugal lies in the North Atlantic, some 400 miles west of the Moroccan coast. An archipelago consisting of the main island of Madeira and its smaller neighbor, Porto Santo, as well as several uninhabited islets, it has a total area of 308 square miles. The first outpost of Portugal's seaborne empire, Madeira (named for its wooded terrain) was discovered in 1420 and promptly cleared for agricultural settlement with a burning off of its forests that took some seven years to complete. Sugar plantations, based on crops imported from Asia, flourished here and became the point from which sugar was introduced into the New World. A wide variety of agricultural products, both of the semitropical and temperate zones, has been cultivated in Madeira, with the production of wine grapes being particularly successful. Madeira wine has carried the name of this island far and wide. It became popular not only in Europe but in the New World, where the long voyage across the Atlantic was believed to have added a particular, desirable flavor. Unlike many other Portuguese acquisitions, Madeira has remained firmly attached to the mother country for more than five centuries, aside from a British occupation between 1807 and 1814 to keep the archipelago from falling into Napoléon's hands. By the beginning of the 21st century the population of Madeira had grown to more than a quarter of a million.

Madrid

Originally a Moorish fortress, Madrid passed under the control of CASTILE in 1082 but was not a major center of Spanish trade or government until PHILIP II made it his capital in 1561. Due to its central location and the monarchy's determination to curb regionalism Madrid gradually developed as the principal city of Spain as well as its seat of government. The BOURBON dynasty was particularly committed to its embellishment with palaces, churches, and other public structures during the 18th century. The citizens of Madrid undertook a fierce resistance

Post office building in Plaza de las Cibeles, Madrid *(Getty)*

to French occupation troops in 1808, and their patriotic uprising was brutally repressed, an episode commemorated in two of GOYA's most famous paintings.

During the SPANISH CIVIL WAR (1936–39) the Republican forces and the civilian population endured prolonged bombardments and aerial attacks by the rebels, not surrendering until March 29, 1939. The city grew steadily in the number of its residents, the prosperity of its commerce, and the impressiveness of its infrastructure in the decades following the end of the austere dictatorship imposed by FRANCISCO FRANCO. Its cultural isolation was ended as it became a center of art, with the magnificent collection at the PRADO gallery being joined by the work of avant-garde painters and sculptors. A glittering nightlife, a dynamic cinema, a newly liberated literary community, and energetic involvement in international affairs reflected its growing sense of being a cosmopolitan European metropolis. Madrid sustained a shocking blow to its self-confidence on March 11, 2004, when a series of bombs placed aboard trains entering the central railroad station killed and wounded almost 200 people. This attack by terrorists helped to bring down the national government, precipitate a withdrawal of Spanish troops from military operations in Iraq, and sour relations with its new ally, the United States.

Maeztu y Whitney, Ramiro de
(1874–1936)

Spanish writer and political theorist
Born in Vitoria to a Basque father and an English mother, Maeztu spent some years of his young manhood working in CUBA to help rebuild the family fortune. His experience in the plantations and among the working class after he returned to Spain gave him a strong sympathy with the need for social justice and political reform. He was, for a time, an anarchist and was detained by the police for his public utterances and early ventures into journalism. He went abroad as a correspondent for several Spanish newspapers in 1909 and lived in the major European capitals, including Berlin. When World War I broke out in 1914 he chose to report the conflict from the Allied side and found himself particularly at home in Great Britain, where his verbal and written command of English was put to good use. After the war the disruption of the old European order and the rise of communism led to a shift in his politics, and he moved toward the Right. In 1923 he hailed the establishment of a virtual dictatorship by General PRIMO DE RIVERA. He was rewarded for his increasingly outspoken conservatism by being named ambassador to ARGENTINA in 1928. His literary-political writings also gained him recognition, including the Luca de Tena Prize and election to the Spanish Royal Academy.

The proclamation of the Second Republic in 1931 accelerated Maeztu's disenchantment with contemporary affairs. He became a conservative activist and theoretician and gained a following among young people as well as the support of disillusioned politicians and military men. His anti-Republican organization, Acción Española, and its journal (which bore the same name) widened his influence. His arguments in favor of Spain's need for regeneration, renewal of its Catholic roots, and leadership in Europe's resistance to Bolshevism attracted Catholic and "Traditionalist" allies. Detained on suspicion after the failed coup of General JOSÉ SANJURJO in 1932, Maeztu was able to travel abroad in 1934 and revisit Germany. There he became an outspoken admirer of Adolf Hitler's authoritarian regime. With the establishment of the left-wing Popular Front government in MADRID early in 1936, Maeztu was denounced as a fascist enemy of the republic. He was jailed despite protests from Britain and Argentina. In July 1936, on the outbreak of FRANCISCO FRANCO's insurrection, Maeztu was taken out of prison and killed by "persons unknown."

Maeztu was neither a consistent nor a particularly original political thinker; however, once he found what he evidently considered his true ideological home, his eloquence and persuasive journalism gave him great influence in shaping the thoughts of those who launched, waged, and won the SPANISH CIVIL WAR. In his early mindset, displayed in *Hacia otra España* (Toward another Spain, 1899), he deplored Spain's shortcomings and urged his country to Europeanize itself and to choose the progressive, modernizing models presented by Britain and Germany. After his transformation Maeztu published, in 1919, *La crisis del humanismo* (The crisis of humanism), in which he completely repudiated the principles he had embraced 20 years earlier. He declared that the ills of modern society were the poisonous fruit of humanism and presented the Enlightenment and marxism as stages in a process that portended disaster for Europe. Spain, he now asserted, was the potential savior of Western civilization, having historically preserved the essential Christian roots of that civilization. Spain, he argued, must renew its commitment to its traditions, reach out to the lands of its former empire, which it had lifted from

barbarism, and resume its rightful place in this age of crisis. These ideas are reiterated and expanded in *Don Quijote, Don Juan y La Celestina* (1926) and *Defensa de la hispanidad* (Defense of Hispanic culture, 1934), in which an increasing emphasis is laid upon the necessity of the Catholic faith to overcome the profoundly sinful nature of humankind. Maeztu's ideas were unwelcome in the aftermath of the Franco dictatorship but still command a following in some circles.

Mafra

Located some 25 miles northwest of LISBON, the palace-monastery-basilica complex at Mafra was built by order of JOHN V between 1717 and 1735. Officially it represented the fulfillment of the king's vow to express his gratitude to God for providing a male heir and to demonstrate his ardent religious feeling. In fact the splendid edifice is equally a gesture of monarchical vanity. Although its conception and general style are reminiscent of EL ESCORIAL in Spain, it is even larger and evokes the grandiosity of Louis XIV's Versailles. John V clearly wished to glory in his wealth, newly derived from the gold and diamonds lately discovered in BRAZIL. The sheer size of the apartments and the splendor of their adornment reflected the king's desire to be perceived as a major figure on the European stage and to remind fellow sovereigns that he, too, presided over a colonial empire.

The German architect Johann Friedrich Ludwig was given a free hand to create the most splendid possible monument of the Portuguese baroque built with colossal quantities of marble (both from Portuguese quarries and imported from Italy). When the suppliers of some of the elegant furnishings of the palace hesitantly warned the king that his requirements would cost a huge amount of money, he promptly responded by sending them twice the amount they had specified. Clearly the scale upon which John the Magnanimous pursued this enterprise was designed to glorify not only God but himself.

Magellan, Ferdinand (Fernão de Magalhães, Fernando de Magallanes) (1480–1521)

Portuguese navigator in the service of Spain

A Portuguese nobleman who had served for more than a decade in his country's East Indian domains, Magellan returned to LIS-BON after a falling-out with the viceroy, AFONSO DE ALBUQUERQUE. On the basis of contacts with Portuguese traders and administrators in the SPICE ISLANDS he developed a plan for reaching those distant outposts by crossing the newly discovered Pacific. When MANUEL I rejected his ideas (1517), Magellan went to Spain where he obtained an audience with CHARLES I and secured a commission to lead a Spanish fleet on an expedition to expand the empire into Asia. Departing with five ships and more than 250 men, he sailed down the east coast of South America seeking a water route through the continent. Some accounts suggest that he had prior knowledge of such a route, which would explain the strenuous Portuguese efforts to prevent his departure. He succeeded in reaching the Pacific through the tortuous passage subsequently known as the Strait of Magellan, near the southern tip of South America. This ocean was previously unexplored. Portuguese

Ferdinand Magellan, 1581 *(Library of Congress)*

charts that he had obtained were based on speculation and proved totally useless. Occupying a third of the globe, large enough to encompass all of the earth's landmasses and 16 times the size of the Atlantic, the Pacific Ocean represented a challenge far greater than that confronted by any earlier explorer, including CHRISTOPHER COLUMBUS. Magellan had already experienced strained relations with his Spanish officers, several of whom he had executed when they threatened mutiny, and one of his ships had deserted him and sailed home while still on the Atlantic coast. His harsh discipline and taciturn authoritarianism continued to alienate his men but served to hold them together throughout a voyage across the most empty area of this ocean, during which they spent four months without sight of land and reduced to near-starvation. Conditions were somewhat relieved when the expedition reached what is now the MARIANA ISLANDS, and after a short stay Magellan proceeded to the archipelago that was designated the PHILIPPINE ISLANDS, after the king's son.

Rather than proceeding directly to the Spice Islands Magellan involved himself in political and religious activity, securing the submission to Spain of one of the Filipino rulers along with the nominal conversion of his subjects to Catholicism. This involved the expedition in military operations to support their new ally against nearby enemies. Ignoring the warnings of his officers, Magellan insisted on leading an attack against the hostile Filipinos in which he was killed, along with a number of his men. What was left of the expedition, by now reduced to two ships, proceeded southwestward, finally reaching the islands of Tidore and Ternate in present-day Indonesia. Despite their battered condition the survivors were able to obtain a large cargo of cloves in exchange for trade goods but dared not remain long because of the reported approach of Portuguese warships. A token force was left behind in the Spice Islands to maintain Spain's claim, while Sebastián Elcano assumed command of the flagship, *Victoria*, and set out across the Indian Ocean to make its way home. The remaining ship at first sought to return via the Pacific route but soon gave up the attempt and remained in the Spice Islands. After many delays and difficulties the *Victoria* finally reached Spain in September 1522, with only 18 crew members left to bring it to harbor.

The short-term results of Magellan's expedition were limited. He himself had perished along with most of his men. His subordinate who had completed the voyage received little material gain from the experience and died a few years later on a sec-ond trip into the Pacific. Spain was unable to maintain its tenuous grip on the Spice Islands and finally ceded its claims there to Portugal (1529) for a nominal payment that scarcely matched the cost of Spain's effort or the potential value of the lucrative Asian spice trade. All this said, the first circumnavigation of the world had been completed, sweeping aside centuries of ignorance and superstition about the size and structure of the globe. Even though Magellan did not personally complete the epic voyage, this, the greatest feat of human persistence and endurance during the age of reconnaissance, immortalizes his name and assures him the posthumous glory that was a prime motive for all conquistadores.

Majorca (Mallorca)

Together with Minorca and several smaller islands Majorca constitutes an archipelago in the western Mediterranean. Known as the BALEARIC ISLANDS (Islas Baleares), they total 1,936 square miles and have a population of about half a million. Successively ruled by different Mediterranean conquerors, Majorca and its dependencies constituted a separate kingdom during the 13th century under a branch of the Aragonese ruling family. Majorca was reunited with ARAGON in 1343. Majorca's prosperity as a trading center declined because of the "discovery" of America, the aggressive competition of the Italian city-states, and periods of social unrest. During much of the 18th century Minorca was separately ruled under British sovereignty, not being returned to Spain until 1802. Minorca again followed a divergent path during the SPANISH CIVIL WAR when it espoused the Loyalist cause until it finally collapsed in February 1939.

Church in Majorca *(Getty)*

Majorca rallied to the revolt led by General FRANCISCO FRANCO and served as a naval base for his Italian allies. In more recent times Majorca has been principally noted for its touristic appeal, with picturesque scenery and a mild climate that draw a steady stream of visitors.

Malacca

This city, dominating the strait of the same name and thereby controlling the most direct sea route from the Indian Ocean to the South China Sea, was the seat of Muslim political and commercial power in Southeast Asia at the beginning of the 16th century. It was captured in 1511 by the great Portuguese empire builder AFONSO DE ALBUQUERQUE. Portugal thus secured a formidable advantage in the entire Indian Ocean region as well as access to the Pacific Rim of Asia. Its dominance in the area was disrupted by the rise of the Dutch Republic as a colonial power. The fall of Malacca to the Dutch in 1642 greatly accelerated Portugal's decline as a force in Asian colonial affairs.

Málaga

Founded by the Phoenicians more that 2,000 years ago, the city of Málaga was a favorite residence of succeeding rulers, including the Romans. Under Muslim rule Málaga became a major seaport of ANDALUSIA until the Christian reconquest (RECONQUISTA) of the region in 1487. In later centuries it was famed for its lush foliage, fine wine, and equable climate. Held by French invaders between 1810 and 1812, Málaga underwent fierce bombing by Franco's forces in 1936, during the SPANISH CIVIL WAR. Today it is the capital of Málaga province, with a population of roughly 550,000 people, and is notable chiefly as a holiday resort.

Malaspina, Alejandro (1754–1810)
Spanish navigator

A younger son of an Italian noble family, Malaspina pursued a career in the Spanish navy, distinguishing himself in the siege of GIBRALTAR during the American Revolution. He participated in several voyages across the Pacific during the 1780s and at the end of that decade was chosen to lead a grand expedition of scientific investigation and administrative survey in that region. The aim was to obtain a detailed knowledge of the natural resources and ethnographical variety of Spain's circum-Pacific empire, as well as gaining insight into the present state and future prospects of her colonies in the area. After several years of preparation, which included selection of experts in many scientific fields, interviews with experienced travelers and scholars, and the construction of two specially designed research vessels, Malaspina embarked at CÁDIZ early in 1789, sailed down the Atlantic coast of South America, and proceeded methodically northward from CHILE to MEXICO, depositing his groups of experts along the way to pursue their investigations and gather material. Having reached Acapulco, he pursued a hitherto confidential mission of reasserting Spanish claims to disputed areas along the Canadian and Alaskan coasts as well as renewing the perennial search for the Northwest Passage through North America. Proceeding on across the Pacific, Malaspina's ships visited the MARIANA ISLANDS and the PHILIPPINE ISLANDS, probed various island groups farther south, then recrossed the vast ocean, making several further stops to acquaint the scientists with the flora, fauna, and native peoples of the islands. Reentering the Atlantic, Malaspina visited the Malvinas archipelago (Falkland Islands) to reassert Spanish claims there and returned home in 1794, after some five years.

Malaspina's voyage, comparable in its extent and significance to those of such other 18th-century navigators as James Cook and Louis-Antoine de Bougainville, not only gained a vast amount of artifacts and scientific specimens as well as a full array of information on the peoples of Spain's Pacific realm; it also provided the astute commander with an opportunity to make detailed analysis of the character of Spanish rule in the region. Malaspina's report on the defects of Spanish colonial administration and the growing disaffection among the Spanish-American populations was all too predictive of the storm of revolution that would soon strike the empire.

Malaspina was well received upon his arrival and promoted to rear admiral, but he soon fell victim to political intrigues. The death of CHARLES III, the enlightened monarch who had initiated Malaspina's voyage, and the departure of his able ministers left Malaspina at the mercy of the dull-witted CHARLES IV and his amoral adviser MANUEL DE GODOY. Malaspina soon found himself in waters that even he could not navigate and was driven into exile, spending his last years in Italy. Scholars have had to wait until the early 21st century to gain a full appreciation of the achievements of his expedition and the complex legacy of the Spanish seaborne experience.

Manila Bay, Battle of (1898)

The first blow struck by the United States in the SPANISH-AMERICAN WAR proved to be the decisive one to remove Spanish colonial power in the Pacific. Alerted by his government that war was about to break out, Commodore George Dewey took his Asiatic Squadron across the China Sea and down the coast of Luzon to launch a surprise attack on May 1, 1898. He found the ships under the command of Admiral Patricio Montojo anchored in Manila Bay and brought them under heavy bombardment. The Spanish ships, with their shorter range of fire, could not hit the Americans. In less than three hours all eight of the Spanish vessels had been sunk or set afire. Their crews had sustained casualties in the hundreds, while the Americans incurred only nine wounded. Dewey maintained a blockade of Manila Bay until the arrival of American naval and army reinforcements enabled the U.S. forces to lay close siege to Manila. Dewey had already enlisted the Filipino nationalist rebels to take the field in support of his enterprise, and Spanish troops in outlying areas of the archipelago were unable to reverse the direction of events. By August Manila had formally surrendered. The cession of the PHILIPPINE ISLANDS to the United States soon followed, although resistance from die-hard Spanish supporters would last for another year. The betrayed nationalist fighters prolonged their war against their new U.S. colonial overlords for several years beyond that.

Manuel I (Manoel I) (1469–1522)
king of Portugal

The sobriquet given to this monarch, "the Fortunate," was well deserved, for he was the beneficiary of a century of Portuguese initiatives aimed at securing a seaborne trade route to the Indies. When Manuel succeeded his cousin John II in 1495, the Cape of Good Hope had already been reached and the first mercantile expedition was already in preparation. The voyage of VASCO DA GAMA (1497–99) opened the way to Portuguese commercial and military domination of the Far East and brought tremendous wealth to Portugal. Manuel and his courtiers were the principal beneficiaries of the spice trade and other sources of enrichment, though his reign also saw the

beginning of a pattern of official corruption and extravagant waste that left a dubious legacy to his successors. Manuel was, however, a patron of the arts and the "Manueline" style in architecture preserves the memory of his lavish tastes.

Manuel was obliged to maintain a precarious balance in his international policy. His own ambition and the achievements of explorers such as PEDRO ÁLVARES CABRAL, who "discovered" BRAZIL in 1500, and soldiers such as FRANCISCO DE ALMEIDA and AFONSO DE ALBUQUERQUE steadily expanded his empire in the Far East. Yet Spain was predominant in Europe, and Manuel had to conciliate her by an agreement to the division of overseas territory, the adoption of Spain's policy of expelling the Jews, and the maintenance of a close dynastic alliance. This last strategy led to his marrying three Spanish princesses in succession. Ultimately the inheritance of Manuel, with all its dazzling wealth and far-flung dependencies, would pass to Portugal's old rival, Spain.

Manuel II (Manoel II) (1889–1932)
king of Portugal

The second son of CHARLES I, Manuel grew up during the tumultuous decades that culminated in the assassination of his father and elder brother in 1908. Barely 19, the young monarch had little prospect of surviving a renewed onslaught from revolutionary republicans who pointed to the oppressive tactics of a conservative government, a long history of corruption in high places, and a generalized poverty that left only a tiny ruling elite to enjoy the wealth generated by the colonial empire. In 1910 Manuel was driven from his throne by an insurrection that proclaimed a republic under the presidency of TEÓFILO BRAGA. Manuel withdrew to a comfortable exile in England, took no interest in a proposed restoration attempt after World War I, and died leaving no successor.

Manuel was the last of the BRAGANÇA dynasty, although kin in the Miguelite line have continued as pretenders. Ironically alluding to the only previous bearer of this royal name, Manuel I, whose virtual foundation of the empire in the early 1500s earned him the nickname "the Fortunate," some have designated Manuel II "the Unfortunate."

Margaret, duchess of Parma
(1522–1586)
Spanish regent of the Netherlands

The illegitimate daughter of CHARLES I (Holy Roman Emperor Charles V) and a Flemish lady, Margaret spent her early years in the Low Countries and was married first to Alessandro dei Medici (1536) and following his assassination to Ottavio Farnese (1538). Although her husband soon succeeded his father as duke of Parma, Margaret demonstrated her commitment to the HABSBURG dynasty by serving her half brother PHILIP II as regent of the Spanish Netherlands from 1559 to 1566. During this critical period she did her best to retain the allegiance of a population increasingly divided over issues of Protestant-Catholic rivalry and autonomist ambitions. Margaret applied the arts of persuasion and diplomacy, seeking to preserve the attachment of the great nobles of the Netherlands to the Habsburgs, invoking their loyalty to her father, the late emperor, and taking advantage of her own childhood ties to the region. When, however, militant Calvinists attacked Catholic churches, she endorsed the use of military force to reestablish order. The king, who had become increasingly dissatisfied with her policy of restraint, dispatched a large force of Spanish troops under the implacable duke of ALBA. Finding herself marginalized by Alba's aggressive tactics and the monarch's approval of them, Margaret resigned her regency and returned to Italy. She had the satisfaction of seeing her son, ALESSANDRO FARNESE, assume the position of governor general in 1578 and vindicate many of her ideas about how to deal with the local population when she paid him a brief visit. Nevertheless, by the time of her death, the country over which she had presided was irretrievably split into the present-day Belgium and the Dutch Netherlands.

Margaret of Austria (1480–1530)
regent of the Spanish Netherlands

As the daughter of Maximilian of Austria (later Holy Roman Emperor Maximilian I) and Marie, duchess of Burgundy, Margaret was at the center of many plans for marriage alliances during the period when Europe's modern state system was taking shape. First betrothed to the heir to the French throne, she was later married briefly to Prince Juan, the only son of ISABELLA of CASTILE and FERDINAND V of ARAGON. Following his demise in 1497 she married the duke of Savoy, who died two years later. The remainder of Margaret's life was devoted to the business of government and statecraft, in which she displayed remarkable intelligence and talent. As regent of the Spanish Netherlands (Burgundy) during the minority of her nephew, CHARLES I of Spain (Holy Roman Emperor Charles V), from 1506 to 1515, and as governor general of the region from 1519 to her death, Margaret was the effective ruler of the richest and most commercially significant region of Europe. She sought to maintain peaceful relations between Spain and France, encouraged cooperation between the Spanish and Austrian branches of the House of HABSBURG, and tried to preserve stable relations with England. A Burgundian by birth and affinity, she understood her people's dependence on a steady supply of English wool for the survival of their textile industry. From the trade negotiations that she carried on with London in the early days of her regency to the "Ladies' Peace" of Cambrai concluded with her former sister-in-law Louise of Savoy (who had become regent of France) in 1529, Margaret displayed a consistent commitment to an orderly pattern of European relations. Affable and willing to compromise when necessary, Margaret was also a hard administrator who was determined to hold the Burgundian inheritance together and curb the pretensions of any internal faction. She chose shrewd and skillful ministers such as the Savoyard Mercurino Gattinara, whom she passed on to her nephew. The pan-European instincts of Emperor Charles V and his councillors were clearly derived from the broad vision of Margaret, whose preference for strong, central government in place of feudalistic remnants appears even more modern when seen in the perspective of a broader European union. Had Margaret's marriage to Prince Juan lasted longer or their child lived, her role as queen consort of Spain and matriarch of a dynasty descended from her might well have guaranteed her a rank in history like that of Elizabeth I of England. Instead she remains a supporting figure in the chronicle of Renaissance Spain.

Maria I (Mary I) (1734–1816)
queen of Portugal

Daughter of JOSEPH I, Maria was married to her father's brother and reigned jointly with him after the king died in 1777. Both the queen and her husband, PETER III, were opposed to the long domination of the chief minister, POMBAL, and supported his enemies in the successful intrigues to end his experiments in enlightened despotism. The death of the queens's consort in 1786 and one of her sons two years later evidently precipitated a mental breakdown. By 1792 her son John (JOHN VI) was directing the affairs of state although he did not assume the regency formally until 1799. Accompanying the rest of the royal family to BRAZIL in 1807, Maria retained the title of queen until her death in 1816.

Maria II (Mary II, Maria da Glória) (1819–1853)
queen of Portugal

The daughter of PEDRO I of Brazil, Maria da Glória had a troubled reign from early childhood, having been proclaimed queen in 1826 upon her father's renunciation of the Portuguese throne. She was subsequently betrothed to her uncle, who usurped the throne two years later; found refuge in England; was restored by the efforts of her father who came from BRAZIL to lead a liberal counter-revolution; and married in 1836 Duke Ferdinand of Saxe-Coburg-Gotha. Although the next few years were beset by frequent political disruptions and attempted military coups, the country made some economic progress, added modestly to its exiguous school system, and even introduced railroad transportation. In 1853, the young queen, who had borne five children, died with two of her sons in an epidemic that swept the capital.

Maria Christina (María Cristina)
(1806–1878)

queen and regent of Spain

A daughter of King Francesco I of Two Sicilies (Naples) and his wife, the infanta Maria Isabella of Spain, Maria Christina married her mother's brother FERDINAND VII in 1829. The fourth wife of that childless monarch, she bore him two daughters, of whom the eldest became Queen ISABELLA II. Much of the short remaining period of her husband's reign was occupied with political quarrels over whether a woman could succeed to the throne. The dispute came to a head in September 1833. Liberals recognized Maria Christina as regent for young Isabella, encouraged in their support by the regent's reputation for liberal sympathies. In the civil war that soon broke out, these *cristinos* were opposed by the *carlistas* (Carlists), who supported the conservative brother of Ferdinand VII, Don Carlos, and insisted that only a male line of succession was legal. During the so-called First Carlist War, not formally ended until 1839, Maria Christina and her daughter were recognized by the new liberal governments in Great Britain and France, while conservative regimes throughout Europe backed Don Carlos.

Maria Christina, confirmed in her regency, continued to preside over Spain until 1843, gradually alienating her former political allies by what they perceived as conservative tendencies. Her position was also weakened by her secret marriage to Agustín Fernando Muñoz, a former guards officer, which was not publicly acknowl-

Queen Maria Christina *(Library of Congress)*

edged until 1843. In 1840, after her one-time champion, General BALDOMERO ESPARTERO, turned against her, she was forced to go into exile in France.

When General RAMÓN NARVÁEZ ousted Espartero in 1843, Maria Christina was allowed to return to Spain, although her daughter was now declared of age. The former regent nevertheless continued to exercise influence until another political upheaval in 1854 brought about her permanent banishment from Spain. She and her husband (now bearing the title duke of Rianzares) and their children returned to France, where they lived out their lives and were joined in exile by Isabella II, who was herself deposed in 1868.

María de Agreda, Sor (María Coronel) (1602–1665)

Spanish mystic

Born María Coronel, she took the name Sor María and that of her native town when she entered the Franciscan order. She was an able administrator, rising to the rank of prioress and, later, abbess. She was also a woman of literary skill and intense religious feeling, combining these qualities in writings that have made her one of Spain's most notable 17th-century mystics. Her most famous work is *La mística ciudad de Dios* (The mystical city of God), published posthumously in 1670 and reprinted over subsequent centuries in many editions. This book is a curious mixture of novel, biography, and mystical rapture. Its central structure is an account of the life of the Blessed Virgin Mary with a highly detailed depiction of the life and times of the Holy Family. The author supplies much information that is not contained in the Gospels, freely inserting such specifics as dates and everyday experiences. Of greater interest to historians is the correspondence carried on between Sor María de Agreda and King PHILIP IV. The monarch broke one of his journeys at her convent in 1643, was pleased with their conversation, and proposed that they maintain an exchange of letters. Their friendly communications lasted for more than 20 years until the nun's death. Philip discussed the doings of the court, reflected on high policy, and asked Sor María's advice on matters of conscience and conduct. She responded with a mixture of semi-mystical piety and pragmatic counsel derived entirely from a naive inexperience that provided a refreshing change of viewpoint for a king undoubtedly overburdened with the input of self-interested advisers. The correspondence, *Cartas* (Letters), published in 1885, affords an intriguing glimpse of an older Spain and the minds of two personalities not unrepresentative of their time.

Mariana Islands (Islas Marianas)

This group of 15 islands in the western Pacific was visited and claimed by FERDINAND MAGELLAN for Spain in 1521. Lying some 1,300 miles east of the PHILIPPINE ISLANDS, this small archipelago (covering a total area of less than 400 square miles) offered a welcome respite for those who had crossed the vast, empty space of the ocean. The looting of several of Magellan's boats, however, led his sailors to call these the Islas de Ladrones (meaning "thieves' islands"), or Ladrone Islands in English. In 1668 Spain took formal possession of the islands, naming them for Queen Mariana, wife of King PHILIP IV. The island of Guam was seized by the U.S. Navy in 1898 during the SPANISH-AMERICAN WAR. In the following year the remaining islands, the most important of them being Saipan and Tinian, were sold by Spain to Germany. They became Japanese possessions after World War I and a UN trust territory of the United States after World War II. Presently the Northern Mariana Islands are a U.S. commonwealth, and Guam is a U.S. territory.

Martí, José (1853–1895)

Spanish colonial rebel

Born in Havana, CUBA, Martí became involved, when barely 16, in the movement that led to the 1868 Cuban insurrection. By 1871 he had served a term in prison and been banished to Spain. If Spanish authorities thought that immersing him in the society of the mother country would cure the young man of his nationalistic inclinations, they were mistaken. He earned a law degree at the University of Zaragoza and published poems and essays. Frustrated by his homeland's status as the last remnant of Spanish imperialism, he wrote about a free and united Western Hemisphere linking all of Spain's former colonial dependencies. During the 1870s Martí lived in a number of Spanish-American countries, teaching, writing, and even serving for a time as a judge in GUATEMALA. From the early 1880s to 1895 he resided in the United States, mostly in New York City, where he founded the Cuban Revolutionary Party and devoted himself to organizing a network of nationalists dedicated to a renewed war of liberation on the island. Martí admired many aspects of society and democratic political life in the United States but feared that country's inevitable pursuit of hemispheric domination. When he returned to Cuba to play a role in the new uprising that began in 1895, his life was tragically cut short in a clash between insurgents and Spanish troops.

In addition to his acknowledged role as the spiritual leader of the Cuban national movement, Martí is recognized as one of the finest poets and essayist of 19th-century Spanish America. Martí's poems are collected in *Ismaelillo* (1882), *Versos libres* (Free verses, 1883), and *Versos sencillos* (Unpretentious verses, 1891).

Martínez de Campos, Arsenio
(1831–1900)
Spanish general

One of the most successful and admired Spanish commanders of the late 19th century, Martínez de Campos was a distinguished graduate of the General Staff College. After serving in various assignments including the abortive Spanish participation in the subjugation of MEXICO in the early 1860s, he was sent to CUBA during the opening stages of the 10-year insurrection that began in 1868. Martínez gradually developed an approach to the rebels that combined vigorous attacks on their strongholds with a humane treatment of civilians and a willingness to grant amnesty to combatants who surrendered. His success gained him rapid promotion and the recognition of his methods as the most promising path to victory. Within a few years Martínez was able to return home in triumph, with Cuba pacified and the laurels of victory mingled with a reputation for humanitarianism that earned him great popularity. Appointed general commanding the forces in CATALONIA, Martínez swept aside the anarchist rebels, abandoned the floundering government of the First Republic, and at the beginning of 1875 proclaimed the restoration of ALFONSO XII. He then played a critical role in ending the Second Carlist War, once again employing both energetic military tactics in conjunction with a strategy of humane and conciliatory treatment of the enemy. During the 1880s Martínez served as minister of war and for a time as president of the Council of State, but his views were too liberal for the conservative authorities, and he was returned to a more limited military role. Sent back to Cuba as military governor in the early 1890s, Martínez confronted a new insurrection with a renewal of his moderate policy of seeking to win the minds and hearts of the Cuban people. Armed rebels were attacked without question, but they were made to understand that there was an alternative to fighting to the death. By 1895 Martínez realized that the government in MADRID would no longer support his gradualist policy, and he resigned, to be replaced by the implacable general VALERIANO WEYLER. Still esteemed for his intelligence and flexibility, Martínez continued to enjoy wide popularity in Spain where he was chosen president of the senate, a post he held until his death.

Martínez de la Rosa, Francisco
(1787–1862)
Spanish statesman and writer
Born in GRANADA, Martínez de la Rosa so distinguished himself as a scholar and teacher at the university there that he was appointed as a professor at an early age. During the attack on Granada launched by forces of JOSEPH I (Joseph Bonaparte), Martínez helped organize the defense of the city. His whole subsequent life was equally divided between public service and intellectual activity. After the expulsion of the French he left Spain during the reactionary rule of FERDINAND VII, returned to serve in the revolutionary government of RAFAEL DEL RIEGO (1820–23), and then traveled abroad again after its fall. During the First Carlist War of the 1830s Martínez led the supporters of ISABELLA II. He withdrew from Spain once again in the early 1840s in protest against the dictatorship of BALDOMERO ESPARTERO and then returned to involve himself in the high politics of the 1850s. During these decades, and almost to the time of his death, Martínez held a wide variety of offices, including minister of state, president of the legislature, and ambassador to Paris and Rome. A moderate liberal who tried to instruct his country in

the art of maintaining a balanced, stable government, he sponsored much legislation that integrated progressive thought with the salutary benefits of monarchical tradition. His policies inevitably earned him the hostility of ultraconservatives and radical reformers. The latter made a number of assassination attempts against him during the Riego period.

In addition to his importance as a political figure Martínez was a notable contributor to Spanish literature. His frequent periods of self-exile were filled with the production of plays, poetry, and historical novels as well as political tracts, didactic essays, and a major analysis of the form and structure of poetics. His most important work was the *Conspiración de Venecia* (Conspiracy of Venice), a play presented in 1834, which is generally considered to mark the beginning of Spanish romanticism. His stature among contemporaries is reflected in his directorship of the Spanish Royal Academy and his election to a number of other learned bodies, including the Academies of San Fernando, History, and Jurisprudence. He was also president of the Atheneum of Madrid and an honorary member of various foreign learned societies.

Martínez Ruiz, José (Azorín)
(1873–1967)
Spanish writer
Modern Spain's most notable essayist and literary critic, Martínez Ruiz was a member of the GENERATION OF '98. He himself gave this name to the group of intellectuals who strove to create new coherence and meaning for Spanish culture at the beginning of the 20th century. Like the other writers in this movement, Martínez Ruiz believed that

the military catastrophe of 1898, when Spain lost the remains of its empire and any lingering claim to great power status, offered an opportunity to renew the country's vitality through a return to its essential identity. Beginning with *El alma castellana* (The Castilian soul, 1900) and continuing in the trilogy of novels *La voluntad* (Will), *Antonio Azorín*, and *Las confesiones de un pequeño filósofo* (Confessions of a small philosopher), published between 1902 and 1904, Martínez Ruiz created a body of work that awakened Spaniards to their literary heritage and the distinctive characteristics of their country and culture.

Borrowing the pen name *Azorín* from his earlier book, the author steadily increased his influence among Spanish readers with compilations of his essays and articles, books such as *La ruta de Don Quijote* (The route of Don Quixote, 1905), *Al margen de los clásicos* (In the margins of the classics, 1915), and *Una hora de España, 1560–1590* (An hour of Spain, 1560–1590, 1924). Although he inspired many imitators, none could match his clarity, perceptiveness, and ease of style. Leaving Spain at the outbreak of the SPANISH CIVIL WAR in 1936, Azorín settled in Paris and returned to his early profession of journalist in articles for the Argentine newspaper *La Nación*. He returned to his native land some 10 years after the war's end and lived quietly until the last years of the Franco regime.

Matute, Ana María (1926–   )
Spanish writer

Matute grew up during the SPANISH CIVIL WAR, as her family moved back and forth between BARCELONA (her birthplace) and MADRID. She spent her adolescence in the grim environment of the postwar Franco regime, with its hunger, gloom, and persistent fears. In this way she absorbed the perspectives and subject matter that would dominate her literary work in adulthood. Much of her fiction presents the anxieties and uncertainties of children, and even her adult characters often preserve the mark of these childhood stresses in later life. Moving away from the social realism that dominated the work of most Franco-era writers, Matute entered the world of semifantasy, in which her juvenile characters saw the stark truths of contemporary Spanish life through eyes of ignorance and inexperienced optimism. In such books as the award-winning *Fiesta al noroeste* (*Celebration in the Northwest*, 1953) and *Los hijos muertos* (*The Lost Children*, 1958), which won the National Critics' Prize and the Miguel de Cervantes Prize in 1958, she revealed her understanding of the interaction between the child and the adult. *Los soldados lloran de noche* (*Soldiers Cry by Night*, 1963) was honored by the Spanish Royal Academy in 1969. It was part of a trilogy that began with *Primera memoria* (*First Memory*, 1959), a novel about children thrust into the adult world by the civil war, and concluding with *La trampa* (*The Trap*, 1969), in which the children of the earlier narrative have grown up.

In 1971 Matute published *La torre vigía* (The watchtower). Set in 10th-century Europe, this novel is a precursor, in its environment and, to some extent, its subject matter, to the magnum opus that she was already contemplating. After 25 years of silence and secrecy as to her plans Matute presented in 1996 *Olvidado Rey Gudú* (Forgotten King Gudu). In an imaginary medieval world of monarchs and dwarfs, half European, half fantastical, Matute had created a sprawling panorama of ideas and emotions that had become over the preceding decades a virtual obsession with her. On an ever-expanding canvas and with an evermore complex interweaving of characters and action she had worked, she later said, with a kind of superstitious fear that if she ever ended the project, she would die. She was delighted to find herself alive and well, and her book, warmly received by critics. Not long afterward she was honored by election to the Spanish Royal Academy, the only woman member at the time.

Medina Sidonia, Alonso Pérez de Guzmán, duque de (1550–1619)
Spanish admiral
Alonso Pérez de Guzmán was the seventh in a line of dukes who were among the highest of the Castilian *grandes,* with a title dating back to the 15th century. Although his personal distinction was unremarkable and his military and naval titles were essentially a reflection of his social status, he succeeded to the command of the ARMADA in 1588. The death of the marqués de SANTA CRUZ in the midst of the preparations for this great enterprise that was aimed at crushing all of Spain's enemies threatened a grand design that was dearest to the heart of PHILIP II. He designated Medina Sidonia as captain general of the coasts of ANDALUSIA and, although the duke had no naval experience, ordered him to take charge of the Armada. Some contemporary accounts suggest that the duke begged to be excused from the task, even pleading that he was subject to seasickness. The king would accept no refusal, for he wanted a man of prestige and wealth to demonstrate the importance of the Armada and assumed

that the duke would rely on the advice of veteran officers. In the actual operations against England during the summer of 1588, Medina Sidonia was overwhelmed by the rapidly changing situation. He rejected the counsel of his senior captains and ordered a retreat northward around the Scottish and Irish coasts that cost him many of his ships.

Far from punishing the duke of Medina Sidonia, the king gave him further assignments, either because he felt some personal guilt for insisting on the mission despite the inexperience of its commander or because the wealth and power of the duke's family in Andalusia was too great to be challenged. Medina Sidonia remained in supreme command of naval defenses in southern Spain, with the additional responsibility of curbing North African corsairs and Turkish raiders. When a large English force attacked and sacked CÁDIZ in 1596, the duke once again demonstrated his ineptitude both in preparing for such an emergency and responding to it once it had occurred. Nevertheless, the duke continued to hold all of his naval titles and responsibilities during the reign of PHILIP III, and his family was closely linked to the duke of LERMA, the all-powerful chief minister of that monarch. As late as the reign of PHILIP IV a subsequent duke of Medina Sidonia was actually involved in a plot to proclaim the independence of Andalusia with himself as king.

Melilla
Located on the Mediterranean coast of MOROCCO, this city was captured by Spain in 1496 and currently encompasses an area of 4.2 square miles. Repeated military and diplomatic attempts by Morocco to regain

the enclave have been rebuffed. The first stage of the 1936 military uprising that led to the SPANISH CIVIL WAR took place in Melilla under the leadership of General FRANCISCO FRANCO. Melilla's population of about 60,000 includes many of the most ardent champions of Spanish nationalism and die-hard supporters of the former Franco regime, whose ardor has only been intensified by the steady pressure of African migrants during the early 21st century trying to use the enclave as a doorway to Europe.

Mendes Leal, José da Silva
(1818–1886)
Portuguese dramatist

A prolific and widely applauded playwright in his day, Mendes Leal's reputation has faded as critics pointed to his numerous borrowings and imitations. During the 1830s he attracted attention with a series of vehement historical romances in the manner of Alexandre Dumas the elder. These were followed by similar productions in the 1840s, which managed to win the praise of his far abler contemporary ALMEIDA GARRETT. Having borrowed from the father, Mendes Leal evidently thought it appropriate to imitate the son, as he brought forth a number of "social dramas" in the style of Dumas the younger during the 1850s. His preference for French fashions in the literary sense continued to be strong, even during the 1860s when he ventured once again into historical drama and comedy. The author's poetical effusions were heavily indebted to Victor Hugo, and both *Cânticos* (1858) and *Poesias* (1859) earned a success that may have owed more to the merits of his model than his own.

Mendes Leal, like many Iberian writers, made frequent excursions into political journalism, as well as actively participating in politics. Various essays, published as pamphlets, and a surprisingly straightforward account of the Crimean War, *História da guerra do oriente* (History of the Eastern War, 1855), are generally considered among his best work.

Mendes Pinto, Fernão (1514–1583)
Portuguese traveler and writer

Born in Montemar-o-Velho in modest circumstances, Mendes Pinto seems to have lived by his wits in his youth and then set out in 1537 to seek his fortune in the vast commercial empire that Portugal was building in Asia. After residing for some time in GOA and other Indian outposts, he spent several decades traveling (by his own account) in virtually every part of the Far East. From Malaya to Cambodia, from present-day Indonesia to China, he observed the people and customs, made and lost several fortunes, and finally decided to return home. He was diverted from this intention by securing the remains of FRANCIS XAVIER, the pioneering Jesuit missionary and an old acquaintance of his. The future saint's remains had been brought to Goa from the place of his death, an island off the coast of China. Mendes Pinto, moved by contrition for his past misdeeds, joined the Society of Jesus himself in a subordinate capacity and traveled to JAPAN with a Portuguese priest who was bound there to assume direction of the order's activities. Four years later he experienced another change of heart and set out again for Portugal, where he arrived with enough left of his wealth to marry and settle down on an estate. He spent the rest of his life working on his major opus, *Peregrinação* (Travels), published posthumously in 1614. This book is one of the few by a Portuguese author of the period to be translated and widely circulated in various European languages. It attracted such attention because of the unique range of Mendes Pinto's observations and opinions on virtually the whole cultural environment of the distant lands of Asia, still little known to Europeans. Later scholars have questioned its value because of obvious flaws and errors introduced in early editions and because of questions about the veracity of the author's tales of his wanderings.

Mendoza, Antonio de (conde de Tendilla) (1490–1552)

Spanish colonial administrator

Member of a long line of Castilian warriors and nobles, Mendoza had fought against domestic rebels in Spain and against Turkish invaders in the Balkans as well as representing his country on diplomatic missions. He was appointed as the first viceroy of NEW SPAIN in 1535. CHARLES I had developed a high opinion of his intelligence and ability and confided to him a mission that involved consolidating competing jurisdictions and curbing ambitious governors. As viceroy Mendoza firmly established his authority and that of his successors in the whole northern area of Spain's dominions in the Americas. This included not only the first colonies in the Caribbean but also the Central American territories and the northern and western regions of New Spain. The lands that encompassed the whole western area of what is now the United States and potentially the PHILIPPINE ISLANDS (as well as the other islands in the Pacific) constituted a responsibility that Mendoza took seriously. He commissioned PEDRO DE ALVARADO to probe the Pacific coast of CALIFORNIA in the early 1540s and sent other expeditions to the Asian shores. In his capital, Mexico City, he had to curb the ambitions and intrigues of local officials and oversee the subjugation of both indigenous and settler rebels to the south. HERNÁN CORTÉS, the original conqueror of New Spain, was deeply resentful of Mendoza's arrival on the scene and made attempts to undermine him or have him recalled to Spain. Mendoza's influence at the royal court thwarted these plots. In his commitment to public works and institutional development, the promotion of trade, and the stabilization of society in New Spain, Mendoza was greatly assisted by JUAN DE ZUMÁRRAGA, the first bishop (and later archbishop) of Mexico City, his friend and collaborator for more than a decade. Mendoza was asked by the king to undertake yet another massive task of taming a raw land and wild spirits when he was nominated viceroy of PERU. Although this position was already considered to outrank that of viceroy of New Spain, Mendoza was at first hesitant to take on fresh burdens. Unable to resist the demands of duty, he set out for Peru in 1551 and boldly confronted the quarreling conquistadores who held sway there. Much remained to be done, however, when death overtook him in 1552.

Mendoza, like his colleague Zumárraga on the ecclesiastical side, was a model civil administrator. His achievements in laying a firm foundation for Spanish government in the New World paralleled those of Zumárraga in firmly establishing the church. Without such able and dedicated administrators the Spanish Empire would not have survived as long and as securely as it did.

Menéndez Pidal, Ramón
(1869–1968)
Spanish scholar

A profound and productive scholar whose career spanned most of the 20th century, Menéndez Pidal was trained at the University of Madrid, where he was a student of MARCELINO MENÉNDEZ Y PELAYO. Like his teacher, he was primarily a student of Spanish medieval literature but ranged widely over the whole of Spanish and European thought, society, and historical experience. Menéndez Pidal first attracted public attention in 1883 when he was awarded a special price by the Spanish Royal Academy for his critical work on the epic poem *Cantar de mío Cid.* That great figure of medieval history and legend would be a reference point throughout his life. He fulfilled his admirers' expectations in 1896 when he won the Spanish Royal Academy of History's award for *La leyenda de los siete infantes de Lara.* Three years later he was named to the professorship of romance philology at the University of Madrid, a position that he would hold for the next four decades. During those years Menéndez played an increasingly important role in the Spanish Royal Academy, of which he became a member in 1902. He was chosen director of the Royal Academy in 1925 and served until 1939. He resumed this office in 1947. He founded the *Revista de filología española* and the Centro de Estudios Históricos, where he trained the rising generation of Spanish historians. He also became well known abroad, traveling and lecturing in Europe and America. His lectures at Johns Hopkins University on medieval Castilian literature were published in 1910.

Among the most significant publications of Menéndez were *Manual de gramática histórica española* (Manual of historical Spanish grammar, 1904), an expanded critical edition of the *Cantar de mío Cid* (1908–12), *Poesía juglaresca y juglares* (Minstrelsy poetry and minstrels, 1924), *Orígenes del español* (Origins of Spanish, 1926), *La España del Cid* (The Spain of El Cid, 1929), and *Romancero hispánico* (Spanish ballads, 1951). These and other writings appeared in numerous editions and remain the standard references on their respective subjects. Menéndez also found time to act as general editor of the multivolume *Historia de España* (History of Spain). When, toward the end of the scholar's life, a Hollywood epic was produced under the title *El Cid,* he was asked to lend his name and fame to the film by giving his imprimatur, so to speak, to the historical and literary accuracy of this cinematic version of the subject to which he had devoted his life. A gentleman of the old school, Menéndez Pidal limited himself to the comment that the actor Charlton Heston presented a fine figure of the medieval hero. On the inevitable compromises made in movie scripts, he offered no comment.

Menéndez y Pelayo, Marcelino
(1856–1912)
Spanish historian and literary critic

It has been said that if the record of the world's intellectual achievements were destroyed in some catastrophe and only the writings of Menéndez y Pelayo survived, the heritage of modern civilization could be reconstructed from his intellectual output alone. At once profoundly learned and boldly outspoken, he dominated the cultural scene of late 19th-century Spain in a way that no single author or artist could. The legends of his erudition attribute to him a mastery of the classics while still a child and an omnivorous acquisition of knowledge during his attendance at several universities that soon outstripped that of his teachers. After receiving his doctorate at the University of Madrid in 1874 he became a member of the faculty and remained professor of Spanish literature for several decades.

In dozens of volumes he explored and analyzed the history and literature of Spain from medieval times to the present, integrating his findings with the contemporary culture of the entire Western world. His personal library of 45,000 volumes was ultimately added to that of the university's, symbolically merging his own intellectual resources into those of the nation.

Menéndez y Pelayo was an ardent Spanish patriot and understood this virtue as being synonymous with his ardent Catholicism; indeed, he held that all Spaniards, even outspoken anticlericals, were fundamentally shaped by their Catholic heritage. This perception enriched and influenced his writings, although some critics complained that it created a profound bias in his work. Menéndez y Pelayo would, in later years, admit to a degree of truth in these accusations, and his later writings are generally more balanced and objective. He also moderated his combative instincts, which he admitted had led him to employ excessive acrimony toward those who failed to agree with him. It was perhaps inevitable that a man who combined encyclopedic scholarship with traditional conservative allegiances should come into conflict with reformist and "progressive" intellectuals. The active career of Menéndez y Pelayo encompassed a period when Spain was passing through socioeconomic upheaval, political disarray, and the collapse of its surviving empire. With so many voices offering prescriptions for change and demanding a "new" Spain, Menéndez y Pelayo seemed to represent an unapologetic champion of the "old" Spain. At the time of his death the controversy was still unresolved, and his writings, as well as his polemics, stood as a massive heritage for 20th-century Spaniards to consider as their changing circumstances would dictate.

Among the more notable works of Menéndez y Pelayo are *Historia de los heterodoxos españoles* (History of heterodox Spaniards, 1880), *La ciencia española* (Spanish science, 1880), *Calderón y su teatro* (Calderón and his theater, 1881), *Historia de las ideas estéticas de España* (History of Spain's aesthetic ideas, 1883–91), and *Orígines de la novela* (Origins of the novel, 1905–10).

Mexico

This name was, at various periods, applied both to the modern country of the same name and to a vast range of territory extending far north of the Rio Grande and encompassing half of the present-day United States. The central region surrounding the modern capital of the country (Mexico City) was ruled on the eve of the Spanish conquest by the Aztec Empire. Following the overthrow of that indigenous regime during the 1520s, the name *Nueva España* (NEW SPAIN) was applied to the entire North American landmass from its farthest northern territories to the Isthmus of Panama. Common usage, however, substituted *Mexico* for the formal designation of New Spain. Spanish rule in this region ended during the early 1820s, and the peoples within its boundaries evolved with changing political developments.

Miguel, prince of Portugal
(1802–1866)
claimant to the throne of Portugal

Second son of King JOHN VI, Dom Miguel, with the rest of the Portuguese royal family, fled to BRAZIL after the French invasion of 1807. The king returned to Portugal with Miguel after the legislature in LISBON demanded that he reside there rather than in Brazil (which had been elevated to the status of equality with Portugal). Miguel became the active leader of the reactionary forces in Portugal and took part in a failed revolt against this father in 1824, prompted by the liberal constitution that John had approved. After John VI's death in 1826, the situation became increasingly complicated. John had recognized the independence of Brazil with his elder son remaining there as Emperor PEDRO I. Now that son was also Pedro IV of Portugal. Pedro promised to abdicate in favor of his daughter Maria da Glória (MARIA II), and to pacify his brother and the Portuguese conservatives he offered Miguel the guardianship of Maria and her hand in marriage when she became of age. Miguel initially accepted this arrangement but repudiated it in 1828 and was proclaimed King Miguel I of Portugal by a legislature under conservative domination. He was recognized as king by the papacy, Austria, Spain (controlled by conservatives at that time), and a number of other states. Maria and her entourage fled to Britain, where her claims were recognized.

Early in 1831 Pedro abdicated the Brazilian throne (in favor of his son by a second marriage) and set out to fight for his daughter's rights. In the civil war that followed Portugal was divided between liberal supporters of Maria and conservatives who felt that the whole structure of Portuguese religion and traditional values was under attack from radicals. Miguel, their king and hero, had presided over fierce persecution of political opponents since 1828 and hoped to prevail in the conflict that now erupted. Pedro, however, rallied with liberals in the AZORES and launched an invasion of the mainland, capturing OPORTO. With British assistance the conservatives were defeated, and Miguel left the country in 1834. The MIGUELITE WAR was officially over, but Miguel, en route to his place of exile, reasserted his claim to the Portuguese crown and denounced his niece and her supporters. The Miguelite claim to the kingship of Portugal was again taken up in arms several times during the 19th century. After the revolution of 1910 that proclaimed a republic and the subsequent extinction of the monarchist line descended from Maria II, the Miguelite pretender asserted his claim with more validity but with equal lack of effect.

Miguelite War (1831–1834)

This Portuguese civil war arose from the complex self-indulgences and ambitions of the BRAGANÇA dynasty. JOHN VI and his family had fled to BRAZIL when France invaded Portugal in 1807. They remained there until 1820, when liberal forces ousted the regency council in LISBON and demanded the king's return. He kept a precarious balance between the forces of the Left and the Right until his death in 1826. His elder son, who had remained in Brazil, chose to become emperor of that newly independent colony as PEDRO I and to pass the Portuguese crown to his daughter Maria da Glória (MARIA II). Pedro's brother, MIGUEL, backed by Portuguese conservatives, insisted that a female could not rule and claimed the succession for himself. He was appeased for a time by Pedro's proposal to have him wed Maria da Glória and exercise a regency during her minority. By 1828, however, the agreement had broken down, and the Traditionalists proclaimed their leader king, as Miguel I, and forced Maria da Glória to flee to Britain. Miguel's supporters (commonly called Miguelites) included aristocratic, clerical, and landowning interests and their rural adherents, principally in the north. As political, religious, cultural, and social conservatives, they were opposed to "modernism" and the "atheism" that they perceived rising up around them. Their political philosophy centered on reversing whatever change had come into the Iberian Peninsula as a result of the French Revolution, particularly the democratic elements of the constitution that had been forced upon John VI. They shared these sentiments with the nascent Carlist movement in Spain and with reactionary factions in Vienna, Berlin, St. Petersburg, and Rome, who also feared a new wave of revolutionary disruption throughout the Continent.

In 1831 Emperor Pedro yielded his throne in Rio de Janeiro to his son and sailed for Europe to take up his daughter's cause. The Miguelite War that followed was waged by the young queen's liberal adherents and the allies whom her father rallied in Britain and France with the aid of the newly installed liberal governments there. They were opposed by Miguel's loyalists, with some indirect help from European conservative governments. Liberal refugees had already established a foothold in the AZORES, where Pedro found a warm welcome, and from this archipelago he launched a series of attacks against the Portuguese mainland. Miguelite warships were defeated off Cape St. Vincent by vessels flying the flag of Maria II and manned by British crews on nominal leave from the Royal Navy. OPORTO was captured in 1832, and Lisbon fell the following year. By 1834 Maria's advisers (her father had died shortly before) won recognition of her title. Their principal inducement was a guarantee of existing rank and privileges to Miguelite army officers and pensions (although not existing jobs) to Miguelite civil servants. Dom Miguel left the country, but his descendants would maintain their pretensions to the throne through the 20th century.

The Carlist uprising in Spain, which arose from a similar conflict over male versus female dynastic succession and antagonistic sociopolitical philosophies, began just as the Miguelite War was drawing to a close. Although there was definite sympathy and evidently some support exchanged between Miguelites and Carlists, they represent parallel rather than intersecting movements in the history of Iberian conservatism.

Millán Astray, José (1878–1954)
Spanish military officer

The career of Millán Astray, one of the most famous Spanish soldiers of the 20th century, began in 1896–97 when he served as a teenage lieutenant in the Philippine insurrection. On the strength of his battlefield experience he was made an instructor of the Infantry School and subsequently spent several years on the faculty of the Staff College. Although Spain was a neutral during World War I, Millán saw ample combat in MOROCCO, where the stability of Spain's political position was deteriorating. In 1919, by now a major, he presented a proposal to his superiors for the creation of the Spanish Foreign Legion. The French Foreign Legion (which had been created originally to fight in Spain during the First Carlist War) had long been engaged in North African colonial conflicts. Millán visited some of their units to gain data and ideas for support of his plan. Although he encountered opposition from vested interests in the army, those whose judgment mattered, from the king to the minister of war, approved his proposal, not the least because it offered an alternative to increasing the number of annual conscripts sent to Morocco. Although the French Foreign Legion had little difficulty in raising volunteers, especially in the postwar period, the Spanish force initially authorized in 1920 was not as successful in recruitment at first. The number of actual foreigners was never very large (most of them being either Portuguese or Cuban). Even after enlistments increased the preponderant number would be Spanish social misfits, ex-criminals, and men driven by economic desperation. Millán, appointed commander of the new unit, with the rank of lieutenant colonel, proved phenomenally successful in transforming these outcasts into a highly disciplined and dedicated body of soldiers. His exhortations to recruits bore a strong resemblance to those a priest might give to sinners: They were going to redeem themselves from everything bad in their past by their selfless sacrifice on the battlefield. He frequently told them that a glorious death would wipe away the bad things they had done up until then. He hailed them as the *novios* (bridegrooms) of death and gave them a battle cry: "*¡Viva la muerte!*" ("Long live death!"). The Foreign Legion, formally known as the TERCIO (in honor of the famed military units of 16th-century Spain), went into action in 1921 and gained rapid renown. Millán helped publicize its operations by arranging for battlefield scenes to be filmed. Victories over Moroccan insurgents and the relief of threatened towns contributed to its positive image. By the late 1920s, when the insurrection was put down, the legion had expanded to six battalions, despite the loss of thousands of men killed or wounded. Millán himself, in the forefront of the fighting, lost an eye and an arm. Eventually he turned over active command of the troops to his fellow Galician, FRANCISCO FRANCO. By the time the SPANISH CIVIL WAR broke out in 1936 the Spanish Foreign Legion was famous (or notorious), and Franco would make full use of its military reputation during the war. Millán, although retired from active duty, continued to advocate his violent personal philosophy, adding to his original slogan a preface that horrified Spanish intellectuals: "*¡Abajo con la inteligencia! ¡Viva la muerte!*" (Down with intelligence! Long live death!). In his later years, Millán Astray, promoted to general, was president of the League of War Wounded.

Miranda, Francisco de (1750–1816)
Spanish colonial rebel

Born in Caracas, VENEZUELA, Miranda became an officer in the Spanish army; took part in the capture of Pensacola in 1781, when Spain was aiding the American revolutionary forces against Britain; and toured the major cities of the United States, meeting with George Washington, Alexander Hamilton, and other leaders. He then traveled throughout continental Europe making a particularly favorable impression on Catherine the Great of Russia. Enlisting in the armies of the French Republic, he fought against her Teutonic enemies, rose to the rank of divisional commander, but was then accused of disloyalty by the Jacobin regime and expelled from France. Miranda now abandoned his career of adventurer at large and spent the next few years in Britain seeking William Pitt's support for the overthrow of Spanish rule in the Americas. He proposed a union of the South American colonies under an emperor descended from the ancient Inca dynasty, with a democratic balance provided by a bicameral legislature. Despite (or, perhaps, because of) the grandiose and unrealistic scope of his vision, with its blending of indigenous and European elements, Miranda succeeded in impressing many of those who listened to him, from Prime Minister Pitt to the future Chilean liberator, BERNARDO O'HIGGINS.

By 1806 Miranda had succeeded in assembling an invasion force that sailed from New York, landed on the Venezuelan coast, and had some initial success before being repulsed. He thus anticipated by several years the general outbreak of colonial revolt that followed the French invasion of Spain in 1808 and the disruption of Spain's central authority. Returning to Venezuela in 1810, after this later rebellion had begun, Miranda joined forces with SIMÓN BOLÍVAR and other rebels. Miranda's initial success on this occasion led to his assumption of dictatorial powers in Venezuela, but mili-

tary setbacks forced him to surrender his principal stronghold to royalist forces under the condition that he might withdraw in safety. Bolívar and his allies now became disgusted with what they saw as Miranda's weakness and treachery, seized him, and handed him over to Spain where he spent his remaining days in a dungeon in CÁDIZ.

Miranda has been rightly described as an international exponent of revolution, an enthusiastic "salesman" of the ideas of the Enlightenment. His ability to charm and (at least temporarily) persuade influential people on three continents to support his schemes has led some historians to see him as more picturesque than substantial. However, once he finally settled on his native land as the focus of his energies, he made a credible contribution to the cause of colonial rebellion. He must be recognized as the great precursor of the struggle for Spanish-American independence.

Miró, Joan (1893–1983)
Spanish painter
Born in CATALONIA and educated in BARCELONA, Miró began his career in Paris in 1919. His early work was naturalistic, but he soon came under the influence of the surrealists and turned to a nonobjective style. He aligned himself with the branch of surrealism known as "psychic automatism," in which the artist worked in a virtual state of unconsciousness. It would later be said that he entered a trancelike state by going without food for a long time or breathing an excess of paint. Whatever the source of his inspiration his unusual images and striking colors gained wide popularity, and his experimentations with various media assured him ongoing attention. He exhib-

ited widely and traveled frequently, becoming one of the best-known Spanish painters of the 20th century. He did not, however, follow the expatriate path of his contemporaries PABLO PICASSO and SALVADOR DALÍ, who lived more or less permanently abroad. Although away from Spain during most of the SPANISH CIVIL WAR and World War II, Miró returned regularly in later years to a village near Tarragona where he had first spent time in his youth. Active throughout an extended old age, he became one of the most recognizable of "modern artists," particularly in the United States, where he had been credited with both introducing abstract expressionism and leading the movement away from it. His paintings are prominently displayed in the major galleries of the world, occupying a particularly prominent place in New York City's Museum of Modern Art. Among Miró's most interesting paintings are *The Farm* (1921–22), *Still Life I* (1922–23). *Still Life II* (1922–23), *The King's Jester* (1926), *Dog Barking at the Moon* (1926), *Circus Horse* (1927), *Portrait of a Young Girl* (1935), *Head of a Woman* (1938), and *Woman and Little Girl in Front of the Sun* (1946).

Mola, Emilio (1887–1937)

Spanish soldier and political conspirator

The son and grandson of army officers, Mola exhibited a strong commitment to the principles and honor of his chosen profession from his days in the military academy onward. The tall, solemn cadet was nicknamed "the Prussian" because of his earnest and formalistic attitude toward all duties and responsibilities. As an officer in the Moroccan campaigns his leadership qualities won him steady promotion, but he was already marked for staff duty. His intellectual gifts and literary skills brought him to the army headquarters in MADRID during the dictatorship of General PRIMO DE RIVERA. By 1930 he had been named director general of security, a role as national police chief that suited his precise and secretive tastes. Mola found the various civilian police forces of Spain to be poorly organized and inefficient, and he applied himself to repairing these deficiencies. He also attempted to curb the rising agitation on the Left that threatened the monarchy. His rigorous methods earned him such unpopularity that the slogan "Kill Mola" was widely heard in 1931. After the proclamation of the Second Republic in that same year Mola continued to serve the new government, being loyal to the nation rather than to the king, but he was transferred to MOROCCO to remove him from the center of political controversy.

By the beginning of 1936, with the Popular Front government poised to introduce a radically left-wing program, Mola was ready to abandon his essentially neutral stance. He had produced a number of memoranda for the scrutiny of senior officers insisting on the army's central position in the survival of the Spanish state. He declared that any movement or individual that challenged the army was an enemy of the state and must be dealt with ruthlessly. At the same time it had not only become necessary to enlist all true Spanish soldiers in the cause of the fatherland but to secure the support of right-minded civilians as well. Mola emerged during this period as the philosopher of what became the Nationalist revolution. He never abandoned, however, his insistence upon the army's primacy in the "crusade" that was about to be launched. He questioned the relevance of a monarchical restoration at any time in the near future and was deeply suspicious of the fascist elements that had surfaced throughout the country. Moreover he recognized personal weaknesses in some of the very generals whom he was obliged to work with as he laid the foundation for the uprising: the impulsiveness of GONZALO QUEIPO DE LLANO in SEVILLE; the egotism of JOSÉ SANJURJO, who was expected to return from exile in LISBON to head the Nationalist regime; and the personal ambition of FRANCISCO FRANCO, whom Mola himself had predicted would play a vital part in leading the Army of Africa over from Morocco to help defeat the Republicans.

As the "revolution" broke out in summer 1936, it met more determined opposition from friends of the republic than Mola had anticipated. His elaborately structured plan for a coordinated national seizure of power failed in many parts of Spain due to vigorous counterblows by the Loyalists or to blunders by military commanders. His own zone of responsibility—including Pamplona and Burgos—was among those harder to control than the rebels had envisioned. Nevertheless, as the first anniversary of the rising neared, notable progress had been made. Yet Franco's assumption of national leadership after Sanjurjo's death in a plane crash was not pleasing at all. Mola, as the "brain" of the national movement, had his own convictions to assert and was undoubtedly encouraged to do so by his admirers. In June 1937 he undertook a short flight to Franco's stronghold in SALAMANCA in order to challenge the increased favoritism shown to monarchists and Falangists at the expense of professional soldiers. His plane crashed, and Mola was killed. His death, in circumstances so similar to that of Sanjurjo a year earlier, removed the only other general who could challenge Franco for mastery of the Nationalist forces. As in the earlier crash, accusations against Franco were made, but no proof has ever been found. Whatever the truth, the death of Mola, the purist of Spanish militarism, left the stage to Franco, the pragmatist.

Moluccas

This group of islands lies at the eastern end of what is now the Indonesian Archipelago, between Celebes and New Guinea. As the Portuguese pursued their course of empire building toward the Pacific shore of Asia, they occupied in 1512 the most important of the islands, rich in cloves and cinnamon, and usually referred to as the SPICE ISLANDS. The Portuguese thus became the masters of the tremendously profitable spice trade that provided Europe with the condiments that enriched and preserved its food. Much of Portugal's wealth during its Golden Age depended upon its mastery of the Moluccas. The arrival in 1521 of Spanish forces from the expedition of FERDINAND MAGELLAN precipitated an armed struggle between the two Iberian colonial powers in which they were supported by local rulers. Portugal's exclusive right to the Moluccas was not recognized by Spain until 1529. Between 1605 and 1621 the new rising colonial power in the East Indies, the Dutch Republic, succeeded in ousting Portugal from the Moluccas and went on to gain dominance over the whole region, which the Netherlands retained until after World War II.

Mombasa

This island off the coast of present-day Kenya was visited by VASCO DA GAMA in 1498 on his voyage to India. Between 1529 and 1698 it was the centerpiece of a Portuguese trade and military-naval dominance in eastern Africa and the Middle East. For varying periods during this span of years Portugal controlled outposts at the entrance to the Red Sea and at the entrance to the Persian Gulf, including Zanzibar, Masqat, Hormuz, and Socotra. Portugal also exercised a transitory dominance of what is now the Cape of Good Hope region in South Africa during the 16th century. These locations were essentially way stations on its trading route to India and the Far East, a region ruled from GOA.

Moneo, José Rafael (1937–)
Spanish architect

Born in NAVARRE, Moneo was educated at the Madrid School of Architecture and worked at the Spanish Academy in Rome from 1963 to 1965, after which he opened his own architectural office in Madrid. Most of his early commissions were in Spain, beginning with the design of a factory in ZARAGOZA in 1967. He went on to create the Museum of Roman Art in Mérida in 1986, the building of the Miró Foundation at Palma de Mallorca in 1992, and the long-discussed extension of the PRADO Museum in Madrid. He also held teaching positions in the University of Barcelona, Princeton University, and, during the 1990s, at Harvard University (where he was for several years chairman of the department of architecture). His growing reputation abroad earned him commissions in Stockholm and in several cities of the United States, including the Davis Art Museum in Wellesley, Massachusetts, and the Museum of Fine Arts in Houston, Texas. Perhaps the most notable achievement in that country was the Cathedral of Our Lady of the Angels in Los Angeles, California, completed in 2002. By then his accomplishments had already earned him the Pritzker Prize, in 1996, generally regarded as architecture's equivalent to the Nobel Prize.

Moneo's admirers have repeatedly praised his ability to combine a sense of the past with the present circumstances of his architectural site and the future purpose of the structure that he is designing. His respect for the past is particularly valued by those who favor the concepts of continuity and integrity as opposed to radical innovation. Furthermore he has consistently exhibited a respect for the need to blend new additions seamlessly with preexisting stages of construction, most notably in his extension of the Prado. This deference to the evolving demands of a historical site has been criticized by some as excessively cautious, and his work has been perceived in some circles as a rebuke to the boldness of architects such as SANTIAGO CALATRAVA, who constantly strive for the "new." Moneo has therefore been presented as a counterbalance to his more daring contemporary. Moneo stated his position clearly when he declared that architecture demands a combination of "beauty and necessity." He has set himself frankly in opposition to the architects who "seek to manifest motion instead of stability," "the ephemeral instead of the perpetual," "the fragmented instead of the whole," and "the fictitious instead of the real."

Moratín, Leandro Fernández de (1760–1828)
Spanish dramatist

Generally esteemed to be the best Spanish dramatist of the neoclassical school,

Moratín was a strong advocate of French cultural models and techniques, with a particular devotion to Molière. The son of a noted playwright and scholar of Spanish literature, Nicolás Fernández de Moratín, Leandro followed in his father's footsteps as regards both of these activities. By 1792 he had already attracted praise from progressives and antagonism from conservatives with his *La comedia nueva* (The new comedy) attacking hack writers who used safe, conventional themes. He came fully into his own in 1806 with the play *El sí de las niñas* (The maidens' consent) in which he condemned the artificiality and narrowness of Spanish social structure and rules of conduct regarding marriage. Having by now been labeled *afrancesado* (supporting French "values"), he inevitably found himself drawn into collaboration with the regime of JOSEPH I (Joseph Bonaparte) that ruled Spain from 1808 to 1814. Moratín somewhat reluctantly accepted an official appointment under the Bonaparte government, thus opening himself to persecution after its fall. After a series of harrowing experiences he fled to France, where he lived for the remainder of his life. While in exile he wrote a significant treatise on the origins of Spanish drama but long remained unhonored in his own country.

A shy and retiring man, despite his bold attacks on the cultural and moral defects of Spain, Moratín was one of a progressive group that strove to lead their country into the era of Enlightenment. Like other intellectuals of his day, he was forced to choose between patriotism and progress, although the latter was rendered an increasingly questionable process under the military dictatorship that grew out of the French Revolution.

Moreto y Cabaña, Agustín
(1618–1669)
Spanish playwright

Son of an Italian merchant and ordained to the priesthood after his university studies, Moreto became a protégé of the archbishop of Toledo. Supported by his patron's grant of a chaplaincy in TOLEDO, Moreto spent the last decades of his life primarily in literary activity. His quiet life contrasted with the eventful and often tumultuous careers of the major Spanish dramatists. Moreto's plays fall into many categories, often deriving from the ideas and models of other authors, including LOPE DE VEGA and CALDERÓN DE LA BARCA. To these works, however, he brought his own distinctive contribution of refined and elegant plot and character treatment. In the polish and suavity of his dramas there is often a foretaste of the 18th-century stage; indeed, his own work was freely borrowed and imitated by French, Italian, and even British writers of the 1700s. While Moreto's historical plays tend to be didactic, reflecting both the viewpoint of Catholic Spain in general and his own priestly outlook, several of his works have an enduring influence. Moreto's most notable plays are *El desdén con el desdén* (Disdain with disdain, 1652) and *El lindo don Diego* (The pretty Don Diego, 1662). In the former, considered his masterpiece, an overly proud young woman has treated her suitors with undeserved contempt. One of them reverses the process, disconcerting her and opening the way to a happy resolution for both of them. In the latter play the protagonist is an absurd and odious fop, Don Diego, whose self-absorption and endless preening are both ludicrous and repulsive. In the end he is tricked into paying court to a woman who is supposedly a rich widow and makes a thorough fool of himself. In both of these plays Moreto makes artful use of comedy and witty dialogue to achieve his moral lesson. He also introduces the figure of the cunning servant who is more than a mere stock image, but actually a major character advancing the resolution of the drama. The clever servingmen of Moreto are, in fact, prototypes of Beaumarchais's Figaro and a long line of similar characters. Although not a dramatist of the highest rank, Moreto is a genial and pleasing playwright, who made his own distinctive contribution of the literature of the SIGLO DE ORO.

Morocco (Marruecos)

Occupying the northwestern corner of Africa and facing the Iberian Peninsula across the Strait of Gibraltar, Morocco and its inhabitants were destined by geographical proximity for warlike interaction with the Spaniards and Portuguese. Following the Arab conquest of this region in the late seventh century, the Moors (or "Moros," as the Spaniards called them) joined, under the banner of Islam, in the invasion of the Iberian kingdoms. As the RECONQUISTA of the Middle Ages drove the intruders back, Spain and Portugal repeatedly attacked Moroccan rulers. Portugal conquered CEUTA in 1415 (the first European colony on the African continent), and Spain took MELILLA in 1497. Both of these cities would be in Spanish hands into the 21st century. The pattern of capture and loss was more varied in the rest of Morocco. Following the annihilation of a Portuguese invading army in the Moroccan desert in 1578 and the acquisition of Ceuta by Spain two years later, Portugal ceased to be a significant presence in North Africa.

Spain's enclaves of Ceuta and Melilla were repeatedly besieged during the 1600s and 1700s. In 1859–60 the Spanish prime minister, General LEOPOLDO O'DONNELL led a major invasion of Morocco to intimidate Spain's old antagonist. After an international conference at MADRID (1885) and subsequent negotiations in the early 1900s Spain emerged as master of a protectorate over western Morocco as well as several disputed provinces collectively referred to as Spanish Sahara.

Beginning in 1911 both Spain and France, which controlled eastern Morocco, were challenged by tribal uprisings in their respective territories. The Spanish conflict in Morocco came to a crisis in 1921 in the BATTLE OF ANUAL, when thousands of Spanish troops were overrun and slaughtered while retreating from their overextended line of fortifications in the interior. Driven back to their coastal outposts, the Spaniards came close to complete disaster, and the political reaction to these events in Spain precipitated the coup d'état of General MIGUEL PRIMO DE RIVERA. By the end of the 1920s the Spaniards, working in cooperation with the French, had regained dominance in Morocco. Fighting in Morocco during World War II between Axis and Allied forces and the emergence of a new Moroccan national movement led to destabilization in the 1950s. By 1956 Spain had followed France in surrendering her protectorate in Morocco, retaining only the Spanish Sahara region, which was reorganized as an "overseas province." The Franco regime, which had launched from Morocco the 1936 military uprising that brought it to power, retained a symbolic link with Morocco and the image of past imperial glory that it represented. Furthermore, discoveries of new iron deposits in the inner desert suggested an economic benefit in the colony's retention. By 1975, in the course of the political and financial reassessment that followed the demise of FRANCISCO FRANCO, the decision was made to surrender Spanish Sahara to Morocco, and an area of over 100,000 sparsely inhabited square miles was given up—the last significant remnant of Spain's empire. Only Ceuta and Melilla, the tiny coastal enclaves now administered as part of Spain remain to preserve a shadow of the past and to keep alive a low level of friction between Spain and Morocco.

Mozambique (Moçambique)

A settlement named Mozambique (Moçambique) was established on the coast of East Africa in the early 1500s and became the nucleus of a Portuguese presence in the region that grew slowly over subsequent centuries as Portugal multiplied its activities in the area around the Indian Ocean. A formal colonial structure did not develop until about 1875 and was achieved by negotiation with the governments of other colonial powers in East Africa. Much of the work of trying to bring in Portuguese settlers and establish plantations was carried on by the Mozambique Company (chartered in 1891). The Mozambique colony was not formally established until 1907 and was divided into two jurisdictions, that of the Portuguese government in the north and the Mozambique Company in the south. This arrangement ended in 1942 when the company's lease expired, and its land was joined with the remainder of the colony. As in ANGOLA the Salazar regime attempted to strengthen the Portuguese presence in

Mozambique and made the colony an "overseas province" in 1951. A nationalist uprising in 1964 came to an end 10 years later when the new democratic government in LISBON called a halt to the fighting. Mozambique was granted independence in 1975.

Murcia

A region of southeastern Spain including the provinces of Murcia and Albacete, this area extends from the Mediterranean coast inland to encompass arid terrain and a zone of irrigated cropland where citrus fruits, grains, and cotton are grown. The first foothold of the Carthaginian Empire in Spain (the city of Cartagena traces its origins to that period), Murcia subsequently became a vassal state of the Moorish caliphate in the eighth century. After passing through various political relationships among the Muslim lords during the RECONQUISTA, Murcia existed as an independent kingdom for a time, eventually absorbed by CASTILE in the late 13th century. The acquisition of Murcia was important to Castile's rising domination in Spain, for it cut off the prospect of Aragonese expansion to the south along the Mediterranean coast. In modern times Murcia was long regarded as a barren, lawless region. From its negative reputation arose the proverbial saying "Kill the king and flee to Murcia," signifying that even the most outrageous crimes would go unpunished in Murcia.

Murillo, Bartolomé Esteban
(1618–1682)
Spanish painter

Born in SEVILLE, at the time the center of Spanish religious enthusiasm and artistic activity, Murillo learned much by studying the technique of the masters in local private collections. After he had transformed his early, somewhat dry style of religious painting into "warm and atmospheric" renditions of scenes from the lives of the saints, he began to secure numerous commissions from churches and monastic communities. His rising stature during the late 1640s and 1650s brought him the presidency of Seville's Academy of Art in 1660. He subsequently displaced FRANCISCO DE ZURBARÁN as the leading painter of religious imagery and developed considerable popularity in genre scenes of urchins and picturesque street folk. His career ended dramatically when he fell from a high scaffold while painting in a church.

Murillo's great appeal lay in a mastery of sweetness and charm of expression and adroit management in his subject matter, whether religious or secular. Through these approaches he was able to win the favor of those who had grown too accustomed to the stark intense imagery of Zurbarán and who were attracted by smiling madonnas, winsome angels, and amusingly picaresque children. Despite the undoubtedly skillful rendering of his sacred themes, such as the images of the Immaculate Conception done in 1665 for the Church of Santa María Blanca in Seville, Murillo would eventually be perceived as too saccharine by modern critics. Nevertheless he and Zurbarán are masters, each in his own way.

N

Narváez, Pánfilo de (1470–1528)

Spanish conquistador

Born near Cuéllar, in Castilla la Vieja, of a gentile family, Narváez evidently spent his youth campaigning against the Muslims in GRANADA and then traveled in the late 1490s to the New World. Under the patronage of DIEGO VELÁZQUEZ DE CUÉLLAR, a townsman who had probably known him since childhood, Narváez took part in the conquest of JAMAICA in 1509 and played a major role in the invasion and occupation of CUBA in 1511. Although described by some contemporaries as an ideal figure of the Spanish conqueror—tall, fair haired, and noble in bearing—others characterized him as reckless and lacking in judgment. The priest BARTOLOMÉ DE LAS CASAS, who knew him well, condemned his harsh treatment of the Indians in Cuba and blamed him for the deteriorating relations between the races. Velázquez saw to it that he received a land grant in Cuba but evidently did not trust him with any major responsibility until 1520, when he was sent to MEXICO to curb the activities of HERNÁN CORTÉS. Velázquez apparently intended to attack and destroy the expedition of Cortés and make himself master of Mexico. Narváez was, however, taken by surprise and lost the first battle between Spanish forces in the New World. Narváez, who was wounded and suffered the loss of an eye, was held prisoner by his rival, while most of his troops joined Cortés.

After returning to Spain and exerting influence at court, Narváez procured the command of a major expedition to invade and conquer FLORIDA. He landed near the present city of Tampa in 1527 and marched into the interior. After suffering many losses in a fierce battle with the Amerindians near what is now Tallahassee, he retreated to the coast with only half of his followers left. These he set to constructing boats to cross the Gulf of Mexico. This attempt failed,

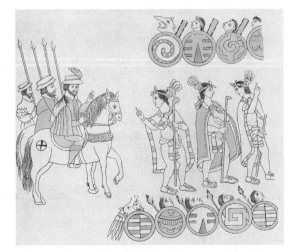

Battle at the water's edge and capture of Pánfilo de Narváez *(Library of Congress)*

however, when his vessels were destroyed in a storm on the coast of TEXAS. Narváez and his companions were drowned or killed by local natives when they struggled ashore. The only survivors of this catastrophe were CABEZA DE VACA and three comrades, who left an amazing record of their wanderings and endurance in the southern deserts of North America.

Narváez seemed to have the makings of a major conquistador. However, like some other promising contemporaries, he lacked the coolness of thought and the flexibility of decision that might have won the confidence of his countrymen and the cooperation of the indigenous folk whom he encountered.

Narváez y Campos, Ramón María (duque de Valencia) (1800–1868)
Spanish soldier and statesman

A professional army officer whose conservative temperament was shaped during the reign of FERDINAND VII, Narváez nevertheless supported the cause of ISABELLA II against the conservative forces during the First Carlist War. His victories in a number of major operations brought him increasing respect and earned him high command. In 1840, however, when the regent, Queen MARIA CHRISTINA, who had moved in a conservative direction fell out with the liberal general BALDOMERO ESPARTERO, Narváez supported the queen mother and followed her into exile in France.

Narváez led the military expedition in 1843 that brought back Maria Christina to the regency and ousted Espartero. Over the next 25 years Narváez held the prime ministership on five separate occasions, as well as serving as ambassador to France in the late 1840s. His conservatism, no longer restrained as it had been during the Carlist War took an increasingly reactionary direction, alienating many of his associates as well as losing him the favor of Maria Christina and Isabella II. Perpetually at odds with other military politicians he was at the helm of government again at the time of his death in April 1868, shortly before Isabella II was driven from the throne.

Navarre (Navarra)

A medieval kingdom occupying territory on both sides of the Pyrenees, Navarre played an important role in the politics of northern Spain during the early centuries of the RECONQUISTA. Dynastic and political alliances linked Navarre at various times with ARAGON, LEÓN, and CASTILE, as well as with the French monarchy. In 1512 Navarre was conquered by FERDINAND V of Aragon who transferred ownership to Castile as a gesture of the increasing integration of the Spanish realms. The trans-Pyrenean districts remained under French control.

Although Navarre remained a subsidiary of Castile throughout its modern history, a separate legal and political structure was preserved until the 19th century, with ISABELLA II of Spain being separately inaugurated as queen of Navarre in 1833. Despite this recognition of Isabella the Navarrese supported the cause of CARLISM in a series of insurrections and rallied to the rebellion of FRANCISCO FRANCO during the SPANISH CIVIL WAR in the hope of reinstating a Carlist pretender.

Although certain districts have a Basque population, Navarre's territory, encompassing more than 4,000 square miles, is not generally considered a part of the BASQUE

PROVINCES. Contemporary Navarre is perhaps best known for the picturesque celebration of the annual feast of San Fermín, in which celebrants (many of them tourists from all over the world) run through the streets of the capital, Pamplona, ahead of a herd of bulls.

Nebrija, Elio Antonio de
(1441–1522)
Spanish humanist

During his lifetime Nebrija fulfilled the dreams that many intellectuals have had throughout the centuries. As a student at Salamanca he became dissatisfied with the archaic and imperfect methods of his teachers and went off to Italy to study at the fountainhead of the "new learning." When he returned to Spain after 10 years he received an appointment at Salamanca, where he introduced the scholarship and subject matter of classical studies in the fields of Latin grammar and rhetoric that he had experienced in Renaissance Italy. His reputation led Cardinal FRANCISCO JIMÉNEZ DE CISNEROS (with whom he collaborated in his production of the Complutensian Bible) to bring him to the new university at Alcalá. There he was, moreover, given ideal conditions, for he was permitted to teach what he wished, or not teach at all but to devote the greater part of his time to writing. At Alcalá Nebrija pursued his mission of transforming the "backward" and "semi-barbarous" state of scholarship in Spain into a condition that could stand comparison with that of other countries. Indeed, Nebrija achieved the ultimate ambition of a learned man— to shape and direct the scholarly life and letters of his country as it entered upon its golden age.

Among Nebrija's major works are *Introductiones latinae* (1481), the first Latin grammar published in Spain; *Interpretation dictionum ex sermone latino in hispaniensem* (1492), the first Latin-Spanish dictionary; *Gramática sobre la lengua castellana* (1492), the first grammar of the Castilian language; *Interpretación de las palabras castellanas en lengua latina* (1495), and *Reglas de ortografía en la lengua castellana* (1517), a Spanish spelling book.

Of his Spanish grammar book Nebrija proudly declared that he had written it so that the language would follow the spread of empire that he foresaw reaching out across the Old World and the New. Perhaps demonstrating the persistence of his youthful frustration with his professors, he also compiled a treatise on the best methods of teaching drawn from the classical writers who had clearly understood their business. Unfortunately this latter work, *De liberis educandis* (1509), remained in manuscript and was not published until nearly 400 years after the author's death.

Netherlands, Revolt of the

Variously known as the Netherlands, the Burgundian provinces, the Low Countries, the 17 duchies, counties, and lordships in northwestern Europe that were the inheritance of the Spanish House of HABSBURG became a source of wealth and of prolonged political turmoil. CHARLES I of Spain (Holy Roman Emperor Charles V) was born in the city of Ghent (now in Belgium) and maintained throughout his life (1500–58) a strong identification with his Burgundian origins. Although he spent an increasing amount of his time in Spain in his later years, he retained the affection and allegiance of his

Netherlandish subjects by his attention to their traditions and distinctive privileges. He understood the languages (Dutch/Flemish in the north, French in the south) and their cultural traits. A cosmopolitan European, he regarded all of his far-flung realms as equally deserving of his attention. PHILIP II did not share his father's perspective, nor did he enjoy the same popularity in the Netherlands. Regarding the 17 provinces as mere colonial dependencies of Spain, he neglected their sense of regional pride and ignored their reserved rights. The onset of the Reformation, particularly in the seven Dutch-speaking provinces of the north, led to religious tensions during the 1560s that were exacerbated by rising nationalist sentiments. Philip's harsh, insensitive treatment of his Dutch subjects provoked a growing number of violent actions by both Calvinist rebels and Spanish soldiers during the 1560s and early 1570s. By 1579 Holland, Zealand, and five allied provinces had established de facto independence, and a full-scale war was being waged by Spain to bring them under submission. Although some of the southern provinces initially shared in the revolt, ethnic, religious, and geopolitical factors ultimately determined their retention by the Spanish monarchy.

By the time of Philip II's death in 1598, the seven provinces of the north, united as the Dutch Republic, were effectively sovereign. Despite periods of truce and various initiatives to effect a compromise, successive Spanish rulers were unable to regain control of the Dutch provinces. Once Spain became embroiled in the Thirty Years' War (1618–48), any chance of restoring the old order was gone. During the latter half of the 17th century the so-called Spanish Netherlands (essentially modern Belgium)

survived as a relic of the old Burgundian realm. After the extinction of the Spanish Habsburg line and the WAR OF THE SPANISH SUCCESSION (1701–14), the area was ceded to Austria, and the Spanish connection with their once proud dominion was at an end.

Netherlands, Spain in the

Through the marriage of the Spanish princess JOANNA (daughter of FERDINAND V and ISABELLA I) to the Habsburg heir Philip (PHILIP I), the immensely valuable and varied territories in northwestern Europe known as the Netherlands passed to Spain at the beginning of the 16th century. Variously designated as the Low Countries, the Burgundian Netherlands, or the Seventeen Netherlands (because they composed 17 autonomous duchies, counties, and lordships), these domains included major maritime, manufacturing, agricultural, and cultural resources. CHARLES I of Spain (Holy Roman Emperor Charles V), who was born in Ghent in 1500, was profoundly representative of this complex and sophisticated region and did his best to integrate it economically while recognizing the distinctive character and reserved rights of his dominions. His successor, PHILIP II, totally Castilian in his sensibilities and priorities, attempted to turn this rich inheritance into a mere possession of imperial Spain. By the 1560s nationalistic and religious issues were already producing violent outbursts in the Netherlands. By 1579 the seven northernmost provinces, largely Dutch speaking, and Protestant, had renounced their allegiance and commenced an armed struggle that would eventually create a sovereign Dutch nation-state. The southern provinces, predominantly French speaking and

Catholic, remained under Spanish control. During the 17th century they would be known as the Spanish Netherlands. At the beginning of the 18th century (after the WAR OF THE SPANISH SUCCESSION) they would be ceded by Spain and designated as the Austrian Netherlands until caught up in the political changes brought on by the French Revolution. It was not until 1830 that the present-day nation-state of Belgium at last came into existence out of what had been the Spanish Netherlands.

New Granada (Nueva Granada)

This Spanish viceroyalty was created in 1718 by detaching the territory encompassing present-day COLOMBIA and PANAMA from the Viceroyalty of PERU. The name had been applied to this area of northwestern South America since the initial Spanish occupation in the 1530s. The structural organization of the new viceroyalty was completed in 1740, when what is present-day VENEZUELA and ECUADOR were included within the jurisdiction of New Granada. This viceroyalty was lost to Spanish rule in 1819, after which its components passed through a series of internal conflicts and an eventual evolution into independent republics.

New Mexico (Nuevo México)

This northward extension of NEW SPAIN included a vast area exceeding the present boundaries of the state of New Mexico in the United States (which itself covers a total of 121,000 square miles). First explored in 1539, Nuevo México contained villages of the Zuni tribe, which were erroneously identified as great cities. Conflated with the

legend of the "Seven Cities of Cíbola," these stories inspired the expeditions of FRANCISCO VÁZQUEZ DE CORONADO (1540) and JUAN DE OÑATE (1598). The latter explorer began Spanish settlement of the region, and its principal town, Santa Fe, was founded in 1609–10. Disturbed by periodic Amerindian uprisings and boundary disputes with TEXAS, which lay to the east, this Spanish colony was surrendered to the independent republic of MEXICO in 1821 and ceded by the Mexicans to the United States in 1848.

New Spain (Nueva España)

With the "discovery" and first phase of occupation of the Americas by the Spanish explorers and conquerors (1492–1540), the political and administrative organization of these new realms became a necessity. There was little serious concern over the question of ownership, and the assumed right of conquest made these lands and their peoples subjects of the Spanish monarchs. This concept of royal acquisition and sovereignty in the so-called Nuevo Mundo (New World) led to the initial organization of these royal dominions into two kingdoms that were regarded as parallel to existing Iberian kingdoms. The lands of the Castilian and Aragonese sovereigns were referred to in official documents as "these kingdoms," and the new realms abroad were described as "those kingdoms." In the absence of the sovereign in "those kingdoms," they were to be governed by viceroys who acted in place of the absentee monarch. Initially there were two of these viceregal entities. The first in regard to discovery and settlement was Nueva España (New Spain). It encompassed all of the Spanish claims north of MEXICO, Mexico itself (with the capital of the viceroyalty located at Mexico City), and the islands of the Caribbean. Central America was also included within New Spain, although PANAMA, despite its contiguous location, was not. Even though they lay across the Pacific the PHILIPPINE ISLANDS as well as various smaller islands far to the west of Mexico were also theoretically part of New Spain. This administrative structure for New Spain survived with little modification until the collapse of Spanish colonial rule in most of the Western Hemisphere during the early 19th century.

PERU, the other viceroyalty created during the first phase of Spanish conquest, would be considered a single "kingdom" until the late 18th century, when the separate Viceroyalties of NEW GRANADA and LA PLATA were carved out of the vastness of South America.

Nicaragua

Nicaragua, like HONDURAS, was first seen by Spaniards during the coastal exploration of the Central American region carried out by CHRISTOPHER COLUMBUS during his final voyage in 1502. Occupation of the region, following the campaigns of HERNÁN CORTÉS and his successors, culminated in the foundation of the cities of León and Granada in 1524. Like the rest of the area, the province of Nicaragua was an administrative dependency of the Captaincy General of GUATE-MALA and, therefore, of the Viceroyalty of NEW SPAIN. Nicaragua was also briefly controlled by the breakaway Mexican empire of AGUSTÍN DE ITURBIDE. From 1823 to 1839 it was a member of the United Provinces of Central America, after which it vigorously asserted total sovereignty despite interference from various interlopers.

O

O'Donnell Joris, Leopoldo (duque de Tetuán) (1809–1867)

Spanish soldier and statesman

Descended from an aristocratic family of Irish Catholic exiles that had already given many notable soldiers to the service of their adopted country, O'Donnell earned rapid promotion during the First Carlist War and became the youngest general in the royal army. When the regent, Queen Mother MARIA CHRISTINA, was forced to leave for France in 1840, O'Donnell was one of those who followed her abroad. He led an unsuccessful invasion attempt in 1841, but when the usurping regime of General BALDOMERO ESPARTERO was overthrown in 1843, O'Donnell's faithful services were rewarded with the governorship of CUBA (1844–48).

In the confused political situation of 1854 O'Donnell turned against his former friend, Maria Christina, who still exercised considerable influence over ISABELLA II. With the support of many civilians who had become disillusioned with the queen mother's now-conservative alignments, O'Donnell organized a military revolt against her. Espartero, once Maria Christina's antagonist, was called out of retirement to defend her but instead formed an alliance with his old opponent, O'Donnell. Out of this series of maneuvers emerged a new administration, with Espartero as prime minister, O'Donnell as war minister, and Maria Christina once again banished. However, the ambitious younger officer could not long be held as a subordinate, and in 1856 O'Donnell supplanted his associate as head of government.

During the next 10 years O'Donnell remained the dominant figure in the political and military leadership of Spain, actually holding the office of premier in 1856, 1858–63, and 1865–66. He even combined the position of chief minister with that of field commander when in 1859–60 he took personal charge of the campaign in MOROCCO that led to the victory at TETUÁN. For this achievement he was created duke of Tetuán, adding to the title count of Lucena that he had been awarded for an earlier battlefield success.

In the perilous world of Spanish military politics O'Donnell was one of the most adroit personalities. Flexible in his beliefs (some said he had no firm principles at all), he apparently created the Liberal Union Party, which reflected a generally moderate stance to serve his own needs rather than those of any faction. In 1866 his brutal treatment of those who had joined in General JUAN PRIM's uprising created an outcry that forced his resignation. O'Donnell died within a year, leaving him no chance to make yet another comeback during the chaos of the next three years when the monarchy was overthrown and Prim was assassinated.

O'Donojú, Juan (1762–1821)
Spanish colonial administrator

Born in SEVILLE, a descendant of the distinguished Irish clan O'Donoghue, O'Donojú followed his family's military tradition and achieved promotion to the rank of general officer during the PENINSULAR WAR. The Regency Council that directed the fight against the Napoleonic invaders made him a member and charged him with the portfolio of minister of war. After the restoration of FERDINAND VII in 1814, O'Donojú was named captain general of ANDALUSIA. He was, however, a covert supporter of the liberal movement in Spain and a leader of the Freemasons, who were particularly strong among dissident officers. After the liberal coup d'état in 1820 O'Donojú was promoted to captain general of NEW SPAIN with full viceregal powers. On arriving in his new domain he found that virtually the whole of the country, outside of Mexico City and a few other large towns, was in the hands of the nationalist rebels.

Although O'Donojú had not been authorized to undertake political negotiations with the insurgents, he established contact with their recognized leader, AGUSTÍN DE ITURBIDE. Himself a former Spanish general, Iturbide had united all the Mexican political factions under his command with the shared goal of achieving independence. Despite its own revolutionary origin the Madrid government had no intention of abandoning its colonial rule in the Americas. O'Donojú, true to his profound commitment to reform and, in any case,

confronted with the realities of the situation on the ground, decided to come to terms with the insurrection in New Spain. He and Iturbide met and concluded the Treaty of Córdoba, which recognized the de facto independence of New Spain. The troops of Iturbide marched unopposed into Mexico City and were saluted from the balcony of the viceregal palace by O'Donojú, who thus formally acknowledged the birth of a sovereign nation. By the time Spain's leaders learned of the rapid rush of events during 1821 and repudiated the Treaty of Córdoba, it was too late for them to affect events. O'Donojú had been appointed a member of the provisional government in MEXICO but died of pneumonia shortly after greeting Iturbide. He was honored as a friend and patron of Mexico's national fulfillment and buried with viceregal honors in the capital city's cathedral.

O'Higgins, Bernardo (1778–1842)
Spanish colonial rebel

Born in Chillán in the colonial province of CHILE, O'Higgins was the son of Don Ambrosio (Ambrose) O'Higgins (1720–1800), a Spanish colonial administrator originally from Ireland who served as governor of Chile from 1778 to 1795 and then as viceroy of PERU from 1795 to 1800. As colonial officials were forbidden to marry residents of their jurisdictions lest their in-laws acquire undue influence, Bernardo was technically illegitimate, though his mother was of a prominent Chilean family. He was fully recognized and supported by his father and sent to Europe for his education. After spending time in England as well as Spain and coming under the influence of the banished South American rebel FRANCISCO DE

MIRANDA, O'Higgins returned to Chile. There he joined the local manifestation of the nationalistic revolt that spread throughout Spanish America in the early 19th century. Elected to the provincial assembly, he played an increasingly important military and political role until the forces under his command were routed by the royalists in 1814. O'Higgins led the remnants of his army across the Andes and formed an alliance with the Argentine leader JOSÉ DE SAN MARTÍN. Three years later they invaded Chile and gained control of that province. O'Higgins was virtual dictator of Chile from 1818 to 1823 and imposed many political and economic reforms on its traditional society. Conservatives objected to his progressive ideas, while liberals found him too authoritarian. In 1824 he abandoned what seemed a hopeless struggle and left Chile forever.

Olavide, Pablo de (1725–1803)
Spanish politician
Born in Lima, PERU, Olavide was appointed a judge in that city at the age of 20. A massive earthquake devastated the city a year later, and the young judge excited indignation by ordering money designated for the reconstruction of a church to be used to rebuild a theater. This early evidence of his "modernist" tendencies led to his being summoned to Spain to account for his actions. Evading punishment, Olavide soon married a rich widow in MADRID and turned her mansion into a center of progressive society. Appointed *intendente* of ANDALUSIA by PEDRO ARANDA, Olavide found new scope for his reformist ideas. His elaborate plan for the reorganization of the educational system published in 1768 won him

the approval of such notable figures of the Spanish Enlightenment as GASPAR JOVELLANOS. Some of Olavide's other ideas, however, were unpalatable to conservatives. He disclosed his plans with his accustomed unreserved frankness to a priest who denounced him to the SPANISH INQUISITION. Tried by the Holy Office, he was condemned in 1778 to be stripped of his rank as a knight of Santiago and sentenced to house arrest. Two years later he escaped to France. Olavide, whose ideas were well known and much admired by the philosophes, was hailed by French intellectuals, and various accounts of his bad treatment by the Inquisition were published. Following the French Revolution and the fall of the monarchy, the National Convention named him an honorary citizen of the French Republic. Still unwisely outspoken, he fell afoul of the Committee of Public Safety and was imprisoned under the Terror, fortunately surviving until the fall of Robespierre (1794). Olavide apparently experienced a surge of prudence and in 1798 published a memoir describing the experiences of a "disillusioned philosophe." This public penance earned a reprieve in Spain, where CHARLES IV repealed the sentence of the Holy Office and restored his property. Returning home, Olavide was offered a government position, but having seen quite enough of the ups and downs of public life, he chose to live quietly until his death in 1803.

Olid, Cristóbal de (c. 1488–1525)
Spanish explorer
Olid came to CUBA as a young soldier of fortune and won the patronage of Governor DIEGO VELÁZQUEZ DE CUÉLLAR. He was

entrusted with a variety of tasks due to his skill in communicating with Indians and sent on a probing voyage down the coast of Central America in 1518. Although acquisition of land grants and status as a colonist in Cuba had rewarded his efforts, Olid eagerly accepted the opportunity to accompany the expedition of HERNÁN CORTÉS in 1519. Velázquez had merely authorized Cortés to investigate the coastal regions of what is now MEXICO, but when Cortés pushed boldly into the interior and took measures that clearly flouted the authority of the governor, Olid wholeheartedly supported his new leader. Olid became the most valuable and reliable lieutenant of Cortés. He fought valiantly in every battle of the campaign to conquer the Aztec Empire, constantly confronting every adversary, including the force sent by Velázquez to restrain Cortés. Olid was designated by Cortés to carry on negotiations with Moctezuma, the Aztec emperor, and was granted the rank of general by the conqueror of Moctezuma's empire. During the early 1520s, as Cortés consolidated his power over the outlying areas of the Aztec realm, Olid continued to play a leading role, despite the jealousy of rivals among Cortés's officers. However, when Olid was sent back to Cuba to gather more men and supplies, he was subverted in his commitment to Cortés by Velázquez. The governor had outwardly reconciled with Cortés and approved his victorious activities in Mexico. He still resented the conqueror of the Aztec, however, and incited Olid to pursue his own ambitions. Olid succumbed to Velázquez's offers of independent authority but remained outwardly loyal to Cortés until he had established himself in what is now HONDURAS. Proclaiming himself master of this territory, Olid defeated several commanders who opposed him, including one sent by Cortés to attack him. But Olid was unwise enough to allow his antagonists what amounted to a form of parole, and they used this freedom of action to capture and execute him.

Few of the conquistadores were as brave in combat or resilient under wounds and adversity as Olid. Yet he was also impulsive, lacking in judgment, and surprisingly guileless. As one of his comrades commented, he was all action without the prudence to balance his actions.

Olivares, Gaspar de Guzmán y Pimentel, conde-duque de (1587–1645)
Spanish statesman

Born into a family of high-ranking nobles in ANDALUSIA, he was a younger son, intended for a career in the church. Educated at the University of Salamanca and granted several ecclesiastical offices while still in his teens, his circumstances changed when his elder brothers died and he became heir to the title and estates. Count of Olivares from 1607, he was subsequently created duke of Sanlúcar but chose to preserve the traditional title under the designation of count-duke of Olivares and was usually referred to by contemporary Spaniards as the *conde-duque*. Olivares lived on a grand scale, indulging his many interests, including horsemanship and bullfighting, but also thought of himself as a literary man and was a patron of notable artists and writers of his day. During the last years of PHILIP III's reign he challenged the dominance of the duke of LERMA. When PHILIP IV ascended the throne in 1621, Olivares replaced Lerma as chief minister and confidant of the monarch.

As the dominant figure in Spanish politics between 1621 and 1643, Olivares was constantly at odds with such major interest groups as the nobility and the clergy. His domestic program, based on uprooting corruption, reducing bureaucracy, and eliminating privilege, was well conceived; however, his honesty and zeal led him to attempt too much too soon so that many of his reforms proved abortive. The external policy of Olivares was totally destructive, for it ignored the need to develop and replenish the economic resources of Spain. With the backing of Philip IV, Olivares chose to renew the war against the Dutch rebels at the expiration of the Twelve Years' Truce (1621) and to become entangled with France over Italian territorial issues. Essentially Olivares and his king wished to revive the grand imperial designs of CHARLES I and PHILIP II, which had, by 1598, exhausted the Spanish nation. The most ambitious concept developed by Olivares was his proposal (1624) for a so-called Union of Arms to rationalize and mobilize the military manpower of the Spanish realms. Had this vision proved practicable, Spain might have fulfilled the potential offered by her imperial dominions; however, Olivares was no more successful at exacting cooperation from the entities that made up the empire than he was in imposing obedience to his domestic reforms. As a result Spain became evermore overcommitted, with the burden falling upon the central kingdom of CASTILE. This was particularly true during the 1630s, as it was drawn into the Thirty Years' War. Olivares, seeking to support the Austrian Habsburgs against a Protestant coalition supported by France, proved no match for the wily French statesman Richelieu. The latter's instigation of revolts in CATALONIA and Portugal (1640) further increased Spain's difficulties.

By 1643 a series of setbacks had so damaged Spain's prestige, to say nothing of its ability to continue its military campaigns, that the enemies of Olivares were able to undermine the king's confidence in the once all-powerful minister. Philip IV eased the departure of Olivares from office by suggesting that his declining health required a period of rest and recuperation. Although Olivares resisted his ouster, he and all his associates were gradually removed from office, and by the time of his death in 1645 he was a broken and tragic figure.

At the height of his influence Olivares seemed to represent the greatness and self-confidence of Spain at its apogee. The famous haughty and dynamic equestrian portrait by DIEGO VELÁZQUEZ suggests a virtual monarch dominating an empire. Far too sure of himself and repeatedly caught off guard by enemies, both foreign and domestic, Olivares finally was toppled from the seat of power, and with his fall there began the decline of the Spanish Empire.

Oñate, Juan de (1550–1626)
Spanish explorer and administrator

Born in NEW SPAIN, a member of one of the founding families of the colony, he was the son of a soldier and administrator who became the richest man in the territory. Juan de Oñate spent his youth campaigning against Indian resisters and Spanish rebels. In 1598 he was designated governor of the unconquered lands to the north of MEXICO and assigned to explore and settle those areas. He led a large expedition of soldiers, civilians, and missionaries, along with thousands of cattle, into what is now TEXAS, near the site of the present El Paso. During the next decade, as the first governor of the region, he pacified many tribes, sponsored the establishment of missions, and founded a number of outposts including San Gabriel in present-day NEW MEXICO, the second-oldest city in the United States. In keeping with his instructions he probed the interior, entering what is now Oklahoma, Kansas, and Missouri and sought access to the Pacific by reaching the Colorado River and sailing down it to the Gulf of California. Following his return to Mexico he was summoned to Spain on charges of having inflicted excessive cruelties on Indians and even some colonists. Although the matter was not settled for many years, Oñate was ultimately exonerated and named inspector of mines in Spain. Shortly before his death he was honored with knighthood in the prestigious military order of Santiago.

Oñate is often referred to as the "last of the conquistadores." Although his career belongs to the period when Spain was consolidating its imperial claims rather than expanding its domains, Oñate shared many of the characteristics of the generation of conquerors who "discovered" and mastered the New World in the first years of the 16th century. Like them, he was a fearless adventurer who went boldly into uncharted territory and persisted in his exertions to the last extremity of his resources. Like them, too, he was a harsh taskmaster and often ruthless in his tactics as he pursued his goal. He represented a breed that was vanishing by the early 1600s, but one that would long be venerated in Spanish lore.

Oporto (Porto)

The second city of Portugal, not only in population (some 500,000) but in pride and self-assertiveness, Oporto was formerly the seat of government. It continues to dominate the north, with a combination of industry and a sense of its distinctive history. As its name proclaims, the city was a center of maritime trade throughout the Middle Ages and the launching place of many expeditions to distant lands of Portugal's Renaissance empire. Its connections with northern Europe were reinforced by the trade in port wine which gave the city particular business and social ties with England from the 17th century onward. Long regarded as the center of conservatism and the object of a prolonged siege during the MIGUELITE WAR (1832), Oporto has followed a more tranquil path in latter days, preserving the ancient structures that have earned it a designation in 1996 as a United Nation's World Heritage Site while erecting new museums and galleries and hosting collections of modern art and festivals of contemporary music.

Opus Dei

This Catholic Church organization, defined as a "personal prelature," was founded in 1928 under the leadership of a Spanish priest, Reverend Josemaría Escrivá de Balaguer. Its title, which signifies "God's work" in Latin, describes the concept that underlies this movement. Although it resembles a religious order in some respects, it contains only a small percentage of ordained priests among its tens of thousands of members throughout the world. Most of these members are lay supporters or affiliates who go about their daily business while adhering to certain general principles. The "numeraries," who constitute the inner core of the organization and most closely resemble what had been traditionally thought of as a religious order, live in communal groups under special vows and carry out various regular devotions and observances. They differ from the conventional members of a religious order, however, in that they maintain no outward show of their status, dressing in "civilian clothing," holding a wide variety of jobs, and sometimes not disclosing their membership in Opus Dei to the general public.

The presence of a large body of committed, often highly educated and professionally trained individuals within the general community had already begun to attract curiosity and even suspicion by the time of the SPANISH CIVIL WAR. During the Franco era it was rumored that half a dozen cabinet ministers and many other high officials of the government were clandestine affiliates of Opus Dei, which led to suspicions about their influence and motives. Comparisons were made to the Freemasons and other secret societies long banned by the church, and some Catholics came to regard the movement as sinister despite its avowed concern with promoting high standards of morality and spiritual values. While Opus Dei was generally perceived as a conservative organization, it clearly favored the positive contributions of modern capitalism to the development and enhancement of Spanish society and it seems to have contributed to the liberalizing tendencies of FRANCISCO FRANCO's later years.

Opus Dei has become a worldwide organization and continues to enjoy the patronage of the papacy, but it has always retained its special relationship with Spain. Although the death of Monsignor Escrivá in 1975 coincided with the beginning of the democratization era, the movement has functioned successfully under his successors and remains unaccepted by its perennial critics. Despite grumbling in some quarters the canonization of Monsignor Escrivá in October 2002 was hailed by many Spaniards as the greatest honor bestowed upon one of their religious leaders since IGNATIUS OF LOYOLA, the founder of the Jesuits (another highly controversial organization), was elevated to the honors of the altar.

O'Reilly, Alexander (Alejandro O'Reilly) (1725–1794)

Spanish general

Born in Dublin, Ireland, O'Reilly followed the peripatetic career of many Irish soldiers of fortune of his day, serving at various times in the armies of Austria and France. In 1760 he entered the Spanish service, where he won the favor of the new king, CHARLES III, by rescuing the monarch during an assassination attempt. O'Reilly served in a number of senior commands, most notably in the New World. There he was sent to evaluate the defensive capacity of CUBA and PUERTO RICO in 1764–65 in the aftermath of the Seven Years' War, and his recommendations led to major improvements in the fortifications and strategic-economic development of both islands. Officers who formed part of his entourage (mostly of Irish origin) played major parts in the strengthening of Spanish rule in the Americas. O'Reilly concluded his mission in the region by a term as governor of LOUISIANA, which had been transferred to Spanish rule in 1763 but remained disorderly under her initial administration. The harsh regime imposed by the general quieted the restless French-speaking population in New Orleans, but his execution of dissidents earned him the nickname of "Bloody O'Reilly" that long survived his departure from Louisiana.

Leading an expedition to Algeria in 1775, O'Reilly encountered reverses that led to the failure of Spain's attempt to reestablish dominance in Muslim North Africa. His enemies, who had bitterly resented the influence of an Irish clique at the royal court led by RICHARD WALL and O'Reilly, did their best to blame him for the Algerian reversal. His friendship with the king protected the general from serious consequences, but he was not entrusted with important duties thereafter. Count O'Reilly, who had received this personal (non-territorial) title in 1785, was called to a more active role at the beginning of Spain's clash with revolutionary France in 1794, but he died just after his arrival to take charge of the Pyrenean frontier.

Orellana, Francisco de (1511–1546)

Spanish explorer and soldier

Orellana joined his fellow townsman FRANCISCO PIZARRO in the conquest of PERU during the 1530s. He was particularly active in operations against the Inca in what is now ECUADOR, where he was a founder of both Quito and Guayaquil.

In 1538 he was appointed second in command to the conqueror's brother, Gonzalo Pizarro, for an expedition into the interior of South America. A large force of Spanish soldiers, Indian bearers, pack animals, and dogs of war set out across the Andes but suffered extreme hardships and heavy losses due to cold and exertion in the high passes. On descending into the eastern lowlands the Spaniards found themselves in a virtually impenetrable jungle, with no sign of the prosperous Indians or the abundant gold and spices that had lured them to the region. Having abandoned most of their

supplies on the journey across the mountains, they were soon near starvation, and the few poverty-stricken natives whom they encountered could only promise that food and gold might be found down the next of a series of rivers that ran through the jungle. On reaching the largest of these streams Orellana suggested that he take several dozen men downriver on a boat that they had constructed to scout out the prospects ahead. Within a few days of leaving the main body he had passed through several increasingly large tributaries of what became an obviously massive waterway, and he resolved to abandon any attempt to return to his chief but rather to sail on in the hope of ultimately reaching the Atlantic. Months of drifting down the great river brought him into contact with many local tribes, some friendly and helpful, others violently hostile. Among those who attacked his craft in canoes were what appeared to be women warriors. Their fancied resemblance to the Amazons of Greek legends would lead to this river being named the Amazon. Finally in August 1541 Orellana and his surviving comrades reached the mouth of the river and sailed up the coast until they reached a Spanish outpost on the northeastern shore of the continent. (Pizarro and the depleted remnants of his expedition had struggled back across the Andes many months before.)

Orellana took ship for Spain to press his case for recognition as a conquistador of the first rank and succeeded in obtaining royal approval for an expedition to explore and claim the region through which he had sailed. Without adequate funding, however, it took him several years to assemble the men, ships, and supplies to return to the mouth of the Amazon. The Portuguese, who had a long-standing dispute with Spain over claims to the area, also did their best to thwart the project. Orellana and his men finally reached South America in 1546, but overwhelmed by a series of diseases and disasters, both the leader and his band of adventurers perished without achieving their reward.

Some chroniclers of the Spanish conquest of the Americas denounce Orellana for betraying his word to Gonzalo Pizarro and dishonorably abandoning his colleagues in their misery. For those who ranked "honor" as the highest virtue his offense was unquestionable. Orellana himself contended that he could not sail back upstream against the current and rightly chose to serve the greater interest of Spain by pressing on into the unknown. However one judges the rectitude of his actions, he achieved one of the greatest voyages in history by sailing down virtually the entire length of the Amazon—the first European do do so—and essentially crossing the South American continent from the Pacific to the Atlantic, a true epic of discovery.

Ortega y Gasset, José (1883–1955)
Spanish philosopher and essayist

Following a family tradition of intellectual activity Ortega y Gasset earned a doctorate in philosophy at the University of Madrid in his 21st year and pursued postgraduate studies at several German universities in the early 1900s. By 1910 he was back in MADRID, where he was awarded a professorship of metaphysics. During the next 25 years he lectured, wrote, and took part in the establishment of a number of intellectual periodicals. He chose to leave Spain at the beginning of the SPANISH CIVIL WAR and spent most of the next decade in various European coun-

tries and ARGENTINA. Returning to Spain in 1945, he established the Institute of Humanities in Madrid three years later and resumed his magisterial role until his death in 1955.

Ortega y Gasset moved away from the neo-Kantian idealism and the abstract philosophical principles of his German training fairly early in his career. He advocated instead a more pragmatic relationship between personal circumstances and philosophical judgments. Far from being narrowly concerned with lofty issues of theory and morality, he wrote frequently on the great questions that bedeviled Western society from the 1930s through the 1950s, frequently addressing problems of political organizations, social relations, and international affairs. One of his most notable series of essays, *La rebelión de las masas* (*The Revolt of the Masses,* 1930), argued that the disruption of the traditional class structure in Europe (and elsewhere) threatened the good order and stability of civilization. He urged the primacy of an educated intellectual class that possessed both the intelligence and the sense of the general good that the masses did not. Viewed as a defense of antidemocratic ideas, Ortega's essay has been praised by political groups toward whom he apparently had no personal sympathy. Arguments both before and after his death, for instance, pitted various factions within the Roman Catholic Church against one another because they saw Ortega as an apologist or as an opponent of Catholic ideology. He did not, it would seem, have any strong religious motivation but, like many Spaniards who saw themselves as citizens of the world, could not avoid being identified with one camp or another. The ideas expressed in the *La rebelión de las masas* are quite similar to those contained in *España invertebrada* (*Invertebrate*

Spain, 1921). In this series of essays Ortega gives very little comfort to any party or allegiance within Spanish society. He blames the divided and ineffectual "particularism" that has kept Spain weak throughout its history on the Visigoth's lack of dynamic leadership, in contrast to that of their Germanic cousins, the Franks. Without a feudal "spine" like that which ultimately produced French unity, Spain remained divided, taking more than 700 years to expel its Muslim invaders and never truly becoming a unified nation-state. Anticipating his assertion in *La rebelión de las masas,* Ortega concludes that because it never developed an effective ruling elite, Spain has remained a land of poor peasants and rich peasants.

It is not surprising that those Spaniards who search for a more "patriotic" side to their greatest 20th-century philosopher have hailed the *Meditaciones del Quijote (Meditations on Quixote,* 1914) as his best work. For Ortega y Gasset in this essay, Quixote is an iconic figure, shaping and imposing his own reality upon the mere objectivity of the other characters, particularly the prosaic Sancho Panza. The self-directed subjectivity of MIGUEL DE CERVANTES's hero, as Ortega would assert in a later edition of this essay, makes the Man of La Mancha a true existential hero. For some critics this recognition of Spain's contribution to the intellectual history of the Western world is the philosopher's most valuable perception.

Ortiz de Retes, Iñigo (fl. ca. 1545)
Spanish explorer

The TREATY OF TORDESILLAS, concluded during the reign of FERDINAND V and ISABELLA I and subsequently modified, divided the world that was being explored by Iberian navigators of the Renaissance between Spain and Portugal in such a way as to grant most of Asia to the king of Portugal. Spaniards continued, however, to seek footholds in the islands along the western shores of Asia. Throughout the 16th century they sent numerous expeditions from NEW SPAIN (MEXICO) to claim not only the PHILIPPINE ISLANDS but also a number of other archipelagoes in that region. They were stoutly resisted by the Portuguese in the MOLUCCAS, but in other parts of the area lying east of those islands and south of the Philippines they made discoveries and explored many islands both by sea and land. Most of their discoveries, including the Admiralty Islands and parts of the Bismark Archipelago, were of minor significance and not effectively claimed. The most important Spanish discovery in the region was what is usually considered the world's largest island. In 1545 the Basque Ortiz de Retes, who had already explored the southern Philippines and fought the Portuguese in the Moluccas, attempted to find a route back across the Pacific to New Spain. He set foot upon the land that he named *Nueva Guinea* (New Guinea). He chose this name because the Melanesian inhabitants were black skinned, resembling, to his eye, the people of Guinea on the west coast of Africa. Ortiz de Retes evidently made an extensive investigation of the northern part of the island. It may have been seen by others before him, and it was certainly visited by others afterward. He was, however, the effective discoverer and name giver to the island presently known as Papua–New Guinea. His exploring activities, like those of several other Spanish expeditions that followed his, were not productive of permanent settlements. By the beginning of the 17th century dominance in the region had passed to the Dutch.

P

Pacheco, Francisco (1564–1654)

Spanish painter and art critic

A competent but not remarkable painter, Pacheco's claim to fame is his role as instructor and theoretician during nearly a century of artistic activity in SEVILLE. Throughout his long life he knew and often taught the leading figures of Spain's Golden Age (SIGLO DE ORO), from EL GRECO to DIEGO VELÁZQUEZ. His account of a visit to the former provides a sympathetic view of the master in his old age, but not approval of his style, which was not understood by the prosaic visitor. As head of Seville's leading academy Pacheco was the instructor of (among many others) Velázquez, who became his son-in-law. A didactic traditionalist, Pacheco was named by the SPANISH INQUISITION to oversee artistic activity in Seville and took a strong position against any religious or moral improprieties in works of art.

Pacheco was clearly very comfortable as a writer. His *El arte de la pintura, su antigüedad y grandeza* (The art of painting, Its antiquity and grandeur), published in 1649, provides not only a valuable overview of the history and techniques of painting but also insights into the way art was comprehended in 17th-century Spain. In addition he assembled a "compendium" of 170 portraits in red and black crayon of "Illustrious and Memorable Men," unfinished at his death. This work combines his skills at portraiture with his comments and judgments on the worthies he most admired. A cheerful, rather than an embittered, conservative, Pacheco reveals an amiable affection for such minor matters as the *bodegones* (still-lifes of kitchen scenes) that some of his contemporaries dismissed as trivial. Although he believed that the proper goal of painting was to inspire religious feelings, he was clearly humanistic enough to enjoy glimpses of ordinary life.

Padilla, Juan de (1490–1521)

Spanish rebel leader

Member of a prominent family in TOLEDO and a member of its city council, Padilla was among the many Castilians who became angered by the behavior of the new king, CHARLES I, in 1518–19. The young monarch surrounded himself with foreign favorites, showed no respect for the Castilian cities, and imposed oppressive taxes to finance his acquisition of the title Holy Roman Emperor. In the early 1520s, with some of his countrymen already in revolt, Padilla became personally aggrieved over the Crown's denial of a property inheritance. He then joined the incipient rebellion and soon became its military commander.

Padilla possessed the personal bravery and tactical skills of a natural warrior but lacked the political cunning to match his military qualifications. He led the insurgent forces through a series of alternating victories and reverses in what came to be known as the "Revolt of the Comuneros" (a reference to the alliance of Castilian communes that defied royal authority). The high point of the revolt came in August 1520, when the insurgents captured the town of Tordesillas, giving them custody of Queen JOANNA, who was still nominally co-ruler of CASTILE with her son, Charles I. The "Prisoner of Tordesillas" had been confined in the castle there for some years due to her alleged mental illness. She received Padilla and his companions in a friendly fashion when they came to pay their respects to her, and they hoped for a time to transform their revolt into an uprising on behalf of the rightful monarch. Joanna refused, however, to sign documents denouncing her son and soon lapsed into a state of total indifference to their wishes.

Padilla continued to lead the rebel forces during the early part of 1521 despite the intrigues directed against him by some local commanders and the defection of a major ally who went over to the king's cause. Padilla was finally encircled and defeated by the ever-increasing troops of Charles and, following his capture, was executed as the arch rebel. Without its ablest military commander, the Revolt of the Comuneros soon collapsed.

Pais, Sidónio (1872–1918)
Portuguese statesman
A former military officer who became a professor of mathematics at the University of Coimbra, Pais joined the republican movement and participated in the bloodless revolution that overthrew King MANUEL II in 1910. During the troubled early years of the new republic he held various cabinet posts and represented Portugal in Germany. Frustrated by the shortcomings of the new regime, he engineered its downfall in 1917. He presided over a provisional government that brought an end to Portugal's disastrous participation in World War I and won election to the presidency in 1918. He ruled dictatorially, anticipating the tactics of ANTÓNIO CARMONA and ANTÓNIO DE OLIVEIRA SALAZAR in the 1920s. Pais, however, enjoyed only a brief tenure of power before being assassinated in December 1918.

Palafox, José de (duque de Zaragoza) (1776–1847)
Spanish general
Born in ZARAGOZA of a prominent family, Palafox served with the Royal Corps of Guards in a series of campaigns in the PENINSULAR WAR and by 1808 held the rank of brigadier. When news of the French seizure of MADRID in early May and the deposition of the Spanish house of BOURBON reached Zaragoza, the senior officers there responded with confusion and delay. In a remarkable display of democracy ARAGON's populace deposed the incumbent leaders and proclaimed Palafox captain general of Aragon. A native son with wide local recognition, he seemed the ideal soldier to respond to the crisis. Showing great energy and determination Palafox organized the defense of the city by combining a small force of regulars with thousands of urban volunteers and peasant militiamen. The French army began a series of massive

bombardments and infantry assaults on Zaragoza in June and continued their siege until August. Palafox seemed to be everywhere, leading sorties, directing counterattacks in threatened positions, raising the spirits of his followers, and famously responding to a French overture to surrender ("capitulation and peace") with the words "war and the knife." As the fighting wore on and the French effected breaches in the city walls, the struggle continued from behind street barricades and rooftops. Palafox's example inspired the emergence of other heroes among the ranks of the citizens, notably Agustina Zaragoza y Domenech, who rallied the defenders of an abandoned battery and drove back the advancing enemy with heavy losses. She was appointed an officer by Palafox, and under the name "Agustina of Aragon" has remained a national hero.

The exhausted and battered invaders withdrew in August, but under the goading of the enraged Napoléon they mounted a new siege in November. Despite Palafox's success in bringing in some additional supplies and reinforcements Zaragoza was gradually overwhelmed by massive attacks and the spread of disease among the hungry and sick defenders. Palafox refused to yield to the overwhelming odds, but while he himself was incapacitated by illness, the city's governing junta accepted terms of surrender, and those still capable of doing so marched out with full military honors from the French in February 1809. Palafox was held prisoner in France until the end of hostilities and was then released to be greeted as the country's greatest warrior and patriot. The restored FERDINAND VII bestowed numerous honors on him including the title *duque de Zaragoza*.

During the First Carlist War of 1834–38, Palafox was in nominal command of the forces supporting Queen ISABELLA II, and his status as a national hero lent major credibility to her cause. After gaining victory Palafox retired amid enduring demonstrations of national admiration.

Panama (Panamá)

Within a decade of being sighted by CHRISTOPHER COLUMBUS on his last voyage in 1502, this area became the focus of intense exploration and settlement activity due to its central position in the Americas. Early conquistadores, such as VASCO NÚÑEZ DE BALBOA realized that Panama was a narrow isthmus linking North and South America and constituting only a minimal obstacle to communication between the Atlantic and the Pacific. The port of Darién (a name sometimes applied to the entirety of Panama) was established in 1510 and soon thereafter Portobelo became the principal transit point for transatlantic trade with the west coast of South America. The city of Panama was subsequently founded on the Pacific side of the isthmus. Despite her proximity to the Central American dependencies of NEW SPAIN and her physical separation from South America, created by mountains and jungles, Panama was considered part of the latter continent and included within the Viceroyalty of PERU. It was transferred in the 18th century to the newly created Viceroyalty of NEW GRANADA. After the dissolution of Spanish rule in the region, Panama remained linked to the successor state of COLOMBIA until it achieved its own independence in 1903. In the following decade the construction of the Panama Canal reestablished its special place in global transportation and communication.

Paraguay

This remote interior region lying at the intersection of Portuguese claims in BRAZIL, Spanish Andean conquests, and penetrations made through the river systems that connect it to the Atlantic was first settled at Asunción in 1538. Spanish presence was largely represented by Jesuit missionaries, who created an elaborate structure of preaching and government among their Guaraní converts between 1605 and 1767. Although they organized an effective militia to resist the depredations of Portuguese slave raiders, the Jesuits were themselves expelled from Paraguay by the Spanish Crown in the late 18th century. Nominally ruled from Buenos Aires under the Viceroyalty of LA PLATA, Paraguay broke away from the Spanish Empire in 1811 and maintained its independence under a succession of local magnates who constituted a dynasty of dictators. The country came close to total destruction in the War of the Triple Alliance (1865–70), the greatest military conflict in the continent's history.

Pardo Bazán, Emilia, condesa de
(1851–1921)

Spanish writer

The leading Spanish female writer of her day and the first Spanish writer to champion naturalism in literature, Pardo Bazán had a strong commitment to her native region, GALICIA, although she spent most of her time in MADRID after her marriage at 18. While still in her 20s she published biographical and critical essays but first attracted widespread attention in 1883 with *La cuestión palpitante* (The burning question). In this series of essays she both praised and partly dismissed Émile Zola as well as some of the more prominent Spanish contemporary writers, drawing a preferential distinction between naturalism and realism. She immediately attracted both praise and denunciation for the boldness of her ideas and the forcefulness of her expression. Among numerous novels her masterpiece is, undoubtedly, *Los pazos de Ulloa* (The manorhouse of Ulloa), published in 1886, with its sequel, *La madre Naturaleza* (Mother nature), which followed in 1887. Set in rural Galicia and enriched by a sense of place as well as by insights into character, the story traces the decline of a gentry family. Pardo Bazán was also the author of short stories that have been described as the best example of this genre produced in 19th-century Spain.

The totality of her work, including novels, short stories, and literary essays, led to official recognition with her appointment in 1916 as a professor at the Central University of Madrid (despite the opposition of some faculty members to having a female colleague). There was stronger and more bitter opposition, however, to her proposed designation to membership in the Royal Academy. Her native city of La Coruña was more generous, erecting a statue to her honor, amid the proliferation of admirals and generals.

Pedrarias Dávila (Pedro Arias de Ávila) (1440–1531)

Spanish colonial administrator

The son of a noble Castilian family, Arias de Ávila (known as Pedrarias) spent his youth at the royal court and his mature years as a soldier in the CONQUEST OF GRANADA (1492) and campaigns against the Muslims in North Africa. He established important connections through marriage and friendships with senior Crown officials. These led to his appointment as governor of the colony of Castilla del Oro (commonly referred to as Darién and corresponding to present-day PANAMA) in 1514. He was almost immediately involved in disputes with various conquistadores, and several of these rivals to his power were executed by his order. The most notable of his victims was VASCO NÚÑEZ DE BALBOA, who had been the first European to reach the Pacific (1513). Balboa had taken great pains to establish friendly and cooperative relations with the natives of the region, but Pedrarias carried out a series of military campaigns that annihilated most of them and reduced the survivors to virtual serfdom. Although Pedrarias essentially destroyed all of the work of his predecessors, he replaced their settlements by a structure of tight administration that assured the stability of the area thereafter. Darién was a zone of intense activity during the era of the Pedrarias regime as it was a transit point for Spaniards seeking gold and glory in South America and anxious to pursue the opportunities opened up by the realization that the Pacific provided a new route to Asia. Pedrarias encouraged trade, commerce, and construction and even made some tentative attempts to create a forerunner of the Panama Canal. He was, however, determined to keep all such activities under his personal control. Suspicion and jealousy governed all of his administrative actions FRANCISCO PIZARRO and his partners were particularly hampered in their efforts to launch the conquest of PERU by the interference of Pedrarias. In 1523 Pedrarias completed the establish-

ment of his personal domination of what is now NICARAGUA by deposing and executing the officer whom he had sent there to complete the conquest. Nicaragua became, in fact, Pedrarias's own stronghold when the new ministers in Spain dismissed him as governor of Darién in 1526. He withdrew to Nicaragua and maintained his authority there until his death five years later.

Pedrarias is remarkable among the founders of Spain's New World empire for the fact that he took up his governorship at an age when most men of his era were dead or retired. In a setting where his rivals were often 30 or 40 years younger, he displayed an adroit cunning and a ruthless brutality that eliminated or at least intimidated all competitors. Although not himself an active explorer, he was constantly alert to new circumstances and eager to take charge of new domains. His founding of what is now Panama City (1519) reflects his perception of the shifting patterns of travel and communication that were replacing the original Spanish focus on the Caribbean. Pedrarias was perhaps the harshest and most frightening figure of his time but certainly must rank high among the conquistadores for transforming mere conquered lands into a foundation for imperial expansion.

Pedro I (Pedro IV of Portugal, Peter I) (1798–1834)

king of Portugal and emperor of Brazil
The son of JOHN VI, the nine-year-old Pedro accompanied his father to BRAZIL in 1807 when the royal family fled the French invasion. Finally returning to LISBON in 1821, John left Pedro in Rio de Janeiro as regent and advised him to join the incipient independence movement and take Brazil for

himself if necessary. Pedro followed this plan in 1822, proclaiming the independence of Brazil with himself as Emperor Pedro I. Portugal recognized Brazilian sovereignty in 1825, but new complications arose in the following year: When John died, his eldest son became Pedro IV, king of Portugal, as well as Pedro I, emperor of Brazil. Pedro attempted to resolve the complexity by designating his daughter Maria da Glória as MARIA II, ruler of Portugal, stipulating that she would marry her uncle Miguel, who was already the idol of the Portuguese conservatives and an active pretender to the throne.

When Miguel and his followers repudiated their original agreement in 1828 and sought to depose Maria da Glória, Pedro handed over Brazil (where his popularity had by now diminished) to his young son, Emperor Pedro II, and returned to Europe to fight for his daughter's rights. During the next several years, Pedro, first from a base in the AZORES and then from OPORTO, led the Portuguese liberals against the Miguelite conservatives (see MIGUELITE WAR). His success in obtaining aid from Great Britain was decisive in their ultimate victory, although Pedro himself died in 1834.

Pedro II   See PETER II.

Pedro III   See PETER III.

Pedro V   See PETER V.

Peninsular War (War of Independence) (1808–1814)

After more than a decade of political maneuvering in the face of the French Rev-

olution, the rulers of Spain and Portugal (CHARLES IV and JOHN VI, respectively) were driven from their thrones when Napoléon sent his armies into the Iberian Peninsula, seizing Portugal in 1807 and Spain in 1808. The French emperor imposed his brother Joseph Bonaparte as King JOSEPH I in MADRID and contemplated dividing Portugal. When Great Britain intervened at the end of 1808, what the British termed the Peninsular War became known in Spain as the War of Independence, aimed at restoring the freedom of the Spanish people from the usurper. The British general Arthur Wellesley (later the duke of Wellington) first succeeded in liberating Portugal and rebuilding the Portuguese army. He then led his Anglo-Portuguese forces into Spain, where he fought a series of fierce but indecisive battles between 1810 and 1814. Spaniards all over the country took up arms to aid in the expulsion of the French, fighting a "little war" (guerrilla) of irregular operations and harassing attacks during the intervals of the major campaigns. Meanwhile, at CÁDIZ, in the unconquered part of southern Spain, the Cortes (see *CORTES*) assembled in 1812 to draw up the nations's first written constitution. While it affirmed the sovereignty of the BOURBON dynasty, it also reflected liberal ideology in its termination of the SPANISH INQUISITION, reduction of aristocratic and clerical power, and greater emphasis on popular representation. By 1814 the French had been completely driven out of Iberia, and FERDINAND VII returned from his captivity in France to pursue what soon became a reactionary rule. The Portuguese monarch would remain in his comfortable refuge in BRAZIL for years to come. While the peninsular operations were a subsidiary dimension of the Napoleonic Wars, they did serve to drain French supplies and manpower badly needed to support Napoléon's campaigns in central and eastern Europe, and the Spanish struggle has been described as a "running sore" that sapped the strength of the French empire. From the Iberian perspective the conflict opened the way to the revolt of most of the Portuguese and Spanish colonies in the New World and a whole new pattern of internal political turmoil in both countries.

Pérez, Antonio (1540–1611)
Spanish political intriguer

Of Aragonese descent (a fact that would later be of vital importance), Pérez was the son of Gonzalo Pérez (1500–66), one of the most important advisers of CHARLES I (Holy Roman Emperor Charles V). Educated in universities both in Spain and abroad, the younger Pérez accompanied his father on many of his journeys as a Spanish diplomat and as a shaper of the broader European policy that the emperor was developing. Although there is evidence that the Spanish king's successor, PHILIP II, detected flaws in the younger Pérez's character and was uncomfortable with him, he found him indispensable due to his level of training and experience. Philip was clearly uneasy about Pérez's illegitimate birth and the fact that his father was in holy orders, although the latter point has been disputed by some historians, who have not found proof that Gonzalo was ever ordained a priest (nor verification of the exact ecclesiastical status of Antonio himself). Apart from these issues that would certainly worry the highly religious king, Philip's own personality—grim and reclusive—was completely at odds with

the outgoing and engaging manner of one to whom he would have to confide matters of the gravest importance. Nevertheless Philip appointed Pérez to succeed his father as secretary of state in 1568. For the next decade he was active at the highest level of HABSBURG government, privy to all of the affairs of state and deeply involved in court intrigues. These pitted the traditional Castilian elite, led by the duke of ALBA, against a more flexible and cosmopolitan group, of which Pérez was a recognized leader.

Pérez's reversal of fortune began in 1578 following the murder of Juan de Escobedo, secretary of JOHN OF AUSTRIA, the king's half brother and governor of the Netherlands. Although there are many versions of what lay behind this event, Pérez was detained and then spent some 10 years in prison charged with a variety of offenses, including an accusation of heresy laid against him by the SPANISH INQUISITION. This murky business was never fully clarified before Pérez contrived to escape from confinement and flee to ZARAGOZA, the capital of ARAGON, where he claimed sanctuary. Pérez made himself a local hero, declaring that he was the victim of unjust persecution and played upon Aragonese fears and suspicions that Philip II was preparing to abolish Aragon's remaining autonomous rights (*fueros*) by force of arms. The presence of Pérez provoked disputes among the Aragonese elite, who engaged in prolonged arguments over how to deal with him. Pérez also managed to incite the regionalist, and even separatist, passions of the lower orders. While being detained in a Zaragoza jail, he was rescued by a riotous crowd that beat off militia men sent to guard him and was hailed as the champion of his people.

Philip II, with his usual deliberate prudence, assembled a large body of troops on the frontier of Aragon, pursued extended negotiations with all interested parties, and then invaded that kingdom. The Castilians were easily victorious and the principal supporters of Pérez were imprisoned or executed. Pérez himself escaped across the border to France, where he spent some time intriguing with local authorities and political exiles from Aragon and Portugal who had gathered there. He was the principal instigator of an incursion by these "renegades" that was crushed within a matter of weeks by Philip's forces.

For the remainder of his life Pérez traveled alternately in France and England, seeking support from Spain's enemies and producing a series of books that contributed to the "Black Legend" (LEYENDA NEGRA) of Spanish infamy. He also detailed his version of various assassinations and other crimes initiated by the king of Spain. As the international political environment changed and the Anglo-Spanish wars came to an end after the death of both Philip II and Elizabeth I of England, Pérez was increasingly marginalized. His venomous charges and his fantastic schemes for attacks on Spain were ignored. King Henri IV of France treated the aging Spaniard kindly and even sought to secure a pardon for him during the last years of Pérez's exile. Spain's leaders would not, however, regard him as anything but an arch traitor whose conduct was beyond forgiveness. Ironically the only remission of guilt that came from Spain was the Inquisition's decision that he had been wrongly convicted of heresy, and this document arrived only after Pérez was dead.

Pérez de Ayala, Ramón (1880–1962)
Spanish writer

Born in ASTURIAS, Pérez de Ayala studied law at the University of Oviedo and philosophy and letters at the University of Madrid. He combined a literary life with a public career. The former had already been recognized by his election to the Spanish Royal Academy in 1928. During World War I he served as a correspondent in various parts of Europe for *La Prensa* of Buenos Aires. After the establishment of the Second Republic he was named ambassador to Britain, a post that he held until 1936. During the SPANISH CIVIL WAR he chose self-exile in Latin America. Aside from a number of poems and essays Pérez de Ayala was best known as a novelist. His early work, beginning in 1903, was well received, but critics found his creations of the 1920s to be his best, full of satirical wit and shrewd philosophical analysis. Distracted and perhaps depressed by the political and military pressures of the 1930s and the post–civil war period, he wrote little until a few years before his death. Pérez de Ayala's early, largely autobiographical novels, dealing with the education, both academic and emotional, of a young man, make up a series of four books published between 1907 and 1913: *Tinieblas en las cumbres* (Darkness at the top), *A.M.D.G.* (To the greater glory of God), *La pata de la raposa* (*The Fox's Paw*), and *Troteras y danzaderas* (Trotters and dancers). Between 1921 and 1926 Pérez de Ayala moved into a mature period of sophisticated development of character and analysis of motivation, interweaving a striking sense of humor that lightened the seriousness of his subject matter. His books of this period included *Belarmino y Apolonio (Belarmino and Apolo-*

nio); Luna de miel, luna de hiel (Honeymoon, Bittermoon); Los trabajos de Urbano y Simona (The labors of Urbano and Simona); *Tigre Juan (Tiger Juan);* and *El curandero de su honra* (The healer of his honor). In the last years of his life, Pérez de Ayala published only a single collection of short fiction, in addition to a few essays and pieces of literary criticism.

Pérez Galdós, Benito (1845–1920)
Spanish novelist

Pérez Galdós (ordinarily referred to as "Galdós") was born in the CANARY ISLANDS and settled in MADRID to study law, which he soon abandoned in favor of journalism. He discovered his true vocation in 1870 when he published the novel *La fontana de oro* (The fountain of gold). Fascinated by the tumultuous and complex experience of his nation in the 19th century, Galdós undertook to trace the years from 1805 to 1875 in a series of historical novels, ultimately totaling 46 titles (the first of them was *Trafalgar,* published in 1873). Divided into groups or series, these *"Episodios nacionales"* were based upon contemporary newspaper accounts, memoirs, and letters used to provide authenticity to the fictional experiences of protagonists who lived through often traumatic events and who in some cases reappeared in more than one novel. Some gaps in the chronological sequence were later filled in by the author, who did not hesitate to focus upon "great men" as the pivotal figures in his stories, as in *Narváez* and *O'Donnell.*

Galdós also wrote a number of novels whose themes were social issues, religious conflicts and class struggle, such as *Doña Perfecta, Nazarín, Misericordia, La familia de*

Benito Pérez Galdós *(Library of Congress)*

León Roch, and *Gloria,* among many others. These *"Novelas contemporáneas"* he distinguished from his *Episodios nacionales.* Not as overtly "political" as his earlier novels, they are not "historical novels," but in their portrayal of Spanish life as he lived it in the late 19th century, they provide a continuity of observation and understanding that moves through what is virtually 100 years of Spanish life. Galdós, in the sweep of his conception and execution, has been compared to such contemporary foreign novelists as Balzac and Dickens, and in sheer output, to Spain's LOPE DE VEGA. Certain commentators have detected a falling off of both energy and skill in the author's later works, which they attribute not only to the aging process but to financial reverses that obliged him to produce his work more rapidly and perhaps more carelessly in order to earn a living. Whatever failings his writings of the early 1900s may exhibit, the total achievement of Galdós is both impressive and, in its way, incomparable. Esteemed primarily as a novelist, Galdós also wrote many plays, which were often derived from his *Novelas contemporáneas* and which were highly successful in their day.

Peru (Perú)

This name, originally applied to a coastal zone on the Atlantic shore of South America, was later used to designate the heartland of the Inca Empire, which beginning in the early 13th century also gained control of what is now Ecuador, Bolivia, and Chile. After initial probes during the 1520s Spaniards launched an invasion and conquest of the Inca lands during the 1530s. From 1542 the designation Viceroyalty of Peru was applied to the whole continent, with the seat of government in Peru proper. During the 18th century some northern and eastern areas of South America were assigned to new, separate viceroyalties. Peru proclaimed its independence from Spain in 1821 but did not win its final victory until 1824. It had to fight one more short war (1866) with the "mother country," however, to establish its full sovereignty.

Pessoa, Fernando António Nogueira (1888–1935)
Portuguese poet

Pessoa spent his youth in Durban, South Africa, where his stepfather was Portuguese consul. The mastery of English that the young man acquired there proved useful after his return in 1905 to Lisbon, where he earned his living as a translator of commercial correspondence. He soon became a participant in the Luso-Brazilian modernist movement, contributing essays to its magazine *Orpheu*. His early poetical work was published in English (beginning in 1918) and did not attract much attention. It was not until the very end of his life that Pessoa ventured into Portuguese, and his book of poetry *Mensagem* (Messages, 1934) did not attract much notice, either. Only after his death, as a series of posthumous books appeared, did his rich imagination and command of the Portuguese language become known and applauded. Particularly striking was his use of figures whom he called "heteronyms," who were in fact alternate manifestations of himself. These other identities are reflected in the titles of his poetical works: *Poesias de Fernando Pessoa* (1942), *Poesias de Álvaro de Campos* (1944), *Poemas de Alberto Caeiro* (1946) and *Odes de Ricardo Reis* (1946). Ironically, in the years following his death Pessoa became, perhaps, the best known of early 20th-century Portuguese poets.

Peter II (Pedro II) (1648–1706)
king of Portugal

The younger son of John IV, Peter was frustrated by the fact that his older brother, Afonso VI, was both mentally and physically incapacitated to the point where his kingship was essentially a mockery. In 1667 Peter deposed Afonso in a coup d'état that enjoyed wide support. Having arranged for the annulment of his brother's nominal marriage to the French princess Marie-Françoise, Peter married the lady. However, he refrained from taking the royal title and governed as regent until Afonso's death in 1683. Both before and after assuming the kingship Peter II guided Portugal through a period of increasing prosperity, in large part derived from the discovery of mineral deposits in BRAZIL. Commercial agreements with Great Britain (particularly the Treaty of Methuen, 1703) benefited the economy but led to Portugal's involvement in the WAR OF THE SPANISH SUCCESSION.

Peter III (Pedro III) (1717–1786)
king of Portugal

Younger son of JOHN V and brother of JOSEPH I, Peter was wed to his niece in one of those marriages to stabilize the dynastic succession that were not uncommon in Iberian royal families. The pair ruled jointly from 1777 until Peter's death in 1786. His widow, MARIA I, due to mental illness, spent most of the next 30 years under a regency.

Peter IV   See PEDRO I.

Peter V (Pedro V) (1837–1861)
king of Portugal

Peter was the son of MARIA II and her consort, Ferdinand of Saxe-Coburg-Gotha, who bore the nominal title King Ferdinand II. On his mother's death, in 1853, he passed under the regency of his father and then was declared of age in 1855. During his brief reign Peter V attracted a certain degree of popularity among those who saw in his youth the promise of better times for Portugal. Even the colonial empire, where new buildings and institutions were named in his honor, reflected this upsurge of

hope. His early death robbed his subjects of their expectations.

Philip I (Felipe el Hermoso, Felipe I de Castilla) (1478–1506)
king of Castile

Born in Bruges (in present-day Belgium), the son of Duchess Marie of Burgundy and Archduke Maximilian of Austria (later Holy Roman Emperor Maximilian I), he succeeded his mother as ruler of the Burgundian Netherlands in 1481. Although much admired by his subjects (who called him "the Handsome") in the prosperous state that lay in a strategic position between France and Germany, he developed into a vain, arrogant, and self-indulgent individual. Assuming that they could manage Philip, Maximilian and FERDINAND V, king of ARAGON, arranged a dynastic alliance uniting Philip with the Spanish princess JOANNA in 1496. The marriage was a tempestuous one due to Joanna's instability and Philip's infidelity; nevertheless, it resulted in six children and established a Habsburg dynasty in Spain, as well as the line of Habsburgs who would rule in Austria for 500 years. Ferdinand and Philip soon became bitter antagonists, first over the younger man's meddling in the delicate relations between Spain and France, then over the question of Philip's claim on the throne of CASTILE.

When ISABELLA I died in 1504 and was succeeded by her daughter Joanna, Ferdinand, who wished to continue the integration of Aragon with Castile, sought to exercise the regency of the latter kingdom. Joanna was willing to accept this arrangement, but her husband insisted that he was now rightful co-sovereign of Castile. Furthermore he suggested that his wife's mental unpredictability required that he be fully in control of her kingdom. Philip, who had spent an increasing amount of time in Castile, had built up a considerable following among those nobles who wished to reverse the centralizing program of Isabella and Ferdinand. In return for their recognition of his title as King Philip I the Habsburg heir regranted to them most of the privileges they had lost during the previous reign. By early 1500 Ferdinand seemed prepared to abandon his claim on the regency, but the sudden death of Philip while celebrating his triumph in Burgos reversed the situation in favor of the Aragonese monarch, who henceforth oversaw Joanna's inheritance.

revolt among crypto-Muslims in Aragon (1569–79) and annihilated the Ottoman fleet at LEPANTO (1571). Throughout this period he employed the full rigors of the SPANISH INQUISITION to "cleanse" Spain and its dependencies of what he regarded as a "Protestant infestation."

Philip was less successful in dealing with the revolt within his hereditary dominions in the Netherlands. Beginning in 1564 and provoked by the spread of Calvinism as well as high-handed Spanish administration, this resistance movement gained in strength over several decades. Philip alternated conciliation with military force but, by the end of his reign, retained only the southern provinces (present-day Belgium), the

Philip II (Felipe II) (1527–1598)
king of Spain

Son of CHARLES I (Holy Roman Emperor Charles V) and Isabella of Portugal, he was greatly influenced by his clerical tutors and by his father's guidance in the duties and responsibilities of a monarch. He obtained experience in the business of waging war and ruling the various Spanish dependencies but never became (as his father had) a commander in the field or a cosmopolitan at home in all parts of Europe. After ascending the throne of Spain in 1556, he rarely left that country and identified almost exclusively with the Castilian heritage. His reign would be devoted to preserving his inheritance and restoring the dominance of the Catholic faith. Among Philip's most notable achievements were his victory over the perennial enemy, France, and his defeat of the Turkish threat in the Mediterranean. After forcing the king of France to abandon his claims in Italy (1559), Philip crushed a

King Philip II *(Library of Congress)*

northern area having become the independent Dutch Republic. In the course of the struggle the old issues with France flared up once more, and by the 1580s Spain was intervening on the Catholic side in that country's civil war. The revolt of the Netherlands also intersected with Anglo-Spanish rivalries. Tensions between Philip and Elizabeth I of England arose from her ambitions in the Spanish-ruled Western Hemisphere and her persecution of Catholics, particularly in Ireland, where Philip supplied covert support to the Irish resistance. By 1585 Elizabeth had dispatched English "volunteers" to aid the Dutch and was recognized as the leader of northern European opposition to Philip's championship of the Counter-Reformation. In 1588 Philip dispatched the "Invincible ARMADA" to invade and conquer England. This great fleet of warships and troop transports was part of a grand design that included a decisive blow against the Dutch rebels and the replacement of the French king by a Catholic protégé of Spain. The plan proved too unwieldy and failed in all its dimensions. In the end Philip was obliged to make peace with France, accept a de facto division of the Netherlands, and leave the unresolved contest with England to his successor.

If the north proved unconquerable, Philip could at least congratulate himself on his political and religious mastery of the south. He completed this during the 1580s by establishing himself as king of Portugal. When the last legitimate member of the AVIZ dynasty died in 1580, Philip laid claim to the crown, citing his mother's royal Portuguese lineage. Although some armed opposition continued for a few years, he was able to establish himself as king of Portugal and, therefore, as ruler of that country's colonial possessions in Africa, Asia, and the Americas. The "personal union" of these two nations that had pioneered in the building of colonial empires made Philip ruler of the greatest realm the world had ever seen. There were even suggestions that he should assume the title of "emperor of the Indies." Although Philip never took his overseas possessions as seriously as those in Europe, they continued to grow throughout his reign as explorers and conquistadores built upon the foundations laid during his father's time. Their principal importance in these later days was as a source of precious metals to finance Philip's wars and grand diplomacy.

According to contemporary observers Philip II derived little visible enjoyment from his vast powers. He was invariably described as gloomy, grim, and so dedicated to his work that he spared scarcely a moment from the business of government. His popular nickname, "the Prudent," was a reflection less of sage caution than of chronic indecisiveness. Reluctant to act in matters that were of tremendous importance, he often delayed until the time was no longer ripe for action. Yet, suspicious of other people's motives, he sought little advice and read all the government documents and annotated all the dispatches for himself, becoming less of a monarch than the chief clerk of an empire.

What happiness that did penetrate the obsessive environment that Philip created for himself in his great monastery-palace of EL ESCORIAL was provided by his family. His first wife, a Portuguese princess, had died soon after the birth of their only child. This son, Charles, for whom he naturally entertained the greatest hopes, had proved a bitter disappointment. He grew into an unstable youth, whose opposition to his father may even have crossed the boundary of treason. Eventually placed under restraint, he died young, leaving only bitter memories and lurid legends that would inspire plays and operas in later centuries. Philip's second marriage, arranged by his father, was equally unhappy in its outcome. If his wife Mary Tudor had given him a son, England and Spain would have been united under a Catholic monarchy. Queen Mary, however, died childless, and Philip was left to make another marriage of political calculation when he wed the French princess Elisabeth of Valois in 1568. Elisabeth died while giving birth to a stillborn son but left Philip two daughters who were the source of great happiness and uncharacteristic playfulness in his paternal role. Philip's fourth wife, the Austrian princess Anne (who was also his niece), left only one surviving child out of five whom she bore him. Upon this younger Philip, the prudent king lavished all his attention and training during the last years of the reign, evidently with little confidence that the boy would prove a capable successor.

At his death in 1598 (a drawn-out and painful affair) Philip II could look back on a reign of some 40 years in which he had achieved much, including the firm mastery of Mediterranean Europe, what proved to be the decisive blow against the Ottoman Turks, and the construction of a global empire that (for all its shortcomings) would endure for centuries. He had nevertheless, failed to roll back the Reformation. For a monarch so devout and dedicated this was surely felt as a defect for which he would have to answer to God. What Philip may not have understood so clearly was his failure to strengthen and stabilize his earthly realm. In pursuing his political vision Philip stunted the economic capacity of Spain and left her a crippled giant prey to the upsurging power of its rivals and the weakness of the kings who would succeed him.

Philip III (Felipe III) (1578–1621)
king of Spain

The youngest son of PHILIP II, he succeeded his father in 1598. Although well trained by his father's councillors, he lacked energy and ambition and soon turned over most of the business of government to his adviser, the duke of LERMA. During the early years of his reign peace was concluded with England (1604) and with the Dutch rebels (1609), and tensions with France were kept in abeyance. Despite the opportunity thus given to reform and energize Spain's decayed economy and inefficient administration, the king did virtually nothing to improve its domestic weaknesses. His chief initiative (urged upon him by church leaders and popular sentiment) was the expulsion of some 500,000 Spaniards of Muslim background who were suspected of secret adherence to Islam or disloyalty. This purge, which began soon after the conclusion of hostilities with the Dutch, was more symbolic than beneficial.

Shortly before his death Philip III renewed warfare in the Netherlands and began the series of confrontations with France that would ultimately lead to Spain's downfall. A pious, passive ruler, Philip III lacked his predecessor's grand vision and energy as well as his successor's flamboyance and vanity. His reign consisted of two decades of wasted time for a country profoundly in need of salutary change.

Philip IV (Felipe IV) (1605–1665)
king of Spain

Son of PHILIP III, he succeeded his father in 1621. A self-indulgent and imprudent monarch, he left the task of government to his *privado* (political favorite) and only took heed of Spain's desperate situation when it was too late to avert military disaster. Unlike his contemporary Louis XIII of France, also an idle and inept monarch, Philip did not have the good sense (or good fortune) to choose a first-class chief minister to manage the country for him. Instead of Richelieu, he had the count-duke of OLIVARES. Both Philip and his favorite were overconfident advocates of aggressive policies. Unlike the pacifistic regime that had preceded them, they made war with the Dutch, the English, and the French, while provoking resentment and revolt within the Iberian Peninsula. Drawn into support for the Austrian Habsburgs on dynastic and religious grounds, Philip IV became involved not only in the Thirty Years' War (1618–48) but in a struggle for mastery of Europe that lasted for still another 11 years. Even before the military disaster at ROCROI (1643) that marked the end of Spanish military hegemony and would forever scar the memory of his reign, Philip had resolved to dispense with the services of Olivares. However, during the second half of his reign he merely substituted one *privado* for another, choosing LUIS DE HARO, the retired favorite's nephew as his new chief minister, with no better results.

Although the king showed somewhat more personal concern and involvement in policy making during these later years, he was not able to effect any real reversal of fortune. Portugal, which had rejected his rule in 1640, was never regained (though he was still seeking to assert control there down to the time of his death). His authority was reestablished in CATALONIA only at great cost, and even in ANDALUSIA he was obliged to struggle against an incipient secession. His rebellious subjects in the Kingdom of Naples were finally beaten down, but the independence of the Dutch had to be conceded in 1648. Even the overseas empire began to slip away when he was obliged to yield JAMAICA to England in 1654.

Exactly a century after his grandfather had established Spain's dominance by forcing a defeated France to surrender its pretensions to European leadership, Philip IV was obliged to sign the humiliating Peace of the Pyrenees in 1559. Not only did he hand over territory to France, he also gave his daughter in marriage to the young Louis XIV, preparing the way for the ultimate accession of the House of BOURBON to the Spanish throne. When the depressed, exhausted, and prematurely aged Philip IV died in 1665, leaving only a sickly boy to succeed him, the once glorious era of Habsburg Spain was virtually at an end.

Thanks to the artistic gifts of DIEGO VELÁZQUEZ, his court painter and greatest of all Spanish artists, Philip IV has established a presence in the minds of subsequent generations that far outweighs his personal capacity or his significance in Spanish history. In numerous portraits of the monarch the arrogant upsweep of his mustache proclaims a self-confidence that was far from justified by performance. The royal family, too, has been immortalized by Velázquez, from the little infantes and infantas to the sinisterly ambitious Don Juan José, the king's bastard son. Even Olivares, in a splendid equestrian study, perpetuates the image of Spanish grandeur that no longer corresponded to reality. Through the genius of an artist whom the king may have considered no more than a servant who painted, Philip IV has long outlasted an empire that he helped to destroy.

Philip V (Felipe V) (1683–1746)
king of Spain

Grandson of Louis XIV of France, he was designated as successor to the Spanish throne in the will of CHARLES II, his great-uncle. The accession of this BOURBON monarch precipitated the political and military opposition of Austria, Great Britain, and the Dutch Republic, who had agreed to a partition of Spanish dependencies upon the extinction of the HABSBURG dynasty in Madrid. In the WAR OF THE SPANISH SUCCESSION (1701–14) Philip, with assistance from France, succeeded in defending his new realm. By 1711 the fighting had spread throughout Europe and overseas, and the British and Dutch had become unwilling to support the Austrian claimant. Eventually the peace settlements confirmed Philip as ruler of Spain and its overseas possessions, though he was obliged to surrender the Belgian and Italian possessions.

Although initially popular among most of his Spanish subjects, the young monarch lost most of the prestige he had gained through vigorous defense of the kingdom by his favoritism to French advisers and his harsh treatment of opponents in ARAGON and CATALONIA. Those who had hoped for modernization of the Spanish administration and economy along French lines were disappointed by Philip's failure to press major reforms, and those who feared loss of privilege were angered by such reforming

efforts as he did make. Perhaps the greatest fault of Philip V was his preoccupation with external ambitions, particularly his designs on the French throne, which he pursued even though he had sworn to make no claim to it. These concerns led to a brief war with France in 1718–20 and an effort to position himself for a claim to the French throne in 1724 when young Louis XV seemed in danger of death. It was perhaps for this reason that he abdicated the Spanish throne in 1724 in favor of his son Louis, alleging that he was weary of the stress of government and wished to devote himself to the quiet pursuit of his religious interests. In any event his resumption of power in Madrid when Louis died suddenly six months later heightened an already-growing reputation for eccentricity.

During his "second reign," Philip V was dominated by his second wife, ISABELLA FARNESE, the last of the ruling line in Parma. Her determination to secure thrones for her sons reinforced the king's own desire to regain the Italian territories that he had been obliged to surrender to Austria. These goals were attained by Spain's successive intervention in the War of the Polish Succession (1733–35) and the War of the Austrian Succession (1740–48). The ultimate result of these military entanglements was the establishment of Bourbon dynasties in the Duchy of Parma and the Kingdom of Naples. Philip, however, did not live to see the final success of these projects, and his mental deterioration in his last years guaranteed that domestic policy continued to be neglected.

For all the expectations created by the arrival in Spain of a promising young ruler and the introduction of a progressive new dynasty, the reign of Philip V proved a disappointment. Although some of his ministers were well chosen, the overall direction of Spanish policy during the first half of the 18th century was retrograde. Spanish policy was focused on the recovery of lost dependencies and the revival of past glories in Europe while the American colonies were neglected, leaving economic opportunities both there and at home to await a later generation of Bourbon reformers.

Philippine Islands (Islas Filipinas)

This vast archipelago lying some 500 miles east of the Asian mainland and including more than 7,000 islands contains a total of more than 115,000 square miles. The archipelago extends more than 1,000 miles from north to south and more than 600 miles east to west, with an abundant wealth of agriculture and mineral resources. This rich prize fell to Spain in 1521 when FERDINAND MAGELLAN claimed the islands for his sovereign after crossing the Pacific. Effective occupation did not begin until 1561, and Manila, the seat of government, was not established until 1571. For the next 300 years Spain clung to possession of this treasure trove, which could be reached only by a long, laborious voyage across two oceans. The Manila Galleon, sailing from Acapulco in NEW SPAIN, made the annual trip that symbolized Spain's determination to hold this most distant outpost of empire. It had to contend with persistent resistance from the "Moros" (the Muslim inhabitants of Mindanao) in the south; European rivalries, including British occupation of Manila in 1762–63; and periodic revolts by the Tagalog-speaking population (a people of Indonesian origin). The Filipino revolutionary movement triumphed in 1898 when the SPANISH-AMERICAN WAR led to the defeat of the colonial forces and the transfer of the islands to the control of the United States. Filipino independence would have to wait for another half-century, but evidence of Spain's long rule of these islands quickly faded away.

Picasso, Pablo (Pablo Ruiz y Picasso) (1881–1973)

Spanish painter

Born in MÁLAGA, the son of a minor painter and art teacher, Picasso had his early training at art schools in Coruña and BARCELONA and spent a few months at the Royal Academy at Madrid. By 1899 he was a member of a circle of young artists in Barcelona who, to some extent, were influenced by native masters such as EL GRECO but were increasingly drawn to new trends in French painting. After 1900 Picasso spent more and more time in Paris, gradually weakening his ties to Barcelona. The first of his famous phases of thematic and stylistic approach to painting, the "blue period," began in Barcelona, but his "rose period" and then the development of cubism occurred as an expatriate. During the first three decades of the 20th century this increasingly famous artist became more identified with France than with his native country, and he lived in Paris or, later, in the south of France during the SPANISH CIVIL WAR and World War II. That Picasso was not entirely divorced from his ancestral roots was dramatically demonstrated, however, in one of his best-known paintings, the massive canvas called *Guernica*. It was inspired by the bombing of the historic seat of BASQUE NATIONALISM by the same name during the war in Spain. The German allies of the Nationalist rebels carried out a murderous aerial assault against

Basque supporters of the Republican cause, killing hundreds. Horrified and indignant, Picasso painted a scene of destruction, mutilation, and death that has become an iconic image of the madness of modern warfare. The painting, according to Picasso's instructions, was never to be displayed in Spain until that country was under a free and democratic government. It remained in New York City's Museum of Modern Art until after the end of the Franco regime and was then returned to hang in a place of honor in MADRID'S PRADO.

Picasso did not live to see the end of dictatorship and the installation of *Guernica* in his native country. He spent the later years of his long life in his chosen French home surrounded by children, grandchildren, friends, and admirers, pursuing his growing interest in sculpture as well as painting, and creating an amazing array of imaginative and distinctive work. For most of the 20th century he had been the ultimate artist in popular imagination, and for all his legendary "temperament," Spaniards remain proud to have nurtured him.

Pineda, Mariana de (1804–1831)
Spanish revolutionary

Destined to be an iconic figure in the history of Spanish radicalism, Pineda was born in GRANADA to an army officer of noble ancestry and his commoner mistress. Orphaned at an early age, she was raised by relatives but soon became virtually the head of her household. Due to her ambiguous social status and her acquaintance with liberal circles in the army she soon developed sympathy with the constitutionalist cause in the years following its repression by FERDINAND VII. Her husband was banished from Spain for his political activities, as was another officer whom she intended to marry after becoming a widow. Her own increasing commitment to the liberal movement involved her carrying messages, forging documents, giving shelter to clandestine meetings, and recruiting new supporters. Although she moved beyond the traditional image of "women's work" in her political activities, she is particularly remembered for embroidering a banner for an intended revolutionary uprising bearing the inscription *"Ley, libertad, igualdad"* ("Law, liberty, equality"). She was detained several times on suspicion of revolutionary activities, and it has been said that the chief judge of Granada was at first so enamored of her that he released her and then so angered by her rejection of him that he persecuted her in a spirit of vengeance. Pineda was ultimately detained on vague charges of sympathy with the enemies of the Crown and communicating with exiled liberals in GIBRALTAR. Particular mention was made in her indictment of the flag that she had embroidered, which was described as a "Masonic banner." Condemned for treason, she was executed in Granada at the age of 27.

Pineda is revered as a martyr of Spanish liberalism. She is particularly remembered in Granada, where the poet-playwright FEDERICO GARCÍA LORCA wrote a drama, *Mariana Pineda,* based on her romantic life and death.

Pintasilgo, Maria de Lurdes (1930–2004)
Portuguese politician

A pioneering feminist, Pintasilgo became Portugal's first woman prime minister in 1979. During the Salazar dictatorship, when women were encouraged to stay at home and educational opportunities were limited, she was able to secure training as a chemical engineer at the University of Coimbra and to win an administrative position in one of the government-controlled corporations that dominated Portuguese industry. Increasingly involved with the Socialist Party, she moved into active politics after the bloodless revolution of 1974 and held several cabinet positions before assuming the premiership. In 1986 she ran for president but was defeated by the Socialist leader MÁRIO SOARES. She subsequently held the informal position of elder stateswoman, called in as a consultant by successive chiefs of state. Her writings on a wide variety of topics made her one of the best-known and most-admired women in Portugal.

Pizarro, Francisco (1475–1541)
Spanish explorer and soldier

The illegitimate son of a Spanish gentleman, Pizarro was a neglected child who spent his youth as an illiterate swineherd. Seeking adventure and fortune he enlisted in an early expedition to the New World and then spent years in present-day COLOMBIA and PANAMA in low-ranking assignments. Although he was a companion of VASCO NÚÑEZ DE BALBOA when the latter discovered the Pacific (1513), he later abandoned him to his fate. It was not until he was nearly 50 that he secured the financial and personal backing to assemble a series of probes down the western coast of South America seeking the fabled empire of the Inca. His early attempts ended in failure, but he succeeded in obtaining a royal decree granting him the governorship of any lands he should seize from the native rulers.

In 1532 Pizarro landed on the shore of what is now PERU with 200 followers and spent time ingratiating himself with the local population, who confirmed the existence of the Inca Empire made up of vast territories in the interior that included many subject and resentful tribes. Marching into the highlands with his soldiers and native allies, Pizarro arranged a meeting with the emperor Atahuallpa, from whom he demanded submission to the Spanish Crown and conversion to Christianity. When this ultimatum was translated to the monarch and indignantly rejected by him, Pizarro's concealed soldiers launched an attack which resulted in the deaths of hundreds of the emperor's followers and the capture of Atahuallpa.

Pizarro had previously learned that Atahuallpa was engaged in a civil war with his brother Huáscar for control of the empire and took full advantage of the situation by playing the rivals off against each other, inciting Inca nobles to mutiny, and encouraging dissent among subject tribes. After promising to release Atahuallpa on payment of a huge ransom in gold and silver, Pizarro broke his pledge and tried the Inca emperor before a formal Spanish-style court for having incited the murder of Huáscar. Atahuallpa was convicted and executed. Pizarro pursued his conquest of the Inca lands, crushing resistance, capturing their principal city, Cuzco, and founding his own capital on the site of present-day Lima.

During the next few years Pizarro and his partner in conquest, Diego Almagro, quarrelled over the division of spoils. Their relatives and adherents introduced a new civil war among the Spaniards when the struggle with the Inca was barely ended. Almagro was killed, but in 1541 his avengers attacked

Pizarro's residence in Lima and slew him, paving the way for the imposition of direct rule by administrators sent out from Spain.

Pizarro's entire life has been described as a second-rate reproduction of the career of HERNÁN CORTÉS. Certainly he seems to have envisioned the conquest of Peru as a reenactment of the conquest of MEXICO (with which it has many parallels). The treachery and violence employed by Pizarro and his associates, however, exceeded even the enormities committed by most conquistadores, and his indifference to the usual standards of honor and dignity shocked even the Spanish authorities who finally put an end to the "Wars of Peru" in the 1540s. Despite his shortcomings Pizarro gained for his country a far vaster empire than that won by Cortés. Virtually the whole of South America was ultimately brought under Spanish rule by the successors of Pizarro. His city of Lima became the seat of a Viceroyalty of Peru that stretched from Panama to Cape Horn.

Pombal, Sebastião José de Carvalho e Melo, marquês de (1699–1782)
Portuguese statesmen

An aristocrat trained in law at the University of Coimbra, the future marquês de Pombal spent the period 1739–49 as a diplomat in London and Vienna. When he returned home, the new king, JOSEPH I, named him secretary of state for foreign affairs and war. In this capacity he was, in effect, chief minister and, indeed, the real ruler of Portugal. During the reign of Joseph I, Pombal presided over a system of enlightened despotism for which the king was merely a figurehead. Pombal was a ruthless reformer who believed that absolute power,

wielded without compromise or mercy, was the best instrument for bringing the Enlightenment to Portugal. He crushed the nobles who conspired against him and his master, expelled the Jesuits from Portugal and its colonies, reduced the Inquisition to total subservience, and introduced a system of state monopolies in all the branches of commerce, waging war, in particular, on the masters of the wine trade. The great earthquake and fire that devastated LISBON in 1755, while he was in the first stage of his reforms, far from disrupting his program was converted into an opportunity to demonstrate his vigor and efficiency in meeting the challenge and in building a more handsome—as well as more secure—capital upon the ruins of the old.

Among Pombal's many achievements were the modernization of the university system, the promotion of new industries, and the strengthening of the armed forces to enhance Portugal's role in the world. He also abolished slavery in Portugal, where it had principally affected Muslim captives. Overseas he paid particular attention to the development of BRAZIL, where he rationalized the administration, promoted the exploitation of natural resources, and sought to strengthen the mercantile bonds between the colony and the mother country.

On the death of Joseph I, Pombal was no longer able to retain his mastery of the Portuguese state. His numerous enemies among the clergy and nobles persuaded the new ruler, MARIA I, that he was guilty of various excesses and usurpations. She removed him from office and banished him from Lisbon, obliging him to spend the last years of his life on his rural estate. After the fall of Pombal many of the enlightened reforms introduced by him were rescinded or allowed to go unenforced, and in many respects Portugal slid backward into her pre-enlightened state.

Ponce de León, Juan (1460–1521)
Spanish explorer and soldier

A member of an aristocratic family, Ponce de León served in his youth as a page at the royal court. During the 1480s he took part in the final stages of the war against the Muslims. He was one of the first Spanish adventurers to travel to the New World, sailing in 1493 on the second expedition of CHRISTOPHER COLUMBUS. Having played an important role in pacifying western HISPANIOLA, he was named governor in the eastern part of the island (the present-day DOMINICAN REPUBLIC). Lured by native accounts of abundant gold in the nearby island of Boriquén (PUERTO RICO), he secured a commission to conquer that land, waged successful campaigns there, and became the first governor. Not satisfied with these accomplishments, he obtained permission to seek out the legendary island of Bimini, which, according to some traditions, contained a fountain of eternal youth. Enriched by his governorship in Puerto Rico, Ponce de León was able to outfit at his own expense an expedition of three ships and 200 men to take possession of that island. Arriving at the coast of present-day FLORIDA on Easter of 1513, he marked the joyous holiday and the lush vegetation of this new land by bestowing the name it has since borne. Although he sailed from his initial landing on the east coast (near modern St. Augustine) through the Florida Keys and part way up the west coast, Ponce de León found the natives violently hostile and the prospect for settlement, enrichment, or even magical springs questionable. He seems also to have concluded that Florida, while probably not "Bimini," was an island. Back in Puerto Rico by 1514 he undertook various missions for the Crown, including an attempted conquest of Guadalupe, where the Caribs proved too fierce to be subdued.

It was not until 1521 that Ponce de León, encouraged by a new decree confirming him as ADELANTADO of Florida, set out again to that territory, this time with a large number of potential settlers, farm animals, and the full intention to plant a permanent colony on the peninsula. Near the site of Tampa, his people were constructing cabins when attacked by an indigenous group, who killed and wounded so many of the Spaniards that the project was abandoned. Finding refuge in CUBA, the aged conquistador succumbed to his wounds, and Florida remained an unfulfilled dream for Spaniards.

One of the earliest arrivals and most vigorous soldier-administrators among the conquistadores, Ponce de León attained a mixed reputation for both benevolence and brutality toward the indigenous population of the Caribbean during the first phase of the conquest. His reputation has been clouded in more recent times by the endlessly repeated story of his Quixotic search for the "Fountain of Youth." This idea played no significant part in the motivations of a practical conquistador driven by the desire for gold and glory.

Porto See OPORTO

Portugal, national identity of

Portugal has been called an arbitrary, or even accidental, country; in fact, there is no particular reason why this portion of the Iberian Peninsula began a separate political existence hundreds of years before a unified Spain emerged. It was recognized as a nation-state in the 12th century, while petty kingdoms covering the greatest part of the Iberian Peninsula were still contending with Moorish invaders or with one another. Students of linguistics assert that Portuguese is no more a distinct language than the dialects spoken in various regions of Spain, and some even describe it as little more than a variant of Galician. Portuguese nationalists sometimes fall back upon the decision by imperial Rome to distinguish between "Hispania" and "Lusitania," a recognition that the land along the Atlantic shore was more remote than the rest of the peninsula. Spain has certainly not seen much merit in Portugal's claim of sovereignty. It has repeatedly laid claim to the smaller country and invaded it on numerous occasions.

And yet Portugal stands apart, even ignoring the origin of its two great rivers, the Douro and the Tagus, which flow westward out of Spain. Would the Germans, they ask, disown the Rhine merely because it rises in another part of Europe? For the Portuguese it is enough that these rivers form estuaries on the Atlantic that encompass Portugal's two largest cities.

Although their country stretches only 360 miles north to south and is nowhere more than 140 miles wide, the Portuguese dwell upon the distinctive characteristics and traditions of its regions. These are the Minho, Trás-os-Montes, the Douro, and the Beiras (Alta, Baixa, and Litoral) in the north and Ribatejo, Estremadura, the ALENTEJO (Alto and Baixo), and the ALGARVE in the southern lowlands. For each they will point

out a particular crop, a local turn of temperament, or some pattern of historical experience that fits into the Portuguese national mosaic but sets its inhabitants apart from the Spaniards. The Portuguese think of their country in terms of the cooler and rainier climate north of the Douro and the warmer environment south of the Tagus, as the terrain slopes down in the southeast toward the Mediterranean. Administrative rearrangements are less important to them than their age-old sense of natural boundaries. Although the near-Atlantic outposts of MADEIRA and the AZORES were acquired at the end of the Middle Ages, most Portuguese think of them as part of the otherwise vanished colonial empire because they have never been a part of that small segment of the European continent that is the age-old land of Portugal. Neither the Roman Empire nor their own world-girdling empire, the integration with Spain that they once endured nor the membership in the European Union that they now enjoy, not even their inclusion in the spiritual abstraction called Christendom, has ever been as important as the fundamental Portuguese identity.

Portuguese Guinea

This West African territory was first touched upon by Portuguese navigators in 1446. Although it contributed to the Portuguese slave trade for the next several centuries, the exact territorial limits were not fixed until the late 19th century, when boundaries were negotiated with neighboring British and French colonies. Portugal was still unable to secure complete mastery in the area until 1915, and there was a serious uprising in 1936. By the time Portuguese

Guinea was formally declared an "overseas province" in 1951, this low-lying agricultural colony consisted of some 14,000 square miles on the mainland and the offshore Bijagos Archipelago, with its capital at Bissau. Anticolonial guerrilla warfare broke out in 1962 as part of the general pattern of insurrection in Portugal's African dependencies. Following the revolution in LISBON in 1974, this territory was granted independence, taking the name Republic of Guinea-Bissau.

Prado, Museo Nacional del

One of the greatest art collections in the world bears the surprisingly prosaic designation of "El Prado," which means originally "the grassy field." Named for a broad stretch of land on the edge of MADRID where some of the great nobles of Spain had built houses, this location was selected by CHARLES III in the late 18th century as the site for a museum of natural history. As an enlightened monarch, he was anxious to promote scientific awareness and learning in his country. By the early 19th century the massive building that had emerged had been redesignated as the repository for the large collection of paintings and sculpture assembled by the Spanish Bourbons. Ironically it was JOSEPH I, the usurper Joseph Bonaparte, who set in motion the process that resulted in the art museum being formally established. It was opened as the Royal Museum by FERDINAND VII in 1819. After the overthrow of ISABELLA II in 1868 the collection was declared the property of the state, and the name was changed to the National Museum, although El Prado remained generally used. Given the checkered career of the Bourbon dynasty in later

days, it is not surprising that they did not seek a reversion of ownership.

The Prado escaped the vicissitudes of foreign invasion and civil strife throughout the modern era, although parts of its collections were moved for safety at certain times. By the beginning of the 21st century it had expanded to include some 8,000 works of art, housed in three distinct units.

The main building of the Prado displays approximately 2,000 paintings and sculptures by what are considered the "old masters." All of the great artists of Spain's Golden Age (SIGLO DE ORO) are exhibited here. The works of DIEGO DE VELÁZQUEZ, the "king" of painters, who painted the royals and courtiers of Spain, are arrayed in dazzling profusion, including his most famous work *Las Meninas*. This great canvas affords a view not only of an infanta and her ladies in waiting but of her parents looking on and the artist himself at work. Spanish painters scarcely less revered than Velázquez are also represented by some of their finest works, as well as masterpieces of Italian, Flemish, and German painting collected by the rulers of earlier times. A short distance away, the Casón del Buen Retiro, a former royal residence, houses 19th-century artworks scarcely less fascinating than those of the Golden Age. The third of these great galleries that house Spain's premier national collections is the Centro de Arte Reina Sofía. Named for the consort of King JUAN CARLOS I and opened in 1986, the center is home to the work of Spain's most famous artists of the 20th century, including PABLO PICASSO and his *Guernica* canvas. This portrayal of a horrendous incident of the SPANISH CIVIL WAR in which the Basques' most revered historical landmark was bombed by Franco's German allies, became a political icon to a degree unattained by any other work of art. Picasso stipulated that it not be displayed in Spain until the dictatorship had been abolished in that country. Its installation in 1992 was a matter of great emotion as well as national pride.

prehistoric discoveries in Iberia

The Iberian Peninsula was for thousands of years a land upon which history was made and from which its inhabitants ventured forth to make dazzling discoveries in other parts of the world. It has only been in recent times that scientists and scholars have looked beneath the surface of Iberia to explore its prehistory and to investigate those, both animal and human, who once roamed its plains and mountains.

Portuguese farmers and traders who, in the course of their work, periodically found gigantic footprints and bizarre fossil remains had no trouble in explaining these things to themselves: Like the inhabitants of other parts of Europe and Asia, they concluded that these were relics of wondrous creatures and fabulous monsters that had once dwelled on earth. Often Portuguese Christians created pious legends to link such remains with biblical times. For instance, on the Atlantic coast, at Cape Espichel, near LISBON, a set of huge tracks leading up from the shore was said to have been left by a gigantic mule who appeared miraculously to save the Virgin Mary from shipwreck. The being was said to have carried her on its back to the top of the cliff. A medieval chapel at the spot, known as the Church of Our Lady of the Mule, commemorated this pious tale.

Seven hundred years later, in 1976, scientists identified the footprints as those of a giant dinosaur of the late Jurassic age. By 1998 enough research had been pursued by paleontologists to inspire an International Dinosaur Conference at Lisbon. Scientists from all over the world gathered to hear reports on a plethora of ancient reptilian remains that had only within recent decades been identified and rescued from the realms of fantasy and ignorant supposition.

Among the discoveries that came to light in the last years of the 20th century were deposits of bones, rock quarries full of fossils, and even dinosaur nests still containing eggs laid millions of years ago, some with embryos still intact. Portugal has in fact emerged as a "showcase" for dinosaur remains, a point celebrated by the government's issuance of a set of postage stamps bearing striking images of some of the prehistoric residents of the country. Thanks to ongoing investigations and careful uncovering of long-ignored sites, visitors can now gaze upon a sauropod trackway located (conveniently for overseas visitors) near the shrine at FÁTIMA. This trackway, at some 300 feet, is the longest ever discovered, and at an estimated 175 million years, they are also "the oldest known wide-gauge sauropod footprints." Portugal has at long last become aware of its Jurassic heritage. Remains such as those identified near Fátima and Lourinha, must, however, contend for official protection with the demands of developers, road builders, and engineers seeking sites for new dams and irrigation projects.

In Spain an awareness of the country's prehistory was stimulated in the 19th century after the great Darwinian debates had roused the consciousness of all Europe. The entrance to a cave system at Altamira, near Santander, in the north of Spain, had been uncovered as early as 1868 by a hunter. During the next decade a local gentleman amateur found animal bones that led him to pursue further investigations and finally to work his way into a cavern that contained an amazing discovery. Not fully revealed and explored until the early 1880s, the Altamira caves were found to contain scores of paintings and etchings on their walls depicting such animals as prehistoric bison and deer. Dating back some 15,000 years, these paintings were amazingly colorful (making use of natural materials to provide vivid reds, violets, and blacks). These images were accompanied by tracings that outlined the hands of the ancient artists. So outstanding was the level of skill and sensibility disclosed by the Altamira paintings that some at first refused to believe that they were authentic. Eventually, after they were authenticated in their dating, they became a national treasure of Spain, guarded against air pollution and temperature change.

During the hundred years that followed the discoveries at Altamira Spain experienced political and military disasters and prolonged dictatorship. In such an environment the history of Spain seemed to many to be the cause of their present miseries, and few could spare the thought for the mysteries of its prehistoric dwellers and the legacy they had left at Altamira. Then, in the 1990s, as Spain was reemerging into the light of modern day, scholars and searchers found their way once again into the subterranean domains where the remains of remote antiquity still lay.

In 1994, at Atapuerca, in the hills of northern Spain, the remains of what are believed to be the oldest human inhabitants of Europe were discovered. As with the findings at Altamira, which disproved the presumed low level of human development that had existed 15,000 years before the cave paintings were found, so the discoveries at Atapuerca dispelled the belief that humankind's earliest evolutionary predecessors had not set foot in Europe until about 500,000 B.C. At Atapuerca the remains of the first Europeans, when subjected to dating technology, doubled that estimate. The first discoveries at Atapuerca gave evidence of extremely early hominid presence in Europe (skulls, bones, and crude implements). A nearby deep crevice proved a much later hominid residence in the same area, which showed prolonged habitation. Moreover it gave substantiation of what had been called "human" behavior. The skeletal remains in this narrow cleft seemed to have been placed there after death in a burial ritual, suggesting an emerging sensibility or, as some have ventured to suggest, an emerging spirituality. Carefully shaped hand axes placed with the bodies disclosed not only a high degree of skilled workmanship but a possible desire to send some product of their lives with them on a journey into the afterlife. Furthermore this group of remains is believed to date from approximately 400,000 B.C. and to represent what has been called the evolutionary "grandfathers" of the Neanderthal species. Some paleontologists believe that these remains are in fact common ancestors of Neanderthals and the first true "modern men."

Atapuerca lies 150 miles north of MADRID. Within its complex of prehistoric remains, Gran Dolina, the site where the initial remains were uncovered, has been, in a sense, "known" since the late 19th century, when a part of the hillside was sheared off during railroad construction. After 100 years of distracting events, discovery of a nearby burial crevice at what has been called "Sima de los Huesos" ("Pit of the Bones") excited even greater scientific interest. A quartzite hand ax lifted from among these bones symbolizes, perhaps even more than the bones themselves, the earliest moment when what might be called a Spaniard applied his skill to the creation of what was both a tool and an expression of feeling.

Prim y Prats, Juan (Joan Prim i Prats; conde de Reus, marqués de los Castillejos) (1814–1870)
Spanish general and statesman

As a young officer this Catalan soldier fought to uphold the succession of ISABELLA II during the First Carlist War. Having established his value to the regime during the next round of political upheaval in the early 1840s, he was successively appointed governor of PUERTO RICO (1847), field commander in Morocco (1859), and leader of a Spanish contingent within the international expedition sent to restore order in MEXICO in 1861.

Back in Spain in 1863 he took part in various attempts against the government of Isabella II. Like many other Spanish officers, Prim had come to believe that her reign had turned into a national scandal, and when she was finally driven into exile in 1868, he emerged as a member of the new leadership. Although the final choice for a replacement ruler, Prince Amadeo of Italy, owed his selection largely to Prim's support, the general was assassinated by political enemies on the eve of the new king's arrival, and virtually the first duty of AMADEO I in Spain was to attend Prim's funeral.

Primo de Rivera, José Antonio
See FALANGE ESPAÑOLA.

Primo de Rivera y Orbaneja, Miguel (marqués de Estella) (1870–1930)
Spanish military leader and statesman

Born to a military family, Primo de Rivera fought against nationalist rebels in CUBA and the PHILIPPINE ISLANDS and against Moroccan opponents of Spain's attempts to establish a protectorate in that country. Thanks to his personal dynamism and family connections he became a general in his 40s. Despite involvement in a number of political controversies he attained the captaincy general in BARCELONA by 1923. He was well placed to take advantage of the multiple problems that beset Spain in its post–SPANISH-AMERICAN WAR era, including socioeconomic upheaval and a sense of marginalization following World War I. The aftermath of the humiliating defeat at ANUAL (June 1921) led ALFONSO XIII to seek a "savior" and Primo de Rivera to proclaim his availability for that role.

On September 13, 1923, Primo de Rivera overturned 50 years of civilian government and democratic process by proclaiming the military takeover of the state. After three months of escalating antagonisms between the cabinet and the high command, and with the clandestine encouragement of officers close to the king, he declared that he was acting against terrorism, financial incompetence, communist threats, impiety, regional extremism, the Moroccan problem, and reckless political opportunism in the Anual investigation. The prime minister could raise virtually no support against the incipient coup d'état (although most of the senior generals remained uncommitted to Primo de Rivera), and Alfonso XIII made it clear that he would not lift a finger to support his ministers. Following their inevitable resignation, Alfonso welcomed the captain general to MADRID and appointed him to head a military directorate with virtually unlimited authority. Primo de Rivera issued a public statement declaring that he was not a dictator and that no one could rightfully call him that. He was simply a man whose comrades had honored him by entrusting him with the mission of saving the fatherland. When a journalist asked him if he was imitating the recent fascist seizure of power in Italy, he responded that there was no need to copy the "great Mussolini." He pointed out that there were splendid precedents in Spanish history for military men intervening to end corruption and mismanagement by politicians. He spoke of nine men who would accomplish as much as possible in 90 days, a seeming promise of limited disruption of constitutional norms that did much to reassure the public.

The regime of Primo de Rivera did in fact turn out to be a dictatorship, and it lasted for years rather than months. Although the military directorate was broadened to include civilian members in 1925, the constitution of 1876 was essentially discarded, and the elected Cortes (see CORTES) dissolved. Under the royal mandate Primo de Rivera ruled by decree, just as despotically as any contemporary dictator. Yet by comparison with most of them he was moderate in his tactics. There was little of the

General Miguel Primo de Rivera *(Library of Congress)*

brutality and persecution of dissidents that characterized, for instance, the Franco tyranny in later decades, to say nothing of those in Russia and Germany. Moreover many of his early programs were constructive. His termination of the war in MOROCCO in 1926 was praised by some as a sensible compromise between imperialism and abandonment, even though it disappointed some of his hard-line military colleagues. True to his oft-repeated pledge, he attacked bureaucratic waste and corruption while seeking to root out the traditional power of the caciques (local political bosses linked to the major parties). He pursued a course of modernization aimed at rendering the administrative apparatus more efficient and productive. In a country often regarded as one of the most backward in western Europe, he spent heavily on roads, bridges, and other public works to facilitate transportation and the growth of commerce.

While the dictator's positive achievements, to say nothing of his program of political stabilization, won the gratitude of the church, industrialists, and the propertied class in general, it was only a matter of time before disgruntled workers and politicians of the Left began agitating against him. There was an abortive uprising in 1929 organized by members of the old Liberal Party. Moreover the anarchist movement, which had deep roots in Spain, retained its capacity for what Primo de Rivera had stigmatized as "terrorism." Perhaps most serious of all was the specter of financial decline that loomed in Spain even before the onset of the worldwide depression.

By January 1930, his prestige fatally diminished, his support among army leaders eroded, and his health failing, Primo de Rivera submitted his resignation to the king. He withdrew to Paris, where he died two months later.

Alfonso XIII attempted to maintain the structure of the directorate under another general, but it soon had to be terminated. In 1931 the king followed the former dictator into exile, and a republic was proclaimed in Madrid. José Antonio Primo de Rivera, the general's son, attained brief political notoriety as founder of the semifascist party the FALANGE ESPAÑOLA in the 1930s, but it was his murder by leftists at the beginning of the SPANISH CIVIL WAR that turned him into an icon during the Franco era, long after his father's dictatorship had been forgotten.

With the passage of time Miguel Primo de Rivera has come to be recognized as one of the most significant figures in Spanish history. Linking the 19th-century tradition of military intervention with the contemporary political trends of 1930s Europe, he paved the way for the great national confrontation of the civil war years, the ascendancy of FRANCISCO FRANCO, and, in a sense, the ultimate triumph of democracy. Some would argue that Primo de Rivera was, despite his denials, indeed a dictator, but a better sort of dictator than Franco, the man often regarded as his political heir.

Puerto Rico

One of the Greater Antilles, with a total area of 3,423 square miles, Puerto Rico was visited by CHRISTOPHER COLUMBUS in 1493 on his second voyage to the New World. It was relatively neglected by Spain until the 17th century and was not fully developed as a colony until the late 1700s when its strategic importance to the defense of Spain's interests in the Caribbean led to the construction of massive fortifications encircling its capital, San Juan. With a strengthened garrison and the increase of a civilian population dedicated to the cultivation of sugar, tobacco, and coffee, Puerto Rico withstood foreign attacks and the revolutionary upheaval that swept the other colonies during the 1820s. During the 19th century, the "ever-loyal island" was free from the revolts that shook CUBA and the PHILIPPINE ISLANDS. Puerto Ricans were rewarded for their stability and moderation by the granting of autonomy in 1897. The statute that made them masters of their own internal affairs had barely gone into effect when the island was occupied by U.S. troops during the Spanish-American War. In December 1898, Puerto Rico was transferred to the ownership of the United States. It took more than 50 years for the island to regain something analogous to the self-government that it had been granted by Spain.

Q

Queipo de Llano, Gonzalo
(1875–1951)
Spanish soldier

An old-fashioned cavalry man who developed a surprising mastery of modern technology, Queipo de Llano became one of the best-known generals of the SPANISH CIVIL WAR without appearing on the battlefields. He first came to the attention of his compatriots in 1913 when, as a lieutenant colonel he led a squadron of horsemen in a charge that routed a much larger force of Moroccan raiders. The episode was made all the more dramatic by occurring at the site of ALCAZARQUIVIR, where Muslim forces had inflicted a decisive defeat on King SEBASTIAN I of Portugal. Ten years later, by now a brigadier general commanding the garrison of CEUTA, he reacted with undisguised hostility to the coup d'état of General MIGUEL PRIMO DE RIVERA. Neglected by the Primo dictatorship, which failed to offer him a promotion, he became deeply embittered and sponsored a journal, *Revista de las tropas coloniales,* which contained thinly veiled attacks on Primo's Moroccan policy. The publication was soon shut down by government order, and Queipo was placed on the inactive reserve list. By 1928 he was calling for the abolition of a monarchy that had allowed power to pass into the unworthy hands of Primo, and even after the latter's resignation in 1930, Queipo conspired against his successor. After the proclamation of the Second Republic in 1931 Queipo was rewarded for his zeal by being given the prestigious command of the First Division, based in MADRID. He was later moved into a seemingly important but actually nominal position as head of the president's military staff. As a prominent advocate of the republic he had expected to be made minister of war. By 1936 his list of grievances had grown and ranged from being passed over for high command in MOROCCO to the slights inflicted upon his in-law Alcalá Zamora by the Popular Front regime. Queipo de Llano joined the conspiracy against the republic being formed by General EMILIO MOLA.

When the revolt of the Spanish army broke out in July 1936, Queipo de Llano, based in SEVILLE, carried out an efficient seizure of power in ANDALUSIA and assumed command of the revolutionary Army of the South. Until December 1938 (when the civil war was drawing to a close) Queipo ruled this region as a virtual independent fiefdom, allied with the rest of the "crusade" led by FRANCISCO FRANCO but following a course very much of his own design. He disliked Franco's increasing reliance on the right-wing political parties and their militias and resisted their attempts to impose control in his zone. In that area he pursued a policy of socioeconomic development, public works, and public welfare that, to some of his allies, seemed dangerously liberal. He was, however, widely popular among the local population and gradually developed national recognition. All of Spain became regular listeners to the general's nightly radio broadcast, tuning in at 10:00 P.M. to hear him alternately berate the personal foibles and political aberrations of the Republican leaders and indulge in a mixture of paternalistic and folksy comments on a wide range of subjects. While most intellectuals considered Queipo's programs vulgar and outlandish, there was no doubt that he achieved a celebrity that was unprecedented in his use of the radio waves. The broadcasts furthermore gave him a recognition level to which he had always aspired.

By the time the war ended in early 1939 Queipo had been deprived of his radio pulpit and stripped of most of the civil authority that he had long held in the south. Worse yet he was passed over for any major recognition in his own professional career. The man who had always insisted that he was a straightforward, plain-spoken soldier and called for military rule in Spain was disgusted to find himself marginalized by fascist politicians and outranked by newly promoted nonentities. As usual he did not keep his opinions to himself, publicly rebuked Franco, and was dismissed from the army. Conciliatory efforts were made on his behalf by more prudent officers, and Franco relented, appointing him head of a special military mission to Italy. Queipo remained in Rome until 1942, increasingly frustrated and embittered by the emptiness of his assignments. He returned to Spain shortly before the collapse of Italy in World War II.

Queipo de Llano fought against many enemies during his career, most of them generated by his own temper and uncontrollable sense of resentment. He persisted in the delusion that "courage" and "forthrightness" would always be honored; instead, he suffered a career of what he perceived as rebuffs and exclusions at the hands of more sophisticated players in military and national politics. He remains an unforgettable figure, however, as the "radio general" of the Spanish civil war.

Quental, Antero de (1842–1892)
Portuguese writer and political activist
Turning against his aristocratic background and Catholic schooling, Quental became an advocate of social reform who denounced the privileged status of the hereditary nobility and the cultural dominance of the church. He was the leading spirit in the so-called Generation of 1870 movement that advocated an inspirational and cleansing mission for Portugal's writers and intellectuals. He expressed his revolutionary passion in *Odes modernas* (Modern odes, 1865) and organized a series of public lectures by like-minded young activists, notably EÇA DE QUEIRÓS. The failure of his agitation to stir feelings of guilt among the ruling class or to rouse the passive masses frustrated and depressed him. He was, moreover, open to the sneering criticisms of those who could point to his own privileged origins. Unable to find spiritual renewal in his Christian roots, he turned to Eastern religions, dabbled in marxism, and, for a time, advocated a pan-Iberian reform movement that would sweep away all the social and cultural dec-

adence that he believed had reduced Portugal and Spain to backward isolationism. His doubts and frustrations are clearly evident in the sonnets that he wrote in his last years. Finally, restless and exhausted in spirit, he committed suicide. For all that he had scorned the overblown romanticism of early 19th-century literature, Quental lived and ended his life like the most romantic of heroes.

Quevedo y Villegas, Francisco de
(1580–1645)

Spanish poet and novelist

Born to a wealthy and well-connected family, Quevedo was an impressive student at the Universities of Alcalá and Valladolid where he demonstrated skill in languages and poetry. His work is said to have been praised by FÉLIX LOPE DE VEGA and MIGUEL DE CERVANTES. Quevedo was, however, a restless and dissatisfied young man whose writing was rather an outlet for his resentment and embitterment that a work of pure art.

A dabbler in political intrigue as well as a critic of contemporary politics, he took part in a series of murky enterprises between 1613 and 1621 related to the viceregal tenure of his patron, the duke of Osuna, in Sicily and Naples. After spending some time in prison at the beginning of PHILIP IV's reign (perhaps due to fiscal irregularities in the administration of Italian revenues), Quevedo succeeded in ingratiating himself with the new king. Unable to restrain his satirical impulses, he offended the monarch and his chief minister, OLIVARES, with a political diatribe in 1639. The result was another period of imprisonment from which he was discharged in 1643 in broken health that soon led to his death.

Quevedo has been praised by critics for his amazing range of knowledge, his stylistic brilliance, and his satirical wit. With so many positive elements in his nature, he was, however, clearly a deeply resentful individual, whose attacks on other writers (most famously LUIS DE GÓNGORA) and inability to stay out of political trouble envenomed his human relationships. Quevedo was apparently tormented by the very breadth of his knowledge and understanding that the age in which he lived was one of decline, when the corruption and futility that underlay the golden façade of imperial Spain was destroying its greatness. He saw not the glory of its past but the sordidness of its present and the futility of its leaders' policies.

His most noted works are unsparing depictions of vice and depravity in which individuals such as the protagonist of his picaresque novel *Historia de la vida del buscon llamado don Pablos* (*Life and Adventures of Don Pablos the Sharper,* 1603–08) lie, cheat, and steal their way through life. Dating from the same early period but not published until the 1620s is satire *Los sueños* (*Dreams*). These volumes constitute a collective variation on the theme of Dante's *Inferno* as the reader is taken on a tour of the most repellent circles of society. Either in genuine moments of religious feeling or from a desire to avoid clerical censorship, Quevedo also wrote works couched in terms of Christian belief such as *Política de Dios* (Polity of God, 1626). It is not clear, however, that he found any prospect of a renovation of society in spiritual transformation. Commentators have called Quevedo the most pessimistic of all Spanish writers but have been unsure as to the source of this emotion. Bad relations with his mother, a crippled leg and weak eyesight, a failed marriage are among the explanations offered. It was, perhaps, simply his unusual capacity for realism that resulted in his mixture of revulsion and artistry.

R

Reconquista (Reconquest)

This term, developed relatively late in Spanish history, relates to the period 711–1492 and to the process by which Iberian Christians regained control of the peninsula from Muslim invaders (usually referred to as Moros, or Moors). The process of reconquest was neither continuous nor fully conscious, except in its later stages. As early as the defeat of the Muslims at the Battle of Covadonga (718) by the king of ASTURIAS, a Christian attempt was being made to halt further conquest by the invaders and recapture a modest amount of lost territory. There was, however, no ongoing drive to resist or repel the Moors. The fractured nature of Iberian political and physical geography made dealings with the local Muslim rulers a matter of regional priorities. There were extended periods of peaceful interaction followed by flare-ups that arose from specific issues. Indeed, Christian warriors venturing across the Pyrenees to promote a "crusade" against Islam in the mid-11th century found that their coreligionists in Iberia were not interested in an all-out onslaught followed by destruction and looting of Muslim towns. They seemed to prefer targeted operations and negotiated settlements. Frustrated by this preference for peaceful coexistence, the French and other would-be combatants soon turned their attention to crusading enterprises in the Middle East.

As for the concept of a grand vision embracing all the Christian people of Iberia in a recovery of the whole territory that had been overrun in the eighth century, there is very little substantial evidence of such an idea in the early Middle Ages. Leaders such as El Cid (Rodrigo Díaz de Vivar), who was later hailed as a champion of Christian liberation, or, in some versions, harmony among all the inhabitants of the peninsula, was essentially a local warlord who fought with or against the Moors according to his needs. When the western area that would evolve into the kingdom of Portugal finally expelled the Moors in the mid-12th century, the leaders of this movement showed little concern for their Spanish neighbors or the remaining Moorish presence in the rest of the peninsula. There were, to be sure, some visionary calls for a crusade, a war of liberation, or a restoration of the old Visigothic realm that preceded the 711 invasion. But these dated mostly from the very early Middle Ages and tended to emanate from the clergy rather than from the pragmatic ranks of lords and fighters.

Irregular and interrupted as the process was, it had produced by the beginning of the 15th century a shift in the balance of power. Thanks to internal quarrels among Muslim rulers and an increasing willingness among Christian kings to cooperate after they had gained control of their own dominions and reduced the number of petty Christian principalities, a clear prospect of victory had opened up. The political and military strength of the Moors had been confined to the area around GRANADA in the extreme south. With reconquest becoming a practicable mission, it began to be talked about as a serious goal. Once again, however, the competing ambitions of Christian monarchs weakened the cause. Instead of pooling their resources for one great final thrust against the Moors, the newly formidable states of CASTILE and ARAGON entered into a protracted struggle for dominance, in which Portugal and even the smaller kingdom of NAVARRE periodically intervened. Internal factionalism, revolts by magnates and their private armies, and the weakness of particular kings all contributed to the survival of Granada as an Islamic enclave.

The final stage of the Reconquista was not launched until the 1480s after ISABELLA I of Castile and her husband, FERDINAND V of Aragon, had become unchallenged rulers of Christian Spain. Their 10-year campaign was slowed by a few Moorish victories, but the implacable determination of the Christians had now been raised to such a pitch by leaders of church and state that scarcely a soldier or civilian could resist rhetorical exhortations to fulfill the demands of faith and patriotism. Isabella was the moving spirit in this enterprise, rallying, recruiting, and funding as her enemies were beaten back and finally forced to capitulate. The queen and her family entered the city of Granada in triumph in January 1492, and after more than seven centuries the Reconquista was accomplished. Over the next five centuries this fight to "liberate" Spain would take on a symbolic significance that far transcended the historical process itself. The Reconquista became the culminating achievement of the "old Spain," just as the "discovery" of the Americas in the same year would mark the beginning of the "new Spain's" attainment of greatness. In the Spanish national mythology the Reconquista would come to be seen as proof of God's special providence and of the destiny that he had marked out for Spain—to rule the world.

Rey, Fernando (Fernando Casado) (1917–1994)
Spanish actor

In a career that spanned more than 40 years, during which he became Spain's best-known film actor and attained international recognition, Rey followed a life path quite different from that anticipated. Born in La Coruña, GALICIA, to a well-to-do family (his original name was Fernando Casado), he was studying architecture in MADRID when the SPANISH CIVIL WAR began. Like his father, an army colonel, he fought for the Second Republic. On the losing side the family was reduced to poverty, and the young man, desperate for employment, answered an advertisement for movie extras in 1940. He progressed from walk-on parts to dubbing for foreign actors to increasingly important roles in the reviving Spanish movie industry. He worked with a series of prominent Spanish directors during the 1950s and '60s and experienced his greatest success in several of LUIS BUÑUEL's acclaimed productions: *Tristana* (1970), *The Discreet Charm of the Bourgeoisie* (1972), and

That Obscure Object of Desire (1977). His other films included Orson Welles's eccentric *Chimes at Midnight* (1966) and Carlos Saura's *Elisa, vida mía* (1977), for which he won the best actor award at the Cannes Film Festival. His roles displayed his full range, from period films, such as *Locura de amor* (1948), in which he played Spanish kings to his memorable appearance as a suave drug kingpin in *The French Connection* (1971) and its sequel (1975). Critics have described him as the epitome of the elegant but world-weary European gentleman, and he was certainly the best-known Spanish actor of his day. Appropriately he was named president of the Spanish Academy of Motion Picture Arts and Sciences in 1992, a title which he retained until the year of his death, in which he was also making what became his final film—the last of 150.

Riego y Núñez, Rafael del
(1784–1823)
Spanish military and political leader

Born in ASTURIAS and educated for the law, Riego joined the royal bodyguard regiment in 1807, fought against the French invaders in the following year as commander of an Asturian unit, and was captured by the enemy. He spent the next five years as a prisoner in France where he appears to have embraced the liberal ideology generated by the French Revolution. After escaping from his captors he joined a force of exiles in Great Britain and returned to Spain to take part in the liberation of his country. Rewarded for his loyalty by a colonelcy under the Bourbon restoration, he soon became disillusioned with the reactionary policies of FERDINAND VII. On January 1, 1820, he launched the first of what would be a long series of *pronunciamientos* (military revolts) in Spanish history by leading his troops in a mutiny at CÁDIZ. Refusing to embark for repressive operations against the rebellious Spanish colonies in the Americas, Riego and his comrades declared their commitment to the liberal constitution of 1812. As he marched north, raising fresh outbursts of mutiny on the way, Riego precipitated a liberal revolution that would introduce the Trienio Constitucional ("Constitutional Trienium"), a period of liberal government in Spain from 1820 to 1823. Even before the forces of Riego and their adherents reached MADRID Ferdinand VII had appointed liberal ministers and vowed to rule in accord with the 1812 constitution. Riego served successively as captain general of GALICIA and ARAGON and was elected president of the Cortes (see CORTES). When the conservative forces of Europe supported an invasion by a French royalist army ("the 100,000 sons of St. Louis") in 1823 to crush Spanish liberalism, Riego led the resistance. Betrayed, captured, and executed, he remained an iconic figure throughout the 19th century, and the song sung by his soldiers in 1820 became known as the "Himno de Riego" (Riego's hymn). During the period of the Second Republic (1931–39) the "Himno de Riego" became Spain's national anthem.

Rivas, Ángel de Saavedra, duque de (1791–1865)
Spanish writer

After fighting against the French invaders of Spain during the PENINSULAR WAR and following the restoration of FERDINAND VII, Saavedra (then still heir to the dukedom of Rivas) was denounced for his liberal sympathies and obliged to flee the country. Living abroad for 10 years (and supporting himself by his skill as a painter) he embraced the literary romanticism then flourishing in most of Europe. At home again in 1834 and now duque de Rivas, he composed the drama *Don Álvaro; o, La fuerza del sino* (*Don Álvaro, or the Force of Fate*), which was premiered in 1835 to tremendous enthusiasm. The play quickly became known throughout the Continent and, among other works, inspired the plot of Verdi's opera *La forza del destino*.

Within a few years of his success with *Don Álvaro* Rivas was forced into exile again because of his political opinions, although by this time he had become a conservative, now the unfashionable point of view. After his second period of exile Rivas settled down to an extended period of public honors and respect, holding several ambassadorships, as well as the presidency of the legislature and the Council of State. At the time of his death he was president of the Spanish Royal Academy.

Although none of the other plays or poems of Rivas possessed the intrinsic merit of *Don Álvaro* or earned the vast applause that it gained, he is regarded as the virtual founder of Spanish romanticism. His *Romances históricos* (Historic ballads, 1841) and *Leyendas* (Legends, 1826–1847) retold many medieval tales and legends in modern literary form. His *El moro expósito* (The foundling Moor, 1834) is a particularly notable rendition of a story growing out of the famous epic of the seven infantes de Lara.

Rocroi, Battle of (1643)

In 1635 the Thirty Years' War (1618–48) had entered its final phase as Spain opened hostilities with France. The Spanish HABSBURG dynasty provided increasingly aggressive support to its Austrian kinsmen and by 1643 seemed to be gaining the advantage. In the spring of that year the governor of the Spanish Netherlands (present-day Belgium) ordered a large-scale attack on northern France. The governor himself, Francisco de Melo (a Portuguese noble in the service of Spain), laid siege to the fortified town of Rocroi, a key defensive position. By late May 1643 more than 20,000 troops were confronting the small garrison of Rocroi. A French force of about equal size advanced under the young duc d'Enghien, moved to the relief of the fortress, and confronted the besiegers across a broad plain flanked by wooded ground that provided cover for flanking attacks. Over several days the Spaniards attempted to hold the French at bay until a major reinforcement could arrive to tip the balance in their favor. Each side scored partial victories, but the deciding moment came when Enghien personally led a daring cavalry maneuver around the flank of the Spanish center, taking the TERCIOS in the rear and forcing them to endure attacks from front and rear simultaneously. The greater part of Spain's troops were killed or captured, including some notable commanders. De Melo escaped to find refuge with the belated reinforcement column but ordered a general retreat.

Although the Franco-Spanish war would continue for several more years, historians generally agree that France's decisive victory at Rocroi marks the end of Spain's long military dominance in Europe and the shift in political mastery of the Continent from Spain to France.

Rodrigo, Joaquín (marqués de los Jardines de Aranjuez) (1901–1999)
Spanish composer

Rodrigo triumphed over blindness that began in childhood to become not only a master of the piano but the leading Spanish composer of his generation. He studied under MANUEL DE FALLA and other masters in Paris and settled permanently in his native land after the SPANISH CIVIL WAR. It was in Spain that he premiered, in 1941, the work that earned him his greatest fame, the *Concierto de Aranjuez,* a concerto for guitar and orchestra inspired by the royal palace and gardens near MADRID. In addition he composed more than 150 other pieces for solo instrument or orchestra, many of them inspired by Spanish folklore and history. The prolific composer also produced film scores, light operas, and dozens of songs as well as venturing into many other musical genres. He was, for more than 30 years, professor of music at the University of Madrid, where he held an academic chair named in honor of his mentor, Falla. The recipient of many honors, he was particularly proud of the title bestowed upon him by King JUAN CARLOS I, in 1991, marqués de los Jardines de Aranjuez (marquis of the Aranjuez Gardens).

Rodrigues, Amália (1920–1999)
Portuguese singer

Millions of people around the world who knew nothing else about Portugal knew the word *fado* ("fate"). The distinctive expression of sorrow, longing, and ultimate hope that for centuries had constituted the nation's characteristic song genre, it survived all the vicissitudes of the 20th century, just as did the Portuguese people. During her long professional career Rodrigues represented the ultimate expression of *fado.* In stage concerts during the 1930s, on the radio in the 1940s, on television (first in the United States) in the 1950s, and in films thereafter, she became, for a global audience, the personification of Portugal's soul. A striking combination of artistic technique and personal presence, the intense, black-clad singer made her last public appearance at the 1998 international exposition in LISBON. Her death in the following year precipitated a heartfelt flood of grief and public tributes. Following her death, marked by three days of national mourning, the assembly voted to place her remains in the National Pantheon in the company of kings and heroes. Although Portugal had long since abandoned monarchy, for her compatriots and international admirers, Rodrigues was not only the "Queen of *Fado*" but also the "Queen of Portugal."

Rodríguez Zapatero, José Luis (1960–   )
Spanish politician

The grandson of an army officer who was executed for refusing to join the Franco uprising, Zapatero (as he is commonly called) came naturally to a position on the Left. A graduate of the University of León and a lecturer there in constitutional law, he was won to the Socialist cause when he attended a speech by the party's then leader, FELIPE GONZÁLEZ. He joined the party in 1979, was elected to parliament (its youngest member) in 1986, and was recognized as an attractive and rising figure, although he had not attained ministerial rank by the time of the Socialists' downfall in 1996. Being unconnected with the scandals and failures of the later González administration was, however, perhaps an advantage, and he brought "clean hands" to the party leadership when he was elected to that office in 2000.

As the Socialists had failed to regain power in the parliamentary election of 2000, Zapatero made promises for the following election that included relief of unemployment, increased support for education, subsidies for new housing, and a pledge to work more sympathetically with regional autonomists. These failed to improve his party's position in local elections; however, in 2004, as the time drew near for the national decision on whether the outgoing conservative leader, JOSÉ MARÍA AZNAR, would be followed by his hand-picked successor, a totally unexpected event changed the political situation. The terrorist attack on railroad passengers in MADRID and its vicinities in March of that year and widespread belief that the incumbent government had tried to shift blame from Islamic militants to Basque separatists led to voter repudiation of Aznar's party and a parliamentary majority for the Socialists and their allies.

Zapatero was installed as prime minister and immediately responded to widespread public demand by withdrawing Spanish forces from the U.S.-led coalition that had occupied Iraq. Zapatero would henceforth have to demonstrate that he was not afraid of Islamic terrorists by vigorously punishing the perpetrators of the Madrid attack. His announced goal of reestablishing Spanish cooperation with the majority of the European Union countries was generally well received and the cooling of relations with Washington did not seem to bother most

Spaniards. The public was less sure about his initiatives on immigration (particularly the ever-mounting number of new arrivals from North Africa), and his proposal to ease the legalization of resident status for illegal residents was widely perceived as imprudent. In any event, when Zapatero responded to the December 2004 earthquake and tsunami disaster in the Indian Ocean region with the largest initial pledge of aid from any country, Spaniards knew that their new prime minister shared at least one characteristic with all of his predecessors: a determination to assert a global presence and a global status for his nation. That he also shared his predecessors' determination to reject the pretensions of BASQUE NATIONALISM was demonstrated in January 2005. In response to a new declaration by the Basque regional legislature of their fundamental right to sovereignty, Zapatero declared that their claim had no basis in law, was a threat to the unity of the Spanish nation, and could only injure the interests of the Basque people.

Rojas, Fernando de (1465–1541)
Spanish writer

The known facts of this author's life are few and much disputed. A university graduate who subsequently practiced law, he is believed to have been of a converso family (his parents were ostensibly forced to abandon Judaism in favor of Christianity). Perhaps due to discrimination he left his original home in CASTILE and settled in Talavera, where he married, prospered, and evidently served for a time as mayor. He is generally acknowledged to be the author of the work known as *La Celestina*. This "dialogue novel" published in 1499 is esteemed by many critics to be second only to the *Don Quixote,* of MIGUEL DE CERVANTES, in the pantheon of Spanish literature. It has been variously described as the first novel published in Spain, or perhaps even anywhere in Europe. It is certainly strikingly different in its use of distinctive characters, each with his or her own language appropriate to social class and role. This alone sets it apart from earlier European literature, mostly versified and undifferentiated in its language. Indeed, it has been hailed as the first truly modern work of literature and the first distinctive literary product of the Renaissance. Scores of Spanish editions were published during the 16th century alone, and it was translated into all the major European languages during that time. Many writers, including William Shakespeare and Cervantes himself, are believed to have been influenced by it.

Originally titled the *Comedia* (later *Tragicomedia*) *de Calisto y Melibea,* after its doomed young lovers, the book soon became known as *La Celestina* after the memorably amoral old woman who facilitates the contact between the lovers and is the true central character of the story. Along with Calisto's servants and their girlfriends, La Celestina provides an insight into the mentality, class conflicts, and personal aspirations of the lower orders in Renaissance Spain, in sharp contrast to the high-flown rhetoric of Calisto and Melibea.

La Celestina (which has sometimes been described as a drama rather than a novel) is not merely the forerunner of modern Spanish literature but a work of originality and distinctive artistic virtues in its own right. It is all the more ironic, therefore, that its author has remained so shadowy a figure.

Rojas Zorrilla, Francisco de
(1607–1648)
Spanish dramatist

Born in TOLEDO, the son of a minor officer, Rojas Zorrilla had an intermittent career as a university student and then settled in MADRID (1631) and devoted himself to literary activities. His facility as a poet first gained him access to court circles, and his ability to work well with others made him the collaborator of CALDERÓN DE LA BARCA and other leading dramatists of the period in a substantial number of works for the stage. In 1635, now working largely on his own, he produced no less than seven plays, and his status, as well as his income, rapidly rose.

Rojas was often regarded as more rigorous in the moral standard reflected in his plays than were some other dramatists, though he could introduce a tolerant note, as when he allowed a seduced wife to be forgiven and reconciled with her husband in *Cada cual lo que le toca* (To each his own), much to the surprise and indignation of many Madrid playgoers. He enjoyed satirizing fools rather than miscreants and is the principal creator of the *figurón* character in the 1645 play *Entre bobos anda el juego* (Gaming among fools). This "pompous fool" type would be a recurrent presence in later Spanish drama, as well as in that of other countries.

Ironically Rojas is best known for *Del rey abajo ninguno* (None below the king), published under circumstances that have raised doubts about its authorship. While his untimely death contributed to the uncertainty, it is now generally accepted that he is the author of this drama in which a nobleman, García del Castañar, living far from the court as a farmer, is affronted by a visiting courtier's attempted seduction of his wife. García has been led to believe that the would-be seducer is the king, traveling incognito, and he must therefore contain his indignation out of deference to the monarch. When García learns the truth, he confronts and slays the courtier, on the ground that no one below the rank of the king himself may ignore the family honor of another. In this classic exposition of the fundamental principles of Spanish society the author expounds one of the basic themes of SIGLO DE ORO drama.

Rueda, Lope de (1510–1565)

Spanish playwright

Born in ANDALUSIA, where he seems to have been apprentice in the goldsmith's trade, Rueda was evidently entranced by visiting Italian companies and embarked upon a life in the theater. Over many decades he traveled across Spain as actor-manager and author. Although he wrote a number of full-length plays based upon the Italian *commedia,* these were only ephemeral in their impact. His chief contribution to Spanish literature was the *paso,* a short play designed to fill the interval between the acts of longer productions or sometimes to be grouped as a series of scenes. They were characterized by stock characters, familiar situations from everyday life, broad humor and slang expressions, and a kind of homely wit/wisdom. Rueda's *pasos* were performed before audiences of every rank, from the monarch down to the proletarian, and represented a kind of national frame of reference for entertainment that lacked the universality and lofty philosophizing of more high-flown drama. Rueda was the creator of a popular theater and the audience for such presentations that made it possible for his more ambitious successors to fulfill their much larger aspirations as playwrights.

There is an ample record of situations, comic figures, and theatrical devices created by Rueda and a plentiful roster of the names and plots of his *pasos.* Many of his basic ideas were borrowed from earlier writers or well-worn comic anecdotes. Exact texts for his compositions, original or otherwise, have not always been preserved. It can be said with some certainty that Rueda's most famous *paso* is *Las aceitunas* (The olives, 1548) in which the arguments between a husband and wife over their prospective earnings from an olive grove whose first trees he has just planted prefigures generations of satire about the folly of fantasizing about wealth that you have yet to acquire.

S

Sá de Miranda, Francisco de
(1481–1558)

Portuguese writer

A major literary figure in the emergence of Renaissance culture in Portugal, Sá de Miranda belonged to a family of northern aristocrats. After attending the University of Lisbon he traveled in Italy, where he acquainted himself with Italian poetic forms, then scarcely known in his native land. He may have taken part in some of the imperial military and commercial enterprises with which most of the Portuguese gentry were then preoccupied but by the late 1520s was devoting himself primarily to writing. His frank criticism of Portuguese society reveals a dissatisfaction with its comparative lack of sophistication and materialism. He saw his own particular mission as the introduction of literary refinements and forms already established in other countries among a population still largely committed to traditional literary forms and subject matter. His *Estrangeiros* (The foreigners, 1527) was evidently the first Portuguese prose comedy in the classical style. His *Cleopatra* (1550), which has survived only in a fragmentary state, was probably the first Portuguese classical tragedy. He also wrote epistolary verse (*Cartas*) and a canzone in the Italian form, "Fabula do Mondego." Most critics regard the eclogue, "Basto," as his finest work, although others favor the *Cartas* or several satires, all of these based upon Italian models. Sá de Miranda was Portugal's "Renaissance man" in the fullest sense of the term.

Sagasta, Práxedes Mateo
(1825–1903)

Spanish statesman

Already active in progressive politics during the 1850s, Sagasta took a leading part, along with General JUAN PRIM, in the overthrow of ISABELLA II in 1868. He served as prime minister under the Italian prince who was elected to replace her as AMADEO I and was also a cabinet member under the First Republic. Sagasta withdrew from public life after the Bourbon restoration of 1875.

Emerging as the leader of the new Liberal Party in 1880, Sagasta returned to the premiership in 1885 and repeatedly held that office in rotation with the conservative chief ANTONIO CÁNOVAS DEL CASTILLO until the latter's death in 1897. Confronted with a deteriorating situation in CUBA, Sagasta offered the rebels there a statute of autonomy but was unable to avert the loss of the island in the catastrophic 1898 war with the United States. Although Sagasta would continue to lead the country until 1902, he inevitably shared the blame for the loss of Spain's remaining colonies with Cánovas, who had done so much to provoke American enmity. Like his conservative rival, Sagasta was also blamed for the cynical policy of rotating Liberals and Conservatives in control of the government that undercut constitutionalism and produced the political sterility that frustrated the development of Spanish democracy.

St. Quentin, Battle of (1557)

This climactic battle of the ITALIAN WARS (1494–1559) was fought in August 1557. The seemingly inexhaustible determination of successive French monarchs to resist Spain's claims to the mastery of Europe had continued through decades of campaigns, truces, and treaties. Henri II had followed in the footsteps of his predecessors by supporting the enemies of CHARLES I in the latter's role as Holy Roman Emperor Charles V. After the emperor's settlement with the German Protestant princes and his weary abdication in 1556, PHILIP II ascended the Spanish throne, and the imperial crown passed to the Austrian branch of the House of HABSBURG. Henri II agreed to a cessation of hostilities but was clearly waiting for an opportunity to renew France's rivalry with Spain. The new pope, Paul IV, offered him such an opportunity when he proposed an alliance to curb Spanish pretensions in Italy. Their plans were disrupted when Philip II launched a powerful attack against French forces, moving to protect the papal dominions. The Spanish monarch then began assembling a large multinational force to deliver a blow that he hoped would eliminate the French challenge once and for all. The army that he assembled in the Burgun-

dian Netherlands in summer 1557 included not only Spanish and Burgundian units but also a large contingent of English troops supplied by his wife, Queen Mary (the Tudor sovereign who had temporarily restored Catholic rule in England). He confided the chief field command to Emmanuele Filiberto, duke of Savoy, and the key role of leading the cavalry spearhead to the count of Egmont (in later years to be one of Philip's chief antagonists in the REVOLT OF THE NETHERLANDS). The Spanish army directed its advance on the northern French city of St. Quentin, to which a part of its forces laid siege. When the greater part of France's available troops had been drawn in to break the siege, they were attacked and overwhelmed by Philip's army on August 9, 1557. The victory was undeniable, with some of the leading French generals among the dead.

To commemorate this victory, on the feast of St. Lawrence, Philip pledged the building of a monastery church in Spain that would later grow into the great church-palace of San Lorenzo de EL ESCORIAL. Although the French attempted to continue the war for a few months more, the completeness of Spain's victory was finally acknowledged in the Treaty of Cateau-Cambrésis in 1559. Philip II had achieved that which his father had never been able to accomplish—Spain's mastery of Europe.

Salamanca

This city in northwestern Spain and the province that surrounds it are part of the old kingdom of LEÓN and are adjacent to Portugal. Inhabited by the Celt-Iberians and seized by Hannibal in the third century B.C. as the western outpost of the Carthaginian

Empire, the city was later captured by the Romans and occupied by Moorish conquerors in the early 700s. After the Christian reconquest (RECONQUISTA) of this region in the 12th century, Salamanca underwent a flurry of construction, including fortifications, towers, public buildings, and the first of its many churches. The medieval cathedral and its adjacent extension, completed in the early 1500s, are the city's most notable monuments, but its greatest fame arises from the university, founded in 1218. For the next four centuries the University of Salamanca ranked with Oxford, Paris, and Bologna as one of the great institutions of learning in all Europe. It had the special character of serving as a channel for the scientific and mathematical learning originating in the Middle East, bringing it to Western peoples. After the expulsion of the Muslims in 1492 and the rise of the SPANISH INQUISITION the intellectual freedom that had characterized Salamanca was steadily eroded by censorship and narrow adherents to Christian orthodoxy.

Salamanca was awakened from two centuries of torpor in 1811 when the duke of Wellington's army clashed with the French near the city. In the aftermath of the battle Salamanca was brutally sacked, and many of her architectural treasures were damaged or leveled. A promising revival of intellectual ferment and freedom occurred during the early years of the 20th century when MIGUEL DE UNAMUNO, Spain's greatest philosopher and rector of the university, cast his own warm glow to match the sunset tint of the ancient stone walls of what he called *"Salamanca dorada"* ("golden Salamanca"). But the onset of the SPANISH CIVIL WAR and Unamuno's own death brought an end to this era. Generalísimo FRANCISCO FRANCO set up his Nationalist headquarters at Salamanca in the early days of the war, and until his death nearly 40 years later the atmosphere remained oppressive. Contemporary Salamanca, however, shows promising signs of an enduring renaissance.

Salazar, António de Oliveira
(1889–1970)
Portuguese statesman

Originally intended for the priesthood, Salazar instead pursued a career in law. He received his doctorate at the University of Coimbra in 1914 and soon joined its faculty. Having earned a reputation as an economic theorist, he was offered the Finance Ministry as early as 1926 but did not accept it until 1928 with the guarantee of a free hand in reconstructing Portugal's disordered affairs. Through a combination of brilliant improvisation and ruthless authoritarianism he balanced the budget and made himself Portugal's indispensable man. In 1932 the president of the republic, realizing his own limitations, appointed Salazar prime minister with virtually unlimited power, a position he would hold for the next 36 years.

A pragmatic rather than dogmatic executive who understood the limitations in which Portugal found itself during the 1930s, Salazar combined Catholic cultural values and socioeconomic conservatism with the kind of nationalistic evocations that had to take the place of vanished glory. Although he founded the National Union as his "official" party in 1930 and crafted a new constitution in 1933 to enshrine his so-called New State, the corporate models upon which they are based fall short of full fascism. While understanding the importance of such interest groups as the church and the landed proprietors, he allowed them only limited access to power. In the same way the army was made to understand that it had to operate within a framework of budgetary and foreign policy reality. Intellectuals chafed under censorship, and leftists experienced harassment from the new secret police, but most Portuguese seemed to accept relative efficiency, as well as modest improvements in the country's infrastructure and industrial production, as a justification of Salazar's harsh medicine. Despite Portugal's evident sympathy with the Franco leadership during and after the SPANISH CIVIL WAR, its neutrality in 1939–45 was not seen in as dark a light as that of Spain's. LISBON served as an escape route for refugees not to mention a base for intelligence operations by all nations, and Salazar eventually made the AZORES available to the United States as an air base. Thus, while Spain was treated as a pariah following World War II, Portugal was admitted as a charter member of the North Atlantic Treaty Organization in 1949. American subsidies and rising prosperity elsewhere in Europe led to steadily expanding investment and an impressive growth in the country's economy through the 1950s.

As a new member of the United Nations (1955), Portugal was confronted by harsh criticism and aggressive pressures to dismantle its empire as Great Britain and France were already doing. Salazar's reply that the latest revision of the Portuguese constitution made the African and Asian outposts "overseas provinces" rather than colonies was greeted with derision and denunciation.

Salazar had committed precious resources to developing the overseas territories, extracting their natural wealth and encour-

aging settlement by European families. The thrust of his policy had been to turn a liability into an asset, transcending the incongruity of a 35,000-square-mile backwater ruling more than 800,000 square miles of mineral and agricultural potential. His greatest legacy to his nation was to have been the conversion of the world's oldest surviving colonial empire into a truly global New State.

For Salazar any concession to anticolonialism was unthinkable. The human and material resources of Portugal were poured into the military repression of revolt in the overseas provinces, disrupting the economic development programs at home that his more progressive advisers had been promoting. In the midst of his African war the dictator suffered a stroke, remaining incapacitated from 1968 until his death in 1970. The "genius" who had ruled the nation for 40 years was laid to rest in the National Pantheon in Lisbon, but his crusade went on.

Salvador   See BAHIA.

Sanjurjo, José (1872–1936)
Spanish soldier and political conspirator
Sanjurjo entered the Spanish army at an early age and fought in the 1898 war with the United States. He rose steadily in rank and reputation during the Moroccan campaigns of the early 1900s. In the aftermath of the disaster at ANUAL he was one of those who "rescued the honor of the army" and helped turn the tide against the insurgents. Sanjurjo was given much of the credit for the ultimate suppression of the rebellion in the Rif region, and journalists nicknamed

him "the Lion of the Rif." Sympathetic to the concept of military strongmen, he supported the dictatorship of General PRIMO DE RIVERA. Although not particularly devoted to the monarchy, he grew increasingly dissatisfied with the Second Republic after its proclamation in 1931. As commander of such paramilitary forces as the Civil Guard and the Border Guard, he found many opportunities to interact with other civilian and uniformed malcontents. In 1932 he took the lead in a mutiny that attempted to overthrow President MANUEL AZAÑA. The rising produced some street fighting in MADRID but quickly collapsed. The episode was already known as "the revolt of General Sanjurjo" when he and fellow conspirators were brought to trial, but although he was, not surprisingly, sentenced to death, the government chose to modify the punishment for the rebels. Sanjurjo's sentence was reduced to life imprisonment, and he was released in 1934 with the implication that he should go abroad.

Established in LISBON, Sanjurjo developed a network of conservative sympathizers extending from the SALAZAR regime of Portugal to the Mussolini dictatorship of Italy. His admirers in Spain saw him as the natural leader of a new and larger insurrection. As the planning moved toward the launching of a grand military revolt in 1936, Sanjurjo became increasingly impatient with FRANCISCO FRANCO, a general whom everyone insisted must be a part of their uprising. The arrogant Sanjurjo responded that the revolt would go ahead with or without "little Franco." When the Spanish army rose against the republic in July 1936, a plane was sent to Lisbon to convey Sanjurjo back home, where he was scheduled to become the chief of the new regime.

Despite warnings that the small plane was dangerously overloaded Sanjurjo insisted upon bringing aboard two large suitcases filled with splendid uniforms appropriate to a national leader. The craft crashed during takeoff, and Sanjurjo was killed. Rumors spread that he had been murdered by Republican agents or even jealous rivals, but the evidence indicates that Sanjurjo was the victim of his own vanity. Within a few months Franco would be proclaimed leader of the "new" Spain, a position he would hold for nearly 40 years, while Sanjurjo was consigned to historical footnotes.

San Martín, José Francisco de (1778–1850)
Spanish colonial rebel

Son of a Spanish military officer and colonial administrator, San Martín was born in the Viceroyalty of LA PLATA (present-day ARGENTINA) but spent his early years in the ancestral homeland. He served as an officer in Spain's campaigns against the North African Moors, the British in the changing alliances of the French revolutionary era, and the Portuguese in 1801. Returning to his birthplace, San Martín was caught up in the Argentine revolutionary movement that began in 1810. In little more that five years he and his fellow rebels had effectively overthrown Spanish rule in Buenos Aires and its adjacent provinces. The outlying provinces, however, were in danger of being attacked and subjugated from the royalist stronghold in PERU. San Martín earned his greatest military laurels by leading an expedition across the Andes and, in 1817, liberating CHILE, which he then handed over to the local nationalist commander, BERNARDO O'HIGGINS. As San

Martín moved on to a final confrontation with the Spaniards in Peru, the situation was complicated by the arrival of the liberator of northern South America, SIMÓN BOLÍVAR. In a meeting (1818) between these two great rebels, the exact content of which has never been revealed, San Martín was persuaded to withdraw, leaving the field to Bolívar. In a remarkable gesture of self-abnegation San Martín left Spanish America and spent the remainder of his life in Europe.

Santa Cruz, Álvaro de Bazán, marqués de (1526–1588)
Spanish admiral

The son of a highly successful and much honored naval commander, Bazán accompanied his father into battle at an early age and soon joined the royal service himself. For nearly 50 years he took part in all the major operations along Spain's Mediterranean and Atlantic coasts, rising steadily in reputation and rank. He was heavily involved in the campaigns against North African corsairs, helped break the siege of Malta in 1565, and delivered a crushing blow to the Turkish fleet at the BATTLE OF LEPANTO (1571). He bore a vast array of well-earned titles, of which marqués de Santa Cruz was only the most lofty. In naval rank he ultimately became admiral of the ocean sea, a title once held by CHRISTOPHER COLUMBUS and (perhaps more personally gratifying) by his own father. After the death of JOHN OF AUSTRIA, the king's half brother, there was no naval officer of comparable status in the service of PHILIP II. He was entrusted with the naval operations that secured the annexation of Portugal in 1580 and defeated all attempts to maintain an anti-Spain resistance in the AZORES. Santa Cruz was naturally selected to organize and lead the "Invincible ARMADA" that was envisioned as overwhelming the British Isles and making possible the triumph of Spain's supporters in France and the Low Countries. As Santa Cruz busied himself with preparations for this great enterprise during the latter part of 1587, the sheer complexity of logistics and a series of unanticipated disruptions in planning provoked Philip's impatience. The king sent his admiral, who had never before received anything but praise and honor for a lifetime of achievements, a harshly worded letter, in effect rebuking him for incompetence. Santa Cruz died suddenly in January 1588. According to traditional belief, the cause was the combined impact of humiliation and indignation.

Santayana, George (Jorge Agustín Nicolás Ruiz de Santillana) (1863–1952)
Spanish philosopher

Born in MADRID under the name Jorge Augustín Nicolás Ruiz de Santillana, Santayana was brought to the United States by his father at the age of nine due to certain family difficulties. He was educated at Harvard, becoming a member of the philosophy faculty and an associate of the leading American thinkers of his day. Although he would refer to himself as an American philosopher, he retained his Spanish citizenship and lived in Europe throughout most of his life, becoming a true cosmopolitan as he resided in Britain, France, and various parts of Italy. Santayana chose a reclusive life, staying for the most part in hotels, establishing no family ties, and in later life

George Santayana *(Library of Congress)*

severing his early academic connections. He sought to pursue his aesthetic and philosophical interests to the exclusion of mundane concerns, taking little interest, for example, in World Wars I and II. A prolific author, whose writings included poetry and a well-regarded novel (*The Last Puritan*, 1935), his primary concern was in the exposition of philosophical theories in the fields of aesthetics, the motivation of human actions and institutions, and variations on the concept of pragmatism. A number of his ideas won wide acceptance, although in later years he was criticized for the seeming contradictions in some of his arguments. For all of his self-proclaimed American

identity, Santayana was very much in a tradition of Spanish humanists that stretched back to the Renaissance. Among Santayana's significant works are *The Sense of Beauty* (1896), *The Life of Reason* (five volumes, 1905–06), *Scepticism and Animal Faith* (1923), *The Realms of Being* (four volumes, 1927–40), and *Dominations and Powers* (1951).

Santiago de Compostela

The most important religious site in Spain and, during the Middle Ages, ranked with Rome and Jerusalem as a destination of pilgrimages, the early history of Santiago de Compostela is interwoven with inconsistent and clearly legendary accounts of its origin. According to the most frequently cited version, Spain was visited shortly after the death of Jesus, by his apostle James, who was the first preacher of Christianity in the Iberian Peninsula. (Santiago is the Spanish equivalent of St. James.) The tradition asserts that the saint returned to the Holy Land, was martyred there, and was then carried back in a sarcophagus, transported by his followers to northwestern Spain. The account tells of a shepherd discovering his burial place hundreds of years later when he noticed a constellation of stars above the location (hence the name *campo stella*, or "field of stars"). The site was certified as a place of veneration by the clergy, and a chapel was erected there by the local ruler. What had been a mere village became, during the early Middle Ages, the major town in the region of GALICIA. After the original chapel was destroyed in a Muslim raid, an impressive cathedral was built in the 11th century to serve as the focus for religious ceremonies and visits by a growing number of pilgrims.

For hundreds of years the prestige of Santiago de Compostela was a source of pride to the Spanish nation, for St. James, whose remains were believed to be in their homeland, was the only one of the apostles to be buried in western Europe. Pilgrims made their way from many lands to pray for miraculous cures and divine blessings at the shrine. At least four distinct routes from various parts of Europe were known as pilgrimage roads to Santiago, the one that led from southern France across the Pyrenees being the most heavily traveled. The city, with its thousands of residents, was centered on the cathedral, which was frequently adorned and extended to accommodate worshippers. But there were also numerous lodging and dining houses as well as many workshops and vendors of relics and pious souvenirs clustered in the heart of the city. During the reign of ISABELLA I and FERDINAND V a university was established, and government buildings and aristocratic townhouses added to the impressiveness of the city. The premier military order of Spain, the Knights of Santiago, took their name and fame from the shrine, which throughout the RECONQUISTA was seen as playing an essential role in the expulsion of the Muslim invaders through the spiritual energies that it focused.

During the early modern period Santiago de Compostela became less of an international gathering place, as the unity of Christendom was shattered during the Reformation and the rivalries within the emerging European state system fed national antagonisms. The pilgrimage route from France still drew pilgrims, but the shrine itself became more intensely identified with Spain and the emotional loyalties of the Spanish people. By the early 21st century, as the population of the city approached 100,000 and political and economic factors affected its viability, there was still a significant flow of visitors, whether drawn by purely religious zeal or by touristic curiosity. Many foreigners committed to the long trek on foot across the mountains, often sleeping at humble youth hostels, to maintain a sense of personal discipline and a dedication to strenuous simplicity.

Santiago de Cuba, Battle of (1898)

This climactic action of the SPANISH-AMERICAN WAR took place at the city that had been the first colonial capital of CUBA (founded by DIEGO VELÁZQUEZ DE CUÉLLAR in 1514) and remained the major commercial and administrative center for the southeastern part of the island. After landing nearly 20,000 troops a few weeks earlier and advancing in conjunction with ongoing attacks by Cuban rebels, the U.S. forces arrived at Santiago on July 1, 1898. Although Spain had a large military presence in Cuba, many of her troops were tied down by action of the *guerrilleros* and exhausted by the seemingly endless struggle waged against them in this tropical climate. The few battles fought by Spanish soldiers against the advancing Americans were vigorously conducted but doomed by inferiority of numbers and firepower. These defensive actions culminated in the Battle for San Juan Hill in which the future American president Theodore Roosevelt gained his military laurels. The senior American commander, General William Shafter, immediately demanded the surrender of the city but was rebuffed by his Spanish antagonists, Linares and Toral. In the meantime the Spanish naval squadron under Admiral PASCUAL CERVERA, which had found shelter in the harbor of Santiago, was ordered to make a sortie against the massive U.S. naval forces waiting offshore. Their doomed effort was commenced on the morning of July 8 and ended within a few hours in the destruction or capture of Cervera's entire squadron. Deprived of covering fire from the Spanish warships and threatened with bombardment by American artillery both on land and sea, the garrison of Santiago yielded, and with it, the entire island of Cuba. The fall of PUERTO RICO in August and the mopping up of American operations in the PHILIPPINE ISLANDS, brought an end to the war. Spain's last imperial outpost in the Caribbean, like those in the Pacific, was no more.

São Tomé and Príncipe (São Tomé e Príncipe)

These two islands in the Gulf of Guinea on the Atlantic coast of Africa were acquired by Portugal during her 15th-century voyages aimed at discovering a water route to the Indies. The islands, with an area of 330 and 42 square miles respectively, were declared an "overseas province" of Portugal in 1951. In 1975, as part of the general abandonment of colonial rule, they became an independent republic.

Saragossa   See ZARAGOZA.

Saramago, José (1922–)
Portuguese writer

Born to a peasant family in the province of Ribatejo, he left school early to support himself as a mechanic and factory hand. Eventually he secured employment as a minor civil servant, moved into journalism and became deputy editor of a newspaper. Saramago was nearly 60 before he began a serious literary career but soon earned praise for his novels, as well as writings in other genres. An ardent but undisciplined communist and a "tolerant atheist," he provoked a controversy in 1991 when he published *O evangelho segundo Jesus Cristo* (*The Gospel According to Jesus Christ*), which conservatives regarded as a blasphemous version of the life of Christ. Disgusted that what he regarded as reactionary views persisted even in postrevolutionary Portugal, he moved to the CANARY ISLANDS. There he was both lionized by the Spanish regional authorities and involved in disputes with local militants. He did not return to Portugal until 1998 when the news that he had been awarded the Nobel Prize in literature made him a national hero. As the first Portuguese recipient of this prize, he has acquired a level of international recognition gained by few of his countryfolk.

Saramago's best-known work is undoubtedly *Baltasar and Blimunda* (1982), a fantastical novel set in 18th-century Portugal in which the protagonists travel widely— sometimes by flying—and institutions are satirized, with special mockery reserved for the church. Saramago also plays with history in *Historia do cerco de Lisboa* (*History of the Siege of Lisbon*, 1984), in which the alteration of one word in an account of a decisive medieval battle alters the entire fate of the nation. In *Todos os nomes* (*All the Names*, 1997) a record keeper becomes obsessed with pursuing one particular individual through mounds of archival material. The setting of *Ensaio sobre la cegueira* (*Blindness*,

1995) is a city (unnamed, as is the country in which it is located) where nearly all the inhabitants loose their eyesight, creating a complex pattern of personal tensions and social breakdown. These and other novels have been described as "magic realism" or even science fiction, but Saramago insists that they should not be assigned arbitrarily to some such genre, as they are all reflections of his consistent perceptions of the human condition. In the same way, whether the setting is specifically Portuguese or unidentified (with even the principal characters never named), he maintains that everything he writes is shaped by his thoughts and feelings about his native land. Perhaps the best guide to the mind and heart of Saramago remains his *Viagem a Portugal* (*Journey to Portugal,* 1981), a fascinating mixture of travel book, cultural history, and reflective memoir in which the author is constantly moving from one level of awareness to another as he travels about the country, recalling her past, commenting on her present and speculating about her future. Significantly he dedicates this volume to ALMEIDA GARRETT, the outstanding literary figure of early 19th-century Portugal, whose blending of political activism with poetic emotionalism may be seen as an anticipation of Saramago's own feelings about the beauties and shortcomings of Portugal.

Sarasate, Pablo de (1844–1908)
Spanish musician and composer
Born in Pamplona and variously hailed as Spain's greatest musician, the greatest violin virtuoso of his time, or the greatest violin virtuoso of all time, Sarasate began performing at age five and gave his first public concert at age eight. By 1859 he had attained an established reputation as a violinist that was dramatically confirmed by his performances during 1861 at the Crystal Palace in London, where all the wonders of the modern world, both in the arts and the sciences, attracted an international audience.

Sarasate's performances were characterized by their melodic and delicate nature that preserved their sheer beauty despite an amazing dexterity in handling his instrument and an unrivaled mastery of technique. A true phenomenon of the age, he traveled widely, attracting new admirers during a concert tour in the United States in 1889 crowned by his triumph in New York City. Some of the greatest composers of the day, including Antonín Dvorák and Camille Saint-Saëns, wrote violin works specifically for him. His own original compositions included the so-called *Zigeunerweisen* (Gypsy airs), perhaps the most frequently performed of his pieces and a perennial favorite of both violin virtuosi and their audiences. Sarasate's career ended amid general mourning when he died while visiting Biarritz in the Basque region of France.

Sartorius, José Luis (conde de San Luis) (1820–1871)
Spanish statesman
Born in SEVILLE to a family of Polish origin and humble circumstances, Sartorius made his way to MADRID as a young man. His quick wits and fertility of imagination gained him a foothold in journalism and won the patronage of JUAN BRAVO MURILLO, an increasingly important political figure. Sartorius was enabled to found a newspaper, *El*

Heraldo (in 1842), which became the mouthpiece of those opposed to the ascendancy of General BALDOMERO ESPARTERO. By 1843 the young editor had been elected to the Cortes (see *CORTES*). By October 1847 he had attached himself to another political general, RAMÓN NARVÁEZ and served as minister of *gobernación* until 1851. Sartorius used the wide range of responsibilities included within his portfolio to pursue reforms in such areas as the development of forestry and the creation of a school of engineering. Modernization of primary education also received his support, as did the upgrading of police training and procedures and the introduction of civil-service legislation to replace patronage by demonstrated competence. He was also responsible for major improvements in Madrid's public works, notably the construction of the Teatro Real. Sartorius won the particular gratitude of Spain's literary community by introducing laws to protect intellectual property rights so that playwrights and poets could secure a return on their writings. A number of those who benefited from his enlightened activities contributed to a volume of tributes that was published in his honor. After a period of political reversal Sartorius ascended to the presidency of the Council of State in 1853, a post he held until the major military coup of July 1854 forced him from office. He introduced a stream of legislation in this new post, including court reform and improvement of communications. The energy and honesty of the young statesman proved more exhausting than impressive to many of his colleagues. Furthermore his self-confidence was perceived by some as vanity or arrogance. Provoked by opposition within the Cortes, the conde de San Luis (the title that had lately been bestowed upon Sartorius) dissolved the legislature. His conduct provoked a series of military revolts during early 1854, and the major rebellion in June of that year forced him from office. Sartorius would subsequently serve as ambassador to Rome and presided over the final parliamentary session of the reign of Queen ISABELLA II (1868).

Fernando Sartorius y Chacón (1869–1926), second count of San Luis, had a more modest political career than his father, although he served as ambassador to LISBON and held ministerial office.

Sebastian I (Sebastião I) (1554–1578)
king of Portugal

After succeeding his grandfather, John III, Sebastian remained under a regency until 1568. Under intense clerical tutelage Sebastian became an ardent champion of Catholicism and a committed advocate of war against Islam. Following several earlier attempts that were abandoned he assembled a crusading army that included most of the available fighting men and many of the nobles of Portugal. He increased this force by hiring mercenaries and even diverted into his service a papal expedition bound to aid the rebels in Ireland when its transports stopped at Lisbon for repairs. Under his personal command the crusaders formed a temporary alliance with one of the rival contenders for the Moroccan throne and marched into the interior of the country to confront the other Moroccan monarch. After a fruitless and exhausting trek through the desert they were attacked and totally defeated in the so-called Battle of the Three Kings at ALCAZARQUIVIR

(August 4, 1578). Sebastian was presumably killed in this encounter and his uncle Henrique was proclaimed king. After the latter's death in 1580, the HOUSE OF AVIZ became extinct, and PHILIP II of Spain took the Portuguese throne.

Sebastian was periodically reported to have escaped death at Alcazarquivir, and pretenders claiming to be the lost king appeared at intervals over many decades. This identification of the lost monarch with Portuguese aspirations for freedom from Spanish rule and the recovery of national dignity persisted as the cult of "Sebastianism" over several centuries and was even transferred to late 19th-century Brazil.

Segovia

Situated on the Castilian plain some 50 miles northwest of MADRID, Segovia was in earlier days a royal residence and more recently has become a favorite place of excursion for those who reside in or have come to visit the modern marvels of the present-day capital. A strategic outpost of the Roman Empire, it preserves the aqueduct built by the former masters of Hispania in the first century A.D. The size and elegance of construction of this monument of antiquity have made it one of Spain's national icons. Segovia fell to the Moors in the early eighth century and by the beginning of the 13th century had succumbed to

The Alcazar of Segovia *(Library of Congress)*

the RECONQUISTA. The walled city that emerged from this period and the towering cathedral are relics of its medieval importance as a seat of government. The fairytale castle known as the Alcazar of Segovia, is, however, the product of 19th-century reconstructive fantasy after the original citadel was destroyed by fire in 1862. In the days when the sovereigns of CASTILE resided there, Segovia was the scene of such notable events as the formal recognition of ISABELLA I as queen in 1474, the agreement between her and her husband, FERDINAND V of ARAGON, as to the sharing of power, and the revolt staged by leading citizens of Segovia in 1477. The deposed mayor of Segovia, Alonso Maldonado, and his ally, the bishop, attempted to hold the daughter of Isabella hostage while her mother was away waging war on the Portuguese. Learning of this conspiracy, accompanied only by two courtiers, she galloped the whole distance from Tordesillas to confront the rebels. The townspeople were so overawed by the outraged mother that they deserted their leaders, who fled from Segovia.

Segovia's proximity to Madrid caused its subordination to the new capital and guaranteed that it would preserve a degree of tranquillity. In the early 18th century the Bourbon kings established a miniature palace of Versailles in La Granja at San Ildefonso, near Segovia. This served as their summer residence for several generations. Segovia itself was sacked by the French invaders during the PENINSULAR WAR and captured by the Nationalists during the SPANISH CIVIL WAR. Spared the devastation brought on so many quarters of Spain during its violent modern history, Segovia survives largely intact as an icon of its past glories.

Segovia, Andrés (1893–1987)
Spanish musician

When Segovia began to study music, the guitar was almost universally dismissed as a vulgar popular instrument, suitable only for entertainment in cafés. Although he originally studied the piano and cello at the music school in GRANADA, he could not be diverted from his instinctive and passionate love for the guitar. No suitable instructor being available, he essentially taught himself to play the instrument. In so doing he not only won respect for the guitar as a serious instrument with potential for highly refined musicality but also transcribed works from the classical repertoire that had originally been written for other instruments. These transcriptions alone amounted to 150 pieces, in addition to his original

Andrés Segovia *(Library of Congress)*

work. As his skills and serious commitment developed, Segovia traveled widely in Europe and South America, becoming by the early 1920s internationally renowned. His influence was projected through a series of pupils who came to Spain to learn from him and who went on to become celebrated musicians. In addition many prominent composers throughout the 20th century created music for the guitar at the instigation of Segovia. He became in effect the apostle of classical guitar music, and the instrument owes its renaissance to his inspiration and advocacy. The "grand old man" continued to perform and teach into his 90s, leaving a unique legacy to Spain and the world.

Serra, Junípero (Miguel José Serra) (1713–1784)

Spanish missionary

Born on MAJORCA, Serra entered the Franciscan order in his youth. After ordination to the priesthood, he took the name Junípero. Serra spent his early clerical career preaching and teaching on Majorca. In 1749 he was sent to NEW SPAIN, where he expanded his activities to working with the Indians.

The long neglect of New Spain's outpost on the Pacific coast had opened the way to Russian colonial settlements in northern CALIFORNIA. JOSE DE GÁLVEZ, the de facto ruler of the viceroyalty, decided in 1769 to dispatch an expedition for the assertion of an effective Spanish presence in California. Father Serra was placed in charge of missionary activity aimed at converting the indigenous peoples of the region. Traveling with other priests, as well as soldiers and civilian colonists, he made the long journey to the western coast of North America and established the Mission of San Diego in 1769. He subsequently established the Missions of San Carlos Borromeo (1770), San Antonio de Padua (1771), San Gabriel Arcangel (1771), San Luis Obispo (1772), San Juan Capistrano (1776), San Francisco de Asís (1776), Santa Clara de Asís (1777), and San Buenaventura (1782). Serra was appointed "president" of the missions in California and supervised the successful conversion and instruction of thousands of Indians. Together with the civilian and military presence established during the period of his religious activity, Serra laid the groundwork for the belated transformation of California from a wilderness into an extension of Spanish colonial civilization and ended the threat of Russian seizure of California.

Serra has been called the "Apostle of California" and recognized as one of the greatest and most successful of Spanish missionaries. His methods, combining religious zeal with practical measures and constant pursuit of his goals, are reminiscent of the career of ST. TERESA OF ÁVILA. Serra has been beatified for his life and work and is a candidate for canonization.

Serrano y Domínguez, Francisco (1810–1885)

Spanish soldier and statesman

Son of a general and trained in the corps of cadets, Serrano received his first commission while still an adolescent and demonstrated his personal courage in the First Carlist War. By 1840 he was already a major general, deputy commander of the VALENCIA region, and member of the Cortes (see *CORTES*). During the next 40 years he would enjoy a remarkable career in the inter-twined worlds of Spanish politics and military life. Following the overthrow of the ESPARTERO regency in 1843 Serrano gained an increasing ascendancy over the young queen ISABELLA II, attaining promotions in both the army and the legislature, with their relationship becoming the object of scandalous rumors. After a series of intrigues Serrano emerged as an ally of LEOPOLDO O'DONNELL when the latter seized control of the government in 1856. Having served as ambassador in Paris, Serrano was made captain general of CUBA in 1860 and while in that post brought about the reoccupation of Santo Domingo (DOMINICAN REPUBLIC) by Spain. For those services Serrano was created duque de la Torre after his return home.

Taking the leadership of the Liberal Union Party following the death of his colleague O'Donnell, Serrano plunged into a new round of political maneuvers that led to his banishment to the CANARY ISLANDS, from which he escaped to lead an insurrection in 1868 against Isabella. Following the deposition of the queen, Serrano became successively head of the provisional government, regent of the realm, and prime minister after the new ruler, AMADEO I, took the throne in 1871.

Although Serrano would continue to play a prominent part in Spanish public life during the 1870s, the ultimate restoration of the Bourbons in 1875 marked the beginning of his eclipse. His previous maneuvers, regarded by some as patriotic initiatives and others as opportunistic treachery, suggested to ALFONSO XII that it was time for the general's retirement. In an era when army leaders kept the country in almost perpetual turmoil, few could compare with Serrano in his perennial readiness to make the destiny of Spain conform to his own desires.

Serveto, Miguel (Michael Servetus) (1511–1553)

Spanish theologian and physician

Born at Villanueva in NAVARRE, this most celebrated Spanish "heretic" of the Reformation era was variously known as Miguel Servet, Michael Servetus, and Michel Villenueve, his pseudonym. He came of a well-to-do family and was able to pursue studies in theology, medicine, and law in France, after mastering Latin, Greek, and Hebrew in Spain. Appointed secretary to the confessor of CHARLES I (Holy Roman Emperor Charles V), he also spent time in Germany, where he met prominent leaders of the Protestant Reformation. A stay in Switzerland stimulated his interest in radical religious ideas but earned him the hostility of local reformers. He returned to France in 1536 and earned a doctorate in medicine. Most of his time thereafter was spent in France practicing as a physician, editing editions of learned works, and writing the excursions into heretical theology that earned him his greatest fame.

An audacious thinker who pursued his philological speculations wherever they took him, Serveto became an anti-Trinitarian who denied the divinity of Christ and published a treatise on a whole series of other "errors" that he found in Christianity. He did not hesitate to quarrel, in person or in writing, with all the leading personalities in both Catholic and Protestant theology. Calvin, in particular, was the object of his scorn and became his implacable enemy.

His books, including *De trinitatis erroribus* (On the errors of the Trinity, 1531), *Dialogorum de Trinitate* (Dialogues on the Trinity, 1532), and *Christianismi restitutio* (Restoration of Christianity, 1553), provoked increasing outrage, as did even those writings that dealt with medical matters. In June 1553 he was arrested by French ecclesiastical authorities, and some of his writings were burned publicly. Serveto, anticipating a similar fate for himself, managed to escape from France. However, with the recklessness that had always characterized his decisions, he chose to flee to Geneva, where his worst enemy, Calvin, exercised a virtual theocratic dictatorship. In a final act of bravado, he entered a church where Calvin was preaching. The latter pointed him out to local officials, and Serveto was imprisoned and tried for heresy. It appears that the judges found the prisoner more reasonable and persuasive than they had expected and were on the point of releasing him when Calvin intervened to introduce new evidence and precipitate a death sentence. Spain's arch heretic was burned at the stake on a hill in Geneva on October 27, 1553.

Seville (Sevilla)

The capital of Spain's southern region, ANDALUSIA, Seville is an ancient city with a

San Telmo Palace in Seville *(Getty)*

proud history. From the half mythical exploits of Hercules and Julius Caesar to the successive conquests of Visigoths, Moors, and Christian kings, Seville played a major role in the early history of the country and was successively the residence of CASTILE's monarchs, the headquarters of the SPANISH INQUISITION, and the first administrative center of Spain's colonial empire. As the wealth of the New World flowed up the Guadalquivir River, a cosmopolitan population of traders, bankers, and adventurers thronged its streets with their fine houses and splendid churches (including the completion of the largest Gothic cathedral in the world). Even after the silting up of the port caused the loss of the city's commercial dominance to CÁDIZ, Seville remained a cultural center whose lively society is portrayed in plays, operas, and novels. Escaping the damage that 19th- and 20th-century civil strife brought to most Spanish cities (although Franco's occupation forces killed many of Seville's citizens), it seemed to dream on in a state of static nostalgia until the 1992 celebrations surrounding the CHRISTOPHER COLUMBUS quincentenary thrust it into the center of world attention and stimulated a burst of modernization. Seville in the 21st century, with a rising economy and nearly 1 million people in and around its boundaries, has entered an era of renewal.

Siglo de Oro (Golden Age)

This term, literally meaning "golden century," refers to Spain's cultural predominance in Europe and has been used in a variety of ways. In the narrowest sense it refers to the 16th century; however, some scholars apply it to the whole period from the marriage of FERDINAND V and ISABELLA I in 1474 to the end of the Spanish HABSBURG dynasty in 1700 and prefer the term *"Golden Era."* Furthermore the age of Spain's greatest cultural achievement is more properly understood to include not only its outstanding literary figures but also its most eminent artists. Without denying the merits of particular masters in later centuries, the conjunction of such names as MIGUEL DE CERVANTES, FÉLIX LOPE DE VEGA, PEDRO CALDERÓN DE LA BARCA, and TIRSO DE MOLINA, as well as GARCILASO DE LA VEGA, FRANCISCO DE QUEVEDO, LUIS DE GÓNGORA, LUIS DE LEÓN, JOHN OF THE CROSS, and TERESA OF ÁVILA, with the artistic genius of DIEGO DE VELÁZQUEZ, EL GRECO, and BARTOLOMÉ ESTEBAN MURILLO during the 1500s and 1600s, not to mention the humanists JUAN LUIS VIVES and ELIO ANTONIO DE NEBRIJA, creates an unparalleled image of genius. Spain's cultural leadership was recognized and acknowledged throughout Europe during this epoch. Its global outreach that attained and explored a New World and, however grudgingly, its predominance in Europe were seen as ratifying Spanish eminence.

Soares, Mário (1924–   )
Portuguese statesman

Son of a prominent lawyer and political opponent of the Salazar dictatorship, Soares was educated at the University of Lisbon and in the Faculty of Law at the University of Paris. He became well known for his defense of victims of political persecution, was himself imprisoned on a number of occasions, and banished to the West African dependency of SÃO TOMÉ in 1968. He took up exile in France two years later where he served as a professor of law at the University of Paris. In the meantime Soares and several colleagues had secretly organized the Portuguese Socialist Party (1964) to plan for the day when dictatorship would end. After the bloodless revolution of 1974 Soares was appointed by the interim military government as foreign minister, with the special duty of planning the independence of Portugal's African provinces. In 1976 he took office as the first prime minister under the new constitution, marking another stage in the democratic evolution of Portugal, after decades of authoritarian rule. When he was chosen president of the republic in 1986, Soares was the first civilian in more than 60 years to hold that office.

Having already gained admission to the European Economic Community for his country, Soares devoted his two successive presidential terms (1986–91 and 1991–96) to developing Portugal's integration into what became the European Union (EU). Closely associated with this enterprise was his promotion of the country's economic development and the reorganization of its finances that would make it an effective member of the international community. After completing his second term Soares devoted himself to a new role as elder statesman. Elected as a Portuguese delegate to the European Parliament in 1999, he served on many of the EU's committees and commissions, becoming an articulate spokesman for the ideals and aspirations of this pan-European body. He also served in leading roles within the European socialist movement, particularly as the breakup of the Soviet satellite empire confronted emerging democracies with the kind of political and economic problems that Por-

tugal had already confronted. Few would deny Soares recognition as the most important political figure to emerge in Portugal since the fall of the dictatorship.

Sorolla y Bastida, Joaquín (1863–1923)
Spanish painter

Overcoming adversity (he was an orphan born in poverty), Sorolla rose by sheer talent to pursue art studies in VALENCIA, Paris, and Rome and to win commissions in portrait painting, including portraits of the Spanish royal family. He was praised by critics, however, for his landscape work in modified impressionistic style. His reputation preceded him to the United States, where he had a one-man show at New York City's Hispanic Society in 1909. He was also commissioned to paint a portrait of the newly inaugurated president, William Howard Taft. On his return to Spain he settled on the Mediterranean coast near Valencia where his studies of the brilliant interplay of light and shadow along the beaches revealed a new dimension of his artistic skills. He was particularly praised for such scenes as *Beaching The Boat, After The Bath* and *Swimmers* (1911–1915).

Soto, Hernando de (1500–1542)
Spanish explorer and administrator

Arriving in the New World while still a teenager, Soto took part in a number of expeditions in and around the Isthmus of Panama, notably the conquest of NICARAGUA. His abilities were recognized by FRANCISCO PIZARRO, who made him second in command during his 1532 expedition to PERU. He soon antagonized his chief by advocating a diplomatic approach to the native peoples and established a friendship with the Inca monarch, Atahuallpa. Pizarro found it expedient to send Soto on a distant mission at the time that Atahuallpa was being killed in violation of previous agreements. Despite these differences Soto played a leading role in the exploration and conquest of the Inca Empire and carried a huge share of the golden spoils home to Spain.

Newly married and with a splendid residence and a grand lifestyle, Soto nevertheless became restless and eager for new challenges in the process of conquering territory for Spain. After reading the account by ÁLVAR NÚÑEZ CABEZA DE VACA of his experiences in FLORIDA and adjacent lands, Soto determined to return to the New World. He converted much of his wealth into financing a large expedition and secured from the Crown the governorship of CUBA as well as the authorization to conquer Florida (which included much of what is now the southeastern United States). After assembling a force of nearly a thousand soldiers and civilians and gathering a great number of horses and supplies in Cuba, he left his wife as acting governor and landed at Espíritu Santo (present-day Tampa) in 1539.

Soto's initial contacts with the Indian tribes of Florida were as unsuccessful as those of PÁNFILO DE NARVÁEZ 10 years earlier. He persisted in his explorations and his search for treasure, encountering almost constant opposition and steadily losing fighting men in clashes with the native population. In the course of the next two years he penetrated what is now Georgia, Tennessee, Alabama, and Arkansas and possibly both Texas and Oklahoma. During his march to the west, he discovered the

Mississippi River and crossed it on boats constructed by his followers (although the mouth of the great river had been sighted by several earlier explorers, Soto was its effective European discoverer). Worn out by wounds and sickness, like the majority of his comrades, Soto died on the bank of the Mississippi in 1542. The survivors sank his body in the river to prevent its desecration by Indians.

Although Soto played a conciliatory role in the conquest of Peru, becoming increasingly unhappy with the brutality of Pizarro's actions, he was unable to retire to a peaceful life with his own share of the Inca treasure. In his later career as ADELANTADO of Florida he adopted many of the harsh and destructive tactics he had previously denounced, and his reputation has become that of a cruel conqueror. Whatever the final judgment on his character, Soto ranks with HERNÁN CORTÉS and Pizarro as one of the great conquistadores for the sheer breadth of his ambitions and his discoveries. His explorations opened up a vast new area of the Spanish Empire in America, and the preserved records of his expeditions added tremendously to European knowledge of North America.

Souza Cardoso, Amadeo de
(1887–1918)
Portuguese artist

The son of a landowning family in northern Portugal, Souza Cardoso pursued preliminary studies aimed at a career in architecture; however, after arriving in Paris in 1906 he soon shifted his attention to painting. Moreover he quickly exchanged the company of Portuguese expatriates for a more cosmopolitan range of artists then working in Paris. He also exchanged the naturalistic tradition of Portuguese painting for the new directions that were opening up before his increasingly sophisticated eyes. After experimenting with primitivism and approaches influenced by his new friend, Amedeo Modigliani, he emerged as an expressionist painter in important exhibits between 1910 and 1914. At the Armory Show in New York City (1913) a total of eight of his works were exhibited alongside those of PABLO PICASSO, Henri Matisse, Georges Braque, and Marcel Duchamp. When these same paintings were exhibited in Chicago three of the eight were purchased by the noted collector Arthur Jerome Eddy: *Saut du Lapin* (*Leap of the Rabbit,* 1911), *Marine pont l'Abbé* (*Marina at Pont L'Abbé,* 1912), *Chateau fort* (*Stronghold,* 1912). *Chateau fort* has attracted particular attention for its integration of cubism and art nouveau. A study in subtle blues and greens, the complex geometric landscape blends with a fantastic castle whose architectural elements recall both the artist's early training and his sensitivity to Portuguese traditions. The Eddy purchases were subsequently donated to the Art Institute of Chicago, which provide an almost unique American venue for the artist's work.

His meteoric artistic career swept him on from figuration through cubism and to exhibits and sales in Germany, as well as a planned first showing in London, but the outbreak of World War I and his marriage compelled his return to Portugal. There his international contacts and growing reputation were less appreciated. He threw himself into support of the nascent avant-garde in his own country, not only among painters, but in the context of the futurist literary movement. This was not the moment, however, when anything labeled "modernist" or "futurist" was likely to find easy acceptance. Souza Cardoso's organization of a show called *Abstractionism,* first in LISBON, then in OPORTO (1916), prompted denunciations for its "radicalism" and its "anticlericalism." He was attacked in print, verbally abused, and even physically assaulted by those who regarded him as a promoter of alien values. The poet FERNANDO PESSOA might have hailed him as "the most celebrated Portuguese vanguard painter" and the critic Almada may have called him "Portugal's first discovery in twentieth century Europe," but the country at large was not ready for him or his ideas. Following his death in the influenza epidemic of 1918, when barely 30 years old, Souza Cardoso sank into relative obscurity among his compatriots. Despite the efforts of his widow and isolated members of the cultural community he remained a marginal presence for some 35 years. It was not until the Salazar regime began seeking international status in the 1950s that he started to receive due attention as an artist of the first rank. His work was assembled in museums, his name was attached to galleries and public buildings, and his status as a pioneer of modern art was proudly celebrated. The new Portuguese icon was honored by major exhibitions in Brussels (1991), MADRID (1998), and Washington, Chicago, and the place where he had enjoyed his first international recognition, New York City (1999–2000). Entering the 21st century, Souza Cardoso appears to have, however belatedly, secured his place not merely as a Portuguese painter but a significant promoter of modernism in the Western world.

Spain and the European powers

The de facto union of CASTILE and ARAGON in 1479 coincided with the emergence of a united France and an England free from feudal divisions. The emergence of three major political powers at the end of the 15th century was followed by a struggle for mastery in Europe that lasted some 500 years. At the beginning of this struggle Spain was clearly dominant. During the ITALIAN WARS (1494–1559) Spain was repeatedly challenged by France, under the leadership of Charles VIII, Louis XII, and, most significant, François I. Despite the persistence of this monarch and his willingness to ally with the Ottoman Empire, Habsburg Spain emerged triumphant, although it was not the great warrior-statesman CHARLES I (Holy Roman Emperor Charles V) but his son, PHILIP II, who finally delivered the death blow to French ambitions when he imposed a humiliating peace on Henri II.

The third major power in Renaissance Europe, England, had aligned itself with Spain under Henry VII and during the early years of Henry VIII. Following the Protestant Reformation the latter and his successor, Edward VI, had maintained an essentially neutral position. Mary I, a Catholic, not only renewed the Spanish alliance but married the future Philip II. After her death in 1558 and the reestablishment of Protestantism in England under her half sister, Elizabeth I, England returned to a posture of neutrality. This was gradually abandoned as Spain's enemies in France (Henri of Bourbon), the Netherlands (William of Orange), and Germany pressed Elizabeth to join them in resisting Philip's use of the Counter-Reformation as an excuse for establishing Spanish hegemony throughout Europe. England's aid to Spain's opponents incited Spanish support to Irish Catholic rebels and the ARMADA's failed invasion of England in 1588.

By the early 1600s Spain and England had arrived at a truce. Spain, still dominant in Europe, was now challenged again by a revived France. The Bourbon kings Louis XIII and Louis XIV and their cunning ministers, Richelieu and Mazarin, proved more than a match for PHILIP IV and his *privado*, the count-duke of OLIVARES. France not only gained ascendancy on the battlefield but incited rebellion among Spain's subjects, notably Portugal which had been subjugated to Spain in 1580 but regained its independence in 1640. By 1700, at the death of the last HABSBURG, the ineffectual CHARLES II, Spain was actually claimed under that monarch's will by a French BOURBON prince.

Louis XIV established his nation's mastery of Europe during the WAR OF THE SPANISH SUCCESSION (1701–14). His grandson was acknowledged as PHILIP V of Spain, and that proud nation was at last obliged to acknowledge its fall from dominance. While the French boast "There are no more Pyrenees!" proved premature, much of the 18th century saw Spanish policy subordinated to that of France. The Bourbon Family Compact led MADRID into repeated clashes with London. The Hanoverian Georges were mere ciphers for parliamentary government in England, but Great Britain was now emerging as a colonial and trading power that rivaled not only France but the global pretensions of Spain. The ablest Spanish Bourbon, CHARLES III, was imprudently drawn into support of his kinsmen in Paris, and Spain's overseas realm began to collapse.

As the era of the French Revolution melted into the Napoleonic era (1789–1815), Spain's weak leaders shifted back and forth between support of the changing regimes in France and affiliation with Britain's crusade against the successive versions of the new European order promulgated from Paris. Napoléon proved the most formidable enemy that Spain had ever yet encountered. His contempt for its ruling dynasty was, perhaps, justified, but his appointment of his brother Joseph Bonaparte as JOSEPH I combined with the ravishing of Spain's resources and the slaughter of its people provoked a national resistance (PENINSULAR WAR). England's intervention, in which the duke of Wellington's liberation of Portugal from French control was followed by the expulsion of the Bonaparte regime from Spain in 1814, permitted the return of the banished FERDINAND VII. The hope of a modern, progressive, and self-respecting Spain that emerged at the beginning of the 19th century proved a delusion, however. By the 1830s the supporters of rival claimants to Ferdinand's throne were slaughtering each other, and the Liberal governments of London and Paris were using Spain as a ploy in their confrontation with the Conservatives who ruled in Vienna, St. Petersburg, and Berlin. In the configuration that emerged from the Congress of Vienna (1814–15), Britain, France, Austria, Russia, and Prussia were recognized as the "Great Powers," and Spain was merely regarded as part of the European miscellany.

By the end of the 19th century Spain's colonial empire had shrunk to a bare remnant. Its politicians and generals had turned the political system into a game of rotation in which monarchy possessed neither authority nor even the prospect of permanency. Its economy was enfeebled, and its society, bitterly divided. Little wonder that the rulers of Europe, whether the old dynasties or the new capitalists, did not take Spain seriously. The ultimate humiliation seemed to come in 1898, when the United States despoiled Spain of all that remained of its empire (SPANISH-AMERICAN WAR).

Spain's neutrality in World War I (1914–18) was less the result of its leaders' prudence than of the Great Powers' indifference to its absence from the battlefield or the conference table. Limping from military disaster in MOROCCO to military dictatorship in the 1920s to an unpopular republic in the early 1930s, Spain plunged into the SPANISH CIVIL WAR in 1936–39. Once again it became the plaything of the great powers although their identities had shifted. Britain and France stood aside while the fascist regimes in Germany and Italy and the Communist regime in Russia intervened supporting one side or the other in Spain while testing weapons and tactics for the European war that would break out in 1939. The United States, which had been indifferent to the European crisis, did not become involved in World War II until 1941.

Adolf Hitler was interested enough in finding a role for Spain in this war to meet with the victorious general FRANCISCO FRANCO. Although the latter would not facilitate a German attack on GIBRALTAR, he did offer Spanish troops and fliers to aid in Hitler's invasion of the Soviet Union in June 1941. The German dictator was disgusted by the duplicity of his Spanish counterpart, who withdrew his troops as soon as difficulties arose in the Russian campaign. Moreover Hitler and Benito Mussolini of Italy, who had both supported Franco's seizure of

Spain, had little respect for that country and its people in general. Yet it was Franco's Spain that survived World War II and Germany and Italy that collapsed. Joseph Stalin of the Soviet Union, who had backed the Spanish Republic, did everything in his power after 1945 to exclude Spain from the community of nations. Britain and France were also resentful of Franco's pro-Axis neutrality but found the United States more ambivalent. In the cold war alignment that quickly emerged after the fall of the fascist powers Washington valued Franco's anti-communism and eventually entered into agreements with him, which the United States induced colleagues in London and Paris to support. Ironically Spain had emerged undamaged from the decline and fall of the European Great Power system. The members of that "club" had either been reduced to underlings of the United States or overshadowed by the new global rivalry of the cold war superpowers who paid more attention to competing ideologies than to traditional European concerns. As a protégé of the United States, Spain was grudgingly readmitted into the Western "family."

Since Franco's replacement by a democratic monarchy in 1975 Spain has played an increasingly important part in the new pattern of European politics, in which the activities of the European Union have replaced the old struggle for mastery. Spain has even reached out into a wider world by reestablishing cultural and commercial contacts with its former colonies. Its participation in international military operations and involvement with the terrorist phenomena of the early 21st century have given Spain a greater visibility and a greater influence than it had known for many generations.

Spain and the Middle East

Spain has had a long and complex relationship with the peoples of the Middle East. In the broadest sense this would even include the period when these regions formed part of the Roman Empire. A new phase began with the rise of Islam and its dominance over most of the modern Middle East, even extending to the Muslim conquest of Spain, from which the "Moors" were not expelled until 1492. Indeed for more than a century after the CONQUEST OF GRANADA Spain continued to war with the Turkish sultan and other Muslim leaders along the shores of the Mediterranean. During the late 19th and early 20th centuries conflict flared up again, particularly in MOROCCO, part of which was subjected to Spanish control. FRANCISCO FRANCO, who had spent much of his military career in North Africa and launched the SPANISH CIVIL WAR from its shores in 1936, sought to bring about a new special relationship between Spain and the governments of the Middle East during his dictatorship (1939–75). All his successors attempted to preserve this relationship by promoting cooperation with countries ranging from Turkey to Algeria, even at the risk of weakening their credentials as proponents of democracy. It was particularly awkward when attempts were simultaneously being made to end Spain's long estrangement from the Jews. Some Muslims did not appreciate the "honest broker" role Spain tried to play at the Madrid Conference in 1991 in working for an Israeli-Palestinian peace. Even the profound and sincere apologies made by King JUAN CARLOS in 1992 for the expulsion of the Jews from Spain in 1492 was taken amiss by some Muslims.

Many of the most awkward moments in post-Franco Spain's efforts to keep the special relationship intact grew out of inevitable friction with Morocco. Geographical proximity, centuries of alternating trade and warfare, and the remnants of colonialism represented by the enclaves of CEUTA and MELILLA were perennial irritants. When King Hassan II of Morocco was succeeded by his son Mohammed VI in 2000, Spain's condolences and expressions of goodwill eased tensions, but its insistence that the enclaves had never actually belonged to Morocco and inflammatory rhetoric on both sides of the Strait of Gibraltar kept bad feelings alive. So, too, did attempts by would-be immigrants to enter Europe via Ceuta and Melilla or by improvised boats crossing the Mediterranean. Many Muslims died in these attempts or were captured and expelled from Spanish territory. Even those who succeeded in finding sanctuary were often obliged to live in poor conditions and to experience more discrimination from ordinary Spaniards than from the Madrid authorities.

Disputes with Morocco would continue with periodic flare-ups over such incidents as rival claims to ownership of a small Mediterranean island and increasing attempts by would-be immigrants (both North African and sub-Saharan) to force their way into the Spanish coastal enclaves. Far more worrisome was the Spanish decision to join the coalition that the United States formed in 2003 to invade Iraq and depose a regime accused of gathering weapons of mass destruction. By dispatching a brigade of Spanish troops to Iraq, Prime Minister JOSÉ MARÍA AZNAR provoked widespread demonstrations in Spain and alienated public opinion throughout the Islamic world. Unfazed by these reactions, Aznar insisted that Spain must join in a war on "global terrorism" and linked the what was now being termed *Islamic terrorism* to the ongoing political violence in Spain that the Basque terrorists of ETA had been waging for decades (see BASQUE NATIONALISM). In March 2004, on the eve of a parliamentary election that was expected to provide a renewed mandate for Aznar's Popular Party and place his hand-picked successor in office despite all the protests against current policies, a shocking act of terrorism struck the Spanish capital. A number of commuter trains approaching Madrid's main railroad terminal were almost simultaneously the target of bombs concealed on board. Nearly 200 people were killed, and hundreds more, injured. The initial reaction of Aznar's administration was to point the finger of guilt at ETA. Public opinion was overwhelmingly against this charge and was furthermore convinced that the regime was lying in order to win the election. The results of the vote were, first of all, the victory of an opposition coalition headed by the Socialists and, secondly, the new government's decision to withdraw Spanish troops from Iraq.

Aznar's successor, Prime Minister JOSÉ LUIS RODRÍGUEZ ZAPATERO, had always opposed Madrid's alliance with Washington and took this as an opportunity to bring the troops home. Some Spaniards, while not enthusiastic about membership in the coalition, complained that Zapatero's decision represented cowardice in the face of terrorism, especially after Islamic sources claimed that the Madrid train bombings were, indeed, a "punishment" for Aznar's affiliation with U.S. president George W. Bush. Spain's international position should not be determined, these commentators argued, by either fear or favor but by rational and honorable principles. Conservatives insisted that initial intelligence had actually suggested an ETA role and continued in later months to insist that ETA had at least given some help to Islamists in what was undeniably a primarily Muslim act of terrorism. Zapatero made some gestures to improve relations with Washington, but these had little effect, and the new Socialist government became increasingly aligned with Paris and Berlin in opposition to U.S. Middle Eastern policy. More serious for Spain than the weakening of its ties with the United States was the growth of a domestic crisis over the Muslim population of the country. Hundreds of thousands of Muslims were living legally in Spain by the end of 2005. Their cultural activities, their religious sites, and their special claims on public institutions were recognized by the authorities. An equal number were believed to have entered the country illegally. At least some of the latter were suspected of ties to the Madrid bombings and with other terrorist actions, including those that had taken place in the United States in 2001 and with those that occurred in Britain in summer 2005. Moreover Muslim confrontations elsewhere in Europe during 2005–06 heightened tensions in Spain. Ranging from protests in Germany, Belgium, and the Netherlands to massive rioting and vandalism in France, these episodes created increasing anxiety. All Europe seemed to be caught up in a "war of civilizations." The Zapatero government sought to ease relations between Islamic and non-Islamic residents while keeping open lines of communication with the Muslim countries of the Middle East. Nevertheless, scarcely a week passed without security forces uncovering some new cell of Islamic militants in Spain. Judicial investigations opened against some of those individuals found evidence linking them to the Madrid attacks or even to the planning and execution of the atrocities in New York and Washington. Spain began to be revealed as having been for some years past a major refuge for planners of Islamist terrorism, rivaling in this regard Italy and Germany (countries which had hitherto been regarded as "soft" on Muslim extremist residents). It was easy for conservatives to make facile references to the medieval struggle between Muslims and Christians in Spain. Islamist extremists made such historical incitements easier by talk of reviving a Muslim caliphate extending from the Persian Gulf to Iberia's coasts. Clearly Spain was moving into a time of crisis.

Spain and the United States

The history of Spain's relations with the United States is, of course, much shorter than the history of Spain in the Americas, which can be traced back to 1492, or in that specific part of the Western Hemisphere that is now the United States, whose local history forms part of Spain's complex record of exploration, theoretical claims, and transient ownership. Putting aside this "prehistory," it is no exaggeration to say that Spain was "present at the creation," for it watched with interest and encouragement the proclamation of the new nation in 1776 and committed itself to direct support for independence in 1779. Like its ally, France, Spain was moved by the practical desire to inconvenience an old enemy, Great Britain, so France and Spain gave military and naval aid to the rebellion. Perhaps Spain's most notable contribution to the Revolutionary

War was the siege of Pensacola and the defeat of the British forces there in 1781. Once the United States had secured recognition as a sovereign nation, the Spanish government assumed a less benign attitude. Although there was a treaty providing for normal diplomatic relations, the new nation was already worried during the 1780s by Spain's control of East and West FLORIDA, the LOUISIANA Territory, and, at least in theory, the greater part of western North America. Spain was perceived by the United States in these early days of the republic in much the same light as Great Britain, being officially at peace with the United States but as much a potential menace along the southeastern borders as the British were along the Canadian and Great Lakes frontier. One of the senior officers of the U.S. Army, General James Wilkinson, was in fact secretly in the pay of MADRID, providing valuable information about his country's political and military policies.

The wars of the French Revolution and Napoléon completely altered this situation. After 1815 the United States no longer saw Spain as a looming menace but rather as a power in decline. The Louisiana Territory, which Spain had retroceded to France, had then been acquired by President Thomas Jefferson, and Florida was sold by Spain to the United States, under pressure, in 1819. Within another decade Spain had been ousted from MEXICO, and the frontiers were now issues between Washington and its Mexican or Amerindian neighbors. American expansionism was not limited, however, to former Spanish colonies, such as TEXAS and CALIFORNIA. By the 1830s there was already talk of intervening in CUBA as a possible zone of expansion for slave-holding interests. The disputes between Wash-

ington and Madrid over the slave ship *Amistad,* the issues raised by the Ostend Manifesto, and the ongoing implications of the Monroe Doctrine of 1823 were merely reminders of Spain's reversal of fortune in a region where it had once predominated. Even the literary activity of such American writers as William H. Prescott and John L. Motley emphasized the darker side of Spain's Golden Age, while George Bancroft presented the rise of American democracy in clear conflict with the perceived Black Legend (LEYENDA NEGRA) of Spanish infamy. Once the Civil War had swept away slavery as an issue, a rising spirit of imperialism, fueled by such prophets of naval power as Alfred Thayer Mahan, turned American eyes upon Spain's remaining colonies in the Caribbean and the Pacific. As early as 1876 George Bancroft, ambassador to Germany, was instructed to pursue secret (and ultimately unsuccessful) negotiations with Spain for the sale of Vieques, a dependency of PUERTO RICO, as a naval base. American sympathy, if not outright support, was extended to Cuban insurrectionists in the 1860s and 1890s. Similar American interest was displayed toward nationalists in the PHILIPPINE ISLANDS during the same period, as American commercial and political interests spread across the Pacific.

Early in 1898 the ambivalences of a century's relations ended in war. The SPANISH-AMERICAN WAR lasted only a few months but resulted in the loss of nearly all of Spain's remaining colonial empire. The Philippines were annexed outright, as was Guam, the most valuable of the MARIANA ISLANDS. Cuba was "liberated" but maintained as a virtual protectorate of the United States for some 60 years. Puerto Rico, transformed since 1898 into a long-sought military and naval base, is still a virtual colony.

During the 20th century, as the United States added insult to injury by activating the implications of the Monroe Doctrine into economic and political domination of Spanish America, Spain remained impotent. Many of its intellectuals hurled diatribes against the United States, but its leaders turned in upon domestic issues that culminated in the SPANISH CIVIL WAR of 1936–39. Individual Americans directed their support to the Loyalists or the Nationalists, but Washington espoused a policy of nonintervention. The latter was replaced by repudiation of FRANCISCO FRANCO when he sided with Adolf Hitler during World War II and cultivation of the Spanish dictator when he shared U.S. hostility toward the Soviet Union during the cold war.

Democratic Spain during the years after 1975 followed a generally pro–United States policy by joining the North Atlantic Treaty Organization and cooperating with the transformation of Europe in the last years of the 20th century. Spain's development of an Iberian outreach in the Americas, including even Puerto Rico, was, for the most part, received benignly by Washington. Since the year 2001, however, Spain and the United States have passed through a period of shifting perceptions and relationships. The support given to U.S. policy in Iraq by Prime Minister JOSÉ MARÍA AZNAR was adroitly linked to his campaign against Basque terrorism as part of America's war against Islamic terrorism. In 2004 the situation changed as Spain experienced a major terrorist event in its own capital that proved to be Islamic terrorist punishment for its aid to the United States. Aznar was superseded by the Socialist leader JOSÉ LUIS RODRÍGUEZ ZAPATERO, Spain's contingent in the coalition forces sent to Iraq was withdrawn, and relations between Madrid and Washington cooled. Both at governmental and popular levels Spain and the United States seemed to have moved into a new pattern of relations that was somehow strangely reminiscent of their relations during the previous two centuries.

Spanish-American War (1898)

This conflict was a product of late 19th-century imperialism that saw the United States pursue its destiny as an emerging great power and Spain, in its period of decline, fall victim to an expansionist spirit in which it had in earlier times been a participant. After several years of mounting denunciation by the United States of harsh Spanish policies in CUBA (a virtual offshore island of the United States), the destruction of the USS *Maine* in Havana Harbor on February 15, 1898, precipitated a confrontation between the two countries. Efforts to avert war were undercut by those who believed that American strategic and commercial interests would be helped by its domination of Cuba. Formal declaration of hostilities took place in late April 1898. Military and naval operations in Cuba resulted in the victory of U.S. forces by late July, while a separate expedition to PUERTO RICO led to the surrender of that island by mid-August. As early as May 1898 U.S. naval forces had destroyed a Spanish squadron at Manila, with Spanish surrender in the PHILIPPINE ISLANDS and other Pacific possessions completed by July. The Treaty of Paris, concluded in December 1898, handed over Puerto Rico, Guam, and the Philippines to the United States and recognized Cuban independence under what amounted to a protectorate exercised from Washington. (For a fuller account of the historical evolution of Spain's relations with the United States see SPAIN AND THE UNITED STATES.)

Spanish civil war (1936–1939)

Like all civil wars, this conflict in Spain arose out of immediate circumstances but, in a deeper sense, from issues that had existed for many generations. Political and military factionalism that developed after the proclamation of the Second Republic in 1931 culminated in the establishment of the Popular Front government in early 1936 and the decision of certain generals to confront this leftist regime. The forces that rallied to support the republic included Communists, Socialists, anarchists, labor unions, and peasant farmers, as well as Basques and Catalans. Despite the wide variety of their interests and fundamental principles all of these felt that their long-term aspirations, ranging from a workers' dictatorship to regional independence could best be achieved under the republic. These "Loyalist" supporters (also called Republicans) were challenged by an equally variegated collection of landowners, capitalists, clericals, and monarchists of several different dynastic allegiances, as well as those who admired fascist ideology and advocates of the military's perennial claim to be the guardian of Spanish integrity.

When General FRANCISCO FRANCO, operating from MOROCCO, launched his revolt in July 1936, he was joined by colleagues who managed to seize control of scattered districts in Spain and its offshore islands. By October he had emerged as the unchal-

This French poster (the translated title is "Help Spain") from a 1937 image draws support for Spain's Republican government under attack by fascists. *(Library of Congress)*

lenged leader of what came to be known as the Nationalist cause and designated chief of state. The struggle raged on through 1937, with gains and losses for both sides, although none of the battles was as brutal and bloody as the initial slaughter of civilians during the opening months of the war that revealed the deep-seated class hatred lying beneath the surface of Spanish society. Gradually the advantage tipped in favor of the Nationalists, who received significant military assistance from Adolf Hitler's Germany and Benito Mussolini's Italy. The Western democracies, despite some initial sympathy for the republic, retreated behind a pledge of nonintervention, and even the support that the Soviet Union gave to the Loyalists was limited and ultimately withdrawn. Thousands of volunteers from Europe and the Western Hemisphere joined the so-called International Brigades that fought for the Loyalist side, but their participation was, in the end, more notable for its romanticism than its practical effect.

By April 1938 the Nationalists had broken through to the Mediterranean, cutting Spain in half from west to east. A process of attrition gradually reduced the territory under the Republican banner until early 1939 saw a collapse of the last defenses in the north and the retreat of thousands of fighters and their dependents across the French frontier. At the beginning of March a grotesque power struggle between Communists and Socialists broke out in the streets of MADRID, as if to justify the worst criticisms of the Nationalists. Within a few weeks the Spanish capital had fallen to Franco's forces; the president of the republic, MANUEL AZAÑA, had abandoned his futile effort to preserve his authority and maintain resistance; and the war was over.

Estimates of those who died in battle, by execution (formal or informal), or from the spread of famine and disease range from 500,000 to 1 million. In the early years of Franco's victorious dictatorship many more would die as prisoners or under the deprivations of the postwar period. The psychological stress of living under an isolationist, reactionary police-state regime took its toll as well, and many did not recover, even after democracy was restored following Franco's death in 1975. Beyond the colossal national trauma endured by the Spanish people the civil war also served to dramatize for the nations of Europe the horrors of modern mass conflict. This "rehearsal" did not, however, prevent Europeans from plunging into World War II only a few months after the Spanish tragedy came to an end.

Propaganda poster issued by Madrid's Defense Committee *(Library of Congress)*

Spanish Guinea (Equatorial Guinea)

This West African territory, claimed by Portugal in 1471, was ceded to Spain in 1778. The colony included a strip of land along the Gulf of Guinea known as Río Muni and the large island of Fernando Poo (or Po) as well as several smaller islands in the Gulf of Guinea, notably Annobón, the Elobeys (Grande and Chico), and Corisco. Spain placed Fernando Poo under British administration in 1829 to permit Great Britain to police more effectively the slave trade. The island was reclaimed by Spain in 1844, and the entire colony (with an area slightly more than 10,000 square miles) was confirmed to Spain by international agreement in 1900. With a relatively small population and modest economic base Spanish Guinea was not deemed worthy of argument when anticolonial criticisms were directed against MADRID. In 1968 it was accorded independence under the name Equatorial Guinea. After the restoration of the monarchy in Spain (1975) this former colony was included in a royal tour of Spanish-speaking areas of the world. The king and queen were greeted with such vociferous enthusiasm and so many demands for a return to Spanish rule that the Madrid government was obliged to make it quite clear that it had no such desire or intention.

Spanish Inquisition

Originally an investigative body established by the papacy to root out heresy, the Inquisition spread from Rome to virtually every country of Catholic Europe during the Middle Ages. In 1479 ISABELLA I successfully petitioned for the establishment of an inquisition in CASTILE. Somewhat reluctantly, because of the sweeping powers stipulated, Rome granted this request, a parallel authorization being given to Isabella's consort, FERDINAND V, for his realm of ARAGON. Each kingdom was to have a council composed of bishops, theologians, and lawyers for the announced purpose of rooting out Jewish converts to Christianity (conversos) who secretly persisted in their original faith. Almost from their beginning these councils functioned as one, commonly known as the Spanish Inquisition. By the early 16th century the mission of the Inquisition had shifted to discovering covert Muslims (Moriscos) and Protestants and its employees included a small army of informers, policemen, and jailers. Totally under government control and functioning as one of the state councils, the Inquisition drew upon ecclesiastics only in matters of doctrinal expertise. Those subjected to interrogation were, in many cases, judged to be the object of frivolous or malicious charges and released, while others were subjected to orders of recantation or minor punishment. Prisoners judged worthy of physical chastisement, including torture or death, were handed over to secular authorities for imposition of such measures. Although the number of capital sentences carried out under the mandate of the Inquisition has never been reliably established, the death penalties imposed over its more than three centuries of existence seem to have been relatively few. The public burnings, however, created a terrifying and lasting impression. The secret procedures of the inquisitorial bodies also contributed to a mysterious and sinister image.

Local tribunals of the Inquisition were established as part of the regular administrative apparatus throughout Spain's overseas empire, as well as in countries temporarily subjected to Spanish dominance, including Portugal. By the mid-18th century the Inquisition was functioning primarily as a court to oversee matters of morality and petty social offenses. These included everything from polygamy, usury, and calumny to smuggling, assumption of false identity, and attempts by priests to seduce penitents. During the Enlightenment, when Rome's Index of Prohibited Books forbade access to almost any "new ideas," the Spanish Inquisition, paradoxically, often limited its censorship role to merely excising a few radical passages.

As one of the most notorious (if not always pernicious) of old regime institutions, the Inquisition was dissolved in 1808 by order of JOSEPH I, the intrusive Bonaparte monarch. Reestablished by the reactionary FERDINAND VII in 1814, the Inquisition was finally abolished in 1834 by the Liberal government that took power after his death.

Spanish Succession, War of the
(1701–1714)

This conflict was precipitated by the death of CHARLES II, the last of the Spanish Habsburg dynasty. Anticipating the extinction of his line, the major European powers drew up two successive partition treaties (1698, 1699) dividing the Spanish realms among themselves. Seeking to preserve the integrity of his inheritance, the dying Charles II dictated a will leaving the undivided Spanish dominions to his great nephew, Philippe, duke of Anjou, the grandson of Louis XIV of France. In November 1700, a few weeks after drawing up this testament, Charles died. Early in 1701 Louis XIV announced that his grandson would accept the sovereignty of Spain and its empire under the designation of PHILIP V. Enraged by the French betrayal of their agreement, the other European powers declared war in an attempt to enforce the partition treaty. By 1702 England, the Dutch Republic, Portugal, and most of the German states were ready to take the field in support of the Austrian archduke Carl's claim to the greater part of Spain's European possessions. France and a few smaller countries backed Philip V, as did most Spaniards. The War of the Spanish Succession was fought during the next decade everywhere from the Spanish Netherlands (present-day Belgium) to southern Germany and northern Italy, with the superior generalship of Britain's duke of Marlborough and Austria's prince Eugène gaining the victory for the Allies in most of the battles. Only in Spain itself did Philip's supporters gain the upper hand and crush a dissident movement in CATALONIA. Sporadic fighting also took place in overseas possessions.

By 1713, due to internal disputes, the coalition had fallen apart and the Treaty of Utrecht, signed by the Dutch and the British, acknowledged Philip's rule over virtually all of the Spanish inheritance, reserving only certain strategic and commercial advantages for his opponents, notably the granting of the ASIENTO to Great Britain. Austria and her German supporters fought on until 1714, when, by the Treaties of Rastadt and Baden, Philip conceded the Belgian provinces and some Italian territory to the Habsburgs but secured recognition as ruler of Spain and its possessions. This war brought a branch of the French BOURBON dynasty to the Spanish throne and initiated a century of French-inspired political and cultural change in Spain.

Spice Islands

This term was variously employed in the early colonial period to describe the entire archipelago now constituting Indonesia and formally referred to as the Dutch East

Indies. More specifically the term was applied to the eastern portion of the archipelago known as the MOLUCCAS. In an even more precise sense it was applied to the islands of Ternate, Tidore, and Ambon, the center for production of spices such as nutmegs, cloves, and mace. These latter products were in tremendous demand among Europeans from the 15th century onward for enhancing the flavor of food and preserving certain perishable products. Portuguese explorers reached the Spice Islands in 1511–12 and established a trading monopoly that was among the principal causes of their country's wealth and influence during the subsequent century. Spanish attempts to seize control of the Spice Islands were beaten off during the 1520s, but the Dutch seized control of the region from Portugal in the early 1600s and retained mastery of the entire East Indies until after World War II.

Spinola, Ambrogio (marqués de los Balbases) (1569–1630)
Spanish general
The most distinguished member of an Italian noble family who provided a number of notable officers to the service of Spain, Spinola placed his considerable personal fortune at the disposal of PHILIP III, raising several thousand troops at his own expense. Appointed to relieve the difficult situation in the Spanish Netherlands, Spinola achieved a great victory at Ostend in 1604. He continued to defeat the Dutch Republic during the next several years, earning the gratitude of the king and a number of titles of honor. Spinola was a well-educated soldier, whose grasp of strategy and tactics and mastery of fortifications were comple-

mented by a shrewd understanding of logistical realities. Perceiving the fiscal limitations that hampered Spain's imperial ambitions, he persuaded the king to negotiate the Twelve Years' Truce (1609–21) in order to provide an opportunity for reorganization and renewal.

The death of Philip III and the downfall of the duke of LERMA and Spinola's other friends at court opened the way for his critics to intrigue against him, but his capture of BREDA (1626) renewed his prestige and gave him the personal support of PHILIP IV. Spinola continued to win laurels in the War of the Mantuan Succession and the early stages of the Thirty Years' War. He was created marqués de los Balbases and appointed governor of the Spanish possessions in northern Italy. Nevertheless, the persistent jealousy of the new king's chief minister, OLIVARES, continued to hamper his services and lower his morale. Many contemporaries believed that his decline in health and eventual death were the result of harassment by enemies at the royal court.

Despite the vicious attacks of those who denounced him as an "outsider," Spinola was described by most of the leading men of the day as a person of the highest integrity and deepest commitment to the interests of the Spanish ruling dynasty. After a series of brilliant soldiers who had led the TERCIOS in a century of great achievements, Spinola stands as the last outstanding general of Habsburg Spain.

Spinola, António Sebastião Ribeiro de (1910–1996)
Portuguese military leader and statesman
Member of an aristocratic family of Italian descent, Spinola was a man of fundamentally conservative views whose military

career brought him into contact with the Fascist regime in Italy and the Nazi regime in Germany of World War II. These tendencies were largely forgotten by the time he rose to national renown in the crises that led to the Portuguese revolution of 1974. Having served with distinction as governor and field commander in PORTUGUESE GUINEA from 1968 to 1972, he returned home to public acclaim and was named deputy chief of the armed forces staff in 1973. His book, *Portugal and the Future,* created a sensation in early 1974 with its assertion that the ongoing campaign against the colonial rebels in Africa was a misguided enterprise, wasteful of blood and treasure. Startling as was this disavowal of national policy by a national hero, Spinola's complaint that the war was undermining the potentials of democratic society in Portugal was even more sensational. There is no evidence that this military celebrity and best-selling author played a part in the bloodless coup d'état that overthrew the dictatorship in April 1974, but Spinola was named provisional president by the revolutionary committee within a few weeks of the event. He initiated a number of moderate reforms and began negotiating a withdrawal from Africa, but the leftward movement of politics led him to resign in September 1974. Spinola's critics have asserted that he showed his true colors when he led a right-wing revolt in March 1975. After the failure of this conservative uprising Spinola played no further role in postrevolutionary Portugal.

Sucre, Antonio José de (1795–1830)
Spanish colonial rebel

Born in VENEZUELA of a well-to-do family, he interrupted his education to join the independence movement while still in his adolescence. For more than a decade he took an active part in a series of political measures and military campaigns aimed at breaking the rule of Spain over NEW GRANADA. He spent several periods in exile and still more time traveling throughout the region to gather recruits and arms for the cause, rising in rank and in the respect of his comrades. First associated with the unsuccessful efforts of FRANCISCO DE MIRANDA, he later joined forces with SIMÓN BOLÍVAR. With this great liberator of South America, he formed a personal and political bond that endured for the remainder of his life. Sucre played a major role in the freeing of ECUADOR and was Bolívar's principal lieutenant in the emancipation of PERU. At the BATTLE OF AYACUCHO (December 9, 1824) he defeated the viceregal forces and received from the Viceroy of Peru what amounted to the ultimate capitulation of Spanish power in the Americas.

Sucre's generous treatment of his opponents after Ayacucho added to his reputation as a man of generosity and humanity whose good judgment and political acumen belied his relative youth. Honored with the title grand marshal of Ayacucho, he was subsequently elected president of the newly independent Upper Peru, which was renamed BOLIVIA in honor of the Liberator. Sucre laid down this title in 1828, after two years, to return to ECUADOR, where he helped defeat aggressive moves by Peru to annex the region. He subsequently devoted his efforts to preserving the breakup of the alliance that held together the components of the old viceroyalty of New Granada. While engaged in these efforts, he was assassinated by political opponents. Sucre has been hailed as the purest and most disinterested of those who fought for South American independence and then sought to preserve the unity of postindependence South America.

T

Tamayo y Baus, Manuel (1829–1898)
Spanish playwright

The son of actors, Tamayo y Baus turned his talents to playwriting at an early age, concentrating at first on adaptations of nondramatic works. He subsequently developed a facility in translating and restructuring the plays as well as novels of foreign-language writers. He eventually began creating his own original plays, ranging over history, moral dilemmas, and romantic comedies. *La locura de amor* (The madness of love, 1855) was inspired by the story of Queen JOANNA, daughter of FERDINAND V and ISABELLA I, and reflected a number of his consistent themes, including a vein of Christian belief that was perhaps becoming somewhat out of fashion among Spanish writers and critics. Despite such reservations many critics have called his *Un drama nuevo* (*A New Drama,* 1867) one of the greatest of Spanish plays and certainly the best of its time. Its subject matter is a love affair within an acting troupe whose leader is known for the role of Yorik, the jester mentioned but never seen in William Shakespeare's *Hamlet.* The plot, which works itself out in a play within a play (both of which end tragically), would inspire Ruggiero Leoncavallo's opera *Pagliacci.* Tamayo y Baus wrote virtually nothing for the stage in his later years, concluding that the melodramatic approach of JOSÉ ECHEGARAY had won the entire attention of Spanish audiences.

Tàpies, Antoni (1923–   )
Spanish painter

A Catalan strongly influenced by the violent experiences of the SPANISH CIVIL WAR era in his native BARCELONA, Tàpies abandoned his earlier studies in law to become a (largely self-taught) painter. In 1946 he became a founder member of the Catalan avant-garde group of artists known as the Dau al Set (seven-sided die). He drew inspiration from surrealism to produce collages of commonplace debris (string, rags, and torn canvas) smeared with paint. By the early 1950s he was holding one-man exhibitions and winning recognition abroad. By 1957 he had moved on to "informalism" as a founder of El Paso group. Although he was no admirer of the Franco regime, the nature of Tàpies's materials and subjects did not bring him into direct confrontation with the censors. Adding a Spanish presence to the general postwar movement of abstract expressionism, he provided the kind of "prestige export" that the government welcomed. One of his best-known works of the period is *Ochre* (1963). Integrating a stark surface of sand and asphalt with daubs of black and white paint, the artist produced an abstraction of his own memories of the civil war period and its aftermath with hints of a "haunting beauty" with the "transcendence of life over circumstance" that critics continue to praise.

Tàpies's work of recent decades has progressed through a still more complex and striking integration of "matter" with canvas to actual use of objects as the "canvas" upon which he paints or attaches other objects, for example, a desk top to which paint and straw has been applied.

Barcelona has honored its native son by housing the collection known as the Tàpies Foundation, which includes several thousand works created by the master. He has been the focal point of exhibits in many countries and the inspiration of abstract artists around the world. His 80th birthday was marked by a grand array of his recent lithographs at a major gallery in Germany. Tàpies was a dominating force in abstract art throughout the latter half of the 20th century. At the beginning of the 21st he is justly hailed as Spain's greatest living artist.

Tercio

This Spanish military formation came into existence during the ITALIAN WARS (1494–1559) and won fame throughout Europe as the instrument by which the kings of Spain attained mastery of the Continent. Its origins are disputed, with some historians claiming that it was based on the ancient Greek phalanx. Its chief characteristics were the tight discipline and coordination imposed upon its troops, who exhibited a remarkable steadiness and alacrity both in defensive and offensive operations. The term *tercio* was derived from the tripartite

division of these infantry units, which contained components of pikemen, musketeers, and swordsmen. The proportion of each component varied over time. So consistent was the performance and so formidable the achievements of the Tercios that the very name attained not only a high level of respect but also a capacity to intimidate by the mere presence of Spanish infantry on the battlefield. Although the number of soldiers in each Tercio and the tactical use of these units evolved over the decades, they retained their preeminence until the mid-17th century. After the Spanish defeat at the BATTLE OF ROCROI (1643) the success of Spanish arms declined, and military ascendancy in Europe gradually passed to France. Changes in the political system as well as weaponry led to the replacement of the Tercios by less distinctive military units resembling those of other conventional European armies during the early 18th century. After the establishment of the Spanish Foreign Legion in 1920 and its dramatic achievements in MOROCCO, the name *Tercio* was revived and bestowed on the legion as a mark of honor and a recognition of its triumphs on the battlefield.

Teresa of Ávila, Saint (1515–1582)
Spanish religious leader and mystic

Born of a well-to-do family named Cepeda and later known variously as Mother Teresa of Jesus or Teresa of Ávila, this most famous of Spanish nuns entered the convent before she was 20 and experienced successive periods of poor health, aridity of religious feeling, and then, beginning in the 1550s, a powerful sense of mystical communion with the divine. This intense spirituality enriched the remainder of her life and undoubtedly helped sustain the active role that she played in the church during the Counter-Reformation.

Like many believers, she had become dissatisfied with the permissive, or even corrupt, state of the religious orders that had developed during the later Middle Ages. Within her own order, the Carmelites, she lamented the abandonment of strict and rigorous rules of contemplation and prayer that had been laid down hundreds of years earlier by the founders of the order. She became an outspoken champion of reform, advocating a return to a strict and simple community observance. In the first of what would be a perpetual campaign to win and hold support from church leaders, she was given permission by Rome to establish at Ávila a convent of Discalced Carmelites (the reference to "unshod" indicating the humility and minimalism of their lifestyle). She was met with fierce opposition from leaders of other religious communities and civil authorities but eventually succeeded in gaining papal authorization to found more than a dozen additional convents of the reform movement in Spain. During the 1560s and '70s Teresa of Ávila became a recognized leader of Catholicism's growing commitment to counteract Protestantism by a revival of Christian values and virtues that had slackened over the centuries. By her writings and her example she evoked a renewed ardor among both clergy and laiety. Her activities, coinciding with the Catholic reform decrees of the Council of Trent, nevertheless met with frequent opposition from those who resented criticism or feared the effects of change. At various moments she was rebuked, ordered to abandon her work, or even subjected to questioning on the authenticity of her spiritual ideas. Undaunted, Teresa did not hesitate to seek and win the backing of the great ones of her time, including the pope and King PHILIP II. She undertook many laborious journeys to argue her case or simply to visit the communities that she had inspired. When she died, worn out by the fatigues of her labor, she could take satisfaction in having achieved her goals.

Teresa of Ávila was canonized in 1622, and in 1970 she was proclaimed a doctor of the church, the first woman to receive this title which recognizes its bearer as one of the fundamental teachers and guides in the practice of the Catholic faith. Teresa of Ávila's legacy lies primarily in her mystical writings, including poetry and the *Moradas, o El castillo interior* (*The Interior Castle*, 1588). Her equally famous *Camino de perfección* (*Way of Perfection*, 1583) and *Vida*, her autobiography, have inspired many to seek a life of virtue. For the Spanish people she has remained an inspirational figure of a different sort—a strong-minded and energetic woman, cheerful and even humorous but irresistible in her determination to do the right thing. She is venerated not merely as a saintly figure but as a true heroine of Spain's Golden Age.

terrorism

A form of political violence characterized by random and ruthless attacks either upon the forces of government or the general public, terrorism is intended to disrupt ordered society and to intimidate those who oppose the aims of the terrorists. Some students of terrorism distinguish between terrorism "from below" and "state terrorism" intended to maintain government authority by extralegal and secret use of force.

Most scholars of the subject also draw a distinction between terrorism and "guerrilla warfare," which is essentially an irregular form of conventional warfare directed by nonuniformed forces of opposition against uniformed soldiers, police, and government representatives. As its name (literally translated as "little war") implies, guerrilla warfare has a particular place in Spanish history, having been most famously employed during the PENINSULAR WAR of 1808–14, when forces loyal to FERDINAND VII attacked individuals and small groups supporting the French-imposed regime of JOSEPH I. Such combatants, properly called *guerrilleros,* are commonly, though incorrectly, referred to in English as "guerrillas."

Terrorism, in its most commonly understood form, was a particular tactic of Spanish anarchists during the late 19th and early 20th centuries in their effort to destabilize and potentially bring down what they considered a corrupt and unjust sociopolitical system. The widespread violence employed by both sides in the SPANISH CIVIL WAR of 1936–39, for all its brutality, is not generally classified as terrorism but rather as an extension of what often degenerated into class warfare. Repressive tactics employed by the regime of FRANCISCO FRANCO during the period 1939–75 are sometimes considered to have been a form of state terrorism, particularly by those who apply that term to the fascist regimes of Adolf Hitler in Germany and Benito Mussolini in Italy.

Beginning approximately in 1969 extreme nationalists in Spain's BASQUE PROVINCES began asserting their demands for independence by attacking Spanish government officials, a process which (accidentally or deliberately) often involved civilian bystanders. By 1999 well over 800 deaths and numerous injuries as well as serious property damage had resulted from Basque terrorism. In 2006 the principal terrorist organization, known as ETA (Euskadi Ta Askatasuna, or Basque Homeland and Liberty) reached a temporary cease-fire agreement with the Spanish government, which it had continued to oppose, even after the establishment of democracy in 1975 (see BASQUE NATIONALISM).

On March 11, 2004, bomb explosions in MADRID's main railroad station and on several suburban train lines killed nearly 200 passengers. The attacks were initially attributed by the authorities to ETA. When evidence emerged that a new terrorist force had appeared in the form of militant Islamists (angered by Spain's support for the U.S. invasion of Iraq) the government of Prime Minister JOSÉ MARÍA AZNAR was widely accused of duplicity and defeated in the general election scheduled for the same week. While ETA terrorism would presumably remain a threat, Spain would henceforth be confronted by a new dimension of this phenomenon.

Tetuán, campaign of (1859)

The main formal military operation of the Spanish army between 1814 and 1898, this Moroccan campaign grew out of repeated attacks by local militants along the borders of Spanish enclaves in North Africa. Despite agreements between the MADRID government and that of the sultans of MOROCCO concluded during the 1840s, the central authorities of the sultanate seemed incapable of restraining their subjects in the disputed areas. By 1859 many in Spain believed that antagonistic elements in Morocco were secretly inciting the border incidents. A rising tide of indignation and patriotic fervor forced the Madrid ministry to declare war in the latter part of the year, and General LEOPOLDO O'DONNELL, the prime minister, took the field in person to lead a formidable military force across the Strait of Gibraltar. A competent leader but unable to accelerate the pace of his preparations or operations, O'Donnell took months to get his forces on the march. In the meantime the nationalist sentiment in Morocco had risen to unexpected heights, and the new sultan had assembled a large army in the interior, near the city of Tetuán. This was an old battleground between Spaniards and Moroccans, destroyed by Castilian invaders in the 15th century and repopulated by Muslim refugees expelled by the edicts of FERDINAND V and ISABELLA I. After a three-week march from CEUTA O'Donnell's force was confronted by some 30,000 fierce but ill-organized tribal warriors who attacked in a frontal assault outside the city. Somewhat more numerous, the Spaniards also had the advantage of firepower and disciplined organization. The Moroccans were defeated with heavy losses. After a few more minor skirmishes, the sultan sued for peace, conceding some additional territory adjacent to the existing Spanish enclaves and recognizing Spanish control in the territory of Ifni along Morocco's Atlantic coast.

General O'Donnell returned to Spain in triumph and was named duke of Tetuán. No Spanish commander since the end of the Napoleonic Wars had achieved a comparable military victory or such popular admiration.

Texas

As part of the gradual movement of Spanish control northward from NEW SPAIN, the region constituting the present state of Texas in the United States was gradually explored and mapped between 1519 and 1684. French claims to the area were first advanced in the late 1600s on the basis of their activities in LOUISIANA. Spain began establishing garrisons at key points mainly as a check to Comanche raids. As a result of the Louisiana Purchase (1803), the United States revived the old French claim to the adjacent area of Texas but abandoned this claim in 1819. Two years later the independence of the republic of MEXICO ended Spanish rule in Texas. This vast area (approximately 262,000 square miles) has subsequently been an independent republic, a part of the United States, a member of the Southern Confederacy, and once again a state in the Union. Its Spanish heritage has been an important factor in its life and culture since the arrival of the Spaniards.

Theotokópoulos, Doménikos   See GRECO, EL.

Thyssen-Bornemisza Museum

A notable extension of Spain's great collections of paintings and sculpture, the Museo Thyssen-Bornemisza forms (albeit unofficially) an extension of the PRADO, and its Buen Retiro and Reina Sofía galleries. It was born of the collecting enthusiasms of several generations of a wealthy German mercantile dynasty whose holdings were ultimately assembled in a Swiss villa after World War II. Baron Hans Heinrich Thyssen-Bornemisza (whose Hungarian mother's family name had been added to that of his father's) had, with the advice of art historians, assembled some 800 paintings and sculptures that embodied the major trends in Western art from the 13th to the 20th centuries. His desire to share the aesthetic and educational potentials of the collection with a wider public led him to seek an arrangement for its proper housing and display in Europe or America. His Spanish-born wife became an important advocate for the Spanish proposal that led to the opening of the Thyssen-Bornemisza Museo in 1992. The greater part of the collection is housed in the former Palacio de Villahermosa in MADRID (near the Prado), while approximately 10 percent of its holdings with special resonance for Catalan cultural history are displayed in a former monastery near BARCELONA.

The works exhibited in the Madrid museum eschew the traditional organization into national schools of art and are arranged to show the transnational influences and developments in the history of Western art. Important trends are illustrated by works produced from the Renaissance to recent decades, both by the famous and lesser-known artists. A distinctive feature of the museum is the presence of representative American artists of the 19th and 20th centuries whose work is infrequently seen in European collections.

Tirso de Molina (Gabriel Téllez)
(c. 1571–1648)
Spanish dramatist

This was the pseudonym of the Mercedarian friar Gabriel Téllez. Often referred to as the principal disciple of FÉLIX LOPE DE VEGA, he is said to have been second only to Lope in the number of his plays, estimated at more than 400, of which only 80 survive. Although he shared the general concern of his contemporaries with reinforcing moral principles and illustrating theological themes, his status as a member of a religious order did not restrain him from taking a lively interest in secular subjects; indeed, the civil authorities eventually ordered him to confine himself to more specifically religious concerns.

His most famous play (written c. 1630) combines an unimpeachably moral message with an excitingly lurid story line. *El burlador de Sevilla y el convidado de piedra* (*The Love Rogue*) introduces one of the most enduring of dramatic characters, Don Juan. Under that name, or as Mozart's Don Giovanni, he has remained a by-word over several centuries for the arrogant seducer who is doomed to a very bad end. Tirso de Molina presents his Don Juan as a literally irresistible conqueror of women, whether they be shepherdesses or aristocrats. Moreover he is willing to commit murder, and the stone guest (*convidado de piedra*) mentioned in the title who comes to confront him is the statue of a man he has slain. The playwright is primarily concerned, however, with an even greater sin: Don Juan's assumption that he can manipulate God's mercy and wipe the slate clean before he dies. As the villain is dragged down to hell, the audience is reminded that one cannot gamble one's fate and assume that one is a more adroit player than God. Tirso de Molina chose to make a similar point, though in reverse, in an earlier (c. 1620) play. The protagonist of *El condenado por desconfiado* (*The Saint and the Sinner*) is Paulo, a saintly hermit who, too presumptuously, asks to be told the circumstances of his death. The devil, disguised as an angel, tells him that he will die like a certain notorious criminal. Paulo thereupon decides to experience all the sinful pleasures that the other man has enjoyed since he is destined to share the same fate. But the criminal, who has the single redeeming virtue of loving his father, is spared, and Paulo ultimately goes to hell for casting aside the profound Christian truth that God can forgive any sinner. Paulo may not be as arrogant as Don Juan, but he has failed to acknowledge God's forgiveness, just as Don Juan has failed to acknowledge the certainty of punishment for the unrepentant.

In the wide range of his subject matter and the sheer volume of his production, as well as his persistent concern with the values of the Catholic heritage, Tirso de Molina is representative of the best achievement of 17th-century Iberian drama. With Lope de Vega and PEDRO CALDERÓN DE LA BARCA, he completes a triumvirate of the SIGLO DE ORO's greatest dramatists.

Toledo

This city in central Spain stands on a high plateau surrounded on three sides by a natural moat of rivers and on the fourth by a double defensive wall. From ancient times it has been a fortress and seat of government. Its name is derived from the Roman *Toletum,* but the site was occupied long before the Romans arrived. Capital of the Visigothic kingdom, Toledo was ruled for several centuries by the Moors and then passed into the hands of the the kings of LEÓN and CASTILE (1085). Toledo became an ecclesiastical as well as political center

View of Toledo from the Alcántara Bridge *(Library of Congress)*

during the Middle Ages, and the archbishop of Toledo is still primate of Spain. His cathedral and many other churches rise above the city, including a converted mosque and synagogue that recall the era of intercommunal tranquillity among the city's inhabitants. Shops and small factories reflect traditional products of Toledo, including the sword blades of such high quality as to earn world renown. Rising above all, the Alcazar, or citadel, built by the Moors rears its impregnable walls and towers.

Even though FERDINAND V and ISABELLA I moved their customary residence to VALLADOLID, their grandson, CHARLES I, chose to spend most of his reign (1516–56) at Toledo. Moved as much by its symbolic air of dominance as by nostalgia, he lent the aura of his title as Holy Roman Emperor to a city already reflecting centuries of majesty.

In later days Toledo would be known for the rigor of its prelates, the genius of its artists (EL GRECO above all), and the air of diminished grandeur so evident to visitors. In 1936, at the outbreak of the SPANISH CIVIL WAR, Toledo once again commanded the attention of all Spain as Republican forces besieged the Alcazar, where army rebels held out in support of General FRANCISCO FRANCO's insurgency. The siege of the ALCAZAR OF TOLEDO became the central drama of the war's opening months, especially because the besiegers held hostage the young son of Colonel Moscardo, the citadel's commander. Moscardo refused to surrender the Alcazar and, when allowed to speak to the youth by telephone, the father urged him to "die like a good Spaniard" and received an equally brave response from his son. Such moments evoked, for both sides in the civil war, the whole history of gran-

Entrance of San Juan de los Reyes Cathedral in Toledo *(Library of Congress)*

deur and misery that constituted their national experience and was enshrined within Toledo's walls.

Tordesillas, Treaty of (1494)

This fundamental allocation between Spain and Portugal of jurisdiction in the newly discovered lands and trade routes of the world was concluded in 1494. Competing claims between these two countries had their origins in the expansionist policies of CASTILE and Portugal dating back to the 14th century. Both kingdoms had designs on trade routes and non-Christian lands lying in or across the Atlantic Ocean or in North Africa and the sub-Saharan region of that continent. Lack of precise geographical information complicated these claims, and attempts to secure papal grants to one or the other claimant merely confused the issue. The report of a successful transatlantic voyage (1492–93) by CHRISTOPHER COLUMBUS focused the dispute and expedited practical resolutions. A new pope, the Spanish-born ALEXANDER VI, declared a preliminary demarcation line in 1493. It ran from the North Pole to the South Pole along a line that assigned all discoveries or acquisitions of non-Christian territories west of that line to Castile (or, in essence, to Spain) and those lying east of the line to Portugal.

The Treaty of Tordesillas, concluded at the Spanish town of that name, confirmed and put into the form of a diplomatic agreement the division of the non-European world into Spanish and Portuguese spheres of influence or conquest. Later papal decrees would grant management of missionary activities to Spanish and Portuguese clergy in their respective zones. The Treaty of Tordesillas itself would be modified several times during subsequent decades. The line of demarcation was shifted westward in 1497–98 to the benefit of Portugal. The latter country did not publicly reveal that it had reached the coast of what is now BRAZIL until 1500, after the revised Tordesillas agreement gave it jurisdiction over what now emerged as a portion of South America. Spain, on the other hand, ventured across the Pacific in the 1520s. The MAGELLAN expedition and other ventures into Asia were opposed by Portugal, which finally conceded the PHILIPPINE ISLANDS to Spain in 1529 by yet another reworking of the Tordesillas agreement. All of these agreements were eventually rendered obsolete when other European countries began venturing into territory originally claimed by Spain or Portugal, adopting the attitude displayed by King François I of France when he remarked that he had found it nowhere written in Father Adam's will that he had left the whole world exclusively to the inheritance of his Spanish and Portuguese descendants.

Torquemada, Tomás de (1429–1498)
Spanish clergyman

A Castilian, born in VALLADOLID, Torquemada became a priest of the Dominican order. His ecclesiastical career was assisted by his uncle, Cardinal Juan de Torquemada (1388–1468), who had significant influence at Rome. His nephew undoubtedly owed his appointment as prior of the Dominican monastery at SEGOVIA to this influence. Tomás developed valuable connections of his own, however, including a friendship with the secretary and treasurer of King FERDINAND V and Queen ISABELLA I. By 1479 he was already well established in the royal favor, extending his influence to other Dominican monasteries and soon becoming confessor to the monarchs.

Inquisitorial tribunals had for some time being operating in Spain but were criticized by the pope in 1482 as poorly managed. In the following year eight new inquisitors were appointed to improve the situation, one of them being Torquemada, who soon acquired an ascendancy over his associates. Within two years he had been named as inquisitor general for the lands of the crown of ARAGON, and by 1487 he was grand inquisitor with jurisdiction over CASTILE as well. During the remaining five years of his life Torquemada laid down the basic principles and practices of the "Holy Office," as the Inquisition was termed, and transformed it into an efficient instrument of the Spanish state. Following the completion of the RECONQUISTA in 1492 Torquemada urged his sovereigns to complete the renewal of Spain by the expulsion of alien religious groups. The Jews were arbitrarily banished in that same year, and the far more numerous Muslim population was placed under notice that it must convert to Christianity within a relatively short time or face expulsion. Aggressive attempts at conversion of the Moors continued, without great success during the remainder of Torquemada's life, but the status of Muslims or crypto-Muslims remained unresolved for decades. Jews, on the other hand, were given little time to choose between conversion or departure. Even those who officially embraced Christianity remained the target of inquisitorial investigation.

Some historians have argued that Torquemada was simply a man of his time for whom matters of law and religion were to be taken seriously and punishment for deviants were to be applied rigorously. Others have denounced him as a monster of fanaticism, obsessed with "cleansing" Spain of all who did not conform to his ideal of perfection. Although he was not the originator of the concept of an inquisition, either in Italy or Spain, he was in effect its founder and its principal ideologue. His brief tenure as grand inquisitor created an image of torture, public executions, secret agents, and mind control that would endure for centuries and become inseparable from the sinister connotations of the term SPANISH INQUISITION. Some commentators have found the supreme irony of Torquemada's particular pursuit of Spain's long-established Jewish community to lie in the fact that he came of a converso family (that is, one that had converted from Judaism generations earlier). His uncle, the cardinal, was able to accept his ancestry and to take a sympathetic interest in his Jewish countryfolk. Torquemada, however, may have been, in the opinion of some analysts, driven by guilt and shame over his origins to an obsessive persecution of those whose bloodline he shared.

Torres Naharro, Bartolomé de
(1476–1530)
Spanish playwright

Like many Spaniards of the Renaissance era, Torres Naharro pursued several careers successively. He was a soldier and spent time as a captive of the Moors. He then became a priest and made his way to Rome, where he met JUAN DEL ENCINA, another Spanish clergyman who had already embarked on a literary path. Both men were influenced by Italian innovations in poetry and poetical drama. Torres Naharro was clearly influenced by his countryman but pursued what is generally regarded as a more sophisticated and sometimes controversial line of dramatic writing. Literary historians have bestowed the title "father of Spanish drama" upon both Encina and Torres Naharro; however, despite the fact that the two men were near contemporaries, it might be more logical, according to some, to call Encina the "grandfather" because he preceded and influenced his friend.

Torres Naharro's earliest work consists largely of frank imitations of *églogas* (eclogues) of Encina, which were themselves derived from Virgilian models. However, when Torres Naharro assembled some of his plays for the volume he titled *Propalladia* (1517—the title is an allusion to Pallas Athena, Greek goddess of wisdom), he included a preface in which he sets forth his own classification of types of drama divided into those based on reality and those derived from imagination yet having a basis in real life. This distinction was not entirely clear, and he would later cross the line himself. He was, nevertheless, attempting to lay a theoretical foundation for a new Spanish drama. Included among the pieces in *Propalladia* was *Comedia soldadesca,* a portrayal of rough and ready military life, undoubtedly derived from his own experience. This volume also included *Comedia Himenea,* a prototype of the "cape and sword" play that introduced a concept of "honor" that became a major theme persisting throughout much of early modern Spanish drama. Torres Naharro is even bolder in *Comedia tinelaria,* in which he portrays the corrupt, immoral, and entertainingly unscrupulous environment of a cardinal's palace viewed from the perspective of the prelate's kitchen and the servants swarming there. These and other plays were performed in the more tolerant atmosphere of papal Rome, but their amorality and lack of discretion scandalized the SPANISH INQUISITION, which forbade their presentation in Spain. The printed text was not published there until the 1540s in altered form. His works as a whole were placed on the Index of Forbidden Books from 1559 and only reappeared in an expurgated form in 1573. One gets a clearer sense of how shocking this playwright's creations were to the censors when it is noted that each of them was preceded by a comic prologue in which peasants, speaking the *sayagués* dialect introduced by Encina for comic effect, descended into gross obscenity.

Both as a theorist and as a playwright Torres Naharro created a pathway to the flourishing drama of the SIGLO DE ORO (Golden Age). He stated norms of structure and theme that continued to influence the thinking of his successors, despite his own willingness to disregard them. He also moved beyond the relatively modest innovations of Encina to present a realistic and sometimes scandalous view of society.

Torres Villaroel, Diego de
(1693–1770)
Spanish writer and adventurer

From his birth in SALAMANCA to his death in the same city, Torres Villaroel passed through a kaleidoscopic variety of activities and occupations. He was, at various times, a youthful runaway, a hermit, a bullfighter, a dancer, a medical student, an astrologer, a self-taught mathematician, a university professor, a priest, a goblin chaser, a social critic and advocate of enlightened reform, a popular idol, and the protégé of several noble ladies. All of these experiences and excursions are recorded in his personal memoir, *Vida,* which was published in 1743 in the guise of a picaresque novel. Those personae not chronicled therein are manifested in the many other books of which he was author during his long life. These revealed the amazing range of his expertise—or at least his interest—and his willingness to share it with the public. Torres has been variously described as a Renaissance man or man of the Enlightenment or a complete charlatan who could win the confidence of influential people as well as credulous commoners by sheer bluff. His first "scientific" publication, for instance, was an almanac that he compiled after limited reading of math texts. His success in predicting certain natural phenomena made him a national celebrity and ended by winning him election to the chair of mathematics at the University of Salamanca over many authentic mathematicians. Whatever the validity of his claims to be a universal genius, he was, at least, a remarkably interesting character and one whose picaro's eye view of 18th-century Spanish life is a useful source for an understanding of that era.

Trafalgar, Battle of (1805)

Only a few years before Napoléon's invasion of Spain precipitated the PENINSULAR WAR, Spain and France, still allies, undertook to clear the English Channel of its naval defenders so that the French emperor's invading forces could overrun the British Isles. Early in 1805 a "combined fleet" under French admiral Pierre de Villeneuve, with the support of Admiral FEDERICO GRAVINA'S "division of observation," undertook to draw off the main British force by feigning a transatlantic expedition. British admiral Horatio Nelson's fleet hastened to the Antilles only to discover that they had been tricked. Meanwhile, the Franco-Spanish armada had reassembled off the European coastline, where a small British force discovered them. Villeneuve allowed the British to escape. Worse yet the enemy took advantage of the onset of fog to capture two Span-

ish ships. With the British Admiralty now alerted and Nelson hastening back from the West Indies, the cross-Channel invasion seemed impossible, and Napoléon furiously dismissed Villeneuve. The admiral ignored his dismissal, however, and set out to provoke a battle with Nelson, hoping to regain imperial favor by a dazzling triumph. The two forces met close to the Spanish coast near Cape Trafalgar. Nelson, in his flagship, *Victory,* launched a bold attack on the Franco-Spanish line, confronting the *Santísima Trinidad,* a 120-gun three-decker, then the largest warship in the world. Beaten back, he repeated the attack and the breaking of the combined fleet's line brought on a general action between individual ships.

The day ended with Nelson dead, Villeneuve captured, and Gravina mortally wounded. Of the 15 major warships in the Spanish contingent, three were sunk, three captured, four run aground, and only five badly damaged vessels limping back to port. In addition to Gravina, Spain also lost two distinguished captains, Antonio Alcalá Galiano and Cosme Churruca, both scientific sailors who had done important work in cartography and hydrography. The Spanish ships and their crews were generously praised by their adversaries for their bravery and heroism. The tragedy of Spain's role in this battle is famously celebrated by BENITO PÉREZ GALDÓS in *Trafalgar,* one of his *Episodios nacionales.*

U

Unamuno, Miguel de (1864–1936)
Spanish writer and philosopher

Spain's leading 20th-century philosopher, Unamuno followed two career paths simultaneously. One was a conventional, if controversial, academic track leading him to a professorship while still in his 20s and the post of rector at the University of Salamanca

Miguel de Unamuno *(Library of Congress)*

a few years later. He held this post for the rest of his life with interruptions caused by his disputes with successive Spanish governments. His outspoken views on Spain's neutrality in World War I led to deposition in 1916 followed by restoration in 1920, but he was banished in 1924 and did not return from France until PRIMO DE RIVERA's dictatorship was ended in 1930. A supporter of the new republic in 1931, he criticized it in 1934, welcomed the military revolt against it in early 1936, denounced the generals a few months later, and was under a form of house arrest when he died in December of that year.

Unamuno's contrarian, sometimes paradoxical public positions led to his being praised as an independent thinker or denounced as an inconsistent curmudgeon. A similar sense of changeability, better characterized as an ongoing struggle to understand human destiny is reflected in his other career path—his literary work. Unamuno distinguished himself as an essayist, poet, and novelist, with occasional excursions into drama and even journalism. All of his writings, as well as his public utterances, were reflections of his evolving personal philosophy. Probably the best known among Unamuno's scores of writings are *En torno al casticismo* (On Castilianism, 1902), *Vida de Don Quijote y Sancho* (*Life of Don Quixote and Sancho*, 1905), *Del sentimiento trágico de la vida* (*The Tragic Sense of Life*, 1913), *Niebla* (*Mist*, 1914), *El Cristo de Velázquez* (The Christ of Velazquez, 1920), and *La agonía del cristianismo* (*The Agony of Christianity*, 1925). His recurring major themes are the human striving for personal identity and the preservation of that identity beyond the limitation imposed by death, and, more particularly, the Spanish character as revealed in its history and cultural manifestations. Unamuno is, thus, alternately preoccupied with universal questions and the immediate crisis forced upon the abstract thinker by the facts of his existence in a particular time and place. For all his "Spanishness" (his Basque origins did not seem to be an issue for him), many Spaniards have found him as baffling as those foreigners who characterize him as impenetrably Castilian. Some have dismissed him as a heretic, while others have praised him as profoundly Christian. What those who know him best would probably affirm is that Unamuno, the eternal student of paradoxes, would have reveled in all of the descriptions of him that have been attempted.

Uruguay

Despite 16th- and early 17th-century exploration and settlement in this region by Spain, constant encroachment from Portuguese-ruled BRAZIL led to competing claims and periodic flare-ups of military action. The area designated as Colonia, including the city of Montevideo, was alternately under Spanish and Portuguese control. Present-day Uruguay was included within the Viceroyalty of LA PLATA from 1776 onward. Known for a time as Banda Oriental, Uruguay followed Buenos Aires in declaring its independence from Spain between 1811 and 1814; nevertheless, Brazil continued to covet the area, formally proclaiming Uruguay as its Cisplatine Province in 1821. Uruguayans rebelled against Brazilian rule in 1825 and finally won general recognition of their sovereignty in 1828.

V

Valdés, Alfonso de (1490–1532)

Spanish official and political writer

The details of Valdés's background are not clear, but his intelligence and skill won him the patronage of CHARLES I (Holy Roman Emperor Charles V), who appointed him to a position in the imperial chancellery in the early 1520s. In this capacity he carried out many assignments relating to Spain's dominant role in the affairs of Europe. These affairs reached a critical stage during 1527 when the ITALIAN WARS (1494–1559) produced a collaboration between Spain's persistent enemy, France, and Pope Clement VII. Failing to persuade the pope to abandon this strategic allegiance, the emperor sent a German army to besiege Rome. The outcome was the capture of the Holy City and a prolonged sack, accompanied by shocking murders and outrages. The general indignation that swept Europe was countered by Valdés in a defense of his master, titled *Diálogo de Lactancio y un arcediano* (Dialogue between Lactancio and an archdeacon). Using the conventional format of a dialogue between a seeker after truth and a knowledgeable person, Valdés exonerated the emperor of all blame, blamed the "Sacco di Roma" on the understandable battle rage of the soldiers, and attempted to show that the pope's advisers bore the true responsibility for what had happened. To this end he quoted various documents allegedly proving the villainy of high-ranking clergymen. Valdés's skillfully composed vindication of the Spanish monarch's honor did not go unchallenged. A papal envoy lodged complaints against him with the Council of Castile and the inquisitor general without success.

Valdés was however living on borrowed time. He had already acquired a reputation as a disciple of Erasmus and had exchanged correspondence with that proponent of ecclesiastical reform. He had gone so far as to write another dialogue, *Diálogo de Mercurio y Carón*, in which he defended the emperor against both foreign and domestic critics through pointed and daring satire. In this essay he was particularly scathing regarding the vanities and improprieties of the clergy. When a campaign against Erasmus was launched at the end of 1529, the Dutch thinker's followers in Spain were vigorously targeted by the SPANISH INQUISITION, and Valdés's name stood high on the list. He was forced to leave Spain to avoid prosecution. He found refuge in Vienna and might have benefited from the patronage and protection of the emperor, but a plague outbreak in 1532 ended Valdés's promising career.

Valdés, Cayetano (1767–1835)
Spanish naval officer and statesman

Joining the navy at an early age, Valdés distinguished himself at the Battle of Cape St. Vincent (1797) and was promoted to the rank of captain at an unusually early age. At TRAFALGAR in 1805 his heroism earned him the rank of rear admiral. When the Franco-Spanish alliance collapsed in 1808 Valdés gave his services promptly to the forces of the anti-Napoleonic junta at CÁDIZ. During the subsequent campaigns that led to the expulsion of the French Valdés displayed his leadership in land warfare, taking command of an army division. As notorious for his liberal political views as his martial prowess, Valdés was removed from his offices by the restored FERDINAND VII in 1814 and spent the next six years confined to prison. The liberal uprising in 1820 restored him to an active role in public affairs, first as military governor of Cádiz and then as a member of the regency that led to the country's resistance to the reactionary counterrevolution of 1823. Valdés was among those condemned to death for his opposition to the absolutist Ferdinand VII but escaped with his life. Having found refuge in GIBRALTAR, Valdés spent the next decade in Great Britain and returned to Spain only after the death of Ferdinand. During his final years many of his honors were restored, and new and grander ones were bestowed upon him by ISABELLA II, including "Great Man of the Nation."

Valdés, Juan de (ca. 1491/1492–1541)
Spanish humanist

Although the year of Valdés's birth is not precisely known, modern scholarship favors 1491 or 1492 and rejects the formerly asserted theory that he and his brother ALFONSO DE VALDÉS were twins. Like his brother, Valdés was a disciple of Erasmus and was clearly influenced by the latter's thinking on the church. His *Diálogo de la doctrina cristiana*, published in 1529, was sufficiently unorthodox to bring him to the attention of the SPANISH INQUISITION. Fleeing a charge of heresy, he found refuge in Italy, eventually settling in Naples, where he would reside for the rest of his life.

Unlike his brother Alfonso, Valdés devoted most of his thinking and writing to religious matters. Although he spoke of a careless life as a student at Alcalá and held no degree in theology, he was clearly a well-read and thoughtful Christian. During the early years of the Reformation crisis he took part in a number of dialogues between Catholic and Protestant thinkers that were sponsored by CHARLES I of Spain (Holy Roman Emperor Charles V). Although he and his fellow conferees could agree on a number of ritualistic or structural points, the discussions always left Valdés supporting the official Catholic doctrinal positions. In his discussions with like-minded Erasmians in the relatively liberal environment of Naples he evidently spoke more freely and even ventured into subjects like the doctrine of justification by faith alone, which church authorities regarded as irredeemably "Lutheran." Valdés produced a number of writings (some of which remained in manuscript until after his death). Widely known and respected, Valdés was one of the most significant Spanish contributors to the great religious debates that eventually left Spain firmly committed to papal Catholicism during the Counter-Reformation era.

Chief among his theological-philosophical books are *Alfabeto cristiano* (*Christian Alphabet*, c. 1537) and *Ciento y diez consideraciones divinas* (*One Hundred Ten Divine Considerations*, c. 1539). In addition Valdés produced his extremely important *Diálogo de la lengua* (Dialogue of the language), which was written in about 1535 but was not published until the 18th century. In it Valdés was dismissive of the famous *Gramática* by ELIO ANTONIO DE NEBRIJA, whom he considered to have been limited in his scope and faulty in his execution. Modern commentators have tended to support Valdés, hailing him as the father of Spanish philology and one of Spain's earliest literary critics, who draws examples from other Castilian writers and evaluates them in an elegant prose style of his own. Had Valdés brought out his own book immediately upon its completion it might well have occupied the place among fundamental expositions of the Spanish language and its origins that was long conceded to Nebrija by scholars of the Iberian Renaissance.

Valdivia, Pedro de (1497–1554)
Spanish explorer

A native of EXTREMADURA, Valdivia joined the army in his youth and fought in the Italian campaigns during the 1520s. Following the temporary cessation of hostilities there he set out to make his fortune in the New World. He spent some time in what is now VENEZUELA and then proceeded to PERU, where he played a prominent role in FRANCISCO PIZARRO's conquest of the Inca heartland. By 1535 he was already a trusted lieutenant of the conqueror, who assigned him the exploration and pacification of the territory to the south.

Like other Spaniards and even the Inca armies before them, Valdivia and his men found the Araucanian tribes of what is now CHILE to be fierce opponents. Every advance was costly to Valdivia, and each foothold that he secured had to be maintained with constant vigilance. Nevertheless, during the 1540s, he was able to plant fortified settlements that would grow into the modern cities of Santiago, Concepción, Valdivia, and others.

Leaving his subordinates to hold the frontier in the south, Valdivia returned to Peru in 1547 with the intention of confirming his authority over the newly conquered lands. He found the country in a state of civil war, with a Spanish-appointed viceroy confronting the rebellious Gonzalo Pizarro, brother and successor of the original conquistador. Valdivia threw his support behind the royal representative, leading a decisive cavalry attack in a crucial battle. The victorious viceroy rewarded him by making him governor of Chile and authorizing him to extend his control there. Returning to Chile in 1549, Valdivia tightened his grip over districts already held and extended his campaign of conquest down to the Bío-Bío River, the farthest practical boundary that could be held. Colonists had begun to settle in Chile and to develop agriculture and stock raising as well as the early stages of a mining industry. Forcing the conquered Indians to work in the mines and taxing them as well soon provoked a massive uprising that devastated several of the settlements in 1553. Overconfidently confronting a large band of Araucanians with a mere 40 soldiers at his back, Valdivia was overwhelmed, and only one of his party survived to carry the story to the nearest fort.

One of the most intelligent, methodical, and successful of the conquistadores, Valdivia's very record of success finally led him to presume too much about his ability to rout the indigenous folk who had already yielded so much of their land to him. He remains, nonetheless, the only one of the conquerors to create under his personal leadership the structure of a Spanish colony that remains a major South American state.

Valencia

This Mediterranean coastal city (with a population of nearly 1 million) was successively ruled by Romans, Visigoths, and Moors, whose mastery was interrupted (1094–99) by the overlordship of Spain's greatest medieval warrior, Rodrigo Díaz de Vivar, known as El Cid. The city and its surrounding territory passed permanently into Christian hands in the late 13th century and was subsequently joined to the lands of the crown of ARAGON as capital of the Kingdom of Valencia. Although maintaining a distinct cultural tradition (with a distinct Valencian language linked to Catalan), Valencia did not become a stronghold of opposition to the centralization program of successive Spanish regimes, as did other regional capitals. The city nevertheless suffered severe damage from bombardment during the PENINSULAR WAR and the SPANISH CIVIL WAR. The recent history of Valencia has been characterized by the growing prosperity of its manufactures, its advantageous use of a wide-range of natural resources, and its historical appeal to the tourists who abound along the Mediterranean coast.

Valera y Alcalá Galiano, Juan
(1824–1905)
Spanish writer

With aristocratic connections and a classical education, Valera was well prepared for a diplomatic career. He served in Rio de Janeiro and Washington, D.C., as well as many European capitals, ultimately becoming ambassador in Vienna. He also held political office, as a deputy in parliament and undersecretary of state and, finally, a senator for life. But Valera was and is best remembered as a literary man. Some recent commentators have called him Spain's best literary critic of the 19th century. Deep in his knowledge of writers, both ancient and modern, and sophisticated in his judgments, he was, at the same time, more generous and sympathetic to newcomers than many of his peers. As a novelist—the role in which he is best known—Valera displayed a similar amiability. In *Pepita Jiménez* (1874), his most famous work, Valera displays a warm sympathy with the dilemmas of his principal characters and a skillful use of both language and setting. These traits are generally also present in *Doña Luz* (1879) and *Juanita la larga* (1895), but some have faulted him for a viewpoint that is too much that of the elegant aristocrat, viewing the world in terms of a philosophical discussion in a salon of gentlefolk. He has nothing to say about the common people and is essentially indifferent to the currents of naturalism running through European literature in his day and affecting other Spanish writers. Even his use of the epistolary form in *Pepita Jiménez* seems to emphasize an old-fashioned gentility as his principal male character, a young seminarian, debates the conflicting demands of a priestly vocation and his growing love for the charming

Pepita. There is, to be sure, a level of psychological insight into the minds of his characters for which Valera has been duly praised; however, Valera, for all the grace and warmth of his Andalusian settings, seems afflicted by an emotional distance not only from his subject matter, but from his era and the "new Spain" that was emerging during his lifetime.

Valladolid

This modern industrial city in central Spain was formerly the capital of CASTILE and the residence of the Spanish royal court from 1454 to 1598. Its points of interest, including churches dating back to the 12th century and the house where CHRISTOPHER COLUMBUS died, reflect a historical experience that culminates in a 17th-century palace. As Spanish monarchs and their courtiers transferred their activities to MADRID, some 100 miles to the southeast, Valladolid was forced into a political decline and is now principally known as a center of light industry.

Valle-Inclán, Ramón María del
(1866–1936)
Spanish writer
One of the most picturesque figures among Spanish writers, this native of GALICIA practiced law, lived the bohemian life in Paris, traveled through MEXICO, and was at various times an estate manager, a teacher, a cattle rancher, and a revolutionary. He was imprisoned for a time for his opposition to the dictator PRIMO DE RIVERA and held various offices under the Second Republic. There was little about Valle-Inclán, however, that could be reduced to prosaic facts

or biographical data. Even his name was partially invented. His manner, dress, and physical appearance were all distinctive and exaggerated, less from eccentricity of mind than from the self-dramatizing impulses of the poseur. Everyone in MADRID knew Don Ramón, with his long straggly beard and hair, his archaic outfits, and his perennial cape.

Valle-Inclán's literary position is also difficult to pin down. Influenced in his early days by French symbolism and later regarded as an exponent of modernism, he has also been considered a proponent of Galician regional culture and an embittered critic of post–1898 Spanish national decline (although not all critics agree in associating him with the GENERATION OF '98). In an early group of novels collectively known as *Sonatas* (1902–05) the author combines intense sensuality with an archaic elegance of style that reveals his mastery of the Spanish language. Ever impatient with subject matter and approaches, Valle-Inclán went through a series of absurdist and bitterly satirical prose writings, indulged in a number of plays notable for their unsparing decadence of subject matter, and in 1926 produced what some critics regard as his finest novel, *Tirano Banderas* (*The Tyrant*)—which others do not accept as a novel at all, but rather a loosely connected set of short stories. This portrayal of the progressive degeneration of a Mexican political leader and the ruin that it brings upon his people is remarkable for its mastery of Mexican vocabulary and setting. A fascinating combination of artistic genius and emotionally unstable decadence, Valle-Inclán is one of the most interesting but difficult figures among modern Spanish literary artists.

Velázquez, Diego Rodríguez de Silva y (1599–1660)

Spanish painter

Born in SEVILLE, the son of a lawyer, Velázquez was apprenticed successively to two well-known Spanish painters of his day, Francisco de Herrera the elder and FRANCISCO PACHECO (who later became both his father-in-law and his biographer). During his early years as an artist Velázquez concentrated on religious and genre themes. In 1622 he moved to MADRID where he benefited from the patronage of the chief minister, OLIVARES, and soon became court painter to PHILIP IV. Many of his best-known paintings were of Olivares and other courtiers and of the king and his family. For more than 30 years Velázquez occupied a privileged and honored place in the service of Philip IV, being granted periods of study and work in Italy (1629–31 and 1649–50). During the latter visit he acted as the king's agent in the selection and purchase of large numbers of Italian masterpieces for the adornment of the royal palaces. Velázquez also received many honors, including membership in the Order of Santiago and appointment as chamberlain (with administrative duties that sometimes interfered in later years with his artistic activities).

Velázquez was acknowledged in his own time as the unrivaled master of virtually every field of painting, including portraits, religious subjects, scenes of everyday live, landscapes, and occasionally mythological figures. Influenced in his earliest days by certain contemporary Spanish painters and perhaps by the Italian Caravaggio, and later benefiting from the advice of Rubens and examining the work of Titian and Tintoretto during his Italian sojourn, Velázquez transcended all of these influences, having some imitators but no equals. His technique became freer and more impressionistic in his mature years, and his handling of color, even more subtle.

Among his most applauded paintings are those of Philip IV, which sympathetically portray the aging of a monarch who was his patron and friend over the decades and of Pope Innocent X who gave Velázquez every assistance during the latter's Roman residence. Among these and other paintings that have won the particular praise of critics over the centuries, undoubtedly Velázquez's most remarkable achievement is the massive canvas known as *Las meninas* (The maids of honor, 1656). The viewer is transported into the artist's studio, where a royal princess and her ladies in waiting are in the foreground, but the true focus of the painting is the king and queen, reflected in a mirror while Velázquez himself is observed working on his canvas. In everything from its coloring to its technical skill and the sheer creativity of the artist's approach, the painting deserves its reputation as one of the enduring achievements of Spanish artistic genius.

Ironically, when the government sought to give Velázquez the ultimate honor of a grandiose tomb to mark the 400th anniversary of his birth in 1999, his actual burial place could not be located. Velázquez was therefore allowed to rest in peace, and a more appropriate honor was bestowed upon his memory by creating the Velázquez Prize as an artistic counterpart to the Cervantes Prize for literary distinction. Thus the greatest painter and the greatest writer of Spain's Golden Age stand together in the pantheon of history.

Velázquez de Cuéllar, Diego
(1460–1524)
Spanish explorer and colonial administrator

Velázquez de Cuéllar was among the first of the conquistadores. He accompanied CHRISTOPHER COLUMBUS on his second voyage (1493). After returning to Europe to fight in the opening stage of the ITALIAN WARS, he traveled to the New World again in the early 1500s, while the center of Spanish presence there was still located in HISPANIOLA. Under the mandate of Diego Columbus, the son of the discoverer, Velázquez undertook the exploration and conquest of CUBA. Between 1510 and 1514 he carried out operations against the native population that included both war and persuasion. In these campaigns he was assisted by many leading members of what had been called the first generation of conquistadores, including PÁNFILO DE NARVÁEZ, PEDRO DE ALVARADO, and (in terms of religion) BARTOLOMÉ DE LAS CASAS. Having pacified Cuba, Velázquez established numerous settlements, many of which survive as towns to the present day and distributed land grants to his principal officers. The jealousy and suspicion of Columbus caused him to interfere with the increasingly independent behavior of his subordinate, but Velázquez had powerful connections at the Spanish Court, and these enabled him to secure a free hand in Cuba and to act as governor from about 1516 onward.

Velázquez dispatched a series of probing expeditions to the North American mainland, including that of JUAN DE GRIJALVA in 1518 and that of HERNÁN CORTÉS, who landed on what is now MEXICO in 1519. The progress of Cortés into the interior of Mexico at first angered Velázquez, who feared that his authority was being ignored, and he dispatched Narváez to supplant Cortés. After Cortés routed Narváez's forces, Velázquez accepted the independent initiatives that were already leading to the conquest of the Aztec Empire. He was confirmed in his own powers by a royal decree of 1519 making him ADELANTADO of Cuba and all lands discovered under his oversight. The suspicious and domineering temperament of Velázquez still did not permit him to work out his differences with Cortés, especially after the latter had completed the conquest of Mexico and opened his own channel of self-promotion to the king of Spain. As a result of these rivalries, Velázquez was actually removed from the governorship of Cuba in 1521, although he regained the post two years later. For the remainder of his life, Velázquez continued to meddle in the activities of the conquistadores (mostly lieutenants of Cortés) who were engaged in the systematic exploration and occupation of Central America.

Velázquez undoubtedly played a pivotal role in moving the Spanish conquest of the Americas from its initial foothold on Hispaniola into the second phase, which involved the islands of the Caribbean and the first penetration into Mexico and Central America. In Cuba he was, in effect, the prime conqueror of what would be Spain's most enduring stronghold in the New World. Despite his military prowess and skill in manipulating officials of the royal government, however, he suffered from a suspicious and contentious temperament that thwarted his ability to achieve the status of a major architect of the Spanish conquest.

Venezuela

Spanish explorers sailing along this stretch of the South American coast in the early 1500s noted the Amerindian dwellings built on stilts in the water and named the area *Venezuela,* or "little Venice," after a fancied resemblance to the Italian city of canals. The first settlement was planted in 1520, and eight years later the greater part of the region was granted to the Welser family of Augsburg, Germany, a banking house that had made extensive loans to CHARLES I. Their agents and conquistadores working either in collaboration or in competition with them explored Venezuela over the next several decades, and by the late 1540s the authority of the Spanish Crown had been established. Venezuela was made subordinate to the Viceroyalty of NEW GRANADA in 1718 and organized as the Captaincy General of Venezuela in 1731. Although Venezuela declared its independence from Spain in 1811, Spanish forces were not finally defeated and ousted until 1821.

Vicente, Gil (1470–1536)
Portuguese playwright

Generally considered Portugal's greatest dramatist, Vicente has also been called the greatest dramatist of Renaissance Europe prior to the advent of William Shakespeare. Little is known with any certainty about his life or the literary influences that shaped his art. His earliest known work was presented in celebration of the birth of the Portuguese prince who later became John III. A significant portion of his 44 plays still extant were evidently produced to mark notable events in the reign of the AVIZ dynasty (including one honoring the marriage of that same prince). Vicente clearly enjoyed the status of

court poet, although some of his productions were intended to mark great achievements in the building of Portugal's overseas empire. He was, thus, also the national laureate of his country in its great Age of Discovery. Vicente's early works show the influence of pastoral and religious productions widely performed in medieval Portugal, and they were followed by a growing awareness of Italian techniques. In his mature period he was ready and able to shift from one genre to the other, displaying a light touch when appropriate but often rising to the eloquence demanded by more serious subjects. He evidently worked almost entirely for private and privileged audiences, eschewing the mass appeal that later playwrights had always to keep in mind. Yet, while he was obliged to respect the dignity of royal and noble patrons, he exhibits satirical wit that did not spare even the foibles of the clergy.

Among Vicente's notable works are *Auto da visitação* (Play of the visitation, 1502), the short play that marks the known beginning of his career; *Auto da fama* (Play of fame, 1515); *Frágua de amor* (*The Forge of Love,* 1524); *Templo de Apolo* (Temple of Apollo, 1526); *Romagem de agravados* (*Pilgrimage of the Aggrieved,* 1533); *Floresta de enganos* (Forest of deceits, 1536); and *Amadís de Gaula* (*Amadis of Gaul,* 1533). In keeping with the close political and cultural ties between the two Iberian kingdoms, Vicente wrote some of his plays in Portuguese, some in Spanish, and others in a mixture of the two languages.

Vieira, António (1608–1697)
Portuguese writer and orator

Born in Portugal, Vieira was taken to BRAZIL by his parents at an early age and educated there. He joined the Jesuit order and gained a reputation as an eloquent teacher and preacher, even before his ordination to the priesthood. He was particularly noted for his ability to communicate effectively with the African and Amerindian segments of the population as well as with those of Portuguese origin. He was prominent in the movement to rally these three groups against the Dutch dominance of northern Brazil. The joint action of the Brazilian peoples was primarily responsible for ousting these intruders and had the further effect of mobilizing them against Spain's overlordship of the Portuguese colonies.

After the Portuguese revolt against the dominance of Spain in 1640 Vieira played a patriotic role and was selected as a member of a delegation sent to LISBON to pledge Brazil's support for the newly proclaimed king, JOHN IV. Vieira quickly won the favor of the monarch and was entrusted by him with diplomatic missions to various countries as well as to the Holy See. Vieira, who had already made himself a champion of the nonwhite inhabitants of Brazil, now became increasingly active as an advocate for the persecuted Portuguese subjects of Jewish origin, who were frequently suspected of clinging to their original faith. His writings and ardent sermons brought him increasingly under the scrutiny of the Portuguese Inquisition and led, during the mid-1660s, to his imprisonment. As this was a period when factional disputes following the death of John IV had deprived him of his former influence at court, he had to wait until the renewed ascendancy of friends in high places won him his freedom.

Vieira spent much of the 1670s in Rome, where his eloquence once again won him a following among the most prominent residents of the Eternal City. But ecclesiastical and political intrigues were beginning to weary him. The latest maneuvers at the royal court of Lisbon, to which he returned for a time, confirmed him in his intention to bid farewell to Europe. Back in Brazil after an absence of some 30 years he found a congenial place of retirement in BAHIA, where he devoted himself to teaching and writing until his death at the age of 90.

Vieira is honored both in Brazil, where he remains a political and cultural icon, and in Portugal. His standing in the Lusitanian pantheon places him as the greatest prose writer of his era, ranked alongside the poet CAMÕES, who flourished a century earlier. His commitment to Sebastianism (the Portuguese messianic belief that King SEBASTIAN did not die in battle in 1578 but waited in a mystical trance for the summons to rescue his country from desperate adversity) was reflected in his support of John IV. The SPANISH INQUISITION found Sebastianism dangerously unorthodox, and modern readers of his writings can only puzzle at its eccentricity. Most of Vieira's writings and the universal acclaim given to his sermons and exhortations make it clear that he was a man of great eloquence and profoundly humane wisdom.

Vieira's principal prose works, some of them published posthumously, include *Sermões* (Sermons, 1679–1748), *Historia do Futuro* (History of the future, 1718) *Cartas* (Letters, 1735–46), and *Arte de Furtar* (The art of stealing, 1652).

Vives, Juan Luis (1492–1540)
Spanish humanist

Vives, who has been called "the glory of VALENCIA," his native city, was born in that "glorious year," 1492, which saw the culmination of the RECONQUISTA of Spain and the voyage of CHRISTOPHER COLUMBUS that began the building of the Spanish Empire. It was, on a more personal level, the year when ELIO ANTONIO DE NEBRIJA launched the Spanish Renaissance with the publication of his famous *Gramática*, the same Nebrija whose chair at Alcalá would be offered upon his death to Spain's greatest living Renaissance scholar, Vives. A darker connection might also be found between the year of Vives's birth and the expulsion of the Jews from Spain, for there are complex questions related to the future humanist's converso origin and the circumstances of his departure from Spain.

Privately educated in at least the fundamentals of both law and medicine, Vives pursued advanced studies in the humanities in Paris (1509–12) then moved on to Bruges, where he became a tutor in a wealthy household whose daughter he would later wed. In the Netherlands he became a friend of Erasmus, whose philosophical and religious ideas he admired, and was urged by his mentor to undertake a treatise on St. Augustine's *De civitate Dei* (1522). This display of his learning brought Vives to the attention of Henry VIII, who had a strong interest in theology, and welcomed him to England. Vives became an adviser to Henry's Spanish-born consort, CATHERINE OF ARAGON, preceptor to her daughter (the future queen Mary I), and a lecturer at Oxford. Vives fell from royal favor when he opposed Henry's plan to divorce his wife, even though the Spanish scholar declined her request to be her trial counsel. After a period of house arrest Vives returned to the Continent, living in France for most of his remaining years.

Despite poor health he devoted himself to study and writing and further enhanced his reputation as a thinker and innovator in the realms of philosophy, education, and what would come to be known as psychology. In a series of publications on the training of both boys and girls he pioneered in the advocacy of schooling for women, the study of the natural world, and the importance of practical subjects such as modern languages. Although only one of his approximately 70 works was originally published in Spanish (Latin being still the universal language of scholarship), he is considered one of the most distinguished of Spain's thinkers and philosophers. His promotion of the inductive method of analysis, inspired by his Erasmian studies, would have great influence on many fields of learning and shape the work of scholars throughout Renaissance Europe. Vives's works include *De ratione studii puerilis* (On the right method of instruction for children, 1523), *De causis corruptarum artium* (On the causes of corruption of the arts, 1531), *De disciplinis* (On education, 1531), *De prima philosophia* (First philosophy, 1531), and *De institutione feminae christianae* (*The Instruction of a Christian Woman*, 1523).

W

Wall, Richard (Ricardo Wall)
(1694–1778)

Spanish statesman

Born in Nantes, France, where his Irish Catholic family had found sanctuary from religious persecution, Wall was raised in Spain, entered the naval service of that country, and won commendation for his role in the Sicilian campaign at the Battle of Cape Passaro (1718–19). He later transferred to the army, fought in Italy, and eventually rose to the rank of lieutenant general. It was as a diplomat, however, that Wall achieved his greatest influence, due to his linguistic skills, polished manners, and personal charm. After serving in a junior capacity in St. Petersburg, he eventually became ambassador to France where he played a key role in negotiating the Treaty of Aix-la-Chapelle (1748). Under FERDINAND VII and CHARLES III he successively served as minister of state and of war. A strong proponent of an Anglo-Spanish alliance (he had spent time as ambassador in London), Wall was nevertheless unable to persuade Charles III to break away from the Bourbon Family Compact. Wall retired in 1763, spending his last years in GRANADA, where his personality and generosity made him a popular and admired local figure.

Weyler y Nicolau, Valeriano
(marqués de Tenerife) (1838–1930)

Spanish soldier

The son of an army surgeon of German origin, Weyler eagerly entered cadet school at the earliest possible age and was a lieutenant by the age of 20. Following duty in Spain and North Africa he made his mark during the 1860s in Caribbean campaigns where he aided in the repression of the Cuban rebellion and operations against those in Santo Domingo who opposed that territory's short-lived return to Spanish rule. There he developed an understanding of irregular warfare and wrote a manual on antiguerrilla operations. Returning to Spain as a colonel in the early 1870s, he distinguished himself in the Second Carlist War and then rose steadily in rank and responsibility, serving as captain general of several regions. (He was made marqués de Tenerife while serving as captain general in the CANARY ISLANDS.) He also held further colonial commands in PUERTO RICO and the PHILIPPINE ISLANDS.

The 1890s found Weyler back in CUBA as captain general, charged with putting down a new insurrection. Grasping the importance to the rebels of their civilian support network, Weyler instituted a plan of "reconcentration." Under this program more than

300,000 Cubans were removed from their rural villages and placed in confined, guarded locations where they could neither aid nor be intimidated by the rebels. Due to inadequate provision of sanitary and health services as well as periodic food shortages, thousands of Cuban peasants died in these camps, creating an international scandal. The United States, soon to intervene in Cuba, was particularly intense in its anti-Spanish protests, with newspapers denouncing "Butcher Weyler" for his atrocities. The assassination of Weyler's strong backer, Prime Minister ANTONIO CÁNOVAS, opened him to denunciation by Spanish Liberals, and he was recalled from his command in 1897.

After the SPANISH-AMERICAN WAR and the virtual loss of Spain's empire Weyler was perceived by many as having been justified in his harsh tactics. Already the recipient of scores of medals and every available military honor, he served three terms as minister of war during the early 1900s, as well as holding successively the titles of commander in chief and chief of the general staff. Once again applying rigorous methods, he crushed the anarchist uprising in CATALONIA during BARCELONA's "Tragic Week" in 1909. When the intrigues of General MIGUEL PRIMO DE RIVERA threatened the government in 1923, Weyler, the senior officer of the army, was the only leader to respond to the prime minister's call for help, even though the coup was already too far advanced to be prevented. In 1929, a year before his death, the venerable general was honored for 75 years of uninterrupted service in the army.

Weyler was an unapologetically brutal commander who subscribed to the idea that war was a serious business and that defeating the enemy was a general's prime duty. Although Spain's critics made his name a by-word for cruelty, his tactics would be widely adopted in the 20th century (as, for instance, by the British in the Boer War of 1899–1902). His uncompromising professionalism was also reflected in his refusal to follow the pattern laid down by 19th-century political generals. When approached about leading a revolt against the regime in 1899, he not only declined but spoke of honor and loyalty with such eloquence that the plotters abandoned their scheme. His willingness to stand against Primo de Rivera was merely the last act in a career of unswerving patriotism.

women's rights in Spain

Spain has produced notable women, from ISABELLA the Catholic and TERESA OF ÁVILA to the fiery (if fictional) Carmen and the even more fiery and definitely real La Pasionaria (DOLORES IBÁRRURI). But, throughout history, the majority of Spanish women have lived lives of obscurity and subjugation. Even women of high social rank have been known chiefly in the context of their family's male leaders. Over the centuries women have been homemakers, child rearers, silent supporters or sufferers, whose only solace outside the bounds of family life has been through religion. Even those who emerged as patriotic fighters or revolutionary zealots did so only briefly, often losing their lives in the process and occasionally gaining a few colorful allusions in popular literature. When demands for women's rights, particularly in the areas of the franchise and personal property, were surging in the United States and some parts of Europe at the beginning of the 20th century, Spain remained unmoved. The birth of the Second Republic in 1931 saw the granting of at least some elements of equality to all citizens, but the clock was turned back eight years later when the republic fell. Only near the end of the FRANCO dictatorship, when some of his more progressive advisers loosened the subjugation of wives to their husbands, was any significant change in prospect.

With the coming of democracy after the dictator's death in 1975 the subject of women's rights became one of the most debated in the "new Spain." Public opinion polls suggested that most men were favorable to reform in this area, although with widely varying levels of tolerance. Not surprisingly women were overwhelmingly interested in improving their situation, although many were ambivalent about possible problems, both moral and material. Perhaps for this reason the question of women's rights remained unresolved for decades. Both those who expected a social revolution to sweep across the Spanish nation and those who anticipated that political and religious traditionalists would mobilize overwhelming opposition to "modernism" encountered instead a complex and confusing process that dragged on through the first 25 years of the "new age." Straightforward change based on fundamental principles of citizenship and constitutional law were relatively easy to achieve. The number of women who became legislators, judges, and even cabinet ministers was significant, although not overwhelmingly impressive. But even the proper political forum for pursuing women's rights created debates. Did women have the best chance for securing their goals through a feminist party, as LIDIA FALCÓN argued, or through activism in the

ranks of the old established parties? The emancipation of women from the long-established rule of male head of household broke down into a multitude of legislative wrangles and court cases, with the general trend toward a woman's rights in matters such as divorce, personal property, relations and responsibilities toward her children, and protection from domestic abuse being positive but slowly established. Opportunities for a full range of educational choices took women along many new career paths, with their access to professions such as law, medicine, and even the military demonstrably improved. In business there were advancements into the executive ranks, although statistically they seemed to be concentrated in certain fields, such as pharmaceuticals, where "the woman's touch" appeared more appropriate. Major corporations and "power-house" industries remained male dominated. The "glass ceiling" was still in place for Spanish women as the 21st century began.

One symbolic achievement appeared in prospect by 2006. Spain had historically ignored the prohibition that existed in many other European monarchies against a female ruler. Both Isabella I and ISABELLA II had to contend with male rivals, but after 500 years the monarchy still appeared to serve a purpose for most Spaniards, and the succession laws still permitted a female monarch. Yet a king's son would always take priority over his older daughters. Thus Juan Carlos I's son, Philip, Prince of Asturias, stood in the line of succession ahead of his two older sisters. When Philip's wife, Princess Letizia, bore their first child, a daughter named Leonor, many Spanish women began agitating for a change in the succession law, similar to one made in recent years by several Scandinavian countries, that guaranteed that a first-born daughter would not be pushed aside by a later-born son. Some Spanish feminists dismissed the whole matter as trivial, as irrelevant as monarchy itself in the modern age. For others the anticipation of the reign of Queen Leonor had a pleasing symbolism that would serve to mark the new fullness of women's rights in Spain.

Z

Zapatero, José Luis Rodríguez See
RODRÍGUEZ ZAPATERO, JOSÉ LUIS.

Zaragoza (Saragossa)

An ancient city located in the province of the
same name in northeastern Spain, it was
originally a settlement of the Celt-Iberians
and then an important trading center for the
Romans. Zaragoza's location on the Ebro
River gave it commercial and strategic importance. Captured by Muslim invaders in 713,
Zaragoza was taken by King Alfonso I of
ARAGON in the 12th century. It was the capital of the Kingdom of Aragon through the
1400s. The site of fighting during the WAR OF
THE SPANISH SUCCESSION (1710), its proximity
to the French frontier and accessibility to
MADRID, lying less than 200 miles to the
southwest, continued to attract invaders.
Zaragoza's most notable battles were fought
during the PENINSULAR WAR when it sustained two major sieges by Napoléon's armies.
Today Zaragoza is the capital of the autonomous region of Aragon, with a population of
roughly 640,000 people, and is due to host
Expo 2008 (the next official World's Fair).

Zaragoza, Battle of (1808–1809)

At the beginning of the PENINSULAR WAR,
the city and province of ZARAGOZA defied
the French invaders and their puppet king,
Joseph Bonaparte (JOSEPH I). A distinguished native of Zaragoza, General JOSÉ
DE PALAFOX was democratically chosen to
lead the defense of ARAGON's ancient capital. Raising a force of urban volunteers and
peasants who marched in from the region
to supplement his small garrison of regular
troops, Palafox kept the BOURBON banner
flying over the city during a series of bombardments and infantry assaults from June
through August 1808. The French attackers withdrew with heavy losses. Goaded
by an infuriated Emperor Napoléon, they
redoubled their attack in November.
Effecting breaches in the walls of the city,
they conducted a street-by-street battle
for the city against the dogged defenders,
who were steadily weakened by casualties
and the outbreak of disease. Palafox had
sworn never to yield, but in February
1809, while he was incapacitated by illness, local government officials surrendered the city to the French. The victors
acknowledged the bravery of their antagonists by permitting the surviving Spanish
fighters to march out with full military
honors. During the next five years, pend-
ing the final expulsion of the invaders
from Spain, the Battle of Zaragoza became
an inspiration for Spanish patriotism and
continued resistance.

zarzuela

This Spanish musical genre dates from the 17th century and takes its name from a royal residence of PHILIP IV near MADRID, La Zarzuela, which was in turn named after the bramble bush (*zarza*) that grew around it. There musical performances were offered before the royal court as early as 1659. The roots of the form have been traced back to the *églogas* (eclogues) of JUAN DEL ENCINA, whose poetic compositions dealing with amorous shepherds were written in the early 1500s. Other components of the zarzuela included folk songs and comic allusions to contemporary themes. Some of the most notable poets and composers of the SIGLO DE ORO, including PEDRO CALDERÓN DE LA BARCA and FÉLIX LOPE DE VEGA and the musician Juan de Hidalgo, contributed to the so-called baroque zarzuela. During the 18th century Italian musical influences interwove with, but did not entirely supplant, Spanish themes. After the distraction of revolution and war during the early 19th century, the "golden age" of zarzuela extended from 1850 to 1950. Many of the greatest works of the genre date from this period, reflecting the genius of composers such as Francisco Barbieri and Federico Chueca as well as the more recent Federico Moreno Torroba, José Serrano, Reveriano Soutillo, and Pablo Sorozabal.

In an era when French, German, and British masters of light opera were active the zarzuela found a special popularity. Its distinctive settings and characters with their unique flavor of social and humorous situations often reflecting life in Madrid won a great following. The middle and upper-middle classes tended to patronize the larger theaters where the *género grande* zarzuelas, often lasting three or four hours, were pre-

sented in lavish style. A more modest, but no less enthusiastic audience flocked to the shorter (and less expensive) productions at the venues of the *género chico* zarzuelas.

The SPANISH CIVIL WAR disrupted both the mood and the taste that had welcomed zarzuela in earlier generations. There were a few attempts to create "dark"-themed zarzuelas in civil war settings, but these had little appeal, and the postwar atmosphere was scarcely more welcoming. In the more positive and prosperous post-FRANCO environment, after 1975, the zarzuela seemed at first to be dismissed as a mere cultural relic of a by-gone age. Yet, more recently a new generation has found charm and gratification in the genre and contributed to its revival. So too have enthusiasts abroad, including a number of Spanish-American countries and the United States. In New York City the Amigos de la Zarzuela has successfully promoted Spanish musical theater in the zarzuela tradition since 1985.

Zea Bermúdez, Francisco (?–1834)
Spanish statesman

After a business career in MÁLAGA, Zea Bermúdez was recruited by the provisional government in CÁDIZ in 1810 to act as a secret agent. Loyal to the exiled FERDINAND VII and resisting the French-supported regime of JOSEPH I (Joseph Bonaparte), the regency in the unoccupied region of Spain favored a general European resistance to Napoléon. Under the guise of a businessman looking for new commercial opportunities in neutral Russia, Zea sounded out officials in St. Petersburg. Early in 1811 he reported to the Spanish leaders that the czar's government was ready to form an alliance with Britain against France. This was welcome news, for Britain's expeditionary force in Spain was already battling against the French invaders. By early 1812 Zea, now with the rank of consul, was back in St. Petersburg successfully negotiating a treaty between Spain and Russia pledging them to a common anti-French policy. As a result of these missions Zea was appointed minister plenipotentiary to Russia during the post-Napoleonic period with oversight of trade negotiations and subsequently was sent to Britain with similar responsibilities.

In 1824, following the fall of the liberal regime that had controlled Spain between 1820 and 1823, Ferdinand VII summoned Zea back from his diplomatic duties to become minister of state at MADRID. Rather than impose a totally repressive policy as some of the king's supporters urged, Zea sought to balance conservative principles with liberal concessions. While insisting on the reaffirmation of royal prerogatives, he diminished the power of reactionary military commanders and guaranteed the pension rights of military men and their families who had supported the fallen liberal administration. The minister's conciliatory actions enraged the hard-line conservatives and provoked a series of conspiracies and threatened coups, forcing him to withdraw from office by October 1825.

In 1832 with Ferdinand VII struggling to secure the succession to his female heir against the opposition of the Carlists, the king brought Zea back to power. The minister established a policy that he christened "enlightened despotism," which was, once again, essentially a compromise between absolute royal power and reformist principles. Zea believed that he could work with the liberals while retaining the support of

all but the most extreme conservatives. Once again he proved overly optimistic.

On the death of Ferdinand VII in 1833 his widow assumed the regency on behalf of the young ISABELLA II. Zea persuaded her to issue a decree asserting the rights of the monarchy but promising no fundamental changes in principles. The minister shuffled his cabinet to no avail and lost the support of the regent when British and French diplomats indicated that they would not support her as long as the present ministry remained in power. Zea realized that he had exhausted all his options. Resigning at the beginning of 1834, he withdrew to France, where he died shortly afterward. Frequently characterized as a man of the ultraright, Zea Bermúdez was in fact a seeker after a balanced system of government who was doomed to failure in a time of uncompromising extremism. With his fall from office the onset of the First Carlist War and years of bloody civil strive became inevitable.

Zorrilla y Moral, José (1817–1893)
Spanish poet and dramatist

The son of a staunch conservative who was a member of FERDINAND VII's inner circle, Zorrilla was educated at a school for young nobles and began his university training under the tutelage of the Jesuits. When he was barely 17 he shocked the ruling circles by joining the liberal critics of the regime. Soon after he won the attention of literary circles in MADRID by delivering an impressive elegy at the funeral of the satirical essayist MARIANO JOSÉ DE LARRA. Building rapidly on the notice he had gained, he published a book of poetry, full of youthful enthusiasm and romantic excess, that was enthusiastically received, as were five other volumes that he completed during the next few years. By the early 1840s he had already developed an alternate field of activity in the writing of plays, which also proved tremendously popular. While some of these stage productions were obviously derivative, including his version of the well-known Don Juan story, Zorrilla's later poems were more mature and balanced in tone than his youthful effusions. They drew upon the history and traditions of "antique" Spain in a way that stirred national pride while contributing to the romantic image of his county that became the accepted version of Spanish life and culture throughout Europe.

Despite the success of both his poetry and plays (or perhaps because of it) Zorrilla's marriage and his finances fell into serious disarray. In 1855 he went abroad, hoping to put his affairs in order, and continued to write prolifically—although remaining persistently insolvent. Returning to Spain in 1866 he adopted a more prudent lifestyle, but it was not until 1889 that he was enabled to enter his golden years with dignity thanks to official recognition as Spain's National Poet, an honor accompanied by a generous pension. While much of his work has been relegated to dusty bookshelves by the changing fashions of the 20th century, Zorrilla remains the quintessential Spanish author of his era, exhibiting a distinctive approach to both character and plot. Startling encounters, overheard conversations, dastardly deeds, and noble sacrifices were among the gratifying experiences that he offered his audiences. His most famous work, *Don Juan Tenorio* (1844), even manges to present the infamous seducer in a romantic light, dis-

tinguishing him from the sinister and sinful character created by TIRSO DE MOLINA. It is Zorrilla's romantic Don Juan that has won the affections of an enduring public, and it is he who still appears upon the stage and even upon the screen. Some of his best known poetical works are *Poesías* (Poems, 1837), *Cantos del trovador*, (Songs of the troubador, 1841), *Recuerdos y fantasias* (Remembrances and fantasies, 1844), *La azucena silvestre* (The wild flower, 1845) and *Granada* (1852).

Zumalacárregui y de Imaz, Tomás de (1788–1835)
Spanish soldier

A Basque officer who joined the resistance to Napoléon's invasion, Zumalacárregui fought with great bravery and skill from 1808 to 1814, displaying particular cunning and ruthlessness in the irregular warfare known as the "guerrilla." After the restoration of FERDINAND VII, Zumalacárregui was one of those officers who supported the absolutist policy of the monarch, in contrast to many who had absorbed liberal principles. He clung to his conservative attitude during the 1820–23 military-backed liberal regime and adhered to the "traditionalist" party that formed around Don Carlos, the king's brother during the final decade of Ferdinand's reign. Zumalacárregui repudiated his late sovereign's wish that his daughter should succeed him as ISABELLA II. In 1834 he became commanding general of the Carlist forces. During the civil war that raged over the next four years, the adherents of the conservative pretender to the throne fought with great determination against that part of the army loyal to the young queen and the British and French troops who were supporters of her liberal government. The Carlists dominated the northern and (for a time) the eastern regions of Spain and enjoyed the support of Europe's conservative monarchies. Zumalacárregui proved a superb leader, both in conventional warfare and in the type of irregular operations that he had conducted with such success during the PENINSULAR WAR. Despite the weight of the forces arrayed against him, the commander's greatest handicap was probably the interference of the titular Charles V in military matters. His preoccupation with political issues (in which he was also deficient) brought the general to the verge of resignation. Finally, however, he laid siege to BILBAO, against his better judgment, because the Carlists felt that it was necessary to capture a major city. Wounded on the field of battle, he was incompetently treated and, following the spread of infection, died of what was originally a less than serious injury.

Many military historians regard Zumalacárregui as Spain's greatest soldier of the 19th century. Due to his unique mastery of both battlefield tactics and the "little war" in which he was able to take advantage of fighting on home ground, he found few rivals who could stand against him. Some critics, on the other hand, have faulted him for rigidity of principle. This trait led him to attack rather than maneuver and to kill prisoners rather than to win them over to his cause.

Zumárraga, Juan de (1468–1548)
Spanish prelate

A Basque priest, prominent in the affairs of the Franciscan order, Zumárraga made the acquaintance of King CHARLES I in 1527. The monarch was impressed by his combination of devoutness and practicality and asked him to become the first bishop of what is now Mexico City. After first modestly demurring Zumárraga agreed to confront what proved a difficult task. It involved not only the consolidation of several temporary ecclesiastical jurisdictions in MEXICO but also confrontation with the harsh and arrogant conduct of the *audiencia,* or governing court, whose members had antagonized virtually everyone in NEW SPAIN. For the next 20 years Zumárraga combined his vision of spiritual leadership with an energetic involvement in building a better human environment in colonial America. He was particularly active in the conversion of the Amerindians, weaning them away from their old blood-thirsty rituals. Admittedly this led him to the destruction of many artifacts and records of pre-Columbian society, but he was preoccupied with implanting a Christian civilization rather than pursuing anthropological research. He sought to protect the native population against the harshness of their conquerors, which often included virtual slavery, and to establish a number of schools particularly intended for them. In the course of his religious activities he frequently clashed with the civil authorities and was at times threatened by local magnates with banishment or worse. His situation improved when a new *audiencia* was appointed and ANTONIO DE MENDOZA was designated first viceroy of New Spain in 1535. The friendly and collaborative relationship between the bishop and the viceroy facilitated many improvements in the state of affairs in Mexico, which had previously preserved much of its wild frontier character. The bishop played an important role in establishing the first printing press in the New World and in publishing the earliest books for an American audience—religious texts in Spanish and indigenous languages, including a book that he wrote. By the late 1540s Zumárraga's work had made such a favorable impression in MADRID and Rome that the pope elevated him to the rank of archbishop. Still sincerely humble he at first tried to refuse the honor but was persuaded that it would serve the best interests of his flock. Zumárraga set an example for those who followed him in the succession of American prelates that only a few could match in the centuries to come.

Zurbarán, Francisco de (1598–1664)
Spanish painter

Born in EXTREMADURA and early apprenticed to a local painter, Zurbarán was already attracting attention with his religious subjects by age 18. Much of his earlier work was executed on commission from churches and monasteries in SEVILLE, whose municipal authorities had designated him "official painter." He subsequently moved to MADRID, where as one of a number of "painters to the king" he completed a series of mythological decorations (the *Labors of Hercules*) for a royal palace. His real skill and taste lay, however, in studies of saints and clergy (both prelates and humble monks). In his last years the solid, austere style that had won him such favor lost ground to the new taste for BARTOLOMÉ ESTEBAN MURILLO's more sentimentalized paintings.

Zurbarán's masterpiece, by general consensus, is *The Apotheosis of St. Thomas Aquinas* (1625), which is still regarded as one of the greatest of Spanish paintings. His studies of St. Peter and St. Jerome and various members and patrons of orders all exhibit an intensity of religious feeling combined with remarkable technical skill. The strength and dignity of his paintings as well as their mastery of color have earned him a transcendent place among the numerous artists who shared the stage with DIEGO RODRÍGUEZ VELÁZQUEZ during Spain's Golden Age (SIGLO DE ORO).

CHRONOLOGY

By the early 15th century the political structure of the Iberian Peninsula has been consolidated into three major kingdoms: Castile, Aragon, and Portugal. After a 700-year struggle (the Reconquest), the once powerful Muslim invaders have been driven back into the region around Granada. Castile and Portugal have already begun probing out into the Atlantic, disputing control of such islands as Madeira, the Azores, and the Canaries. Aragon, concentrating on the Mediterranean, has taken control of the Balearics and established a dynastic presence in southern Italy.

1469

Marriage of Isabella, heiress of Castile, to Ferdinand, heir of Aragon, marking the first step in the creation of a unified Spanish nation-state.

1474

Death of Enrique IV of Castile. His half sister, Isabella, takes the throne, declaring Enrique's daughter, Joanna, to be illegitimate. Isabella is supported by most of the Castilian nobles. Afonso V of Portugal, who has married Joanna, invades Castile to assert her claim but is defeated at the Battle of Toro.

1479

Ferdinand succeeds to the throne of Aragon. Now sovereign in their respective kingdoms, he and Isabella begin the next stage in the creation of the Spanish state. Their policies include strengthening of the towns at the expense of the feudal aristocracy, creating a bureaucracy for the management of finance, establishment of armed forces at their disposal, and arrangements with the church that give them power over the appointment of prelates and the use of the Inquisition as an instrument of ideological control.

1482

Portugal, continuing its exploration of the African coast, establishes a trading post at Mina on the Gold Coast (Ghana).

1484–85

King John II of Portugal (1481–95) intensifies the pace of exploration. Diogo Cão reaches the mouth of the Congo River.

1488

Bartolomeu Dias rounds the southern tip of Africa (Cape of Good Hope) and sails some distance up the continent's east coast, proving that India is accessible by a water route.

1492

Fall of Granada, last stronghold of the Moors in Spain. Isabella, aided by the Inquisition, begins a program of religious "purification": All Jews in her kingdom (between 150,000 and 200,000) are ordered to convert to Christianity or leave. The same order is imposed upon Muslims in 1502. For the time being these policies are not enforced in Aragon.

1492–93

Christopher Columbus, sailing under authority from Castile, crosses the Atlantic, seeking an all-water route to Asia that will rival the Portuguese. He "discovers" America, touching at the island he names Hispaniola (present-day Haiti and the Dominican Republic). On three subsequent voyages he will reach other islands in the Caribbean and the South American mainland in what is now Venezuela.

1494

Treaty of Tordesillas, in which Spain and Portugal agree on a division of newly discovered lands outside Europe.

Beginning of the Italian Wars (to 1559). Ferdinand of Aragon intervenes to prevent French conquest of his Neapolitan kin's territory, and a struggle for mastery of the rich but politically divided Italian peninsula evolves into a protracted struggle between France and Spain. Shifting alliances and periodic truces keep these wars (which soon extended far beyond Italy) at the center of European politics until Spain emerges as the dominant power.

1495–1521

King Manuel I of Portugal, presiding over the great age of political and economic expansion in Asia, Africa, and America, comes to be known as "the Great" or "the Fortunate." The riches that flow into Lisbon from control of Far Eastern trade foster an extravagant royal lifestyle and patronage of the arts. In 1497 he marries the eldest daughter of Ferdinand and Isabella, marking the start of a Portuguese-Spanish dynastic alliance that will be renewed over several generations. In that same year he expels the Jews from Portugal, as a gesture of solidarity with his in-laws.

1497–99

Vasco da Gama leads an expedition to India, opening up Portugal's contact with the Far East.

1500–01

Pedro Cabral, commanding a fleet of 13 ships, follows up on da Gama's voyage by opening trade with India. En route he crosses the Atlantic at its narrowest width and touches the coast of South America, discovering Brazil in spring 1500.

1501–12

Spanish colonization of Cuba, Puerto Rico, and (abortively) Florida.

1501–1600

During the 16th century both Spain and Portugal, drawing upon the fruits of war and conquest, emerge into the full light of the Renaissance. Spain, which had established its first printing press in Valencia in 1477, had already produced a Castilian grammar that was the first vernacular grammar in any language (Antonio de Nebrija, 1492) and one of its greatest works of literature, Fernando de Rojas's *La Celestina* (1499). An abundant flow of writers, artists, and religious thinkers would continue on through the generations to come. Portugal would move away from foreign influences to produce such literary masterpieces as *Os Lusíadas* (1572), Luíz Vaz de Camões's epic account of his countrymen's overseas voyages, as well as the masterpieces of Manueline art and architecture that adorn churches and palaces.

1504

Isabella of Castile dies. Her daughter, Joanna, succeeds her with Philip of Habsburg as king-consort (Philip I).

1505

Portuguese establish forts on the coast of East Africa and western India, beginning their colonial presence in these regions.

1506

Philip I dies, and Joanna is confined on grounds of insanity. Her father, Ferdinand of Aragon, assumes control of Castile.

1509–11

During a pause in the Italian Wars, Spain wages a successful campaign against the Muslim rulers of North Africa, gaining dominance in that region.

1510

Goa, on the west coast of India, becomes capital of the Portuguese realm in the Far East.

1511

Portuguese gain control of Malacca, leading to their dominance of trade with Siam (Thailand), the Spice Islands (in present-day Indonesia), and China.

1513

Vasco Núñez de Balboa crosses the Isthmus of Panama and sights the "Great South Sea" (Pacific Ocean).

1516

Ferdinand V dies. He is succeeded by his grandson, the son of Philip I and Joanna.

1516–56

Charles I's accession completes the de facto union of Castile and Aragon. In 1519 he succeeds his Habsburg grandfather, Emperor Maximilian I, as ruler of the Holy Roman Empire.

1518–21

Hernán Cortés, setting out from Cuba, leads an expedition to Mexico and conquers the Aztec Empire. His lieutenants and successors will use Mexico as a base from which to explore and extend Spanish claims over North America (Viceroyalty of New Spain).

1519–22

Ferdinand Magellan leads an expedition to find access for Spain to the trade of Asia. After unsuccessful attempts to find a water route through the American landmass, he rounds the tip of South America and sails across the Pacific. He reaches and names the Philippine Islands but is killed in a fight with the inhabitants. One of his ships sails on to Spain, completing the first voyage around the world.

1520–21

Angered by lack of respect from their Flemish-born young monarch and by his preoccupation with German affairs, many of the towns (*comunidades*) of Castile rebel against Charles. Although he defeats the uprising, with the aid of the aristocracy, Charles will henceforth pay due deference to the Castilian town's folk and their traditional prerogatives. He will, in fact, spend most of his reign ingratiating himself with his Spanish subjects and establishing mutual bonds of affection that turn him into one of the most "Spanish" of kings.

1521–57

John III, king of Portugal, continues the overseas expansion and domestic grandeur of his predecessor. He maintains a close political collaboration with Spain, cemented by dynastic marriages. An ardent Catholic, he sponsors the establishment of the Inquisition in Portugal (1536).

1529

Treaty of Saragossa revises the Tordesillas agreement by conceding the Philippine Islands to Spain, although Portugal retains control of the Spice Islands and the rest of its trading empire in Asia.

Treaty of Cambrai marks a temporary cessation of war between Spain and France, although it will be resumed at intervals for the next 30 years. Meanwhile Charles I must deal with the ongoing Turkish threat to Spanish dominance in North Africa and the western Mediterranean. In addition he is obliged to cope with the spread of the Reformation (religious war in the Holy Roman Empire, 1531–47) and a separate Turkish threat to the southeastern frontier of the Holy Roman Empire.

1530–32

Beginning of first serious attempts by Portugal to colonize its territory in Brazil.

1531–36

Francisco Pizarro, setting out from Panama, lands on the coast of Peru and conquers the Inca Empire. Subsequent exploration and conquest will establish Spanish domination over all of South America (Viceroyalty of Peru) except Portuguese-ruled Brazil.

1542

First Portuguese contact with Japan.

1549

Bahia is founded as seat of government for Brazil. Jesuit missionaries arrive to undertake the conversion of the native population; they will play an important part in the expansion and consolidation of Portuguese rule.

1556

Worn out by the burden of his multiple responsibilities and the struggle to maintain Spanish dominance throughout Europe, Charles I abdicates, passing the Holy Roman Empire to his brother (Austrian Habsburg line). Spain, with all its possessions in Europe and overseas, goes to his son (Spanish Habsburg line). Charles dies in 1558.

1556–98

Philip II, king of Spain, will spend his reign attempting to succeed where his father failed: defeating France, repulsing the Turks, and halting the spread of Protestantism.

1557

Portuguese fort is established at Macao on the coast of China, opening a commercial and colonial presence that will endure for more than 400 years.

1557–78

Sebastian I, king of Portugal, grandson of John III, is a minor, who reigns under a regency until he comes of age. Obsessed with the idea of a crusade against the Moors, he assembles an army that drains the human and material resources of his country and takes it into Morocco.

1559

With the Treaty of Cateau-Cambrésis the wars of Italy end in the defeat of France. Spain emerges as the supreme power in Europe.

1560

Madrid becomes the permanent capital of Spain.

1563

Philip begins construction of the massive palace-monastery El Escorial, which will serve as the royal residence and nerve-center of the Spanish Empire.

1567

Outbreak of revolt in the Netherlands. Tension had been building in this northern dependency ever since the accession of Philip II, who lacked his father's tact in dealing with the religious and ethnic sensibilities of the inhabitants. An ongoing war will drain Spanish resources for some 80 years, ending with the independence of the Dutch-speaking, mainly Protestant provinces and confirmation of Spanish rule in what will later become Belgium.

1569–71

The Moriscos, converted Muslims who were long suspected of allegiance to Islam, rebel against Philip's oppressive regime. Their resistance is harshly repressed, and many flee to Muslim territory in the Mediterranean. The last remnant of this population is expelled in 1609.

1571

Battle of Lepanto (off the western coast of Greece) marks a decisive Spanish victory over the Turkish fleet and confirms Spanish ascendancy in the Mediterranean.

1578

Battle of Alcazarquivir. Sebastian, the king of Portugal, and most of his followers are killed in the North African desert.

1578–80

Henrique I, great-uncle of the slain Portuguese king, cardinal and grand inquisitor, is the last ruler of the House of Aviz.

1580

Philip II of Spain, claiming the Portuguese inheritance through his mother, occupies Lisbon against weak resistance. He is proclaimed king of Portugal under the name Philip I. Between 1580 and 1640 Spain and Portugal share a common sovereign, and Portugal's empire is exploited for Spanish benefit.

1587

English attack on Cádiz marks the first direct clash between Philip II and Elizabeth I of England. Hostility had been building for some years due to England's support of the Dutch rebels and European Protestantism in general, as well as her countrymen's attacks on Spanish shipping in the West Indies. The Anglo-Spanish rivalry is thus a part of the Counter-Reformation struggle and of the growing imperial competition between the Iberian kingdoms and northern European countries.

1588

The "Invincible Armada," sent to conquer England, is defeated in the Channel. Despite further threats to the British Isles, nothing more is accomplished, and peace is concluded in 1604.

1589

Spanish intervention in the civil-religious war being waged in France. Like his campaigns against the English and the Dutch, this is part of Philip II's grand strategy against his northern European rivals; however, Spain's French allies are defeated, and peace is concluded in 1598.

1598–1621

King Philip III of Spain, after a brief attempt to continue his father's policies, concludes peace with England and a truce with the Dutch rebels, and devotes himself largely to religious matters. His chief adviser, the duke of Lerma, manages the administration, combining personal corruption with neglect of the economy, and initiates a period of decline.

1621–65

Philip IV, king of Spain, is not as passive as his father but lacks the grand vision of his grandfather. Philip is obliged to deal with the consequences of their respective policies. He and his chief minister, Count-Duke Olivares, find themselves beset by a host of challenges in Europe and overseas, which ultimately prove too much to handle.

1622

Spain's renewed war with France, initially over a minor border problem, gradually becomes a new round in the struggle for mastery in Europe. After the expiration of Spain's truce with the Dutch Republic, war is resumed in the Netherlands. This and the war with France become international during the 1630s as part of the Catholic-Protestant conflict in Germany (Thirty Year's War, 1618–48), with Spain supporting the Austrian Habsburgs and France backing the Protestant cause.

1640

Portugal breaks with Spain. Like the Catalan rising that begins the same year and a later (failed) revolt in Naples, this challenge to Madrid's control is provoked by France. After 60 years of "tyranny" as well as devastating attacks on their colonies by Spain's enemies, widespread support among the Portuguese for the reestablishment of full independence leads to the proclamation of the duke of Bragança as king of Portugal. Spain will refuse to recognize Portuguese sovereignty until 1669.

1640–56

John IV, first ruler of the Bragança dynasty, spends most of his reign successfully resisting Spanish attempts to regain control of Portugal. In 1654 the Dutch, who had invaded northern Brazil while it was under Spanish overlordship, are expelled, although other Portuguese losses to Spain's enemies are never recovered.

1640–59

Revolt in Catalonia is provoked by the fiscal and administrative policies of Olivares and the king's failure to respect the traditional rights and privileges of the principality. Aided by France, the Catalans are able to prolong their resistance and ultimately secure redress of most of their grievances.

1643

Battle of Rocroi. Spanish field forces are defeated by the French. This victory ends a century and a half of Spanish military dominance in Europe and sets the stage for the rise of France to supremacy on the Continent.

1656–67

Afonso VI is king of Portugal. The early years of his reign, under a regency, are marked by repeated Portuguese victories over the Spanish invaders, which finally results in the recognition of Portugal independence. Furthermore, Portugal's status is enhanced by the marriage of Princess Catalina, sister of the king, to Charles II of England (1662), strengthening the relationship between the two countries. These glory days are followed by the increasingly dissolute and eccentric behavior that leads to Afonso's deposition by his brother Peter. Afonso VI is banished to the Azores, where he dies in 1683.

1659

Treaty of the Pyrenees ends the war between Spain and France. Philip IV is obliged to surrender border territories in the Spanish Netherlands and the Pyrenean region and agree to the marriage of his daughter María Teresa to Louis XIV of France.

1665–1700

Charles II, king of Spain, the only surviving son of Philip IV, is four years old at his accession. Even after coming of age he remains under the guidance of advisers due to physical and mental disabilities. During his reign Spain participates in a number of European coalitions designed to block the rising power of Louis XIV but accomplishes little and loses several valuable territories. When his declining health and lack of a direct heir induces his allies to plan the partition of the Spanish Empire, Charles is provoked into drawing up a will leaving his entire inheritance to Philippe, duke of Anjou, grandson of Louis XIV and the Spanish princess María Teresa (and therefore his own great-nephew). Thus, the last of the Spanish Habsburgs rejects the claims of his Austrian kinsmen and paves the way for a general European war.

The extinction of the Spanish Habsburg dynasty marks the end of an age of cultural as well as political dominance in Europe. Termed the *Siglo de Oro* in Spanish (literally "golden century"), Spain's Golden Age actually spans a period of some two centuries during which the achievements of Spanish writers, artists, and thinkers command the attention and stimulate the imagination of the Western world. Among the greatest of these are Miguel de Cervantes, the creator of *Don Quixote;* Mateo Alemán, master of the picaresque genre; the Renaissance poets Juan Boscán and Garcilaso de la Vega; and the baroque poets Luis de Góngora and Francisco de Quevedo. Poetical impulses and mystical visions inspire John of the Cross and Teresa of Ávila, as well as Luis de León. Drama, from England to Italy, is influenced by the playwrights Félix Lope de Vega, Pedro Calderón de la Barca, and Tirso de Molina (who gives the world the eternal archetype Don Juan). Among Europe's greatest painters of the 1600s are El Greco, Diego Velázquez, Bartolomé Murillo, and Francisco de Zurbarán. In Portugal Nuno Gonçalves is the central figure in the school of Renaissance painting. There is also a group of accomplished poets of whom Luíz Vaz de Camões attains the status of national icon, albeit posthumously. Within a few years of Camões's death his country passes under Spanish dominance and is overshadowed culturally as well as militarily by Spain throughout the 16th century.

1683–1706

Peter II, after serving as regent since his brother's ouster, assumes the kingship upon Afonso's death. Peter is dedicated to strengthening the English connection and ratifies the Treaty of Methuen of

1703, which establishes an advantageous trade relationship. Allied with England during the War of the Spanish Succession, Portugal suffers a brief invasion by French and Spanish troops in 1704; however, an Anglo-Portuguese force stages a counterinvasion of Spain in 1706, and Portugal has the glory of occupying Madrid for a brief period.

1700–46

Philip V, the 17 year-old grandson of Louis XIV of France, becomes king of Spain. He is challenged by an anti-French coalition that includes England, the Dutch Republic, and the Holy Roman Empire. Their candidate for the throne is Archduke Carl of the Austrian Habsburg line.

1701–14

War of the Spanish Succession. Although much fighting takes place in other parts of Europe or in overseas colonies, there are several major battles in Spain itself, with Archduke Carl temporarily capturing both Barcelona and Madrid. After the breakup of the coalition Philip V is able to secure recognition as king. Britain retains control of Gibraltar and Minorca as well as access to the Spanish colonial market for African slaves. Philip is also obliged to surrender the Spanish Netherlands and certain possessions in Italy to his Austrian rival.

1706–50

King John V of Portugal spends his early years under the regency of his father's sister, the Dowager Queen Catherine of England. John is the beneficiary of a tremendous influx of wealth from the hitherto unproductive colony of Brazil, where diamonds and gold deposits are discovered in rapid succession. A self-indulgent and dissolute monarch, he wastes much of these new revenues on grandiose constructions, such as the palace at Mafra, and encourages his courtiers to imitate the lifestyle of Louis XV's court at Versailles. After a brief intervention in the War of the Spanish Succession, Portugal avoids further foreign entanglements during his reign.

1714–24

Philip V initiates the so-called Bourbon Reforms, including modernization of the bureaucracy, consolidation of power (abolition of Catalan rights of local government), improvement of infrastructure, and promotion of mining and manufacturing. However, much effort is wasted on attempts to secure control of France during the minority of his young relative Louis XV, although it had previously been agreed that the two countries would never be united.

1724

Perhaps feeling overworked, Philip abdicates in favor of his eldest son. Louis I dies after only six months, and Philip resumes the throne.

1725–46

The latter part of Philip's reign is occupied by Spanish participation in a series of wars, usually involving an alliance with France against Great Britain and Austria. The chief result of these efforts is the establishment of junior branches of the Spanish Bourbon dynasty in Naples and Parma.

1746–59

King Ferdinand VI of Spain, the second son of Philip V, continues both his father's reforms and the policy of military support to France. A relatively weak figure, Ferdinand fails to enhance the prestige of the Bourbons, either in Spain or abroad.

1750–77

King Joseph I of Portugal, a passive figure, surrenders the business of government to his chief minister, Sebastião José de Carvalho e Mello, marquês de Pombal. Playing the role of an enlightened despot, Pombal introduces a wide range of reforms in Portugal and the colonies that affect everything from administration and education to trade and agriculture. When challenged by conservative nobles and clergy he responds with brutal repression.

1755

Catastrophic earthquake at Lisbon destroys much of the city, and thousands perish in the accompanying fires and tidal wave. Pombal's energetic response to the disaster and his program of reconstruction does much to confirm his role as the strongman of the government.

1759–88

Charles III, king of Spain, third son of Philip V, is an able practitioner of enlightened despotism. He continues the reforms of administration and economy at home and in the colonies.

1761

Portuguese support for Britain during the Seven Years' War leads to a Spanish invasion, repulsed with difficulty.

1763

As the result of its participation in the Seven Years' War, Spain loses Florida to Britain but takes over the vast Louisiana region from France.

1767

As part of his program of strengthening despotic power over church and state, Charles III expels the Jesuits from all Spanish dominions (they had already been banished from the Portuguese realms in 1759). The order will subsequently be dissolved by the papacy and not reestablished until 1814.

1777–1816

Maria I is queen of Portugal. Her mother, the widowed regent, arranged for her to marry the late king's brother, who rules jointly as Peter III until his death in 1786. Pombal's influence is quickly subverted, and his dismissal follows.

1779

Spain renews hostilities against Great Britain by joining in the American Revolution. As a result Spain regains Florida (1783).

1788–1808

Charles IV, king of Spain, a pale shadow of his father, spends his entire reign responding to the disruptions growing out of the French Revolution (1789).

1792

Queen Maria I becomes insane (an infirmity that also affected her father in his last years), and her son, Prince John, assumes the regency of Portugal, a position he will hold for the next 24 years. John is a champion of conservative values and re-presses everything that seems to reflect the revolutionary spirit of the age.

1793

The French Republic declares war on Spain. Spain allies itself with Great Britain and launches an invasion of southern France.

1795

After suffering a series of defeats, Spain becomes an ally of France.

1797

A combined Spanish-French fleet is defeated off Cape St. Vincent. Great Britain captures Trinidad and attacks Puerto Rico.

1800

Spain returns Louisiana to France, which is now under the rule of Napoléon Bonaparte.

1801

War of the Oranges. Spain, instigated by France, invades Portugal and forces John to secure his country's survival by promising to sever all trade and political ties with Great Britain.

1805

In the Battle of Trafalgar, combined Spanish and French fleets are defeated by Britain's Lord Nelson off Cape Trafalgar (Spain). Napoléon's plans for an invasion of the British Isles are permanently disrupted.

1807

Portugal becomes the object of further plotting by Napoléon and the Spanish first minister, Manuel de Godoy. The country

is to be divided, with Godoy receiving a third of it as a personal principality in return for his collaboration. The royal family escapes from Lisbon aboard British warships, just ahead of an invading French army. The queen, the regent, and his children find refuge in Rio de Janeiro.

While his forces overrun Portugal, Napoléon decides to resolve a dispute in the Spanish royal family in his own favor. Charles IV is declared deposed by his son, who proclaims himself Ferdinand VII. Napoléon invites both to confer with him in France but then places Charles, Ferdinand, and their family in custody and installs his own brother, Joseph Bonaparte, on the Spanish throne (Joseph I).

1808

The British invade Portugal and force the French to withdraw. A series of popular uprisings and military actions in Spain seem to be about to force the French out of that county as well. Napoléon, however, personally leads a new army into Spain, captures Madrid, and secures his brother in firm domination of the north.

1809

A British army under Sir John Moore crosses Portugal into Galicia to divert Napoléon's attention from the conquest of southern Spain. At the Battle of Corunna, Moore is killed, and the British are forced to retreat. Napoléon, having demonstrated to his generals how to deal with the Spanish situation, returns to France. Despite a number of French successes, the arrival of additional British troops in Portugal under Sir Arthur Wellesley (later duke of Wellington) and widespread popular re-

sistance (guerrilla warfare) deny victory
to the French invaders.

1810–11

The struggle between the Anglo-Portuguese
troops and their Spanish allies on the one
side and the French on the other continues to sway back and forth.

1812

An assembly loyal to Ferdinand VII meets at
Cádiz in the unoccupied region of the
south and proclaims a constitution. This
document—a landmark in Spanish and,
indeed European, history—gives the first
written guarantees of popular representation, ministerial responsibility, and freedom of speech and assembly. It represents
the first upsurge of liberalism in Spain—a
delayed response to the revolutionary
spirit of the age. Meanwhile, in a series of
hard-fought battles, Wellington drives the
French northward, forcing Joseph
Bonaparte to abandon Madrid and retreat
to the line of the Ebro River. By the end
of 1813 the French have withdrawn from
Spain. Wellington pursues them across
the Pyrenees but leaves his Spanish allies
behind, fearing that they would "take a
terrible revenge" upon their enemies.

1814

Ferdinand VII returns from exile in France,
thus marking the end of the Peninsular
War, and begins a reign as king of Spain
that will last until 1833. Although he has
promised to respect the 1812 constitution, he soon rallies conservative forces,
including the aristocracy and the church,
and restores absolutism. During the next
six years a series of revolts by civilian and
military liberals is crushed.

1814–19

Independence movement in Spanish colonies (beginning as early as 1810 in Mexico) grows out of long-standing grievances
against the mother country and the opportunities for local initiatives presented
by the Peninsular War. Ferdinand, fearing loss of revenue from the American
dependencies and encouraged by anti-
revolutionary governments in Europe,
dispatches troops to fight the colonial
rebels.

1820

Mutiny of troops (at Cádiz) who refuse to
embark for South America. They march
on Madrid, are joined by other rebels,
and enter the capital in triumph. Ferdinand is compelled to restore the constitution and rule under liberal domination
until 1823.

Portuguese revolution, inspired by the uprising in Spain, overthrows the regency.
This council has governed Portugal since
the flight of the royal family to Brazil in
1807 and cooperated with the British
during the Peninsular War. The royal
family's preference for Brazil over Portugal as a residence had created increasing
tension since the end of the war. The new
king, John VI (who succeeded his mother
in 1816), has elevated Brazil to equal
stature with Portugal and shows no interest in returning to Lisbon.

1822

The liberals, now controlling Portugal, institute a constitution largely modeled on
that of the liberal regime in Spain. John
VI is urged to return to Portugal.

During his time in Brazil the king has come
to understand the complex nature of

nationalist aspirations there and realize that a separation is probably inevitable. John VI returns to Portugal but first urges his eldest son, Peter, to seize leadership of the nascent movement and proclaim himself monarch rather than have the Braganças entirely excluded from Brazil. Brazil proclaims independence, and Peter assumes the title emperor of Brazil.

1823

Back in Portugal, John VI finds himself under pressure to undercut the liberal components of the constitution, and his second son, Miguel, actually rallies a conservative revolt against the liberal government.

An invasion force ("the 100,000 Sons of St. Louis") is sent into Spain by the restored French Bourbon monarchy, acting as the agent of the conservative Holy Alliance powers. The Spanish liberals are defeated, and Ferdinand is restored to full authority. The Constitution of 1812 is once again abolished, and he governs despotically for the remainder of his reign.

Proclamation of the Monroe Doctrine (December 2) by the United States is a warning against European interference with the independence of any former Spanish colony in the Americas. It is reinforced by Great Britain, which wishes to secure free access to trade in that region. All hope of regaining Spain's empire in the Western Hemisphere now disappears. Only Cuba and Puerto Rico remain Spanish outposts, Florida having been sold to the United States in 1819.

1826

John VI dies, leaving the throne to Peter of Brazil, who becomes King Peter IV of Portugal. Peter, in turn, revises the constitution back into a liberal framework. To complicate matters further, he declines to return to Lisbon, hands over the succession there to his daughter Maria da Glória (Maria II), and names his brother, Miguel (who is at political odds with him), to be regent for the child queen.

1826–53

Maria II is queen of Portugal, but early in 1828 a conservative coup, led by Miguel, forces the queen and her principal supporters to take refuge in Great Britain. This development precipitates the Miguelite War, in which liberals and conservatives struggle for dominance.

1831

Emperor Pedro I of Brazil transfers his throne to his young son (Pedro II) and returns to Europe to aid his daughter's cause. With assistance from the new liberal governments of Great Britain and France he mounts an invasion of Portuguese territory. In 1834 a Quadruple Alliance is formed by the adherence of the liberal regime in Spain, which fears the collaboration of Miguelites with their own Carlist enemies. Miguel is defeated and forced to leave Portugal. He and his descendants are nevertheless regarded as the rightful kings by subsequent generations of "Miguelites."

1833–68

Isabella II, the eldest surviving child of Ferdinand VII, is proclaimed heir in June and succeeds her father to the Spanish throne upon his death in September. Ferdinand's repudiation of the Salic law (introduced by the French Bourbons during the reign of Philip V) thwarts the claim of the king's brother Carlos, who refuses to acknowledge Isabella as the legal sovereign.

1834

Queen Mother Maria Christina, regent for her daughter, seeks support against the conservative followers of Carlos by proclaiming the Estatuto Real. This royal constitution introduces such innovations as a bicameral parliament (Cortes), a reformed bureaucracy, and a new administrative structure in the provinces but retains strong executive powers in the hands of the sovereign. By failing to reinstate the full provisions of the 1812 constitution, Maria Christina splits the liberals whom she had sought to rally to her support. Some (moderates) agree to back the young queen, but others (progressives) insist on having the 1812 guarantees fully restored.

1834–39

First Carlist War. When the young queen's uncle, Carlos, proclaims himself the rightful ruler of Spain, the country is thrown into a civil conflict. The Carlist armies are recruited from conservative factions, supported by church leaders and by such regions as Catalonia, Navarre, Aragon, and the Basque provinces, who fear the new regime's centralist plans. The *cristinos* (supporters of the regent, Maria Christina) include liberals of various allegiances, anticlericals, and those who fear the reactionary spirit of the Holy Alliance era. Each side is supported by the conservative and liberal blocs among the European powers.

1836–38

Aided by British volunteers and soldiers of the newly formed French Foreign Legion, the supporters of Isabella gradually overcome the Carlists, and Carlos is forced to leave the country, without renouncing his claim. Together with the parallel war in Portugal this conflict transforms the Iberian Peninsula into a battleground of competing European ideologies.

1837

After bitter disputes between the moderates and the progressives, the regent is forced to accept a new constitution, which integrates some of the features of the 1812 constitution.

1840

General Baldomero Espartero, with the support of the progressives, forces Maria Christina to leave the country and assumes the regency. In 1841 he crushes a *cristino* uprising.

1842

Espartero carries out a bloody suppression of a revolt in Barcelona, where the Catalans have proclaimed an independent republic, demonstrating their continuing desire for national autonomy.

1843

General Ramón Narváez ousts the Espartero regime. Although the queen mother is permitted to return, Isabella II is declared of age and the management of government is assumed by Narváez as de facto ruler.

1846

Marriage of Isabella II to her cousin Francisco de Asís, duke of Cádiz, and the simultaneous marriage of her younger sister Luisa Fernanda to a French prince precipitate an international crisis (the "Affair of the Spanish Marriages"), due to the competing interests of Great Britain and France.

1851

Spanish treaty (Concordat) with the Vatican grants the Catholic Church extensive powers in education and censorship in return for Rome's abandonment of claims to confiscated ecclesiastical property.

1853–61

Peter V, king of Portugal, succeeds his mother, Maria II, after she and other members of the royal family die in an epidemic. He is succeeded, after a short, uneventful reign, by his brother Louis.

1854–63

Spain experiences a period of military coups (*pronunciamientos*) in which control of government alternates among Leopoldo O'Donnell, Baldomero Espartero, and Ramón Narváez.

1861

Spain reoccupies Santo Domingo on Hispaniola. After a period of internal unrest and economic disruption, it abandons the territory in 1865.

1861–89

During the reign of Louis I, king of Portugal, political stability is maintained by a compact between the conservatives and liberals who manage the vote in such a way as to hold a parliamentary majority and control of the government in alternating periods. A republican opposition, stimu-lated by the disgust of the intellectuals and labor leaders with this closed system, emerges during the 1880s.

1864

Narváez, supported by conservatives, intensifies authoritarian and Catholic policies and provokes a united front of opposition by liberals.

1864–66

Attempts by Spain to reassert its dominance in former colonial areas continue. Claims on Peruvian offshore islands are followed by a naval war with Chile. These activities have no positive outcome.

1868

Following the death of Narváez an upsurge of liberal activity weakens the position of a discredited conservative administration. The queen's infatuation with Carlos Marfori, an actor whom she has appointed as minister of state, provokes an outburst of scandalous newspaper articles. That diminishes respect for her among the military. Uprisings in September, led by generals Francisco Serrano and Juan Prim, bring on a full-scale revolution. When forces loyal to her are defeated Isabella II flees to France. Under the presidency of Serrano and the guiding influence of Prim, a provisional government is established, and it quickly repeals much conservative legislation and diminishes the power of the church.

1869

After a debate in the newly summoned constituent Cortes it is decided to preserve the monarchy in Spain. Serrano, now regent, and Prim, now chief minister, offer the crown to various European princes, who decline the offer. Leopold of Hohenzollern-Sigmaringen (the Catholic branch of the Prussian royal family) accepts the kingship, exciting French protests. Although he subsequently withdraws his name from consideration, the dispute over his candidacy leads to the Franco-Prussian War of 1870–71.

1871–73

Amadeo I is king of Spain. A son of the king of Italy, the prince accepts the throne of Spain but encounters general hostility and even violence (assassination of Prim, revolts by Carlists and Catalans). Finding his position impossible to sustain, he abdicates, leaving Spain to face its unresolved problems.

1873–74

First Republic. Taking advantage of the void left by Amadeo's abdication, the Cortes rejects monarchy in favor of a republican experiment. This decision has been made possible by a temporary majority of left-wing delegates, who immediately fall to disputing over whether the republic shall be centralized or loosely federal. In the midst of this debate the Second Carlist War breaks out, as conservatives in the north reject the entire political process. Emilio Castelar is chosen as president to direct the fight against the Carlists but resigns in January 1874. Serrano then takes charge but is confronted by rival officers who wish to restore the Bourbons. In November a declaration by Isabella's son Alfonso that he supports constitutional monarchy brings him the support of various political parties.

1875–85

Alfonso XII is king of Spain. The rallying of both military commanders and civilian politicians to the dynasty is caused as much by anger over the First Republic's incoherent blundering as by any knowledge of Alfonso himself. Although the republic collapses with scarcely any resistance (December 1874–January 1875), the war with the Carlists continues until February 1876. Alfonso and his advisers soon begin to adjust their policies to what they perceive as political necessity. In order to win over Catholics (the pope had hailed the Carlist pretender as legitimate king of Spain), many of the church's privileges revoked by previous liberal governments are restored. A new constituent Cortes (July 1876) approves a revised constitution that preserves the structure of the constitutional monarchy that Alfonso has promised to uphold but limits suffrage and gives ultimate power to the monarchy. Royal absolutism is modified in practice by an agreement between the two major political blocs that soon emerge. The Conservatives (under Antonio Cánovas del Castillo) and the Liberals (under Práxedes Mateo Sagasta) agree on a system of rotation in control of the ministry similar to that developed in Portugal. Although anything resembling a democratic political process is impossible, stagnation is widely accepted as preferable to the constant plotting and fighting of the previous few decades. The king himself, although possessing a degree of personal charm and tact in dealing with the public, gradually loses favor with Spaniards due to a series of corruption scandals at the royal court.

1886–1931

Alfonso XIII is king of Spain. Following the death of Alfonso XII in 1885, his pregnant wife, María Cristina, serves as regent until the birth of their son, Alfonso XIII (May 17). She continues in that office until he comes of age in 1902. The situation strengthens the position of the ministerial leaders, who continue to strike a balance between political extremes.

1889–1908

King Charles I of Portugal is an arrogant and self-indulgent monarch who stimulates growing resentment by his high-handed behavior and luxurious lifestyle. On the other hand his reign sees considerable economic development, exploitation of colonial resources in Africa, and an increase in public works, cultural activities, and international image building.

1890

In a concession to liberal principles and public agitation universal voting rights are restored in Spain. Such concessions also reflect the growth of a middle class based on commercial and industrial development during the years of domestic tranquillity. At the same time the increase of manufacturing in such cities as Barcelona and Bilbao leads to the growth of an industrial proletariat, labor unrest, and the revival of an anarchist movement that had been in abeyance since the collapse of the First Republic. Stimulated by parallel developments in other European countries, Spanish militants carry out a series of bombings and attacks on officials (assassination of Cánovas, 1897) during the 1890s that are met by repressive tactics from the security forces. The regional movements in Catalonia and the Basque provinces continue to express their own aspirations.

1895

Long after the remnants of the Spanish Empire have ceased to be more than an occasional distraction from domestic politics, a revolutionary movement breaks out in Cuba. Although Spain's other surviving Caribbean possession, Puerto Rico, is persuaded by timely concessions to remain loyal, nationalists in the Philippines soon launch their own war of independence. Spain finds itself embroiled in a major expenditure of blood and treasure as it attempts to deal with these insurrections, both of which engage the attention of expansionists in the United States.

1898

War between Spain and the United States, precipitated by an incident in Cuba (explosion that sinks the USS *Maine*), soon becomes a general American onslaught against what is perceived as a weak and decadent relic of European colonialism. After four months of fighting Spain agrees to a cease-fire and in December cedes Puerto Rico and Guam outright to the United States, along with the Philippines, whose indigenous rebels struggle on against their erstwhile liberators from the United States until 1902. Cuba is recognized as an independent republic in 1902. The loss of this war and of most of Spain's colonies has a profoundly adverse effect on the nation's morale.

During the 200 years stretching from the extinction of the Spanish Habsburg dynasty to the loss of Spain's last imperial outpost, the nation's cultural life undergoes changes that parallel the great reversal of fortune in its political life. The 18th century, broadly speaking, reflects the overwhelming influence of the new Bourbon monarchy and the hegemony of France in most dimensions of intellectual activity. The new regime in Madrid establishes institutions based on French models, including the Royal Academies of Language and History and the National Library. In the theater French influence is reflected in the plays of Leandro Fernández de Moratín and his contemporaries, while "fabulists" such as Félix M. Samaniego and Tomás Iriarte are inspired by the tales of La Fontaine. José Cadalso, in his *Cartas marruecas,* imitates Montesquieu's *Lettres persannes.* Gaspar Melchor de Jovellanos, jurist and advocate of enlightened reform, is a champion of progressive French principles who is obliged during his later years to take part in his country's resistance to invasion by French armies.

Although the artists of 18th-century Spain are less numerous and impressive than those of the Siglo de Oro, Francisco de Goya y Lucientes adorns its closing decades with powerfully insightful portraits of the royal family and follows with the brutally intense drawings contained in his series the *Disasters of War* during the struggle against Napoléon. In the realm of music Father Antonio Soler offers a wide range of instrumental and vocal compositions both in the form of religious and secular themes. During the 19th century French influence continued to predominate despite the fact that the first three decades had been taken up with the national military struggle against France and its political aftermath.

Romanticism came late to Spain but found expression in the plays of the duke of Rivas (*Don Álvaro*) and José Zorrilla (*Don Juan Tenorio*). José de Espronceda and Gustavo Adolfo Bécquer represent contrasting poetic responses to romantic influences, the former filled with exuberance and passion, the latter reflecting quiet, deep feeling. Mariano José de Larra, a writer of deep emotion, becomes caught up in his country's seemingly endless struggle. Although he commits suicide at 36, he profoundly influences the future Generation of '98. During the latter part of the 19th century the currents of realism sweep over Spain, involving such novelists as Benito Pérez Galdós (*Doña Perfecta, Episodios Nacionales*), Emilia Pardo Bazán (*Los Pazos de Ulloa*), Juan Valera (*Pepita Jiménez*), and Vicente Blasco Ibáñez (*La Barraca, Los cuatro jinetes del apocalipsis*).

In Portugal, as in Spain, the 18th century's cultural scene is dominated by external influences, particularly those emanating from France. Likewise, the following century (after the end of the Napoleonic Wars and the subsidence of dynastic quarrels) sees the successive influence of romanticism and realism. João Baptista de Almeida Garrett, poet and playwright, is a major force in shaping a Portuguese literary identity, an enterprise continued by Alexandre Herculano. Toward the end of the century José Maria Eça de Queirós achieves international renown with his perceptive novels portraying the realities of his country's changing social structure (*Os Maias* and *O crime do Padre Amaro*).

1909

A decade of growing political and social unrest in Spain culminates in the great revolt in Barcelona, which is put down with brutal force.

1910

After the ouster of Manuel II, who became king in 1908, a republic is proclaimed in Portugal.

1914–18

World War I. Although Spain remains neutral, Portugal joins the Anglo-French alliance, hoping to improve its international status and acceptance of the new republican government. It suffers severe financial and manpower losses with little resulting benefit.

1923–30

Following a humiliating defeat of the Spanish forces in Morocco and in response to growing socioeconomic unrest at home, King Alfonso XIII confers dictatorial powers upon General Miguel Primo de Rivera.

1928–32

Emergence of António de Oliveira Salazar as political strongman in Portugal. First as finance minister then as prime minister he restructures the national revenue system and moves on to create an authoritarian regime, combining elements of the Italian Fascist concepts with Portuguese Catholic traditionalism.

1931

Alfonso XIII leaves Spain in the aftermath of elections that favor the parties of the Left. The Second Republic is proclaimed.

1933

Proclamation of the "New State" in Portugal. Under this regime, although a symbolic presidency continues, the republic is transformed into a dictatorship, with Salazar ruling the country for the next 35 years.

1936–39

Spanish civil war is initiated by a revolt of army commanders opposed to the republic's increasing concessions to radical and autonomist demands. The military rebels are supported by Carlists, monarchists, and a wide range of conservative groups. The republic rallies some units of the armed forces and the national police, as well as the party militias of the anarchists and various marxist organizations. Long-standing class hatreds produce acts of revenge and numerous atrocities. General Francisco Franco emerges as the dominant leader of the Nationalists and receives armed assistance from the German and Italian dictatorships. Although volunteers from many countries arrive to aid the Loyalists (Republicans), Western democratic governments decline to intervene, and the Soviet Union's aid to the republic is limited by calculation of its own advantages.

1938

Although the Salazar regime in Portugal is generally supportive of the Spanish Nationalists, some Portuguese residents of border districts give aid and shelter to fleeing refugees as the republic begins to collapse.

1939

With the defeat of the Republicans, General Franco assumes the position of leader (El Caudillo) of the Spanish state, establishing a dictatorship that will last until his death in 1975.

1939–45

World War II. Spain remains neutral, although Franco is clearly sympathetic to the Axis Powers. Salazar also proclaims neutrality, but he eventually allows U.S. and British air forces to use the Azores for patrol operations.

1940

In the aftermath of the civil war Franco consolidates his power by creating a one-party system in which the "National Movement" (built around the fascist-like Falange) holds all government offices.

1945–55

The Franco regime is ostracized for its pro-Axis sympathies but gradually brought back into the international system by U.S. cold war policy needs. Portugal, never as resented as Spain, soon becomes a regular participant in Western affairs.

1955

Spain and Portugal become active members of the United Nations.

1960–68

Salazar seeks to develop Portugal's national wealth by intensified exploitation of natural resources in the African colonies. Resistance movements in these territories are met with military force, and Portugal embarks upon a series of African campaigns that create growing bitterness and financial strain at home.

1965–70

Franco begins a process of political and economic "liberalization" that produces growing boldness among the critics of his regime and a rising standard of living.

1968

Salazar suffers a paralyzing stroke and can no longer carry out his duties, although he remains nominal prime minister.

1970

Salazar dies and is replaced as head of government by his associate Marcelo Caetano.

1971–74

A slowdown in the Spanish economic "boom" provokes disputes among hard-line and moderate cliques within the Franco government as the leader's declining health raises questions about the future.

1974

Carnation Revolution in Portugal is a bloodless military coup, symbolized by the red flowers inserted in the soldiers' gun barrels. The Caetano government is overthrown, and within a year a provisional administration has opened negotiations for ending the war in Africa (a major cause of the army's revolt) and granting independence to the colonies.

1975

Death of Franco. He is succeeded by the Bourbon prince (a grandson of Alfonso XIII) he groomed to restore the monarchy. King Juan Carlos I soon makes clear his commitment to democracy rather than Francoism.

1976

Portugal emerges from a period of political instability, establishing a democratic constitution.

1978

Adoption of a democratic constitution in Spain. The Cortes, elected by universal suffrage and working with a prime minister who can command a majority of its votes, will henceforth include all political persuasions.

1981

Reactionary groups within the army and police seize the Cortes chamber and threaten to topple the new parliamentary system. The king, putting aside his merely symbolic duties as chief of state, rallies the support of the nation and demands the obedience of the armed forces to the constitution. The collapse of this coup marks the end of any serious threat to the "new Spain."

1982–96

The Socialist Party, under Felipe González, wins three successive national elections in Spain. Moving toward an increasingly centrist position González leads Spain into the North Atlantic Treaty Organization, which his party had previously opposed. His economic policies are a mixture of socialist theory and pragmatic capitalism. Although presiding over a new "boom" in national prosperity and a rejection of all restrains on personal liberties, he gradually loses support through his inability to deal with autonomist demands.

1986

Portugal is admitted to the European Union in recognition of a decade of economic and political stability.

1992

Spain marks the quincentenary of the 1492 voyage of Columbus that led to the creation of her transatlantic empire. Elaborate celebrations take place at Madrid and Seville. These are linked to the 1992 Olympic Games staged at Barcelona. The tremendous expenditures on the beautification of these cities and the enhancement of transportation facilities is justified on grounds of national prestige.

1996

Socialists win Portuguese national elections, taking the presidency (Jorge Sampaio) and the prime ministership (António Guterres).

1996–2004

José María Aznar, leader of the conservative Popular Party becomes prime minister and is subsequently reelected with an increased majority. Spain, now a member of the European Union, commits itself to an active role in world affairs, including a special involvement in Spanish America. Like his Socialist predecessor, Aznar is bedeviled by economic instability and controversies over regionalism.

1999

Portugal hands over its last remaining colony, Macao, to China.

2000

Portugal and Brazil celebrate the 500th anniversary of the European discovery of Brazil.

Despite the political convulsions of its 20th-century history Spain's cultural achievements lead some to speak of a new Siglo de Oro. Spain produces five winners of the Nobel Prize in literature: José Echegaray (1904), Jacinto Benavente (1922), Juan Ramón Jiménez (1956), Vicente Aleixandre (1977), and Camilo José Cela (1989), as well as major poets, such as Antonio Machado and Federico García Lorca. The philosopher-essayists Miguel de Unamuno and José Ortega y Gasset win international renown, as does the expatriate George Santayana (Jorge Ruiz de Santillana). Among artists, Pablo Picasso, a founder of cubism, towers above all others, though the painters Joan Miró and Salvador Dalí make important contributions to modern art, as does the sculptor Eduardo Chillida. Composers of distinction include Enrique Granados, Manuel de Falla, Isaac Albéniz, and Joaquín Rodrigo, and the composer-cellist Pablo (Pau) Casals is honored on both sides of the Atlantic. So, too, are performers such as the tenors Plácido Domingo, José Carreras, and Alfredo Kraus and the sopranos Montserrat Caballé and Victoria de los Ángeles. Among film directors Luis Buñuel is one of the giants of 20th-century cinema and is followed in the post-Franco era by the acute Carlos Saura and the outrageous Pedro Almodóvar (winner of an Academy Award in Hollywood). The twin burdens of cultural isolation and political repression weigh heavily on Portugal during most of the 20th century. The pioneering modernist painter Amadeo de Souza Cardoso receives his due recognition only in the 1990s. The Nobel Prize in literature is awarded to the maverick Communist anticlerical novelist José Saramago only at the end of the century (1998), making him the first Portuguese recipient of this honor and acknowledging not only the virtues of his work but the felicities of his language.

2001

After a brief cease-fire the Spanish government is forced to resume its conflict with the Basque nationalist organization ETA, which has been carrying on a campaign of terroristic violence for more than 30 years.

2003

Prime Minister Aznar, pledging support for the U.S. invasion of Iraq as part of the "war on terror," orders the dispatch of Spanish troops to aid in the occupation of the country. The force, designated the "Plus Ultra" Brigade (in reference to the motto of imperial Spain), will eventually grow to some 1,300 soldiers.

2004

On March 11 a series of explosions at the principal railroad station in Madrid and on board commuter trains entering the city kills nearly 200 people and wounds hundreds of others. The Aznar government at first attributes this terrorist attack to Basque militants but subsequently admits that the evidence points to Islamist groups. In the election to the Cortes that takes place, as scheduled, a few days later, Aznar's hand-picked successor and the Popular Party are defeated, evidently because voters believe the administration has lied about the source of the bombing.

2005

As Socialist prime minister José Luis Rodríguez Zapatero approaches the first anniversary of his administration, he is faced by many urgent concerns. Among them are a deterioration in U.S.-Spanish relations following the withdrawal of the Spanish contingent from Iraq and continuing evidence of Islamic terrorist plotting among Spain's large Muslim population. Even more urgent is the threat to national unity posed by ETA bombings and a new spirit of defiance among Basque regional leaders that eschews violence but presents autonomist demands that threaten the fabric of the constitution.

Perhaps distracted by their own constitutional problems, Spaniards give only a lukewarm support to the European Union constitution. In a referendum designed to place Spain in a leadership role on the march to European unity, a mere 40 percent of eligible voters go to the polls, although the majority affirm the pan-European charter.

José Socrates is appointed prime minister of Portugal, his Socialist Party having gained control of parliament in the February election. He replaces Pedro Santana Lopes of the Social Democrats whose four-month tenure had been generally rejected by politicians and businesspeople for its incompetence and had lost the confidence of the nation's president Jorge Sampaio. Although Socrates promises to restore economic and social stability that have badly deteriorated since 2000, his announced policies do not differ markedly from those of his predecessor.

2006

The sudden promise of a cease-fire and serious negotiations from ETA is at first received with skepticism in Madrid, given the failure of earlier peace plans. Prime Minister Rodriguez Zapatero, nevertheless, pursues contacts with Basque politicians throughout 2006. A major stumbling block is the concept of "Basque nation" as distinguished from an autonomous region within Spain. Furthermore, the question of Basque "homeland" areas lying within France seems insoluble. The Basque initiative also stimulates new demands from Catalonia and other regions, as well as arousing conservative nationalists' fears over the unity of the Spanish state.

A continuing investigation of plotting by Islamic militants within Spain is accompanied by the steady growth of a Muslim presence in the country. As many as 100,000 "refugees" enter Spain during 2006. Some of these cross the Strait of Gibraltar on rafts or try to force their way through barriers at Ceuta and Melilla, Spain's North African enclaves. A new tactic is the launching of decrepit overloaded boats from Senegal and adjacent African territories in the hope of reaching the Canary Islands. Spain seeks the help of European and African Muslim countries in stopping this tide of newcomers.

In December, Spain and Morocco make a curiously incongruous announcement that they are actively exploring the construction of a tunnel beneath the Strait of Gibraltar. Such a route connecting Africa to Europe had been discussed periodically for more than 30 years, with enthusiastic projections of technological and natural resource flow being the main advantage. Now a series of engineering calculations suggest that several parallel railroad tunnels could be blasted through the Mediterranean seabed within a practical time frame and a cost-effective system of financing. The question immediately arises as to whether Spain (and, indeed, the rest of Europe) wishes to confront the social and political implications of linking the two continents.

APPENDIXES

APPENDIX I
Rulers and Statesmen of Spain and Portugal

APPENDIX II
Maps

RULERS AND STATESMEN OF SPAIN AND PORTUGAL

Rulers of Spain

Union of Castile and Aragon

Isabella I (of Castile), 1474–1504, ruled jointly with Ferdinand II (of Aragon).

Ferdinand II (of Aragon), 1474–1504, ruled jointly with Isabella I as Ferdinand V of Castile; 1504–16, ruled Aragon; 1506–16, ruled Castile as regent.

House of Habsburg

Joanna (the Mad), 1504–06, ruled Castile only (jointly with Philip I in 1506). Daughter of Ferdinand and Isabella.

Philip I (the Handsome), 1506, ruled Castile jointly with Joanna. Son of Holy Roman Emperor Maximilian I.

Charles I, 1516–56 (Holy Roman Emperor Charles V, 1519–56), ruled a united Spain. Son of Joanna and Philip I. (His grandfather Ferdinand V of Aragon exercised effective control of Spain until 1516).

Philip II, 1556–98. Son of the preceding. (Portugal was joined to the union in 1580.)

Philip III, 1598–1621. Son of the preceding.

Philip IV, 1621–65. Son of the preceding. (Portugal becomes independent in 1640.)

Charles II, 1665–1700. Son of the preceding.

House of Bourbon

Philip V, 1700–24. Great-nephew of the preceding; grandson of Louis XIV, hence first king of the Spanish branch of the French house of Bourbon.

Louis I, 1724. Son of the preceding, who had abdicated.

Philip V, 1724–46. Resumes the throne upon the preceding's death.

Ferdinand VI, 1746–59. Son of the preceding.

Charles III, 1759–88. Brother of the preceding.

Charles IV, 1788–1808. Son of the preceding.

Ferdinand VII, 1808. Son of the preceding.

House of Bonaparte

Joseph I (Joseph Bonaparte), 1808–1813. Brother of Napoléon, who invades the Iberian Peninsula.

Bourbon Restoration

Ferdinand VII, 1813–33. Restored to the throne after the preceding is deposed.

Isabella II, 1833–68. Daughter of the preceding.

House of Savoy

Amadeo I, 1871–73. Prince of the Italian house of Savoy installed by Spanish military leaders three years after the overthrow of the preceding.

First Republic

1873–73. Established after abdication of the preceding.

Bourbon Restoration

Alfonso XII, 1875–85. Son of Isabella II.

Alfonso XIII, 1885–1931. Posthumous son of the preceding. His mother, Maria Christina of Austria, serves as regent until 1902.

Second Republic
1931–39. Established after the preceding leaves the country, without abdicating.

Nationalist Government
1939–75. Following the civil war of 1936–39 General Francisco Franco presides over the "Spanish State" as El Caudillo (leader) until his death.

Constitutional Monarchy
Juan Carlos I, 1975– . By prearrangement the grandson of Alfonso XIII replaces Franco's administration under a renewed constitutional monarchy.

Presidents of Spain*

Name	Took Office
Francisco Martínez de la Rosa	January 15, 1834
José María Queipo de Llano Ruiz de Saravia, count of Toreno	June 7, 1835
Miguel Ricardo de Álava	September 14, 1835
Juan Álvarez Mendizábal	September 25, 1835 (acting)
Francisco Javier Istúriz	May 15, 1836 (acting)
José María Calatrava	August 14, 1836
Baldomero Espartero	August 18, 1837
Eusebio Bardají y Azara	October 18, 1837
Narciso Heredia y Begines de los Ríos	December 16, 1837
Bernardino Fernández de Velasco	September 6, 1838
Evaristo Pérez de Castro	December 9, 1838
Antonio González y González	July 20, 1840
Valentín Ferraz	August 12, 1840
Modesto Cortázar	August 29, 1840 (acting)
Vicente Sancho	September 11, 1840
Baldomero Espartero	September 16, 1840
Joaquín María Ferrer y Echevarría	May 10, 1841
Antonio González y González	May 20, 1841
José Ramón Rodil y Campillo	June 17, 1842
Joaquín María López	May 9, 1843
Álvaro Gomez Becerra	May 19, 1943
Joaquín María López	July 23, 1843
Salustiano Olózaga	November 20, 1843
Luis González Bravo	December 5, 1843

*Being a constitutional monarchy, the government of Spain is headed by a prime minister, but the official title in Spanish is *presidente del gobierno*, literally "president of the government."

Presidents of Spain (continued)

Name	Took Office
Ramón María Narváez y Campos, duke of Valencia	May 3, 1844
Manuel Pando Fernández de Pineda	February 12, 1846
Ramón María Narváez y Campos, duke of Valencia	March 16, 1846
Francisco Javier Istúriz	April 5, 1846
Carlos Martínez de Irujo	January 28, 1847
Joaquín Francisco Pacheco y Gutiérrez Calderón	March 28, 1847
Florencio García Goyena	September 12, 1847
Ramón María Narváez y Campos, duke of Valencia	October 4, 1847
Serafín María de Sotto	October 19, 1849
Ramón María Narváez y Campos, duke of Valencia	October 20, 1849
Juan Bravo Murillo	January 14, 1851
Federico Roncali	December 14, 1852
Francisco Lersundi y Hormaechea	April 14, 1853
Luis José Sartorius	September 19, 1853
Fernando Fernández de Córdova	July 17, 1854
Ángel de Saavedra, duke of Rivas	July 18, 1854
Baldomero Espartero	July 19, 1854
Leopoldo O'Donnell Joris	July 14, 1856
Ramón María Narváez y Campos, duke of Valencia	October 12, 1856
Francisco Armero Peñaranda	October 15, 1857
Francisco Javier Istúriz	January 14, 1858
Leopoldo O'Donnell Joris	June 30, 1858
Manuel Pando Fernández de Pineda	March 2, 1863
Lorenzo Arrazola	January 17, 1864
Alejandro Mon y Pidal	March 1, 1864
Ramón María Narváez y Campos, duke of Valencia	September 16, 1864
Leopoldo O'Donnell Joris	June 21, 1865
Ramón María Narváez y Campos, duke of Valencia	July 10, 1866
Luis González Bravo	April 23, 1868
José Gutiérrez de la Concha	September 19, 1868
Francisco Serrano y Domínguez	October 3, 1868
Juan Prim y Prats	June 18, 1869
Juan Bautista Topete y Carballo	December 27, 1870 (acting)
Francisco Serrano y Domínguez	January 4, 1871
Manuel Ruiz Zorrilla	July 24, 1871
José Malcampo y Monge	October 5, 1871
Práxedes Mateo Sagasta	December 21, 1871
Francisco Serrano y Domínguez	May 26, 1872
Manuel Ruiz Zorrilla	June 13, 1872

Name	Took Office
Estanislao Figueras y Moragas	February 12, 1873
Francisco Pi y Margall	June 11, 1873
Nicolás Salmerón Alonso	July 18, 1873
Emilio Castelar y Ripoll	September 7, 1873
Francisco Serrano y Domínguez	January 2, 1874
Juan Zavala y de la Puente	February 26, 1874
Práxedes Mateo Sagasta	September 3, 1874
Antonio Cánovas del Castillo	December 31, 1874
Joaquín Jovellar Soler	September 12, 1875
Antonio Cánovas del Castillo	December 2, 1875
Arsenio Martínez Campos y Antón	March 7, 1879
Antonio Cánovas del Castillo	December 9, 1879
Práxedes Mateo Sagasta	February 8, 1881
José Posada Herrera	October 13, 1883
Antonio Cánovas del Castillo	January 18, 1884
Práxedes Mateo Sagasta	November 27, 1885
Antonio Cánovas del Castillo	July 5, 1890
Práxedes Mateo Sagasta	December 11, 1892
Antonio Cánovas del Castillo	March 23, 1895
Marcelo Azcarraga y Palmero	August 8, 1897 (acting)
Práxedes Mateo Sagasta	October 4, 1897
Francisco Silvela le Vielleuze	March 4, 1899
Marcelo Azcárraga y Palmero	October 23, 1900
Práxedes Mateo Sagasta	March 6, 1902
Francisco Silvela le Vielleuze	December 6, 1902
Raimundo Fernández Villaverde	July 20, 1903
Antonio Maura Montaner	December 5, 1903
Marcelo Azcárraga y Palmero	December 16, 1904
Raimundo Fernández Villaverde	January 27, 1905
Eugenio Montero Ríos	June 23, 1905
Segismundo Moret y Prendergast	December 1, 1905
José López Domínguez	July 6, 1906
Segismundo Moret y Prendergast	November 30, 1906
Antonio Aguilar Correa	December 4, 1906
Antonio Maura Montaner	January 25, 1907
Segismundo Moret y Prendergast	October 21, 1909
José Canalejas Méndez	February 9, 1910
Manuel García Prieto	November 12, 1912 (acting)
Álvaro Figueroa Torres	November 14, 1912
Eduardo Dato Iradier	October 27, 1913
Álvaro Figueroa Torres	December 9, 1915

Presidents of Spain *(continued)*

Name	Took Office
Manuel García Prieto	April 19, 1917
Eduardo Dato Iradier	June 11, 1917
Manuel García Prieto	November 3, 1917
Antonio Maura Montaner	March 22, 1918
Manuel García Prieto	November 9, 1918
Álvaro Figueroa Torres	December 5, 1918
Antonio Maura Montaner	April 15, 1919
Joaquín Sánchez de Toca	July 20, 1919
Manuel Allendesalazar Muñoz de Salazar	December 12, 1919
Eduardo Dato Iradier	May 5, 1920
Gabino Bugallal Araujo	March 8, 1921 (acting)
Manuel Allendesalazar Muñoz de Salazar	March 13, 1921
Antonio Maura Montaner	August 14, 1921
José Sánchez Guerra	March 8, 1922
Manuel García Prieto	December 7, 1922
Miguel Primo de Rivera y Orbaneja	September 15, 1923
Dámaso Berenguer Fusté	January 30, 1930
Juan Bautista Aznar Cabañas	February 18, 1931
Niceto Alcalá-Zamora Torres	April 14, 1931
Manuel Azaña Díaz	October 14, 1931
Alejandro Lerroux García	September 12, 1933
Diego Martínez Barrio	October 8, 1933
Alejandro Lerroux García	December 16, 1933
Ricardo Samper Ibáñez	April 28, 1934
Alejandro Lerroux García	October 4, 1934
Joaquín Chapaprieta Torregrosa	September 25, 1935
Manuel Portela Valladares	December 14, 1935
Manuel Azaña Díaz	February 19, 1936
Augusto Barcía Trelles	May 10, 1936
Santiago Casares Quiroga	May 13, 1936
Diego Martínez Barrio	July 19, 1936
José Giral Pereira	July 19, 1936
Francisco Largo Caballero	September 4, 1936
Juan Negrín López	May 17, 1937
Francisco Franco Bahamonde	January 30, 1938
Luis Carrero Blanco	June 8, 1973
Torcuato Fernández-Miranda Hevia	December 20, 1973
Carlos Arias Navarro	December 29, 1973

Name	Took Office
Fernando de Santiago y Díaz de Mendívil	July 1, 1976
Adolfo Suárez González	July 3, 1976
Leopoldo Calvo-Sotelo Bustelo	February 25, 1981
Felipe González Márquez	December 1, 1982
José María Aznar López	May 4, 1996
José Luis Rodríguez Zapatero	April 17, 2004

Rulers of Portugal

House of Aviz
John I, 1385–1433.
Edward I, 1433–38. Son of the preceding.
Afonso V, 1438–81. Son of the preceding.
John II, 1481–95. Son of the preceding.
Manuel I, 1495–1521. Cousin of the preceding.
John III, 1521–57. Son of the preceding.
Sebastian I, 1557–78. Grandson of the preceding.
Henrique I, 1578–80. Great-uncle of the preceding.

Spanish Rule

Philip I (II of Spain), 1580–98.
Philip II (III of Spain), 1598–1621. Son of the preceding.
Philip III (IV of Spain), 1621–40. Son of the preceding.

House of Bragança
John IV, 1640–56.
Afonso VI, 1656–67. Son of the preceding.
Peter II, 1667–1706. Brother of the preceding; ruled as regent until 1683.
John V, 1706–50. Son of the preceding.
Joseph I, 1750–77. Son of the preceding.
Peter III, 1777–86. Brother of the preceding; joint reign with Maria I.
Maria I, 1777–1816. Daughter of Joseph I; joint reign with Peter III until his death.
John VI, 1816–26. Son of the preceding; ruled as regent since 1792.
Peter IV, 1826. Son of the preceding.
Maria II, 1826–28. Daughter of the preceding.
Miguel, 1828–34. Brother of Peter IV; ruled as regent from 1827 then usurped the throne.
Maria II, 1834–53. Restored to the throne.
Peter V, 1853–61. Son of the preceding; under the regency of his father until 1855.
Louis I, 1861–89. Brother of the preceding.
Charles I, 1889–1908. Son of the preceding.
Manuel II, 1908–10. Son of the preceding.

Presidents of Portugal

Name	Office
Teófilo Braga (provisional)	1910–11
Manuel José de Arriaga	1911–15
Teófilo Braga	1915
Bernardino Machado	1915–17
Sidónio Pais	1917–18
João do Canto e Castro (provisional)	1918–19
António José de Almeida	1919–23
Manuel Teixeira Gomes	1923–25
Bernardino Machado	1925–26
Provisional government	1926
António Oscar de Fragoso Carmona	1926–51
Antonio de Oliveira Salazar (prime minister, acting head of state)	1951
Francisco Craveiro Lopes	1951–58
Amórico de Deus Rodrigues Tomás	1958–74
António de Spinola	1974
Francisco da Costa Gomes	1974–76
António Ramalho Eanes	1976–86
Mário Alberto Nobre Lopes Soares	1986–96
Jorge Fernando Branco de Sampaio	1996–2006
Aníbal António Cavaco Silva	2006–

Prime Ministers of Portugal

Name	Years in Office
Teófilo Braga	1910–11
João Chagas	1911
Augusto de Vasconcelos	1911–12
Duarte Leite	1912–13
Afonso Costa	1913–14
Álvaro de Castro	1913–1924
Rodrigues Gaspar	1924
José Domingues dos Santos	1924–25
Vitorino Guimarães	1925
António Maria da Silva	1925
Domingos Pereira	1925
António Maria da Silva	1925
José Mendes Cabeçadas	1926
Gomes da Costa	1926
Óscar Fragoso Carmona	1926–28
Vicente de Freitas	1928–29

Name	Years in Office
Ivens Ferraz	1929–30
Domingos Oliveira	1930–32
António de Oliveira Salazar	1932–68
Marcello Caetano	1968–74
Adélino da Palmo Carlos	1974
Vasco dos Santos Gonçalves	1974–75
José Pinheiro de Azevedo	1975–76
Mário Soares	1976–78
Alfredo Nobre da Costa	1978
Carlos de Mota Pinto	1978–79
Maria de Lurdes Pintassilgo	1979
Francisco Sá Carneiro	1979–80
Francisco Pinto Balsemão	1989–83
Mário Soares	1983–85
Aníbal António Cavaco Silva	1985–95
António Manuel de Oliveira Guterres	1995–2002
José Manuel Durão Barroso	2002–04
Pedro Santana Lopes	2004–05
José Sócrates Carvalho Pinto de Sousa	2005–

APPENDIX II

MAPS

Empire of Charles V

Spanish Explorations of South America, 1524–1542

Spanish Explorations of Middle America, 1513–1543

Overseas Empires of Spain and Portugal, ca.1550

Spanish Armada, 1588

Spanish Rule in Europe, 1580–1714

Spain and Portugal in the Americas, 1750

Peninsular War (War of Independence), 1808–1814

Spanish Civil War, 1936–1939

Former Colonies of Spain and Portugal

Spain and Portugal

EMPIRE OF CHARLES V

SPANISH EXPLORATIONS OF SOUTH AMERICA, 1524–1542

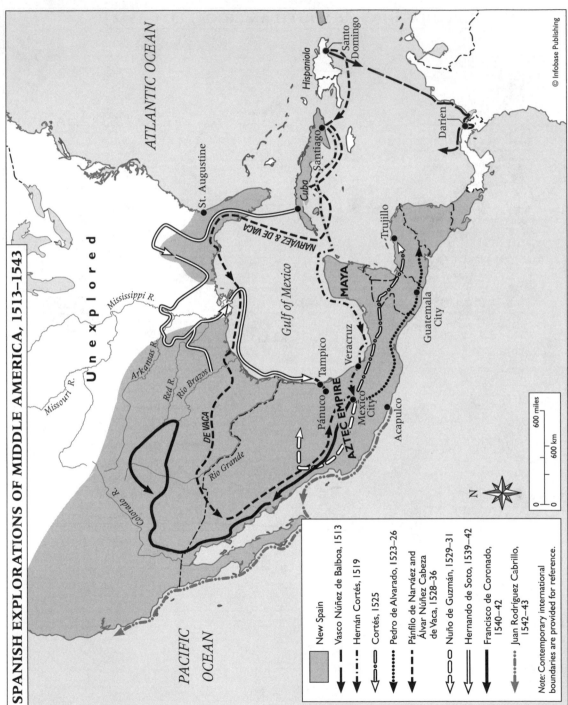

SPANISH EXPLORATIONS OF MIDDLE AMERICA, 1513–1543

ATLANTIC OCEAN

PACIFIC OCEAN

Unexplored

Gulf of Mexico

Mississippi R.
Missouri R.
Arkansas R.
Red R.
Rio Brazos
Rio Grande
Colorado R.

St. Augustine
Cuba
Santiago
Hispaniola
Santo Domingo
Darien
Trujillo
Guatemala City
Acapulco
Mexico City
Veracruz
Tampico
Pánuco
AZTEC EMPIRE
MAYA
DE VACA
NARVÁEZ & DE VACA

N

600 miles
600 km

© Infobase Publishing

New Spain
Vasco Núñez de Balboa, 1513
Hernán Cortés, 1519
Cortés, 1525
Pedro de Alvarado, 1523–26
Pánfilo de Narváez and
Álvar Núñez Cabeza
de Vaca, 1528–36
Nuño de Guzmán, 1529–31
Hernando de Soto, 1539–42
Francisco de Coronado,
1540–42
Juan Rodríguez Cabrillo,
1542–43

Note: Contemporary international
boundaries are provided for reference.

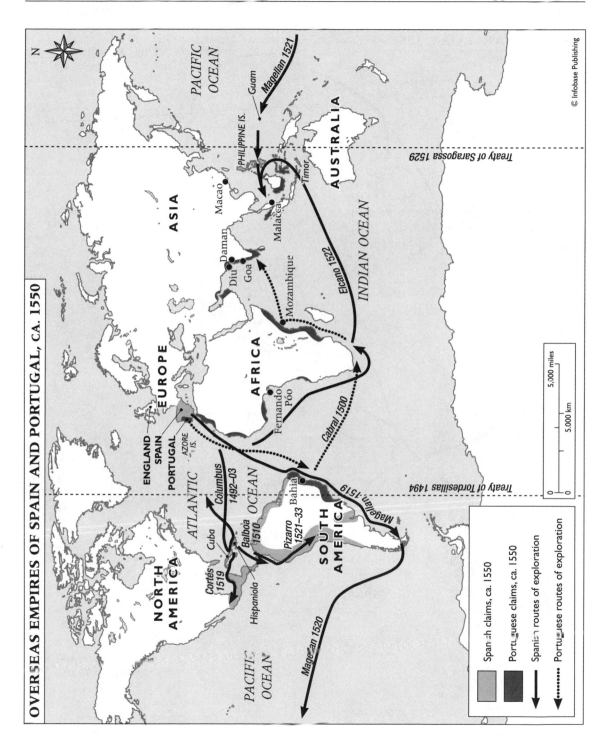

OVERSEAS EMPIRES OF SPAIN AND PORTUGAL, CA. 1550

© Infobase Publishing

N

PACIFIC
OCEAN

Magellan 1521

Guam

PHILIPPINE IS.

Macao

Daman

Diu

Goa

Malacca

Timor

AUSTRALIA

Treaty of Saragossa 1529

Elcano 1522

INDIAN OCEAN

Mozambique

ASIA

EUROPE

AFRICA

Fernando
Póo

Cabral 1500

ENGLAND
SPAIN
PORTUGAL

AZORE
IS.

ATLANTIC
OCEAN

Columbus
1492–03

Cuba

Cortés
1519

Hispaniola

Balboa
1510

Pizarro
1521–33

SOUTH
AMERICA

Bahia

Treaty of Tordesillas 1494

Magellan 1519

Magellan 1520

NORTH
AMERICA

PACIFIC
OCEAN

5,000 miles

5,000 km

0

0

Spanish claims, ca. 1550

Portuguese claims, ca. 1550

Spanish routes of exploration

Portuguese routes of exploration

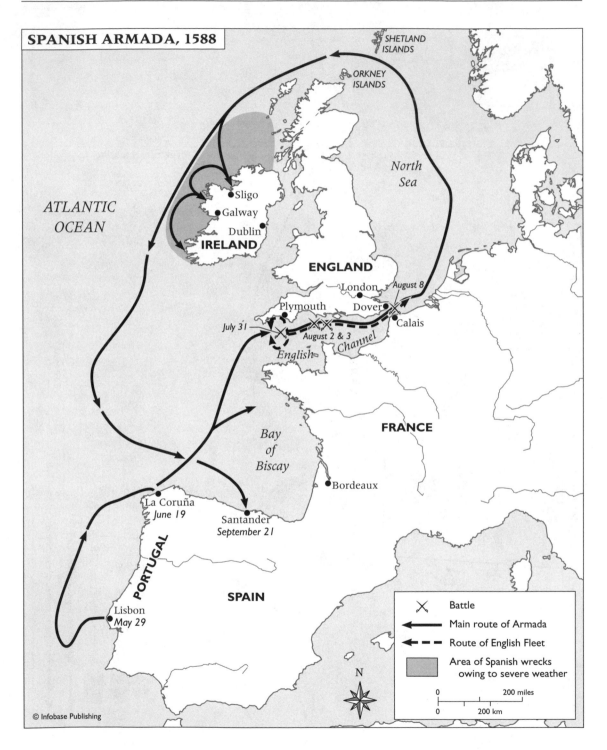

SPANISH ARMADA, 1588

SHETLAND ISLANDS

ORKNEY ISLANDS

North Sea

ATLANTIC OCEAN

Sligo

Galway

Dublin

IRELAND

ENGLAND

London

Plymouth

Dover

August 8

Calais

July 31

August 2 & 3

English

Channel

FRANCE

Bay of Biscay

Bordeaux

La Coruña
June 19

Santander
September 21

PORTUGAL

SPAIN

Lisbon
May 29

N

✕   Battle

←   Main route of Armada

◀---   Route of English Fleet

      Area of Spanish wrecks
      owing to severe weather

0   200 miles
0   200 km

© Infobase Publishing

SPANISH RULE IN EUROPE, 1580–1714

	Spanish Habsburg territory
	Austrian Habsburg territory
1678	Date of loss of territory

0   350 miles
0   350 km

SCOTLAND

IRELAND

ENGLAND

London

North Sea

Hamburg

Berlin

POLAND

ATLANTIC OCEAN

UNITED PROVINCES

Brussels
NETHERLANDS
1713

HOLY ROMAN EMPIRE

Prague

Kraków

Paris

Vienna

Pressburg

Orléans

Franche-Comté
1678

AUSTRIA

HUNGARY

Pest

Bay of Biscay

FRANCE

Milan
MILAN
1714

REPUBLIC OF VENICE

MANTUA

OTTOMAN EMPIRE

Bordeaux

Adriatic Sea

PORTUGAL
1668

SPAIN

Catalonia

PAPAL STATES

Lisbon

Madrid

Barcelona

Rome

Naples

KINGDOM OF NAPLES
1714

BALEARIC IS.

SARDINIA
1714

Minorca
1713

Tangier
Ceuta

Gibraltar
1713

Mediterranean Sea

Palermo

SICILY
1713

Oran

N

© Infobase Publishing

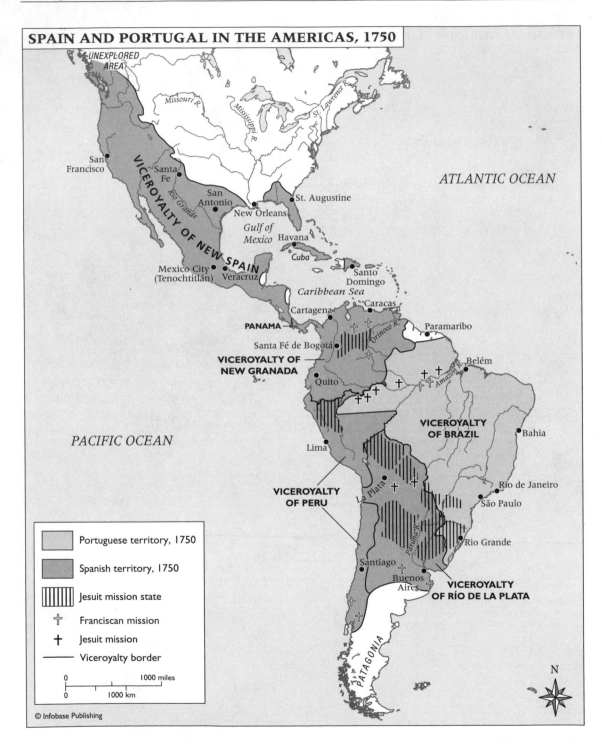

SPAIN AND PORTUGAL IN THE AMERICAS, 1750

UNEXPLORED AREA

Missouri R.

Mississippi R.

St. Lawrence R.

San Francisco

Santa Fe

Rio Grande

San Antonio

New Orleans

St. Augustine

Gulf of Mexico

Havana

VICEROYALTY OF NEW SPAIN

ATLANTIC OCEAN

Mexico City (Tenochtitlán)

Veracruz

Cuba

Santo Domingo

Caribbean Sea

Cartagena

Caracas

Orinoco R.

Paramaribo

PANAMA

Santa Fé de Bogotá

VICEROYALTY OF NEW GRANADA

Belém

Amazon R.

Quito

PACIFIC OCEAN

VICEROYALTY OF BRAZIL

Bahia

Lima

Rio de Janeiro

VICEROYALTY OF PERU

La Plata

São Paulo

Paraná R.

Rio Grande

Santiago

Buenos Aires

VICEROYALTY OF RÍO DE LA PLATA

PATAGONIA

N

Portuguese territory, 1750

Spanish territory, 1750

Jesuit mission state

Franciscan mission

Jesuit mission

Viceroyalty border

0   1000 miles

0   1000 km

© Infobase Publishing

PENINSULAR WAR (WAR OF INDEPENDENCE), 1808–1814

N

Bay of Biscay

FRANCE

La Coruña
1809
El Ferrol

Santander

Oviedo

Vitoria
1808 Fr, 1813 Br

Bilbao

Bayonne

Toulouse
1814

P Y R E N E E S

Astorga

Burgos
1808

Pamplona

Tudela
1808

Ebro R.

PORTUGAL

Valladolid

Zaragoza

Barcelona

Duero R.

Porto

Almeida

Salamanca
1812

Madrid

SPAIN

Tarragona

Tortosa

Busacco
1810

Ciudad Rodrigo

Mondego
Bay

Tagus (Tajo) R.

Talavera
de la Reina
1809

Ocaña
1809

BALEARIC IS.

Vimeiro
1808

Abrantes

Valencia

Majorca

Lisbon

Badajoz

Guadiana R.

Júcar R.

Ibiza

Formentera

Torres
Vedras

La Albuera
1811

Córdoba

Bailén
1808

Segura R.

Guadalquivir R.

Murcia

Cape St.
Vincent
1797

Seville
1808–1810

Granada

Almería

Cartagena

Mediterranean Sea

Cádiz
from 1810

Málaga

0   100 miles

Trafalgar
1805

Gibraltar (U.K.)

0   100 km

ATLANTIC
OCEAN

Cádiz
from 1810

Seat of Spanish provisional
government, with date

British victory

Area held by France,
1812–1813

© Infobase Publishing

Center of Spanish revolt

International boundary, 1812

French victory

Spanish victory

British campaign

French campaign

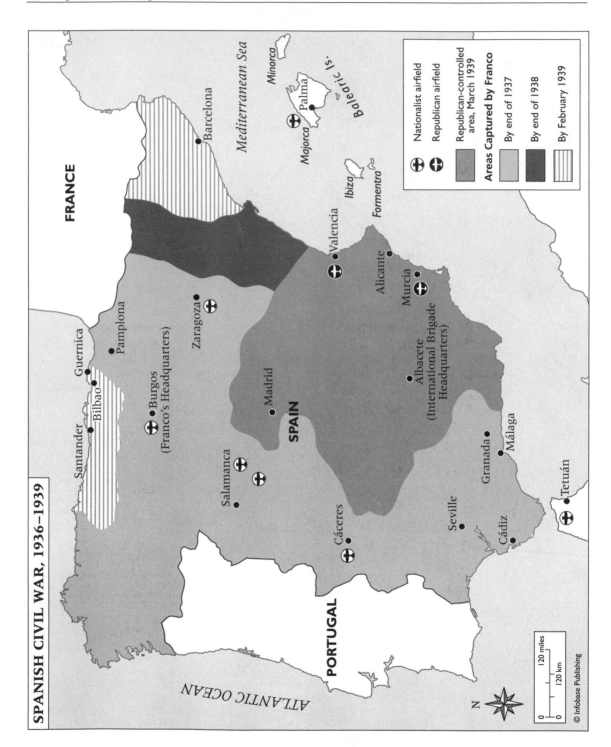

SPANISH CIVIL WAR, 1936–1939

FRANCE

Mediterranean Sea

Minorca

Palma

Majorca

Balearic Is.

Barcelona

Ibiza

Formentra

Valencia

Alicante

Murcia

Albacete
(International Brigade
Headquarters)

Pamplona

Guernica

Santander

Bilbao

Zaragoza

Burgos
(Franco's Headquarters)

Madrid

SPAIN

Salamanca

Cáceres

Granada

Málaga

Seville

Cádiz

Tetuán

PORTUGAL

ATLANTIC OCEAN

N

Nationalist airfield
Republican airfield

Areas Captured by Franco
Republican-controlled
area, March 1939
By end of 1937
By end of 1938
By February 1939

120 miles
120 km

© Infobase Publishing

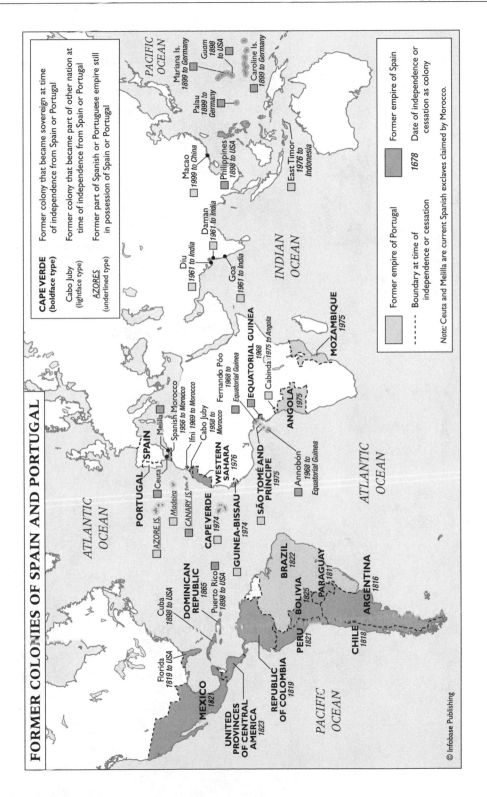

FORMER COLONIES OF SPAIN AND PORTUGAL

CAPE VERDE (boldface type) — Former colony that became sovereign at time of independence from Spain or Portugal

Cabo Juby (lightface type) — Former colony that became part of other nation at time of independence from Spain or Portugal

AZORES (underlined type) — Former part of Spanish or Portuguese empire still in possession of Spain or Portugal

Former empire of Portugal

Former empire of Spain

1678 Date of independence or cessation as colony

- - - - Boundary at time of independence or cessation

Note: Ceuta and Melilla are current Spanish exclaves claimed by Morocco.

© Infobase Publishing

PACIFIC OCEAN

ATLANTIC OCEAN

INDIAN OCEAN

Mariana Is. *1899 to Germany*
Guam *1898 to USA*
Palau *1899 to Germany*
Caroline Is. *1899 to Germany*

Macao *1999 to China*
Philippines *1898 to USA*
East Timor *1976 to Indonesia*

Daman *1961 to India*
Diu *1961 to India*
Goa *1961 to India*

MOZAMBIQUE *1975*

Spanish Morocco *1956 to Morocco*
Ifni *1969 to Morocco*
Cabo Juby *1958 to Morocco*

Fernando Póo *1968 to Equatorial Guinea*
EQUATORIAL GUINEA *1968*
Cabinda *1975 to Angola*

ANGOLA *1975*

PORTUGAL   SPAIN
Melilla
Ceuta
AZORE IS.
Madeira
CANARY IS.

WESTERN SAHARA *1976*

CAPE VERDE *1974*
GUINEA-BISSAU *1974*
SÃO TOMÉ AND PRÍNCIPE *1975*
Annobón *1968 to Equatorial Guinea*

Cuba *1898 to USA*
DOMINICAN REPUBLIC *1865*
Puerto Rico *1898 to USA*
Florida *1819 to USA*

MEXICO *1821*
UNITED PROVINCES OF CENTRAL AMERICA *1823*
REPUBLIC OF COLOMBIA *1819*

BRAZIL *1822*
PERU *1821*
BOLIVIA *1825*
PARAGUAY *1811*
CHILE *1818*
ARGENTINA *1816*

ATLANTIC OCEAN
PACIFIC OCEAN

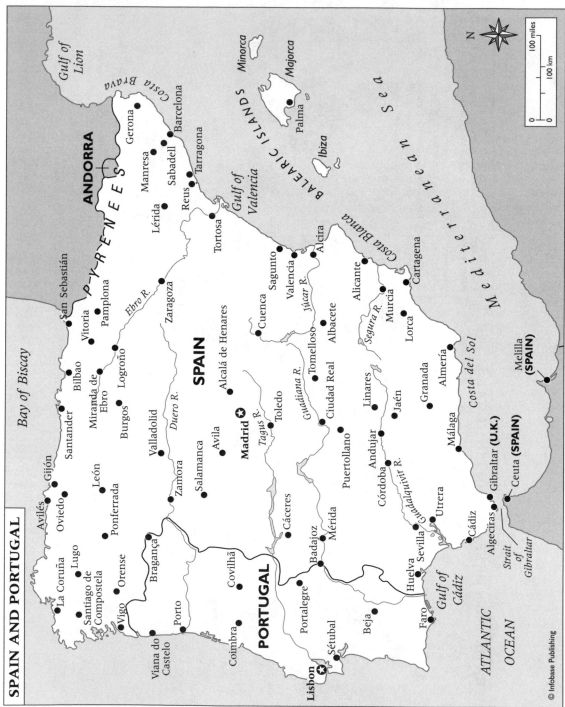

SPAIN AND PORTUGAL

Gulf of Lion

Costa Brava

ANDORRA

PYRENEES

Gerona

Manresa

Barcelona

Sabadell

Tarragona

Reus

Lérida

Tortosa

Minorca

Majorca

Palma

Ibiza

BALEARIC ISLANDS

Gulf of Valencia

Mediterranean Sea

N

100 miles

100 km

0

0

Bay of Biscay

San Sebastián

Vitoria

Pamplona

Ebro R.

Zaragoza

Cuenca

Sagunto

Valencia

Júcar R.

Alcira

Costa Blanca

Alicante

Cartagena

Segura R.

Murcia

Lorca

Melilla (SPAIN)

SPAIN

Alcalá de Henares

Madrid ✪

Tagus R.

Toledo

Guadiana R.

Tomelloso

Albacete

Ciudad Real

Jaén

Granada

Almería

Costa del Sol

Málaga

Miranda de Ebro

Logroño

Burgos

Duero R.

Valladolid

Zamora

Salamanca

Avila

Santander

Bilbao

Gijón

Avilés

Oviedo

León

Ponferrada

Lugo

La Coruña

Santiago de Compostela

Vigo

Orense

Bragança

Covilhã

Viana do Castelo

Porto

Coimbra

PORTUGAL

Portalegre

Sétubal

Beja

Faro

Cáceres

Badajoz

Mérida

Puertollano

Córdoba

Andújar

Linares

Guadalquivir R.

Utrera

Sevilla

Huelva

Cádiz

Algeciras

Gibraltar (U.K.)

Ceuta (SPAIN)

Strait of Gibraltar

Gulf of Cádiz

ATLANTIC OCEAN

Lisbon ✪

© Infobase Publishing

BIBLIOGRAPHY

Acker, Thomas. *The Baroque Vortex: Velázquez, Calderón and Gracián under Philip IV.* New York: Peter Lang, 2002.

Aguilar, Paloma. *Memory and Amnesia: The Role of the Spanish Civil War in Transition to Democracy.* Translated by Mark Oakley. New York: Berghan Books, 2002.

Alpert, Michael. *A New International History of the Spanish Civil War.* New York: St. Martin's Press, 1994.

Anderson, James M. *The Spanish Civil War: A History and Reference Guide.* Westport, Conn.: Greenwood Publishing, 2003.

Aronson, Theo. *Royal Vendetta: The Crown of Spain, 1829–1965.* Indianapolis: Bobbs-Merrill, 1966.

Artola, Miguel, ed. *Enciclopedia de historia de España.* Madrid: Alianza, 1993.

Bachoud, André. *Franco.* Barcelona: Juventud, 1998.

Bell, A. F. *Castilian Literature.* Oxford: Clarendon Press, 1938.

Birmingham, David. *A Concise History of Portugal.* Cambridge: Cambridge University Press, 1993.

Bleiberg, Germán. *Diccionario de historia de España,* 2d ed. 3 vols. Madrid: Ediciones de la Revista de Occidente, 1968.

———, and Julián Marías. *Diccionario de literatura española.* 2d ed. Madrid: Ediciones de la Revista de Occidente, 1953.

Boxer, C. R. *The Portuguese Seaborne Empire.* New York: Knopf, 1960.

Brenan, Gerald. *The Spanish Labyrinth.* Cambridge: Cambridge University Press, 1965.

Brown, G. G. *A Literary History of Spain: The Twentieth Century.* New York: Barnes and Noble Books, 1974.

Brown, Jonathan, and J. H. Elliott. *A Palace for a King: The Buen Retiro and the Court of Philip IV.* New Haven, Conn.: Yale University Press, 1980.

Calleja, José María. *Contra la barbarie: Un alegato en favor de las víctimas de ETA.* Madrid: Tema de Hoy, 1997.

Cantarino, Vicente. *Civilización y cultura de España.* New York: Macmillan, 1988.

Carr, E. H. *The Comintern and the Spanish Civil War.* London: Macmillan, 1984.

Carr, Raymond. *Spain, 1808–1975.* Oxford: Clarendon Press, 1982.

———. *Spain, a History.* New York: Oxford University Press, 2000.

———, and Juan Pablo Fussi. *Spain, Dictatorship to Democracy.* London: Allen and Unwin, 1979.

Cassan, Patrick. *Le pouvoir français et la question basque (1981–1993).* Paris: L'Harmattan, 1997.

Cattell, D. *Soviet Diplomacy and the Spanish Civil War.* Berkeley: University of California Press, 1957.

Clark, Robert P. *Negotiating with ETA: Obstacles to Peace in the Basque Country, 1975–1988.* Reno: University of Nevada Press, 1990.

Cortada, James, ed. *Historical Dictionary of the Spanish Civil War (1936–1939)*. Westport, Conn.: Greenwood Press, 1982.

———. *Spain in the Twentieth Century: Essays on Spanish Diplomacy, 1898–1978*. Westport, Conn.: Greenwood Press, 1979.

Cowlley, Olivia Lorrillard, ed. *Let's Go, Spain and Portugal*. New York: St. Martin's Press, 2000.

Coyle, Laura, ed. *At the Edge: A Portuguese Futurist: Amadeo de Souza Cardoso*. Lisbon: Gabinete das Relaçoes Internacionais, 1999.

Crow, John. *Spain: The Root and the Flower*. Berkeley: University of California Press, 1985.

Delgado, I. *Portugal e a guerra civil de Espanha*. Lisbon: Publicacãos Europa-America, 1980.

Díaz-Plaja, Fernando, and William W. Cressey. *La España que sobrevive*. Washington, D.C.: Georgetown University Press, 1997.

Domínguez Ortiz, Antonio. *Las clases privilegiadas en la España del antiguo régimen*. Madrid: Istmo, 1973.

Duffy, James. *Portugal in Africa*. Baltimore: Penguin Books, 1963.

Edwards, J. *The British Government and the Spanish Civil War*. London: Macmillan, 1979.

Elliott, J. H. *Imperial Spain*. New York: Meridian, 1962.

Falcón, Lidia. *Memorias políticas (1959–1999)*. Barcelona: Planeta, 1999.

———. *La razón feminista*. Madrid: Vindicación Feminista, 1983.

Fernández-Armesto, Felipe. *Ferdinand and Isabella*. New York: Taplinger Publishing, 1975.

Fossi, M., and J. Palafox. *España, 1808–1992*. Madrid: Alba, 1993.

Fuentes, Carlos. *Buried Mirror: Reflections on Spain and the New World*. New York: Houghton Mifflin, 1992.

Gallagher, Tom. *Portugal, a Twentieth-Century Interpretation*. Manchester, U.K.: Manchester University Press, 1983.

García Durán, Juan. *La guerra civil española, fuentes: Archivos, bibliografía y filmografía*. Barcelona: Crítica, 1985.

García Hernán, Henrique. *Políiticos de la monarquia hispánica (1469–1700): Ensayo y diccionario*. Madrid: Funcación Histórica Tavera, 2002.

Garnier, Christine. *Salazar in Portugal*. New York: Farrar, Straus and Young, 1954.

Gazarian Gautier, Marie-Lise. *Interviews with Spanish Writers*. Elmont Park, Ill.: Dalkey Archive Press, 1991.

Goodwin, R. M. *The Spanish Army, 1956–1996*. London: Hyde, 1997.

Graff, Marie Louise. *Culture Shock! Spain*. Portland, Oreg.: Graphic Arts Center, 1997.

Graham, Robert. *Spain: A Nation Comes of Age*. New York: St. Martin's Press, 1984.

Green, Otis H. *Spain and the Western Tradition*. 4 vols. Madison: University of Wisconsin Press, 1968.

Hanke, Lewis. *The Spanish Struggle for Justice: The Conquest of America*. Boston: Little, Brown, 1965.

Harrison, Joseph. *An Economic History of Modern Spain*. New York: Homes and Meier, 1978.

Harvey, Robert. *Portugal: Birth of a Democracy*. New York: St. Martin's Press, 1978.

Hernández Giménez, Félix. *Estudios de geografía histórica española*. Madrid: Ediciones Polifemo, 1994.

Holt, Edgar. *The Carlist Wars*. London: Methuen, 1980.

Hooper, John. *The New Spaniards*. New York: Penguin, 1990.

Hughes, Robert. *Barcelona*. New York: Vintage, 1993.

Jackson, Gabriel. *Historian's Quest: A Twenty-Year Journey into the Spanish Mind.* New York: Alfred A. Knopf, 1969.

Jepson, Tim. *Exploring Portugal.* New York: Fodor, 1998.

Kamen, Henry. *Empire: How Spain Became a World Power, 1492–1763.* New York: Harper Collins, 2003.

———. *Philip of Spain.* New Haven, Conn.: Yale University Press, 1998.

Kaplan, Marion. *The Portuguese: The Land and Its People.* New York: Viking, 1991.

Kay, Hugh. *Salazar and Modern Portugal.* London: Eyre and Spottiswoode, 1970.

Kurlansky, Mark. *The Basque History of the World.* New York: Walker, 1999.

Livermore, H. V. *A New History of Portugal.* Cambridge: Cambridge University Press, 1976.

Lomax, Derek W. *The Reconquest of Spain.* London: Longman, 1978.

López-Davalillo, Julio. *Atlas histórico de España y Portugal.* Madrid: Editorial Síntesis, 1999.

Lynch, John. *Bourbon Spain, 1700–1808.* Oxford: Blackwell, 1993.

Mangini, Shirley. *Las modernas de Madrid: Las grandes intelectuales españolas de la vanguardia.* Barcelona: Península, 2001.

Marías, Julián. *Los españoles.* Madrid: Revista de Occidente, 1971.

———. *Understanding Spain.* Ann Arbor: University of Michigan Press, 1999.

Martin, Benjamin. *The Agony of Modernization: Labor and Industrialization in Spain.* Ithaca, N.Y.: Cornell University, 1990.

Maxwell, K., ed. *The Press and the Rebirth of Iberian Democracy.* Westport, Conn.: Greenwood Press, 1983.

Medina Domínguez, Alberto. *Exorcismos de la memoria: Políticas y poéticas de la melancolía en la España de la transición.* Madrid: Ediciones Libertarias, 2001.

Menéndez Pidal, Ramón. *Historia de España.* Madrid: Espasa-Calpe, 1995.

Merriman, R. B. *The Rise of the Spanish Empire.* 2d ed. 4 vols. New York: Cooper Square Publishers, 1962.

Miller, Townsend. *Henry IV of Castile.* Philadelphia: J. B. Lippincott, 1972.

Morrison, R. J. *Portugal: Revolutionary Change in an Open Economy.* Boston: Auburn House, 1981.

Newton, Michael, and Peter Donaghy. *Institutions of Modern Spain.* Cambridge, Mass.: Harvard University Press, 1998.

Nowell, Charles E. *Portugal.* Englewood Cliffs, N.J.: Prentice Hall, 1973.

Oliveira Marques, A. H. de. *History of Portugal.* New York: Columbia University Press, 1976.

Opello, Walter. *Portugal: From Monarchy to Pluralist Democracy.* Boulder, Colo.: Westview Press, 1991.

Ortiz-Griffin, Julia L., and William D. Griffin. *Spain and Portugal Today.* New York: Peter Lang, 2003.

Partington, Helen, ed. *Insight Guide to Spain.* London: Langenscheidt, 1999.

Payne, Stanley. *A History of Spain and Portugal.* 2 vols. Madison: University of Wisconsin Press, 1973.

———. *Politics and the Military in Modern Spain.* Stanford, Calif.: Stanford University Press, 1967.

———. *Spanish Catholicism: A Historical Overview.* Madison: University of Wisconsin Press, 1984.

Pérez Díaz, Víctor. *The Return of Civil Society: The Emergence of Democratic Spain.* Cambridge, Mass.: Harvard University Press, 1998.

Perriam, Chris. *Stars and Masculinities in Spanish Cinema: From Banderas to Bardem.* New York: Oxford University Press, 2003.

Porter, Darwin, and Danforth Price. *Portugal*. New York: Macmillan, 1996.

Powell, T. *Mexico and the Spanish Civil War*. Albuquerque: University of New Mexico Press, 1980.

Pratt, Dale. *Signs of Science: Literature, Science, and Spanish Modernity since 1868*. West Lafayette, Ind.: Purdue University Press, 2001.

Preston, Paul, ed. *The Evolution and Decline of the Franco Regime*. New York: Barnes and Noble Books, 1976.

————. *Franco*. New York: Basic Books, 1994.

Resina, Joan Ramón, ed. *Disremembering the Dictatorship: The Politics of Memory in the Spanish Transition to Democracy*. Amsterdam and Atlanta, Ga.: Rodopi, 2000.

Robinson, R. A. H. *Contemporary Portugal: A History*. London: Allen and Unwin, 1979.

Ross, Christopher. *Contemporaary Spain*. London: Arnold, 1997.

Russsell, Peter Edward, ed. *Spain: A Companion to Spanish Studies*. London: Methuen, 1973.

Salmon, K. G. *The Modern Spanish Economy: Transformation and Integration into Europe*. London: Pinter, 1995.

Santana, Francisco, and Eduardo Sucena, eds. *Diccionario da historia de Lisboa*. Lisbon: C. Quintas, 1994.

Sanz Villanueva, Santos. *Historia de la literatura española: El siglo XX*. Barcelona: Ariel, 1984.

Saramago, José. *Journey to Portugal*. Translated by Amanda Hopkinson and Nick Caistor. New York: Harcourt, 2000.

Serrão, Joel, ed. *Dicionário de história de Portugal*. Porto, Portugal: Livraria Figuerinhas, 1981.

Shergold, N. D. *A History of the Spanish Stage from Medieval Times until the End of the Seventeenth Century*. Oxford: Clarendon, 1967.

Shubert, Adrian. *Death and Money in the Afternoon: A History of the Spanish Bullfight*. New York: Oxford University Press, 2000.

Spitzmesser, Ana M. *Narrativa posmoderna española*. New York: Peter Lang, 1999.

Stanton, Edward. *Handbook of Spanish Popular Culture*. Westport, Conn.: Greenwood Press, 1999.

Summerhill, Stephen, and John A. Williams. *Sinking Columbus: Contested History, Cultural Politics and Mythmaking During the Quincentenary*. Gainesville: Florida University Press, 2000.

Thomas, Hugh. *Conquest*. New York: Simon and Schuster, 1993.

————. *The Spanish Civil War*. New York: Harper and Brothers, 1961.

Ticknor, George. *History of Spanish Literature*. 3 vols. New York: Harper and Brothers, 1863.

Vincent, Mary, and R. A. Stradling. *Cultural Atlas of Spain and Portugal*. New York: Facts On File, 1994.

Way, Ruth. *A Geography of Spain and Portugal*. London: Methuen, 1962.

Wheeler, Douglas L. *Historical Dictionary of Portugal*. Metuchen, N.J.: Scarecrow Press, 1993.

Wiarda, Howard J. *Corporation and Development in Portugal*. Amherst: University of Massachusetts Press, 1977.

Wilkinson, Julia, and John King. *Portugal*. London: Lonely Planet, 2001.

Williams, Patrick. *Philip II*. New York: Palgrave, 2001.

Boldface page numbers indicate primary discussions. *Italic* page numbers indicate illustrations.

A

Abarca de Bolea, Pedro Pablo (conde de Aranda). *See* Aranda, Pedro Pablo Abarca de Bolea, conde de
Abd el-Krim 87
abstract expressionism 203, 382–383
Abstractionism (art exhibit) 367
Acción Española 261
Aceitunas, Las (Rueda) 347
A cidade e as serras (Eça de Queirós) 171
acting 341–342. *See also* drama
adelantado **69,** 99, 327
Adoration of the Holy Name of Jesus, The (El Greco) 216
Afghanistan 63, 64
Afonso de Bragança 111
Afonso V (king of Portugal and Algarve) 80–81
Afonso VI (king of Portugal) 23, **69,** 316, 317, 424c
Afonso XII (king of Portugal) 176
Africa 8, 55–56
    Angola 86–87
    asiento 92
    Carnation Revolution 132, 133
    Charles I (king of Portugal) 117
    Dias, Bartolomeu 167
    Gama, Vasco da 199
    immigrants in Portugal 226–227
    Las Casas, Bartolomé de 248, 249
    Mombasa 285–286
    Morocco 288–289
    Mozambique 289
    Portuguese Guinea 328–329

Salazar, António de Oliveira 351
    Soares, Mário 365
    Spanish Guinea 376–377
agrarian reform 242
agriculture 78
Agudeza y arte de ingenio (Baltasar) 212
Águila, Don Juan del 245
Aguirre, Lope de **69–70**
Aix-la-Chapelle, Treaty of 406
Alarcón y Mendoza, Juan Ruiz de **70–71**
Alas, Leopoldo (Clarín) **71–72**
Alba, Fernando Álvarez de Toledo, duque de **72,** 173, 313
Albéniz, Isaac Manuel Francisco 62, **73,** 439c
Alberoni, Giulio 26, **73–74,** 231
Alberti, Rafael **74**
albolistas 170
Albuquerque, Afonso de **74–75,** 206, 263, 265, 267
Alcalá Galiano, Antonio 393
Alcalá-Zamora y Torres, Niceto 94
Alcazar of Toledo, siege of the **75–76,** 389
Alcazarquivir, Battle of **76–77,** 336, 358–359, 423c
Aleixandre, Vicente 62, **77,** 438c
Alemán, Mateo **77–78,** 424c
Alentejo **78**
Alexander VI (pope) **78–79,** 173, 390
Alfonso I (king of Aragon) 410
Alfonso XII (king of Spain) 40, *79,* **79,** 434c
    Amadeo I (king of Spain) 84
    Bourbon 110
    Cánovas del Castillo, Antonio 130
    Carlism 131
    Castelar y Ripoll, Emilio 134

Martínez de Campos, Arsenio 272
    Serrano y Domínguez, Francisco 362
Alfonso XIII (king of Spain) 40, 44–46, **79–80,** *80,* 433c, 434c, 436c
    Anual, campaign of 87
    Azaña, Manuel 94
    Bourbon 110
    Isabella II (queen of Spain) 230
    Juan Carlos I (king of Spain) 243
    Primo de Rivera y Orbaneja, Miguel 332–334
Algarve **80–81**
Algeria 304
Alhambra 213
Almagro, Diego 325
Almansa, Battle of **81**
Almeida, António José de **81**
Almeida, Francisco de **82,** 267
Almeida Garrett, João Baptista da Silva Leitão, visconde de **82,** 357, 435c
Alta California 125
Altamira caves 330–331
Altamira Crevea, Rafael **82–83**
Alva, duque de. *See* Alba, Fernando Álvarez de Toledo, duque de
Alvarado, Pedro de **83–84,** 120–121, 160, 277, 402
Álvarez de Castro, Mariano 204–205
Álvarez de Toledo, Fernando (duke of Alba). *See* Alba, Fernando Álvarez de Toledo, duque de
Amadeo I (king of Spain) 39, **84–85,** 433c
    Cánovas del Castillo, Antonio 129
    Castelar y Ripoll, Emilio 134
    Espartero, Baldomero 176
    Prim y Prats, Juan 332

Sagasta, Práxedes Mateo 348
Serrano y Domínguez, Francisco
    362
America 7, 29, 38–39. *See also*
  Central America; South America
  adelantado 69
  Aguirre, Lope de 69–70
  Charles I (king of Spain) 147–
    148
  Charles III (king of Spain)
    150–151
  Columbus, Christopher 157
  Coronado, Francisco Vázquez
    de 159
  Dominican Republic 168
  encomienda 173
  Federmann, Nikolaus 182
  Ferdinand V (king of Aragon and
    united Spain) 183
  Ferdinand VII (king of Spain) 186
  Las Casas, Bartolomé de 248
  Leyenda Negra 251
  Louisiana 255–256
  Miranda, Francisco de 283
  Narváez, Pánfilo de 291–292
  New Spain 295
  Ponce de León, Juan 327
  Soto, Hernando de 366
  Spain and Portugal in the
    Americas (1750) 458*m*
  Velázquez de Cuéllar, Diego 402
American Indians. *See* Native
  Americans
American Revolution 30
  Aranda, Pedro Pablo Abarca de
    Bolea, conde de 88
  Cadalso, José 121
  Charles III (king of Spain) 150
  Florida 191
  Louisiana 255–256
  Malaspina, Alejandro 265
  Miranda, Francisco de 282–283
  Spain and the United States
    372–373
Amigos de la Zarzuela 411
Amistad 373
Ana Mendoza de la Cerda (princess
  of Éboli) 170
anarchism 44, 85, 189, 190, 334,
  385
Andalusia **85**
  Alberti, Rafael 74

Bailén, Battle of 97
Cádiz 121–122
Calleja del Rey, Félix María 125
Córdoba 157–158
García Lorca, Federico 200
Jiménez, Juan Ramón 236
John of Austria 239
John of the Cross, Saint 240
Machado, Antonio 257
O'Donojú, Juan 298
Olavide, Pablo de 299
Philip IV (king of Spain) 321
Queipo de Llano, Gonzalo 336
Seville 363–364
Andorra **85–86**
Ángeles, Victoria de los **86,** 439*c*
Anglo-Spanish Wars 314
Angola 55, **86–87,** 112, 169
Anne (princess of Austria) 320
anticolonialism 87, 108–109, 283,
  329
Anual, campaign of 45, 80, **87–88,**
  288, 332, 351
Apotheosis of St. Thomas Aquinas, The
  (Francisco de Zurbarán) 415
Arab empire 158, 199
Aragon 3, 5, 9, **88**
  Balearic Islands 99
  Barcelona 99
  Catalonia 137
  Charles I (king of Spain) 147
  Ferdinand V (king of Aragon and
    united Spain) 183
  Granada, conquest of 213–214
  Labrador, Pedro Gómez Labrador,
    marqués de 246
  Majorca 264
  Palafox, José de 308–309
  Pérez, Antonio 313, 314
  Philip I (king of Castile) 317
  Reconquista 341
  Spanish Inquisition 377
  Torquemada, Tomás de 390
  Valencia 399
  Zaragoza 410
  Zaragoza, Battle of 410
Aranda, Pedro Pablo Abarca de
  Bolea, conde de 30, **88–89,** 299
Arauca 398
architecture 122–123, 202–203,
  286
Argentina **89,** 261, 352

Arias de Ávilia, Pedro. *See* Pedrarias
  Dávila
Arias Navarro, Carlos **89**
Arizona **90**
Armada 13, **90–91,** 423*c*, 456*m*
  Lepanto, Battle of 250
  Medina Sidonia, Alonso Pérez de
    Guzmán, duque de 275
  Philip II (king of Spain) 319
  Santa Cruz, Álvaro de Bazán,
    marqués de 353
  Spain and the European powers
    368
  Trafalgar, Battle of 393
Armory Show 367
Army of Africa 194
Arroz y tartana (Blasco Ibáñez) 106
art 62
  Bilbao 106
  Chillida, Eduardo 152–153
  Dalí i Domènech, Salvador 164
  Fernandes, Vasco 187
  González, Julio 210
  Goya y Lucientes, Francisco José
    de 211–212
  Greco, El 216–217
  Gris, Juan 218–219
  Miró, Joan 283–284
  Murillo, Bartolomé Esteban
    289–290
  Pacheco, Francisco 307
  Picasso, Pablo 323–324
  Prado, Museo Nacional del
    329–330
  Sorolla y Bastida, Joaquín 365
  Souza Cardoso, Amadeo de
    366–367
  Tàpies, Antoni 382–383
  Thyssen-Bornemisza Museum
    386–387
  Velázquez, Diego Rodríguez de
    Silva y 401
  Zurbarán, Francisco de 415
art criticism 307
*Arte de la pintura, su antigüedad y
  grandeza, El* (Pacheco) 307
Arthur (prince of Wales) 139, 140
Art of Worldly Wisdom, The (Baltasar)
  212–213
Asencio Torrado, José **91**
Asia 74, 75, 148, 167, 390
asiento **91–92,** 378

Asturias **92,** 249
Asturias ministers' revolt 194
Atahuallpa 325, 366
Atapuerca 331–332
audiencia 414
Augsburg, Religious Peace of 148
Augustine, Saint 405
Augustín I (emperor of Mexico) 234
Austria 233
Austrian Succession, War of the 322
Avellaneda, Alonso Fernández de 144
Aviz, House of 7, 12, 76, **93,** 319, 359, 423*c*
Ayacucho, Battle of **93,** 380
Aymara 109
Azaña, Manuel **94,** 352, 376
Aznar López, José María 59–60, 63, **94–95,** 438*c,* 439*c*
  Basque nationalism 103
  Rodríguez Zapatero, José Luis 345
  Spain and the Middle East 371
  Spain and the United States 374
  terrorism 385
Azores 7, 63, **95–96,** 280, 281, 351
Azorín. *See* Martínez Ruiz, José
Aztec Empire 83–84, 160, 172, 217, 279, 300

B

Bach, Johann Sebastian 134
Baden, Treaty of 378
Bahia **97,** 422*c*
Bailén, Battle of **97–98**
Baja California 121, 125
Balboa, Vasco Núñez de 10, **98–99,** 309, 311, 325, 421*c*
Balearic Islands **99,** 264
Balmas, Antonio Oliver 157
Baltasar and Blimunda (Saramago) 356
Banco de San Carlos 118
Bancroft, George 373
Bando de España 171
Barcelona **99–100,** 138, 202, 382, 383, 387, 431*c,* 436*c*
Baroja, Pío **100–101**
Basque Homeland and Freedom. *See* ETA

Basque nationalism 54, 59, 60, 64–65, **101–103,** 439*c,* 440*c*
  Arias Navarro, Carlos 89
  Aznar López, José María 94–95
  Basque provinces 103
  Catalonia 139
  Falcón, Lidia 179–180
  Madariaga, Salvador de 259
  Picasso, Pablo 323–324
  Rodríguez Zapatero, José Luis 345
  terrorism 385
Basque provinces **103–104,** 106, 292–293
Basques 210
Bastida, Gustavo Adolfo Domínguez Bastida. *See* Bécquer, Gustavo Adolfo
Bautista de Toledo, Juan 175
Bécquer, Gustavo Adolfo 42, **104,** 435*c*
Belalcázar, Sebastián de **104–105,** 182, 237
Belgium 230
Benavente y Martínez, Jacinto 62, **105–106,** 438*c*
Benedictine order 182
Berwick, duke of 81
Bilbao 101, 104, **106,** 152, 414
Black Legend. *See* Leyenda Negra
Blasco Ibáñez, Vicente **106–107,** 435*c*
Blue Division 51, **107–108**
Boabdil 214–215
Bodas de sangre (García Lorca) 201
Böhl von Faber, Cecilia. *See* Caballero, Fernán
Boleyn, Anne 140
Bolívar, Simón *108,* **108–109**
  Ayacucho, Battle of 93
  Bolivia 109
  Boyacá, Battle of 110
  Colombia 154
  Miranda, Francisco de 283
  San Martín, José Francisco de 353
  Sucre, Antonio José de 380
Bolivia 109, **109,** 380
Bonaparte, Joseph. *See* Joseph I (king of Spain)
Borja, Rodrigo de. *See* Alexander VI (pope)

Bougainville, Louis-Antoine de 266
Bourbon 25–28, **109–110,** 430*c,* 435*c*
  bullfighting 114
  Cánovas del Castillo, Antonio 129
  Carlism 130–131
  Catalonia 137
  Charles IV (king of Spain) 151
  Espartero, Baldomero 176
  Ferdinand VII (king of Spain) 186
  Godoy, Manuel de 207
  Isabella II (queen of Spain) 229
  Italy, Spain in 233
  Iturbide, Agustín de 234
  Joseph I (king of Spain) 241
  Labrador, Pedro Gómez Labrador, marqués de 246
  Louis I (king of Spain) 254–255
  Madrid 260
  Philip IV (king of Spain) 321
  Philip V (king of Spain) 322, 323
  Prado, Museo Nacional del 329
  Riego y Núñez, Rafael del 342
  Segovia 360
  Spanish Succession, War of the 378
  Zaragoza, Battle of 410
Bourbon Family Compact 368
Bourbon-Parma line 231
Bourbon Reforms 185, 242
Boyacá, Battle of **110**
Braga, Teófilo **110–111,** 268
Bragança 41–42, **111,** 424*c*
  Aviz, House of 93
  Brazil 113
  Catherine of Bragança 140–141
  John IV (king of Portugal) 238
  Lisbon 252
  Manuel II (king of Portugal) 268
  Miguelite War 280
Bravo Murillo, Juan **111–112,** 357
Brazil 8, 32, **112–113,** 420*c,* 422*c,* 424*c,* 426*c,* 429*c*–430*c,* 438*c*
  Bahia 97
  Cabral, Pedro Álvares 120
  immigrants in Portugal 226
  John V (king of Portugal) 238
  John VI (king of Portugal) 239
  Joseph I (king of Portugal) 241
  Miguel, prince of Portugal 280

Miguelite War 280
Pedro I (king of Portugal and emperor of Brazil) 311–312
Peter II (king of Portugal) 317
Pombal, Sebastião José de Carvalho e Melo, marquês de 326
Tordesillas, Treaty of 390
Uruguay 395
Breda, siege of **113,** 379
Britain. *See* England; Great Britain
Buenos Aires 89, 247
Buero Vallejo, Antonio **113–114**
bullfighting **114–116,** *115, 116,* 201
Buñuel, Luis 62, **116–117,** 164, 341
Burgundy 147, 192
Burial of Count Orgaz, The (El Greco) 217
Burlador de Sevilla y el convidado de piedra, El (Tirso de Molina) 387
Bush, George W. 63, 371

C

Caballero, Fernán **118**
Caballero de Olmedo, El (Lope de Vega Carpio) 254
Cabarrús, Francisco conde de **118–119**
Cabeza de Vaca, Álvar Núñez **119,** 158, 292
Cabral, Pedro Álvares 97, **119–120,** *120,* 167, 267, 420*c*
Cabrillo, Juan Rodríguez **120–121**
Cadalso, José **121,** 435*c*
Cádiz 35, **121–122,** 125, 160, 312, 364, 423*c*, 429*c*
Cádiz, Constitution of 186
Caetano, Marcelo 55, 56, 60, 132–133, 437*c*
Calatrava, Santiago **122–123,** 286
Calderón, Rodrigo **123–124**
Calderón de la Barca, Pedro **124,** 287, 346, 411, 424*c*
Calicut 120
California 121, **124–125,** 198, 361
Calleja del Rey, Félix María **125–126**
Calpe 205
Calvin, John 362, 363
Camões, Luíz Vaz de **126–127,** 404, 420*c*, 424*c*

Campoamor y Campoosorio, Ramón de **127–128**
Campos de Castilla 258
Camprubí, Zenobia 236
Canary Islands 64, *128,* **128–129,** *129,* 145, 153, 194, 356, 362
Cánovas del Castillo, Antonio 40, **129–130,** 348, 349, 407, 433*c*, 434*c*
Cape Passaro, Battle of 406
Cape St. Vincent, battle of 397
Cape Verde Islands 8, **130**
Capitulation of Breda, The (Velázquez) 113
Caprichos, Los (Goya) 211
Carew, Sir George 245
Carlism 36, 39–40, **130–131,** 431*c*, 436*c*
  Espartero, Baldomero 176
  Falange Española 179
  Isabella II (queen of Spain) 230
  Labrador, Pedro Gómez Labrador, marqués de 246
  Maria Christina (queen and regent of Spain) 270
  Miguelite War 281
  Navarre 292
  Zea Bermúdez, Francisco 412
  Zumalacárregui y de Imaz, Tomás de 413–414
Carlist War, First 36–37
  Bilbao 106
  Carlism 130–131
  Isabella II (queen of Spain) 230
  Maria Christina (queen and regent of Spain) 270
  Martínez de la Rosa, Francisco 273
  Narváez y Campos, Ramón María 292
  O'Donnell Joris, Leopoldo 297
  Palafox, José de 309
  Prim y Prats, Juan 332
  Serrano y Domínguez, Francisco 361
  Zea Bermúdez, Francisco 412
Carlist War, Second 39, 79, 106, 131, 272, 406
Carlos. *See* Charles *entries*
Carmelites 240, 384
Carmona, António Óscar de Fragoso **131–132**

Carnation Revolution 56, 60, **132–133,** 169, 226, 437*c*
Carreras, José 167, 439*c*
Carrero Blanco, Luis 89, 102
Carthaginian Empire 289, 349–350
Casa de Bernarda Alba, La (García Lorca) 201
Casa de Contratación 192
Casals, Pablo 62, **134,** 215, 439*c*
Castaños, Francisco 97, 98
Castelar y Ripoll, Emilio **134–135,** 433*c*
Castelo Branco, Camilo (visconde de Correia Botelho) **135–136**
Castile 3, 5, 7, 9, 11, 18–20, **136,** 421*c*
  Andalusia 85
  Aragon 88
  Asturias 92
  Basque nationalism 101
  Bilbao 106
  Canary Islands 128
  Catalonia 137
  Charles I (king of Spain) 147
  Cisneros, Francisco Jiménez de 153, 154
  Ferdinand V (king of Aragon and united Spain) 183
  Fernández de Córdoba, Gonzalo 188
  Floridablanca, José Moñino, conde de 191
  Garcilaso de la Vega 202
  Gaudí i Cornet, Antonio 202
  Gibraltar 205
  Granada, conquest of 213–214
  Haro, Luis de 221–222
  Isabella I (queen of Castile) 227
  Joanna (queen of Castile) 238
  La Mancha 246–247
  León 249
  Machado, Antonio 257, 258
  Murcia 289
  Olivares, Gaspar de Guzmán y Pimentel, conde-duque de 301
  Padilla, Juan de 307
  Pérez, Antonio 313, 314
  Philip I (king of Castile) 317, 318
  Philip II (king of Spain) 318
  Reconquista 341
  Segovia 359–360
  Seville 364

Spanish Inquisition 377
Toledo 388
Tordesillas, Treaty of 389
Torquemada, Tomás de 390
Valladolid 400
Castilla del Oro 311
Castro, Eugénio de **136**
Castro y Bellvís, Guillén de **136–137**
Catalan 137
Catalan nationalism 138–139
Catalonia 59, 94, 99–100, **137–139,** 204, 321, 378, 424*c*, 431*c*
Cateau-Cambrésis, Treaty of 232, 349
Catherine of Aragon 9, **139–140,** *140*, 405
Catherine of Bragança **140–141**
Catholicism. *See* Roman Catholic Church
Catholic Reformation 240
Cela, Camilo José 62, **141–142,** 438*c*
Celestina, La (Rojas) 345–346
Central America 10. *See also specific countries, e.g.:* Nicaragua
    Alvarado, Pedro de 83–84
    Belalcázar, Sebastián de 104
    Columbus, Christopher 156
    Cortés, Hernán 160
    New Spain 296
    Spanish Explorations of Middle America (1513–1543) 453*m*
Cerignola, Battle of **142–143,** 188
Cervantes Saavedra, Miguel de 24, 136, *143,* **143–145,** 246–247, 250, 424*c*
Cervera y Topete, Pascual **145–146,** 356
Ceuta **146,** 288, 336, 371
Ceylon 82, **146**
Charlemagne 85
Charles I (king of Portugal) 41–42, **146–147,** 434*c*
    Éboli, Ruy Gómez de Silva, prince of 170
    Escorial, El 175
    Farnese, Alessandro 180
    Ferdinand V (king of Aragon and united Spain) 185
    Fonseca, Juan Rodríguez de 192
    Franche-Comté, Spain in the 192

Garcilaso de la Vega 202
Habsburg 220
Italian Wars 232
Italy, Spain in 233
Charles I (king of Spain; Holy Roman Emperor Charles V) 9–11, **147–148,** 421*c,* 422*c*
    Alba, Fernando Álvarez de Toledo, duque de 72
    Catherine of Aragon 140
    Cisneros, Francisco Jiménez de 154
    Cortés, Hernán 160
    Empire of Charles V 452*m*
    Federmann, Nikolaus 181
    Habsburg 220
    Italian Wars 232
    Joanna (queen of Castile) 238
    John of Austria 239
    Las Casas, Bartolomé de 248
    Magellan, Ferdinand 263
    Manuel II (king of Portugal) 267
    Margaret, duchess of Parma 268
    Margaret of Austria 268, 269
    Mendoza, Antonio de 277
    Netherlands, Revolt of the 293–294
    Netherlands, Spain in the 294
    Padilla, Juan de 307
    St. Quentin, Battle of 349
    Serveto, Miguel 362
    Toledo 389
    Valdés, Alfonso de 396
    Valdés, Juan de 397
    Venezuela 403
    Zumalacárregui y de Imaz, Tomás de 414
    Zumárraga, Juan de 414
Charles II (king of England) 140, 141, 185, 220
Charles II (king of Spain) 21–22, 25, **148–149,** *149,* 368, 378, 424*c*
Charles III (king of Spain) 28–31, **149–151,** 427*c*
    Aranda, Pedro Pablo Abarca de Bolea, conde de 88
    Bourbon 110
    Cabarrús, Francisco conde de 118
    Floridablanca, José Moñino, conde de 191
    Gálvez, Bernardo de 198, 199

Gálvez, José de 197–199
Godoy, Manuel de 208
Isabella Farnese (queen consort of Spain) 231
Italy, Spain in 233
Jovellanos, Gaspar Melchor de 242
Louisiana 255
Malaspina, Alejandro 266
O'Reilly, Alexander 303
Prado, Museo Nacional del 329
Spain and the European powers 368
Wall, Richard 406
Charles IV (king of Spain) 28, 31, 33, 34, *151,* **151–152,** 427*c,* 428*c*
    Aranda, Pedro Pablo Abarca de Bolea, conde de 88
    Bourbon 110
    Cabarrús, Francisco conde de 118
    Ferdinand VII (king of Spain) 185
    Floridablanca, José Moñino, conde de 192
    Godoy, Manuel de 207
    Goya y Lucientes, Francisco José de 211
    Jovellanos, Gaspar Melchor de 243
    Labrador, Pedro Gómez Labrador, marqués de 246
    Louisiana 256
    Malaspina, Alejandro 266
    Olavide, Pablo de 299
    Peninsular War 312
Charles V (Holy Roman Emperor). *See* Charles I (king of Spain)
Charles V (king of Spain) 36, 37, 130–131, 270, 413
Charles VII (king of Spain) 40, 131
Charles VIII (king of France) 188, 232
Chibchas 237
Chile **152,** 298–299, 352, 398, 432*c*
Chillida, Eduardo 62, **152–153,** 439*c*
China 257
Christianity. *See also* Roman Catholic Church
    encomienda 174
    Goa 206

Granada, conquest of 213–215
Isabella I (queen of Castile) 228–229
Japan, Portuguese presence in 235
Reconquista 340–341
Santiago de Compostela 354–355
Serveto, Miguel 362
Churruca, Cosme 393
Cid, El. *See* Vivar, Rodrigo Díaz de
Cid, Le (Corneille) 136
cinema 62
   Buñuel, Luis 116–117
   Dalí i Domènech, Salvador 164
   Domingo, Plácido 167
   Rey, Fernando 341–342
   Tamayo y Baus, Manuel 382
   Tirso de Molina 387–388
   Torres Naharro, Bartolomé de 391–392
Cisneros, Francisco Jiménez de **153–154,** 228, 293
Ciudad de Guatemala 219
Civil War (U.S.) 373
Clarín. *See* Alas, Leopoldo
Clásicos y modernos (Azorín) 204
Clement VII (pope) 396
cold war 53, 370, 374
Colmena, La (Cela) 141
Colombia 104, 110, **154,** 237, 295, 309
Colonia 29
colonialism 29–30, 35, 40–41, 55
   Albuquerque, Afonso de 74–75
   Almeida, Francisco de 82
   Angola 86–87
   asiento 91
   Ayacucho, Battle of 93
   Bolívar, Simón 108–109
   Brazil 112–113
   Cabeza de Vaca, Álvar Núñez 119
   California 125
   Canary Islands 128
   Cape Verde Islands 130
   Carnation Revolution 132, 133
   Ceylon 146
   Charles I (king of Portugal) 147
   Charles III (king of Spain) 150–151
   Chile 152
   Costa Gomes, Francisco da 162
   Dominican Republic 168

Eanes, António dos Santos Ramalho 169
East Timor 169–170
encomienda 173–174
Ferdinand VII (king of Spain) 186
Fonseca, Juan Rodríguez de 192
Former Colonies of Spain and Portugal 461*m*
Gálvez, José de 198–199
Honduras 224
immigrants in Portugal 226
Iturbide, Agustín de 233–234
Jamaica 235
Jiménez de Queseda, Gonzalo 237–238
La Plata, Viceroyalty of 247
Las Casas, Bartolomé de 249
Leyenda Negra 251
Louisiana 255–256
Macao 257
Malacca 265
Manuel II (king of Portugal) 267
Mendoza, Antonio de 277
Mexico 279–280
Moluccas 285
Mozambique 289
New Spain 295–296
Oñate, Juan de 301–302
Philip II (king of Spain) 319
Philippine Islands 323
Portuguese Guinea 328–329
Puerto Rico 334
Salazar, António de Oliveira 351
San Martín, José Francisco de 352–353
São Tomé and Príncipe 356
Seville 364
Spain and the European powers 369
Spanish Guinea 376–377
Spice Islands 378–379
Sucre, Antonio José de 380–381
Velázquez de Cuéllar, Diego 402
Zumárraga, Juan de 414
Columbus, Christopher 7, 8, 10, **154–157,** *155, 156,* 419*c*–420*c*
   Belalcázar, Sebastián de 104
   Costa Rica 162
   Cuba 162
   Dominican Republic 168
   Ferdinand V (king of Aragon and united Spain) 183

Fonseca, Juan Rodríguez de 192
   Hispaniola 223
   Honduras 224
   Isabella I (queen of Castile) 228–229
   Jamaica 235
   Magellan, Ferdinand 263
   Nicaragua 296
   Ponce de León, Juan 327
   Puerto Rico 334
   Tordesillas, Treaty of 390
   Valladolid 400
   Velázquez de Cuéllar, Diego 402
   Vives, Juan Luis 405
Columbus, Diego 156
communism 259, 261
Communist Party 225
Compañía de Comercio de Filipinas 118
Comte, Auguste 110
Comuneros, Revolt of the 307
Concierto de Aranjuez (Rodrigo) 344
Conde, Carmen **157**
Condenado por desconfiado, El (Tirso de Molina) 387–388
Congress of Vienna 246
conquistadores
   adelantado 69
   Aguirre, Lope de 69–70
   Alvarado, Pedro de 83–84
   Balboa, Vasco Núñez de 98–99
   Cortés, Hernán 160–162
   Ecuador 172
   Fonseca, Juan Rodríguez de 192
   Las Casas, Bartolomé de 249
   Narváez, Pánfilo de 291–292
   Oñate, Juan de 302
   Orellana, Francisco de 304
   Pedrarias Dávila 310–311
   Pizarro, Francisco 325–326
   Soto, Hernando de 365–366
   Valdivia, Pedro de 398
Conservative Party 130
Conspiración de Venecia (Francisco Martínez de la Rosa) 273
constitutionalism 324
Constitution of 1812 122
conversos 377, 391
Cook, James 266
Córdoba **157–158,** *158*
Córdoba, Treaty of 298

Coronado, Francisco Vázquez de
158–159, 295
cortes 5, 18, 22, 36, 45, **159–160,**
431*c*, 438*c*
  Bravo Murillo, Juan 111
  Cádiz 122
  Carlism 130
  Ferdinand VII (king of Spain) 186
  González Márquez, Felipe 210
  Peninsular War 312
  Riego y Núñez, Rafael del 342
  Sartorius, José Luis 358
Cortés, Hernán 10, **160–162,** *161,*
421*c*
  Alvarado, Pedro de 83, 84
  Cabrillo, Juan Rodríguez 120
  California 124–125
  Charles I (king of Spain) 148
  El Salvador 172
  Fonseca, Juan Rodríguez de 192
  Guatemala 219
  Mendoza, Antonio de 277
  Narváez, Pánfilo de 291
  Nicaragua 296
  Olid, Cristóbal de 300
  Velázquez de Cuéllar, Diego 402
Cortot, Alfred 134
Coruña, La 197
Costa Gomes, Francisco da **162**
Costa Rica **162**
Counter-Reformation 12, 90–91,
319, 368, 384
Covadonga, Battle of 92, 340
Criticón, El (Baltasar) 212
Cromwell, Oliver 141
Crusades 358
Cuba 40–41, **162–163,** 430*c*, 434*c*
  Alfonso XII (king of Spain) 79
  Alvarado, Pedro de 83
  Cabrillo, Juan Rodríguez 120
  Cánovas del Castillo, Antonio
  130
  Cervera y Topete, Pascual 145–
  146
  Columbus, Christopher 156
  Cortés, Hernán 160
  Grijalva, Juan de 217
  Louisiana 256
  Martí, José 271
  Martínez de Campos, Arsenio
  272
  Narváez, Pánfilo de 291

Olid, Cristóbal de 299–300
O'Reilly, Alexander 303
Sagasta, Práxedes Mateo 348
Santiago de Cuba, Battle of
355–356
Serrano y Domínguez, Francisco
362
Soto, Hernando de 366
Spain and the United States 373
Spanish-American War 374, 375
Velázquez de Cuéllar, Diego 402
Cuban Revolutionary Party 271
cubism 209, 218, 323
Cuestión palpitante, La (Pardo Bazán)
310

D

Dalí i Domènech, Salvador 62, 117,
164–165, 439*c*
Damão and Diu 132, **165**
Daríen 309, 311
Darío, Rubén 127, **165–166,** 236
Dau al Set 382
Del rey abajo ninguno (Rojas Zorrilla)
346–347
Desastres de la guerra, Los (Goya) 211
Desdén con el desdén, El (Moreto)
287–288
Dewey, George 266
Diálogo de Lactancio y un arcediano
(Valdés) 396
Diálogo de la doctrina cristiana
(Valdés) 397
Diálogo de Mercurio y Carón (Valdés)
396
Dias, Bartolomeu 8, **166–167,** 419*c*
dinosaurs 330
diplomacy 73
División Azul. *See* Blue Division
Domingo, Plácido **167–168,** 439*c*
Dominican Republic **168,** 224, 362
Dominicans 390–391
Don Alfonso Carlos 131
Don Álvaro; o, La fuerza del sino
(Rivas) 343
Don Carlos. *See* Charles V (king of
Spain)
Don Carlos Hugo 131
Don Jaime 131
Don Juan de Austria. *See* John of
Austria

Don Juan Tenorio (José Zorrilla y
Moral) 413
Don Quijote [Quixote] *de la Mancha*
(Cervantes) 144–145
Don Quijote [Quixote] *de la Mancha*
(theater adaptation) 137
drama
  Alarcón y Mendoza, Juan Ruiz
  de 70–71
  Almeida Garrett, João Baptista da
  Silva Leitão, visconde de 82
  Benavente y Martínez, Jacinto
  105–106
  Buero Vallejo, Antonio 113–114
  Calderón de la Barca, Pedro 124
  Castro y Bellvís, Guillén de
  136–137
  Cervantes Saavedra, Miguel de
  143–144
  Echegaray y Eizaguirre, José
  171–172
  Encina, Juan del 172–173
  García Lorca, Federico 200–201
  Lope de Vega Carpio, Félix
  253–254
  Mendes Leal, José da Silva 276
  Moratín, Leandro Fernández de
  286–287
  Moreto y Cabaña, Agustín
  287–288
  Pérez Galdós, Benito 316
  Rivas, Ángel de Saavedra, duque
  de 343
  Rojas Zorrilla, Francisco de
  346–347
  Rueda, Lope de 347
  Tirso de Molina 387–388
  Unamuno, Miguel de 394–395
  Vicente, Gil 403
  Zorrilla y Moral, José 412–413
Drama nuevo, un (Tamayo y Baus)
382
Dumas, Alexandre 276
Dupont, Pierre 98
Dutch East Indies 378–379

E

Eanes, António dos Santos Ramalho
169, **169**
East Africa 289
East Timor 61, **169–170**

Éboli, Ruy Gómez de Silva, prince of 170, **170**
Eça de Queirós, José Maria 42, **170–171,** 337, 435c
Echegaray y Eizaguirre, José 62, **171–172,** 438c
Ecuador 84, 104, **172,** 304, 380
Edward VI (king of England) 368
églogas 411
Egmont, duke of 349
Elcano, Sebastián 264
El Dorado 70, 237
El Greco. *See* Greco, El
Elisabeth of Valois 320
Elizabeth I (queen of England) 90, 140, 245, 319, 368
El Salvador 84, **172**
Emmanuele Filberto, duke of Savoy 349
Empire of Charles V 10, 452m
Encina, Juan del **172–173,** 391, 411
encomienda **173–174,** 174
engineering 122–123
England 14. *See also* Great Britain
    Almansa, Battle of 81
    Armada 90
    Catherine of Bragança 140–141
    Gibraltar 205
    Jamaica 235
    John VI (king of Portugal) 239
    Lerma, Francisco Gómez de Sandoval y Rojas, duque de 251
    Oporto 302
    Spain and the European powers 368
    Trafalgar, Battle of 393
English Channel 90–91, 393
Enlightenment, The 30–31
    Aranda, Pedro Pablo Abarca de Bolea, conde de 88
    Charles III (king of Spain) 149–150
    Feijoo, Benito Jerónimo 183
    Gálvez, Bernardo de 198
    Gálvez, José de 199
    Jovellanos, Gaspar Melchor de 242
    Leyenda Negra 252
    Miranda, Francisco de 283
    Moratín, Leandro Fernández de 287

Pombal, Sebastião José de Carvalho e Melo, marquês de 326
    Spanish Inquisition 378
Enrique IV (king of Castile). *See* Henry IV (king of Castile)
"Enterprise of England" 90–91
environmental issues in Spain and Portugal **174–175**
Equatorial Guinea. *See* Spanish Guinea
Erasmus 396, 397, 405
Escobedo, Juan de 313
Escorial, El **175–176,** 319, 349, 423c
Escrivá de Balaguer, Josemaría 302, 303
Escuela Moderna 190
España invertebrada (Ortega y Gasset) 305–306
Espartero, Baldomero **176,** 431c, 432c
    Bravo Murillo, Juan 111
    Maria Christina (queen and regent of Spain) 270
    Martínez de la Rosa, Francisco 273
    Narváez y Campos, Ramón María 292
    O'Donnell Joris, Leopoldo 297
    Sartorius, José Luis 358
    Serrano y Domínguez, Francisco 362
Espronceda, José de 42, **176–177,** 435c
ETA (Euskadi Ta Askatasuna; Basque Homeland and Freedom) 59, 63, 64, 439c, 440c
    Aznar López, José María 95
    Basque nationalism 102, 103
    Catalonia 139
    Spain and the Middle East 371, 372
    terrorism 385
European Union (EU) 61, 63, 438c, 440c
    Aznar López, José María 95
    environmental issues in Spain and Portugal 174
    González Márquez, Felipe 210
    Herculano de Carvalho e Araújo, Alexandre 222
    Rodríguez Zapatero, José Luis 345

Soares, Mário 365
    Spain and the European powers 370
Euskadi Ta Askatasuna. *See* ETA
exploration 7–8, 10. *See also* conquistadores
    adelantado 69
    Alvarado, Pedro de 83–84
    Argentina 89
    Balboa, Vasco Núñez de 98–99
    Belalcázar, Sebastián de 104–105
    Cabeza de Vaca, Álvar Núñez 119
    Cabral, Pedro Álvares 119–120
    Cabrillo, Juan Rodríguez 120–121
    Canary Islands 128
    Colombia 154
    Columbus, Christopher 154–157
    Coronado, Francisco Vázquez de 158–159
    Cortés, Hernán 160–162
    Cuba 162
    Dias, Bartolomeu 166–167
    Federmann, Nikolaus 182
    Florida 191
    Fonseca, Juan Rodríguez de 192
    Gálvez, José de 198
    Gama, Vasco da 199
    Grijalva, Juan de 217–218
    Isabella I (queen of Castile) 228–229
    Jiménez de Queseda, Gonzalo 237–238
    Lisbon 252
    Magellan, Ferdinand 263
    Malaspina, Alejandro 265
    Olid, Cristóbal de 299–300
    Oñate, Juan de 301–302
    Orellana, Francisco de 304–305
    Ortiz de Retes, Iñigo 306
    Pizarro, Francisco 325–326
    Ponce de León, Juan 327
    Soto, Hernando de 365–366
    Uruguay 395
    Velázquez de Cuéllar, Diego 402
Extremadura **177**

F

Fábula de Polifemo y Galeata (Góngora) 209
fado 344

Falange Española *178,* **178–179,** 195, 232, 334

Falcón, Lidia **179–180,** 408

Falkland Islands 266

Falla, Manuel de 62, **180,** 344, 439*c*

Familia de Pascual Duarte, La (Cela) 141

Farnese, Alessandro **180–181,** 268

Farnese, Ottavio 268

fascism 178, 179, 194, 375, 380

Fátima **181**

Federmann, Nikolaus 104, **181– 182,** 237

Feijoo, Benito Jerónimo **182–183**

Felipe. *See* Philip *entries*

feminism 179–180, 324–325

Ferdinand (duke of Saxe-Coburg-Gotha) 269

Ferdinand I (Holy Roman Emperor) 148

Ferdinand I (king of Portugal) 93

Ferdinand V (king of Aragon and united Spain) 5–9, **183–185,** *184,* 419*c*–421*c*

  Aragon 88

  Balboa, Vasco Núñez de 99

  Cerignola, Battle of 142

  Cisneros, Francisco Jiménez de 153, 154

  Columbus, Christopher 156

  Fernández de Córdoba, Gonzalo 188

  Granada 213

  Granada, conquest of 214

  Guevara, Antonio de 219

  Habsburg 220

  Haro, Luis de 221–222

  Henry IV (king of Castile) 221– 222

  Ignatius of Loyola, Saint 225

  Isabella I (queen of Castile) 227–229

  Italian Wars 232

  Italy, Spain in 233

  Joanna (queen of Castile) 238

  Margaret of Austria 268

  Navarre 292

  Philip I (king of Castile) 317, 318

  Reconquista 341

  Santiago de Compostela 355

  Segovia 360

  Spanish Inquisition 377

Tetuán, campaign of 386

Torquemada, Tomás de 390

Ferdinand VI (king of Spain) 27– 28, 110, 183, **185,** 231, 427*c*

Ferdinand VII (king of Spain) 34– 36, **185–187,** *186,* 428*c*–431*c*

  Bailén, Battle of 97

  Bourbon 110

  Calleja del Rey, Félix María 125

  Carlism 130

  Charles IV (king of Spain) 151–152

  Espartero, Baldomero 176

  Godoy, Manuel de 207–208

  Goya y Lucientes, Francisco José de 211

  Isabella II (queen of Spain) 229

  Joseph I (king of Spain) 242

  Labrador, Pedro Gómez Labrador, marqués de 246

  Maria Christina (queen and regent of Spain) 270

  Martínez de la Rosa, Francisco 273

  Narváez y Campos, Ramón María 292

  O'Donojú, Juan 298

  Palafox, José de 309

  Peninsular War 312

  Pineda, Mariana de 324

  Prado, Museo Nacional del 329

  Riego y Núñez, Rafael del 342

  Rivas, Ángel de Saavedra, duque de 342

  Spain and the European powers 369

  Spanish Inquisition 378

  Valdés, Cayetano 397

  Wall, Richard 406

  Zea Bermúdez, Francisco 411, 412

  Zumalacárregui y de Imaz, Tomás de 413

Fernandes, Vasco **187**

Fernández de Córdoba, Gonzalo 142–143, **187–188**

Fernández de Enciso, Martín 98

Fernández Silvestre, Manuel 87

Fernández y González, Manuel 106, **188–189**

Fernando. *See* Ferdinand *entries*

Fernando Casado. *See* Rey, Fernando

Fernando de Noronha **189**

Ferrelo, Bartolomé 121

Ferrer, Francisco **189–190**

Fialho de Almeida, José Valentim **190–191**

First Republic 134–135, 348

Fitzjames, James (duke of Berwick) 81

Flanders 230–231

Florida 30, **191,** 427*c*

  Cabeza de Vaca, Álvar Núñez 119

  Charles III (king of Spain) 150

  Gálvez, Bernardo de 197–198

  Louisiana 256

  Narváez, Pánfilo de 291

  Ponce de León, Juan 327

  Soto, Hernando de 366

  Spain and the United States 373

Floridablanca, José Moñino, conde de 30, 88, **191–192**

Foix, Germaine de 185

Fonseca, Juan Rodríguez de **192**

Former Colonies of Spain and Portugal 461*m*

France 11, 20, 21, 33, 34, 42, 45

  Alberoni, Giulio 73

  Almansa, Battle of 81

  Aranda, Pedro Pablo Abarca de Bolea, conde de 88

  asiento 92

  Basque nationalism 101, 103

  Bourbon 109, 110

  Buñuel, Luis 117

  Casals, Pablo 134

  Cerignola, Battle of 142–143

  Charles I (king of Spain) 147

  Charles IV (king of Spain) 152

  Córdoba 158

  cortes 159–160

  Dalí i Domènech, Salvador 164

  Dominican Republic 168

  Espartero, Baldomero 176

  Ferdinand VII (king of Spain) 187

  Fernández de Córdoba, Gonzalo 188

  Ferrer, Francisco 189

  Florida 191

  Gálvez, Bernardo de 197

  Garcilaso de la Vega 202

  Gerona, siege of 204–205

  Godoy, Manuel de 207

Goya y Lucientes, Francisco José de 211
Gravina y Nápoli, Federico Carlos 215–216
Haro, Luis de 221
Hispaniola 224
Isabella Farnese (queen consort of Spain) 231
Italian Wars 232
Italy, Spain in 233
John IV (king of Portugal) 238
John VI (king of Portugal) 239
Joseph I (king of Spain) 241, 242
Larra, Mariano José de 247
Leyenda Negra 252
Louisiana 255, 256
Miranda, Francisco de 283
Olavide, Pablo de 299
Peninsular War 312–313
Philip II (king of Spain) 318, 319
Philip V (king of Spain) 322
Picasso, Pablo 323, 324
Riego y Núñez, Rafael del 342
Rocroi, Battle of 343
St. Quentin, Battle of 349
Serveto, Miguel 362–363
Soares, Mário 364–365
Souza Cardoso, Amadeo de 366–367
Spain and the European powers 368, 370
Texas 386
Trafalgar, Battle of 393
Valdés, Alfonso de 396
Zea Bermúdez, Francisco 411–412
Francesco I (king of Naples) 270
Franche-Comté, Spain in the **192–193**
Franciscans 361
Francis Xavier, Saint **193,** 235
Franco, João 147
Franco Bahamonde, Francisco, and regime 47–49, 51–54, 179, **193–196,** *194,* 436c–437c
   Alberti, Rafael 74
   Aleixandre, Vicente 77
   Anual, campaign of 87
   Asencio Torrado, José 91
   Barcelona 100
   Baroja, Pío 101
   Basque nationalism 102

Basque provinces 103
Blue Division 107, 108
Buero Vallejo, Antonio 113–114
bullfighting 114–115
Buñuel, Luis 117
Carlism 131
Casals, Pablo 134
Catalonia 138
Cela, Camilo José 141
Chillida, Eduardo 152
Conde, Carmen 157
environmental issues in Spain and Portugal 174
Juan Carlos I (king of Spain) 243–244
Largo Caballero, Francisco 247
Madariaga, Salvador de 259
Madrid 261
Maeztu y Whitney, Ramiro de 262
Majorca 264–265
Melilla 276
Millán Astray, José 282
Mola, Emilio 285
Morocco 288–289
Navarre 292
Opus Dei 303
Primo de Rivera y Orbaneja, Miguel 334
Queipo de Llano, Gonzalo 336, 337
Salamanca 350
Sanjurjo, José 352
Spain and the European powers 369–370
Spain and the Middle East 370
Spain and the United States 374
Spanish civil war 375, 376
terrorism 385
Toledo 389
women's rights in Spain 408
François I (king of France) 232
Fray Luis. *See* León, Luis de
French Revolution
   Bolívar, Simón 108
   Dominican Republic 168
   Olavide, Pablo de 299
   Peninsular War 312
   Riego y Núñez, Rafael del 342
   Spain and the European powers 369
   Spain and the United States 373

Frente Popular 94
Freud, Sigmund 164
Fuenteovejuna (Lope de Vega Carpio) 253

G

Gabriel Téllez. *See* Tirso de Molina
Galicia **197,** 310, 354–355
Gálvez, Bernardo de **197–198**
Gálvez, José de **198–199,** 361
Galway, earl of 81
Gama, Vasco da 8, 119, 127, **199,** 267, 285, 420c
Ganivet, Ángel **199–200**
García Lorca, Federico 62, **200–201,** 324, 439c
Garcilaso de la Vega **201–202**
Garrett, Almeida 276
Gattinara, Savoyard Mercurino 269
Gaudí i Cornet, Antonio **202–203,** *203*
Gaviota, La (Caballero) 118
Gehry, Frank 106
Generation of '27 74, **203,** 209
Generation of '98 61–62, **204,** 435c
   Baroja, Pío 101
   Darío, Rubén 165
   Ganivet, Ángel 200
   Generation of '27 203
   Jiménez, Juan Ramón 236
   Machado, Antonio 257, 258
   Martínez Ruiz, José 273
   Valle-Inclán, Ramón María del 400
Generation of 1870 337
Germany 107, 181, 232, 380
Gerona, siege of **204–205**
Gibraltar 26, 51, **205,** 440c
Gibraltar, siege of 121, 125, 192, 265
Giner de los Ríos, Francisco 83, **205–206,** 257, 258
global warming 175
Goa 55, 74, 132, 165, **206,** 421c
Godoy, Manuel de (príncipe de la Paz, duque de Alcudia) 31, 33, **206–208,** 428c
   Aranda, Pedro Pablo Abarca de Bolea, conde de 88–89
   Charles IV (king of Spain) 151, 152

Floridablanca, José Moñino, conde de 192
  Jovellanos, Gaspar Melchor de 243
  Louisiana 256
  Malaspina, Alejandro 266
Golden Age. *See* Siglo de Oro
Gomes da Costa, Manuel de Oliveria 132
Gómez de Silva, Ruy (prince of Éboli). *See* Éboli, Ruy Gómez de Silva, prince of
Góngora y Argote, Luis de 203, **208–209,** 424*c*
González, Julio **209–210**
González Márquez, Felipe 58, 59, 94, 102–103, **210–211,** 344, 438*c*
González Pérez, José Victoriano. *See* Gris, Juan
Goya y Lucientes, Francisco José de 42, **211–212,** 261, 435*c*
Goyescas 215
Gracián, Baltasar **212–213**
Gramática (Vives) 405
Granada 6, 7, *213,* **213**
  Castile 136
  Cisneros, Francisco Jiménez de 153
  García Lorca, Federico 201
  Narváez, Pánfilo de 291
  Pineda, Mariana de 324
  Reconquista 341
  Segovia, Andrés 360
  Sucre, Antonio José de 380
Granada, conquest of **213–215,** 419*c*
  Almeida, Francisco de 82
  Andalusia 85
  Ferdinand V (king of Aragon and united Spain) 183
  Isabella I (queen of Castile) 228
  Pedrarias Dávila 310
  Spain and the Middle East 370
Granados, Enrique 62, **215,** 439*c*
Gravina y Nápoli, Federico Carlos **215–216,** 393
Great Britain 34. *See also* England
  Aranda, Pedro Pablo Abarca de Bolea, conde de 88
  Argentina 89
  asiento 92
  Charles III (king of Spain) 150

Florida 191
Gálvez, Bernardo de 197
Goa 206
Godoy, Manuel de 207
Gravina y Nápoli, Federico Carlos 216
Joseph I (king of Portugal) 241
Leyenda Negra 252
Peninsular War 312
Spain and the European powers 368, 370
Spain and the United States 373
Greco, El **216–217,** 307, 389, 424*c*
Grijalva, Juan de 83, **217–218,** 402
Gris, Juan **218–219**
Guam 271, 373
Guardia de Corps 207
Guatemala 84, **219,** 248
Guernica 48–49, 102
Guernica (Picasso) 323, 329–330
guerrilla warfare 312, 329, 385, 413
Guevara, Antonio de **219**
Guinea 55
guitar 360–361
Guzmán, Fernando de 70
Guzmán de Alfarache (Alemán) 77–78

H

Habsburg 9–24, **220,** 422*c*, 424*c*
  Bourbon 109
  Catalonia 138
  Charles II (king of Spain) 148–149
  Franche-Comté, Spain in the 192
  John of Austria 239–240
  Leyenda Negra 252
  Margaret, duchess of Parma 268
  Margaret of Austria 269
  Netherlands, Revolt of the 293
  Olivares, Gaspar de Guzmán y Pimentel, conde-duque de 301
  Pérez, Antonio 313
  Philip I (king of Castile) 317, 318
  Philip V (king of Spain) 322
  Rocroi, Battle of 343
  St. Quentin, Battle of 349
  Spain and the European powers 368
  Spanish Succession, War of the 378
  Spinola, Ambrogio 379

Hannibal 349–350
Haro, Luis de 20, **220–221,** 321
Hassan II (king of Morocco) 371
Hemingway, Ernest 115
Henri Bourbon 181
Henri II (king of France) 232, 349, 368
Henri IV (king of France) 314
Henrique I (king of Portugal) 93
Henry IV (king of Castile) 221, **221–222,** 227, 419*c*
Henry the Navigator (prince of Portugal) 7
Henry VII (king of England) 140
Henry VIII (king of England) 140, 368, 405
Herculano de Carvalho e Araújo, Alexandre **222–223,** 435*c*
heresy 363
Herrera, Fernando de **223**
Herrera, Juan de 175
hidalgo 16, **223**
Hidalgo, Juan de 411
Hidalgo, Father Miguel 125
Hidalgo family 207
Hispaniola 223, **223–224,** 432*c*. *See also* Dominican Republic
  Alvarado, Pedro de 83
  Balboa, Vasco Núñez de 98
  Columbus, Christopher 156
  Dominican Republic 168
  encomienda 173
  Ponce de León, Juan 327
  Velázquez de Cuéllar, Diego 402
Historia de España y de la civilización española (Altamira) 83
History of Portugal (Herculano) 222
Hitler, Adolf 51
  Blue Division 107, 108
  Franco Bahamonde, Francisco 195
  Maeztu y Whitney, Ramiro de 262
  Spain and the European powers 369
  Spain and the United States 374
  Spanish civil war 375
Holy Alliance 187
Holy League 250
Honduras **224,** 300
House of Austria 220
Huáscar 325

Hugo, Victor 276
humanism 183, 190, 262, 293, 397, 404–405
Hussein, Saddam 63

I

Ibárruri, Dolores **225,** 407
Ideárium español (Ganivet) 200
Ignatius of Loyola, Saint 193, **225–226**
Ilhas do Cabo Verde. *See* Cape Verde Islands
illegal immigration 64
illustrators 219
immigrants in Portugal **226–227**
immigration 146, 226, 276, 440c
Inca Empire 84, 109, 172, 316, 325, 366
Independence, War of. *See* Peninsular War
India 8, 82, 169, 206
Indian Ocean 82, 167, 265
Indians, American. *See* Native Americans
Indies, Council of the 192
Indonesia 169–170
Industrial Revolution 100
Ingenioso hidalgo don Quixote de la Mancha, El (Cervantes) 144–145
Innocent X (pope) 401
Inquisition. *See* Spanish Inquisition
Institución Libre de Enseñanza 205–206
International Brigades 376
"international style" 203
Invincible Armada. *See* Armada
Iraq War (2003–) 63, 95, 345, 371, 374, 439c
Ireland 14, 204, 245
Isabella (princess of Portugal) 147
Isabella (queen consort of Spain) 27
Isabella Clara Eugenia (princess of Spain, archduchess of Austria) **230–231,** 407
Isabella Farnese (queen consort of Spain) 73, **231–232,** 322
Isabella I (queen of Castile) 5–8, **227–229,** *228,* 419c, 420c
  Cisneros, Francisco Jiménez de 153
  Columbus, Christopher 155, 157

Ferdinand V (king of Aragon and united Spain) 183
Fernández de Córdoba, Gonzalo 188
Fonseca, Juan Rodríguez de 192
Granada 213
Granada, conquest of 214, 215
Guevara, Antonio de 219
Habsburg 220
Haro, Luis de 221–222
Joanna (queen of Castile) 238
Margaret of Austria 268
Philip I (king of Castile) 317, 318
Reconquista 341
Santiago de Compostela 355
Segovia 360
Spanish Inquisition 377
Tetuán, campaign of 386
Torquemada, Tomás de 390
women's rights in Spain 408
Isabella II (queen of Spain) 36–39, **229–230,** 430c–432c
  Bourbon 110
  Bravo Murillo, Juan 111
  Carlism 131
  Castelar y Ripoll, Emilio 134
  Espartero, Baldomero 176
  Ferdinand VII (king of Spain) 187
  Maria Christina (queen and regent of Spain) 270
  Martínez de la Rosa, Francisco 273
  Narváez y Campos, Ramón María 292
  Navarre 292
  O'Donnell Joris, Leopoldo 297
  Palafox, José de 309
  Prado, Museo Nacional del 329
  Prim y Prats, Juan 332
  Sagasta, Práxedes Mateo 348
  Sartorius, José Luis 358
  Serrano y Domínguez, Francisco 362
  Valdés, Cayetano 397
  women's rights in Spain 408
  Zea Bermúdez, Francisco 412
  Zumalacárregui y de Imaz, Tomás de 413
Islam 11, 15–16, 200. *See also* Muslims
Islamic terrorism 62–64, 139, 345, 372, 385. *See also* Madrid train bombings (2004)

Islas Canarias. *See* Canary Islands
Italian Wars **232,** 420c–422c
  Alba, Fernando Álvarez de Toledo, duque de 72
  Alexander VI (pope) 78
  Catherine of Aragon 140
  Cerignola, Battle of 142–143
  Ferdinand V (king of Aragon and united Spain) 184
  Fernández de Córdoba, Gonzalo 188
  Italy, Spain in 233
  St. Quentin, Battle of 349
  Spain and the European powers 368
  Tercio 383
  Valdés, Alfonso de 396
  Velázquez de Cuéllar, Diego 402
Italy 73, 173, 188, 231, 322, 380
Italy, Spain in 231, **232–233**
Iturbide, Agustín de 125, 162, 219, **233–234,** *234,* 296, 298

J

Jamaica **235,** 291, 321
James, Saint 354, 355
James II (king of England) 141
Japan 276
Japan, Portuguese presence in **235–236,** 422c
Jefferson, Thomas 373
Jesuits
  Alberoni, Giulio 73
  Aranda, Pedro Pablo Abarca de Bolea, conde de 88
  Buñuel, Luis 116
  Charles III (king of Spain) 150
  Floridablanca, José Moñino, conde de 191
  Francis Xavier, Saint 193
  Gracián, Baltasar 212
  Ignatius of Loyola, Saint 226
  Japan, Portuguese presence in 236
  Paraguay 310
  Pombal, Sebastião José de Carvalho e Melo, marquês de 326
Jews 183, 213, 228, 370, 377, 391
Jiménez, Juan Ramón 62, **236–237,** 438c

Jiménez de Quesada, Juan Ramón 181–182

Jiménez de Queseda, Gonzalo 104, 154, 182, **237–238**

Joanna (queen of Castile) 9, **238,** 419*c*, 421*c*
  Ferdinand V (king of Aragon and united Spain) 184
  Habsburg 220
  Netherlands, Spain in the 294
  Padilla, Juan de 307
  Philip I (king of Castile) 317

João. *See* John *entries*

John I (king of Portugal) 93, 111

John II (king of Castile) 183, 221, 227

John III (king of Portugal) 403

John IV (king of Portugal) 22, 23, 111, 112, **238,** 269, 404, 424*c*

John of Austria 143, 180, *239,* **239–240,** 250, 353

John of the Cross, Saint **240,** 424*c*

John V (king of Portugal) 31–32, **238–239,** 241, 252, 262, 426*c*

John VI (king of Portugal) 37, **239,** 280, 311–312, 427*c*–430*c*

José. *See* Joseph *entries*

Joseph I (king of Portugal) 32, *241,* **241,** 427*c*
  Espartero, Baldomero 176
  Godoy, Manuel de 207
  Goya y Lucientes, Francisco José de 211
  Maria I (queen of Portugal) 269
  Pombal, Sebastião José de Carvalho e Melo, marquês de 326

Joseph I (king of Spain) 34, **241– 242,** 428*c*, 429*c*
  Bailén, Battle of 97, 98
  Cabarrús, Francisco conde de 119
  Charles IV (king of Spain) 151
  Ferdinand VII (king of Spain) 186
  Jovellanos, Gaspar Melchor de 243
  Martínez de la Rosa, Francisco 273
  Moratín, Leandro Fernández de 287
  Peninsular War 312
  Prado, Museo Nacional del 329

Spain and the European powers 369

Spanish Inquisition 378

Zaragoza, Battle of 410

Zea Bermúdez, Francisco 411

journalism
  Darío, Rubén 165
  Falcón, Lidia 179–180
  Herculano de Carvalho e Araújo, Alexandre 222
  Larra, Mariano José de 248
  Maeztu y Whitney, Ramiro de 261
  Mendes Leal, José da Silva 276
  Pérez de Ayala, Ramón 314
  Pérez Galdós, Benito 315
  Sartorius, José Luis 357–358

Jovellanos, Gaspar Melchor de 118, 119, **242–243,** 435*c*

Juana. *See* Joanna (queen of Castile)

Juan Carlos I (king of Spain) 54, 57, **243–244,** 437*c*
  Arias Navarro, Carlos 89
  Bourbon 110
  Catalonia 139
  Cela, Camilo José 141
  Franco Bahamonde, Francisco 195–196
  Madariaga, Salvador de 259
  Prado, Museo Nacional del 329
  Rodrigo, Joaquín 344
  Spain and the Middle East 370

Juan de la Cruz. *See* John of the Cross, Saint

Justin, Count of Nassau 113

K

Karl (archduke of Austria) 81, 138, 378

Kennedy, John F. 134

Kingdom of the Two Sicilies 233

Kinsale, Battle of **245**

Krause, Karl 205

Krausismo 205

L

Labors of Hercules (Francisco de Zurbarán) 415

labor unions 225

Labrador, Pedro Gómez Labrador, marqués de **246**

Ladies' Peace 232

La Mancha **246–247**

La Plata, Viceroyalty of 89, 109, **247,** 310

Largo Caballero, Francisco **247**

Larra, Mariano José de **247–248,** 435*c*

Las Casas, Bartolomé de 217, **248– 249,** 291, 402

Las Palmas 128

League of Augsburg, War of the 149

League of Nations 83, 259

León 92, **249,** 349–350, 388

León, Luis de **249–250,** 424*c*

Leo X (pope) 173

Lepanto, Battle of 11, **250,** 423*c*
  Cervantes Saavedra, Miguel de 143
  Farnese, Alessandro 180
  John of Austria 239–240
  Philip II (king of Spain) 318
  Santa Cruz, Álvaro de Bazán, marqués de 353

Lerma, Francisco Gómez de Sandoval y Rojas, duque de 17–18, 123, **250–251,** 300, 320, 379, 424*c*

letrillas 209

Leyenda Negra 11–12, 249, **251– 252,** 314, 373

Liberal Party 334, 348

libertarianism 190

Lisbon 32, **252–253,** 427*c*
  Carnation Revolution 133
  John IV (king of Portugal) 238
  John V (king of Portugal) 238
  Joseph I (king of Portugal) 241
  Pombal, Sebastião José de Carvalho e Melo, marquês de 326
  Salazar, António de Oliveira 351
  Sanjurjo, José 352

Liszt, Franz 73

literary salons 223

literature 62. *See also* drama; poetry
  Alas, Leopoldo 71–72
  Alemán, Mateo 77–78
  Almeida Garrett, João Baptista da Silva Leitão, visconde de 82
  Baroja, Pío 100–101
  Blasco Ibáñez, Vicente 106–107

Braga, Teófilo 110–111
Caballero, Fernán 118
Cabeza de Vaca, Álvar Núñez 119
Cadalso, José 121
Cánovas del Castillo, Antonio 129–130
Castelo Branco, Camilo 135–136
Cela, Camilo José 141–142
Cervantes Saavedra, Miguel de 143–145
Conde, Carmen 157
Darío, Rubén 165–166
Eça de Queirós, José Maria 170–171
Falcón, Lidia 179–180
Feijoo, Benito Jerónimo 182–183
Fernández y González, Manuel 188–189
Fialho de Almeida, José Valentim 190–191
Ganivet, Ángel 199–200
García Lorca, Federico 201
Generation of '98 204
Gracián, Baltasar 212–213
Herculano de Carvalho e Araújo, Alexandre 222
Jiménez, Juan Ramón 236–237
Jovellanos, Gaspar Melchor de 242–243
Larra, Mariano José de 247–248
León, Luis de 249–250
Machado, Antonio 257
María de Agreda, Sor 271
Martínez Ruiz, José 273–274
Matute, Ana María 274
Menéndez Pidal, Ramón 278
Menéndez y Pelayo, Marcelino 278–279
Moratín, Leandro Fernández de 286–287
Moreto y Cabaña, Agustín 287–288
Nebrija, Elio Antonio de 293
Ortega y Gasset, José 305–306
Pardo Bazán, Emilia, condesa de 310
Pérez de Ayala, Ramón 314–315
Pérez Galdós, Benito 315–316
Quental, Antero de 337–338
Quevedo y Villegas, Francisco de 338–339

Rivas, Ángel de Saavedra, duque de 342–343
Rojas, Fernando de 345–346
Sá de Miranda, Francisco de 348
Santayana, George 353–354
Saramago, José 356–357
Torres Villaroel, Diego de 392–393
Unamuno, Miguel de 394–395
Valdés, Alfonso de 396
Valdés, Juan de 397–398
Valera y Alcalá Galiano, Juan 399
Valle-Inclán, Ramón María del 400
Vieira, António 404
Locura de amor, La (Tamayo y Baus) 382
Lope de Vega, Félix 411
Lope de Vega Carpio, Félix 136, **253–254,** 287, 387, 424*c*
Louis I (king of Portugal) 146, **254,** 432*c*
Louis I (king of Spain) 27, **254–255,** 426*c*
Louisiana 151, 207, **255–256,** 303, 373, 427*c,* 428*c*
Louisiana Purchase 386
Louis XII (king of France) 142, 188, 232
Louis XIII (king of France) 368
Louis XIV (king of France) 137, 149, 321, 368, 378
Louis XV (king of France) 322
Loyalists 91, 117, 375, 376
Ludwig, Johann Friedrich 262
Luís. *See* Louis *entries*
Lusiads, The (Camòes) 199

M

Macao 61, 116, **257,** 422*c,* 438*c*
Machado, Antonio 62, **257–258,** 439*c*
Machado, Manuel **258–259**
Madariaga, Salvador de **259–260**
Madeira 7, **260**
Madrid *260,* **260–261,** 422*c*
   Alberti, Rafael 74
   Aranda, Pedro Pablo Abarca de Bolea, conde de 88
   Asencio Torrado, José 91

Barcelona 100
Bécquer, Gustavo Adolfo 104
bullfighting 115
Catalonia 138
Cervantes Saavedra, Miguel de 143
Jiménez, Juan Ramón 236
Sartorius, José Luis 357–358
Segovia 360
Spanish civil war 376
Thyssen-Bornemisza Museo 387
Madrid, Treaty of 232
Madrid Conference (1991) 370
Madrid train bombings (2004) 63, 439*c*
   Aznar López, José María 95
   Basque nationalism 103
   Madrid 261
   Rodríguez Zapatero, José Luis 345
   Spain and the Middle East 371, 372
   Spain and the United States 374
   terrorism 385
Maeztu y Whitney, Ramiro de **261–262**
Mafra 31–32, 238–239, **262–263,** 426*c*
Magellan, Ferdinand 10, **263–264,** 271, 285, 323, 390, 421*c*
Mahan, Alfred Thayer 373
Maine, USS 40–41, 162, 374
Majorca **264–265,** *265*
Malacca **265,** 421*c*
Málaga 91, 198, **265**
Malaspina, Alejandro **265–266**
Malaysia 82
Maldonado, Alonso 360
Malintzin (Doña Marina) 160
Mallorca. *See* Majorca
Malvinas archipelago 266
Manila Bay, Battle of 41, **266–267**
Manila Galleon 323
Manoel. *See* Manuel *entries*
Mantuan Succession, War of the 379
Manuel I (king of Portugal) **267,** 420*c*
   Albuquerque, Afonso de 74
   Aviz, House of 93
   Cabral, Pedro Álvares 119
   Dias, Bartolomeu 167

Gama, Vasco da 199
Magellan, Ferdinand 263
Manuel II (king of Portugal) 42,
    111, 132, **267–268,** 308, 436*c*
Margaret, duchess of Parma 180,
    268
Margaret of Austria 232, **268–269**
Margarita of Austria 123
Maria Christina (queen and regent
    of Spain) 40, 44, 79, 176, **270,**
    292, 297, 431*c*, 434*c*
Maria da Glória. *See* Maria II (queen
    of Portugal)
María de Agreda, Sor **271**
Maria I (queen of Portugal) 32,
    239, **269,** 317, 326, 427*c*
Maria II (queen of Portugal) 37, 38,
    269–270, 430*c*
    Azores 96
    Brazil 113
    Miguel, prince of Portugal 280
    Miguelite War 281
    Pedro I (king of Portugal and
        emperor of Brazil) 312
Maria Isabella 270
Maria Luisa of Parma 151, 152,
    207–208
María Luisa Teresa (queen of Spain)
    208
Mariana Islands 263, **271,** 373
Marinero en tierra (Alberti) 74
Marísa Luisa (queen of Spain)
    207–208
Martí, José **271–272**
Martínez de Campos, Arsenio
    272–273
Martínez de la Rosa, Francisco **273**
Martínez Ruiz, José (Azorín) 127,
    204, **273–274**
Martyrdom of St. Maurice, The (El
    Greco) 216
Mary. *See also* Maria *entries*
Mary I (queen of England) 140,
    320, 368
Mary of Burgundy 317
Mary Tudor. *See* Mary I (queen of
    England)
Massue, Henri de (earl of Galway)
    81
Matute, Ana María **274–275**
Maximilian I (Holy Roman
    Emperor) 154

Maya 84
Medici, Alessandro dei 268
Medina Sidonia, Alonso Pérez de
    Guzmán, duque de 90, **275**
Meditaciones del Quijote (Ortega y
    Gasset) 306
Mediterranean Sea 99
Melilla 87, **275–276,** 288, 371
Melo, Francisco de 343
Memorias políticas 179–180
Mendes Leal, José da Silva **276**
Mendes Pinto, Fernão **276–277**
Mendoza, Antonio de **277–278,**
    414
Menéndez Pidal, Ramón **278**
Menéndez y Pelayo, Marcelino
    278, **278–279**
Meninas, Las (Velázquez) 329, 401
Methuen Treaty 141, 317
Mexico 10, **279–280,** 421*c*. *See also*
    New Granada
    Alvarado, Pedro de 83–84
    Boyacá, Battle of 110
    Buñuel, Luis 117
    Cabrillo, Juan Rodríguez 120
    Calleja del Rey, Félix María
        125–126
    Cortés, Hernán 160
    Gálvez, Bernardo de 198
    Grijalva, Juan 217
    Iturbide, Agustín de 233–234
    Las Casas, Bartolomé de 248
    Martínez de Campos, Arsenio
        272
    Narváez, Pánfilo de 291
    New Mexico 295
    O'Donojú, Juan 298
    Olid, Cristóbal de 300
    Spain and the United States 373
    Texas 386
    Zumárraga, Juan de 414
Mexico City 167
Middle Ages 99, 116, 302, 354–
    355, 389
Middle America, Spanish
    Explorations of (1513–43) 453*m*
Miguel, prince of Portugal 37, 38,
    222, 239, **280,** 281, 312, 430*c*
Miguelite War 82, 95–96, 280,
    280–281, 302, 312, 430*c*
Milanese 233
Millán Astray, José **281–282**

mining 78, 173
Minorca 99
Miranda, Francisco de **282–283,**
    298–299, 380
Miró, Joan 62, 164, **283–284,** 439*c*
missionaries
    Arizona 90
    California 125
    Francis Xavier, Saint 193
    Gálvez, José de 198
    Ignatius of Loyola, Saint 226
    Japan, Portuguese presence in
        235
    Las Casas, Bartolomé de 248
    Serra, Junípero 361
Mississippi River 255
Mística ciudad de Dios, La (Sor Maria
    de Agreda) 271
Mocedades del Cid, Las (Castro y
    Bellvís) 136
Moctezuma 16, 83, 217, 300
Mohammed VI (king of Morocco)
    371
Mola, Emilio **284–285,** 336
Moluccas **285,** 306, 379
Mombasa **285–286**
Moneo, José Rafael **286**
Monroe Doctrine 373, 374
Montojo, Patricio 266–267
Montserrat (González) 210
Moors
    Asturias 92
    Cádiz 122
    Cisneros, Francisco Jiménez de
        153
    Córdoba 158
    Fernández de Córdoba, Gonzalo
        188
    Granada 213
    Isabella I (queen of Castile) 228
    Morocco 288
    Reconquista 340–341
    Salamanca 350
    Segovia 359
    Spain and the Middle East 370
    Toledo 388
    Torquemada, Tomás de 391
Moratín, Leandro Fernández de 42,
    286–287, 435*c*
Morelos, José 125
Moreto y Cabaña, Agustín **287–288**
Moriscos 15–16, 377

Morocco 45, **288–289,** 436c, 440c
  Alcazarquivir, Battle of 76
  Almeida, Francisco de 82
  Anual, campaign of 87–88
  Aviz, House of 93
  Camões, Luíz Vaz de 127
  Ceuta 146
  Millán Astray, José 282
  Primo de Rivera y Orbaneja,
    Miguel 333
  Sanjurjo, José 351–352
  Sebastian I (king of Portugal) 358
  Spain and the European powers
    369
  Spain and the Middle East 370,
    371
  Spanish civil war 375
  Tercio 383
  Tetuán, campaign of 385–386
Moros 323
Moscardo, José 75, 76
Motley, John L. 373
Movimiento (film) 122
Mozambique 55, 169, **289**
Mühlberg, Battle of 72
Muñoz, Agustín Fernando 270
Muñoz Grande, Augustín 107
Murcia **289**
Murillo, Bartolomé Esteban **289–**
  290, 415, 424c
Museo Guggenheim de Arte
  Contemporáneo 106
Museo Thyssen-Bornemisza. *See*
  Thyssen-Bornemisza Museum
music 62
  Albéniz, Isaac Manuel Francisco
    73
  Ángeles, Victoria de los 86
  Casals, Pablo 134
  Domingo, Plácido 167–168
  Encina, Juan del 172–173
  Falla, Manuel de 180
  Granados, Enrique 215
  Rodrigo, Joaquín 344
  Rodrigues, Amália 344
  Sarasate, Pablo de 357
  Segovia, Andrés 360–361
  zarzuela 411
Muslims
  Algarve 80
  Andalusia 85
  Ceuta 146

Cisneros, Francisco Jiménez de
  153, 154
Ferdinand V (king of Aragon and
  united Spain) 183
Gibraltar 205
Granada 213
Granada, conquest of 213
Isabella I (queen of Castile) 228
Lepanto, Battle of 250
Malacca 265
Málaga 265
Philip III (king of Spain) 320
Philippine Islands 323
Ponce de León, Juan 327
Reconquista 340–341
Santiago de Compostela 355
Spain and the Middle East 370,
  372
Spanish Inquisition 377
Tetuán, campaign of 386
Torquemada, Tomás de 391
Mussolini, Benito 369, 375
My First Forty Years (Domingo) 167
mysticism 271

N

Nación, La (newspaper) 165
Naples 232, 241, 321
Napoléon Bonaparte 33, 34
  Bailén, Battle of 97, 98
  Charles IV (king of Spain) 151
  Ferdinand VII (king of Spain)
    186
  Gerona, siege of 204
  Godoy, Manuel de 207
  Joseph I (king of Spain) 241, 242
  Labrador, Pedro Gómez Labrador,
    marqués de 246
  Louisiana 256
  Palafox, José de 309
  Peninsular War 312, 313
  Spain and the European powers
    369
  Spain and the United States 373
  Trafalgar, Battle of 393
  Zaragoza, Battle of 410
Napoleonic Wars 88, 112, 168,
  312–313
Narváez, Pánfilo de *161, 291,*
  291–292
  Cabeza de Vaca, Álvar Núñez 119

Cabrillo, Juan Rodríguez 120
Cortés, Hernán 160
Florida 191
Grijalva, Juan 217
Louisiana 255
Velázquez de Cuéllar, Diego
  402
Narváez y Campos, Ramón María
  292, 358, 431c, 432c
Nationalists 75–76, 107, 113, 194,
  284–285, 375, 376
National Movement 195
National Union 350
Native Americans
  asiento 91
  Dominican Republic 168
  Ecuador 172
  encomienda 173
  Hispaniola 223
  Las Casas, Bartolomé de 248–
    249
  Narváez, Pánfilo de 291
  Serra, Junípero 361
  Soto, Hernando de 366
NATO. *See* North Atlantic Treaty
  Organization
naturalism 71, 165, 171
Naváez, Ramón 270
Navarre 9, 131, 185, 193, **292–293,**
  341
navigation. *See* exploration
Nebrija, Elio Antonio de **293,** 398,
  405
Nelson, Horatio 393
Netherlands 23
  Ceylon 146
  Farnese, Alessandro 181
  Goa 206
  Isabella Clara Eugenia 230–231
  Japan, Portuguese presence in
    236
  Olivares, Gaspar de Guzmán y
    Pimentel, conde-duque de 301
  Philip III (king of Spain) 320
  Philip IV (king of Spain) 321
  Spice Islands 379
Netherlands, Revolt of the 12–13,
  15, 18, **293–294,** 423c
  Alba, Fernando Álvarez de
    Toledo, duque de 72
  Breda, siege of 113
  John of Austria 240

Lerma, Francisco Gómez de
Sandoval y Rojas, duque de 251
Philip II (king of Spain) 318–319
Netherlands, Spain in the **294–295,**
379
New Granada 110, 158, 159, **295**
New Granada, Viceroyalty of 110,
154, 172, 295, 309
New Guinea 306
New Mexico 90, **295,** 302
New Orleans 197, 255, 256, 303
New Spain 10, **295–296**
Alemán, Mateo 77
Arizona 90
California 125
Calleja del Rey, Félix María 125
Cortés, Hernán 161–162
Cuba 162
Gálvez, Bernardo de 197
Gálvez, José de 198
Mexico 279–280
New Mexico 295
Nicaragua 296
O'Donojú, Juan 298
Ortiz de Retes, Iñigo 306
Serra, Junípero 361
Texas 386
New Spain, Viceroyalty of 172
New World 7–8. *See also* America;
specific New World regions
Nicaragua **296,** 311, 365
Nine Years' War 21
Niza, Fray Marcos de 158
Nobel Prize (Literature) 62, 438*c*–
439*c*
Aleixandre, Vicente 77
Benavente y Martínez, Jacinto 105
Cela, Camilo José 142
Echegaray y Eizaguirre, José 171
Jiménez, Juan Ramón 236–237
Saramago, José 356
Noches lúgubres (Cadalso) 121
North Africa 45
Alcazarquivir, Battle of 76–77
Anual, campaign of 87–88
Cisneros, Francisco Jiménez de
154
Morocco 280–289
Pedrarias Dávila 311
Santa Cruz, Álvaro de Bazán,
marqués de 353
Tetuán, campaign of 385–386

North America 301–302
North Atlantic Treaty Organization
(NATO) 63, 64, 96, 210, 351, 374,
438*c*

O

Ochre (Tàpies) 382–383
O'Connor, Rodrigo 90
O crime do Padre Amaro (Eça de
Queirós) 171
O'Donnell Joris, Leopoldo 129,
176, 288, **297–298,** 362, 386, 432*c*
O'Donojú, Juan **298**
O'Higgins, Bernardo 283, **298–299,**
352
Olavide, Pablo de **299**
Olid, Cristóbal de **299–300**
Olivares, Gaspar de Guzmán y
Pimentel, conde-duque de 18–20,
300–301, 424*c*
Haro, Luis de 220
Lerma, Francisco Gómez de
Sandoval y Rojas, duque de
251
Philip IV (king of Spain) 321–322
Quevedo y Villegas, Francisco
de 338
Spain and the European powers
368
Spinola, Ambrogio 379
Velázquez, Diego Rodríguez de
Silva y 401
O locura o santidad (Echegaray y
Eizaguirre) 172
Olvidado Rey Gudú (Matute) 274–
275
Olympic Games (Athens, 2004)
122
Olympic Games (Barcelona, 1992)
100, 438*c*
Oñate, Juan de 295, **301–302**
One Hundred Thousand Sons of St.
Louis 187
O'Neill, Hugh, earl of Tyrone 245
O Panorama (journal) 222
opera 86, 167–168
Oporto 38, 280, 281, **302**
Opus Dei **302–303**
Oranges, War of the 239
O'Reilly, Alexander 255, **303–304**
Orellana, Francisco de **304–305**

*Origine e establecimento da inquisicã*o
em *Portugal, Da* (Herculano) 222
Ortega y Gasset, José 62, **305–306,**
439*c*
Ortiz de Retes, Iñigo **306**
Os Lusíadas (Camões) 127
Os Maias (Eça de Queirós) 171
Ostend 379
Osuna, duke of 338
Ottoman Empire 15, 250, 368
Overseas Empires of Spain and
Portugal (c. 1550) 455*m*

P

Pacheco, Francisco **307**
Pacific Ocean 98, 99, 263, 265–
266
Padilla, Juan de **307–308**
Pais, Sidónio **308**
Palafox, José de (duque de
Zaragoza) **308–309,** 410
paleontology 330–332
Panama 295, **309–310,** 311
Panama Canal 309–311
Papal States 78
Paraguay 119, **310**
Pardo Bazán, Emilia, condesa de
310, 435*c*
Paris, siege of 181
Paris, Treaty of (1898) 374
Paris World Exhibition 210
Parma 233
Partido Socialista Obrero Español
(PSOE). *See* Socialist Workers
Party of Spain
Paul IV (pope) 349
Pavarotti, Luciano 167
Pavia, Battle of 232
Pedrarias Dávila 99, 162, **310–311**
Pedrell, Felipe 73
Pedro. *See also* Peter *entries*
Pedro I (king of Portugal and
emperor of Brazil) 37, 112–113,
239, 269, 280, 281, **311–312,**
430*c*
Pedro II (emperor of Brazil) 113, 312
Pedro IV (king of Portugal). *See*
Pedro I (king of Portugal and
emperor of Brazil)
Peines del viento (Chillida) 152–153
Pelayo 92

Peninsular War 34, **312–313,** 428*c*–
    429*c*, 457*m*
  Bailén, Battle of 98
  Cádiz 122
  Córdoba 158
  Espronceda, José de 177
  Extremadura 177
  O'Donojú, Juan 298
  Palafox, José de 308
  Segovia 360
  Valencia 399
  Zaragoza 410
  Zaragoza, Battle of 410
  Zumalacárregui y de Imaz, Tomás
    de 414
Pepita Jiménez (Juan Valera y Alcalá
    Galiano) 399–400
Pérez, Antonio 170, **313–314**
Pérez, González. *See* Gris, Juan
Pérez de Ayala, Ramón **314–315**
Pérez Galdós, Benito *315,* **315–316,**
    393, 435*c*
Peribáñez y el comendador de Ocaña
    (Lope de Vega Carpio) 253–254
Persistence of Memory, The (Dalí) 164
Peru 10, 29, **316,** 432*c*
  Aguirre, Lope de 69–70
  Ayacucho, Battle of 93
  Belalcázar, Sebastián de 104
  Chile 152
  La Plata, Viceroyalty of 247
  Mendoza, Antonio de 277
  New Granada 295
  New Spain 296
  Orellana, Francisco de 304
  Pizarro, Francisco 325–326
  San Martín, José Francisco de
    352
  Soto, Hernando de 365–366
  Sucre, Antonio José de 380
Peru, Viceroyalty of 89, 172, 309,
    316
Peruvian War of Independence 93
Pessoa, Fernando António Nogueira
    316, 367
Peter II (king of Portugal) 23, 69,
    141, 238, **316–317,** 424*c*–425*c*
Peter III (king of Portugal) 239,
    269, **317**
Peter V (king of Portugal) 254, **317,**
    432*c*
Philip (prince of Asturias) 92

Philip I (king of Castile) 9, **317–
    318,** 420*c*, 421*c*, 423*c*
  Cisneros, Francisco Jiménez de
    153
  Ferdinand V (king of Aragon and
    united Spain) 184
  Habsburg 220
  Joanna (queen of Castile) 238
  Netherlands, Spain in the 294
Philip I (king of Portugal). *See* Philip
    II (king of Spain)
Philip II (king of Spain) 11–13, 17,
    318, **318–320,** 422*c*, 423*c*
  Aguirre, Lope de 70
  Alba, Fernando Álvarez de
    Toledo, duque de 72
  Alcazarquivir, Battle of 76
  Aragon 88
  Armada 90, 91
  Aviz, House of 93
  Bragança 111
  Charles I (king of Spain) 148
  Éboli, Ruy Gómez de Silva, prince
    of 170
  Escorial, El 175
  Farnese, Alessandro 180, 181
  Ferdinand V (king of Aragon and
    united Spain) 185
  Greco, El 216
  Habsburg 220
  Isabella Clara Eugenia 230, 231
  Italian Wars 232
  John IV (king of Portugal) 238
  John of Austria 239, 240
  Kinsale, Battle of 245
  Lerma, Francisco Gómez de
    Sandoval y Rojas, duque de 251
  Madrid 260
  Margaret, duchess of Parma 268
  Medina Sidonia, Alonso Pérez de
    Guzmán, duque de 275
  Netherlands, Revolt of the 294
  Netherlands, Spain in the 294
  Pérez, Antonio 313, 314
  St. Quentin, Battle of 349
  Santa Cruz, Álvaro de Bazán,
    marqués de 353
  Sebastian I (king of Portugal) 359
  Spain and the European powers
    368
  Spinola, Ambrogio 379
  Teresa of Ávila, Saint 384

Philip III (king of Spain) 13–18,
    320, 423*c*–424*c*
  Armada 91
  Calderón, Rodrigo 123
  Habsburg 220
  Kinsale, Battle of 245
  Lerma, Francisco Gómez de
    Sandoval y Rojas, duque de 251
  Medina Sidonia, Alonso Pérez de
    Guzmán, duque de 275
  Olivares, Gaspar de Guzmán y
    Pimentel, conde-duque de 300
  Spinola, Ambrogio 379
Philip IV (king of Spain) 18–21,
    321–322, 424*c*
  Breda, siege of 113
  Calderón, Rodrigo 123
  Calderón de la Barca, Pedro 124
  Catalonia 137
  Habsburg 220
  Haro, Luis de 220
  Isabella Clara Eugenia 231
  Italy, Spain in 233
  Lerma, Francisco Gómez de
    Sandoval y Rojas, duque de 251
  Louis I (king of Spain) 255
  María de Agreda, Sor 271
  Mariana Islands 271
  Medina Sidonia, Alonso Pérez de
    Guzmán, duque de 275
  Olivares, Gaspar de Guzmán y
    Pimentel, conde-duque de 300,
    301
  Quevedo y Villegas, Francisco
    de 338
  Spain and the European powers
    368
  Spinola, Ambrogio 379
  Velázquez, Diego Rodríguez de
    Silva y 401
  zarzuela 411
Philippine Islands 10, 40, 41, **323,**
    422*c*, 434*c*
  Magellan, Ferdinand 264
  Manila Bay, Battle of 267
  Mariana Islands 271
  Millán Astray, José 281
  New Spain 296
  Ortiz de Retes, Iñigo 306
  Spain and the United States 373
  Spanish-American War 374
  Tordesillas, Treaty of 390

Philip V (king of Spain) 26, 27,
    322–323, 426*c*
  Aragon 88
  Bourbon 109, 110
  Catalonia 138
  Charles II (king of Spain) 149
  Ferdinand VI (king of Spain) 185
  Isabella Farnese (queen consort
    of Spain) 231
  Louis I (king of Spain) 254
  Spain and the European powers
    368
  Spanish Succession, War of the
    378
philosophy 205–206, 212–213,
    305–306, 353–354
Picasso, Pablo 62, 164, 209, **323–
    324,** 329, 439*c*
pilgramages 181
Pillars of Hercules 205
Pineda, Mariana de **324**
Pintasilgo, Maria de Lurdes **324–
    325**
Pitt, William 283
Pizarro, Francisco 10, **325–326,**
    422*c*
  Alvarado, Pedro de 84
  Belalcázar, Sebastián de 104, 105
  Charles I (king of Spain) 148
  Orellana, Francisco de 304
  Pedrarias Dávila 311
  Soto, Hernando de 365–366
  Valdivia, Pedro de 398
Pizarro, Gonzalo 304, 305, 398
Plácido, Ana 135
Platero y yo (Jiménez) 237
plays. *See* drama
Plessis, Armand-Jean du. *See*
  Richelieu, Cardinal
poetry
  Alberti, Rafael 74
  Aleixandre, Vicente 77
  Almeida Garrett, João Baptista da
    Silva Leitão, visconde de 82
  Bécquer, Gustavo Adolfo 104
  Camões, Luíz Vaz de 126–127
  Campoamor y Campoosorio,
    Ramón de 127–128
  Castro, Eugénio de 136
  Conde, Carmen 157
  Darío, Rubén 165
  Espronceda, José de 176

García Lorca, Federico 200–201
Garcilaso de la Vega 201–202
Generation of '27 203
Góngora y Argote, Luis de
    208–209
Herrera, Fernando de 223
Jiménez, Juan Ramón 236–237
John of the Cross, Saint 240
Jovellanos, Gaspar Melchor de
    242
León, Luis de 250
Machado, Antonio 257
Machado, Manuel 258
Pessoa, Fernando António
    Nogueira 316
Quevedo y Villegas, Francisco de
    338–339
Zorrilla y Moral, José 412–413
Polish Succession War 322
Pombal, Sebastião José de Carvalho
    e Melo, marquês de 32, 241, 269,
    326–327, 427*c*
Ponce de León, Juan 191, **327**
Popish Plot 141
Popular Front 284, 375
Popular Party 94, 95, 103, 371
Portugal, map of 462*m*
Portugal, national identity of
    327–328
Portugal and the Future (Spinola)
    380
Portuguese Guinea 169, **328–329**
Portuguese Inquisition 222, 404
Portuguese Socialist Party 365
Porvenir de España, El 200
Prado, Museo Nacional del 261,
    324, **329–330,** 386–387
prehistoric discoveries in Iberia
    330–332
Prescott, William H. 252, 373
Primo de Rivera, José Antonio 52,
    178, 334
Primo de Rivera y Orbaneja, Miguel
    45–46, **332–334,** 333, 436*c*
  Alfonso XIII (king of Spain) 80
  Anual, campaign of 87–88
  Largo Caballero, Francisco 247
  Maeztu y Whitney, Ramiro de
    261
  Mola, Emilio 284
  Morocco 288
  Queipo de Llano, Gonzalo 336

Sanjurjo, José 352
Unamuno, Miguel de 394
Valle-Inclán, Ramón María del
    400
Weyler y Nicolau, Valeriano 407
Prim y Prats, Juan 39, 84, 297, 298,
    332, 348, 432*c*, 433*c*
Propalladia (Torres Naharro) 392
Protestant Reformation 226
Protestants 232, 377
Provincias Vascongadas. *See* Basque
  provinces
PSOE. *See* Socialist Workers Party
  of Spain
Puerto Rico 41, **334–335,** 428*c*,
    430*c*, 434*c*
  Casals, Pablo 134
  Jiménez, Juan Ramón 236
  O'Reilly, Alexander 303
  Ponce de León, Juan 327
  Spain and the United States
    373–374
  Spanish-American War 374
Pujol, Jordi 138, 139
Pyrenees, Peace of the 221, 321

Q

al-Quaeda 63
Queipo de Llano, Gonzalo 285,
    336–337
Quental, Antero de **337–338**
Quevedo y Villegas, Francisco de
    338–339, 424*c*
Quivira 255

R

Rafael del Riego, Revolt of 233
Rastadt, Treaty of 378
Rebelíon de las Masas, La (Ortega y
  Gasset) 305
Reconquista 3, **340–341**
  Andalusia 85
  Asturias 92
  Castile 136
  Córdoba 158
  Isabella I (queen of Castile) 229
  León 249
  Málaga 265
  Morocco 288
  Murcia 289

Navarre 292
Salamanca 350
Santiago de Compostela 355
Segovia 360
Torquemada, Tomás de 391
Reding, Theodor von 98
Reformation 72, 293–294, 320, 355
religion 383–384
*Reloj de príncipes o libro áureo del
emperador Marco Aurelio* (Guevara)
219
Renaissance 3–24
Alexander VI (pope) 78–79
Aragon 88
Cabeza de Vaca, Álvar Núñez
119
Camões, Luíz Vaz de 126–127
Catalonia 137
Cisneros, Francisco Jiménez de
153, 154
Encina, Juan del 173
Ferdinand V (king of Aragon and
united Spain) 185
Garcilaso de la Vega 202
León, Luis de 249
Lisbon 252
Oporto 302
Sá de Miranda, Francisco de 348
Siglo de Oro 364
Spain and the European powers
368
Torres Naharro, Bartolomé de
391–392
Republican Evolutionist Party 81
Republicans 113–114, 117, 376. *See
also* Loyalists
Revolutionary War (U.S.). *See*
American Revolution
Rey, Fernando **341–342**
Reyes Católicos 214
Richelieu, Cardinal 301, 368
Riego y Núñez, Rafael del 35, 36,
273, **342**
Rimas (Bécquer) 104
Rivas, Ángel de Saavedra, duque de
342–343, 435c
Robespierre, Maximilien-François-
Marie-Isidore 299
Rocroi, Battle of 321, **343,** 383,
424c
Rodrigo, Joaquín 62, **344,** 439c
Rodrigues, Amália **344**

Rodríguez Zapatero, José Luis 63,
64, 95, 103, 139, **344–345,** 371,
372, 374, 439c, 440c
Rojas, Fernando de **345–346,** 420c
Rojas Zorrilla, Francisco de **346–
347**
Roman Catholic Church 6–7,
11–13, 29, 43
Charles I (king of Spain) 148
Cisneros, Francisco Jiménez de
153, 154
Falange Española 178
Fátima 181
Ignatius of Loyola, Saint 226
Japan, Portuguese presence in
236
John of the Cross, Saint 240
Kinsale, Battle of 245
Magellan, Ferdinand 264
Opus Dei 302–303
Santiago de Compostela 354–355
Spanish Inquisition 377–378
Teresa of Ávila, Saint 383–384
Toledo 389
Torquemada, Tomás de 390–391
Romancero gitano (García Lorca) 201
Roman Empire 85, 114, 158, 350,
359, 370
romanticism 104, 171, 176, 189,
273
Romero, Pedro 114
Roosevelt, Theodore 355
Rubén Darío Archive 165
Rueda, Lope de **347**
Russia 107–108

S

Sá de Miranda, Francisco de **348**
Sagasta, Práxedes Mateo 40, 130,
348–349, 433c
Sagrada Familia (church) 202–203
St. Quentin, Battle of 175, 232, **349**
Saint-Saëns, Camile 215
Salamanca **349–350**
Salazar, António de Oliveira, and
regime 49–52, 54–56, **350–351,**
436c, 437c
Angola 87
Azores 96
Carmona, António Óscar de
Fragoso 132

Carnation Revolution 132, 133
Costa Gomes, Francisco da 162
environmental issues in Spain
and Portugal 174
Lisbon 252
Mozambique 289
Pintasilgo, Maria de Lurdes
324–325
Soares, Mário 364
Souza Cardoso, Amadeo de 367
Salic law 229
Salvador. *See* Bahia
Sampaio, Jorge 440c
San Juan Hill, Battle of 355
Sanjurjo, José 262, 285, **351–352**
San Martín, José Francisco de 299,
352–353
San Salvador 156
Santa Cruz, Álvaro de Bazán,
marqués de **353**
Santa Cruz de Tenerife 128
Santana Lopes, Pedro 440c
Santayana, George 62, **353–354,**
354, 439c
Santiago de Compostela **354–355**
Santiago de Cuba, Battle of 41,
145, **355–356**
Santo Domingo. *See* Dominican
Republic
São Tomé and Príncipe **356,** 364
Saragossa. *See* Zaragoza
Saramago, José 62, **356–357,** 439c
Sarasate, Pablo de **357**
Sartorius, José Luis **357–358**
satire 121, 190, 209, 212, 248, 396
Scott, Sir Walter 82
sculpture 152–153, 209–210, 219
Sebastian I (king of Portugal) 76,
93, **358–359,** 422c, 423c
Sebastianism 404
Second Republic 46–47
Alberti, Rafael 74
Barcelona 100
Basque nationalism 101
Basque provinces 103
Catalonia 138
Franco Bahamonde, Francisco
194
García Lorca, Federico 201
Ibárruri, Dolores 225
Largo Caballero, Francisco 247
Machado, Antonio 257

Madariaga, Salvador de 259
Mola, Emilio 284
Queipo de Llano, Gonzalo 336
Rey, Fernando 341
Sanjurjo, José 352
Spanish civil war 375
Segovia **359–360**
Segovia, Andrés 62, **360–361**
Selim II (Ottoman sultan) 250
September 11, 2001 terrorist attacks
62–63, 123
Serna y Hinojosa, José de la 93
Serra, Junípero 125, **361**
Serrano y Domínguez, Francisco
361–362, 432c–433c
Serveto, Miguel **362–363**
Seven Years' War 30, 32, 121, 150,
197, 241, 255
Seville 223, 307, 363, **363–364**
Sforza dynasty 233
Shafter, William 355
Shakespeare, William 403
Sicily 232–233
Siglo de Oro 4, 23–24, **364,** 424c
bullfighting 114
Gama, Vasco da 199
Garcilaso de la Vega 202
Herrera, Fernando de 223
Leyenda Negra 252
Moluccas 285
Moreto y Cabaña, Agustín
287–288
Pacheco, Francisco 307
Prado, Museo Nacional del 329
Rojas Zorrilla, Francisco de
346–347
Teresa de Ávila, Saint 384
Tirso de Molina 387–388
Torres Naharro, Bartolomé de
392
zarzuela 411
Zurbarán, Francisco de 415
Silva, Gómez da 170
Sixty Years' Tyranny 111, 238
slavery
Angola 86
asiento 91–92
Brazil 112
encomienda 174
Hispaniola 223–224
Jamaica 235
Las Casas, Bartolomé de 248–249

Pombal, Sebastião José de
Carvalho e Melo, marquês de
326
Portuguese Guinea 328
Spain and the United States 373
Spanish Guinea 377
Smoker, The (Gris) 218
Soares, Mário 60–61, 325, **364–365**
social commentary
Baroja, Pío 100–101
Cadalso, José 121
Eça de Queirós, José Maria 171
Goya y Lucientes, Francisco José
de 211
Gracián, Baltasar 212–213
Pérez Galdós, Benito 315
Quental, Antero de 337–338
Sá de Miranda, Francisco de 348
Socialist Party (Portugal) 325, 365
Socialist Party (Spain) 58, 210, 247
Socialist Workers Party of Spain
(PSOE) 58, 59, 210
social realism 141, 201
Society of Jesus. *See* Jesuits
Socrates, José 440c
Soledades (Góngora y Argote) 209
Sor María. *See* María de Agreda, Sor
Sorolla y Bastida, Joaquín **365**
Soto, Hernando de 191, **365–366**
Sousa, Tomé de 97
South America 29–30, 38–39. *See
also specific countries, e.g.:* Brazil
Ayacucho, Battle of 93
Balboa, Vasco Núñez de 98
Belalcázar, Sebastián de 104, 105
Bolívar, Simón 108–109
Boyacá, Battle of 110
Cabeza de Vaca, Álvar Núñez 119
Cabral, Pedro Álvares 120
Charles I (king of Spain) 148
Espartero, Baldomero 176
La Plata, Viceroyalty of 247
Miranda, Francisco de 283
Orellana, Francisco de 304–305
Pizarro, Francisco 325–326
San Martín, José Francisco de
352–353
Spanish explorations of (1524–
1542) 453m
Souza Cardoso, Amadeo de 62,
366–367, 439c

Soviet Union 107–108, 225, 369,
370, 374, 376
Spain and Portugal (map) 462m
Spain and Portugal in the Americas
(1750) 458m
Spain and the European powers 7,
20, 39, 246, **368–370**
Spain and the Middle East **370–372**
Spain and the United States **372–374,** 434c
Spanish-American War 40–41,
374–375, 434c
Blasco Ibáñez, Vicente 106
Cervera y Topete, Pascual 145–146
Cuba 162–163
Ganivet, Ángel 200
Generation of '98 204
Leyenda Negra 252
Manila Bay, Battle of 266
Mariana Islands 271
Philippine Islands 323
Picasso, Pablo 323–324
Puerto Rico 335
Sagasta, Práxedes Mateo 348–349
Santiago de Cuba, Battle of
355–356
Spain and the European powers
369
Spain and the United States 373
Weyler y Nicolau, Valeriano 407
Spanish-American writers 165
Spanish Armada. *See* Armada
Spanish civil war 47–49, **375–376,**
436c, 460m
Alberti, Rafael 74
Alcazar of Toledo, siege of the
75–76
Aleixandre, Vicente 77
Alfonso XIII (king of Spain) 80
Arias Navarro, Carlos 89
Asencio Torrado, José 91
Asturias 92
Azaña, Manuel 94
Barcelona 100
Basque nationalism 101
Basque provinces 103
Bilbao 106
Blue Division 107
Buero Vallejo, Antonio 113
Buñuel, Luis 117

Carlism 131
Casals, Pablo 134
Catalonia 138
Cela, Camilo José 141
Dalí i Domènech, Salvador 165
Falange Española 178, 179
Franco Bahamonde, Francisco 194
González Márquez, Felipe 210
Ibárruri, Dolores 225
Jiménez, Juan Ramón 236
Largo Caballero, Francisco 247
Machado, Manuel 258
Madariaga, Salvador de 259
Madrid 261
Maeztu y Whitney, Ramiro de 262
Majorca 264–265
Málaga 265
Martínez Ruiz, José 274
Matute, Ana María 274
Melilla 276
Millán Astray, José 282
Mola, Emilio 285
Navarre 292
Opus Dei 303
Ortega y Gasset, José 305
Pérez de Ayala, Ramón 314
Primo de Rivera y Orbaneja, Miguel 334
Queipo de Llano, Gonzalo 336–337
Rey, Fernando 341
Salamanca 350
Sanjurjo, José 352
Segovia 360
Seville 364
Spain and the European powers 369
Spain and the Middle East 370
Spain and the United States 374
Tàpies, Antoni 382
terrorism 385
Toledo 389
Valencia 399
zarzuela 411
Spanish Explorations of Middle America (1513–1543) 453m
Spanish Explorations of South America (1524–1542) 453m
Spanish Foreign Legion 282
Spanish Guinea **376–377**

Spanish Inquisition 11–12, 29, 35, **377–378,** 419c, 421c
Charles III (king of Spain) 150
Cisneros, Francisco Jiménez de 153
Ferdinand V (king of Aragon and united Spain) 183
Ferdinand VII (king of Spain) 186
Ignatius of Loyola, Saint 225–226
Leyenda Negra 251
Olavide, Pablo de 299
Pacheco, Francisco 307
Peninsular War 312
Pérez, Antonio 313, 314
Philip II (king of Spain) 318
Pombal, Sebastião José de Carvalho e Melo, marquês de 326
Salamanca 350
Seville 364
Torquemada, Tomás de 390–391
Torres Naharro, Bartolomé de 392
Valdés, Alfonso de 396
Valdés, Juan de 397
Vieira, António 404
Spanish Netherlands 343, 379
Spanish Rule in Europe (1580–1714) 459m
Spanish Succession, War of the 25, 26, 31, **378,** 426c
Almansa, Battle of 81
Aragon 88
asiento 92
Barcelona 100
Bourbon 109
Catalonia 137
Gibraltar 205
Italy, Spain in 233
John V (king of Portugal) 238
Netherlands, Revolt of the 294
Netherlands, Spain in the 295
Peter II (king of Portugal) 317
Philip V (king of Spain) 322
Spain and the European powers 368
Zaragoza 410
Spice Islands 84, 263, 285, **378–379,** 421c
Spinola, Ambrogio 113, 169, **379**

Spinola, António Sebastião Ribeiro de 56, 133, **379–380**
Spiritual Exercises (Ignatius of Loyola) 226
Sri Lanka. *See* Ceylon
Stalin, Joseph 370
state terrorism 385
Still-Life (Gris) 218
Sucre, Antonio José de 93, **380–381**
surrealism 164, 203, 210, 283–284

T

Taft, William Howard 365
Taliban 63
Tamayo y Baus, Manuel **382**
Tàpies, Antoni **382–383**
Ten Years' War 162
Tercio 142–143, 282, 343, 379, **383**
Teresa of Ávila, Saint 240, **383–384,** 407, 424c
terrorism 59, 60, 62–64, **384–385,** 439c. *See also* Madrid train bombings (2004)
Arias Navarro, Carlos 89
Basque nationalism 102–103
Canary Islands 128–129
Catalonia 139
Spain and the Middle East 371–372
Tetuán, campaign of 297, **385–386**
Texas 119, 301–302, **386**
theater. *See* drama
theology 362–363
Theotokópoulos, Doménikos. *See* Greco, El
Thibaud, Jacques 134
Thirty Years' War 21
Habsburg 220
Haro, Luis de 221
Isabella Clara Eugenia 230
Netherlands, Revolt of the 294
Olivares, Gaspar de Guzmán y Pimentel, conde-duque de 301
Philip IV (king of Spain) 321
Rocroi, Battle of 343
Spinola, Ambrogio 379
Three Kings, Battle of the 358–359
Three Tenors 167
Thyssen-Bornemisza, Hans Heinrich 386–387

Thyssen-Bornemisza Museum **386–387**
Tirano Banderas (Valle-Inclán) 400
Tirso de Molina **387–388,** 413, 424c
Tokugawa shogunate 236
Toledo 75–76, 240, *388,* **388–389,** *389*
Tordesillas, Treaty of 79, 306, **389–390,** 420c
Torquemada, Tomás de **390–391**
Torres Naharro, Bartolomé de **391–392**
Torres Villaroel, Diego de **392–393**
tourism 174
trade 8, 29–30
    Alentejo 78
    Almeida, Francisco de 82
    Andalusia 85
    asiento 91–92
    Barcelona 99, 100
    Bilbao 106
    Cabarrús, Francisco conde de 118
    Cádiz 122
    Cape Verde Islands 130
    Ceuta 146
    Columbus, Christopher 155
    Cuba 162
    Dias, Bartolomeu 167
    Florida 191
    Gama, Vasco da 199
    immigrants in Portugal 226
    Japan, Portuguese presence in 235–236
    Lisbon 252
    Moluccas 285
    Oporto 302
    Peter II (king of Portugal) 317
    Seville 364
    Spice Islands 379
    Tordesillas, Treaty of 389–390
Trafalgar, Battle of 33, 151, 207, 216, **393,** 397, 428c
Tragic Week 190
Trent, Council of 384
Trienio Constitucional 342
Triple Alliance, War of the 310
Tudor dynasty 140
Turkey 184, 232, 250
Twelve Years' Truce 113, 231, 379
Tyrone, earl of 245

U

Uceda, duke of 251
Ulloa, Antonio de 255
Ulster 245
Unamuno, Miguel de 62, 200, 350, *394,* **394–395,** 439c
Union of India 165
United Nations 86, 132, 195, 351
United Provinces of the Río de La Plata 89
United States 63–64. *See also* Spain and the United States; Spanish-American War
    Altamira Crevea, Rafael 83
    Arizona 90
    Aznar López, José María 95
    Calatrava, Santiago 123
    Casals, Pablo 134
    Cuba 162–163
    Darío, Rubén 165
    Gálvez, Bernardo de 197
    García Lorca, Federico 201
    Leyenda Negra 252
    Louisiana 256
    Miranda, Francisco de 283
    Moneo, José Rafael 286
    New Mexico 295
    Philippine Islands 323
    Puerto Rico 335
    Rodríguez Zapatero, José Luis 345
    Santayana, George 353, 354
    Santiago de Cuba, Battle of 355, 356
    Sarasate, Pablo de 357
    Sorolla y Bastida, Joaquín 365
    Spain and the European powers 369, 370
    Spain and the Middle East 371, 372
    Texas 386
Upper Peru 380
Ursúa, Pedro de 70
Uruguay 29, **395**
Utrecht, Treaty of 81, 378

V

Valdés, Alfonso de **396,** 397
Valdés, Cayetano **397**
Valdés, Juan de **397–398**
Valdivia, Pedro de **398–399**
400, 4⌐⌐
Valladolid **400**
Valle-Inclán, Ramón María del
Vedel, Jean 98
Velázquez, Diego Rodríguez de Silva y 18, **401,** 424c
    Olivares, Gaspar de Guzmán y Pimentel, conde-duque de 301
    Pacheco, Francisco 307
    Philip IV (king of Spain) 321
    Prado, Museo Nacional del 329
    Zurbarán, Francisco de 415
Velázquez de Cuéllar, Diego 160, 162, 299, **402**
Vendôme, duke of 73
Venezuela 108–109, 156, 181–182, 283, 380, **403**
Venice 82
Verdad sospechosa, La (Alarcón y Mendoza) 71
Vespucci, Amerigo 97
Viagem a Portugal (Saramago) 357
Vicente, Gil **403**
Viceroyalty. *See specific vicroyalty, e.g.:* La Plata, Viceroyalty of
Victòria dels Àngels. *See* Ángeles, Victoria de los
Vida (Torres Villaroel) 392
Vida es sueño, La (Calderón de la Barca) 124
Vieira, António **403–404**
Vieques, Puerto Rico 373
View of Toledo (El Greco) 217
Villeneuve, Pierre de 393
Virgin Mary 181
Visigoths 388
Vivar, Rodrigo Díaz de 399
Vives, Juan Luis **404–405**
Voltaire 88

W

Wall, Richard 30, 304, **406**
"war on terror" 63, 371, 374, 439c
Wellesley, Arthur (duke of Wellington) 312, 350, 369
West Africa 86–87, 328–329
Weyler y Nicolau, Valeriano 130, 273, **406–407**
Wilkinson, James 373

women's rights in Spain 179–180, **407–409**
World Trade Center attacks. *See* September 11, 2001 terrorist attacks
World War I 44–45, 49, 436*c*
  Alfonso XIII (king of Spain) 80
  Almeida, António José de 81
  Altamira Crevea, Rafael 83
  Benavente y Martínez, Jacinto 105
  Braga, Teófilo 110
  Gibraltar 205
  González, Julio 209
  Granados, Enrique 215
  Maeztu y Whitney, Ramiro de 261
  Mariana Islands 271
  Millán Astray, José 282
  Pais, Sidónio 308
  Pérez de Ayala, Ramón 314
  Souza Cardoso, Amadeo de 367
  Spain and the European powers 369

World War II 51–52, 437*c*
  Azores 96
  Blue Division 107–108
  Dalí i Domènech, Salvador 165
  Franco Bahamonde, Francisco 194
  Gibraltar 205
  Largo Caballero, Francisco 247
  Lisbon 252
  Morocco 288
  Salazar, António de Oliveira 351
  Spain and the European powers 369, 370
  Spain and the United States 374
  Spinola, António Sebastião Ribeiro de 380

X

Xavier, Francis 276

Y

Yerma (García Lorca) 201

Z

Zapatero, José Luis. *See* Rodríguez Zapatero, José Luis
Zaragoza 88, 173, 308–309, 313, **410**
Zaragoza, Battle of **410**
Zaragoza, Treaty of 10
Zaragoza y Domenech, Agustina 309
zarzuela **411**
Zea Bermúdez, Francisco **411–412**
Zigeunerweisen (Sarasate) 357
Zorrilla y Moral, José **412–413,** 435*c*
Zumalacárregui y de Imaz, Tomás de **413–414**
Zumárraga, Juan de 277, **414–415**
Zurbarán, Francisco de 290, **415,** 424*c*